750.

FEDERAL ADMINISTRATIVE LAW

A Study of the Growth, Nature, and Control
of Administrative Action

By

RINEHART JOHN SWENSON

PROFESSOR OF GOVERNMENT
NEW YORK UNIVERSITY

THE RONALD PRESS COMPANY ⟋ NEW YORK

344
S974f

Library of Congress Catalog Card Number: 52–9466

PRINTED IN THE UNITED STATES OF AMERICA

PREFACE

Out of the welter of competing interests, desires, and requirements of our complex society today, increasing demands are being made on government to provide various services on national, state, and local levels. Government is becoming more and more a matter of administration, and in consequence a considerable body of administrative law has developed to implement legislative policies and to complement judicial justice. In accordance with the "rule of law" the regular courts oversee and control the administrative process—a task which they have found increasingly difficult to discharge. The case or lawsuit method to redress grievances arising out of administrative action is poorly adapted to the determination of issues involving broad public policies: often these questions are less concerned with jurisprudence than with highly technical points in economics, finance, engineering, medicine, and other fields of learning. Yet, administrative discretion must be properly channeled. Hence, it is imperative to continue to formalize administrative action into a coherent body of law, supervised by special courts of limited jurisdiction that are presided over by judges with specialized training and knowledge. This is the underlying thesis of the book.

The volume deals with the growth, nature, and control of administrative action. It traces the evolution of American thinking and practice in a changing economy and society from a philosophy of "rugged individualism" to that of the modern "service state" with its "big government" and bureaucracy. The forms of administrative action and the means of their enforcement are examined. The relations of the constitutional separation of powers and of the Anglo-American rule of law to the development of administrative law in the United States are explored at some length, and a detailed and extensive consideration is given to the review of administrative action by the regular courts. Finally, attention is called to the role of the Congress in supervising administration.

The scope of this book is limited almost wholly to the federal government. References to State laws, judicial decisions, and administrative practices are for the purpose of supporting or clarifying federal law or explaining federal-State relations. The approach is mainly that of a legal study, relating administrative law to the

iii

causes and procedures which determine its form and substance. Thus, the volume provides a textbook for the increasing number of courses on administrative law offered on both undergraduate and graduate levels. It should also be of interest to public administrators, judges, lawyers, and all who are concerned with the functions present-day government is assuming.

The materials for this book have been discussed and criticized by successive groups of students, and I wish to express my appreciation to them for their constructive comments. I wish also to acknowledge my debt to Mr. Laird Dunbar for painstakingly checking the manuscript against the sources; to Miss Mary Conley for typing the manuscript; to my wife Aagot for performing various onerous tasks in connection with the preparation of the manuscript for the printer, reading proof, and preparing the index; and to the various publishers who graciously consented to the use of materials previously published. All shortcomings and errors are mine alone.

RINEHART JOHN SWENSON

New York
July, 1952

CONTENTS

CHAPTER   PAGE

1   FROM LAISSEZ FAIRE TO BUREAUCRACY   3

2   THE PLACE OF ADMINISTRATION IN THE CONSTITU-
TIONAL TRICHOTOMY   33

3   THE ADMINISTRATIVE PROCESS   60

4   ENFORCEMENT OF ADMINISTRATIVE ACTION .   .   .   123

5   THE RULE OF LAW: THE DOCTRINE OF STATE IM-
MUNITY   156

6   THE RULE OF LAW: THE LIABILITY OF PUBLIC
OFFICERS   182

7   JUDICIAL PROCESSING OF ADMINISTRATIVE ACTION   .   212

8   LIMITATIONS OF JUDICIAL CONTROL OF THE ADMINIS-
TRATIVE PROCESS   274

9   GOVERNMENT BY AGENCY OR GOVERNMENT BY LAWSUIT   304

10   CONGRESSIONAL SUPERVISION OF THE FEDERAL ADMINIS-
TRATIVE PROCESS   325

TABLE OF CASES   355

INDEX OF NAMES   369

INDEX OF SUBJECTS   372

FEDERAL
ADMINISTRATIVE LAW

Chapter 1

FROM LAISSEZ FAIRE TO BUREAUCRACY

The Constitution radiates distrust of government. The Americans of 1787 were individualists. The New World was fertile soil for the doctrines of the Protestant Reformation, of John Locke, and of Adam Smith—all of which stressed the importance of individual self-determination in religious, political, and economic behavior. The "natural" right of the individual to acquire and hold private property was the central idea of the laissez faire doctrine. When the individual added his labor to the gifts of nature, he created something that was his own, his property. The chief, if not the sole, function of government was to protect this property right in labor and things by making it possible for the individual to follow his own self-interest in free competition with every other individual. Hence the best government was one which governed least. "The great and chief end, therefore, of men uniting into commonwealths, and putting themselves under government," said John Locke, "is the preservation of their property." [1]

In keeping with this current of thought, laissez faire was adopted by the framers of the Constitution as a rule of political action—the "natural rights" of the individual were protected (1) by an elaborate check and balance system, intended to reduce government action to a minimum, and (2) by incorporating a bill of rights in the fundamental law.

But whatever can be said for the applicability and usefulness of the laissez faire doctrine to the United States of the eighteenth and the first half of the nineteenth centuries must necessarily be revised when considered in relation to the highly industrialized United States of today. In the modern world all individual rights are held subject to the paramount right of society to regulate them in the interest of the whole. Today the individuality of the citizen is conditioned by his membership in organizations. The individual deals with, competes

[1] *Of Civil Government, Two Treatises* ("Everyman's Library," E. P. Dutton & Co., Inc., New York, 1924), Bk. II, chap. ix, p. 179. Also see "For the political society is instituted for no other end, but only to secure every man's possession of the things of this life." John Locke, *The Second Treatise of Civil Government and a Letter Concerning Toleration* (Basil Blackwell, Ltd., Oxford, 1946), p. 153.

with, great impersonal concerns, not with other individuals. Employers are incorporated; employees are unionized. In that sense production and labor are "socialized." The factory system has created large-scale employers and a large class of workers whose sole capital is the labor of their hands. Self-interest, perhaps not enlightened self-interest, has pitted these two groups against each other in an uncompromising and destructive industrial war. Boycotts, strikes, lockouts, picketing, intimidation, and rioting are the news of the day from the labor front. These activities involve mass, not individual, action. Within the ranks of business, unregulated competition leads to cutthroat competition—price fixing, rebating, blacklisting, espionage, manipulation, coercion, and conspiracy. Cutthroat competition leads to monopoly which, in turn, means the elimination of competitors and the creation of big businesses. Mass production and large-scale wholesaling, jobbing, and retailing, involving large sums of capital, have largely replaced the handicrafts. Individual enterprise is not free in an industrial society which requires large capital outlays in order to engage in effective competition. And the right of the individual to contract—in part, the essence of individualism—is without meaning unless the contracting parties stand on a plane of bargaining equality. Hence laissez faire today is little more than a catch phrase employed by those who believe in the principle of self-government for business and oppose public regulation as unwarranted interference with individual initiative. Industrial individualists appear to forget that today "the individual is caught in a great confused nexus of all sorts of complicated circumstances, and that to let him alone is to leave him helpless as against the obstacles with which he has to contend." [2]

With the revolutionary or evolutionary change that has taken place in the economic life of America has come a corresponding change in philosophy. The individualistic concept of freedom has of necessity given way to a social concept. Freedom does not mean social isolation—to be left alone. To be free from disease, from malnutrition, from criminal and immoral influences, from unwholesome housing, from the terrors of unemployment, from unfair methods of business competition, and from the fear of the poorhouse—such freedom is more important in modern society than to be left alone. The individual does not always know his own interests best; and if he does, he cannot be left free to pursue them to his neighbor's disadvantage.

[2] Woodrow Wilson, *The New Freedom* (Doubleday, Page & Co., New York, 1913), p. 284.

In other words, the change from the handcraft stage to the factory system of production not only affected the economic status of the individual, but it conditioned his attitude toward his government—it converted him from the theory and practice of rugged individualism to a view of the state as a service institution. When the interests of the labor class created by the factory system came into conflict with the profit motive of the employer class, the government was forced to assume the role of arbiter. The result was an extensive list of factory and labor laws with appropriate enforcement machinery. The factory system further urbanized America and so brought into existence privately owned and operated urban utilities upon which the public became dependent for essential services. Again, the government was constrained to intercede to protect the public interest, and State and federal regulatory commissions were created to that end. Further, urbanization created or multiplied governmental services relating to police, fire, and health protection. This normal expansion of the public service has been greatly stimulated by national crises, of which the depression following World War I was an example par excellence. In an effort to repair the ravages of a devastating war, the national government instituted a comprehensive recovery program which involved the organization of administrative agencies on a scale which would have seemed fantastic only a decade before, but which lost much of its fearsome impressiveness when compared to the administrative organization created during World War II.

Our administrative system is machine-made. While American life was predominantly rural, the family was largely self-sufficient and self-contained, and the government was essentially a local policeman standing guard over the individual's "natural rights." These rights were defined by the legislature and enforced by the courts in private actions for damages or for relief in equity. That is, the principal means of law enforcement was trial by court and jury. The administrative hierarchy is a by-product of the application of steam to production. The machines that made locomotives, automobiles, and radios also made cities, corporations, immigration, and the stock exchange and forced the citizen to make repeated calls upon the "policeman" for new protective services.

This interest in government on the part of the general public is both the result and the cause of a shift in the conception of the functions of government from that of a big policeman to that of a powerful promoter of society's welfare. . . . Rugged individualism, in the sense of the fullest possible opportunity for development of American men and women, will, one hopes, always continue to be the ultimate aim of

American society. But "rugged individualism," as a theory of political non-action and as a practice of hands off by government, has been dead in England since the days of Gladstone and Disraeli, and in this country was buried by Theodore Roosevelt beyond resurrection even by Harding and Coolidge.[3]

The Federal Bureaucracy

The growth of government services, or at least activities, may be gauged not only by the increase in personnel but also by the rising cost of government. The following statistical data will illustrate this expansion.[4]

Year	Population (000)	National Income ($100,000)	No. Employed by National Government	Total Governmental Expenditure ($000,000)	Per Capita Governmental Expenditure	Per Capita National Income
1913[5]	96,512	31,909	469,879	725	7.51	330.62
1920	105,711	65,928	691,116	6,482	60.85	623.66
1925	114,867	73,067	548,077	3,530	30.73	636.10
1930	122,775	72,729	595,456	3,994	32.53	577.40
1935	127,172	54,946	815,789	7,376	58.00	437.62
1940[5]	131,699	75,706	1,119,641	10,071	76.46	574.84

The number of listed government agencies and personnel varies with the purposes for which the listing is made; the critics are invariably more generous than the defenders and the apologists. A Citizens National Committee Inc. reported 428 federal agencies on June 30, 1944, and an average number of civilian employees in the executive branch of 2,932,704 for the fiscal year 1944.[6] Senator Harry F. Byrd, chairman of the Congressional Joint Committee on Non-Essential Federal Expenditures, said in November, 1945:

> The Federal Government had 554,000 civilian employees in 1933, compared with 975,000 on Armistice Day in 1918. But we now have about 3,000,000 as of last August, not including about 700,000 outside the United States, as against 933,000 before the war in August, 1939.[7]

[3] Felix Frankfurter, *Law and Politics* (Harcourt, Brace & Co., Inc., New York, 1939), p. 240.

[4] Data from Department of Commerce, *Statistical Abstract of the United States* (Government Printing Office, Washington, D.C., 1941) ; *Basic Statistics* (Standard Statistics Corporation, New York, 1938), Vol. LXXXVIII, No. 9, pp. 51–52; and *Current Statistics* (January, 1942).

[5] The year 1913 is considered a normal year, with an index number 100 in statistical studies; 1940 is the year before the creation of the new war agencies.

[6] Federal Agencies, *Publication No. 333* (Washington, D.C., 1944), p. 4.

[7] *New York Times,* November 2, 1945, p. 9.

The Civil Service Commission put the total number of employees of the federal executive departments at the end of January, 1949, at 2.1 million. This figure includes 195,000 working outside continental United States. In addition, there were 7,500 employed by the legislative branch, 3,500 by the judicial branch, and more than 25,000 in various government corporations. About three-fourths of all federal civilian workers were employed by three agencies in 1949: 750,000 in the three military departments; 200,000 in the Veteran's Administration; and 500,000 in the Post Office Department.[8] There is not much likelihood that these services will be reduced in the near future.

The Hoover Commission reported:

> As a result of depression, war, new needs for defense, and our greater responsibilities in the foreign field, the Federal Government has become the most gigantic business on earth. In less than 20 years the number of its civil employees has risen from 570,000 to over 2,100,000. The number of bureaus, sections, services, and units has increased fourfold to over 1,800. Annual expenditures have increased from about $3,600,-000,000 to over $42,000,000,000. The national debt per average family has increased from about $500 to about $7,500.[9]

The total annual salaries paid to federal civilian employees has risen from approximately $1 billion to $5.7 billion in twenty years.[10] Personnel skills number over 15,000, or two-thirds the number required for all private enterprise.[11] The cost of all government— federal, State, and local—increased from about $3 billion in 1913 to about $55 billion in 1948.[12]

Fifty years ago these figures would have seemed astronomical. Small·wonder that thrifty citizens have become budget conscious and not a little disturbed over the trend away from the tradition of laissez faire.

In the modern world, governmental functions are so vast and complicated that democratically organized legislative bodies are not qualified even to initiate many public policies. Many legislative measures are framed by "experts" or technicians outside the legislative chambers and are merely evaluated by the lawmakers. Many legislative policies are conditioned by data which technicians alone

[8] Nona Brown in *New York Sunday Times,* March 20, 1949.
[9] *The Hoover Commission Report on Organization of the Executive Branch of the Government* (McGraw-Hill Book Co., Inc., New York, 1949), p. 14.
[10] *Ibid.,* p. 109.
[11] *Ibid.*
[12] *Ibid.,* p. 492.

are qualified to find. Hence the innumerable independent, semi-independent, and ex officio offices and boards and commissions in the federal and State services. Not only has science multiplied administrative services, but it has revolutionized the methods, the techniques, of administration. In short

> Administrative tribunals . . . did not come because any one wanted them to come. They came because there seemed to be no other practical way of carrying on the affairs of government and discharging the duties and obligations which an increasingly complex social organization made it necessary for the government to perform.[13]

Indeed, as Duguit pointed out, civilization itself is simply the growth and satisfaction of all kinds of needs and, consequently, "governmental intervention becomes normally more frequent with the growth of civilization simply because government alone can make civilization a thing of meaning." [14] And government is necessarily administered by men.

Thus technology is applied to the art of government, a development that is the inevitable result of social progress. Whether, in turn, technology as inevitably induces an incrustation of the vices of bureaucracy in the government service is a matter of public concern [15] —a concern which centers largely on devising instruments of control that can reduce arbitrary administrative action to a minimum without interfering with the independence of the administrative agency in all the matters essential to the purposes for which the agency exists.

Bureaucracy: "Administrative Lawlessness"? [16]—In common usage the term *bureaucracy* has an invidious connotation; it is a word

[13] Marvin B. Rosenberry, "Administrative Law and the Constitution," 23 *American Political Science Review* (February, 1929), 32, 35.

[14] Léon Duguit, *Les Transformations du Droit* (1913), trans. by Frida and Harold Laski as *Law in the Modern State* (B. W. Huebsch, New York, 1919), p. 45.

[15] *Cf.* James Burnham, *The Managerial Revolution* (The John Day Co., Inc., New York, 1941); F. O. Lowden, "Permanent Officials in the National Administration of the United States," 21 *American Political Science Review* (August, 1927), 529–36; H. J. Laski, "Limitations of the Expert," 162 *Harper's* (December, 1930), 101–10; John Dickinson, "Administrative Law and the Fear of Bureaucracy," 14 *American Bar Association Journal* (1928), 513, 597 ff.; C. J. Friedrich, "Responsible Government Service Under the American Constitution," *Problems of the American Public Service* (McGraw-Hill Book Co., Inc., New York, 1935); James Hart, *An Introduction to Administrative Law* (F. S. Crofts & Co., New York, 1940), chap. v; M. E. Dimock and H. K. Hyde, *Bureaucracy and Trusteeship in Large Corporations* (Government Printing Office, Washington, D.C., 1940), Parts II, III; Harvey Pinney, "Administocracy, Inc.," 19 *Social Forces* (March, 1941), 402–9.

[16] For the shortcomings of bureaucracy see the following: Gordon Hewart, *The New Despotism* (Cosmopolitan Book Corp., New York, 1929); J. M. Beck, *Our*

of reproach applied particularly to the federal administrative service. Less commonly, it is used as the collective name for all the administrative vices of large-scale organization. It refers to the methods employed and the kind of work performed by the administrative hierarchy, rather than to the form of administrative organization. A bureaucrat is an officer who acts arbitrarily, performs useless or objectionable work, and wastes public funds; bureaucracy is the sum of these afflictions to society.

In the technical sense a bureaucracy is a hierarchical, large-scale administrative organization, having a professional personnel, and based upon the principle of specialization. In and of itself it is not a conspiracy against the common weal, but an administrative system to achieve certain objectives in a systematic and economic manner. Thus regarded, bureaucracy may be said to inhere in all large organizations, and the evils usually attributed to the former should more properly be ascribed to the latter.

But however regarded, bureaucracy is not peculiar to public administration alone; it is fully as common in the church, a political party, and great business corporations. The evils associated with bureaucratic public administration are no less evident in business ad-

Wonderland of Bureaucracy (The Macmillan Co., New York, 1932); C. K. Allen, *Bureaucracy Triumphant* (Oxford University Press, London, 1931); Martin Abbotson, *Bureaucracy Run Mad* (Watts & Co., London, 1940); W. M. Kiplinger, *Washington Is Like That* (Harper & Bros., New York, 1942); Louis Ludlow, *America Go Bust* (The Stratford Co., Boston, 1933); A. T. Mason, *Bureaucracy Convicts Itself* (The Viking Press, Inc., New York, 1941); L. Sullivan, *The Dead Hand of Bureaucracy* (Bobbs-Merrill Co., New York, 1940); *Bureaucracy Runs Amuck* (Bobbs-Merrill Co., New York, 1944); H. W. Sumners, "American Capacity for Self-Government Is Being Destroyed by Bureaucracy," 30 *American Bar Association Journal* (January, 1944), 3 ff.; G. E. Outland, "New Personal Devil Bureaucracy," 109 *New Republic* (October 25, 1943), 561–63; J. C. O'Mahoney, "Declining Power of the States; Bureaucracy Is the Road to State Socialism," 9 *Vital Speeches* (February 1, 1943), 226–28; J. Kluttz, "To Washington an 'E' for Inefficiency," 41 *Reader's Digest* (December, 1942), 43–47; A. A. Hood, "Shall Industry or Bureaucracy Plan Our Economic Environment," 9 *Vital Speeches* (May 1, 1943), 425–33; F. M. Dixon, "Crossroads Democracy: Concentration of Power Is Dangerous," 9 *Vital Speeches* (February 1, 1943), 236–40; H. Bratter, "Bureaus Have Nine Lives," 31 *Nation's Business* (June, 1943), 30 ff.

For less critical and more sympathetic, and perhaps more objective, views on bureaucracy see: C. J. Friedrich and T. Cole, *Responsible Bureaucracy: A Challenge to Better Management* (Harvard University Press, Cambridge, Mass., 1932); H. S. Commager, "The Bugaboo of Bureaucracy," 42 *Scholastic* (May 3, 1943), 7; H. J. Laski, "Bureaucracy," *Encyclopedia of the Social Sciences* (The Macmillan Co., New York, 1930), Vol. III, pp. 70–73; F. M. Marx, "Bureaucracy," in R. Peel and J. S. Roucek (eds.), *Introduction to Politics* (Thomas Y. Crowell Co., New York, 1941), chap. xix; E. B. Stason, "If Men Were Angels: A Review," 41 *Michigan Law Review* (October, 1942), 269–75; C. M. Wiltse, "The Representative Function of Bureaucracy," 35 *American Political Science Review* (June, 1941), 510–16.

ministration, and in applying correctives to these evils, government and business are about equally handicapped. Furthermore, as our political and economic activities become more and more interdependent and interrelated, the acts of the government and of business bureaucrats may be equally affected with a public interest. When, therefore, "big business" makes an issue of governmental regimentation it is often a case of the pot calling the kettle black.

In truth, political bureaucracy is an outgrowth of industrial bureaucracy. The modern economic system produced the conditions —the factory system, urban utilities, monopolies—which made regulatory agencies necessary. Governmental bureaucracy, i.e., a comprehensive and systematic administration, is not necessarily undemocratic. In fact, it may be the means by which democracy may hope to reconcile liberty and private enterprise. The government must either operate or regulate our industrial system. There is no liberty in a society governed by the jungle law of cutthroat competition. Economic laws do not operate for the common good in a highly industrialized laissez faire society. Popular government must devise controls to protect private enterprise against monopoly or perish for its failure. The modern industrial system and the modern bureaucratic state are, therefore, interrelated and interdependent phenomena. Both systems are more or less infested with dry-rot fungus calling for remedial, but not destructive, measures.

There are important differences between public and private administration, differences which cancel out some common comparisons. One of the current fallacies is that businessmen and business methods would make the government more efficient and less costly. But the qualifications for a successful business executive are much narrower than are the qualifications for a good government executive. The latter should have knowledge of political science, economics, sociology, and business, without being essentially an expert in those fields, or at least without administering as an expert, because public administration is politics, statecraft. Anything he does is news, for he is a servant of the public. He lives in a house without walls, in an atmosphere of potential attack from within and without, which conditions his actions. The partisan opposition, the news-conscious press, the favor-seeking group, the muckraker, and the disgruntled subordinate are as pitiless as the klieg lights of publicity. On the other hand, the public has little interest in most of the activities of the business executive. To satisfy the profit motive of his public, the stockholders, the business executive needs to be competent only in the management of the specialized affairs of his plant. Business administration is authoritative, public administration is democratic; these characteristics make for stricter discipline in the former, a fact often mistaken for efficiency. The power to command is not always an element of strength, nor is action by compromise necessarily a confession of weakness.

Further, as Felix Frankfurter [17] so aptly reminds us: "Certainly the undramatic Reports of the United States Supreme Court reveal authoritatively that business and finance have their ample quota of favoritism, sharp practices, incompetence, and failures."

The relatively higher cost of public administration over business administration is due not to different standards of efficiency but to basic differences in objectives. The one is organized for *service,* the other for *profit.* For example, when postal rates are fixed, costs are incidental to securing a wide distribution of reading matter. Freedom to print has little meaning unless there is also freedom to read. And to mete out justice at a profit would be a strange practice in a democracy. Paradoxically, liberty and justice are dear, yet without price. To secure the one and to insure the other are the chief ends of government.

Also, as the government executive works *for* the public he must give much of his time to inquiries and complaints addressed to him by innumerable individuals and organizations and to defending himself and his subordinates against public criticism. Almost any charge of misfeasance or malfeasance leads to investigation by the public prosecutor or a legislative committee. All this interferes with the expedition, if not with the ultimate effectiveness, of the administrative process and makes for costly administration. A single federal department receives 13 million pieces of mail and handles 13 million telephone messages each year.[18] The public pays for this labor. The Post Office Department is one of the world's largest businesses. It employs over 500,000 persons, operates more than 10,000 trucks, manages 24,000 buildings, handles around 40 billion pieces of mail and over 800 million transactions in such special services, as money orders, C.O.D. mail, and postal savings. It contracts for tens of billions of dollars yearly for rail, ship, air-line, and trucking transportation; it sells around $300 million in money orders, and operates the Postal Savings System with about 4 million depositors having total accounts of over $3.4 billion.[19] The extended investigations by

[17] *Law and Politics,* p. 245.
[18] The Department of Agriculture. P. H. Appleby, *Big Democracy* (Alfred A. Knopf, New York, 1945), p. 25.
[19] *The Hoover Commission Report,* p. 219.

congressional committees, such as the Dies Committee on Un-American Activities and the Byrd Committee on Administrative Management, are at public expense. The Hoover Commission spent around $2 million. There seems to be no escape from this kind of government costs in a democracy. They are the democratic ways of achieving free institutions.

Constructively the administrative bureaucracy gives functional representation to important interests or groups in their relations with the President and Congress. Thus agriculture, commerce, and labor are represented by executive departments, and other interests are represented by such agencies as the United States Fish Commission, the Bureau of Animal Industry, the United States Maritime Commission, the Bituminous Coal Commission, the Office of Education, the Children's Bureau, and the Social Security Board. These agencies are official intermediaries between the interest group and the government, as opposed to extralegal lobbies which function largely under cover and not always in the public interest.[20]

The Indictment.—Bureaucracy is indicted on many counts. To some of these it pleads guilty, but to others it demurs. Some of the more serious criticisms may be considered briefly.

1. *The bureaucrat is not responsive to public criticism and demands.* He is insulated from the public by hierarchical layers of responsibility; only the head of the pyramid is exposed to public opinion. This independence may result in arrogance and arbitrariness and is regarded as antidemocratic.

It is the possession of discretionary power rather than political isolation that may result in arbitrary action, and the former is not peculiar to bureaucratic organization but is the common possession of all important administrative officers. Furthermore, the division of labor, which is the basis of bureaucratic organization, allows for specialization and concentration of effort in dealing with highly technical administrative problems. A career bureaucracy, as distinguished from a patronage bureaucracy, provides trained and experienced administrators who give continuity and system to the service, without which a large organization would fall apart. Also, the independence which results from isolation is a protection to professional standards, and the hierarchical system of authority necessarily fixes *internal responsibility* and puts a premium on loyalty to the organization.

[20] *Cf.* C. M. Wiltse, "The Representative Function of Bureaucracy," 35 *American Political Science Review* (June, 1941), 510–16.

2. *The administrative hierarchy tends to become a loose federation of practically independent and even competing units.* This results from the segregation inherent in large-scale organization, the different types of pressures to which the various agencies are subjected, and the jealousies generated by feudal loyalties and competitive and combative instincts. The result of this malcoordination is jurisdictional squabbles, overlapping functions, and disintegration rather than integration of policy: hence the persistent demand for "reorganization" of the executive branch.

In 1936 President Roosevelt appointed a Committee on Administrative Management which submitted its final report in 1937,[21] recommending consolidation of all federal agencies in twelve executive departments, thus placing the federal administrative service under the management of the President acting through department heads, except that judicial functions were to be exercised by independent "judicial sections" within the agencies. In February, 1939, the Attorney General, at the request of the President, appointed the Attorney General's Committee on Administrative Procedure to investigate the "need for procedural reform in the field of administrative law." In January 1941, the Committee submitted an elaborate report describing, among other things, "the defects found in the rule-making and adjudicatory aspects of the administrative process, and recommendations for the correction of these defects." [22] Under the Reorganization Act of 1939,[23] a number of the President's Reorganization Plans were approved and made effective by congressional resolution.[24] But World War II not only interrupted further reorganization, it aggravated the problem by greatly increasing the administrative service.

In 1947 Congress made provision for the organization of the Commission on Organization of the Executive Branch of the Government, the Hoover Commission.[25] This Commission made its report in 1949, recommending extensive overhauling of the executive branch.[26] The work of that branch was found to be poorly integrated.

[21] President's Committee on Administrative Management, *Report and Special Studies* (Washington, 1937).

[22] *Administrative Procedure in Government Agencies, S. Doc. No. 8,* 77th Cong., 1st Sess., p. iv. Similar investigations have been made in some of the States. In 1942 the "Benjamin Report," *Administrative Adjudication in the State of New York* was issued.

[23] Act of April 3, 1939, 53 *Stat.* 561, 5 *U.S.C.A.* § 133.

[24] 53 *Stat.* 813, 5 *U.S.C.A.* § 133s, 54 *Stat.* 1231, 1238, 5 *U.S.C.A.* §§ 133u, 133v.

[25] *Public Law 162,* 80th Cong., 1st Sess., approved July 7, 1947.

[26] *The Hoover Commission Report on Organization of the Executive Branch of the Government* (McGraw-Hill Book Co., Inc., New York, 1949).

An analysis of the federal government made by the Congressional Joint Committee on Non-Essential Federal Expenditures showed 22 agencies or units in 11 departments and independent establishments dealing with housing, 27 agencies in 12 departments and independent establishments dealing with standards and inspection, and 24 agencies and independent establishments dealing with agriculture.[27] The Hoover Commission concluded that some of the departments are loose confederations of independent bureaus and agencies, resulting in much duplication and overlapping of work. In many cases there may not be a duplication of functions, but several agencies dealing with different phases of a problem may be poorly integrated.

3. *The bureaucracy tends to build up an elaborate and unwieldy body of rules, to enmesh administration in "red tape," to overemphasize nonessential detail.* This may be the product of overspecialization and overemphasis on the scientific method, a by-product of professionalism; or it may be due in part to the natural desire of the bureaucrat to protect himself against attack through the creation of a detailed record of his activities; or it may be a case of efficiency gone into reverse, the result of an attempt to standardize all procedures in order ultimately to deal more expeditiously with a great volume of business.

On the other hand, red tape may stand "for firm insistence on statutory principle, equality before the law, orderly procedure, and careful weighing of all relevant facts."[28] It may be used to "check" and so to enforce administrative responsibility and integrity. It is found in business as well as in government administration.

4. *The vast activities of the bureaucracy have established a parens patriae relationship between the state and its people.* It is said that the individual is becoming a dependent, a public charge. Bureaucracy means too much government, too much ordering of private life, and too much intervention in the affairs of business. This is contrary to the individualistic spirit of our people and to the guaranties of civil liberty. The logical goal of bureaucracy is a completely managed economy—state socialism.

Critics of big government are likely not to distinguish between a managed and a *planned* economy—almost any form of regulation is interference with so-called natural or economic laws and results in the "enslavement" of the individual. So it would seem to be one of the articles of faith of the National Association of Manufacturers that "under economic planning . . . all of us would become mere

[27] *New York Times,* November 2, 1945, p. 9.
[28] F. M. Marx, "Bureaucracy," in Roy Peel and J. S. Roucek (eds.), *Introduction to Politics* (Thomas Y. Crowell Co., New York, 1946), p. 413.

puppets of a centralized bureaucracy."[29] But to Stuart Chase, ". . . the conception of economic planning is science supervising a people's housekeeping. Not its morals, not its play, not its loves or its living. Science is to be only a good cook, making sure we have enough to eat."[30] Even the National Association of Manufacturers might find it hard to survive in a world where "natural laws" have full play— in a survival of the fittest economy, where man had not interfered with, diverted, or controlled such "natural laws" as gravitation and the propagation of animal and plant life. An unplanned society is a chaotic society. Planning is but the application of reason to individual and social problems; it is an expression of man's rationality. An unregulated system of private enterprise would be unthinkable, and regulation that is not related to a plan of economic behavior is not government by law but by "catch as catch can." It is not planning per se but the abuse of planning that leads to the "creeping paralysis" of paternalism.

However, to the extent that the American people become dependent upon government subsidies and services, they lose their economic independence and they tend to become sharecroppers of the state, and so they are deprived of the most effective weapon of democracy—the power of criticism.

5. *Many criticisms of bureaucracy relate to the person of the bureaucrat.* (a) A bureaucrat is credited with possessing a keen appreciation of the disutility of labor, a characteristic acquired through forced idleness resulting from overstaffing. The much caricatured WPA worker is supposed to typify the federal service, a service harboring needless employees. This condition is represented as making for gross inefficiency and waste. (b) The bureaucracy is built on political patronage rather than on the merit system of recruitment. The so-called emergency agencies are especially open to nepotism and spoils. The bureaucrat is not an expert but a spoilsman; he is, in short, incompetent. This criticism, particularly in so far as it calls attention to the need for more bona fide experts in the government service, is too well founded to be ignored. A greater sense of professionalism, such as prevails in courts of law, would improve the administrative service materially.[31] (c) If the bureaucrat is not a

[29] Robert G. Whalen (compiler), "Planned Economy," *New York Times Magazine,* February 13, 1949, p. 16.

[30] *Ibid.*

[31] This criticism applies as well to bureaucracy in business. Robert A. Brady observes: "Above foreman ranks, the story is somewhat different. A line somewhat similar to that found in governmental circles between 'civil service' and 'political appointees' seems to run between the two lower levels of business staff on the one hand and the directorial and upper managerial ranks on the other. Here, as has

spoilsman he is an impractical academician, a "brain truster" engaged in theoretical planning at public expense. Baiting the college-trained men in the administrative service has been a chief indoor sport of "practical" politicians and businessmen for many years. College training is not a substitute for honesty, courage, or intelligence, but it implements these virtues, and it supplies the technical and scientific training required in many of the government services.

The Federal Welfare Government

The Federal Grants-in-Aid Program.[32]—Congress may lay and collect taxes to provide for the "general welfare of the United States."[33] The Constitution does not specifically authorize Congress to appropriate the moneys collected by taxes, but this power is necessarily implied. The "general welfare" is not limited to the enumerated powers of Congress, but embraces a large variety of matters which are not susceptible of specification or definition—matters which must lie within the discretion of Congress. It has been generally assumed that there are no known limitations on the spending power of Congress, save the general requirement that public moneys must be spent for a "public" not a "private" purpose, a distinction that seems to have little practical value.[34]

Since the foundation of the nation, sharp differences of opinion have persisted as to the true interpretation of the phrase [the "general welfare"]. Madison asserted it amounted to no more than a reference to the other powers enumerated in the subsequent clauses of the same section; that, as the United States is a government of limited and enumerated powers, the grant of power to tax and spend for the general national welfare must be confined to the enumerated legislative fields committed to the Congress. In this view the phrase is mere tautology,

---

been pointed out, the evidence seems to show that 'position,' 'pull,' 'family,' 'contacts,' 'family wealth,' 'nepotism,' 'sinecure,' 'indulgences,' and the like are becoming increasingly important." *Business As a System of Power* (Columbia University Press, New York, 1943), p. 302.

[32] For a survey of the federal grants-in-aid system see Paul Studenski and E. J. Baikie, "Federal Grants-in-Aid," 2 *National Tax Journal* (September, 1949), 193–214. For more comprehensive treatment see A. F. MacDonald, *Federal Aid* (Thomas Y. Crowell & Co., New York, 1928) ; V. O. Key, *Administration of Federal Grants to States* (Committee on Public Administration, Social Science Research Council, Chicago, 1937) ; H. J. Bittermann, *State and Federal Grants-in-Aid* (Report of the Committee on Grants-in-Aid, Council of State Governments 1949) ; Joint Committee on Reduction of Non-Essential Federal Expenditures, *Federal Subsidies and Federal Grants-in-Aid, S. Doc. No. 13,* 80th Cong., 1st Sess. (February, 1947).

[33] *Constitution,* Art. I, Sec. 8.

[34] *Cf.* Edward S. Corwin, "The Spending Power of Congress," 36 *Harvard Law Review* (March, 1923), 548 ff.

for taxation and appropriation are or may be necessary incidents of the exercise of any of the enumerated legislative powers. Hamilton, on the other hand, maintained the clause confers a power separate and distinct from those later enumerated, is not restricted in meaning by the grant of them, and Congress consequently has a substantive power to tax and to appropriate, limited only by the requirement that it shall be exercised to provide for the general welfare of the United States. Each contention has had the support of those whose views are entitled to weight. This court has noticed the question, but has never found it necessary to decide which is the true construction. Mr. Justice Story, in his Commentaries, espouses the Hamiltonian position. We shall not review the writings of public men and commentators or discuss the legislative practice. Study of all these leads us to conclude that the reading advocated by Mr. Justice Story is the correct one. While, therefore, the power to tax is not unlimited, its confines are set in the clause which confers it, and not in those of section 8 which bestow and define the legislative powers of the Congress. It results that the power of Congress to authorize expenditure of public moneys for public purposes is not limited by the direct grants of legislative power found in the Constitution.[35]

Yet difficulties are left when the power is conceded. The line must still be drawn between one welfare and another, between particular and general. Where this shall be placed cannot be known through a formula in advance of the event. There is a middle ground or certainly a penumbra in which discretion is at large. The discretion, however, is not confided to the courts. The discretion belongs to Congress, unless the choice is clearly wrong, a display of arbitrary power, not an exercise of judgment. This is now familiar law. . . . Nor is the concept of the general welfare static. Needs that were narrow or parochial a century ago may be interwoven in our day with the well-being of the nation. What is critical or urgent changes with the times.[36]

Since the earliest years of the Constitution, the Congress has aided individuals and business, directly and indirectly, through protective tariffs, land grants, and subsidies from the Treasury. The protective tariff system has diverted untold sums from the consumers to the manufacturers, on the theory that the general welfare is promoted when industry is encouraged and strengthened. Congress is vested with power to dispose of and make all needful rules and regulations with respect to the public lands.[37] This "power is subject to no limi-

[35] *United States v. Butler,* 297 U.S. 1, 65–66, 56 S. Ct. 312, 319, 80 L. Ed. 477 (1936).
[36] Mr. Justice Cardozo in *Helvering et al. v. Davis,* 301 U.S. 619, 640–41, 57 S. Ct. 904, 908–9, 81 L. Ed. 1307, 1315 (1937).
[37] *Constitution,* Art. IV, Sec. 3, par. 2.

tations." [38]   Land has been granted outright either to specified classes of persons such as adult citizens or heads of families, soldiers, or railway companies, or for specified purposes as in the case of swampland grants and school sites.   The purpose of the government has been twofold: "to develop the resources of the country; and to secure a class of small proprietors in the belief that such a class made a good economic basis for democratic government." [39]

Grants of public lands for educational purposes dates from colonial days and was provided for in the Ordinance of 1787.   Later Congress continued the policy by making substantial grants to the States. The Morrill Act of 1862 [40] was the first important milestone in the development of the federal aid system.   By this Act, States with public lands received grants equivalent to 30,000 acres for each Senator and Representative in Congress; States without public lands received the equivalent in land scrip.   Proceeds from the sale of these lands were to be invested and the interest used for educational purposes, on condition that the institutions receiving aid should include in their curricula instruction in military science.   The Hatch Act of 1887 [41] appropriated $15,000 annually to each State to establish an agricultural experiment station for research in connection with a land-grant college.   The Morrill Act of 1890 [42] authorized the Secretary of the Interior to withhold the allotment of funds provided by the Hatch Act from any State which did not fulfill the conditions of the grant.   This Act further provided funds to colleges for resident instruction in agriculture, mechanics arts, English, mathematics, and physical and natural and economic sciences with special reference to their application in the industries of life.   The Adams Act of 1906 [43] granted additional funds for research in agricultural industries; the Smith-Lever Act of 1914 [44] established a system of county agents and provided for agricultural extension work; and the Smith-Hughes

---

[38] *Gibson v. Chonteau,* 13 Wall. 92, 94, 20 L. Ed. 534, 536 (1871).

[39] Frank J. Goodnow, *Social Reform and the Constitution* (The Macmillan Co., New York, 1911), p. 316.

[40] Act of July 2, 1862, 12 *Stat.* 503, c. 130, 7 *U.S.C.A.* §§ 301–5, 307–8.

[41] Act of March 2, 1887, 24 *Stat.* 440, c. 314, 7 *U.S.C.A.* §§ 362, 363, 365, 368, 377–79. The grant was increased by various acts to $60,000 annually in 1940. 43 *Stat.* 970, c. 308, 7 *U.S.C.A.* § 370.

[42] Act of August 30, 1890, 26 *Stat.* 417, c. 841, 7 *U.S.C.A.* §§ 321–28.

[43] Act of March 16, 1906, 34 *Stat.* 63, c. 951, 7 *U.S.C.A.* §§ 369, 375.

[44] Act of May 8, 1914, 38 *Stat.* 372, c. 79, 7 *U.S.C.A.* §§ 341–48. This Act established the principle of matched funds, the principle upon which present grants-in-aid are modeled. The regulatory power of the Secretary of Agriculture over experimental colleges was increased by the Bankhead-Jones Act of 1935 (49 *Stat.* 436, 7 *U.S.C.A.* §§ 343d, 427) and the Cooperative Farm Forestry Act of May 18, 1937 (50 *Stat.* 188, c. 226, 16 *U.S.C.A.* § 568b).

Act of 1917 [45] provided funds for the teaching of trade and industrial subjects and home economics under the supervision of the Federal Bureau for Vocational Study. The power of Congress to make and enforce conditions in relation to grants of public lands was upheld by the Supreme Court,[46] thus opening the way for federal participation in certain State activities which, although nation-wide in effect, are reserved to the States by the Constitution.

Federal aid to highway construction has metamorphosed from a grant in the act admitting Ohio into the Union in 1802 of 5 per cent of the proceeds from the sale of public lands within its borders for the construction of public roads. A total of 3,250,000 acres of land were granted to the States to aid the construction of "wagon roads." [47] In 1893 Congress appropriated $10,000 to enable the Secretary of Agriculture to investigate methods of road construction throughout the United States and to prepare publications on the subject for use in agricultural colleges and experiment stations. The present road construction program had its beginning in the Post Office Appropriation Act of 1913 which provided $500,000 for the improvement of post roads. This was followed by the Federal Aid Road Act of 1916,[48] which laid the groundwork for subsequent road legislation. It required all States that wished to share in a $75 million appropriation to establish highway departments, match federal money, and accede to a rather detailed control. The Act was administered by the Department of Agriculture, as was the Federal Highway Act of 1921,[49] which required the Secretary of Agriculture and the State highway departments jointly to designate a system of interstate and intercounty roads as a federal highway system for future development. These acts were vaguely related to the program of agricultural experimentation, but were authorized under the constitutional grant of power "To establish . . . post roads." In addition several hundred million dollars have been appropriated for road improvement as part of a program for the emergency relief of unemployment.[50]

[45] Act of February 23, 1917, 39 *Stat.* 929, c. 114, 20 *U.S.C.A.* §§ 11–28.
[46] *Ervien v. United States,* 251 U.S. 41, 40 S. Ct. 75, 64 L. Ed. 128 (1919).
[47] B. H. Hibbard, "Land Grants," *The Encyclopedia of the Social Sciences* (The Macmillan Co., New York, 1933), Vol. IX, p. 35.
[48] Act of July 11, 1916, 39 *Stat.* 355, c. 241, 16 *U.S.C.A.* § 503, 23 *U.S.C.A.* § 48.
[49] Act of November 9, 1921, 42 *Stat.* 212, c. 119, 23 *U.S.C.A.* §§ 1–4, 6–25.
[50] In 1930, $80 million; $120 million in 1932. See *Public Roads Administration and Its Work* (Rev. September, 1939), Public Roads Administration Publication, p. 13. The National Industrial Recovery Act of 1933 (48 *Stat.* 195, c. 90) provided $400 million; the Hayden-Cartwright Act of June 8, 1938 (16 *U.S.C.A.* § 460b), $200 million; the Emergency Relief Appropriation Act of 1935 (49 *Stat.* 115, 15 *U.S.C.A.* § 728), $200 million.

These forms of federal aid were not "viewed with too much alarm." After all, the protective tariff system was as American as Henry Clay—or the International Harvester Trust. It protected American industries from competition with the "decadent" economy of the Old World. Tariff walls were the stout dikes that held back floods of cheap goods and cheap labor and so preserved the American standard of living. That is well-established American practice. Dating from 1796 the system is one of our most treasured institutional antiques—the perambulator of several generations of infant industries. As for the public lands—the national government could do no better than to return them to the States (or their citizens) from whence they derived. Whether the beneficiaries were railroads, schools, or homesteaders, all helped to populate and develop the new States. That, too, was as it should be. That, too, was not paternalism—just good nationalism. These activities of the government were promotional, not merely protective, to be sure, but they were not as yet related to the concept of the service state, with its big government and its bureaucracy. Big government did not become a matter of serious concern before the Recovery Program of Franklin D. Roosevelt's first administration projected the national government deeply into the affairs of the States and of citizens. With totalitarianism at large in the world, the growing activities of the government have taken on a sinister aspect to many Americans; they seem to spell concentration of power in a paternalistic national government which will cancel out the States as self-governing entities and the citizens as free moral agents.

It is the extension of the grants-in-aid program to the social field that has given the general welfare clause of the Constitution new if not lost horizons. In 1918 Congress passed the Soldiers Rehabilitation Act [51] providing for the vocational rehabilitation of disabled soldiers, sailors, and marines. In 1920 the Kenyon-Fess Act [52] extended rehabilitation aid to persons injured in industry or otherwise. This was followed by various acts continuing grants of funds to the States for vocational rehabilitation, and in 1935 this program was incorporated in the Social Security Act.[53] In order to receive funds under this Act, a State is required to cooperate with the Federal Board in the administration of the Act, match the funds received, and submit to federal supervision of its rehabilitation plan.

[51] Smith-Sears Bill, Act of June 27, 1918, 40 *Stat.* 617, c. 107. See J. A. Kratz, *Vocational Rehabilitation of the Physically Handicapped* (Vocational Education Bulletin No. 190, Education Office, U. S. Department of Interior).

[52] Act of June 2, 1920, 41 *Stat.* 735, c. 219, 29 *U.S.C.A.* §§ 31–44.

[53] Act of August 14, 1935, 49 *Stat.* 620, c. 531, 42 *U.S.C.A.* § 301 ff.

Through the Federal Board for Vocational Education [54] the national government aided the States in establishing vocational schools and classes and in giving instruction in agricultural trade, industrial, and commercial subjects. Again the federal funds were matched and spent by the States under fairly close federal supervision in respect to school equipment, courses of study, methods of instruction, and qualifications of teachers.

Through the Federal Public Health Service [55] Congress has liberally subsidized the State public health programs. In 1921 the Sheppard-Towner Act [56] granted aid for maternal and infant care. Participating States were required to match federal funds and provide an agency to cooperate with the Federal Children's Bureau [57] in the administration of the Act. Under the Venereal Disease Act of 1918 [58] and amendments, Congress has authorized expenditures ($12.5 million for the fiscal year 1943 alone) to assist States and their political subdivisions in the control of venereal disease. In general, the Public Health Service, under the Public Health Service Act [59] assists States, counties, health districts, and other political subdivisions of the State in establishing and maintaining public health services, subject to conditions and requirements prescribed by Congress.

The federal general welfare program is now largely concentrated in the Federal Security Agency.[60] Grouped in this Agency are those agencies of the national government whose primary function is to promote social and economic security, educational opportunity, and health, such as the Social Security Board, the Office of Education, the Public Health Service, and the Office of Vocational Rehabilitation. The grants-in-aid to the States, administered by the above agencies,

[54] This Board consisted of the Secretaries of Agriculture, Commerce, and Labor and U. S. Commissioner of Education and three citizen members. Act of February 23, 1917, 39 *Stat.* 929, c. 114, 20 *U.S.C.A.* §§ 11–28; Act of June 2, 1920, 41 *Stat.* 735, c. 219, 29 *U.S.C.A.* §§ 31–44; Act of June 8, 1936, 49 *Stat.* 1488, c. 541.

[55] The Public Health Service originated in an Act of Congress of July 16, 1798 (1 *Stat.* 605, c. 77), creating marine hospitals for the care of American merchant seamen. It is now a part of the Federal Security Agency.

[56] Act of November 23, 1921, 42 *Stat.* 224, c. 135, 42 *U.S.C.A.* §§ 161–74.

[57] Created by Act of April 9, 1912, 37 *Stat.* 79, 42 *U.S.C.A.* §§ 191–93. The Bureau was given general jurisdiction of federal laws relating to maternal and child welfare under the Social Security Act of 1935 (49 *Stat.* 620, 629, 42 *U.S.C.A.* §§ 701–31) and the Fair Labor Standards Act of 1938, relating to child labor (52 *Stat.* 1060, 29 *U.S.C.A.* §§ 201–19).

[58] Act of July 9, 1918, 40 *Stat.* 845, c. 143, 42 *U.S.C.A.* §§ 24, 28, 50 *U.S.C.A.* § 172.

[59] Act of July 1, 1944, 58 *Stat.* 682, 42 *U.S.C.A.* §§ 241–72.

[60] Created by President's Reorganization Plan I, April 25, 1939, in accordance with the Reorganization Act of 1939, 53 *Stat.* 561, 5 *U.S.C.A.* § 133.

make up a substantial part of the national budget.[61] These grants reached a peak of $2.9 billion in 1939, largely because of unemployment relief.[62] Since the national government must necessarily fix minimum standards for the State programs it helps to finance, it exercises a measure of control over State administration of the subsidized services.

Is this federal grant-in-aid program an insidious invasion of the reserved powers of the States? And will it weaken, if not eventually destroy, the federal system? The problem is not constitutional, but political and economic. Allegations that Congress invades the rights of the States when it makes *conditional* grants-in-aid, because the ulterior motive of Congress is to induce or bribe the States to yield a portion of their "sovereign" rights, have been held to present a political and not a justiciable issue. When the Maternity Act of 1921 was challenged because, among other objections, it "imposed upon the States an illegal and unconstitutional option either to yield to the federal government a part of their reserved rights or lose their share of the moneys appropriated," the Supreme Court observed:

> Probably it would be sufficient to point out that the powers of the state are not invaded, since the statute imposes no obligation but simply extends an option which the state is free to accept or reject. But we do not rest here. . . .
>
> In the last analysis, the complaint of the plaintiff state is brought to the naked contention that Congress has usurped the reserved powers of the several states by the mere enactment of the statute, though nothing has been done and nothing is to be done without their consent; and

[61]   FEDERAL AID TO STATE AND LOCAL GOVERNMENTS
(Amounts in millions of dollars)

	1947–48 (Actual)	1948–49 (Estimated)	1949–50 (Estimated)
Veterans services and benefits..................	85.0	29.5	13.6
Social welfare, health, and security.............	891.8	1,155.8	1,359.0
Housing and community facilities..............	53.9	25.5	13.3
Education and general research................	37.1	36.7	323.3
Agriculture and agricultural resources..........	64.1	61.9	62.9
Other natural resources (forest fire, private forestry cooperation, wild life restoration).......	11.5	20.8	18.4
Transportation and communication.............	333.6	470.1	517.7
Labor (unemployment compensation administration and public employment offices)...........	133.1	129.5	138.0
District of Columbia........................	12.0	12.0	12.0
Total grants-in-aid......................	1,622.1	1,941.8	2,458.2
Shared revenues.........................	16.0	21.3	21.8

Compiled from *United States Budget, 1949–1950*, pp. 1369–73, by Paul Studenski and E. J. Baikie in "Federal Grants-in-Aid," 2 *National Tax Journal* (September, 1949), 196.

[62] *New York Sun*, March 18, 1949, p. 6.

it is plain that that question, as it is thus presented, is political, and not judicial in character, and therefore is not a matter which admits of the exercise of the judicial power.[63]

The Court has also sustained, in all essential details, the Social Security Act of 1935. In *Steward Machine Co. v. Davis*,[64] the validity of the payroll tax imposed under Title IX of the Act was challenged on the ground, among others, that "its purpose was not revenue, but an unlawful invasion of the reserved powers of the states; and that the states in submitting to it have yielded to coercion and have abandoned governmental functions which they are not permitted to surrender."[65] It was contended that the proceeds from this tax, while not earmarked in any way, were *intended* to be applied to grants-in-aid to States for unemployment compensation under Title III. Therefore, the tax and the benefits were inseparable parts of a scheme to coerce the States in violation of the Tenth Amendment. But "The tax is not void," said Mr. Justice Cardozo for the Court, "as involving the coercion of the States in contravention of the Tenth Amendment or of restrictions implicit in our federal form of government."[66]

> The assailants of the statute say that its dominant end and aim is to drive the state Legislatures under the whip of economic pressure into the enactment of unemployment compensation laws at the bidding of the central government. . . .
>
> Who then is coerced through the operation of this statute? Not the taxpayer. He pays in fulfilment of the mandate of the local legislature. Not the state. Even now she does not offer a suggestion that in passing the unemployment law she was affected by duress. . . . to hold that motive or temptation is equivalent to coercion is to plunge the law in endless difficulties. The outcome of such a doctrine is the acceptance of a philosophical determinism by which choice becomes impossible.[67]

One of the questions in *Carmichael v. Southern Coal & Coke Co.*[68] was whether the Unemployment Compensation Act of Alabama was "invalid because its enactment was coerced by the action of the Federal Government in adopting the Social Security Act." Mr. Justice Stone, speaking for the majority of the Court, said:

[63] *Massachusetts v. Mellon* and *Frothingham v. Mellon,* 262 U.S. 447, 480, 483, 43 S. Ct. 597, 598, 599, 67 L. Ed. 1078, 1082, 1083 (1923).

[64] 301 U.S. 548, 57 S. Ct. 883, 81 L. Ed. 1279 (1937). Mr. Justice Sutherland, Mr. Justice Van Devanter, Mr. Justice McReynolds, and Mr. Justice Butler dissented.

[65] 301 U.S. at 578, 57 S. Ct. at 887, 81 L. Ed. at 1286.

[66] 301 U.S. at 585, 57 S. Ct. at 890, 81 L. Ed. at 1290.

[67] 301 U.S. at 587, 588, 590, 57 S. Ct. at 891, 892, 81 L. Ed. at 1292.

[68] 301 U.S. 495, 57 S. Ct. 868, 81 L. Ed. 1245 (1937).

As the Social Security Act is not coercive in its operation, the Unemployment Compensation Act cannot be set aside as an unconstitutional product of coercion. The United States and the State of Alabama are not alien governments. They coexist within the same territory. Unemployment within it is their common concern. Together the two statutes now before us embody a cooperative legislative effort by state and national governments for carrying out a public purpose common to both, which neither could fully achieve without the cooperation of the other. The Constitution does not prohibit such cooperation.[69]

The constitutional question aside, is the federal political system endangered by the increasing activities of the national government? There is no indication that the States are in process of liquidation. On the contrary, the increase in State expenditures in recent years indicates that the States are expanding rather than restricting their operations. This is due in part to the matching of federal grant-in-aid funds. Federal grants supplied around 1 per cent of State and local revenues in 1930, 5 per cent in 1940, about 15 per cent in 1948–49, and "In a few years, if the present trends prevail, they may supply 20 to 25 per cent of those revenues." [70] But the fact remains that the police power is an unplumbed reservoir of State power. State budgets in recent years have shown a marked increase, due to urgent demands of expanding educational needs, liberalized welfare programs, highway projects, and aid to local governments. On the other hand, federal power has expanded into areas either vacated or ineffectively covered by State legislation. Industry is largely nationalized, and so, largely removed from State control. And the unequal distribution of wealth among the States makes the burden of adequate public services greater than the poorer States can bear. Therefore, a considerable portion of the responsibility for social and regulatory legislation has been shifted to the national government, which accounts for much of the rapid growth in federal administration. As the Hoover Commission pointed out:

Our Government today is very different in structure and in operation from that envisioned by the founding fathers. From a number of small semi-autonomous agricultural States, we have become a highly industrialized far-flung nation. We have become a world power with interests and responsibilities throughout the globe.

As we have grown as a nation, so have we grown as independent States; and government today—all of our governments—is a large so-

[69] 301 U.S. at 526, 57 S. Ct. at 880, 81 L. Ed. at 1262. Mr. Justice McReynolds, Mr. Justice Sutherland, Mr. Justice Butler, and Mr. Justice Van Devanter dissented.
[70] Studenski and Baikie, "Federal Grants-in-Aid," *loc. cit.*, p. 197.

cial and economic mechanism designed to serve and operate for the welfare of the people.[71]

The grant-in-aid is a device for federal-State cooperation under the Constitution. It tends to raise and to equalize the quality of public services in the States by introducing national administrative standards and by financial support for the programs of the poorer States. But grant-in-aid programs should be coordinated, and related to the special requirements of the several States and to the national tax structure. Further, haphazard and injudicious use of grants may tempt States to commit themselves to continuing and accumulating expenditures which may overtax their economies. Overextended public assistance programs will put private enterprise in jeopardy. Private initiative does not thrive under the enervating weight of burdensome federal, State, and local budgets. The Hoover Commission concluded:

> The development of cooperative government, based largely upon grants-in-aid, has had a far-reaching effect upon the executive branch.
>
> It has enlarged the executive branch, requiring great expansion in many departments and the establishment of new administrative agencies.
>
> It has increased national taxes.
>
> And it has been responsible to some extent for the rapid development and extension of that fourth area of Government, known as the "regional area," serviced in large part by Federal regional offices.
>
> Whether measured in terms of organizational set-up, personnel, or expenditures, a very large part of the executive and administrative task of the Federal Government is concerned with problems, functions, and services involving Federal-State relations.[72]

Direct Federal Aid.—Conditional grants-in-aid to States as a means of relieving the unemployed, the needy aged, and dependent and crippled children is a roundabout way "to provide for the general welfare." The first child labor case [73] and the AAA case [74] attempted

[71] *Hoover Commission Report,* p. 491.

[72] *Ibid.,* p. 495. Note also the following, "On the one hand, the Federal grants bind the Federal Government and the states in a new type of relationship, never dreamed of by the founders of our constitutional system. The essence of this new relationship is intergovernmental cooperation—a concept which gives new meaning and strength to federalism and increases its adaptability to new conditions. On the other hand, the grants also introduce dictation by the Federal Government to the states—a condition heretofore absent from their relationship but now threatening the spirit of federalism and distorting it into a semi-centralism. These weaknesses in the Federal grant system must be corrected and the whole system thoroughly overhauled, if serious damage to the fabric of our government is to be avoided and maximum benefit from the grant system realized." Studenski and Baikie, *loc. cit.,* p. 193.

[73] *Hammer v. Dagenhart,* 247 U.S. 251, 38 S. Ct. 529, 62 L. Ed. 1101 (1918).

[74] *United States v. Butler,* 297 U.S. 1, 56 S. Ct. 312, 80 L. Ed. 477 (1936).

to establish the untenable doctrine that the Tenth Amendment limits Congress in the exercise of a granted power. In the first case a congressional regulation of the interstate transportation of goods from factories where children under fourteen years were employed was held invalid as an invasion of the reserved commerce power of the States. In the second case a similar limitation was imposed upon the taxing and spending powers of Congress. The net result of these two decisions was a ruling that the States alone have the constitutional power to do that which by the very nature of things they cannot and will not do. Both cases involved regulatory acts of Congress which acted directly upon parties within the States—they did not channel the federal power through the States.

The Act [75] held invalid in the AAA case levied a tax on processors of basic agricultural products and appropriated the proceeds derived from the tax "to be available to the Secretary of Agriculture for expansion of markets and removal of surplus agricultural products." [76] Whatever its wisdom, the Act was designed to save agriculture from pending ruin. It aimed to raise prices of agricultural commodities through a system of crop control. Only farmers who cooperated in the control program were to receive benefits. The "welfare" of agriculture as an industry was to be "provided for" by way of direct aid to individual farmers. The Court held that the tax and the appropriation were "interwoven strands in a scheme to coerce farmers to curb production," [77] and that the result was a regulation of crop production in violation of the Tenth Amendment. The regulation, said Mr. Justice Roberts for the majority of the Court, was not in fact voluntary, since the price of refusal to comply with the government's program was a loss of benefits, and "The power to confer or withhold unlimited benefits is the power to coerce and destroy." [78] But even if "the plan were one for purely voluntary co-operation, it would stand no better so far as federal power is concerned. At best, it is a scheme for purchasing with federal funds submission to federal regulation of a subject reserved to the States." [79]

[75] Agricultural Adjustment Act of May 12, 1933, 48 *Stat.* 31, c. 25, 7 *U.S.C.A.* §§ 601–59.

[76] 48 *Stat.* 38, § 12(b).

[77] Phraseology from T. R. Powell, "The Processing Tax and the Social Security Act," 5 *Brooklyn Law Review* (January, 1936), 129.

[78] 297 U.S. at 71, 56 S. Ct. at 321, 80 L. Ed. at 491.

[79] 297 U.S. at 72, 56 S. Ct. at 322, 80 L. Ed. at 491–92. Senator G. W. Norris, speaking in the United States Senate on February 12, 1936, said in regard to the decision in *United States v. Butler:* "Mr. President, if that decision shall stand a large portion of the laws which Congress has enacted during the past hundred years are absolutely unconstitutional. The law giving relief from the effects of the boll

Thus, while Congress could make *unconditional gifts* to farmers, it could not *"impose conditions reasonably adapted to the attainment of the end which alone would justify the expenditure."* [80] "This," said Mr. Justice Stone, "is a contradiction in terms." [81] Also, the majority doctrine is not consistent with the supremacy clause of the Constitution in that the spending power of Congress is subordinated to a reserved power of the States.

United States v. Butler has not been expressly overruled, but Congress, for all practical purposes, reenacted the invalidated act in the Agricultural Adjustment Act of 1938,[82] which *technically* met the objections to the earlier Act by omitting the processing tax and basing congressional authority on soil conservation and marketing control. Both acts had the same purpose and effect, crop reduction and parity of farm prices and income. The Act authorizes the Secretary of Agriculture to make acreage allotments for soil-depleting crops, such as cotton, corn, wheat, tobacco, and rice. The Secretary may use various measures to "encourage" cooperation by the farmer. He may make conditional grants to the States, thereby encouraging the States to undertake crop control as part of a national plan. Or he may make grants or payments to farmers on condition that they conform "with farming practices which the Secretary finds tend to effectuate any one or more of the purposes" of the Act.[83] Crop control through acreage allotments is enforced by means of marketing quotas. These quotas are approved by a two-thirds vote of farmers, making cooperation *voluntary,* and the quotas relate to produce *marketed,* not *grown.*

The Act was attacked in *Mulford v. Smith* [84] as "a statutory plan to control agricultural production and, therefore, beyond the powers delegated to Congress." But the Court held that the Act controls marketing, not production. Said Mr. Justice Roberts:

---

weevil, the law providing relief for grasshopper sufferers, the law providing relief for those injured by earthquake, by wind, by storm, by hurricane, by drought, by dust storm, are likewise, everyone of them, unconstitutional. Every provision in the laws creating and providing for the Bureau of Reclamation, upon which a large part of the West depends for its prosperity, is unconstitutional. In fact, there is nothing left of the Agricultural Department. It is all gone, all unconstitutional; and, by fair implication, a great many of the other activities of the Government, almost too numerous to mention, outside of the Agricultural Department, will have to fall."

[80] 297 U.S. at 85, 56 S. Ct. at 327–28, 80 L. Ed. at 498. Mr. Justice Stone dissenting, joined by Mr. Justice Brandeis and Mr. Justice Cardozo. Italics supplied.

[81] *Ibid.*

[82] Act of February 16, 1938, 52 *Stat.* 31, c. 30, 7 *U.S.C.A.* § 1281, 16 *U.S.C.A.* § 590o and p.

[83] *Ibid.,* 16 *U.S.C.A.* § 590h(d).

[84] 307 U.S. 38, 59 S. Ct. 648, 83 L. Ed. 1092 (1939).

The statute does not purport to control production. It sets no limit upon the acreage which may be planted or produced and imposes no penalty for the planting and producing of tobacco in excess of the marketing quota. It purports to be solely a regulation of interstate commerce, which it reaches and effects at the throat where tobacco enters the stream of commerce—the marketing warehouse. . . . Any rule, such as that embodied in the Act, which is intended to foster, protect and conserve that commerce, or to prevent the flow of commerce from working harm to the people of the nation, is within the competence of Congress. . . . The motive of Congress in exerting the power is irrelevant to the validity of the legislation.[85]

Farmers have drawn heavily upon the Federal Treasury not only through the Agricultural Adjustment Administration,[86] but also the Farm Credit Administration,[87] the Farmers Home Administration,[88] and the Federal Crop Insurance Corporation.[89] Veterans of the armed forces receive substantial assistance, through the Veterans' Administration,[90] for pensions, insurance, medical care, and education.[91] The legality and propriety of the latter expenditures have not been seriously questioned. Workers are aided not only by grants-in-aid

[85] 307 U.S. at 47, 48, 59 S. Ct. at 652, 83 L. Ed. at 1099, 1100. Mr. Justice Butler, dissenting, said: "Mere inspection of the statute and Secretary's regulations unmistakably disclose purpose to raise price by lessening production. Whatever may be its declared policy or appearance, the enactment operates to control quantity raised by each farmer. It is wholly fallacious to say that the penalty is not imposed upon production. The farmer raises tobacco only for sale. Punishment for selling is the exact equivalent of punishment for raising tobacco."

[86] Created pursuant to the Agricultural Adjustment Acts of May 12, 1933, 48 *Stat.* 31, 7 *U.S.C.A.* § 601, Act of February 16, 1938, 52 *Stat.* 31, 7 *U.S.C.A.* § 1281. Consolidated into Production and Marketing Administration, August 18, 1945.

[87] Authorized by Federal Farm Loan Act of July 17, 1916, as amended; the Cooperative Marketing Act of July 2, 1926; the Agricultural Marketing Act of June 15, 1929, and amendments; the Emergency Farm Mortgage Act of May 12, 1933; the Farm Credit Acts of June 16, 1933, June 3, 1935, and August 19, 1937; the Federal Farm Mortgage Corporation Act of January 31, 1934. Transferred to Department of Agriculture, April 25, 1939.

[88] Act of August 14, 1946, 60 *Stat.* 1064, 7 *U.S.C.A.* § 1014 ff.

[89] Act of February 16, 1938, 52 *Stat.* 72, 7 *U.S.C.A.* § 1501. Under the Homestead Act of 1862 and subsequent land acts, farmers, ranchers, and timbermen received over 200 million acres of public lands. Henry Steele Commager, "Appraisal of the Welfare State," *New York Times Magazine*, May 15, 1949, p. 10.

[90] Created by Executive Order 5393, July 21, 1930, under authorization of Congress of July 3, 1930, 46 *Stat.* 1016, 38 *U.S.C.A.* § 11.

[91] An estimated average of 235,000 persons each month received vocational rehabilitation training in the fiscal year 1948, at a cost of $287 million. For the same period an estimated average monthly number of 2.2 million persons were assisted under the general education program. This program cost more than $2.7 billion in the fiscal year 1949. The disability compensation and pension programs of the Veterans' Administration are currently costing around $2 billion each year. The Administration will spend an estimated $5.3 billion in the fiscal year 1950. The fed-

to States from the Unemployment Trust Fund, but Title II of the Social Security Act [92] also provides for a federal compulsory contributory old-age benefit system. This is wholly a federal project, administered entirely by the Social Security Board. Title VIII of the Act provides for "contributions" in the form of an "income tax" on employees and an "excise tax" on employers. These taxes are collected by the Bureau of Internal Revenue and the moneys are deposited in the Treasury along with other tax receipts. They are not earmarked in any way. Title II sets up an Old-Age Reserve Account under the custodianship of the Secretary of the Treasury, who is required to invest the moneys in the account in United States government obligations. It has been estimated that the reserve will reach about $32.8 billion by 1970,[93] which, since the funds are invested in government bonds, simply means that the government will owe this amount to the Old Age Reserve Account.[94]

In *Helvering v. Davis* [95] the Court considered the validity of the contributory old-age taxes. The challengers of the statute claimed that the taxes were levied for the payment of old-age benefits under Title II, and that Title II was void as an invasion of powers reserved to the States by the Tenth Amendment. But the Court held that the scheme of benefits created by the provisions of Title II is not forbidden by the Tenth Amendment. Mr. Justice Cardozo, speaking for the Court, said:

> Whether wisdom or unwisdom resides in the scheme of benefits set forth in Title II, is not for us to say. The answer to such inquiries must come from Congress, not the courts. Our concern here as often is with power, not with wisdom. Counsel for respondent has recalled to us the virtues of self-reliance and frugality. There is a possibility, he says, that aid from a paternal government may sap those sturdy virtues and breed a race of weaklings. If Massachusetts so believes and shapes her laws in that conviction, must her breed of sons be changed, he asks,

---

eral government gives varying degrees of medical care to around 24 million persons, of whom about 18.5 million are veterans, at a cost of nearly $2 billion in 1949. *Hoover Commission Report*, pp. 336, 337, 359, 370, 373.

Veterans of the Revolutionary War, the War of 1812, the Mexican War, and the Civil War received land grants of "fully 68,000,000 acres." Hibbard, "Land Grants," *loc. cit.*, p. 33.

[92] Act of August 14, 1935, 49 *Stat.* 620, c. 531, 42 *U.S.C.A.* c. 7 (Supp.).

[93] United States House of Representatives, Committee on Ways and Means, *The Social Security Bill, H.R. Rep. No. 615*, 74th Cong., 1st Sess. (1935), p. 6.

[94] "For the calendar year 1948, the collections of Old-Age and Survivors' Insurance approximated $1,688,000,000, and disbursements $550,000,000. The accumulated funds on August 31, 1948, were $10,388,000,000." *Hoover Commission Report*, p. 444.

[95] 301 U.S. 619, 57 S. Ct. 904, 81 L. Ed. 1307 (1937).

because some other philosophy of government finds favor in the halls of Congress? But the answer is not doubtful. One might ask with equal reason whether the system of protective tariffs is to be set aside at will in one state or another whenever local policy prefers the rule of laissez faire. The issue is a closed one. It was fought out long ago. When money is spent to promote the general welfare, the concept of welfare or the opposite is shaped by Congress, not the states. So the concept be not arbitrary, the locality must yield.[96]

The government has been no less generous to private industry. Protective tariffs have not only provided consumer subsidies for American manufacturers, but they have deprived the Treasury of vast sums of customs duties that would have been collected under a freer trade policy. Between 1850 and 1871 the railroads received, from federal and State governments, 167.8 million acres, or 262,238 square miles, as gifts from the public domain.[97] During this period Congress made eighty grants to the States to aid railroads, but in the 1860's the railroads received direct grants from Congress—four transcontinental railroads (the Union Pacific, the Northern Pacific, the Atlantic and Pacific, and the Texas and Pacific) received charters and large tracts along their rights of way from the national legislature.[98] As a result of the abuses growing out of this reckless policy, land grants for internal improvements were discontinued in 1871.

The federal government owns or is financially interested in about 100 business enterprises which are engaged directly or indirectly in lending money, guaranteeing loans and deposits, writing insurance, producing and selling electric power and fertilizer, operating railroads and ships, purchasing and selling farm commodities, and smelting and selling metals.[99] The government has more than $20 billion invested in these enterprises.[100] In addition it guarantees about $90 billion of deposits and mortgages, and it has written nearly $40 billion life insurance.[101] Forty different agencies are engaged in making loans to various private enterprises, involving investments of around $4.8 billion.

[96] 301 U.S. at 644, 645, 57 S. Ct. at 910, 81 L. Ed. at 1317. Mr. Justice McReynolds and Mr. Justice Butler dissented.

[97] Hibbard, "Land Grants," loc. cit., p. 35. According to Henry Steele Commager, "The Federal Government subsidized the construction of Western railroads to the tune of about 180 million acres of public land, while states added additional tens of millions." New York Times Magazine, May 15, 1949, p. 10.

[98] Hibbard, "Land Grants," loc. cit.

[99] Hoover Commission Report, p. 377.

[100] Ibid.

[101] Ibid.

According to a tabulation by the Budget Bureau, the United States government subsidized private business and farmers to the amount of more than $15.1 billion in the fifteen-year period 1934–48.[102] This includes $643 million for the food and cotton stamp plans of 1939–43 and the school-lunch program of 1936–40 and 1947–49. Not included are indirect or hidden subsidies that covered "crop insurance losses, low grazing fees on public lands, postal deficits, aids to aviation, flood control works, public power developments, housing developments, government loans to business, payments to veterans, and pensions." [103]

The preceding discussion presents an incomplete picture of the activities of the national government. It is intended only to explain in part, not to justify, the phenomenal growth of our administrative bureaucracy. It pictures the emergence of our federal welfare government from its laissez faire cocoon. The incubation process started with the projection of a program of internal improvements in the administration of John Quincy Adams. The Granger regulatory laws of the 1870's, Theodore Roosevelt's Square Deal, Woodrow Wilson's New Freedom, Franklin Roosevelt's New Deal, and Harry Truman's Fair Deal are stages of development. The national elections since 1932 would seem to indicate that the New Deal stage, with modifications, has been generally accepted by the electorate. The welfare government of our day has replaced, inevitably and irrevocably, the laissez faire government of our fathers. Will it, in turn, as inevitably lead to a completely managed economy, as feared by its critics? Paternalism, socialism, and totalitarianism are no longer mere bogies to frighten our people into an acceptance of the status quo. They are realities in a world of which the United States has become an integral part. Our only effective defense against alien ideologies is to make our democracy work. Our house must be put in order, integrated, and disciplined. Waste is democracy's greatest hazard. Incentive-destroying taxes resulting from democratically organized and overextended government, and the fearsome waste resulting from political and industrial strife may well liquidate private enterprise and force the democratic process into receivership and a managed society.

There is an undisciplined spirit abroad—an acquisitive, demanding spirit that neither measures the relativity of values nor reckons social costs. It might be well to remind ourselves that

[102] Peter Edson, *New York World-Telegram,* May 11, 1949, p. 37.
[103] *Ibid.*

Self-government is not a mere form of institutions, to be had when desired, if only proper pains be taken. It is a form of character. It follows upon the long discipline which gives a people self-possession, self-mastery, the habit of order and peace and common counsel, and a reverence for law which will not fail them when they themselves become the makers of law: the steadiness and self-esteem of political maturity. And these things cannot be had without long discipline.[104]

Big Government and Democracy.—Every law that has enlarged the dominion of the government has also added a new section to the administrative hierarchy. Under the stimulus of freedom our democracy has grown so big and so complex that many fear we shall lose that very freedom which made us great. To meet the challenge of big government to the traditional American way of life, we can do a number of things. We can modernize our government. We can make necessary and desirable adjustments in the constitutional pattern in respect to the distribution of governmental powers. The executive branch can be thoroughly overhauled, and every unnecessary agency dismantled. Government services can be subjected to acid tests of utility, and nonessential activities can be discontinued. This could reduce the national budget by several billions of dollars and materially help to fortify public confidence in the soundness of our economy.

But with all practical reductions in services and personnel, we are committed to big government, and today "the bulk of government is administration."[105] Consequently, problems of administrative procedure and control, the domain of administrative law, bulk large in the immediate future. The survival of democracy may well depend upon an orderly development of administrative law and tribunals to give effective direction to the administrative process. Executive justice must be coordinated with, not assimilated to, judicial justice. There seems to be no better way to reconcile necessary government and liberty. The problem that has plagued democracy since its birth, and whose solution has now become imperative, still is:

Must a government of necessity be too *strong* for the liberties of its own people, or too *weak* to maintain its own existence?[106]

---

[104] Woodrow Wilson, *Constitutional Government in the United States* (Columbia University Press, New York, 1911), p. 52.

[105] C. E. Merriam, *The New Democracy and the New Despotism* (McGraw-Hill Book Co., Inc., New York, 1939), p. 255.

[106] Abraham Lincoln, Message to Congress, July 4, 1861, in James D. Richardson (comp.), *Messages and Papers of the Presidents* (Bureau of National Literature and Art, Washington, D.C., 1910), Vol. V, p. 3224.

Chapter 2

THE PLACE OF ADMINISTRATION IN THE CONSTITUTIONAL TRICHOTOMY

The Constitutional Separation of Governmental Powers

The attempt, particularly by the judiciary, to adhere to a constitutional pattern distributing the powers of government amongst three independent and coequal departments has impeded the normal growth of administration and of administrative law in the United States.

Locke [1] and Montesquieu,[2] whose political ideas are imbedded in the framework of the American Constitution, conceived of the separability of both governmental departments and functions, but the two divisions did not coincide—they provided for departmental independence but did not require complete functional separation. The framers of the Constitution appear to have been more concerned with departmental than with functional separation, since their prime motive seems to have been to create a system of governmental checks rather than a system for the most effective division of labor.[3] A separation of powers was insurance against tyranny. Not only would such a separation place limited power in any one department, but it would also reduce all government to a minimum by creating a three-way counterirritant.

[1] John Locke, *Of Civil Government* ("Everyman's Library"; E. P. Dutton & Co., Inc., New York, 1924).

[2] Baron de Montesquieu, *The Spirit of the Laws,* trans. by Thomas Nugent (Hafner Publishing Co., New York, 1949). *Cf.* J. T. Brand, "Montesquieu and the Separation of Powers," 12 *Oregon Law Review* (April, 1933), 175–200.

[3] See James Madison, *The Debates in the Federal Convention of 1787* (International Edition, ed. by Gaillard Hunt and James B. Scott; Oxford University Press, New York, 1920); and later *The Federalist* (see Nos. 42, 43, 48, 51). The debates in the Constitutional Convention generally support the conclusion of Mr. Justice Brandeis, "The doctrine of the separation of powers was adopted by the Convention of 1787 not to promote efficiency, but to preclude the exercise of arbitrary power. . . ." *Myers v. United States,* 272 U.S. 52, 293, 47 S. Ct. 21, 85, 71 L. Ed. 160, 242 (1926). But see the lengthy majority and minority opinions by Mr. Chief Justice Taft and Mr. Justice McReynolds, respectively, in *Myers v. United States* relying on the same early sources and reaching opposed conclusions.

33

James Madison voiced the prevailing distrust of government when he said in *The Federalist:*

> The accumulation of all powers, legislative, executive, and judiciary, in the same hands, whether of one, a few, or many, and whether heredi-tary, self-appointed, or elective, may justly be pronounced the very defi-nition of tyranny.[4]

James Wilson, one of the strongest supporters of departmental in-dependence, said:

> The separation of the departments does not require that they should have separate objects but that they should act separately tho' on the same objects. It is necessary that the two branches of the Legislature should be separate and distinct, yet they are both to act precisely on the same object.[5]

No ideological or scientific separation could have been contem-plated, since the English pattern had evolved from traditions that were the product of opportunism rather than of a deliberate plan, and it made no differentiation beyond a "specialization of functions." More likely the framers of our Constitution accepted the current English and colonial departmental distribution of powers, rather than the definition of the lexicographers, when they employed the terms legislative, executive, and judicial. The departmental separa-tion was intended to serve two main purposes: (1) to prevent hasty or immoderate action contrary to the doctrines of natural law, and (2) to give all social groups their proper places and influence in government.[6] Separation of powers under State constitutions during the Revolution was heavily weighted in favor of the legislature, and the government created by the Articles of Confederation was a single legislative body. These State legislatures used their powers freely and in a manner that threatened vested interests in property and commerce. The delegates to the Constitutional Convention (and many of the delegates to State ratifying conventions) were men of

---

[4] *The Federalist* (Modern Library, Inc., New York, 1941), No. 47, p. 313.

[5] James Madison, *The Debates in the Federal Convention of 1787,* p. 299.

[6] John Adams, the most prolific of early American writers on the separation of powers (see his *Defense of the Constitution of the United States*), held that every state must have: (1) a first magistracy, representing the monarchial class or ele-ment, (2) a senate or little council, representing the aristocratic class, and (3) a larger assembly, representing the democratic element. The judicial function was not represented in his classification, but later he regarded the judiciary as an important check upon the "larger assembly," the House of Representatives. See Charles E. Merriam, *A History of American Political Theories* (The Macmillan Co., New York, 1903), pp. 139–40; Raymond G. Gettell, *History of Political Thought* (Cen-tury Co., New York, 1924), p. 331.

property who insisted upon the separation of powers in the national government as a safeguard against contemporary legislative tyranny and the "follies of democracy."

But judicial construction has attempted to identify departmental and functional separation through the corollary doctrine that delegated power cannot be redelegated: *delegata potestas non potest delegari.*

> It is believed to be one of the chief merits of the American system of written constitutional law [said Mr. Justice Miller] that all the powers entrusted to government, whether state or national, are divided into three grand departments, the executive, the legislative, and the judicial. That the functions appropriate to each of these branches of government shall be vested in a separate body of public servants, and that the perfection of the system requires that the lines which separate and divide these departments shall be broadly and clearly defined. It is also essential to the successful working of this system that the persons entrusted with power in any one of these branches shall not be permitted to encroach upon the powers confided to the others, but that each shall by the law of its creation be limited to the exercise of the powers appropriate to its own department and no other.[7]

According to the doctrine of the nondelegation of powers, a precise distinction among legislative, executive, and judicial functions and powers is the basis for decisions in "cases or controversies" which may limit materially public authority in the interest of private rights. The authority of an executive or administrative officer to act under a given statute may well depend upon a judicial finding that he is not exercising "delegated" legislative or judicial power. The merits of the statute or of the administrative action may have no bearing on the judicial decision. As, therefore, administrative law deals with *proper* administrative action, that is, action authorized by statute *and by the Constitution,* it is necessary to examine the nature of administration and its relation to the legislative, executive, and judicial powers.

The Constitution recognizes, without defining or distinguishing, "legislative powers," "executive power," and "judicial power," but it neglects to mention *administration.* It refers to "the executive departments," "officers of the United States," "civil officers of the

[7] *Kilbourn v. Thompson,* 103 U.S. 168, 190, 26 L. Ed. 377, 387 (1891). See also *Field v. Clark,* 143 U.S. 649, 12 S. Ct. 495, 36 L. Ed. 294 (1892); *United States v. Grimaud,* 220 U.S. 506, 31 S. Ct. 480, 55 L. Ed. 563 (1911); *J. W. Hampton, Jr. & Co. v. United States,* 276 U.S. 394, 48 S. Ct. 348, 72 L. Ed. 624 (1928); P. W. Duff and H. E. Whiteside, "Delegata Potestas non Potest Delegari," 14 *Cornell Law Quarterly* (1929), 168, 195–96.

United States," and "executive and judicial officers"; but it does not mention any *administrative* office or officer. The clear implication is that administration was assimilated to one or more of the three departments. There was surprisingly little discussion of this matter by the fathers of the Constitution, but Hamilton definitely associated administration with the executive department [8] where, functionally, it belongs. Furthermore, the President is *de facto* director of national administration by virtue of the constitutional duty to see that the laws are faithfully executed, and by grace of Congress when organizing administrative departments and agencies. So while the legislative power creates, the executive power supervises and directs administrative agencies.[9]

It is possible to define "broadly" if not "clearly" the "lines which separate" the three departments of government, but it is not possible to distinguish the executive and administrative functions or to separate administration from any department. The men who designed the Constitution did not trouble to define the powers they had "separated." It almost seems that they evaded the issue, for the recorded discussion of the subject adds more mystification than clarification. Even Mr. Chief Justice Marshall, as late as 1825, did not offer a better explanation than the following:

> The difference between the departments undoubtedly is, that the legislature makes, the executive executes, and the judiciary construes the law; but the maker of the law may commit something to the discretion of the other departments, and the precise boundary of this power is a subject of delicate and difficulty inquiry, into which a court will not enter unnecessarily.[10]

Such generalizations served well enough perhaps so long as governments confined their activities to the traditional protective func-

---

[8] Alexander Hamilton said: "The administration of government, in its largest sense, comprehends all the operations of the body politic, whether legislative, executive, or judiciary; but in its most usual, and perhaps in its most precise signification, it is limited to executive details, and falls peculiarly within the province of the executive department. The actual conduct of foreign negotiations, the preparatory plans of finance, the application and disbursement of the public moneys . . . the arrangement of the army and navy . . . these, and other matters of a like nature, constitute what seems to be most properly understood by the administration of government." *The Federalist,* No. 71, p. 469.

On the other hand, W. F. Willoughby asserts that a "distinction between the executive and administrative powers is, in fact, clearly made in our federal constitution itself." *The Government of Modern States* (Rev. ed.; D. Appleton-Century Co., New York, 1936), p. 220.

[9] The Budget and Accounting Act of 1921, 42 *Stat.* 20, 31 *U.S.C.A.* § 11, in large measure made the President the "working head" of the administration.

[10] *Wayman v. Southard,* 10 Wheat. 1, 46, 6 L. Ed. 253, 263 (1825).

tions, but the growth of administration following upon the industrial expansion of the latter half of the nineteenth century led to more restrictive judicial definitions of political power and ultimately brought the judiciary into open conflict with the other departments of government. In extending its regulatory powers to business, the Congress created administrative agencies with broad powers of rule-making and adjudication. The judiciary, mindful of its conservative traditions and of its role as protector of the rights of property, under-took to insulate business against the operation of this regulatory legislation by invoking the doctrine of the separation of powers to preclude Congress from delegating *legislative* or *judicial* powers to administrative agencies. Thus the judiciary put it squarely up to the courts to define legislative and judicial power whenever an admin-istrative action is challenged in a private law litigation charging un-constitutional delegation of power.

Constitutionally, a distinction may be drawn here between "power" and "function." The former relates to the ambit of departmental authority, which is a mixture of functions; the latter is included in the former and refers to the undefined grants of "the legislative power," "the executive power," and "the judicial power of the United States" found in the opening sentences of Articles I, II, and III—it relates to a *type* rather than to a *grant* of power. An uncon-stitutional delegation of power may involve, therefore, either a rela-tively simple construction of an enumerated power or it may call for a functional definition of "legislative," "executive," or "judicial."

In defining these functions, the utterances of lawyers and laymen alike are hopelessly at odds, particularly in State jurisdictions.[11] The confusion extends to disagreement whether there are three or more or less functions of government. Léon Duguit held that as sover-eignty is not divisible there could be only *one* governmental power. Of the tripartite division he said:

> That conception of a sovereign power, one in three powers, is a metaphysical conception analogous to the Christian mystery of the Trinity . . . which is inadmissible in a truly positive construction of public law.[12]

[11] See John Dickinson, *Administrative Justice and the Supremacy of Law* (Har-vard University Press, Cambridge, 1927), pp. 4–5; Frank J. Goodnow, *The Prin-ciples of the Administrative Law of the United States* (G. P. Putnam's Sons, New York, 1905), pp. 31–42; Thomas R. Powell, "Separation of Powers: Administrative Exercise of Legislative and Judicial Power," 27 *Political Science Quarterly* (1912), 215–38.

[12] *Manual de Droit Constitutionel* (1907), p. 331, quoted by John A. Fairlie, "The Separation of Powers," 21 *Michigan Law Review* (1927), 393, 420.

Locke and Montesquieu provided for three departments, but their functional classification of powers into legislative, executive, and federative ("the executive in respect to things dependent on the law of nations") is essentially a dual one. The judicial and administrative functions were included in the executive.[13] Likewise, Thomas Paine held that the judiciary was part of the executive, and that there were but *two* functions of government, namely the creation and the execution of the law.[14] Frank J. Goodnow divided governmental powers into *politics* and *administration*.

> Politics has to do with policies or expressions of the state will. Administration has to do with the execution of these policies.[15]

Furthermore,

> It is impossible to assign each of these functions to a separate authority, not merely because the exercise of governmental power cannot be clearly apportioned, but also because, as political systems develop, these two primary functions of government tend to be differentiated into minor and secondary functions. The discharge of each of these minor functions is entrusted to somewhat separate and independent governmental organs.[16]

Herman Finer makes a similar classification:

> . . . we see that to a complete act of government two things are necessary: to resolve and to execute; that is, to determine that certain things shall be done and then to cause people to do them.[17]

This appears to be the view also of modern French writers in administrative law—they deny the inherent separation of the judicial from the executive powers.[18] Then there is the classical tripartite classification of both functions and departments, and a number of writers have discovered five or more governmental functions through the analysis of modern governments.[19] W. F. Willoughby insists

[13] Locke, *op. cit.,* pp. 190–92; Montesquieu, *op. cit.,* Bk. XI, chap. vi, p. 151.

[14] Gettell, *op. cit.,* p. 298.

[15] Goodnow, *op. cit.,* p. 6.

[16] Frank J. Goodnow, *Politics and Administration* (The Macmillan Co., New York, 1900), p. 16.

[17] *The Theory and Practice of Modern Government* (Henry Holt & Co., New York, 1949), p. 109.

[18] *Cf.* R. K. Gooch, "Modern French Views in the Separation of Powers," 38 *Political Science Quarterly* (1923), 578 ff.

[19] For the views of Woolsey, Sidgwick, Dealey, and Gettell, see Fairlie, "The Separation of Powers," *loc. cit.,* pp. 393–436.

upon a fivefold division—executive, legislative, judicial, administrative, and electoral.[20]

It should be remarked that there is no necessary relation between the classifications of governmental functions and departments and that our difficulties result largely from a forced marriage of these classifications under immutable constitutional provisions. A realistic distribution of powers among governmental departments should recognize not only functional differences, but social requirements and official capacities, too; it should, in short, be governed by political expediency rather than constitutional mandate. A practical rather than a legalistic basis for the separation of powers was recognized by Mr. Chief Justice Taft when he said:

> In determining what it [Congress] may do in seeking assistance from another branch, the extent and character of that assistance must be fixed according to common sense and the inherent necessities of the governmental co-ordination.[21]

When we search the record for definitions of terms, the confusion thickens. Mr. Justice Holmes distinguished the legislative and judicial functions as follows :

> A judicial inquiry investigates, declares, and enforces liabilities as they stand on present or past facts and under laws supposed already to exist. That is its purpose and end. Legislation, on the other hand, looks to the future, and changes existing conditions by making a new rule, to be applied thereafter to all or some part of those subject to its power.[22]

According to William Bondy, an act is "legislative in nature"

> . . . which in effect establishes a rule of civil conduct irrespective of the manner in which, or the body by which, it is enacted, . . .

[20] *Op. cit.,* p. 217. Kenneth C. Davis observes that "The label logic of separation-of-powers classification is too often specious. Why should a particular function of some agency be legislative or judicial? Why not recognize that the categories are largely survivals of governmental processes having little in common with the administrative process, and that a modern function may be somewhat judicial and somewhat legislative but neither wholly one nor wholly the other?" "The Requirement of Opportunity to be Heard in the Administrative Process," 51 *Yale Law Journal* (1942), 1093, 1113–14. See also K. C. Davis, "Separation of Functions in Administrative Agencies," 61 *Harvard Law Review* (1948), 390, 612.

[21] *J. W. Hampton, Jr. and Co. v. United States,* 276 U.S. 394, 406, 48 S. Ct. 348, 351, 72 L. Ed. 624, 629 (1928).

[22] *Prentis v. Atlantic Coast Line,* 211 U.S. 210, 226, 29 S. Ct. 67, 69, 53 L. Ed. 150, 158 (1908). Said Mr. Justice Field: "The distinction between a judicial and a legislative act is well defined. The one determines what the law is, and what the rights of parties are, with reference to transactions already had; the other prescribes what the law shall be in future cases arising under it." *Central Pacific R. v. Gallatin* (Sinking Fund Cases), 99 U.S. 700, 761, 25 L. Ed. 496, 516 (1879).

Any act which tends, no matter how indirectly, to the enforcement of a law, or the enforcement of a superior command, is executive in its nature. . . .

Power to hear and to determine, or power to ascertain facts and to apply the law to the facts when ascertained, is judicial in its nature.[23]

Frederick Green makes the following distinctions:

Legislation is the creation by the state of a right (including an authority, a privilege, or an immunity), duty, or status not dependent on the existence of a previous right, duty, or status.

Adjudication is the imposition of a specific duty *in personam,* or of a liability, or the granting of a right or status which is dependent on a previous right, or duty, in that it is imposed by way of giving effect to a right or duty determined to exist or to have existed, or by way of redress or punishment for its violation.

Administration probably cannot be so clearly defined. It consists in a management of public affairs and includes all state action not part of a process of legislation or adjudication which affects rights or involves the use of adverse force. It cannot be closely defined, because, . . . it may slightly overlap the legislative field . . . and . . . the judicial field.[24]

These definitions are rationalizations of the prevailing separation of powers and fail to make sharp distinctions in kind. Obviously, Bondy's definition of "executive" power includes the "judicial" power, and Green's characterization of "administration" embraces the "executive" and partakes of the legislative and judicial powers. And Holmes' definition of legislative and judicial functions describes rather well the mixed duties and powers of an administrative agency.

The distinctions drawn between legislation and adjudication are fairly realistic. Legislation determines rights and duties *in futuro* while adjudication determines rights and duties under existing rules of law; the former shapes public policy, the latter aids in the execution of that policy; the one is creative, the other is declaratory. But the executive power defies definition in terms of a functional separation of powers, and certainly no satisfactory distinction between executive and administrative functions, offices, or officers has been or can be made in theory or in practice. W. F. Willoughby asserts that

[23] *The Separation of Governmental Powers* (Columbia University Press, New York, 1896), pp. 70–71.
[24] "Separation of Governmental Powers," 29 *Yale Law Journal* (1920), 369, 373–74.

Due largely to the unfortunate use of the words "executive" and "administrative" as almost interchangeable terms, the chief executives of our governments are very generally regarded by the public as being the custodians of administrative authority. In this the public is wholly in error. In most, if not all political systems, and especially in those of our own country, *a clear distinction is made between executive power and administrative power.* The executive power, or rather function, is that of representing the government as a whole and of seeing that all of its laws are properly complied with by its several parts. The administrative function is that of actually administering the law as declared by the legislative, and interpreted by the judicial, branch of the government. This distinction is usually made by declaring the executive function to be essentially political in character; that is, one involving the exercise of judgment in its use; and the administrative function to be one concerned with the putting into effect of policies and the carrying out of orders as determined or given by other organs.[25]

But this is oversimplification. The executive power is "political" but so is the legislative power.[26] And the implication that the executive power is discretionary and administration ministerial would vest most of the executive power in administrative agencies. All the constitutional powers of the President are discretionary. Are they, therefore, executive and political? The ordinance, veto, and treaty-making powers are legislative. The pardoning power and the power to review judgments of courts martial are judicial and, therefore, not political. To add further to the prevailing confusion, W. W. Willoughby holds that the functions of the chief executive are "of two kinds—political and administrative." [27] This view is shared, evidently, by James Hart who concludes that the executive power consists of two distinct classes of powers: "(1) certain political powers of a discretionary nature . . . ; (2) the executive function in the general sense of administration of the laws, . . . which . . . is relative to the laws and involves only such discretion as is expressed or implied in the laws themselves." [28]

The early American theory of the executive function was that of aiding the legislature in the execution of the laws; that is, it was

[25] *Principles of Public Administration* (Johns Hopkins Press, Baltimore, 1927), pp. 10–11. Italics supplied.

[26] "The judicial power is vested in one supreme court, and in such inferior courts as Congress may ordain and establish: the political power of the government, in the other two departments." *Georgia v. Stanton,* 6 Wall. 50, 71, 18 L. Ed. 721, 723 (1868).

[27] *The Constitutional Law of the United States* (Baker, Voorhis & Co., Inc., New York, 1929), Vol. III, p. 1479.

[28] "The Bearing of Myers v. United States upon the Independence of Federal Administrative Tribunals," 23 *American Political Science Review* (1929), 657, 666.

administrative. The Constitutional Convention established an independent executive department with enlarged powers, but the injunction that the President "shall take care that the laws be faithfully executed" was intended to make him (and inevitably made him) the head of the national administration. In *Williams v. United States* the Court said:

> The President's duty in general requires his superintendence of the administration; yet this duty cannot require of him to become the administrative officer of every department and bureau, or to perform in person the numerous details incident to services which, nevertheless, he is, in the correct sense, by the Constitution and laws required and expected to perform. This cannot be, 1st, Because, if it were practicable, it would be to absorb the duties and responsibilities of the various departments of the government in the personal action of the one chief executive officer. It cannot be, for the strongest reason, that it is impracticable—nay, impossible.[29]

So closely are the executive powers identified with the national administration that the President does not only "superintend," but he acts largely through subordinate officers, and such delegation of powers does not violate the constitutional separation of powers for the obvious reason that *the national administration is the executive department*. Consequently, in *Runkle v. United States* it was said:

> There can be no doubt that the President, in the exercise of his executive powers under the Constitution, may act through the head of the appropriate executive department. The heads of the departments are his authorized assistants in the performance of his executive duties, and their official acts, promulgated in the regular course of business, are presumptively his acts. That has many times been decided by the court. Here, however, the action required of the President [to review proceedings of courts martial under the war powers] is *judicial in its character,* not *administrative*.[30]

Here "executive" and "administrative" are interchangeable terms—the "executive powers" which the President may delegate to the "head of the appropriate executive department" are "administrative" as distinguished from "judicial" functions which may not be delegated. This is common practice in legal literature—the "executive departments" are also the "administrative departments," and the heads of

[29] 1 How. 290, 296, 11 L. Ed. 135, 138 (1843).
[30] 122 U.S. 543, 557, 7 S. Ct. 1141, 1146–47, 30 L. Ed. 1167, 1171 (1887). Italics supplied. See also *United States v. Eliason,* 16 Pet. 291, 10 L. Ed. 968 (1842); *Jones v. United States,* 137 U.S. 202, 11 S. Ct. 80, 34 L. Ed. 691 (1890). Since the acts of the heads of departments are regarded as the acts of the President, an appeal does not lie, generally, from the former to the latter.

the departments are at once "executive" and "administrative" chiefs. The effort made, therefore, by the Supreme Court in *Humphrey's Executor v. United States* [31] to distinguish between executive and administrative offices is as superficial as it is sterile. Said Mr. Justice Sutherland for the Court:

> A postmaster is an executive officer restricted to the performance of executive functions . . . such an officer is merely one of the units in the executive department and, hence, inherently subject to the exclusive and illimitable power of removal by the Chief Executive. . . .

But a Federal Trade Commissioner is a member of

> . . . an administrative body created by Congress to carry into effect legislative policies embodied in the statute in accordance with the legislative standard therein prescribed, and to perform other specified duties as a legislative or as a judicial aid. Such a body cannot in any proper sense be characterized as an arm or as an eye of the executive. Its duties are performed without executive leave and, in the contemplation of the statute, must be free from executive control. . . . To the extent that it exercises any executive function—as distinguished from executive power in the constitutional sense—it does so in the discharge and effectuation of its quasi-judicial and quasi-legislative powers, or as an agency of the legislative or judicial departments of the government. [32]

So, in order to circumvent the judicial theory of constitutional limitations under the doctrine of the separation of powers, it becomes necessary to distinguish "executive function" from "executive power in the constitutional sense," and to employ the "weasel" terms "quasi-judicial" and "quasi-legislative."

> Such labour'd nothings, in so strange a style,
> Amaze the unlearn'd, and make the learned smile. [33]

Was the Post Office Department *not* "created by Congress to carry into effect legislative policies embodied in the statute"? The Departments of State and Defense are especially close to the President since they are his agents in carrying on our foreign relations and in executing the military powers; but since Congress shares these powers with the President, these departments are also "arms" of the legislature carrying out legislative policy. The other executive departments, however, are essentially legislative aids—they are engaged in carrying out important legislative programs. The Department of Agricul-

---

[31] 295 U.S. 602, 55 S. Ct. 869, 79 L. Ed. 1611 (1935).

[32] 295 U.S. at 627, 628, 55 S. Ct. at 874, 79 L. Ed. at 1690.

[33] Alexander Pope, *Essays on Criticism* (The University Press, Cambridge, 1917), Pt. II, p. 126.

ture, for instance, is definitely carrying out more important legislative policies than is the Federal Trade Commission. As to the independent agencies, such as the Federal Trade Commission, are they "administrative" simply because Congress has not included them among the executive departments? And would they become "executive" if Congress should elect to convert them into "offices" in the executive departments?

The Supreme Court has held that the fixing of "reasonable prices" by the Bituminous Coal Commission and the fixing of "reasonable rates" by the Interstate Commerce Commission (under the Interstate Commerce Act) and by the Secretary of Agriculture (under the Packers and Stockyards Act) "cannot be differentiated legally." [34] But under the doctrine of the Humphrey's case the acts of the commissions would be *administrative* and that of the Secretary, *executive*.

Furthermore, what "common ground of any substance" exists between such administrative (as distinguished from executive) agencies as "the Works Progress Administration and the Federal Trade Commission, the National Youth Administration and the Interstate Commerce Commission, the Bituminous Coal Commission and the Civilian Conservation Corps?" [35] Are they "administrative" only because they "must be free from executive control," despite the constitutional mandate that the President shall "take care that the laws be faithfully executed"?

The doctrine of the separation of powers requires that "the executive power" shall be independent of legislative control (although not necessarily of judicial control, as will appear later). Therefore, it is necessary to separate administrative from executive functions in order to give Congress the desired jurisdiction over the former. If "the divine right of powers to be separated" must be respected, it would be more consistent with the facts to limit the separation to the powers specifically enumerated in the Constitution than to attempt departmental separation along strict functional lines, and to admit that modern government requires extensive delegations of legislative and judicial powers to administrative agencies. The Constitution gives Congress the power to create executive or administrative agencies. The power to create implies the power to prescribe their duties, powers, and tenure and this is in no proper sense an invasion of the President's "executive" power. The division of labor argu-

---

[34] *Sunshine Anthracite Coal Co. v. Adkins,* 310 U.S. 381, 398, 60 S. Ct. 907, 914, 84 L. Ed. 1263, 1273 (1940).

[35] James M. Landis, *The Administrative Process* (Yale University Press, New Haven, 1938), p. 22.

ment is the justification for departmental separation, but the insistence upon functional separation of powers often results in confusion and stalemate in government. Delegation of power is by judicial leave, camouflaged by a *quasi*. As to the factual situation, Judge Rosenberry has said:

> At an early time it was recognized that in practice a complete separation of powers was not possible, and it soon became apparent that no satisfactory definition of executive, legislative, or judicial power could be made. While jurists have a fairly clear conception of what was meant by these terms, and while they can be defined for some purposes, all attempts to make a comprehensive, all-inclusive, accurate definition have failed. As a matter of fact, the powers have never in actual practice been scientifically or completely separated. They are overlapping, and of necessity must be so. An executive officer must, in the performance of his statutory duties, construe and apply the law. When courts reach out and by means of a receiver operate a great system of railways, they are discharging administrative and executive duties which have historically found their way into the judicial department. Most constitutions reserve to legislatures in express terms the right to exercise certain kinds of judicial power.[36]

Administrative officers are the agents of any one or of all of the three departments of government; they have such delegated powers as the departments cannot exercise intelligently or effectively. Administration cuts across the separation of powers and bridges the departmental division; it is "the art and science of management applied to the affairs of the state." [37]

The Doctrine of Nondelegation of Power—Quasi-Power— Legislative Standards

The Constitution of the United States does not contain a distributing clause. But Article I vests "all legislative powers" in "a Congress of the United States"; Article II grants "the executive power" to "a President of the United States"; and Article III confers "the judicial power of the United States" upon "one Supreme Court" and "such inferior courts as the Congress may from time to time ordain and establish." This vesting of separate powers in separate departments was held early to be exclusive so that neither department might exer-

[36] Marvin B. Rosenberry (then Acting Chief Justice, Supreme Court of Wisconsin), "Administrative Law and the Constitution," 23 *American Political Science Review* (1929), 33.

[37] L. E. White, "Public Administration," *Encyclopedia of the Social Sciences* (The Macmillan Co., New York, 1930), Vol. I, p. 440.

cise the proper functions of the other.[38]　To this doctrine of the separation of powers has been assimilated as a corollary the well-known maxim *delegata potestas non potest delegari.*[39]　Mr. Chief Justice Taft stated the doctrine of "the divine right of powers to be separated" [40] as follows:

> The Federal Constitution and State Constitutions of this country divide the governmental power into three branches. The first is the legislative, the second is the executive, and the third is the judicial, and the rule is that in the actual administration of the government Congress or the Legislature should exercise the legislative power, the President or the State executive, the Governor, the executive power, and the Courts or the judiciary the judicial power and in carrying out that constitutional division into three branches it is a breach of the National fundamental law if Congress gives up its legislative power and transfers it to the President, or to the Judicial branch, or if by law it attempts to invest itself or its members with either executive power or judicial power.[41]

[38] *Wayman v. Southard,* 10 Wheat. 1, 42, 6 L. Ed. 253, 262 (1825). See also William Bondy, *The Separation of Governmental Powers* (Columbia University Studies in History, Economics, and Public Law, Vol. V; Columbia University Press, New York, 1896). Felix Frankfurter and James M. Landis, "Power of Congress Over Procedure in Criminal Contempts in 'Inferior' Federal Courts: a Study in Separation of Powers," 37 *Harvard Law Review* (1924), 1010 ff.

[39] ". . . This maxim, which originated with the glossators, was introduced into English law through the misreading of Bracton, developed there as a doctrine of agency, was established by Coke in English public law in decisions forbidding the delegation of judicial power and found its way into the writings of English and American publicists in the guise of a fundamental principle of free government." Eleanor Bontecou, "Delegation of Powers," *Encyclopedia of the Social Sciences* (The Macmillan Co., New York, 1930–35), Vol. V, p. 66. "Far from being a principle of constitutional law, it seems that the maxim has little, if any, application to the distribution of the work of government by the legislature. There is no mention of it in any American Constitution, nor any remote reference to it. The whole doctrine, insofar as it is asserted to be a principle of constitutional law, is built upon the thinnest of implication, or is the product of the unwritten constitution." P. W. Duff and H. E. Whiteside, "Delegata Potestas non Potest Delegari," 14 *Cornell Law Quarterly* (1929), 168, 195–96. See also, C. T. Carr, *Delegated Legislation* (The University Press, Cambridge, 1921); J. P. Comer, *Legislative Functions of National Administrative Authority* (Columbia University Press, New York, 1927).

[40] ". . . until Montesquieu misread the English system in that most famous chapter of his *Esprit des Lois* (Book XI, chap. vi) the divine right of powers to be separated had hardly been asserted." William A. Robson, *Justice and Administrative Law* (The Macmillan Co., London, 1928), pp. 17–18.

[41] *J. W. Hampton, Jr. & Co. v. United States,* 276 U.S. 394, 406, 48 S. Ct. 348, 351, 72 L. Ed. 624, 629 (1928).

"It is believed to be one of the chief merits of the American system of written constitutional law, that all the powers intrusted to government, whether state or national, are divided into three grand departments, the executive, the legislative, and the judicial. That the functions appropriate to each of these branches of government shall be vested in a separate body of public servants, and that the perfection of the system requires that the lines which separate and divide these

In an earlier case the Chief Justice pointed out:

> Complete independence and separation between the three branches, however, are not attained, or intended, as other provisions of the Constitution and the normal operation of government under it easily demonstrate. By affirmative action through the veto power, the Executive and one more than one-third of either House may defeat all legislation. One-half of the House and two-thirds of the Senate may impeach and remove the members of the Judiciary. The Executive can reprieve or pardon all offenses after their commission, either before trial, during trial, or after trial, by individuals, or by classes, conditionally or absolutely, and this without modification or regulation by Congress. . . . Negatively, one House of Congress can withhold all appropriations and stop the operation of Government. The Senate can hold up all appointments, confirmation of which either the Constitution or a statute requires, and thus deprive the President of the necessary agents with which he is to take care that the laws be faithfully executed.[42]

The verbal constitutional exceptions to the doctrine of the separation of powers, however, has not proved adequate, and it has become

---

departments shall be broadly and clearly defined. It is also essential to the successful working of this system that the persons intrusted with power in any one of these branches shall not be permitted to encroach upon the powers confided to the others, but that each shall by the law of its creation be limited to the exercise of the powers appropriate to its own department and no other. To these general propositions there are in the Constitution of the United States some important exceptions. One of these is, that the President is so far made a part of the legislative power, that his assent is required to the enactment of all statutes and resolutions of Congress.

"This, however, is so only to a limited extent, for a bill may become a law notwithstanding the refusal of the President to approve it, by a vote of two thirds in each house of the Legislature.

"So also, the Senate is made a partaker in the functions of appointing officers and making treaties, which are supposed to be properly executive, by requiring its consent to the appointment of such officers and the ratification of treaties. The Senate also exercises the judicial power of trying impeachments, and the House of preferring articles of impeachment.

"In the main, however, that instrument . . . has blocked out with singular precision, and in bold lines, in its three primary articles, the allotment of power to the executive, the legislative, and the judicial departments of the government. It also remains true, as a general rule, that the powers confided by the Constitution to one of these departments cannot be exercised by another." Mr. Justice Miller in *Kilbourn v. Thompson*, 103 U.S. 168, 190–91, 26 L. Ed. 377, 387 (1880).

"It may be stated then, as a rule inherent in the American constitutional system, that, unless otherwise expressly provided or incidental to the powers conferred, the legislature cannot exercise either executive or judicial power; the executive cannot exercise either legislative or judicial power. . . ." *Springer v. Philippine Islands*, 277 U.S. 189, 201–2, 48 S. Ct. 480, 482, 72 L. Ed. 845, 849 (1928).

See also, *Field v. Clark*, 143 U.S. 649, 12 S. Ct. 495, 36 L. Ed. 294 (1892); *United States v. Grimaud*, 220 U.S. 506, 31 S. Ct. 480, 55 L. Ed. 563 (1911).

[42] *Ex parte Grossman*, 267 U.S. 87, 119–20, 45 S. Ct. 332, 336–37, 69 L. Ed. 527, 535 (1925).

imperative to ease the rule against the delegations of power. The complex problems of modern legislation and administration have led to the creation of a large number of boards and commissions to which have been delegated both legislative and judicial functions. But the judiciary could not recognize this delegation of power as such without abandoning the Latin maxim; so they cast about for a new formula which would permit the legislatures to disregard the prohibition against the delegation of power whenever the courts should deem it desirable and necessary. Such a device is found in the rule that legislative, executive, or judicial power may be delegated only when "softened by a quasi." [43]

Thus, "If Congress shall lay down by legislative act an intelligible principle to which the person or body authorized to fix such rates is directed to conform, such legislative action is not a forbidden delegation of legislative power." [44] And "Congress may declare its will, and after fixing a *primary* standard, devolve upon administrative officers the 'power to fill up the details' by prescribing administrative rules and regulations." [45] That is ". . . the legislature must declare the *policy of the law* and fix the *legal principles* which are to control in given cases; but an administrative body may be invested with the power to ascertain the facts and conditions to which the policy and principles apply." [46] If the statute fixes a "primary standard" or "intelligible principle" or "appropriate standards" [47] the power delegated is *quasi-legislative* and the delegation is constitutional.

This may be just another way of saying that Congress may delegate legislative power when "necessary and proper" to carry into effect a delegated power, inasmuch as a delegation is generally sustained by the Court when otherwise a power vested in Congress

---

[43] Mr. Justice Holmes, dissenting, *Springer v. Philippine Islands,* 277 U.S. 189, 210, 48 S. Ct. 480, 485, 72 L. Ed. 845, 853 (1928); *Plymouth Coal Co. v. Pennsylvania,* 232 U.S. 531, 544, 34 S. Ct. 359, 362, 58 L. Ed. 713, 719 (1914).

[44] *J. W. Hampton, Jr. & Co. v. United States,* 276 U.S. 394, 409, 48 S. Ct. 348, 352, 72 L. Ed. 624, 630 (1928).

[45] *United States v. Shreveport Grain Co.,* 287 U.S. 77, 85, 53 S. Ct. 42, 44, 77 L. Ed. 175, 179 (1932). Italics supplied. "The legislature cannot delegate its power to make a law; but it can make a law to delegate a power to determine some fact or state of things upon which the law makes, or intends to make, its own action depend." Quoted from *Locke's Appeal,* 72 Penn. St. 498 (1873) with approval in *Field v. Clark,* 143 U.S. 649, 694, 12 S. Ct. 495, 505, 36 L. Ed. 294, 310 (1892).

[46] *Mutual Film Corp. v. Industrial Commission,* 236 U.S. 230, 245, 35 S. Ct. 387, 392, 59 L. Ed. 552, 560 (1915). Italics supplied.

[47] "Exercising its rate-making authority, the legislature has a broad discretion. It may exercise that authority directly, or through the agency it creates or appoints to act for that purpose in accordance with *appropriate standards.*" *St. Joseph Stock Yards Co. v. United States,* 298 U.S. 38, 50, 56 S. Ct. 720, 725, 80 L. Ed. 1033, 1040–41 (1936). Italics supplied.

"could not be efficaciously exerted." [48] Furthermore, Congress does not divest itself of power so delegated—the power is subject to recall at the pleasure of Congress.[49]

But whether a statute contains an "appropriate" *standard* is for a court to decide. An examination of the statutes and of the cases makes it rather too obvious that any or no standard is adequate when a court chooses to sustain the law. A few examples will suffice to demonstrate how innocuous are these so-called legislative standards. The Tariff Act of 1890 [50] authorized the President to suspend by proclamation the provision of the Act relating to the free introduction of certain products from foreign states which imposed duties upon products of the United States which the President "may deem to be reciprocally unequal and unreasonable." The Act was held to fix an adequate legislative standard.[51] The Tariff Act of 1922 [52] empowered the President to increase or decrease duties up to 50 per cent of those fixed by the statute, upon ascertaining that the latter duties did not equalize the cost of production in the United States and competing countries. In ascertaining such costs the President should consider "in so far as he finds it practicable" certain enumerated matters and "any other advantages or disadvantages in competition"; and he should secure, although he was not required to follow, the advisory assistance of the Tariff Commission. The Supreme Court found herein an "intelligible standard." [53] It should be noted that the President, after finding the necessary facts, was not required to act thereon. A similar discretion conferred upon the President by the National Industrial Recovery Act was found to be fatally defective in *Panama Refining Co. v. Ryan.*[54]

[48] *Buttfield v. Stranahan*, 192 U.S. 470, 496, 24 S. Ct. 349, 355, 48 L. Ed. 525, 526 (1904).

[49] *Clark Distilling Co. v. West Maryland Railroad*, 242 U.S. 311, 326, 37 S. Ct. 180, 185, 61 L. Ed. 326, 338 (1917).

[50] Act of October 1, 1890, 26 *Stat.* 567, 612, c. 1244, § 3.

[51] *Field v. Clark*, 143 U.S. 649, 12 S. Ct. 495, 36 L. Ed. 294 (1892). Mr. Chief Justice Fuller and Mr. Justice Lamar held in part: "This certainly extends to the executive the exercise of those discretionary powers which the Constitution has vested in the law-making department. It unquestionably vests in the President the power to regulate our commerce with all foreign nations which produce sugar, tea, coffee, molasses, hides, or any other such articles; . . ." 143 U.S. at 699, 12 S. Ct. at 507, 36 L. Ed. at 312.

[52] Act of September 21, 1922, 42 *Stat.* 858, 941, c. 356, Tit. III, 315.

[53] *J. W. Hampton, Jr. & Co. v. United States*, 276 U.S. 394, 48 S. Ct. 348, 72 L. Ed. 624 (1928).

[54] 293 U.S. 388, 55 S. Ct. 241, 79 L. Ed. 446 (1935). Sec. 9(c) of the National Industrial Recovery Act, 48 *Stat.* 195, 200, 15 *U.S.C.A.* § 709(c), authorized the President to prohibit the transportation in interstate commerce of any petroleum produced in excess of State quotas. The Court held that the Act gave the President

Under the Emergency Price Control Act of 1942 [55] the Administrator was authorized to fix commodity prices and rents during the wartime emergency. The prices and rents should be "fair and equitable" and should "effectuate the purposes" of the Act. Regulations conforming to these legislative "standards" were held valid—they did not involve an unconstitutional delegation of the legislative power of Congress.[56] "It is enough," said the Court, "to satisfy the statutory requirements that the Administrator finds that the prices fixed will tend to achieve that standard and will conform to those standards, and that the courts in an appropriate proceeding can see that substantial basis for these findings is not wanting." [57] Mr. Justice Roberts, dissenting, concluded that the "supposed standards for the Administrator's guidance" were illusory and that the "Act sets no limits upon the discretion or judgment of the Administrator." [58] A comparison he said, of the "standards" in the National Recovery Act,

. . . with those of the present Act and perusal of what was said concerning them in *A. L. A. Schechter Poultry Corp. v. United States,* . . . leaves no doubt that the decision is now overruled. There, as here, the "code" or regulation, to become effective, had to be found by the Executive to "tend to effectuate the policy" of the Act.[59]

A statute which authorized the President to prohibit the export of war supplies whenever he "determines it is necessary and in the interest of national defense" [60] was held to provide an "adequate standard" so as not to amount to an improper delegation of legislative power.[61] Under the Renegotiation Act [62] the Secretary of War, or the War Contracts Adjustment Board, was empowered to deter-

---

unqualified discretion to prohibit or not to prohibit transportation of "hot oil" in interstate commerce—it did "not state whether or in what circumstances or under what conditions the President is to prohibit the transportation" of hot oil. The Tariff Act of 1922 states the circumstances under which the President may raise or lower rates, but this is of no legal significance so long as the President's findings are conclusive and when he is free to ignore his own findings. Furthermore, prior to the Panama Refining Company case the Court had not required the President to make *any findings.*

[55] 56 *Stat.* 24, 50 *U.S.C.A.* (App.) § 901 *et sqq.*

[56] *Yakus v. United States,* 321 U.S. 414, 64 S. Ct. 660, 88 L. Ed. 834 (1944); *Carter v. Bowles,* 56 F. Supp. 278 (D.C.W.D.S.C., 1944); *Bowles v. Willingham,* 321 U.S. 503, 64 S. Ct. 641, 88 L. Ed. 892 (1944).

[57] *Yakus v. United States,* 321 U.S. 414, 423, 64 S. Ct. 660, 667, 88 L. Ed. 834, 848.

[58] 321 U.S. at 449, 451, 64 S. Ct. at 679, 680, 88 L. Ed. at 862, 863.

[59] 321 U.S. at 452, 64 S. Ct. at 680, 88 L. Ed. at 863.

[60] 54 *Stat.* 714 (1940), 50 *U.S.C.A.* (App.) § 701; 61 *Stat.* 133 (1947), 50 *U.S.C.A.* (App.) § 1191.

[61] *United States v. Rosenberg,* 150 F. (2d) 788 (C.C.A. 2d, 1945).

[62] Act of April 28, 1942, 56 *Stat.* 226, 245, 246, c. 247; Act of October 21, 1942, 56 *Stat.* 798, 982–85, c. 619; Act of July 1, 1943, 57 *Stat.* 347, 348, c. 185; Act of

mine "excessive profits" in connection with the renegotiation of government war contracts. This authority was challenged as an "unconstitutional exercise of legislative power by an administrative official instead of a mere exercise of administrative discretion under valid legislative authority." [63] The Supreme Court held that the statutory term "excessive profits" prescribed "an intelligible principle" and did not constitute an unconstitutional delegation of legislative power. The legislative "standard" can be stated in broad and general terms.

> It is not necessary that Congress supply administrative officials with a specific formula for their guidance in a field where flexibility and the adaptation of the congressional policy to infinitely variable conditions constitute the essence of the program. . . . Standards prescribed by Congress are to be read in the light of the conditions to which they are to be applied.[64]

The Housing and Rent Act of 1947 [65] authorized the Housing and Rent Expediter to remove rent controls in any defense rental area if *in his judgment* the need therefor no longer existed by reason of new construction or satisfaction of demand in other ways. This broad grant of discretionary power was upheld by the Supreme Court.[66]

Several of the laws considered above involved the effective use of the war power. It appears that the Court may permit a broader delegation of legislative power in "time of crisis," particularly a war emergency, than at other times. Said Mr. Justice Burton:

> In time of crisis nothing could be more tragic and less expressive of the intent of the people than so to construe their Constitution that by its own terms it would substantially hinder rather than help them in defending their national safety.[67]

July 14, 1943, 57 *Stat.* 564, 565, c. 239; Act of February 25, 1944, 58 *Stat.* 21, 78–93, c. 63; Act of June 30, 1945, 59 *Stat.* 294, 295, c. 210.

[63] *Lichter v. United States,* 334 U.S. 742, 68 S. Ct. 1294, 92 L. Ed. 1694 (1948). Also, *Spaulding v. Douglas Aircraft Co.,* 154 F. (2d) 419 (C.C.A. 9th, 1946).

[64] *Lichter v. United States,* 334 U.S. at 785, 68 S. Ct. at 1316, 92 L. Ed. at 1726.

[65] Act of July 1, 1947, 61 *Stat.* 196, 50 *U.S.C.A.* (App.) § 1891 *et sqq.*

[66] *Woods v. Cloyd W. Miller Co.,* 333 U.S. 138, 68 S. Ct. 421, 92 L. Ed. 596 (1948).

[67] *Lichter v. United States,* 334 U.S. at 780, 68 S. Ct. at 1314, 92 L. Ed. at 1723. Mr. Justice Frankfurter on another occasion said: "The validity of action under the war power must be judged wholly in the context of war. That action is not to be stigmatized as lawless because like action in time of peace would be lawless." *Korematsu v. United States,* 323 U.S. 214, 224, 65 S. Ct. 193, 198, 89 L. Ed. 194, 203 (1944).

But are there degrees of crises? Is a war emergency of a higher order than an economic emergency, even if the latter may threaten to destroy the nation's economy? Is this evaluation of emergencies a justiciable issue? The following judicial comment would seem to reject the "crisis" argument. Mr. Chief Justice Hughes, speaking for a unanimous Court in the Schechter case said:

> Extraordinary conditions may call for extraordinary remedies. But the argument necessarily stops short of an attempt to justify action which lies outside the sphere of constitutional authority. *Extraordinary conditions do not create or enlarge constitutional power.*[68]

And in 1948, Mr. Justice Douglas said:

> The question of the constitutionality of action taken by Congress does not depend on recitals of the power which it undertakes to exercise.[69]

In *Varney v. Warehime* [70] a federal court specifically ruled:

> In the exercise of its war powers, the Congress must observe the prohibition against the delegation of legislative power to executive officers. In this respect, the Congress has no greater wartime power than it has peacetime power.[71]

The Federal Narcotic Drug Act [72] provides that possession of narcotic drugs shall be deemed sufficient evidence for conviction of violating the Act unless the defendant explains such possession to the "satisfaction of the jury." This was held not to delegate legislative power unlawfully even though the jury is free to accept or reject an explanation of a defendant for *any* or *no* reason.[73] Section 11(b)(2) of the Public Utility Holding Company Act of 1935 directed the Securities and Exchange Commission to see that the corporate structures of any company did not "unduly or unnecessarily complicate the structure" or "unfairly or inequitably distribute voting power among security holders." In *American Power & Light Co. v. Securi-*

---

[68] *A. L. A. Schechter Poultry Corp. v. United States,* 295 U.S. 495, 528, 55 S. Ct. 837, 842, 79 L. Ed. 1570, 1579 (1935). Italics supplied.

[69] *Woods v. Cloyd W. Miller Co.,* 333 U.S. at 144, 68 S. Ct. at 424, 92 L. Ed. at 602.

[70] 147 F. (2d) 238 (C.C.A. 6th, 1945).

[71] 147 F. (2d) at 244. Note also that ". . . even the war power does not remove constitutional limitations safeguarding essential liberties." *Home Building & Loan Association v. Blaisdell,* 290 U.S. 398, 426, 54 S. Ct. 231, 235, 78 L. Ed. 413, 422 (1933).

[72] Act of June 7, 1924, 43 *Stat.* 657 (1924), 21 *U.S.C.A.* § 174.

[73] *Gonzales v. United States,* 162 F. (2d) 870 (C.C.A. 9th, 1947).

ties and Exchange Commission [74] it was urged that Section 11 was an unconstitutional delegation of legislative power in that the quoted phrases were undefined, meaningless in themselves, and did not connote any historically defined concepts. But Mr. Justice Murphy, speaking for the Court, said that the challenged phrases "cannot be said to be utterly without meaning, especially to those familiar with corporate realities," and further:

> These standards are certainly no less definite in nature than those speaking in other contexts in terms of "public interest," "just and reasonable rates," "unfair methods of competition" or "relevant factors." The approval which this Court has given in the past to those standards thus compels the sanctioning of the ones in issue. . . .
> *The judicial approval accorded these "broad" standards for administrative action is a reflection of the necessities of modern legislation dealing with complex economic and social problems.* [75]

The Interstate Commerce Commission and State railroad and public service commissions have the essentially legislative function of prescribing just and reasonable maximum and minimum rates and charges for railroads and other utilities as well as just, fair, and reasonable classifications, regulations, and practices to be observed *in futuro.* [76] The Supreme Court has held repeatedly that "the function of rate-making is *purely legislative* in its character, *and this is true, whether it is exercised directly by the legislature itself or by some subordinate or administrative body, to whom the power of fixing rates in detail has been delegated. The completed act derives its authority from the legislature and must be regarded as an exercise of the legislative power."* [77] Speaking specifically of the powers of the Interstate Commerce Commission, the Court has said:

[74] 329 U.S. 90, 67 S. Ct. 133, 91 L. Ed. 103 (1946).

[75] 329 U.S. at 104, 105, 67 S. Ct. at 142, 91 L. Ed. at 115, 116. Italics supplied.

[76] Sec. 152, Interstate Commerce Act, as amended provides: "(2) In the exercise of its power to prescribe *just* and *reasonable* rates the Commission shall initiate, modify, establish or adjust such rates so that carriers as a whole . . . will, *under honest, efficient and economical management and reasonable expenditures* for maintenance of way, structures and equipment, earn an aggregate annual net railway operating income equal, as nearly as may be, to a *fair return* upon the aggregate value of the railway property of such carriers and held for and used in the service of transportation." Italics supplied. 41 *Stat.* 488, c. 91.

[77] *Knoxville v. Knoxville Water Co.,* 212 U.S. 1, 8, 29 S. Ct. 148, 150, 53 L. Ed. 371, 378 (1909). Italics supplied. See also the following: *"The rate-making power is a legislative power* and necessarily implies a range of legislative discretion. We do not sit as a board of revision to substitute our judgment for that of the legislature, or of the commission lawfully constituted by it. . . ." *Simpson v. Shepard,* 230 U.S. 352, 433, 33 S. Ct. 729, 754, 57 L. Ed. 1511, 1555 (1913). Italics supplied.

". . . prescribing rates for the future is an act legislative, and not judicial, in kind. . . . It pertains, broadly speaking, to the legislative power. The legislature

When . . . the Commission declares a specific rate to be the reasonable and lawful rate for the future, it speaks as the legislature, and its pronouncement has the force of a statute. . . . in declaring a maximum rate the Commission is exercising a delegated power legislative in character. . . . The action of the Commission in fixing such rates for the future is subject to the same tests as to its validity as would be an act of Congress intended to accomplish the same purpose. . . . when it prescribed a maximum reasonable rate for the future, it was performing a legislative function. . . . *Congress . . . in effect, vests in the Commission the power to legislate in specific cases as to the future conduct of the carrier.*[78]

And in another instance :

The problem of fixing reasonable prices for bituminous coal cannot be differentiated legally from the task of fixing rates under the Interstate Commerce Act (41 *Stat.* 484, 49 U.S.C.A. § 15) and the Packers and Stockyards Act (42 *Stat.* 166, 7 U.S.C.A. § 211). The latter provide the standard of "just and reasonable" to guide the administrative body in the rate-making process. The validity of that standard . . . the appropriateness of the criterion of the "public interest" in various contexts . . . the legality of the standard of "unreasonable obstruction" to navigation . . . all make it clear that there is a valid delegation of authority in this case. . . . Delegation by Congress has long been recognized as necessary in order that the exertion of legislative power does not become a futility. . . . But the effectiveness of both the legislative and administrative processes would become endangered if Congress were under the constitutional compulsion of filling in the details beyond the liberal prescription here. Then the burdens of minutiae would be apt to clog the administration of the law and deprive the agency of that flexibility and dispatch which are its salient virtues.[79]

---

may act directly, or . . . it may commit the authority to fix rates to a subordinate body. . . . it was final as a legislative act within the Commission's authority. . . . *The order of the Railroad Commission in fixing rates was a legislative act, under its delegated power.* It had 'the same force as if made by the legislature.' " *Louisville & Nashville R. R. v. Garrett,* 231 U.S. 298, 305, 308, 318, 34 S. Ct. 48, 51, 52, 56, 58 L. Ed. 229, 239, 240, 244 (1913). Italics supplied.

"The order . . . in effect prescribed maximum rates for the service. It was, therefore, a legislative order ; and under the Fourteenth Amendment plaintiff was entitled to an opportunity for a review in the courts of its contention that the rates were not compensatory." *Oklahoma Operating Co. v. Love,* 252 U.S. 331, 335, 40 S. Ct. 338, 339–40, 64 L. Ed. 596, 598 (1920).

[78] *Arizona Grocery Co. v. Atchison, Topeka & Santa Fe Ry.,* 384 U.S. 370, 386, 387, 388, 389, 390, 52 S. Ct. 183, 185, 186, 76 L. Ed. 348, 354, 355, 356 (1932). Italics supplied.

[79] Mr. Justice Douglas in *Sunshine Anthracite Coal Co. v. Adkins,* 310 U.S. 381, 398, 60 S. Ct. 907, 914, 915, 84 L. Ed. 1263, 1273–74 (1940).

Why, then, has there not been an unlawful delegation of legislative power to these regulatory commissions? Because the words of the Court do not always mean what they seem to mean. What they *presumably* mean is: inasmuch as legislative power cannot be delegated, the rate-making power of commissions is not strictly legislative but *quasi-legislative,* because the statutes under which they operate declare *adequate legislative standards* which direct and control the discretion of the commissioners, who really are administrative officers.[80] What they *actually* mean is: a legislature may delegate some legislative functions; the extent of such delegation is to be determined by the courts in accordance with an unpredictable rule requiring a legislative standard; and the Supreme Court, the final arbiter, will use a sound discretion in discovering an adequate legislative standard, to the end that legislative power may be delegated only when necessary and proper to carry into effect some legislative purpose which meets with the approval of the Court.

The Supreme Court summarizes, in effect, the above cases in the following manner:

> What is done by the Tariff Commission and the President in changing the tariff rates to conform to new conditions is in *substance* a delegation, *though a permissible one,* of the legislative process. . . . the kind of hearing assured by the statute to those affected by the change is a hearing of the same order as had been given by congressional committees when the legislative process was in the hands of Congress and no one else. . . . Much is made by the petitioner of the procedure of the Interstate Commerce Commission when regulating the conduct or

---

[80] In *Plymouth Coal Co. v. Pennsylvania,* 232 U.S. 531, 544, 34 S. Ct. 359, 362, 58 L. Ed. 713, 719 (1914), the determination by a State mine inspector, together with the engineers of adjoining mine owners, of the thickness of the coal barrier between the mines, was held to be "quasi-legislative." In the *Intermountain Rate Cases,* 234 U.S. 476, 490, 34 S. Ct. 986, 993, 58 L. Ed. 1408, 1424 (1914), the rate-making function of the Interstate Commerce Commission is referred to as "administrative." In *United States v. Grimaud,* 220 U.S. 506, 518, 521, 31 S. Ct. 480, 483, 484, 55 L. Ed. 563, 568, 569 (1911), the powers of the Secretary of Agriculture in the administration of the National Forest Reserves was held to be administrative: "In making these regulations the officers did not legislate. They did not go outside of the circle of that which the act itself had affirmatively required to be done, or treated as unlawful if done. . . . But the authority to make administrative rules is not a delegation of legislative power, nor are such rules raised from an administrative to a legislative character because the violation thereof is punished as a public offense." In *Reagan v. Farmers' Loan and Trust Co., No. 1,* 154 U.S. 362, 397, 399, 400, 14 S. Ct. 1047, 1054, 1055, 38 L. Ed. 1014, 1023, 1024 (1894), the Court held that a State railroad commission performs "mere administrative work" and spoke of the "merely administrative duty of framing a tariff of rates for carriage," but such a tariff is an "act of quasi legislation." See also, *Buttfield v. Stranahan,* 192 U.S. 470, 24 S. Ct. 349, 48 L. Ed. 525 (1904).

the charges of interstate carriers, and that of the Public Service Commissions of the states when regulating the conduct or the charges of public service corporations. . . . There is indeed this common bond that *all alike are instruments in a governmental process which according to the accepted classification is legislative,* not judicial.[81]

The purpose of a legislative standard in a statute is to control the discretion of the executive or administrative agent or agency charged with the administration of the law. But such accepted standards as, "if, in its [board of health] opinion, it is necessary for the public health or safety," [82] "an unreasonable obstruction to the free navigation of such waters," [83] "reasonable variations," [84] "undue or unreasonable restraint of trade," [85] and "just and reasonable rates" and "fair return," [86] the "public interest, convenience or necessity," [87] "generally fair and equitable" rents,[88] are far too indefinite to have other than a moral effect upon the administrative agencies concerned —they cannot control, in any legal sense, the discretion of such agencies. The *real* purpose of the Supreme Court in requiring a legislative standard, then, is not to place intelligible limits upon administrative discretion, but to supply that Court with formulas by which it may control and direct the discretion of administrative agents. Such a judicial expedient can be justified only on the assumption that the Supreme Court is better qualified than, for example, the Interstate Commerce Commission to regulate the railroads.

---

[81] *Norwegian Nitrogen Products Co. v. United States,* 288 U.S. 294, 305, 317–18, 53 S. Ct. 350, 354, 359, 77 L. Ed. 796, 802, 808 (1933). Italics supplied.

[82] *Massachusetts Rev. Laws,* 1902, c. 75, 137; sustained in *Jacobson v. Massachusetts,* 197 U.S. 11, 25 S. Ct. 358, 49 L. Ed. 643 (1905).

[83] River and Harbor Act of March 3, 1899, c. 425, 18, 30 *Stat.* 1121, 1153; sustained in *Union Bridge Co. v. United States,* 204 U.S. 364, 27 S. Ct. 367, 51 L. Ed. 523 (1907).

[84] Pure Food and Drug Act of 1906, as amended by the Act of March 3, 1913, c. 117, 37 *Stat.* 732, 21 *U.S.C.* § 10; sustained in *United States v. Shreveport Grain Co.,* 287 U.S. 77, 53 S. Ct. 42, 77 L. Ed. 175 (1932).

[85] Sherman Law of July 2, 1890, § 1, 26 *Stat.* 209, forbade contracts or combinations "in restraint of trade." In *Standard Oil Co. v. United States,* 221 U.S. 1, 31 S. Ct. 502, 55 L. Ed. 619 (1911) the Court held that only such contracts or combinations which restrained trade "unduly" were forbidden. As so construed the Act was held not to be void on account of indefiniteness in *Nash v. United States,* 229 U.S. 373, 376–78, 33 S. Ct. 780, 781, 57 L. Ed. 1232, 1235–36 (1913).

[86] Interstate Commerce Act of 1887, as amended, § 15a, 41 *Stat.* 488, c. 91.

[87] Federal Communications Act of 1934, 48 *Stat.* 1064, 47 *U.S.C.A.* §§ 301, 303, 307, 309, 310, 312. Applied in *Federal Communications Commission v. Pottsville Broadcasting Co.* 309 U.S. 134, 138, 60 S. Ct. 437, 439, 84 L. Ed. 656, 659 (1940); *National Broadcasting Co. v. United States,* 319 U.S. 190, 216, 63 S. Ct. 997, 1009, 87 L. Ed. 1344, 1362 (1943).

[88] Emergency Price Control Act of 1942, 56 *Stat.* 23, § 2(b), 50 *U.S.C.A.* § 902(b).

The quasi-power fiction serves no useful purpose,[89] nor have the courts promoted good government by belaboring and distorting the doctrine of the nondelegation of power into meaning that to delegate is to surrender power. A delegated power is exercised at the pleasure of the delegating authority. Since the Congress holds its powers in trust under the Constitution, it may not grant in perpetuity any of these powers; but a delegation that is revocable at the pleasure of Congress does not violate either the letter or spirit of the Constitution and is presumptively calculated to effectuate the purposes of that instrument. Repeal or recall is a matter of procedure, not of power. Provision for recall has been made in a number of statutes, but even in the absence of such a specific provision the power is necessarily implied. As recall by *bill* or *joint resolution* requires Presidential approval, Congress has used the *concurrent resolution,* which does not, according to practice, require the approval of the President.[90] In the Reorganization Act of 1939,[91] Congress reserved the right to veto by "concurrent resolution," any reorganization plan proposed by the President. Subsequently, Congress made provision for the recall, by "vote or resolution," of the powers delegated to the President by the Lend Lease Act, the First War Powers Act, the Emergency Price Control Act, the Stabilization Act, and the War Disputes Act.[92] Congress could, of course, accomplish the same purpose by bill, which, if disapproved by the President, could be passed over the veto. But since the original delegation is made, and must be so made,

[89] "In the committee's opinion, nothing is to be gained by the continued use of the rather clumsy expressions 'quasi-legislative,' and 'quasi-judicial' in speaking of administrative tribunals as above defined. It is better frankly to recognize the fact that the Supreme Court of the United States has sanctioned extensive delegations of legislative and judicial power to executive and independent agencies." The Committee ". . . defines an administrative tribunal as an agency, either part of the executive branch or independent of all three branches, authorized to exercise legislative or judicial powers." From Report of the Special Committee on Administrative Law to the American Bar Association, *Reports of American Bar Association, 1934,* p. 541.

[90] According to the House Manual ". . . in the modern practice, concurrent resolutions have been developed as a means of expressing fact, principles, opinions, and purposes of the two Houses. . . . A concurrent resolution . . . is not sent to the President for approval unless it contains a proposition of legislation, which is not within the scope of the modern form of concurrent resolution." *H.R. Doc. No. 700,* 75th Cong., 3rd Sess., § 396. See also A. C. Hinds, *Precedents of the House of Representatives,* Vol. IV, § 3483; *S. Rep. No. 1335,* 54th Cong., 2d Sess. (Jan. 26, 1897).

[91] Act of April 3, 1939, 53 *Stat.* Pt. 2, 561 ff. For a discussion of this new technique see J. D. Millett and L. Rogers, "The Legislative Veto and the Reorganization Act of 1939," 1 *Public Administration* (1941), 176–89.

[92] Edward S. Corwin, *Total War and the Constitution* (Alfred A. Knopf, New York, 1947), p. 45.

either in specific terms or by implication, contingent upon the continued approval of the Congress, any device by which Congress expresses an official opinion would seem to be a constitutional method of recall.

It has been argued that congressional recall of delegated power by means of the "concurrent resolution" is not constitutional.[93] But the following opinion by Edward S. Corwin would seem to be a more correct view of the matter:

> It is generally agreed that Congress, being free not to delegate power, is free to do so on certain stipulated conditions, as, for example, that the delegation shall terminate by a certain date or upon the occurrence of a specified event, the end of a war, for instance. Why, then, should not one condition be that the delegation shall continue only so long as the two houses are of opinions that it is working beneficially? . . .
>
> It is generally agreed, too, that the maxim that the legislature may not *delegate* its powers signifies at the very least that the legislature may not *abdicate* its powers. Yet how, in view of the scope that legislative delegations take nowadays, is the line between *delegation* and *abdication* to be maintained? Only, I suggest, by rendering the delegated powers recoverable without the consent of the delegate; and for this purpose the concurrent resolution seems to be an available mechanism, and the only one.[94]

There has been some concern expressed in regard to the practice of legislators and judges acting as agents of the executive branch. Some recent examples of this practice is the participation by Senators Connolly and Vandenberg in the proceedings of the San Francisco Conference of the United Nations and the later meeting of the United Nations in London, the investigation of the Pearl Harbor disaster by Mr. Justice Roberts, and the prosecution of the war criminals in the Nuremberg trials by Mr. Justice Jackson. This blending of functions is "viewed with alarm" by many members of the bar in particular. The New York Bar Association issued this warning:

> This situation would seem open to question because the Senate is intended to be the body to protect the people from an improvident treaty that may have been negotiated by the executive. The fact that the San Francisco treaty received overwhelming support, and the fact that only two Senators were at San Francisco, do not remove the danger— the two Senators held strategic positions in the Senate, and, further-

[93] Howard White, "The Concurrent Resolution in Congress," 25 *American Political Science Review* (1941), 886–89.
[94] Corwin, *op. cit.*, pp. 46–47.

more, a trend usually develops gradually. The duty of the lawyer is to war at the threshold.[95]

But the Senate action on the League of Nations covenant is the kind of protection the people can expect from a partisan Senate that is not invited to participate in the formulation of an important treaty. In that historic instance the "check and balance system" actually "worked" at the eventual cost of another world war. A responsible, rather than a frustrated, government is best calculated to serve the ends of democracy. Cooperation—not distrust, jealousy, and obstruction—engendered by the theory of "checks," is a necessary condition if government is to serve the purposes for which it is ordained and established.

[95] New York Bar Association, *Lawyer Service Letter No. 104* (August 14, 1945). Congress generally has disapproved the practice of designating members of Congress to represent the United States at diplomatic and international conferences. Presumably such posts are not "offices." See *S. Rep. No. 563,* 67th Cong., 2d Sess. (March, 1922). President Madison appointed Senator James A. Bayard and Speaker Henry Clay to represent the United States at the Conference of Ghent at the close of the War of 1812. Before serving, however, they resigned from Congress. In 1898 President McKinley included three Senators in the Peace Commission to the Paris Conference which concluded the Spanish-American War. There was considerable Senate opposition to the appointments. But President Wilson was criticized for *not* taking Senators to Paris to help draft the Treaty of Versailles. In 1921 President Harding appointed Senators Lodge and Underwood as Commissioners to the Washington Arms Conference, and he later appointed a Senator and a Representative on the World War Foreign Debt Settlement Commission. Again these appointments aroused some critical discussion in the Senate. President Hoover put Senators Reed and Robinson on the American Delegation at the London Naval Conference without much Senate opposition. *Cf.* Royden J. Dangerfield, *In Defense of the Senate* (University of Oklahoma Press, Norman, 1933), pp. 29–293; Lindsay Rogers, *The American Senate* (Alfred A. Knopf, New York, 1926), pp. 65 ff.; D. F. Fleming, *The Treaty Veto of the American Senate* (G. P. Putnam's Sons, New York, 1930), pp. 27–32; George F. Hoar, *The Autobiography of Seventy Years* (New York, 1903), Vol. II, pp. 47 ff.

Chapter 3

THE ADMINISTRATIVE PROCESS

Through the years the Congress, the courts, and the administrative agencies have jointly built up the administrative process as we know it today. This development has been slow, without centralized direction, and retarded by distrust and ancient departmental vested rights. The judiciary has been particularly reluctant to share the adjudicating function. As a result, administrative bodies developed different and often overlapping and confusing procedures and forms for taking action. The tremendous expansion of administration, largely as a result of the two world wars, focused attention not only upon the need for administrative reorganization, but also upon the need for the standardization of terms and, within sound limits, of procedures.

Administrative agencies have functioned by making rules and regulations, decisions, proclamations, orders, awards, or decrees.[1] Any given agency has employed one or more of the above-mentioned forms of administrative action. Some of these forms are essentially administrative (decisions) or executive (proclamations) or judicial (orders, decrees, awards) or legislative (rules and regulations) although there has been no clear distinction in use. Historically, these forms represent different administrative objectives, for each of which an appropriate procedure was developed. The resulting diversity of procedure, generally defended by the administrators, has been criticized severely by both laymen and lawyers. The criticisms of the lawyers were crystallized in the Administrative Procedure Act of 1946 which reduced all administrative action to *rules* and *orders*.

Forms of Administrative Action

Rule-Making.—The enforcement of almost all the laws passed by Congress depends upon the rules which some administrative body has to make. This rule-making process is commonly referred to as

[1] For a detailed classification of forms of administrative action, see F. F. Blachly and Miriam Oatman, *Federal Regulatory Action and Control* (The Brookings Institution, Washington, D.C., 1940), chap. iv; and F. F. Blachly and Miriam Oatman, *Administrative Legislation and Adjudication* (The Brookings Institution, Washington, D.C., 1934), chaps. ii, v, vi.

"filling in legislative details," but the "details" are an integral part of the statute and are enforceable as such in courts of law. These rules may implement statutes carrying out the political, proprietary, fiscal, benefactory, and police functions of the government, or they may relate to the regulation of such diverse interests as public utilities, banking, insurance, finance, industry, the professions, and the public health and morals.

This delegation of a substantial part of the legislative power was the inevitable result of extending legal control over economic and social interests growing out of the vast changes brought about by industry during the nineteenth century.

The Administrative Procedure Act of 1946 defines *rule* and *rulemaking* as follows:

> "Rule" means the whole or any part of any agency statement of general or particular applicability and future effect designed to implement, interpret, or prescribe law or policy or to describe the organization, procedure, or practice requirements of any agency and includes the approval or prescription for the future of rates, wages, corporate or financial structures or reorganizations thereof, prices, facilities, appliances, services or allowances therefor or valuations, costs, or accounting, or practices bearing upon any of the foregoing. "Rule making" means agency process for the formulation, amendment, or repeal of a rule.[2]

The Act thus recognizes two general types of rules: those which "implement, interpret, or prescribe law or policy," and those which "describe the organization, procedure, or practice requirements of any agency." The former generally relate to the application of the substantive provisions of some statute to individuals. They may give meaning to such general legislative standards as "reasonable rates" and "unfair methods of competition"; or supply the facts upon which the application of a law is conditioned; or prescribe classification of persons, organizations, or things affected by a statute. In these in-

[2] Act of June 11, 1946, *Public Law 404*, c. 324, Sec. 2(c), 79th Cong., 2d Sess. (1946), 5 *U.S.C.A.* §§ 1001–11 (1950).

"The definition of a rule is not limited to substantive rules, but embraces interpretive, organizational and procedural rules as well. Of particular importance is the fact that 'rule' includes agency statements not only of general applicability but also those of particular applicability applying either to a class or to a single person. In either case, they must be of *future effect,* implementing or prescribing future law. Accordingly, the approval of a corporate reorganization by the Securities and Exchange Commission, the prescription of future rates for a single named utility by the Federal Power Commission, and similar agency actions, although applicable only to named persons, constitute rule making." *Attorney General's Manual on the Administrative Procedure Act* (United States Department of Justice, Washington, D.C., 1947), p. 13.

stances the agencies are associated with Congress in the formulation and carrying into effect of legislative policy.

The second class of rules are designed to give uniformity and certainty to the administration of law. They are of two types: (1) rules of a managerial nature, such as regulations governing national parks, subsidies, veterans' benefits, and the like; and (2) rules governing the adjudication of cases.

Adjudication.—All administrative adjudication is now made by the "order." The Administrative Procedure Act gives the following definition of order and adjudication:

> "Order" means the whole or any part of the final disposition (whether affirmative, negative, injunctive, or declaratory in form) of any agency in any matter other than rule making but including licensing. "Adjudication" means agency process for the formulation of an order.[3]

License and licensing, which is included in the above definition of order, is in turn defined as:

> "License" includes the whole or part of any agency permit, certificate, approval, registration, charter, membership, statutory exemption, or other form of permission. "Licensing" includes agency process respecting the grant, renewal, denial, revocation, suspension, annulment, withdrawal, limitation amendment, modification, or conditioning of a license.[4]

Presumably "sanctions" and "reliefs" are also subsumed by the *order*, since they are not in terms or in reason included in rule, the only other form of administrative action.[5]

[3] Sec. 2(d).

[4] Sec. 2(e). Accordingly, "adjudication" is intended to include such proceedings as:

"1. Proceedings instituted by the Federal Trade Commission and the National Labor Relations Board leading to the issuance of orders to cease and desist from unfair methods of competition or unfair labor practices, respectively.

"2. The determination of claims for money, such as compensation claims under the Longshoremen's and Harbor Workers' Compensation Act, and Claims under Title II (Old Age and Survivors' Insurance) of the Social Security Act.

"3. Reparation proceedings in which the agency determines whether a shipper or other consumer is entitled to damages arising out of the alleged *past* unreasonableness of rates.

"4. The determination of individual claims for benefits, such as grants-in-aid and subsidies.

"5. Licencing proceedings, including the grant, denial, renewal, revocation, suspension, etc. of, for example, radio broadcasting licences, certificates of public convenience and necessity, airman certificates, and the like." *Attorney General's Manual on the Administrative Procedure Act,* pp. 15–16.

[5] For an examination of *sanctions* see Chapter 4.

Thus, Frederick F. Blachly and Miriam E. Oatman observe:

Instead of confining the use of the order, as has been customary, to situations where the government forces, compels, withholds, punishes, or otherwise takes compulsory action, the new law enlarges its scope in a seemingly haphazard way to include even situations where the government acts in a favorable way toward the individual, as in granting pensions, lending money, giving benefits, granting subsidies, providing insurance, making parity payments, granting permits and so on. At the same time, the fixing of wage and rate schedules is defined as a rule or regulation. The purpose of the changes, in addition to a desire for "simplification" which has resulted in a wild confusion of categories, was obviously to extend to its utmost boundaries the subject matter of judicial review.[6]

Administrative Procedure

Notice and Hearing as Due Process of Law.—In addition to statutory provisions for notice and hearing, the Constitution provides that no person shall be deprived of his life, liberty, or property without due process of law. The modern concept of due process is traceable to the conflict between the doctrine of absolutism practiced by the Tudors and Stuarts (who prostituted justice in the courts of Star Chamber and High Commission) and the theory pressed by Lord Coke that the common law, being natural law, was superior to the law of King and Parliament. While it is not likely that the early American settlers were familiar with Coke's view of the common law, "Their religious, political, and economic inclinations led to conclusions not unlike Coke's. Nor is it surprising that a hearty welcome was accorded to Coke's theories about the common law when they were brought to America by the professional lawyers."[7] Black-

[6] "Sabotage of the Administrative Process," 6 *Public Administration Review* (1946), 224. For types of administrative orders see the following.

Cease and desist orders: Federal Trade Commission Act of 1914, § 5(b)(g), 15 *U.S.C.A.* § 45(b)(g).

Orders stopping, permitting, or refusing sales, acquisitions, or entry or continuance in business: Securities Act of 1933, §§ 5(a), 8(b)(d)(e), 15 *U.S.C.A.* §§ 77e(a), 77h(b)(d)(e); Interstate Commerce Act, § 20a(2)(3), 49 *U.S.C.A.* §§ 20a(2)(3), 206(a)(b), 49 *U.S.C.A.* §§ 306(a)(b), 307(a), 308(a), 312(a); Public Utility Holding Company Act of 1935, § 9(a), 10(a)(b)(c)(d), 15 *U.S.C.A.* §§ 79i(a), 79j(a)(b)(c)(d); Securities Exchange Act of 1934, § 15(a)(b), 15 *U.S.C.A.* § 78o(a)(b); Communications Act of 1934, §§ 301, 307(a)(b)(d), 308(a)(b), 309(a), 47 *U.S.C. Supp.* §§ 301, 307(a)(b)(d), 308(a)(b), 309(a).

Orders requiring affirmative acts, such as payment of money: Interstate Commerce Act, § 16(1)(2), 49 *U.S.C.A.* § 16(1)(2); National Labor Relations Act of 1935, § 10(c), 29 *U.S.C.A.* § 160(c).

[7] Walter Gellhorn, *Administrative Law, Cases and Comment* (The Foundation Press, Inc., Brooklyn, 1947, 2d ed.), p. 231.

stone's *Commentaries* had wide circulation in America before the Constitution was framed, and Blackstone shared Coke's views on the fundamental nature of the common law.

The original Constitution did not contain the due process clause, since it did not contain a formal Bill of Rights—largely because the States already had Declarations of Rights in their constitutions. Some of these Declarations had due process clauses, and in all of the States the common law was in force. In construing the due process clauses of the Fifth and Fourteenth Amendments to the Constitution, our courts have held that the words were "intended to convey the same meaning as the words, 'by the law of the land,' in Magna Charta." [8] To the same effect is the statement:

> The "due process of law," by which Congress is limited in the Fifth Amendment, and the states by the Fourteenth Amendment, is equivalent to the "law of the land," and is intended to protect the citizen against arbitrary action, and secure to all persons equal and impartial justice under the law.[9]

The Constitution did not define *due process* but assumed that its meaning had already been established by law and custom. In truth, the Bill of Rights was not intended to make new law, but rather to secure the inviolability of existing legal principles. "Due process," therefore, is not identical with "judicial process." Thus, administrative process has been customary process and so, due process, in levying and collecting taxes. Also, the procedure in a military court is not judicial procedure but it is due procedure. In short, "The Fifth Amendment guarantees no particular form of procedure; it protects substantial rights." [10] And, "The requirements imposed by that guaranty [the due process clause of the Fifth Amendment] are not technical, nor is any particular form of procedure necessary." [11]

LEGISLATIVE AND JUDICIAL ACTION DISTINGUISHED. Due process of law does not require notice and hearing as a condition antecedent to administrative legislation. If the action taken, whether by a legislature or an administrative agency, is categorized as "legislative," preliminary notice and hearing is not required. If, however, the administrative determination is "judicial," notice and hearing must precede the determination. There is fairly general judicial ac-

[8] *Murray's Lessee, et al. v. Hoboken Land and Improvement Co.,* 18 How. (56 U.S.) 272, 276, 15 L. Ed. 372, 374 (1856).

[9] *United States v. Yount,* 267 Fed. 861, 863 (D.C.W.D. Pa., 1920).

[10] *National Labor Relations Board v. Mackay Radio & Telegraph Co.,* 304 U.S. 333, 351, 58 S. Ct. 904, 913, 82 L. Ed. 1381 (1938).

[11] *Inland Empire Dist. Council v. Millis,* 325 U.S. 697, 710, 65 S. Ct. 1316, 1323, 89 L. Ed. 1877 (1945).

ceptance of this rule in principle, but there is considerable difference of opinion as to whether a given action is legislative or judicial.[12]

The rule was stated concisely by the New Jersey Court of Errors and Appeals in reference to administrative prescription of minimum milk prices for the milk industry, as follows:

> In the absence of a specific constitutional or statutory requirement thereof, notice of proceedings before the subordinate body exercising, as here, the administrative function is not requisite to valid action by that body. Nor is a hearing required in the absence of a provision therefor in the organic or statutory law. The due process clause of the Fourteenth Amendment imposes no such requirement; and, for obvious reasons, the like clauses in the state Constitution bear the same construction. . . .
>
> Such regulation is purely a legislative function; and, even when exercised by a subordinate body, upon which it is conferred, the notice of hearing essential in judicial proceedings is not indispensable to a valid exercise of the power. If the regulation undertaking is arbitrary or unreasonable, and, in the case of rates and charges imposed upon a business clothed with a public interest, confiscatory, relief may be had in the courts. A judicial review of administrative proceedings, in notice, satisfies the demand of the due process clauses.[13]

The reason for the rule was thus aptly explained by Mr. Justice Holmes:

> Where a rule of conduct applies to more than a few people it is impracticable that every one should have a direct voice in its adoption. The Constitution does not require all public acts to be done in town meeting or an assembly of the whole. . . . There must be a limit to individual argument in such matters if government is to go on.[14]

The difference in the constitutional effect of due process in the judicial and legislative processes has been generally recognized by courts. For example, the Supreme Judicial Court of Massachusetts has held:

> . . . where the law is general and the question is whether under it the defendants are committing a nuisance, the facts are determined by judicial action; on the other hand, the determination of the same facts is legislative in case the Legislature decides to make the thing a nuisance

---

[12] *Cf.* Bernard Schwartz, "Procedural Due Process in Federal Administrative Law," 25 *New York University Law Review* (July, 1950), 552–78; K. C. Davis, "The Requirement of Opportunity to be Heard in the Administrative Process," 51 *Yale Law Journal* (1942), 1093 ff.

[13] *State ex rel. State Board of Milk Control v. Newark Milk Co.*, 118 N.J. Eq. 504, 522–23, 179 Atl. 116, 126–27 (1935).

[14] *Bi-Metallic Investment Co. v. State Board of Equalization*, 239 U.S. 441, 445, 36 S. Ct. 141, 142, 60 L. Ed. 372, 375 (1915).

per se. And where it is legislative it is final and no hearing is necessary; and where, as is the case here, it is made in the exercise of the police power, no compensation is due. The delegation of such legislative powers to a board is going a great way. But the remedy is by application to the Legislature if a remedy should be given. In our opinion it is within the constitutional power, and the court can give no remedy.[15]

A similar distinction was made by the Supreme Court in respect to the exercise of eminent domain in condemnation cases.

Where the intended use is public, the necessity and expediency of the taking may be determined by such agency and in such mode as the State may designate. They are legislative questions, no matter who may be charged with their decision, and a hearing thereon is not essential to due process in the sense of the Fourteenth Amendment. . . . But it is essential to due process that the mode of determining the compensation be such as to afford the owner an opportunity to be heard.[16]

And a similar construction applies in tax assessment cases:

There is no constitutional command that notice of the assessment of a tax, and opportunity to contest it, must be given in advance of the assessment. It is enough that all available defenses may be presented to a competent tribunal before exaction of the tax and before the command of the state to pay become final and irrevocable.[17]

To the same effect the Supreme Court has held:

. . . where the legislature of a State, instead of fixing the tax itself, commits to some subordinate body the duty of determining whether, in what amount, and upon whom it shall be levied, and of making its assessment and apportionment, due process of law requires that at some stage of the proceedings *before the tax become irrevocably fixed,* the taxpayer shall have an opportunity to be heard, of which he must have notice, either personal, by publication, or by a law fixing the time and place of the hearing.[18]

---

[15] *Commonwealth v. Sisson,* 189 Mass. 247, 254, 75 N.E. 619, 622 (1905).

[16] *Bragg v. Weaver,* 251 U.S. 57, 58–59, 40 S. Ct. 62, 63, 64 L. Ed. 135, 137 (1919).

[17] *Nickey v. Mississippi,* 292 U.S. 393, 396, 54 S. Ct. 743, 744, 78 L. Ed. 1323, 1326 (1934). Also, *Hagar v. Reclamation District,* 111 U.S. 701, 4 S. Ct. 663, 28 L. Ed. 569 (1884). "It is not essential to due process of law that the taxpayer be given notice and hearing before the value of his property is originally assessed; it being sufficient if he is granted the right to be heard on the assessment before the valuation is finally determined." *McGregor v. Hogan,* 263 U.S. 234, 237, 44 S. Ct. 50, 51, 68 L. Ed. 282, 283 (1923).

[18] *Londoner v. Denver,* 210 U.S. 373, 385–86, 28 S. Ct. 708, 714, 52 L. Ed. 1103, 1112 (1908). Italics supplied.

The Supreme Court has held repeatedly that "the function of rate-making *is purely legislative in its character, and this is true, whether it is exercised directly by the legislature itself or by some subordinate or administrative body, to whom the power of fixing rates in detail has been delegated. The completed act derives its authority from the legislature and must be regarded as an exercise of the legislative power.*" [19] Accordingly, the Interstate Commerce Commission and State railroad and public service commissions exercise an essentially legislative function in prescribing, for railroads and other utilities, just and reasonable maximum and minimum charges to be observed *in futuro;* and due process of law does not require notice and hearing in advance of the initiation of such legislative orders, but *opportunity for a hearing before a rate order goes into effect* must be given.[20] It would seem that a hearing before a reviewing court would satisfy due process. An order cannot be enforced, if challenged on constitutional grounds, except by judicial process. It is common *statutory practice,* however, to require a hearing in rate-making.

Similarly, the Emergency Price Control Act of 1942 [21] was held not to violate the Fifth Amendment because it did not make provision for a hearing to landlords before the order or regulation fixing rents became effective, since judicial review of the order was provided.[22] Congress, said the Court, would not have been under necessity to give notice and hearing before it acted, had it decided to fix rents on a national basis; and it need not make that requirement when it delegates the task to an administrative agency.[23] Likewise, when the President and the Tariff Commission change tariff rates by authority of the tariff acts [24] they exercise delegated legislative power, and the

---

[19] *Knoxville v. Knoxville Water Co.,* 212 U.S. 1, 8, 29 S. Ct. 148, 150, 53 L. Ed. 371, 378 (1909). Italics supplied. In *Louisville & Nashville R. Co. v. Garrett,* 231 U.S. 298, 305, 308, 318, 34 S. Ct. 48, 51, 52, 56, 58 L. Ed. 229, 240, 244 (1913), it was held that a rate order is legislative while a reparation order is judicial. Fixing a "reasonable rate" by a State railroad commission was held to be "eminently a question for judicial investigation" requiring a hearing, in *Chicago, M. & St. P. Ry. Co. v. Minnesota,* 134 U.S. 418, 457, 458 (1890). See also *United States v. Baltimore & Ohio R. Co.,* 293 U.S. 454, 55 S. Ct. 268, 79 L. Ed. 587 (1935).

[20] *United States v. Illinois Central R. Co.,* 291 U.S. 457, 54 S. Ct. 471, 78 L. Ed. 909 (1934). Zoning regulations were held to be "legislative" in *Lexington v. Bean,* 272 Mass. 547, 172 N.E. 867 (1930). Minimum wage regulations were "judicial" in *McGrew v. Industrial Commission,* 96 Utah 203, 85 P. (2d) 608 (1938), *Western Union Telegraph Co. v. Industrial Commission of Minnesota,* 24 F. Supp. 370 (D. Minn., 1933), but "legislative" in *Associated Industries v. Industrial Welfare Commission,* 185 Okla. 177, 90 P. (2d) 899 (1939), *Spokane Hotel Co. v. Younger,* 113 Wash. 359, 194 Pac. 595 (1920).

[21] 56 *Stat.* 23, 50 *U.S.C. App.,* § 901 *et sqq.*

[22] *Bowles v. Willingham,* 321 U.S. 503, 64 S. Ct. 641, 88 L. Ed. 892 (1944).

[23] *Ibid.*

[24] Act of 1922, 42 *Stat.* 858, 941, c. 356, § 315.

hearing provided for by statute to those affected by the change is a hearing of the same order as is given by a congressional committee in aid of the legislative process.[25]

This distinction between the "legislative" and "judicial" processes is solely for the purpose of deciding if notice and hearing is required *before* the administrative determination is made. Legislative action once taken can be challenged on the grounds that it is *ultra vires* or that its effect is to deprive a person of life, liberty, or property without due process of law. Opportunity to test the legality of an administrative rule before it becomes final is all that is required by due process of law. The source of a legislative rule is of no consequence when it is challenged under the due process clause.

According to Judge Cooley "It is a fundamental rule that in judicial or quasi judicial proceedings, affecting the rights of the citizen, he shall have notice and be given an opportunity to be heard before any judgment, decree, order, or demand shall be given and established against him." [26] That is, ". . . it is essential to the validity of any proceeding by which the property of any individual is taken that notice must be given at some time and in some form before the final adjudication." [27]

Some courts, federal and State, have held that a statute is unconstitutional which does not provide *specifically* for notice and hearing prior to a determination which conclusively and finally disposes of individual property rights.[28] *Stuart v. Palmer* [29] seems to have furnished the yardstick for this rule in the following dictum:

> It is not enough that the owners may by chance have notice, or that they may as a matter of favor have a hearing. The law must require notice to them, and give them a right to a hearing and an opportunity to be heard. It matters not upon the question of the constitutionality of such a law, that the assessment has, in fact, been fairly

[25] *Norwegian Nitrogen Products Co. v. United States,* 288 U.S. 294, 53 S. Ct. 350, 77 L. Ed. 796 (1933).

[26] Thomas McIntyre Cooley, *The Law of Taxation* (4th ed., Callaghan & Co., Chicago, 1924), Vol. III, p. 2253; *Inland Empire District Council, etc. v. Millis,* 325 U.S. 697, 65 S. Ct. 1316, 89 L. Ed. 1877 (1946).

[27] *Pittsburgh, C. C. & St. L. Ry. Co. v. Backus,* 154 U.S. 421, 425–26, 14 S. Ct. 1114, 1116, 38 L. Ed. 1031, 1036 (1894).

[28] FEDERAL CASES: *Central of Georgia R. Co. v. Wright,* 207 U.S. 127, 28 S. Ct. 47, 52 L. Ed. 134 (1907); *Coe v. Aamons Fertilizer Works,* 237 U.S. 413, 35 S. Ct. 625, 59 L. Ed. 1027 (1915); *Wuchter v. Pizzuti,* 276 U.S. 13, 48 S. Ct. 259, 72 L. Ed. 446 (1928).

STATE CASES: *Stuart v. Palmer,* 74 N.Y. 183 (1878); *Kunz v. Sumption,* 117 Ind. 1, 19 N.E. 474 (1889). See Gellhorn, *op. cit.,* pp. 352–61, for discussion of cases. See also *Dation v. Ford Motors Co.,* 22. N.W. (2d) 252 (Mich. 1946).

[29] 74 N.Y. 183 (1878).

apportioned. The constitutional validity of a law is to be tested, not by what has been done under it, but by what may, by its authority, be done. The Legislature may prescribe the kind of notice and the mode in which it shall be given, but it cannot dispense with all notice.[30]

The more reasonable rule *implies* notice and hearing when the statute is silent, on the theory that a statute should be taken to be constitutional "unless the contrary plainly and palpably appears," since a statute which clearly excludes a hearing in the above situation would not be due process of law.[31] The following extract is an amplification:

> . . . if the statute purported to authorize the imposition of the burden without notice to the defendant and opportunity to be heard, it would be unconstitutional. But express statutory requirement for such notice and hearing is not essential for the reason that the constitutional requirement that there shall be notice and opportunity to be heard is a part of the law governing the railroad commissioners. As the statute is silent on the subject, the presumption is that the Legislature intended for the commissioners to comply with the Constitution, not to violate it.[32]

This opinion has been fortified by decisions of the Supreme Court. In two cases involving the Securities Exchange Act [33] the Court held that the Act was not unconstitutional because it did not make express provision for notice and hearing.[34] The Commission had given notice and an opportunity for a hearing. Said Mr. Justice Murphy for the majority:

> That the statute does not expressly insist upon what in fact has been given the security holders is without constitutional relevance under these circumstances. Wherever possible, statutes must be interpreted in accordance with constitutional principles. Here, in the absence of definite contrary indications, it is fair to assume that Congress desired that § 11(b)(2) be lawfully executed by giving appropriate notice and opportunity for hearing to all those constitutionally entitled thereto. And when that assumption is added to the provisions of § 19, it be-

[30] 74 N.Y. at 188.

[31] *Kaoru Yamataya v. Fisher,* 189 U.S. 86, 23 S. Ct. 611, 47 L. Ed. 721 (1903), the Japanese Immigrant Case; *Toombs v. Citizens Bank,* 281 U.S. 643, 50 S. Ct. 434, 74 L. Ed. 1088 (1930); *Paulsen v. Portland,* 149 U.S. 30, 13 S. Ct. 750, 37 L. Ed. 637 (1893); *Bratton v. Chandler,* 260 U.S. 110, 43 S. Ct. 43, 67 L. Ed. 157 (1922).

[32] *Railroad Commissioners v. Columbia, N. & L. R. Co.,* 82 S.C. 418, 422–23, 64 S. E. 240, 242 (1909).

[33] Act of June 6, 1934, 48 *Stat.* 881.

[34] *American Power and Light Co. v. Securities and Exchange Commission, Electric Power & Light Corp. v. Securities and Exchange Commission,* 329 U.S. 90, 67 S. Ct. 133, 91 L. Ed. 260 (1946).

comes quite evident that the Commission is bound under the statute to give notice and opportunity for hearing to consumers, investors and other persons whenever constitutionally necessary.[35]

A similar conclusion was reached by a circuit court in regard to the Renegotiation Act: [36]

> . . . there is not merit in the contention that in the exercise of such an administrative power the word "hearing" is not mentioned. The word "renegotiation" implies a hearing. Here there was a hearing and the absence of statutory requirement is immaterial.[37]

In short, the presumption is that the statute *requires* an administrative hearing, and that an administrative action without hearing is a violation of the statute. If notice and hearing cannot be presumed from the statute, it is not enough that *in fact* notice was given and a hearing was held, since "A notice not authorized by law is in legal contemplation no notice." [38] But this rule should apply only when the legislative intent *not to grant notice* is reasonably discernible from the terms of the statute, and such an intent should not be read into a statute that is merely silent as to notice. In such a situation the administrative action, not the statute, should be invalidated. There would seem to be no good reason why a court should not accept an administrative construction which would make a statute valid, while rejecting a construction which would make the statute invalid.

Statutory Procedural Requirements: Rule-Making.—The procedure followed in administrative rule-making is necessarily less formal than in statute-making. It does not require a committee stage, or "three readings" on three different days, and it is not subject to the veto power. The entire procedure takes place within the agency, and it may be (1) left to the discretion of the agency or (2) prescribed by statute.

Since the primary purpose of legislative procedure is to inform the law-makers, not to protect private rights, this procedure is essentially discretionary. As indicated in preceding pages, in the absence of constitutional or statutory prescriptions, "due process" does not require notice and hearing *prior* to enactment of a rule of law; that "process" is served when any person affected by the *application* of the rule has his "day in court," which may be an administrative or a judicial hear-

---

[35] 329 U.S. at 107–8, 67 S. Ct. at 143–44, 91 L. Ed. at 100.

[36] Act of April 28, 1942, 56 *Stat.* 245, as amended, 56 *Stat.* 982 (1942), 57 *Stat.* 347 (1943).

[37] *Spaulding v. Douglas Aircraft Co.*, 154 F. (2d) 419, 426 (C.C.A. 9th, 1946).

[38] *Kunz v. Sumption*, 117 Ind. 1, 3, 19 N.E. 474, 475 (1889).

ing. In practice, legislative procedure has varied greatly according to agency and subject matter. It may involve investigation, research, consultation, conference, and hearings, all with a view to enlighten the rule-maker and to permit private interests to participate in the formulation of regulations which affect them.

Since 1900 a considerable number of statutes have prescribed that certain rules should issue only "after hearing" or "after full hearing." [39] A number of agencies have voluntarily, and in the absence of statutory requirements, held hearings prior to the formulation of rules and regulations.[40] These hearings have been announced pub-

[39] Safety Appliance Act of March 2, 1903, 32 *Stat.* 943, c. 976, 45 *U.S.C.A.* § 9 (1935), and Act of April 14, 1910, 36 *Stat.* 298, c. 160, 45 *U.S.C.A.* § 12 (1935); Boiler Inspection Act of February 17, 1911, 36 *Stat.* 914, c. 103, 45 *U.S.C.A.* §§ 21–29, 31–34, and Act of May 29, 1917, 40 *Stat.* 101, c. 23, 49 *U.S.C.A.* § 1 (14) (1934); the Plant Quarantine Act of August 20, 1912, 37 *Stat.* 315–19, c. 308, 7 *U.S.C.A.* §§ 159–61 (1935); the Food, Drug and Cosmetic Act of June 25, 1938, 52 *Stat.* 1055, 21 *U.S.C.A.* § 371; the Federal Alcohol Administration Act of August 29, 1935, 49 *Stat.* 981, c. 814, 27 *U.S.C.A.* § 205(f) (Supp. 1939); the Fair Labor Standards Act of June 25, 1938, 52 *Stat.* 1064, c. 676, 29 *U.S.C.A.* § 208(d) (Supp. 1939); the Agricultural Marketing Agreements Act of June 3, 1937, 50 *Stat.* 246, as amended, 50 *Stat.* 563, 7 *U.S.C.A.* § 608b–f; and others.

The Federal Seed Act of August 9, 1939, 53 *Stat.* 1275, 7 *U.S.C.A.* §§ 1551–1610, provides for a public hearing prior to promulgation of rules but does not prescribe a particular procedure and does not provide for judicial review.

The Commodity Exchange Act of June 15, 1936, 49 *Stat.* 1491, 7 *U.S.C.A.* § 8, provides for judicial review of the Commission's orders to determine if they were "issued without due notice and a reasonable opportunity having been afforded . . . for a hearing, or infringes the Constitution . . . or beyond the jurisdiction of said commission."

The Federal Food, Drug, and Cosmetics Act of June 25, 1938, 52 *Stat.* 1040, 1055, 21 *U.S.C.A.* § 371, provides that "The Administrator shall base his order [legislative order] only on substantial evidence or record at the hearing and shall set forth as part of the order detailed findings of fact on which the order is based." The order is made subject to review by the Circuit Court of Appeals. The Railway Mail Pay Act of 1916, 39 *U.S.C.A.* §§ 523–68, authorized the Interstate Commerce Commission to fix "fair and reasonable rates" for carriers transporting mails *after notice and hearing.*

[40] Among the important agencies voluntarily consulting with the interests they regulate are the Federal Reserve Board, the Federal Communications Commission, the Securities and Exchange Commission, the United States Maritime Commission, the Civil Aeronautics Authority, the Bituminous Coal Division, the Bureau of Biological Survey, the Secretary of Agriculture, the Interstate Commerce Commission, the Children's Bureau, and many others.

However, even in cases where the statute may not require a hearing, the Supreme Court has ". . . indulged in talk to the effect that the promulgation of such regulations in order to have validity must be buttressed by findings of fact." James M. Landis, *The Administrative Process* (Yale University Press, New Haven, 1938), p. 148, citing *Panama Refining Co. v. Ryan,* 293 U.S. 388, 55 S. Ct. 241, 79 L. Ed. 446 (1935); *Schechter Poultry Corp. v. United States,* 295 U.S. 495, 55 S. Ct. 837, 79 L. Ed. 1570 (1935); *United States v. Baltimore & Ohio R. R. Co.,* 293 U.S. 454, 55 S. Ct. 268, 79 L. Ed. 587 (1935). Mr. Landis adds, "How far this suggestion should be taken seriously is a matter of considerable doubt."

licly, so that any interested party may attend and testify, but they have not been formalized, since the purpose was to permit business interests to share in making rules for the future and not to determine rights under existing rules or laws. Legislative hearings relate to rules which affect the property rights of a business or businesses in a general way, such as the fixing of rates and wages, and the prescription of commodity standards and trade and marketing practices. They are investigatory and nonadversary, not judicial.

The Administrative Procedure Act attempts to formalize and standardize administrative procedure.[41] It prescribes three types of rule-making procedures: (1) discretionary, (2) administrative, and (3) adjudicatory.

DISCRETIONARY PROCEDURE. The areas of rule-making for which a particular procedure does not seem to have been provided, and so appears left to administrative discretion, are "(1) any military, naval, or foreign affairs function of the United States or (2) any matter relating to agency management or personnel or to public property, loans, grants, benefits, or contracts."[42] The areas comprehended under (1) belong by tradition and the Constitution to the Chief Executive (subject to certain legislative checks), and the exercise of these powers involves a large degree of secrecy. Accordingly public hearings prior to the making of rules relating to military and foreign affairs would not serve a public purpose. The remaining areas under (2) affect private rights only indirectly. They relate largely to the proprietary and benefactory powers of the government. A formal procedure, requiring notice and hearing, in making rules for the administration of these services would not serve a useful purpose. The above areas of public power are the safest for a free play of administrative discretion.

Also included in discretionary procedure are interpretative rules, general statements of policy, rules of agency organization, procedure, and practice, or "any situation in which the agency for good cause finds (and incorporates the finding and a brief statement of

[41] The American Bar Association is advocating greater uniformity in administrative procedure. See Arthur T. Vanderbilt, "Administrative Procedure: Shall Rules Before Agencies Be Uniform?" 24 *American Bar Association Journal* (1948), 869 ff.; Administrative Practitioners Bill, *H. R. Doc. No. 2657*, 80th Cong., 1st Sess. (1947). For general comments on the Act see Ray A. Brown, "The Federal Administrative Procedure Act," 1947 *Wisconsin Law Review* (January, 1947), 66–87; Nathaniel L. Nathanson, "Some Comments on the Administrative Procedure Act," 41 *Illinois Law Review* (September–October, 1946), 368–422; George Warren (ed.). *The Federal Administrative Procedure Act and the Administrative Agencies* (New York University School of Law, New York, 1947).

[42] Sec. 4.

the reasons therefore in the rules issued) that notice and public procedure thereon are impracticable, unnecessary, or contrary to the public interest." [43] The extent of administrative discretion under this provision will depend upon the conclusiveness of the agency "finding" of public convenience or interest.

ADMINISTRATIVE PROCEDURE. Except as noted in the preceding paragraphs, and except where a hearing is prescribed by statute (requiring adjudicatory procedure, as discussed in the next section), the Act requires the publication in the Federal Register of General Notice which shall include "(1) a statement of the time, place, and nature of public rule-making proceedings; (2) reference to the authority under which the rule is proposed; and (3) either the terms or substance of the proposed rule or a description of the subjects and issues involved." [44] Interested persons must be given "an opportunity to participate in the rule-making through submission of written data, views, or arguments" with or without the opportunity to be present. After consideration of "all relevant matter presented," the agency shall incorporate in the rules adopted a statement of their basis and purpose.[45]

This provision of the Act would seem to burden the rule-making process with impossible requirements. Thousands of persons are "interested," for example, in the rules made by the Housing Administration. Are all of them to be given "an opportunity to participate" in the making of these rules? Considering the number of agencies, the number of rules made, and the number of "interested persons," the time required for publication, notice, and consideration of "all relevant matter presented" will make effective administration impossible, if the provisions of the Act are complied with literally.

ADJUDICATORY PROCEDURE. "Where rules are required by statute to be made on the record after opportunity for an agency hearing," the Act prescribes a judicialized procedure—the same procedure as is required for true administrative adjudication.[46] Thus, agency hearings are required only when provision therefor already is made in statutes in particular cases.

Some rule-making proceedings are partly adversary in nature. A rule may affect the interests of opposed or competing groups—employer v. employee, large v. small businesses, producer v. consumer,

[43] Sec. 4(a).
[44] *Ibid.*
[45] Sec. 4(b).
[46] *Ibid.*

buyer v. seller—it may work to the benefit of one group and to the disadvantage of another. In these circumstances it may be desirable to hold public hearings at which the affected interests appear as adversary parties for the purpose of protecting their rights by submitting and rebutting evidence. Such hearings are now held, either with or without statutory requirements. However, as these proceedings involve complex issues and many diverse parties, the procedure is likely to be both cumbersome and costly and may delay unduly the work of the rule-making agency. Furthermore, the parties are not "adversary" in the sense of a judicial case or controversy. In a legislative proceeding the private parties aim to inform and to influence the action of the rule-makers. In a judicial proceeding the parties merely seek a declaration of rights under existing law. The legislative and judicial processes differ in purpose and effect. Each has developed a procedure best adapted to its purposes. Neither should be required to adopt the procedure of the other. Congress may have been over-hasty, therefore, in prescribing adversary rule-making procedure under the Administrative Procedure Act.

Statutory Procedural Requirements: Adjudication.—The Administrative Procedure Act does not require administrative notice and hearing—it merely provides that "in every case of adjudication *required by statute* to be determined on the record after opportunity for an agency hearing" certain procedural requirements shall be observed.[47] After noting certain exceptions, the Act makes the following provisions:

> Persons entitled to notice of an agency hearing shall be timely informed of (1) the time, place, and nature thereof; (2) the legal authority and jurisdiction under which the hearing is to be held; and (3) the matters of fact and law asserted. . . .[48]
>
> The agency shall afford all interested parties opportunity for (1) the submission and consideration of facts, arguments, offers of settlement, or proposals of adjustment where time, the nature of the proceeding, and the public interest permit, and (2) to the extent that the parties are unable so to determine any controversy by consent, hearing, and decision upon notice. . . .[49]

That is, "hearing, and decision upon notice" is required only when the parties are unable to settle the controversy by mutual consent. This informal procedure is not only best adapted, in most cases, to protect the interests of the parties, but it is made necessary by the large volume of business performed by many agencies.

[47] Sec. 5. Italics supplied.
[48] Sec. 5(a).
[49] Sec. 5(b).

The Act further provides that *when a hearing is prescribed by statute:*

> There shall preside at the taking of evidence (1) the agency, (2) one or more members of the body which comprises the agency, or (3) one or more examiners appointed as provided in this Act; *but nothing in this Act shall be deemed to supersede the conduct of specified classes of proceedings in whole or part by or before boards or other officers specially provided for, by or designated pursuant to statute.*[50]

To the end that an investigating or prosecuting officer shall not influence the operations of the hearing and deciding officers, the Act requires that the officers who preside at the taking of evidence must make the decision or recommend decision in the case. Save for the disposition of ex parte matters, the hearing officers may not consult any person or party, except openly and upon notice to all parties nor may they be made subject to the supervision of prosecuting officers.[51]

The presiding or hearing officers are empowered to:

> . . . (1) administer oaths and affirmations, (2) issue subpenas authorized by law, (3) rule upon offers of proof and receive relevant evidence, (4) take or cause depositions to be taken whenever the ends of justice would be served thereby, (5) regulate the course of the hearing, (6) hold conferences for the settlement or simplification of the issues by consent of the parties, (7) dispose of procedural requests or similar matters, (8) make decisions or recommend decisions in conformity with section 8, and (9) take any other action authorized by agency rule consistent with this Act.[52]

Except as statutes provide otherwise, the burden of proof is placed upon the proponent of a rule or order. Any evidence may be admitted but every agency is required to provide for the exclusion of irrelevant and unduly repetitious evidence, and no sanction may be imposed or rule or order issued except as supported by reliable, probative, and substantial evidence. Any party may present his case or defense by oral or documentary evidence, and may conduct cross examination. But in rule-making or determining claims for money or benefits or applications for initial licenses, an agency may adopt procedures for the submission of all or part of the evidence in written form so far as the interest of any party will not be prejudiced

---

[50] Sec. 7(a). Italics supplied.
[51] Sec. 5(c).
[52] Sec. 7(b).

thereby.[53] Every interested party in any agency proceeding is entitled to appear in person or by counsel.[54] The transcript of the evidence taken together with the papers filed is made the exclusive record for decision, and, upon payment of costs, is made available to all parties.[55]

Opinion is divided as to the legislative intent in Sections 5 and 7 (a) of the Act. Mr. Justice Jackson, speaking for the majority of the Supreme Court, has admitted, "We do not know. The legislative history is more conflicting than the text is ambiguous." [56] But the Attorney General, basing his deduction on the legislative history of the Act, concluded:

> It will be noted that the formal procedural requirements of the Act are invoked only where agency action "on the record after opportunity for agency hearing" is *required by some other statute*. The legislative history makes clear that the word "statute" was used deliberately so as to make sections 5, 7 and 8 applicable only where Congress has otherwise *specifically* required a hearing to be held. . . . Mere statutory authorization to hold hearings (e.g., "such hearings as may be deemed necessary") does not constitute such a requirement. In cases where a hearing is held, although not required by statute, but as a matter of due process or agency policy or practice, sections 5, 7 and 8 do not apply.[57]

In line with this construction of the Act, the Solicitor of the Post Office Department and the Court of Appeals for the District of Columbia have held that the procedural provisions of Section 5 of the Act are not applicable to postal fraud order proceedings by the Postmaster General, since the fraud order statutes do not require a hearing but merely provide that the Postmaster General may act "upon evidence satisfactory to him." [58] Said Judge Proctor:

> The fraud order statutes do not in terms require a hearing. Therefore, we think, they do not come within the scope of the procedural provisions of the Administrative Procedure Act.[59]

A number of federal courts have held that the Administrative Procedure Act does not apply to hearings held under the Immigration Laws, since, they do not require a statutory hearing.[60] But in *Eisler*

---

[53] Sec. 7(c).   [54] Sec. 6(a).   [55] Sec. 7(d).

[56] *Wong Yang Sung v. McGrath,* 339 U.S. 33, 49, 70 S. Ct. 445, 454, 94 L. Ed. 616, 628 (1950).

[57] *Attorney General's Manual on the Administrative Procedure Act,* p. 41. Italics supplied.

[58] See Bernard Schwartz, "Administrative Law," *1949 Annual Survey of American Law* (New York University School of Law, New York, 1949), pp. 169–70.

[59] *Bersoff v. Donaldson,* 174 F. (2d) 494 (D.C. Cir., 1949).

[60] *Wong Yang Sung v. Clark,* 80 F. Supp. 235 (D.C., 1948), 174 F. (2d) 158 (D.C. App., 1949) ; *Yanish v. Wixon,* 81 F. Supp. 499 (N.D. Cal., 1948) ; *United*

v. Clark,[61] Justice Goldsborough held that ". . . the Courts have read due process into the Act, that due process requires a hearing, and that therefore hearing is an integral part of the Deportation Act; in fact, just as much as if the Act itself in words stated that a hearing should be held." [62] This view of the Act was subscribed to by the Supreme Court in *Wong Yang Sung v. McGrath* [63] where Mr. Justice Jackson said:

> We think that the limitation to hearings "required by statute" in § 5 of the Administrative Procedure Act exempts from that section's application only those hearings which administrative agencies may hold by regulation, rule, custom, or special dispensation; not those held by compulsion. We do not think the limiting words render the Administrative Procedure Act inapplicable to hearings, *the requirement for which has been read into a statute by the Court in order to save the statute from invalidity.* They exempt hearings of less than statutory authority, not those of more than statutory authority. We would hardly attribute to Congress a purpose to be less scrupulous about the fairness of a hearing necessitated by the Constitution than one granted by it as a matter of expediency.
>
> Indeed, to so construe the Immigration Act might again bring it into constitutional jeopardy. When the Constitution requires a hearing, it requires a fair one, one before a tribunal which meets at least currently prevailing standards of impartiality.[64]

States v. Watkins, 170 F.(2d) 1009 (2d Cir., 1948) ; *Ex parte Wong So Wan,* 82 F. Supp. 60 (N.D. Cal., 1948) ; *In re United States,* 82 F. Supp. 36 (S.D.N.Y., 1948).

[61] 77 F. Supp. 610 (D.D.C., 1948).

[62] *Ibid.,* at 611. "What Justice Goldsborough is doing here is to interpret the words *required by statute* in Section 5 of the APA as synonymous with *required by law.* But the Act does not purport to govern hearings *required by law;* indeed, those words were used in early drafts of the Administrative Procedure Bill, and a deliberate change was made in the final draft so as to refer only to hearings 'required by statute.' The learned Justice would, therefore, seem to go too far in his interpretation of the statute, however much one may sympathize with his desire to hold the procedure in deportation cases — which may result 'in loss of both property and life; or of all that makes life worth living'—to the level required by the APA." Bernard Schwartz, "Administrative Law," *1948 Annual Survey of American Law* (New York University School of Law, New York, 1948), pp. 159–60.

[63] 339 U.S. 33, 70 S. Ct. 445, 94 L. Ed. 616 (1950).

[64] 339 U.S. at 50, 70 S. Ct. at 454, 94 L. Ed. at 628. Italics supplied. Mr. Justice Reed, dissenting, said: "The Court, it seems to me, has disregarded a Congressional exemption of certain agencies, including the Immigration and Naturalization Service, from some of the requirements of the Administrative Procedure Act. Such judicial intrusion into the legislative domain justifies a protest." 339 U.S. at 53, 70 S. Ct. at 455, 94 L. Ed. at 630. Mr. Justice Reed pointed out that no one had questioned the constitutionality of the administrative hearing given the petitioner in the instant case.

In other words, the procedural requirements of the Administrative Procedure Act are applicable, anything in the Act to the contrary notwithstanding, in all cases requiring, in the opinion of the Court, a hearing by virtue of the due process clause of the Constitution.

On the other hand, since *entry* by an alien into the United States is a *privilege,* not a vested right, Congress may prescribe conditions of entry and *entrust to executive officers the duty of specifying the procedures* for carrying out the congressional intent, "because the power of exclusion of aliens is also inherent in the executive department of the sovereign." [65] Shortly after the decision in the Wong Yang case, Congress provided that "proceedings under laws relating to the exclusion or expulsion of aliens shall hereafter be without regard to the provisions of Sections 5, 7 and 8 of the Administrative Procedure Act," [66] thus nullifying the effect of the decision.

What Constitutes Notice and Hearing

Notice and Pleading.—A person entitled to an administrative hearing must be given such specific notice of the time and place of the hearing and of the charges against him as will enable him to formulate a defense.[67]

An elementary and fundamental requirement of due process in any proceeding which is to be accorded finality is notice reasonably calculated, under all the circumstances, to appraise interested parties of the pendency of the action, afford them an opportunity to present their objections. . . . The notice must be of such a nature as reasonably to convey the required information, . . . and it must afford a reasonable time for those interested to make their appearance, ...[68]

Before a license may be suspended for fraud or misrepresentation, the licensee must have notice of the particular acts charged as con-

---

[65] *United States v. Shaughnessy,* 338 U.S. 537, 543, 70 S. Ct. 309, 313, 94 L. Ed. 317 (1950). Said Mr. Justice Minton: "At the outset we wish to point out that an alien who seeks admission to this country may not do so under any claim of right. Admission of aliens to the United States is a privilege granted by the sovereign United States Government. Such privilege is granted to an alien only upon such terms as the United States shall prescribe. It must be exercised in accordance with the procedure which the United States provides." 338 U.S. at 542.

[66] *Public Law 843,* Chap. 3, 81st Cong., 2d Sess. (1950).

[67] *Brahy v. Federal Radio Commission,* 59 F. (2d) 879 (App. D.C., 1932); *Alton & Southern R. v. Commerce Commission,* 316 Ill. 625, 147 N.E. 417 (1925); *Liquor Shop v. O'Connell,* 273 App. Div. 68, 70, 75 N.Y.S. (2d) 411, 413 (1st Dept., 1947).

[68] *Mullane v. Central Hanover Bank and Trust Co.,* 339 U.S. 306, 314, 70 S. Ct. 652, 657, 94 L. Ed. 865, 873 (1950).

stituting fraud or misrepresentation.[69] Preciseness of notice also requires that the administrative action taken shall be based upon evidence or information that lies within the scope of the issues as set forth in the published notice; [70] except, that the issues may be enlarged, the pleadings amended, both before and during the hearing, provided ample time is allowed the parties to prepare their case. Amendments may be made during the hearing at the request of the parties, and continuance is necessary only if one of the parties claims to be surprised thereby.[71] It would appear, too, that an agency may amend the pleadings so as to make them conform to the proof to which no objection has been taken; [72] otherwise the pleadings would control the evidence, whereas the evidence should shape or reshape the pleadings. On the other hand:

> The function of the complaint is solely to advise the respondent of the charges made, so that he may have due notice and full opportunity for a hearing thereon. It does not purport to set out the elements of a crime like an indictment or information, nor the elements of a cause of action like a declaration at law or a bill of equity. All that is requisite in a complaint before the Commission [Federal Trade Commission] is that there be a plain statement of the thing claimed to be wrong so that the respondent may be put upon his defense. . . .
>
> The complaint here under consideration stated clearly that an unfair method of competition had been used by respondents, and specified what it was, namely, refusing to sell cotton ties unless the customer would purchase with each six ties also six yards of bagging. *The complaint did not set out the circumstances which rendered this tying of bagging to ties an unfair practice. But this was not necessary.* The complaint was similar in form to those filed with the Interstate Commerce Commission on complaints to enforce prohibition of "unjust and unreasonable charges" or of "undue or unreasonable preference or advantage" which the Act to Regulate Commerce imposes. *It is unnecessary to set forth why the rate specified was unjust or why the preference specified is undue or unreasonable, because these are matters not of law but of fact to be established by the evidence.*[73]

[69] *Abrams v. Dougherty,* 60 Cal. App. 297, 212 Pac. 942 (1922).

[70] *Carl Zeiss, Inc. v. United States,* 76 F. (2d) 412 (1935).

[71] *Jefferson Electric Co. v. National Labor Relations Board,* 102 F. (2d) 949 (C.C.A. 7th, 1939) ; *Harris v. Hoage,* 66 F. (2d) 801 (App. D.C., 1939).

[72] *Earl W. Baker & Co. v. Maples,* 155 Okla. 105, 8 P. (2d) 46 (1932) ; *Brahy v. Federal Radio Commission,* 59 F. (2d) 879 (App. D.C., 1932) ; *National Licorice Co. v. National Labor Relations Board,* 309 U.S. 350, 60 S. Ct. 569, 84 L. Ed. 799 (1940).

[73] Mr. Justice Brandeis, dissenting, in *Federal Trade Commission v. Gratz,* 253 U.S. 421, 430–31, 40 S. Ct. 572, 575–76, 64 L. Ed. 993, 997 (1920). Italics supplied.

A notice received in any manner other than that prescribed by the statute, is not legal notice.[74] Exceptions are made for minor irregularities and when the only person who is entitled to the notice appears, which generally validates a defective notice.

In proceedings against a class of persons, such as a labor union or a chamber of commerce, notice may be served upon representative members of that class.

> When procedure against a class is proper in judicial proceedings, there would seem no reason why the same thing should not be done in less formal hearings, such as this [by the Federal Trade Commission], provided always that the conditions are such as to make the class representation rule applicable. . . . These necessary conditions are (1) a common or general interest and (2) such number of individuals as to make it impracticable to bring all of them before the court.[75]

Notice to the duly constituted officers of an organization generally is sufficient to bind the members.[76]

In actions against real property, such as assessments for improvements or foreclosure of liens for unpaid taxes, notice by publication is fairly common.

> The Constitution, . . . does not require that *personal notice* of a proceeding be given to one whose property, situated within this commonwealth, is sought to be affected, and when no personal judgment against him is sought. *Substituted notice* in such a case is sufficient, if it be reasonably probable that it will reach the person interested, and apprise him of what is going on, and will afford him an opportunity to come in and defend his property. . . . As was pointed out by Mr. Justice McKenna in Ballard v. Hunter (204 U. S. 241) and by Mr. Justice Miller in Huling v. Kaw Valley Railway (130 id. 559), the duty rests upon the owner to keep himself informed concerning his real property. If he fails to do so, and notice affecting his lands, given by such publication as is usually required in like cases, fails to reach him, it is his misfortune, and he must suffer the consequences. The public is charged with knowledge of the provisions of all statutes, and is required to take notice of the procedure therein specified.[77]

In tax proceedings, however, if a tax increase is not confined to certain individuals but affects taxpayers generally, notice by publication

---

[74] *H. F. Wilcox Oil & Gas Co. v. Walker,* 168 Okla. 355, 32 P. (2d) 1044 (1934). See Gellhorn, *op. cit.,* pp. 392–95 for cases.

[75] *Chamber of Commerce v. Federal Trade Commission,* 13 F. (2d) 673 (C.C.A. 8th, 1926).

[76] *Estes v. Union Terminal Co.,* 89 F. (2d) 768 (C.C.A. 5th, 1937).

[77] *Buffalo v. Hawks,* 226 App. Div. 480, 483, 484–85, 236 N.Y. Supp. 89, 93, 95 (1929), affirmed 251 N.Y. 588, 168 N.E. 438 (1929). Italics supplied.

is all that is required; [78] and, in either situation, personal notice is not necessary if the statute fixes the time and place for the meeting of the board of assessors or of equalization.[79]

In a proceeding for judicial settlement of accounts by a trustee of a common trust fund, statutory notice by newspaper publication setting forth the name and address of the trust company, the name and date of the establishment of the common trust fund, and a list of all participating estates, trusts, or funds, is sufficient to satisfy due process as to those beneficiaries whose interests or whereabouts cannot with due diligence be ascertained, but not as to known beneficiaries of known place of residence.[80]

Hearing.—GENERAL PREREQUISITES. The courts have conceded that administrative hearings of necessity may be informal—that they are not governed by the common law rules of evidence.[81] But this informality is tempered by the tendency of judges "to amalgamate their notions of due process with the procedure to which their own experience has habituated them," so that administrative procedure "must approximate the formal methods from which it was hoped there would be escape." [82]

Said Mr. Chief Justice Hughes:

> . . . if these multiplying agencies deemed necessary in our complex society are to serve the purposes for which they are created and endowed with vast powers, they must accredit themselves by acting in accordance with cherished judicial tradition embodying the basic concepts of fair play.[83]

From Utah came the following echo:

> For these agencies, which necessarily multiply in our complex society, —to serve the purposes for which they are created and endowed with

[78] *Bi-Metallic Investment Co. v. State Board of Equalization*, 239 U.S. 441, 36 S. Ct. 141, 60 L. Ed. 372 (1915) ; *Draffen v. City of Paducah*, 215 Ky. 139, 284 S.W. 1027 (1926).

[79] *Pittsburgh, Cincinnati & Chicago & St. L. Ry. Co. v. Backus*, 154 U.S. 421, 14 S. Ct. 1114, 38 L. Ed. 1031 (1894).

[80] *Mullane v. Central Hanover Bank and Trust Co.*, 339 U.S. 306, 70 S. Ct. 652, 94 L. Ed. 865 (1950).

[81] *Interstate Commerce Commission v. Baird*, 194 U.S. 25, 24 S. Ct. 563, 48 L. Ed. 860 (1904) ; *National Labor Relations Board v. Donnelly Garment Co.*, 330 U.S. 219, 236, 67 S. Ct. 756, 765, 91 L. Ed. 854, 867 (1947) ; *National Labor Relations Board v. Grieder Machine, T. & D. Co.*, 142 F. (2d) 163 (C.C.A. 6th, 1944) ; *National Labor Relations Board v. T. W. Phillips Gas & Oil Co.*, 141 F. (2d) 304 (C.C.A. 3d, 1944) ; *Bridges v. Wixon*, 144 F. (2d) 927 (C.C.A. 9th, 1944).

[82] Gellhorn, *op. cit.*, p. 441.

[83] *Morgan v. United States*, 304 U.S. 1, 22, 58 S. Ct. 773, 778, 82 L. Ed. 1129 (1938).

such vast power, they must accredit themselves by acting in harmony with the inbred concepts of fair play and the cherished traditions of a cautious, deliberate and judicious determination of the questions affecting people's rights or liberties.[84]

And the Senate Committee on the Judiciary in its report on the Administrative Procedure Act said that "the standards and principles of probity and reliability of evidence must be the same as those prevailing in courts of law or equity in nonadministrative cases." But in the next sentence the Committee admits that

> There are no real rules of probity and reliability even in courts of law, but there are certain standards and principles—usually applied tacitly and resting mainly upon common sense—which people engaged in the conduct of responsible affairs instinctively understand and act upon. They may vary with the circumstances and kind of case, but they exist and must be rationally applied. These principles, under this subsection, are to govern in administrative proceedings.[85]

A fairly comprehensive statement of "the fundamentals ordinarily requisite to a fair hearing leading to adverse action against an individual" is found in the Final Report of the Attorney General's Committee on Administrative Procedure:

> Before adverse action is to be taken by an agency, whether it be denying privileges to an applicant or bounties to a claimant, before a cease-and-desist order is issued or privileges or bounties are permanently withdrawn, before an individual is ordered directly to alter his method of business, or before discipline is imposed upon him, the individual immediately concerned should be apprised not only of the contemplated action with sufficient precision to permit his preparation to resist, but, before final action, he should be apprised of the evidence and contentions brought forward against him so that he may meet them. He must be offered a forum which provides him with an opportunity to bring his own contentions home to those who will adjudicate the controversy in which he is concerned. The forum itself must be one which is prepared

---

[84] *McGrew v. Industrial Commission,* 96 Utah 203, 225, 85 P. (2d) 608, 618 (1938).

An administrative hearing "must conform to fair practices as they are known in Anglo-Saxon jurisprudence. . . . Orders by administrative boards, after hearings, can be justified only by the adherence of the hearing officers to basic principles and standards, which constitute the genius of our jurisprudence. Such principles and standards are designed to protect the life, liberty and property of the individual in accordance with the American standard. They are the 'inexorable safeguard' of quasi-judicial procedure." *Takeo Tadano v. Manney,* 160 F. (2d) 665, 667 (C.C.A. 9th, 1947).

[85] *S. Rep. No. 752,* 79th Cong., 1st Sess., p. 22.

to receive and consider all that he offers which is relevant to the controversy.[86]

Furthermore, the "forum," the regulatory agency, must be impartial in its composition. "If a partial, biased, and prejudiced Commissioner participates in a judicial or quasi-judicial proceeding the ends of justice and the due-process requirements of the Constitution alike would be defeated. As the Commission is a tribunal of last as well as first resort as to findings of fact, it must, to serve the ends of justice, be free from passion, prejudice, or personal hostility." [87] Under the Bituminous Coal Conservation Act of 1935,[88] a code was formulated by the Commission which provided, among other things, that wage agreements negotiated between representatives of more than two-thirds of the mine owners by tonnage and of more than a majority of the mine workers in any district or group of districts, should be binding upon all code members of such district or districts. In holding this unlawful the Supreme Court stated:

> The power conferred upon the majority is, in effect, the power to regulate the affairs of an unwilling minority. This is legislative delegation in its most obnoxious form; for, it is not even delegation to an official or an official body, presumptively disinterested, but to private persons whose interests may be and often are adverse to the interests of others in the same business. . . . The delegation is so utterly arbitrary, and so clearly a denial of rights safeguarded by the due process clause of the Fifth Amendment, that it is unnecessary to do more than refer to decisions of this court which foreclose the question.[89]

When, however, the Act was amended to provide for regulation by a commission of five, two of which were to be experienced mine opera-

[86] *Administrative Procedure in Government Agencies, S. Doc. No. 8,* 77th Cong., 1st Sess. (1941), p. 62. And said Mr. Justice Lamar in *Interstate Commerce Commission v. Louisville & Nashville R.R. Co.,* 227 U.S. 88, 93–94, 33 S. Ct. 185, 187–88, 57 L. Ed. 431, 434 (1913): "But the more liberal the practice in admitting testimony, the more imperative the obligation to preserve the essential rules of evidence by which rights are asserted or defended. In such cases the Commissioners cannot act upon their own information, as could jurors in primitive days. All parties must be fully apprised of the evidence submitted or to be considered, and must be given opportunity to cross-examine witnesses, to inspect documents, and to offer evidence in explanation or rebuttal. In no other way can a party maintain its rights or make its defense. In no other way can it test the sufficiency of the facts to support the finding; for otherwise, even though it appeared that the order was without evidence, the manifest deficiency could always be explained on the theory that the Commission had before it extraneous, unknown, but presumptively sufficient information to support the finding."

[87] *In re Segal and Smith,* 5 F.C.C. 3, 11–12 (1937).

[88] 49 *Stat.* 991, 15 *U.S.C.A.* § 801 *et sqq.*

[89] *Carter v. Carter Coal Co.,* 298 U.S. 238, 311, 56 S. Ct. 855, 873, 80 L. Ed. 1160, 1189 (1936).

tors and two experienced mine workers,[90] the Court did not raise any constitutional objection.[91]

An agency examiner is not to be deemed "biased," and hence disqualified, by reason of prior adverse rulings and findings. Such a disqualifying rule, explained the Supreme Court, is not applied in judicial proceedings, and

> We find no warrant for imposing upon administrative agencies a stiffer rule, whereby examiners would be disentitled to sit because they ruled strongly against a party in the first hearing. The Board might have gone beyond the legal compulsions and ordered the new evidence to be heard before a new Examiner who could report with a mind wholly free from prior litigious embroilments. The Board might have been well advised also to allow greater leeway in admitting evidence not strictly relevant. It takes time to avoid even the appearance of grievances. But it is time well spent, even though it is not easy to satisfy interested parties, and defeated litigants, no matter how fairly treated, do not always have the feeling that they have received justice. In any event we are not the advisers of these agencies. And we have no right to upset their orders unless they fall afoul of legal requirements.[92]

In a case involving a charge of prejudgment by the New York State Civil Service Commission, the State Supreme Court held that

> It is well settled, that where the Legislature vests in a particular officer or administrative agency the sole power of investigation and decision, the Legislature's purpose cannot be defeated by disqualification of the designated officer or agency on the ground of alleged prejudgment or bias.[93]

The fact that the Federal Trade Commission, in its official reports, expresses opinions, as the result of ex parte investigations, with respect to the legality of certain trade practices, does not preclude the Commission from acting in subsequent unfair trade practices proceedings where the respondents are free to rebut by evidence and argument the conclusions previously arrived at by the Commission: otherwise the "experience acquired from their work as commissioners would be a handicap instead of an advantage," and investigations

---

[90] Act of 1937, 50 *Stat.* 72, 15 *U.S.C.A.* § 833(c).

[91] *Sunshine Anthracite Coal Co. v. Adkins,* 310 U.S. 381, 60 S. Ct. 907, 84 L. Ed. 1263 (1940).

[92] *National Labor Relations Board v. Donnelly Garment Co.,* 330 U.S. 219, 236–37, 67 S. Ct. 756, 765, 91 L. Ed. 854, 867 (1947).

[93] *Kaney v. Civil Service Commission,* 190 Misc. 944, 947–48, 77 N.Y.S. (2d) 8, 13 (Sup. Ct., 1948).

by the Commission as required by law would immunize "the practices investigated, even though they are 'unfair,' from any cease and desist order by the Commission or any other governmental agency." [94]

Nor does the concentration of functions in an agency make the agency "biased" so as to render it incapable of giving a fair hearing. In regard to the concentration of functions in the Alcohol Tax Unit of the Bureau of Internal Revenue a federal court observed:

> It is of course true that the charge originated in, was investigated, prosecuted, heard, and decided by the agency charged with the administration of the Act. But this adjudicatory plan is encompassed within the Congressional enactment, is not repugnant to constitutional concepts, and the remedy for the evil, if it be called evil, does not therefore lie in the courts.[95]

But in another case, a state court said:

> Where a *disqualified* member of a tribunal, which is composed of two or more persons and which exercises judicial or quasi-judicial power, acts as a member of a tribunal notwithstanding his disqualification, such action makes a decision of the tribunal void or at least voidable at the instance of a party aggrieved who has made timely protest to the jurisdiction of the tribunal as constituted. It appears that in England, and in some states in this country, the decision by a tribunal so constituted is void, while in other states it is only voidable.[96]

The denial of a fair hearing, and so of due process of law, is not established by proving merely that the decision was wrong. "This is equally true whether the error consists in deciding wrongly that evidence introduced constituted legal evidence of the fact, or in drawing a wrong inference from the evidence," unless the error is "so flagrant as to convince a court that the hearing had was not a fair one." [97]   Also, the fact that the members of an administrative agency which finally decided the case did not hear the witnesses, nor the argument, and did not prepare the findings of fact nor the conclusions of law, does not constitute a denial of due process of law.[98]

[94] *Federal Trade Commission v. Cement Institute,* 333 U.S. 683, 702, 701, 68 S. Ct. 793, 804, 803, 92 L. Ed. 1010, 1035, 1034 (1948).

[95] *Levers v. Berkshire,* 159 F. (2d) 689, 693 (C.C.A. 10th, 1947). See also *Fahey v. Malonee,* 332 U.S. 245, 256, 67 S. Ct. 1552, 1557, 91 L. Ed. 2030, 2040 (1947).

[96] *Narragansett Racing Association, Inc. v. Kiernan,* 59 R.I. 90, 112, 194 Atl. 692, 701 (1937). Italics supplied.

[97] *United States ex rel. Tisi v. Tod,* 264 U.S. 131, 133, 44 S. Ct. 260, 261, 68 L. Ed. 590, 591 (1924).

[98] *Lacomastic Corp. v. Parker,* 54 F. Supp. 138 (D.C. Md., 1944).

In some situations notice and hearing prior to administrative action is not practicable. Courts agree that the police power "justifies the 'abatement, by summary proceedings, of whatever may be regarded as a public nuisance,'" [99] although there is a tendency to apply this rule strictly. [100] This deviation from the usual procedure requiring notice and hearing is permissible because the administrative action is not final. If the property abated is not in fact a nuisance, the owner may resort to equity for an injunction or to law for damages. [101] Furthermore, notice and hearing on the administrative level is not necessary if there is a right to a full hearing *de novo* in a court to determine the legality of an order. [102]

The courts distinguish, also, between a *hearing* and a *preliminary investigation* to determine whether the facts justify a decision to hold a hearing or to bring suit for injunctive relief. Investigations of this kind are analogous to grand jury proceedings, and are not governed by the procedural requirements for a *hearing*. [103] An investigation, unlike a hearing, makes no determination or decision between the parties for there are no parties. A similar distinction is made between a hearing before an investigating body, such as the Tariff Commission, and a regulatory agency, such as the Interstate Commerce Commission. The first type of agency merely advises, while the other ordains; therefore, the traditional forms of hearing appropriate to the latter are unknown to the former. [104]

The exercise of some governmental powers, such as foreign affairs, involves a large degree of secrecy, and so may require that public hearings be dispensed with in the interest of public security. It has been held, by way of example, that the alien wife of a citizen (a war veteran) may be excluded without hearing and solely upon a finding by the Attorney General that her admission would be prejudicial to the interests of the United States. [105] The admission or exclusion of aliens is a fundamental act of sovereignty, which not only stems from legislative power but is inherent in the executive

[99] *Application of Barkan,* 189 Misc. 358, 359, 71 N.Y.S. (2d) 267, 269 (1947).

[100] *Cox v. Cox,* 400 Ill. 291, 79 N.E. (2d) 497 (1948).

[101] *City of Newburgh v. Park Filling Station,* 273 App. Div. 24, 26, 75 N.Y.S. (2d) 439, 441 (1947).

[102] *Jordan v. American Eagle Fire Insurance Co.,* 169 F. (2d) 281 (App. D.C., 1948).

[103] *In re Securities and Exchange Commission,* 84 F. (2d) 316 (C.C.A. 2d, 1936); *Consolidated Mines of California v. Securities and Exchange Commission,* 97 F. (2d) 704 (C.C.A. 9th, 1938).

[104] *Norwegian Nitrogen Products Co. v. United States,* 288 U.S. 294, 53 S. Ct. 350, 77 L. Ed. 796 (1933).

[105] *United States v. Shaughnessy,* 338 U.S. 537, 70 S. Ct. 309, 94 L. Ed. 317 (1950).

power to control the foreign affairs of the nation. The action of an executive officer under such authority is final and conclusive. Three Justices condemned the procedure as "abhorrent to free men." Mr. Justice Jackson, dissenting, said:

> Security is like liberty in that many are the crimes committed in its name. The menace to the security of this country, be it great as it may, from this girl's admission is as nothing compared to the menace to free institution inherent in procedures of this pattern. In the name of security the police state justifies its arbitrary oppressions on evidence that is secret, because security might be prejudiced if it were brought to light in hearings. The plea that evidence of guilt must be secret is abhorrent to free men, because it provides a cloak for the malevolent, the misinformed, the meddlesome, and the corrupt to play the role of informer undetected and uncorrected.[106]

The right to a hearing may be waived, and failure of a party to request a hearing as provided by statute or by administrative regulations constitutes a waiver.[107] Legal hearing has been accorded when due notice has been given, but the interested party does not appear on advice of the counsel.[108]

DUTY TO HEAR EVIDENCE. In the first Morgan case,[109] Mr. Chief Justice Hughes said:

> The requirement of a "full hearing" has obvious reference to the tradition of judicial proceedings in which evidence is received and weighed by the trier of the facts. The "hearing" is designed to afford the safeguard that the one who decides shall be bound in good conscience to consider the evidence, to be guided by that alone, and to reach his conclusion, uninfluenced by extraneous considerations which in other fields might have play in determining purely executive action. The "hearing" is the hearing of evidence and argument. If the one who determines the facts which underlie the order has not considered evidence or argument, it is manifest that the hearing has not been given.[110]

This does not mean that the deciding officer must necessarily be the hearing officer, but that he who decides must have given due

---

[106] 338 U.S. at 551, 70 S. Ct. at 317, 94 L. Ed. at 328–29; Mr. Justice Black and Mr. Justice Frankfurter joined in this dissent. Mr. Justice Douglas and Mr. Justice Clark did not take part in the case.

[107] *Direct Realty Co. v. Porter,* 157 F. (2d) 434 (C.C.A., 1946).

[108] *Ranke v. Michigan Corp. and Securities Commission,* 317 Mich. 304, 26 N.W. (2d) 898 (1947).

[109] *Morgan v. United States,* 298 U.S. 468, 56 S. Ct. 906, 80 L. Ed. 1288 (1936).

[110] 298 U.S. at 480–81, 56 S. Ct. at 911, 80 L. Ed. at 1295. The rules laid down in the Morgan case were rejected in *State v. Board of Commissioners,* 184 P. (2d) 577, 590 (Wash., 1947).

consideration to the evidence by whomsoever it may have been taken.[111] What constitutes due consideration is unclear, but obviously the deciding officer is not required to hear or read *all* the evidence. Said the District Court in reference to the decision in the first Morgan case:

> The Supreme Court has not said that it was the duty of the Secretary of Agriculture to hear or read *all* the evidence and, *in addition thereto,* to hear the oral arguments and to read and consider briefs. If the Supreme Court had said that it would have meant that the Packers and Stockyards Act . . . cannot be administered. . . .
>
> Consider that in this very case the transcript of the oral testimony fills 13,000 pages. . . . A narrative statement of just a part of the oral testimony fills 500 pages. Learned counsel for plaintiffs assert indeed that they do not mean to contend that the Secretary personally must have read all of this mass of testimony. Such a contention could not be maintained. Let it be frankly stated now that the judges of this court, whose duty it was to consider the case de novo (since it involved constitutional issues), did not read all this testimony. We think, moreover, that it may be predicted with some assurance that all this testimony will not be read by the justices of the Supreme Court when, as they must, consider the cases on the merits.[112]

To what extent the Administrative Procedure Act has modified the ruling in the first Morgan case awaits judicial determination. Section 7(a) provides for presiding or hearing officers, and Section 7(b) defines the duties and powers of these officers.[113]

In view of the broad powers here granted, the reasoning of a California court interpreting the procedural provisions of the State Administrative Procedure Act would seem applicable. This court held that the Morgan cases "cannot be interpreted to mean that, where a fair trial is required by the statute before a fair and impartial hearing officer who is required by the statute to weigh and appraise the evidence and prepare a proposed decision, the Legislature cannot provide that the administrative agency may adopt his proposed decision

---

[111] In ruling that the Rent Administrator of the District of Columbia could not adopt a determination of a minimum service standard by a trial examiner without personally examining the evidence on which the examiner had based his conclusion, the District Court said: "This does not mean that the Administrator may not avail himself of the assistance of examiners to hear, analyze and sift evidence and make recommendations, but it does mean that the one on whom final responsibility for the determination is imposed must consider and appraise the evidence which justifies the determination." *Sager v. Parker*, 55 Atl. (2) 349, 351 (D.C., 1947).

[112] *Morgan v. United States*, 23 F. Supp. 380, 382 (1937). Italics supplied.

[113] *Public Law No. 404*, 79th Cong., 2d Sess. For the provisions of Sections 7(a) and 7(b) see page 75.

without reading the record." [114] And a New York court refused to apply the rule of the first Morgan case to the proceedings of the State Labor Relations Board, holding that

> Personal examination by each member of the Labor Relations Board of all the testimony as a prerequisite to a determination is not an essential. For many reasons such a reading of all of the record might be a labor of supererogation. . . . The members of the Labor Relations Board are entitled to avail themselves of the services of competent assistants in the sifting and analyzing of the proof.[115]

If a hearing agency excludes relevant evidence, the injured party is not entitled to have that evidence introduced in court but only to have it taken by the agency, which is the tribunal of first resort; [116] nor may a reviewing court modify the agency order to conform to the excluded evidence, but must remand the matter to the agency for its determination prior to formulating its order.[117]

A refusal to *hear* testimony offered by an interested party is not due process, and on appeal a court will remand the case to the agency with instructions to admit the evidence.[118] But if the evidence is admitted, and the agency *asserts* that the evidence was duly considered, the courts will sustain an order against the charge that the agency did not take the evidence into account in reaching its findings. Mr. Justice Frankfurter has said:

> It is a grave responsibility to conclude that in admitting the testimony of the Company's employees, the Board [National Labor Relations Board] went through a mere pretense of obedience to the Court's direction, and heard the testimony with a deaf ear and a closed mind. In the light of the authority with which Congress has endowed the Board, and with due regard to the conscientiousness which we must attribute to another branch of the Government, we cannot reject its explicit avowal that it did take into account evidence which it should have considered unless an examination of the whole record puts its acceptance beyond reason.[119]

[114] *Hohreiter v. Garrison,* 184 P. (2d) 323, 333 (Cal., 1947).

[115] *Labor Relations Board v. Greif Realty Corp.,* 272 App. Div. 928, 71 N.Y.S. (2d) 91, 92 (2d Dept., 1947).

[116] *Consolidated Edison Co. v. National Labor Relations Board,* 305 U.S. 197, 59 S. Ct. 206, 83 L. Ed. 126 (1938).

[117] *Phelps Dodge Corporation v. National Labor Relations Board,* 313 U.S. 177, 61 S. Ct. 845, 85 L. Ed. 1271 (1941).

[118] *Donnelly Garment Co. v. National Labor Relations Board,* 123 F. (2d) 215 (C.C.A. 8th, 1941).

[119] *National Labor Relations Board v. Donnelly Garment Co.,* 330 U.S. 219, 229, 67 S. Ct. 756, 762, 91 L. Ed. 854, 863 (1947).

While the exclusion of competent, relevant, and material evidence may vitiate an administrative determination, the mere admission of irrelevant or unreliable evidence is "not to be taken as a prejudicial error,"[120] since an administrative hearing is compared with an equity proceeding in the courts (where there is no jury to be influenced by the improper evidence). It is the proper use rather than the improper admission of such evidence that may be questioned.[121]

> In the conduct of quasi-judicial hearings administrative agencies are not legally bound by the exclusionary rules of evidence which limit admissibility in judicial proceedings. To put the matter another way, the mere admission of evidence that would be excluded by the legal rules of evidence, whether on grounds of incompetency, irrelevancy or immateriality, will not vitiate the proceedings.[122]

In a leading case in the Supreme Court, Mr. Chief Justice Hughes said:

> The companies urge that the Board [Labor Board] received "remote hearsay" and "mere rumor." The statute provides that "the rules of evidence prevailing in courts of law shall not be controlling." The obvious purpose of this and similar provisions is to free administrative boards from the compulsion of technical rules so that the mere admission of matter which would be deemed incompetent in judicial proceedings would not invalidate the administrative order. . . . But this assurance of a desirable flexibility in administrative procedure does not go so far as to justify orders without a basis in evidence having rational probative force. Mere uncorroborated hearsay or rumor does not constitute substantial evidence.[123]

As to deportation proceedings, the Supreme Court in a five-to-four opinion set aside a deportation order on the ground that the Attorney General had admitted and considered hearsay evidence, which was contrary to common law, and so not due process.[124] In a vigorous dissent, Mr. Justice Stone said:

[120] *S. Rep. No. 752,* 79th Cong., 1st Sess., p. 22. "The mere admission by an administrative tribunal of matter which under the rules of evidence applicable in judicial proceedings would be deemed incompetent does not invalidate its order." *United States v. Abilene & So. Ry. Co.,* 265 U.S. 274, 288, 44 S. Ct. 565, 569, 68 L. Ed. 1016, 1022 (1924).

[121] *Vajtauer v. Commissioner of Immigration,* 273 U.S. 103, 106, 47 S. Ct. 302, 304, 71 L. Ed. 560, 563 (1927).

[122] *Commissioner's Report on Administrative Adjudication in the State of New York* (1942), p. 171.

[123] *Consolidated Edison Co. v. National Labor Relations Board,* 305 U.S. 197, 229–30, 59 S. Ct. 206, 217, 83 L. Ed. 126, 140 (1938).

[124] *Bridges v. Wixon,* 326 U.S. 135, 65 S. Ct. 1443, 89 L. Ed. 2103 (1945).

That the evidence would be inadmissible in a criminal proceeding is irrelevant here, since a deportation proceeding is not a criminal proceeding. . . . And no principle of law has been better settled than that the technical rules for the exclusion of evidence, applicable in trials in courts, particularly the hearsay rule, need not be followed in deportation proceedings, ... The only objections that can be taken to the evidence in such proceedings are not to its admissibility, but to its probative value.[125]

But there is the following qualification:

. . . where evidence was improperly received and where but for that evidence it is wholly speculative whether the requisite finding would have been made. Then there is deportation without a fair hearing which may be corrected on habeas corpus.[126]

So hearsay evidence may be considered if it merely corroborates other competent evidence,[127] or if the order is supported by other evidence of recognized probative character;[128] but an order which is based solely upon hearsay evidence will not be sustained.[129]

There are persuasive arguments in favor of this rule. Not only are the judicial rules of evidence too technical for application by non-lawyers, but they are not adapted to the administrative process, which, unlike the judicial process, is concerned with the formulation and execution of public policy.[130]

An administrative adjudication must rest upon evidence appearing in the record of the hearing, otherwise it is not possible for an appellate court to review the law and the facts and intelligently decide that the findings of the agency are supported by the evidence.[131] Furthermore, "Nothing can be treated as evidence which is not introduced as such," [132] and so an order which rested in part upon data

---

[125] 326 U.S. at 175–76, 65 S. Ct. at 1462, 89 L. Ed. at 2126–27.

[126] 326 U.S. at 156. Hearsay evidence has been held competent in State courts: *Case v. Michigan Liquor Control Commission*, 314 Mich. 632, 23 N.W. (2d) 109 (1946); *Scales v. Texas Liquor Control Board*, 192 S.W. (2d) 466 (1946).

[127] *Johnson v. Employment Security Commission*, 32 N.W. (2d) 786 (Iowa, 1948); *Cia. Mexicana de Gas v. Federal Power Commission*, 167 F. (2d) 804 (5th Cir., 1948).

[128] *Lambing v. Consolidated Coal Co.*, 54 Atl. (2d) 291 (Pa., 1947).

[129] *Kinney v. Employers' Retirement System*, 176 P. (2d) 775 (Cal., 1947); *In re Schmidt*, 68 F. Supp. 765 (N.D. Cal., 1946); *Twibill v. Federal Shipbuilding Co.*, 56 Atl. (2d) 602 (N.J., 1948).

[130] See 326 U.S. at 171–80 for discussion.

[131] *Ohio Bell Telephone Co. v. Public Utilities Commission of Ohio*, 301 U.S. 292, 57 S. Ct. 724, 81 L. Ed. 1093 (1937).

[132] *United States v. Abilene & Southern Ry. Co.*, 265 U.S. 274, 288, 44 S. Ct. 565, 569, 68 L. Ed. 1016, 1023 (1924).

taken from the annual reports of the plaintiff, but not formally put in evidence, was held void.[133] But more recently the Court said:

> Due process, of course, requires that commissions proceed upon matters in evidence and that parties have opportunity to subject evidence to the test of cross-examination and rebuttal. But due process deals with matters of substance and is not to be trivialized by formal objections that have no substantial bearing on the ultimate rights of parties. The process of keeping informed as to regulated utilities is a continuous matter with commissions. We are unwilling to say that such an incidental reference as we have here to a party's own reports, although not formally marked in evidence in the proceeding, in the absence of any showing of error or prejudice constitutes a want of due process.[134]

Also, administrative tribunals in common with courts may take "official" or "judicial" notice of facts within their general expert knowledge, facts not found, therefore, in the record. To this effect the Supreme Court has held:

> It is true that ordinarily an administrative agency will act appropriately, in a proceeding of this sort, upon the record presented and such matters as properly may receive its attention through "official notice." It is also true that this Court, in appropriate instances, has limited the use of the latter implement in order to assure that the parties will not be deprived of a fair hearing. . . . But in doing so it has not undertaken to make a fetish of sticking squarely within the four corners of the specific record in administrative proceedings or of pinning down such agencies, with reference to fact determinations, even more rigidly than the courts in strictly judicial proceedings. On the contrary, in the one case as in the other, the mere fact that the determining body has looked beyond the record proper does not invalidate its action unless substantial prejudice is shown to result.[135]

In short

> Administrative agencies like the Federal Trade Commission have never been restricted by the rigid rules of evidence . . . rules which bar certain types of evidence in criminal or quasi-criminal cases are not controlling in proceedings like this where the effect of the Commission's order is not to punish or to fasten liability on respondents for past

[133] *Ibid.*

[134] *Market Street R. Co. v. Railroad Commission of California,* 324 U.S. 548, 562, 65 S. Ct. 770, 777, 89 L. Ed. 1171, 1182 (1945).

[135] *United States v. Pierce Auto Freight Lines, Inc.,* 327 U.S. 515, 529–30, 66 S. Ct. 687, 695, 90 L. Ed. 821, 832 (1946). Also, *Reconstruction Finance Corp. v. Denver & Rio Grande Western R.R.,* 328 U.S. 495, 516, 66 S. Ct. 1282, 1293, 90 L. Ed. 1400, 1414–15 (1946).

conduct but to ban specific practices for the future in accordance with the general mandate of Congress.[136]

TENTATIVE REPORTS. In the second Morgan case,[137] an administrative proceeding in which the deciding officer did not make the findings was found to be "fatally defective" because the complainants had not been given a "tentative report." Mr. Chief Justice Hughes again speaking for the Court said:

> The right to a hearing embraces not only the right to present evidence but also a reasonable opportunity to know the claims of the opposing party and to meet them. The right to submit argument implies that opportunity; otherwise the right may be but a barren one. Those who are brought into contest with the Government in a quasi-judicial proceeding aimed at the control of their activities are entitled to be fairly advised of what the Government proposes and to be heard upon its proposals before it issues its final command. . . .
>
> The Government adverts to an observation in our former opinion that, while it was good practice—which we approved—to have the examiner, receiving the evidence in such a case, prepare a report as a basis for exceptions and argument.[138] We could not say that that particular type of procedure was essential to the validity of the proceeding. That is true, for, as we said, what the statute requires "relates to substance and not to form." . . . But what would not be essential to the adequacy of the hearing if the Secretary himself makes the findings is not a criterion for a case in which the Secretary accepts and makes as his own the findings which have been prepared by the active prosecutors of the Government, after an ex parte discussion with them and without according any reasonable opportunity to the respondents in the proceeding to know the claims thus presented and to contest them. That is more than an irregularity in practice; it is a vital defect.[139]

---

[136] *Federal Trade Commission v. Cement Institute,* 333 U.S. 683, 705–6, 68 S. Ct. 793, 805–6, 92 L. Ed. 1010, 1037 (1948).

[137] *Morgan v. United States,* 304 U.S. 1, 58 S. Ct. 773, 82 L. Ed. 1129 (1938).

[138] In the "former opinion" the Court rejected the complaint of the brokers that they were entitled to a tentative report. Such a report was not "essential to the validity of the hearing" and "the statute does not require it." Said the Solicitor General (now Mr. Justice Jackson) in his petition for reargument: ". . . the issue as to a tentative report was eliminated from the case. Two years later—after a second trial in the District Court upon a different procedural issue and a second appeal on that issue—the Court now revives the questions of a tentative report and holds that the failure of the Secretary of Agriculture to serve such a report, five years previously, was a 'vital defect.'" Quoted by Gellhorn, *op. cit.,* p. 718. In *Consolidated Edison Co. v. National Labor Relations Board,* 305 U.S. 197, 228, 59 S. Ct. 206, 216, 83 L. Ed. 126, 139 (1938) the Court said that "It would have been better practice for the Board to have directed the examiner to make a tentative report with an opportunity for exceptions and argument therein." But the Court did not require a tentative report.

[139] 304 U.S. at 18–22, 58 S. Ct. at 776–78. 82 L. Ed. at 1132–34.

This principle is incorporated in Section 8(a) of the Administrative Procedure Act to the extent that

Whenever the agency makes the initial decision without having presided at the reception of the evidence, such officers [the subordinate hearing officers] *shall first recommend a decision except that in rulemaking or determining applications for initial licenses* (1) in lieu thereof the agency may issue a tentative decision or any of its responsible officers may recommend a decision or (2) any such procedure may be omitted in any case in which the agency finds upon the record that due and timely execution of its functions imperatively and unavoidably so requires.

The requirement of a tentative or intermediate report or decision has some obvious drawbacks, as pointed out in the *Commissioner's Report on Administrative Adjudication in the State of New York:*

While the merits of the examiner-report procedure are apparent, its utility as a procedure of general application is limited by several factors. It is apparent, first, that its most successful operation often requires not only high qualifications on the part of the trial examiner but also diligence in the preparation of his report. The difficulty of drafting a satisfactory report increases as questions of policy or of the exercise of discretion, or difficult questions of law, or complicated questions of fact, enter into the determination to be made; but even in the absence of such questions the preparation of a wholly satisfactory intermediate report is likely to be difficult. To the extent that the intermediate report falls short of what it should be, the argument before the deciding body will tend to degenerate into an argument about the report rather than about the merits of the case. If the intermediate report does not at least raise all the relevant issues (whether or not it decides them all correctly), and if the final decision is on some ground untouched in the intermediate report, reargument after the final decision may be necessary. Apart from such problems as to the adequacy of intermediate reports, the examiner-report procedure involves substantial delay in adjudication.[140]

FINDINGS. Since an administrative order which affects private rights must be based upon "substantial evidence," the officer or agency making the order must make "findings" embodying such evidence. The absence of "the basic or essential findings required to support an agency's order renders it void." [141] This is an administrative duty owed in the first place to the parties affected in that it enables them

[140] P. 229.

[141] *State of Florida v. United States*, 282 U.S. 194, 51 S. Ct. 119, 75 L. Ed. 291 (1931); *State of North Carolina v. United States*, 325 U.S. 507, 65 S. Ct. 1260, 89 L. Ed. 1760 (1945); *United States v. Baltimore & Ohio R. Co.*, 293 U.S. 454, 55 S. Ct. 268, 79 L. Ed. 587 (1935).

to judge for themselves whether or not the decision rests upon the evidence, and so whether or not to ask for a rehearing or for judicial review. The findings thus tend to assure the parties of considered action by the deciding officer. In the second place they are a necessary basis for an intelligent judicial review. "We must know what a decision means," the Supreme Court has said, "before the duty becomes ours to say whether it is right or wrong." [142] In a case involving the conviction of a draftee for failure to report for induction, a Circuit Court of Appeals held that ". . . since the conclusions of the board of appeal are necessarily based upon the written record, omission of material facts deprives the registrant of his right to an adequate consideration of his case on appeal and amounts to a denial of due process by the local board which invalidates its classification and order of induction into the armed services." [143] In the matter of ratemaking by the Interstate Commerce Commission, the Court has emphasized the need for "sufficient explication to enable the parties and ourselves to understand, with fair degree of assurance, why the Commission acts as it does." [144] And in the Chenery Corporation case the Supreme Court restated the rule as follows:

When the case was first here,[145] we emphasized a simple but fundamental rule of administrative law. That rule is to the effect that a reviewing court, in dealing with a determination or judgment which an administrative agency alone is authorized to make, must judge the propriety of such action solely by the grounds invoked by the agency. If those grounds are inadequate or improper, the court is powerless to affirm the administrative action by substituting what it considers to be a more adequate or proper basis. To do so would propel the Court into the domain which Congress has set aside exclusively for the administrative agency.

We also emphasized in our prior decision an important corollary of the foregoing rule. If the administrative action is to be tested by the basis upon which it purports to rest, that basis must be set forth with such clarity as to be understandable.[146]

[142] *United States v. Chicago, M., St. P. & P. R. Co.,* 294 U.S. 499, 511, 55 S. Ct. 462, 467, 79 L. Ed. 1023, 1032 (1935). See also *Howard Hall Co. v. United States,* 315 U. S. 495, 498–99, 62 S. Ct. 732, 734, 86 L. Ed. 986, 990 (1942).

[143] *Smith v. United States,* 157 F. (2d) 176, 182 (C.C.A. 4th, 1946).

[144] *Eastern-Central Motor Carriers Association v. United States,* 321 U.S. 194, 211–12, 64 S. Ct. 499, 508, 88 L. Ed. 668 (1944). Also, *State of Alabama v. United States,* 325 U.S. 535, 65 S. Ct. 1274, 89 L. Ed. 1779 (1945) ; *State of North Carolina v. United States,* 325 U.S. 507, 65 S. Ct. 1260, 89 L. Ed. 1760 (1945) ; *Inland Motor Freight v. United States,* 60 F. Supp. 520, 524 (D.C.E.D. Wash., 1945).

[145] *Securities and Exchange Commission v. Chenery Corp.,* 318 U.S. 80, 63 S. Ct. 454, 87 L. Ed. 626 (1943).

[146] *Securities and Exchange Commission v. Chenery Corp.,* 332 U.S. 194, 196, 67 S. Ct. 1575, 1577, 91 L. Ed. 1995, 1999 (1947).

Likewise :

> Congress has made a grant of rights to carriers such as appellee. Congress has prescribed statutory standards pursuant to which those rights are to be determined. Neither the Court nor the Commission is warranted in departing from those standards because of any doubts which may exist as to the wisdom of following the course which Congress has chosen. Congress has also provided for judicial review as an additional assurance that its policies are executed. That review certainly entails an inquiry as to whether the Commission has employed those statutory standards. If that inquiry is halted at the threshold by reason of the fact that it is impossible to say whether or not those standards have been applied, then that review has indeed become a perfunctory process. If, as seems likely here, an erroneous statutory construction lies hidden in vague findings, then statutory rights will be whittled away. An insistence upon the findings which Congress has made basic and essential to the Commission's action is no intrusion into the administrative domain. It is no more and no less than an insistence upon the observance of those standards which Congress has made "prerequisite to the operation of its statutory command." . . . Hence that requirement is not a mere formal one. Only when the statutory standards have been applied can the question be reached as to whether the findings are supported by evidence.[147]

To effectuate the above ends the Administrative Procedure Act provides that

> All decisions (including initial, recommended, or tentative decisions) shall become a part of the record and include a statement of (1) findings and conclusions, as well as the reasons or basis therefor, upon all the material issues of fact, law or discretion presented on the record; . . . .[148]

This provision does not require the filing of formal opinions, except in the limited sense that the agency shall give "the reasons or basis" for its decisions. Written opinions give substance to administrative law.

In *City of Yonkers v. United States,*[149] the Supreme Court held invalid an order of the Interstate Commerce Commission on the dubious ground that the Commission failed to make a *finding of the facts upon which its jurisdiction depended.* The majority ruled that it is not the duty of courts to

---

[147] *United States v. Carolina Carriers Corp.,* 315 U.S. 475, 489, 62 S. Ct. 722, 729–30, 86 L. Ed. 971, 982–83 (1942).

[148] Sec. 8(b).

[149] 320 U.S. 685, 64 S. Ct. 327, 88 L. Ed. 400 (1944).

. . . supply the requisite jurisdictional findings which the Commission did not make and to which it even failed to make any reference. . . . The insistence that the Commission make these jurisdictional findings before it undertakes to act not only gives added assurance that the local interests for which Congress expressed its solicitude will be safeguarded. It also gives to the reviewing courts the assistance of an expert judgment on a knotty phase of a technical subject.[150]

Three dissenting justices [151] took the sounder view that the Court should not reverse the order unless it was *in fact* outside the Commission's jurisdiction. "We should judge a challenged order of the Commission by, 'the report, read as a whole,' . . . and by the record as a whole out of which the report arose." [152] The requirement of administrative findings "is merely part of the need for courts to know what it is that the Commission has really determined in order that they may know what to review." [153] To require "jurisdictional" findings is to insist on "an empty formalism" and is "a reversion to seventeenth century pleading which required talismanic phrases." [154] The ruling of the Court

> In effect, . . . remits the controversy to the Interstate Commerce Commission on the ground that the Commission did not make a formal finding, described as "jurisdiction," . . . . The Commission may very well now formally make such a finding . . . and the weary round of litigation may be repeated to the futile end of having this Court then, forsooth, express an opinion on the merits opposed to that of the Commission and the District Court. This danger, if not likelihood of thus marching the king's men up the hill and then marching them down again seems to me a mode of judicial administration to which I cannot yield concurrence.[155]

The minority view in the above case is in line with a ruling by a District Court to the effect that it is not necessary for the President in issuing an executive order to refer specifically to a statutory provision authorizing the order—it is sufficient that he actually acted under authority of an existing statute.[156]

There is, also, judicial argument to the effect that the findings of an administrative rate-making agency—specifically the Federal Power

---

[150] 320 U.S. at 691–92, 64 S. Ct. at 330, 331, 88 L. Ed. at 404.
[151] Mr. Justice Frankfurter, Mr. Justice Reed, and Mr. Justice Jackson.
[152] 320 U.S. at 695, 64 S. Ct. at 333, 88 L. Ed. at 406.
[153] 320 U.S. at 694, 64 S. Ct. at 332, 88 L. Ed. at 406.
[154] 320 U.S. at 698, 64 S. Ct. at 334, 88 L. Ed. at 407.
[155] 320 U.S. at 693–94, 64 S. Ct. at 332, 88 L. Ed. at 405. Mr. Justice Frankfurter.
[156] *Toledo, P. & W. R. R. v. Stover*, 60 F. Supp. 587 (D.C.S.D. Ill., 1945).

Commission—"should set forth with explicitness the *criteria* by which it is guided in determining that rates are 'just and reasonable.' " [157] To hold that a given rate is reasonable just because the Commission has said that it is reasonable is to make judicial review,

> . . . a costly, time-consuming pageant of no practical value to anyone. If on the other hand we are to bring judgment of our own to the task, we should for the guidance of the regulators and the regulated reveal something of the *philosophy,* be it legal or economic or social, which guides us. We need not be slaves to a formula but unless we can point out a rational way of reaching our conclusions they can only be accepted as resting on intuition or predilection. I must admit that I possess no instinct by which to know the "reasonable" from the "unreasonable" in prices and must seek some *conscious design* for decision.[158]

That is, the "philosophy" or "conscious design" which should guide the court when reviewing a rate order, should be also the "criteria" which should guide the Commission; and the "criteria" must be set forth in the findings if the court is to be able to discharge its duty.

REHEARINGS. A petition for a rehearing before an administrative body is addressed to its own discretion. This rule is applied almost universally in federal courts, even when the petition is based upon the contention that the record is "stale" and that, therefore, a fresh record is important. In *Interstate Commerce Commission v. Jersey City* [159] the Supreme Court said:

> One of the grounds of resistance to administrative orders throughout federal experience with the administrative process has been the claims of private litigants to be entitled to rehearings to bring the record up to date and meanwhile to stall the enforcement of the administrative order. Administrative consideration of evidence—particularly where the evidence is taken by an examiner, his report submitted to the parties, and a hearing held on their exceptions to it—always creates a gap between the time the record is closed and the time the administrative decision is promulgated. . . . If upon the coming down of the order litigants might demand rehearings as a matter of law because some new circumstance has arisen, some new trend has been observed,

---

[157] Mr. Justice Frankfurter, dissenting, in *Federal Power Commission v. Hope Natural Gas Co.,* 320 U.S. 591, 627–28, 64 S. Ct. 281, 300, 88 L. Ed. 333, 358 (1944). Italics supplied.
[158] Mr. Justice Jackson, dissenting, in *Federal Power Commission v. Hope Natural Gas Co.,* 320 U.S. at 645, 64 S. Ct. at 308, 88 L. Ed. at 367–68. Italics supplied.
[159] 322 U.S. 503, 64 S. Ct. 1129, 88 L. Ed. 1420 (1944).

or some new fact discovered, there would be little hope that that administrative process could ever be consummated in an order that would not be subject to reopening. It has been almost a rule of necessity that rehearings were not matters of right, but were pleas to discretion. And likewise it has been considered that the discretion to be invoked was that of the body making the order, and not that of a reviewing body.[160]

There has been only one exception to this rule,[161] and in that case the "Court promptly restricted that decision to its special facts, . . . and, it stands virtually alone." [162] And "Except in the single instance, it has been held consistently that rehearings before administrative bodies are addressed to their own discretion. . . . Only a showing of the clearest abuse of discretion could sustain an exception to that rule." [163]

THE RIGHT TO CROSS-EXAMINATION. The Administrative Procedure Act provides that "Every party shall have the right to present his case or defense by oral or documentary evidence, to submit rebuttal evidence, and to conduct such cross-examination as may be required for a full and true disclosure of the facts." [164] Presumably this provision relates to the cross-examination of witnesses, which is regarded as a fundamental element of a fair hearing,[165] and not of the deciding officers.

The ruling in the first Morgan case [166] suggests that any administrative order or rule may be challenged in a court on the ground of insufficient consideration of the evidence, and that the deciding officer

[160] 322 U.S. at 514–15, 64 S. Ct. at 1134–35, 88 L. Ed. at 1428.

[161] Atchison, Topeka & Santa Fe R. R. v. United States, 284 U.S. 248, 52 S. Ct. 146, 76 L. Ed. 273 (1932).

[162] 322 U.S. at 515, 64 S. Ct. at 1135, 88 L. Ed. at 1429.

[163] United States v. Pierce Auto Freight Lines, Inc., 327 U.S. 515, 535, 66 S. Ct. 687, 697, 90 L. Ed. 821, 834 (1946).

[164] Sec. 7(c).

[165] In a fraud order proceeding before the Postmaster General the respondents sought to question the government's witnesses, medical specialists, concerning statements favorable to respondents found in certain medical books. The questions were not permitted, on the ground that the government's experts did not regard the books in question as authoritative. This was held to be prejudicial error, even though the memorandum of the fact-finding official indicated that he had read the excluded materials and would have made the same adverse findings if the materials had been admitted. Reilly v. Pinkus, 338 U.S. 269, 70 S. Ct. 110, 94 L. Ed. 63 (1949). In re Friedel, 269 App. Div. 890, 56 N.Y.S. (2d) 148 (1945).
"Cross examination of adverse witnesses is a matter of right in every trial of a disputed issue of fact. . . . That right, of course, can be exercised before administrative fact-finding tribunals, and denial thereof by such a tribunal is error of law." Friedel v. Board of Regents, 296 N.Y. 347, 352, 73 N.E. (2d) 545, 547 (1947). But, "Once the right has been accorded, the extent of cross-examination rests largely in the discretion of the tribunal, whose exercise thereof is not reviewable unless abused." Ibid., at 548.

[166] Morgan v. United States, 298 U.S. 468, 56 S. Ct. 906, 80 L. Ed. 1288 (1936).

may be required to answer innumerable questions as to the weight given to the testimony of each witness, the number of pages of briefs and exhibits read, his attitude towards the parties, his economic philosophy, and so on *ad inifinitum*. That is precisely what happened when the case went back to the District Court for retrial.[167] The Secretary of Agriculture appeared in person at the trial and was questioned at length regarding the procedure by which he arrived at the conclusions of his rate order. However, in the fourth Morgan case [168] the Supreme Court expressed its unqualified disapproval of the questioning and heckling of the Secretary in the proceedings in the District Court. Said Mr. Justice Frankfurter:

> But the short of the business is that the Secretary should never have been subjected to this examination. The proceeding before the Secretary "has the quality resembling that of a judicial proceeding." . . . Such an examination of a judge would be destructive of judicial responsibility. We have explicitly held in this very litigation that "it was not the function of the court to probe the mental processes of the Secretary." . . . Just as a judge cannot be subjected to such a scrutiny, . . . so the integrity of the administrative process must be equally respected. . . . It will bear repeating that although the administrative process has had a different development and pursues somewhat different ways from those of the courts, they are to be deemed collaborative instrumentalities and the appropriate independence of each should be respected by the other.[169]

Prior to the above case, the Ford Motor Company in attacking an order of the National Labor Relations Board, sought, through its attorney Frederick H. Wood (who also represented the brokers in the Morgan cases),

> . . . to have the Court interrogate the Board on how it made up its mind in the Ford case. One of these proposed interrogations contained a most scurrilous and offensive innuendo. Mr. Wood proposed to inquire of the Board whether in deciding the Ford case it had consulted John L. Lewis, Homer Martin, Ben Cohen, or Thomas Corcoran. In this double-barrelled slander constructed out of whole cloth, Mr. Wood intimated that the Board in deciding a highly important case took council with interested labor leaders and with two government attorneys who are known to enjoy the confidence of the President of the United States.[170]

[167] *Morgan v. United States,* 23 F. Supp. 380 (1937).

[168] *United States v. Morgan,* 313 U.S. 409, 61 S. Ct. 999, 85 L. Ed. 1429 (1941).

[169] 313 U.S. at 422, 61 S. Ct. at 1004–5, 85 L. Ed. at 1435–36.

[170] Statement by E. S. Smith, Member of National Labor Relations Board, quoted by Gellhorn, *op. cit.,* p. 723. The Supreme Court sustained the Board in *Ford Motor Co. v. National Labor Relations Board,* 305 U.S. 364, 59 S. Ct. 301, 83 L. Ed. 221 (1938).

Closely related to the right to cross-examine is the right to oral argument. The latter is not an inherent element of procedural due process in all judicial or quasi-judicial determinations of questions of law—this right varies from case to case in accordance with different circumstances. Congress has wide discretion in prescribing the procedures to be followed in both judicial and administrative proceedings.[171]

The Granting and Revoking of Licenses

It has been suggested that the original determination in the granting of a license, relief, or other benefit is predominantly an executive function; but that a subsequent determination to alter the terms of the license, permit, or grant to the disadvantage of the beneficiary is an exercise of the judicial function.[172]

But the New York courts have held (not without dissents, however) that

> The powers of the members of the board of health *being administrative merely,* they can *issue* or *revoke* permits to sell milk in the exercise of their best judgment, upon or without notice, based upon such information as they may obtain through their own agencies, and their action is not subject to review either by appeal or by certiorari.[173]

An applicant does not have a constitutional right *to* a license and so may not demand, except as a statutory right, a hearing upon his application. A licensee, however, may acquire a right within the protection of the due process clause.

Judicial opinion has divided licenses into "privilege" and "property" categories and has required a judicialized revocation procedure only for the latter category. The distinction between a "privilege" and a "property" license seems to depend upon questions of "respectability" and the "amount" invested.[174] According to Roger R. Tuttrup:

> If a given occupation be calculated to serve some useful purpose advantageous to the general public or any considerable number thereof, and if the pursuit of such occupation affords but a slight, if any, opportunity for the infliction of general and substantial injury to the public health, safety, morals, or convenience, then a license to

[171] *Federal Communications Commission v. WJR, the Goodwill Station,* 337 U.S. 265, 70 S. Ct. 1097, 93 L. Ed. 1353 (1950).
[172] American Bar Association, *Report* (1937), p. 240.
[173] *People ex rel. Lodes v. Department of Health of City of New York,* 189 N.Y. 187, 194, 82 N.E. 187, 189 (1907), citing cases. Italics supplied.
[174] *Cf.* Gellhorn, *op. cit.,* pp. 273–83.

engage in such occupation confers upon its holder a right which cannot be divested without notice to him and opportunity for him to be heard; but if an occupation be one which serves no socially useful purpose or which affords opportunity to jeopardize or injure the health, safety, morals, or convenience of large numbers of people, then a license to engage therein is, at most, a mere privilege, and is subject, due cause being shown, to summary revocation in the public interest.[175]

So a permit to sell milk in the City of New York "cannot be treated as property in any legal or constitutional sense, but was a mere license revocable by the power that was authorized to issue it."[176] And the Supreme Court of Illinois has held: "Whether the right to practice medicine or law is property, in the technical sense, it is a valuable franchise, and one of which a person ought not to be deprived, without being offered an opportunity, by timely notice, to defend it."[177]

The Administrative Procedure Act prescribes a judicialized procedure for the *granting* as well as the *revocation* of licenses. A hearing may be dispensed with in revoking a license only "in cases of willfulness or those in which public health, interest, or safety requires otherwise."[178] This permits summary revocation in the specified cases and seems to leave the questions of "willfulness" or "public health, interest, or safety" to the judgment of the licensing authorities. It is a compromise between the rule of law and administrative discretion.

It may be questioned whether *summary suspension,* pending a hearing prior to revocation, would not give adequate protection to the public and greater safeguards to private interests. Summary revocation is arbitrary action even when exercised wisely; and the administrative hearing would give the licensee his "day in court" and relieve him in most cases of the longer and costlier appeal to judicial justice if he feels that the revocation of his license is contrary to law.

In requiring the same procedure for the granting as for the revocation of licenses, Congress goes contrary to accepted practice. Proceedings leading to the issuing of a license or permit are not unlike rule-making proceedings in that the main purpose is to inform the licensing officers. Such officers ordinarily are not required to proceed as courts do in cases between parties—they do not have power to

---

[175] "Necessity of Notice and Hearing in Revocation of Occupational Licenses," 4 *Wisconsin Law Review* (1927), 180. Quoted by Gellhorn, *op. cit.,* pp. 276–77.

[176] See footnote 173 *supra.*

[177] *People to Use of State Board of Health v. McCoy,* 125 Ill. 289, 297, 17 N.E. 786, 788 (1888).

[178] Sec. 9(b).

summon witnesses, administer oaths, or to compel the giving of testimony. When passing on an application for a license, the officers ascertain and determine public *interests,* not *pre-existing rights of the petitioner.* When a hearing is held and evidence is taken,

> The object of evidence in such cases is to inform the conscience of the court [court of sessions granting liquor licenses], so that it may act intelligently and justly in the performance of a public duty. Whilst the act in deciding in such cases is quasi-judicial, the difference between the granting and withholding of a license and the decision of a question between parties to a private litigation is manifest.
>
> . . . inasmuch as the object of evidence in such examinations is merely to inform the conscience and judgment of the officer, such evidence may be taken in any way that is reasonably sufficient for that purpose. The officer is not governed by the rules of litigious evidence, and his decisions are not to be arbitrary merely because they are founded upon information which a court would hold not to be evidence at all.[179]

Res Judicata in Administrative Proceedings

Are the doctrines of *res judicata* and *stare decisis* applicable in administrative proceedings? The two doctrines are not the same. Under *stare decisis* a decision becomes a precedent to be followed in like cases in the future, but precedents may be and frequently are overruled. *Res judicata,* however, gives finality to a decision as between the parties involved and so may not be disturbed. *Res judicata* is based upon the theory that it is in the interest of the litigant not to be vexed twice in regard to a particular cause and that it is further in the interest of the state that there be an end to litigation.[180] To constitute a matter *res judicata,* (1) the tribunal deciding the issue must have had jurisdiction over the person and subject matter; (2) there must be identity of parties,[181] subject matter, and of the cause of action; and (3) there must have been a final determination of the issues on the merits.[182] The decision must be valid. Gross

[179] *United States ex rel. Roop v. Douglass,* 19 D.C. 99, 114, 115 (1890). Also *Dodd et al. v. Francisco et al.,* 68 N.Y. Law 490 (1902).

[180] "There are no maxims of the law more firmly established, or of more value in the administration of justice than the two which are designed to prevent repeated litigation between the same parties in regard to the same subject or controversy, namely: *Interest reipublicae, ut sit finis litium,* and *Nemo debet vexari pro una et eadam causa.".* *United States v. Throckmorton,* 98 U.S. 61, 65, 25 L. Ed. 93, 95 (1878). And see Reginald Parker, "Administrative Res Judicata," 40 *Illinois Law Review* (1945), 56 ff.

[181] Except proceedings *in rem* when the adjudication attaches to the *res.*

[182] *Noble v. Union River Logging R. R. Co.,* 147 U.S. 165, 13 S. Ct. 271, 37 L. Ed. 123 (1893).

error as to the facts or misconstruction of law justifies revocation of a prior decision.[183]

The experts do not agree as to the applicability of *res judicata* to the administrative process.[184] This disagreement is due in large measure to the fact that administration cuts across the traditional tripartite separation of governmental functions. The judicial decisions follow a flexible pattern in the matter of the binding effect of administrative determinations. Explicit provisions in the governing statute are controlling; but in the absence of a clear statutory intent, *res judicata* is applicable only to *judicial,* not *legislative* or *administrative* actions. "The rule of estoppel by judgment obviously applies only to bodies exercising judicial functions; it is manifestly inapplicable to legislative action." [185] To apply the rule to a rate order of the Interstate Commerce Commission, as an example, would plainly defeat the purposes of the Commerce Act.[186]

A statute may confer a *continuing jurisdiction* upon the administrative agency, that is, the agency may be vested with continuing authority to review, modify, or rescind its own decisions in the public

---

[183] *Johnson v. Towsley,* 13 Wall. 72, 83–87, 20 L. Ed. 485, 486–88 (1871); *Woodworth v. Kales,* 26 F. (2d) 178, 181 (C.C.A. 6th, 1928).

[184] "Summing up the opinions *pro* and *contra* we feel entitled to say that the better and nowadays prevailing view is in favor of *res judicata* with regard to administrative decisions." Parker, "Administrative Res Judicata," *loc. cit.,* p. 78.

"The only workable test by which to ascertain whether or not an administrative decision has all or some of the effects of *res judicata* is the legislative intent to be gathered from the statutes which created the agency whose decision is in issue. Most of the federal cases employ this approach." E. H. Shopflocker, "Doctrine of *Res Judicata* in Administrative Law," 17 *Wisconsin Law Review* (1942), 198.

An administrative decision is "free from the principles of stare decisis and res judicata." F. Trowbridge von Baur, *Federal Administrative Law* (Callaghan & Co., Chicago, 1942), p. 162, § 183.

"All final judicial decisions are *res judicata* as to the cause of action and the matters actually adjudicated. This determination is a judicial or quasi judicial decision. Therefore, it binds the parties as if it were the judgment of a court of law. Conversely, if the determination is considered legislative or merely administrative, it is res judicata neither in subsequent court litigation nor in collateral proceedings." N. K. Gregory, "Administrative Decisions as Res Judicata," 29 *California Law Review* (1941), 741, 749–50.

[185] *Arizona Grocery Co. v. Atchison, Topeka & Santa Fe Ry. Co.,* 284 U.S. 370, 389, 52 S. Ct. 183, 186, 76 L. Ed. 348, 356 (1932).

[186] *State Corporation Commission of Kansas v. Wichita Gas Co.,* 290 U.S. 561, 568–70, 54 S. Ct. 321, 324–25, 78 L. Ed. 500, 504–5 (1934); *Prentis v. Atlantic Coast Line Co.,* 211 U.S. 210, 29 S. Ct. 67, 53 L. Ed. 150 (1908); *Skinner & Eddy Corp. v. United States,* 248 U.S. 557, 570, 39 S. Ct. 375, 380, 63 L. Ed. 772, 780 (1919); *Great Northern Ry. Co. v. Sunburst Oil & Refining Co.,* 287 U.S. 358, 362, 53 S. Ct. 145, 148, 77 L. Ed. 360, 365 (1932); *Chicago, B. & Q. R. R. v. United States,* 60 F. Supp. 580 (D.C.E.D., 1945); N. K. Gregory, "Administrative Decisions as Res Judicata," 29 *California Law Review* (1941), 741–43; E. N. Griswold, "Res Judicata in Federal Tax Cases," 46 *Yale Law Review* (1937), 1320 ff.

interest.[187] Thus the National Labor Relations Act makes *res judicata* inapplicable to a decision of the National Labor Relations Board.[188] When the Board ruled that the Baltimore Transit Company was not subject to the provisions of the National Labor Relations Act, and when subsequent decisions by the Supreme Court made it clear that the Board's construction of the Act was erroneous, the reviewing court held that the Board was not bound by its decision, since the principle of equitable estoppel may not be applied so as to deprive the public of the benefits of a statute because of a mistaken action by public officials.[189]

The Federal Trade Commission is given complete control over its decision for a period of 60 days, during which an aggrieved party may apply for judicial review.[190] But, when the Commission decided, after hearing, that a given product was *not* proscribed by the Food, Drug, and Cosmetics Act, the reviewing courts ruled that the Commission's finding, if supported by evidence, was conclusive not only upon the courts but upon the Government itself, since the Commission was in privy with the Government as its agent.[191] The Interstate Commerce Commission may "suspend or modify its own orders upon notice." [192] That is, the Commission may, upon request or on its own motion, correct any order still under its control.[193] The Secretary of Agriculture has a continuing power under the Meat Inspection Act [194] to determine whether a trade-name is deceptive, so that he may disapprove a name which he has previously approved.[195] Administrative orders concerning the public lands are subject to revision so long as the land remains under the jurisdiction of the Department

[187] *Federal Trade Commission v. Raladam Co.,* 316 U.S. 149, 152, 62 S. Ct. 966, 968, 86 L. Ed. 1336, 1340–41 (1942) ; *Wallace Corp. v. National Labor Relations Board,* 141 F. (2d) 87 (C.C.A. 4th, 1944) ; *National Labor Relations Board v. Atkins & Co.,* 147 F. (2d) 730 (C.C.A. 7th, 1945) ; *Chiquita Mining Co., Ltd. v. Commissioner,* 148 F. (2d) 306 (C.C.A. 9th, 1945) ; *Grandview Dairy, Inc. v. Jones,* 61 F. Supp. 460, 462 (D.C.E.D.N.Y., 1945).

[188] 49 *Stat.* 449, § 10(d) (1935), 29 *U.S.C.A.* § 160(d).

[189] *National Labor Relations Board v. Baltimore Transit Co.,* 140 F. (2d) 51 (C.C.A. 4th, 1944). Certiorari denied, 321 U.S. 795, 64 S. Ct. 848, 88 L. Ed. 1084 (1944).

[190] 52 *Stat.* 111, § 3(b), 15 *U.S.C.A.* § 45b (1939).

[191] *United States v. Willard Tablet Co.,* 141 F. (2d) 141 (C.C.A. 7th, 1944).

[192] 34 *Stat.* 591 (1906), 49 *U.S.C.A.* § 16(6) (1946). See *Baldwin, Trustees v. Scott County Milling Co.,* 307 U.S. 478, 59 S. Ct. 943, 83 L. Ed. 1409 (1939).

[193] *Louisville & Nashville R. Co. v. Sloss-Sheffield Iron Co.,* 269 U.S. 217, 46 S. Ct. 73, 70 L. Ed. 242 (1925) ; *Froeber-Norfleet, Inc. v. Southern Ry.,* 9 F. Supp. 409 (N.D. Ga., 1934).

[194] 34 *Stat.* 1256.

[195] *Brougham v. Blanton Mfg. Co.,* 249 U.S. 495, 501, 39 S. Ct. 363, 366, 63 L. Ed. 725, 731 (1919).

of Interior.[196]   The granting or denying by the Federal Communications Commission of an application for a license does not preclude a subsequent contrary ruling,[197] since the decision of the Commission is governed by findings of "public interest, convenience and necessity," [198] except that a license lawfully granted may not be revoked except for violations of law, since the licensee acquires a vested interest therein.[199]   Under the Federal Longshoremen's and Harbor Workers' Compensation Act,[200] the Deputy Commissioner is authorized to modify or terminate compensation on the ground of a "change in conditions or because of a mistake in a determination of fact" within one year after the award.

It has been held in a number of cases that decisions of the Immigration and Naturalization Service are not *res judicata.*[201]

> The doctrine of res adjudicata does not apply to decisions of administrative tribunals even when, as here, a question of citizenship is involved,—with the rather curious result that, although the petitioner on his admission in 1922 became a citizen of this country and entitled to the rights of a citizen, he was not entitled to re-enter the country after having left it, without again establishing his citizenship de novo.[202]

Continuing jurisdiction is generally admitted where no adverse interests of other parties are affected.[203]   But an administrative decision cannot be revoked or rescinded if it has the effect of vesting a

[196] *West v. Standard Oil Co.,* 278 U.S. 200, 211, 214, 218, 49 S. Ct. 138, 140, 142, 143, 73 L. Ed. 265, 270, 271, 273 (1929) ; *Lane v. Darlington,* 249 U.S. 331, 39 S. Ct. 299, 63 L. Ed. 629 (1919).

[197] *Federal Communications Commission v. Pottsville Broadcasting Co.,* 309 U.S. 134, 60 S. Ct. 437, 84 L. Ed. 656 (1940).

[198] 48 *Stat.* 1085 (1934), 47 *U.S.C.A.* § 309 (1946).

[199] *Brougham v. Blanton Mfg. Co.,* 243 Fed. 503 (C.C.A. 8th, 1917). Under the Administrative Procedure Act the granting or revoking of a license is a judicial not an administrative act. Patent applications are held not *res judicata. Jeffrey Mfg. Co. v. Kinsgland,* 179 F. (2d) 35 (C.A.D.C., 1950).

[200] 44 *Stat.* 1424, 1437 (1927), 33 *U.S.C.A.* § 922 (1946), as amended 52 *Stat.* 1167 (1938), 33 *U.S.C.A.* § 922 (1946).

[201] *Flynn ex rel. Ham Loy Wong v. Ward,* 95 F. (2d) 742 (C.C.A. 1st, 1938) ; *Mock Kee Song v. Cahill,* 94 F. (2d) 975 (C.C.A. 9th, 1938) ; *Jung Yen Loy v. Cahill,* 81 F. (2d) 809 (C.C.A. 9th, 1936). The decision of the Supreme Court in *Wong Yang Sung v. McGrath,* 339 U.S. 33, 70 S. Ct. 445, 94 L. Ed. 616 (1950) holding that immigration proceedings must conform to procedural requirements of the Administrative Procedure Act may have some bearing on the decisions in the above cases.

[202] *Flynn ex. rel. Ham Loy Wong v. Ward,* 95 F. (2d) 742, 743 (C.C.A. 1st, 1938).

[203] *Beley v. Naphtali,* 169 U.S. 353, 354, 18 S. Ct. 354, 42 L. Ed. 775 (1898) ; *In re Pollock,* 257 Fed. 350 (S.D.N.Y., 1918).

substantial right—such as title to land,[204] a right of way,[205] a trade name,[206] a visa,[207] a compensation award,[208] or money payments.[209] The granter has remedy, however, in equity for fraud or error.[210] The issue in the above cases is one of due process of law rather than of *res judicata*.

In tax cases, decisions by the Commissioner of Internal Revenue (with some exceptions)[211] and by the Tax Court, and its predecessor the Board of Tax Appeals (although it was not a court)[212] are *res judicata*.[213] This is an area of administrative action where the legal maxim underlying the doctrine of *res judicata* is clearly pertinent— it means security to both taxpayer and government. So tax decisions or orders are *judicial* for the purpose of *res judicata*. It would seem that "the vast, undisclosed range" of due process would cover the situation as well.

To rest the rule of *res judicata* on a functional division of administrative powers is a rather uncertain criterion. The Administrative Procedure Act divides administrative action into legislative *rules* and judicial *orders*. Does it follow that all orders are *res judicata,* save

[204] *Stone v. United States,* 2 Wall. 525, 17 L. Ed. 765 (1864) ; *Lane v. Watts,* 234 U.S. 525, 34 S. Ct. 965, 58 L. Ed. 1440 (1914).

[205] *Noble v. Union River Logging R.R.,* 147 U.S. 165, 13 S. Ct. 271, 37 L. Ed. 123 (1893).

[206] *Brougham v. Blanton Mfg. Co.,* 243 Fed. 503 (C.C.A. 8th, 1917) ; *United States v. Willard Tablet Co.,* 141 F. (2d) 141, 143 (C.C.A. 7th, 1944).

[207] *United States ex rel. Strachey v. Reimer,* 101 F. (2d) 267, 269–70 (C.C.A. 2d, 1939).

[208] *United Fruit Co. v. Pillsbury,* 55 F. (2d) 369, 370 (N.D. Cal., 1932).

[209] *Butte, Anaconda & Pacific Ry. Co. v. United States,* 290 U.S. 127, 135–36, 142, 54 S. Ct. 108, 109–10, 112, 78 L. Ed. 222, 224–25, 228 (1933) ; *United States v. Great Northern R. Co.,* 287 U.S. 144, 151–52, 53 S. Ct. 28, 30–31, 77 L. Ed. 223, 228–29 (1932).

[210] *Waddell v. United States,* 25 Ct. Cl. 323, 7 L.R.A. 861 (1890).

[211] *Blair v. Commissioner of Internal Revenue,* 300 U.S. 5, 57 S. Ct. 330, 81 L. Ed. 465 (1937) ; *Burnet v. Porter,* 283 U.S. 229, 51 S. Ct. 416, 75 L. Ed. 996 (1931) ; *McIlhenny v. Commissioner of Internal Revenue,* 39 F. (2d) 356 (C.C.A. 3rd, 1930) ; *Tonningsen v. Commissioner of Internal Revenue,* 61 F. (2d) 199 (C.C.A. 9th, 1932).

[212] *Old Colony Trust Co. v. Commissioner of Internal Revenue,* 279 U.S. 716, 725, 49 S. Ct. 499, 502, 73 L. Ed. 918, 926 (1929).

[213] *American S. S. Co. v. Wickwire Spencer Steel Co.,* 8 F. Supp. 562, 566 (S.D.N.Y., 1934) ; *Backus v. United States,* 59 F. (2d) 242, 258 (Ct. Cl., 1932) ; *Tait, Collector v. Western Maryland Ry.,* 289 U.S. 620, 53 S. Ct. 706, 77 L. Ed. 1405 (1933) ; *Continental Petroleum Co. v. United States,* 87 F. (2d) 91 (C.C.A. 10th, 1936; *Pelham Hall Co. v. Hassett,* 147 F. (2d) 63, 66 (C.C.A. 1st, 1945) ; Griswold, "Res Judicata in Federal Tax Cases," *loc. cit.* An administrative decision or order does not constitute a precedent for courts dealing with similar problems, *United States v. American Sheet & Tin Plate Co.,* 301 U.S. 402, 57 S. Ct. 804, 81 L. Ed. 1186 (1937) ; *Dobson v. Commissioner of Internal Revenue,* 320 U.S. 489, 502, 64 S. Ct. 239, 247, 88 L. Ed. 248, 258 (1943).

those excepted by statute? Or will a court apply its own construction of *judicial* when the intent of the enabling statute is not clear? To complicate the problem further, administrative adjudication is said to be only quasi-judicial, and an "administrative body," such as the Federal Trade Commission, is said to act "in part quasi legislatively and in part quasi judicially," while an "executive officer," such as a postmaster, "is restricted to the performance of executive functions." [214] Obviously the matter of *res judicata* in administrative proceedings needs clarification.

If an administrative case is not "closed by final action, the proceedings of an officer of a department are as much open to review or reversal by himself or his successor as are the interlocutory decrees of a court open to review upon the final hearing." [215] However, when an administrative order has been submitted to a court for enforcement and a decree to that effect has been issued, the administrative proceeding "has ended and has been merged in a decree of a court" and this action is "final"; and the agency cannot, in the absence of specific statutory authority, recall the proceeding for further hearing and action.[216] The rule, and the reasons for it, governing in this situation has been stated by the Supreme Court as follows:

> Until the transcript of a case is filed in court, the Board [National Labor Relations Board] may, after reasonable notice, modify any finding or order in whole or in part. After the case has come under the jurisdiction of the court, either party may apply to the court for remand to the Board. There is no dearth of discretion or opportunity for its exercise, but opportunities should not be unlimited. . . .
>
> Finality to litigation is an end to be desired as well in proceedings to which an administrative body is a party as in exclusively private litigation. The party adverse to the administrative body is entitled to rely on the conclusiveness of a decree entered by a court to the same extent that other litigants may rely on judgments for or against them.[217]

But Mr. Justice Murphy, dissenting,[218] held that

> If at any time *before the decree is executed* the Board becomes convinced that the remedy as tentatively approved by the court will no longer serve the statutory purposes, reason and justice dictate that the

[214] *Humphrey's Executor v. United States,* 295 U.S. 602, 55 S. Ct. 869, 79 L. Ed. 1611 (1935).

[215] *City of New Orleans v. Paine,* 147 U.S. 261, 266, 13 S. Ct. 303, 306, 37 L. Ed. 162, 164 (1893); *Wilbur v. United States,* 281 U.S. 206, 50 S. Ct. 320, 74 L. Ed. 809 (1930).

[216] *Mine Workers v. Eagle-Picher Co.,* 325 U.S. 335, 65 S. Ct. 1166, 89 L. Ed. 1649 (1945).

[217] 325 U.S. at 341, 340, 65 S. Ct. at 1169, 1168, 89 L. Ed. at 1155, 1154.

[218] Concurring: Mr. Justice Black, Mr. Justice Douglas, and Mr. Justice Rutledge.

Board should have the opportunity to reconsider the matter. Whether the inadequacy of the remedy be due to inadvertence, negligence, fraud or other reasons, there is no recognizable public or private interest in executing such a remedy. . . . We are concerned, . . . with the attempt of an administrative agency to effectuate the policies set forth in a Congressional mandate. Until those policies are effectuated through the enforcement and execution of statutory remedies, the agency and the courts should coordinate their efforts to realize the plain will of the people.[219]

Apparently the rule of the majority in the above case does not apply if the agency has specific statutory authority to modify its order after it has become final either through failure to appeal or by court order.[220]

Administrative Tribunals

The legal professions in England and the United States have been slow to recognize administrative law as a separate body of law, and even now their chief concern is with its limitations. This is in keeping with the traditions of the "rule of law" [221] and the doctrine of the separation of powers. It has been long a boast of Anglo-Americans that the highest officer and the lowliest citizen are subject to the same rule of law in the same court of justice. Equality before the law has been at once a statement of legal principle and a political slogan, but, like many other credos, without proper implementation it can become a mere shibboleth. Equality assumes that functionary and citizen are equally liable for tortious conduct. No such equality exists in any state. For torts committed in the name of the state— for his official acts—the officer, both in England and the United States, is not responsible to the courts under the doctrine of state immunity. His responsibility, therefore, is not as an officer but as a private person acting outside his official authority.

The "rule of law" in the strict sense precludes "executive" or "administrative justice" except as a preliminary step, or unless administrative tribunals are recognized as courts of law. "Judicial justice" means that issues of a justiciable nature are determined *finally* by courts. Under the doctrine of the separation of powers a judicial

---

[219] 325 U.S. at 356, 65 S. Ct. at 1175–76, 89 L. Ed. at 1163. Italics supplied.

[220] *American Chain and Cable Co. v. Federal Trade Commission,* 142 F. (2d) 909 (C.C.A. 4th, 1944).

[221] "From the very beginning the administrative tribunal has faced the hostility of the legal profession." Robert H. Jackson, "The Administrative Process," 5 *Journal of Social Philosophy* (1940), 146.

decision cannot be subjected to review by any of the other branches of government, except in the limited sense of the pardoning power. The role of executive justice is conditioned, therefore, by the definition of *courts*.

There is a basic difference between judicial and executive justice which makes it difficult to accept "a day in an agency" as "a day in court" within the meaning of the rule of law. A court of law is presumed to be impartial—an agency is not. It is the function of administration to "effectuate the purposes of the law," to implement and to activate the law, not merely to apply existing law to individual situations. While a court deals with *cases,* specific controversies, an agency often deals with situations involving groups of conflicting interests, often broad public interests: industry v. labor, railroads v. shippers, brokers v. investors, or producer v. consumer.

> Administrative tribunals do not have that independence from government which is one of the traditionally prized guarantees of the justice administered by our common-law courts. Their adjudications, taking place as very part and parcel of the process of government, are exposed to the influence of all the political forces which act upon government.[222]

Classification of Courts.—Article III of the Constitution vests "the judicial power of the United States" in one Supreme Court and such inferior courts as Congress may establish. In accordance with the dogma of the separation of powers and the ancillary precept that a delegated power cannot be redelegated, it would appear that the *judicial power of the United States* is vested *exclusively* in courts created under Article III—except as otherwise specifically provided in the Constitution, such as vesting the impeachment power in Congress and the pardoning power in the President. But under the doctrine of *McCulloch v. Maryland*,[223] the Congress has an *implied power* to set up federal courts as *appropriate means* to carry into effect a delegated power.

The courts created under Article III are called *constitutional courts,* and those established under the implied powers of Congress are *legislative courts.* The former may exercise *judicial* power only; the latter may be given *judicial* as well as *nonjudicial* powers. Speaking for the Court in the Bakelite case, Mr. Justice Van Devanter said:

[222] John Dickinson, *Administrative Justice and the Supremacy of Law* (Harvard University Press, Cambridge, Mass., 1927), p. 36.
[223] 4 Wheat. 316, 4 L. Ed. 579 (1819).

While Article III of the Constitution declares, in section 1, that the judicial power of the United States shall be vested in one Supreme Court and in "such inferior courts as the Congress may from time to time ordain and establish," and prescribes, in section 2, that the power shall extend to cases and controversies of certain enumerated classes, it long has been settled that Article III does not express the full authority of Congress to create courts, and that other Articles invest Congress with powers in the exertion of which it may create inferior courts and clothe them with functions deemed essential or helpful in carrying those powers into execution. But there is a difference between the two classes of courts. Those established under the specific power given in section 2 of Article III are called constitutional courts. They share in the exercise of the judicial power defined in that section, can be invested with no other jurisdiction, and have judges who hold office during good behavior, with no power in Congress to provide otherwise. On the other hand, those created by Congress in the exertion of other powers are called legislative courts. Their functions are always directed to the execution of one or more of such powers and are prescribed by Congress independently of section 2 of Article III; and their judges hold office for such term as Congress prescribes, whether it be a fixed period of years or during good behavior.[224]

To justify this classification of the federal courts as *constitutional* and *legislative,* it was necessary to hold that the judicial function exercised by the legislative courts is not a part of "the judicial power of the United States" within the meaning of Article III of the Constitution, a little matter which Mr. Chief Justice Marshall attended to with characteristic directness.[225] But as legislative courts exercise judicial power under the authority of the United States, it follows that the grant of judicial power in Article III is not exclusive.

This distinction between constitutional and legislative courts has given the Supreme Court no end of embarrassment. The Court of

[224] *Ex parte Bakelite Corp.,* 279 U.S. 438, 449, 49 S. Ct. 411, 412–13, 73 L. Ed. 789, 793 (1929). See also, *Williams v. United States,* 289 U.S. 553, 567, 568, 53 S. Ct. 751, 755, 756, 77 L. Ed. 1372, 1377, 1378 (1933); *United States v. Coe,* 155 U.S. 76, 15 S. Ct. 16, 39 L. Ed. 76 (1894); *Ex parte Cooper,* 143 U.S. 472, 12 S. Ct. 453, 36 L. Ed. 232 (1892).

[225] Speaking of the courts of the Territory of Florida, the Chief Justice said: "These courts, then, are not constitutional courts, in which the judicial power conferred by the constitution on the general government, can be deposited. They are incapable of receiving it. They are legislative courts, created in virtue of the general right of sovereignty which exists in the government, or in virtue of that clause which enables congress to make all needful rules and regulations, respecting the territory belonging to the United States. The jurisdiction with which they are invested, is not a part of that judicial power which is defined in the 3d article of the constitution, but is conferred by congress, in the execution of those general powers which that body possesses over the territories of the United States." *American Insurance Co. v. Canter,* 1 Pet. 511, 546, 7 L. Ed. 242, 257 (1828).

Claims was created by Congress in 1855 [226] to examine and determine, but in a purely advisory capacity, the validity of claims against the United States. Later the judges of this court were given life tenure and were granted authority to render judgments, which judgments were made reviewable by the Supreme Court, but payment of the adjudged claims was left to the discretion of Congress and the Secretary of the Treasury.[227] This act, to all intents and purposes, created an "inferior court" under Article III of the Constitution. But the Supreme Court refused to review a decision of the Court of Claims on the ground that the latter was not acting judicially but as an advisory agency of Congress, since its judgments were not final but were subject to the veto of the Congress—in short, the Court of Claims was a legislative court.[228] Later the Court of Claims was regarded as a constitutional court,[229] and more recently again as a legislative court whose judicial power is not derived from the Judiciary Article of the Constitution but from the Congressional power to "pay the debts . . . of the United States." [230] However, *final* decisions of the Court of Claims (as distinguished from judgments which are subject to executive or congressional approval) are reviewable by the Supreme Court; [231] and, under the Federal Tort Claims Act of 1946 [232] the Court of Claims is given concurrent appellate jurisdiction with the United States Circuit Courts of Appeals (constitutional courts) to review judgments of United States District Courts (constitutional courts) in claims cases, with the written consent of all the appellees.

The United States Customs Court, created in 1926 [233] as successor

[226] Act of February 24, 1855, 10 *Stat.* 612, 28 *U.S.C.A.* c. 7; amended by Tucker Act of March 3, 1887, 24 *Stat.* 505; supplemented and re-enacted by *Judicial Code,* § 145, 28 *U.S.C.A.* § 250. *Judicial Code* § 24 (20), 28 *U.S.C.A.* § 41 (20), confers concurrent jurisdiction on United States District Courts of all claims not exceeding $10,000.

[227] Act of March 3, 1863, 12 *Stat.* 765, 768, c. 92, § 14, 28 *U.S.C.A.* § 241.

[228] *Gordon v. United States,* 2 Wall. 561, 17 L. Ed. 921 (1865). This was Mr. Chief Justice Taney's last judicial utterance. Also, *In re Sanborn,* 148 U.S. 222, 13 S. Ct. 577, 37 L. Ed. 429 (1893).

[229] *Kansas v. United States,* 204 U.S. 331, 27 S. Ct. 388, 51 L. Ed. 510 (1907).

[230] *Williams v. United States,* 289 U.S. 553, 53 S. Ct. 751, 77 L. Ed. 1372 (1933). In *United States v. Sherwood,* 312 U.S. 584, 587, 61 S. Ct. 767, 770, 85 L. Ed. 1058 (1941) the Court said: "The Court of Claims is a legislative, not a constitutional court. Its judicial power is derived not from the Judiciary Article of the Constitution [Article III], but from the Congressional power 'to pay the debts . . . of the United States,' [Article I, 8, cl. 1] which it is free to exercise through judicial as well as non-judicial agencies."

[231] *De Groot v. United States,* 5 Wall. 419, 18 L. Ed. 700 (1867); *United States v. Jones,* 119 U.S. 477, 7 S. Ct. 283, 30 L. Ed. 440 (1886).

[232] 60 *Stat.* 843-47 (1946).

[233] Act of May 28, 1926, 44 *Stat.* 669, c. 411, 28 *U.S.C.A.* § 296.

to the powers and duties of the former Board of General Appraisers,[234] has been held to be an executive agency whose functions are largely quasi-judicial but of such a nature as to be susceptible of performance by executive, but not by strictly judicial, officers.[235] The Court of Customs Appeals, organized under the Payne-Aldrich Act of 1909,[236] changed to the Court of Customs and Patent Appeals in 1929,[237] with jurisdiction to review on appeal decisions by the Customs Court, is a legislative court since it "was created by Congress in virtue of its power to lay and collect duties on imports and to adopt any appropriate means of carrying that power into execution."[238] Its decisions affecting patents and trade-marks are not reviewable by the Supreme Court since such decisions are administrative and not judicial,[239] but some of its judgments and decrees are subject to review.[240]

The Board of Tax Appeals, although not called a court, differed from the other legislative courts only in respect to tenure of office. Its sole function was to hear and decide cases, to review decisions of the Commissioner of Internal Revenue. "It is an executive or administrative board, upon the decision of which the parties are given an opportunity to base a petition for review to the courts after an administrative inquiry of the Board has been had and decided."[241] The Board has been converted into the Tax Court of the United States, a regular legislative court.[242]

The status of the District Court and the Court of Appeals for the District of Columbia has been especially uncertain.

The courts of the District of Columbia were given jurisdiction, under an Act of 1913,[243] to review orders of the Public Utilities Commission of the District, both as to law and fact, and to amend valua-

---

[234] Act of June 10, 1890, 26 *Stat.* 136.

[235] *Ex parte Bakelite Corp.,* 279 U.S. 438, 49 S. Ct. 411, 73 L. Ed. 789 (1929).

[236] Act of August 5, 1909, 36 *Stat.* 91–108, c. 6.

[237] Act of March 2, 1929, 45 *Stat.* 1475. c. 488, 28 *U.S.C.A.* § 301.

[238] *Ex parte Bakelite Corp.,* 279 U.S. 438, 458, 49 S. Ct. 411, 416, 73 L. Ed. 789, 797 (1929).

[239] *Laughlin v. Robertson,* 284 U.S. 652, 52 S. Ct. 32, 76 L. Ed. 553 (1931).

[240] Judicial Code § 195 as amended by Tariff Act of 1930, 46 *Stat.* 590, c. 497, § 647, 28 *U.S.C.A.* § 308.

[241] *Old Colony Trust Co. et al. v. Commissioner of Internal Revenue,* 279 U.S. 716, 725, 49 S. Ct. 499, 502, 73 L. Ed. 918, 926 (1929).

[242] Created by 53 *Stat.* 158, as amended by 56 *Stat.* 957, 26 *U.S.C.A.* § 1100: "The Board of Tax Appeals (hereinafter referred to as the 'Board') shall be continued as an independent agency in the Executive Branch of the Government. The Board shall be known as The Tax Court of the United States and the members thereof shall be known as the presiding judge and the judges of The Tax Court of the United States."

[243] Act of March 4, 1913, 37 *Stat.* 974, 988, c. 150, § 8, par. 64.

tions, rates, and regulations established by the Commission. In 1923 the latter was held to be a legislative function authorized under Article I, Section 8, Clause 17, of the Constitution. Congress, said the Court, has a dual authority over the District of Columbia, and "may clothe the courts of the District not only with the jurisdiction and powers of federal courts in the several States but with such authority as a State may confer on her courts." [244] But a provision of the above act was held unconstitutional which allowed appeal to the Supreme Court from the legislative rulings of the courts of the District. Citing *Muskrat v. United States*,[245] the Court said:

> The principle there recognized and enforced on reason and authority is that the *jurisdiction* of this Court and *of the inferior courts of the United States ordained and established by Congress under and by virtue of the third article of the Constitution* is limited to cases and controversies in such form that the judicial power is capable of acting on them and *does not extend* to an issue of constitutional law framed by Congress for the purpose of invoking the advice of this Court without real parties or a real case, or *to administrative or legislative issues or controversies.*[246]

It seems to follow that the courts of the District are *not* created under Article III, a conclusion supported by Mr. Chief Justice Taft in the Postum Cereal Company case in 1927 when he said:

> The distinction between the jurisdiction of this Court, . . . and . . . courts of the District, is shown in the case of *Keller v. Potomac Electric Company*, . . . There it is pointed out that, while Congress in its constitutional exercise of exclusive legislation over the District may clothe the courts of the District not only with the jurisdiction and powers of the federal courts in the several States but also with such authority as a State might confer on her courts, . . . and so may vest courts of the District with administrative or legislative functions which are not properly judicial, *it may not do so with this Court or any federal court established under Article III of the Constitution.*[247]

This is in agreement with the language used in the Bakelite case to the effect that *constitutional courts* "share in the exercise of the judicial power defined in" Article III, Section 2, and *"can be invested with*

---

[244] Mr. Chief Justice Taft in *Keller v. Potomac Electric Power Co.*, 261 U.S. 428, 443, 43 S. Ct. 445, 448, 67 L. Ed. 731, 736 (1923).

[245] 219 U.S. 346, 31 S. Ct. 250, 55 L. Ed. 246 (1911).

[246] *Keller v. Potomac Electric Power Co.*, 261 U.S. 428, 444, 43 S. Ct. 445, 449, 67 L. Ed. 731, 737 (1923). Italics supplied.

[247] *Postum Cereal Co. v. California Fig Nut Co.*, 272 U.S. 693, 700, 47 S. Ct. 284, 286, 71 L. Ed. 478, 481 (1927). Italics supplied. See also *Federal Radio Commission v. General Electric Co.*, 281 U.S. 464, 50 S. Ct. 389, 74 L. Ed. 969 (1930).

no other jurisdiction," [248] and, therefore, the District of Columbia courts, having been invested with "other jurisdiction," must be *legislative courts.* But in 1933 the Supreme Court faced a dilemma. The Appropriation Act of 1932 [249] made provision for certain reductions in the salaries of judges (and of other federal officers). If the District of Columbia courts were constitutional courts, created under Article III, the judges of these courts would not be subject to the salary reduction under the rule of *Evans v. Gore;* [250] but if they were constitutional courts, they could not be invested with legislative and administrative functions on authority of the Keller, Bakelite, and Postum Cereal cases. Mr. Justice Sutherland was equal to the occasion. The courts of the District were held to be created under Article III, and the District judges were accordingly exempted from the operation of a general federal economy statute which affected all other federal employees except judges of constitutional courts, by judicial dispensation. The language of the Postum case was explained away thus:

> Taken literally, this seems to negative the view that the superior courts of the District are established under Art. 3. But the observation, read in the light of what was said in the Keller case in respect of the dual power of Congress in dealing with the courts of the District, should be confined to federal courts in the states as to which no such dual power exists; and thus confined, it is not in conflict with the view that Congress derives from the District clause distinct powers in respect of the constitutional courts of the District which Congress does not possess in respect of such courts outside the District.[251]

The District of Columbia courts are *constitutional* not *legislative* courts, but, *unlike all other constitutional courts,* they may be invested with functions which only legislative courts may exercise. In creating and defining the jurisdiction of the courts of the District, Congress is not limited by Article III, as it is in dealing with the other constitutional courts, because "the clause giving *plenary power of legislation over the District* enables Congress to confer such jurisdiction in addition to the federal jurisdiction which the District courts exercise under Art. 3, notwithstanding that they are recipients of the judicial power of the United States under, and are constituted in virtue of, that article." [252]

---

[248] *Ex parte Bakelite Corp.,* note 224, *supra.*
[249] Act of June 30, 1932, 47 *Stat.* 382, 401–2, c. 314, §§ 105, 106, 107.
[250] 253 U.S. 245, 40 S. Ct. 550, 64 L. Ed. 887 (1920).
[251] *O'Donoghue v. United States,* 289 U.S. 516, 551, 53 S. Ct. 740, 750, 77 L. Ed. 1356, 1371 (1933).
[252] 289 U.S. at 546, 53 S. Ct. at 748–49, 77 L. Ed. at 1368. Italics supplied.

However, the power of Congress over the other territories is also "plenary," but the courts of these territories are legislative courts.[253] Speaking of the territorial governments established by Congress, the Supreme Court said in *Benner v. Porter:* "They are legislative governments, and their courts legislative courts. *Congress, in the exercise of its powers in the organization and government of the Territories, combining the powers of both the federal and State authorities."* [254] In *Mormon Church v. United States,* the Court again held: "The power of Congress over the Territories of the United States is general and *plenary,* arising from and incidental to the right to acquire the territory itself, and from the power given by the Constitution to make all needful rules and regulations respecting the territory or other property belonging to the United States." [255] And in *National Bank v. County of Yankton:* "It [Congress] may do for the Territories what the People, under the Constitution of the United States, may do for the States." [256] That is, Congress possesses a "plenary" and "dual authority" over *all* the territories of the United States. But Mr. Justice Sutherland distinguished the District of Columbia from the other territories—the former is a permanent territory, while the latter look to statehood [257]—thus qualifying "plenary power" as to the latter.

"Gossamer distinctions" are used to implement our governmental trichotomy. With reference to the distinctions between constitutional and legislative courts, James M. Landis makes the following comment:

> *Legal sophistication* of this character has led some commentators to classify agencies such as the Board of Tax Appeals, the Court of Customs and Patent Appeals, and even the Court of Claims as "administrative tribunals." But distinctions that relate merely to the inviolability of judicial salaries, the absence of life tenure for judges, the power and tendency to apply different and more flexible procedural rules, the right to admit and consider evidence that would be rejected under a strict application of common law principles, all seem insufficient to alter the essential fact that the agency is still a court that is "passively" adjudicating the merits of such conflicting claims as may be presented to it.[258]

[253] *American Insurance Co. v. Canter,* 1 Pet. 511, 7 L. Ed. 242 (1828).
[254] 9 How. 235, 242, 13 L. Ed. 119, 122 (1850). Italics supplied.
[255] 136 U.S. 1, 42, 10 S. Ct. 792, 802, 34 L. Ed. 478, 490–91 (1889). Italics supplied.
[256] 101 U.S. 1, 129, 133, 25 L. Ed. 1046, 1047 (1880).
[257] *O'Donoghue v. United States,* 289 U.S. 516, 551, 53 S. Ct. 740, 77 L. Ed. 1356 (1933).
[258] *The Administrative Process* (Yale University Press, New Haven, 1938), p. 20. Italics supplied.

Accordingly, the judicial power of the United States is exercised by three categories of tribunals:

1. *Constitutional Courts.* The constitutional courts are the Supreme Court, the Federal Circuit Courts of Appeals, the Federal District Courts, and the District Court and the Court of Appeals of the District of Columbia.

2. *Legislative Courts.* The legislative courts include the Court of Claims, the Customs Court, the Court of Customs and Patent Appeals, the Tax Court, consular courts, and the territorial courts. *Some* of these courts, such as the territorial courts, exercise *pure judicial* power, albeit not a part of "the judicial power of the United States" within the meaning of Article III. *All* exercise, or may be authorized to exercise, certain functions (such as the adjudication of claims for damages by individuals against the government, or claims for revenue by the government against individuals) which should also be classified as *strictly judicial,* if the distinction between constitutional and legislative courts is valid, since these functions are shared by the legislative courts and the constitutional federal district courts and the District of Columbia courts. And *all* the legislative courts either exercise, or may be authorized to exercise administrative powers, usually on review of decisions by administrative agencies.[259] Decisions of this type are not supposed to be subject to review by constitutional courts except on questions of law.

All these courts, except the consular and territorial courts, are *administrative courts.*

3. *Administrative Agencies or Tribunals.* Any administrative agency exercising judicial power may be regarded as an administrative tribunal. Administrative agencies settle innumerable disputes on the basis of law and fact. These proceedings have the earmarks of cases or controversies, and the procedure and resulting orders are essentially judicial; but in deference to the doctrine of the separation of powers, administrative adjudication is only "quasi-judicial" since an administrative decision or order affecting private rights is not final; nor can the agency, theoretically, apply a criminal penalty prescribed by law or punish for contempt.[260]

Administrative tribunals differ from legislative and constitutional

[259] *Muskrat v. United States,* 219 U.S. 346, 31 S. Ct. 250, 55 L. Ed. 246 (1911); *Ex parte Bakelite Corp.,* 279 U.S. 438, 49 S. Ct. 411, 73 L. Ed. 789 (1929); *Willing v. Chicago Auditorium Association,* 277 U.S. 274, 48 S. Ct. 507, 72 L. Ed. 880 (1928); *Fairchild v. Hughes,* 258 U.S. 126, 129, 42 S. Ct. 274, 66 L. Ed. 499 (1922); *Keller v. Potomac Electric Co.,* 261 U.S. 428, 444, 43 S. Ct. 445, 67 L. Ed. 731 (1923); *Postum Cereal Co. v. California Fig Nut Co.,* 272 U.S. 693, 47 S. Ct. 284, 71 L. Ed. 478 (1927).
[260] See Chapter 4.

courts in that they often combine the exercise of legislative, executive, and judicial powers: a single agency may act as rulemaker, prosecutor, and judge.

Citing the Federal Trade Commission, the Interstate Commerce Commission, and the State public service commissions as examples, a federal judge observed:

> The spectacle of an administrative tribunal acting as both prosecutor and judge has been the subject of much comment, and efforts to do away with such practice have been studied for years. . . . But it has never held that such procedure denies constitutional right. On the contrary, many agencies have functioned for years, with the approval of the courts, which combine these roles.[261]

Proposals for a Federal Administrative Court.—In 1929, Senator Norris of Nebraska introduced in the Senate a bill which provided for the merging of all existing legislative (administrative) courts into a single United States Court of Administrative Justice.[262] The bill proposed to transfer to the new court (1) the five judges of the Court of Claims and the five judges of the Court of Customs Appeals, and (2) the jurisdiction of the Court of Claims, the Court of Customs Appeals, the Board of Tax Appeals, and of the Supreme Court of the District of Columbia to grant writs of mandamus and injunction against officers and employees of the United States, and of the United States District Courts to entertain suits against the United States. The bill did not become law.

In 1933 the American Bar Association created a Special Committee on Administrative Law to inquire into the practicality and desirability (1) of divorcing quasi-judicial functions from quasi-legislative and executive functions in some or all of those administrative tribunals in which a combination of functions now exists; (2) of concentrating the quasi-judicial functions in an independent body having the character of an administrative court with appropriate branches and divisions and assisted by examiners or commissioners, its decisions to be subject to judicial review; and (3) of concentrat-

---

[261] *Brinkley v. Hassig*, 83 F. (2d) 351, 356–57 (C.C.A., 1936). Also, *Federal Trade Commission v. Klesner*, 280 U.S. 19, 50 S. Ct. 1, 74 L. Ed. 138 (1929); *Farmers' Live Stock Commission v. United States*, 54 F. (2d) 375 (D.C.E.D. Ill., 1931). While lawyers generally condemn the administrative process as one which combines law-maker, prosecutor, and judge, they can find no fault with the judicial use of the contempt power, where one individual, the judge, acts as lawyer, jury, and judge.

[262] *S. 5154*, 70th Cong., 2d Sess. (1929); *Cong. Rec.*, 70th Cong., 2d Sess., Vol. LXX, Pt. 1, pp. 1030–33.

ing the quasi-legislative and executive functions under executive officers responsible to the President.[263]

That same year, 1933, Senator Logan introduced a bill for a Federal Administrative Court, similar to but more elaborate than the Court proposed by Senator Norris.[264] O. R. McGuire, a member of the Special Committee on Administrative Law of the American Bar Association, said of the Logan Bill:

> It is proposed in the bill to transfer to that court [the Administrative Court] the five judges of the Court of Claims and the five judges of the Court of Customs and Patent Appeals and to add five more judges, making a court of fifteen judges, with authority to sit in divisions of three for the purpose of hearing cases and in divisions of five for the purpose of determining motions for new trials. This would, in effect, result in five courts for the hearing of cases, or three courts for the purpose of new trials. The advantages are obvious of such a system in establishing justice between the citizen and his Government; in preventing conflicts in decisions; and in securing expeditious reviews of administrative decisions in the class of cases within the jurisdiction of that court.[265]

The Logan Bill died in committee. But the Bar Association continued to press for action. In its 1934 *Report* it recommended the creation of a Federal Administrative Court with appropriate branches and divisions; or, failing this, an appropriate number of independent tribunals similar to the Court of Claims and the Court of Customs and Patent Appeals.[266] The Bar Association's interest in a Federal Administrative Court reflected the interest of lawyers generally in segregating the judicial function from the legislative and executive functions, and making administrative action subject to judicial review on law and fact.

In the spring of 1935 the Special Committee presented a draft of a bill to the Executive Committee of the Bar Association, but since the latter "asked to be excused from having the bill introduced at the then pending session of Congress," the Select Committee did not have the bill introduced and did not make a formal report at the annual meeting of the Association.[267] In 1936 the Special Committee completed the draft of a new bill which was delivered to Senator

---

[263] American Bar Association, *Report* (1933), Vol. LVIII, p. 415.

[264] *S. 1835*, 73rd Cong., 1st Sess. (1933).

[265] "Proposed Reforms in Judicial Reviews of Federal Administrative Action," 19 *American Bar Association Journal*, 471, 473.

[266] American Bar Association, *Report* (1934), Vol. LIX, pp. 539, 540.

[267] *Report of the Special Committee on Administrative Law* (1936), pp. 246–47.

Logan who introduced it in the Senate in January, 1936.[268] The identical bill was introduced in the House by Representative Celler in April, 1936.[269] These bills, like their predecessors, proposed the establishment of a single Federal Administrative Court incorporating several existing legislative courts and the judicial functions of federal administrative agencies. The bills died on the adjournment of Congress.[270]

The following year, in 1937, the President's Committee on Administrative Management proposed the transfer of the adjudicating functions of existing administrative agencies to independent "judicial sections," in effect, special administrative courts.[271] And that year the Bar Association abandoned its proposal for an over-all administrative court and concentrated on the improvement and standardization of administrative procedure and the extension of review of administrative action by the ordinary courts of law.[272]

In 1938, Senator Logan, shifting position somewhat, introduced a bill for the creation of a United States Court of Appeals with exclusive jurisdiction to review on appeal all final decisions and orders, now subject to review by the federal courts, of the most important federal administrative officers and agencies.[273] This bill differed from the Logan-Celler Bill [274] in that it did not propose to merge existing legislative courts, or to transfer to the new Court the adjudicating powers of the agencies: it merely provided for a high court of appeals to review the more important administrative decisions. No action was taken on the measure by the Congress, but in 1939 its proposals were substantially embodied in two new bills, which also failed to get Congressional approval. Congress, like the Bar Association, now turned to the simpler problem of revising administrative procedure and in December, 1940, passed the Logan-Celler Bill,[275] later known as the Walter-Logan Bill. This bill was sponsored by

[268] *S. 3787*, 74th Cong., 2d Sess.

[269] *H.R. 12297*, 74th Cong., 2d Sess.

[270] *Cf.* D. C. Bular, "A United States Administrative Court," 26 *Georgetown Law Journal* (1936), No. 4; L. G. Caldwell, "A Federal Administrative Court," 84 *University of Pennsylvania Law Review* (1936); O. R. McGuire, "The Need for a Federal Administrative Court," 5 *George Washington Law Review* (1936–37).

[271] President's Committee on Administrative Management, *Report with Special Studies* (Government Printing Office, Washington, D.C., 1937).

[272] American Bar Association, *Report* (1937), Vol. LXII, pp. 805–7, L. L. Jaffe, "Invective and Investigation in Administrative Law," 52 *Harvard Law Review* (1939), pp. 1201 ff.

[273] *S. 3676*, 75th Cong., 3d Sess. (1938).

[274] Representative Celler introduced *H.R. 234* on January 3, 1939. This was reintroduced later as *H.R. 4235* and as *S. 916*.

[275] *S. 915*, *H.R. 4236* (later replaced by *H.R. 6324*), 76th Cong., 3d Sess. (1940).

the American Bar Association and drafted by its Special Committee on Administrative Law. The bill contained gross infirmities. It prescribed a single, impossibly rigid procedure for rule-making and subjected almost every administrative action to judicial review, on questions of law and fact, and for almost any conceivable reason. It proposed a sterilization of the administrative process. It met with severe criticism,[276] including an indignant veto message by President Roosevelt,[277] which was sustained by the House.[278]

In 1941, bills based upon the majority and minority reports of the Attorney General's Committee on Administrative Procedure, were introduced in both Houses of Congress.[279] World War II intervened to postpone serious consideration of the problem. Some bills on the subject appeared in 1944,[280] but received little attention. Meanwhile the Bar Association and the supporters of the Walter-Logan Bill assumed direction of the Congressional campaign to formalize and standardize administrative procedure, to separate adjudication from rule-making, and to extend judicial control over administrative action; and in 1945 the McCarran-Summers Bill [281] was placed before the Congress. After some revision [282] the measure was passed and approved by the President on June 11, 1946.[283] This is the Federal Administrative Procedure Act of 1946.[284]

This is a lawyer's law, conceived by lawyers and dedicated to the proposition that justice is the exclusive business of lawyers. It falls far short of solving the problem raised in the administrative court bills: the problem of providing executive justice with adequate judicial machinery for the guidance and control of administrative discretion. "The Act thus," said Mr. Justice Jackson, "represents a long period of study and strife; it settles long continued and hard-fought contentions, and enacts a formula upon which opposing social

---

[276] Cf. Alfred Jaretzki, Jr., "The Administrative Law Bill: Unsound and Unworkable," 2 *Louisiana Law Review* (1940), 294; Ashley Sellers, "Administrative Law — The Extent to Which S. 915 or H.R. 4236 Would Affect the Work of the Department of Agriculture," 7 *George Washington Law Review* (1939), 819, 923; F. F. Blachly in *Hearings Before the Sub-Committee Number 4 of the Committee on the Judiciary on H.R. 6324*, 76th Cong., 1st Sess. (1939).

[277] Message of Dec. 18, 1940, *H.R. Doc. No. 986*, 76th Cong., 3d Sess. (1940).

[278] 86 *Cong. Rec.*, 13953 (1940).

[279] *S. 675, H.R. 4782* (Majority Report); *S. 674, H.R. 4238* (Minority Report). *Report of the Attorney General's Committee on Administrative Procedure, S. Doc. No. 8*, 77th Cong., 1st Sess. (1941).

[280] *H.R. 4314, H.R. 5081, H.R. 5237, S. 2030*, 78th Cong., 2d Sess. (1944).

[281] *S. 7* and *H.R. 1203*, 79th Cong., 1st Sess. (1945).

[282] *S. Doc. No. 248*, 79th Cong., 2d Sess. (1945), pp. 175, 190–91, 233, 248–49; *S. Rep. No. 752*, 79th Cong., 1st Sess. (1945), pp. 37–45.

[283] 92 *Cong. Rec.*, 2167, 5668, 5791, 6706 (1946).

[284] 60 *Stat.* 237, 5 *U.S.C.A.* § 1001 *et sqq.*

and political forces have come to rest. It contains many compromises and generalities and, no doubt, some ambiguities. Experience may reveal defects." [285] The record reveals more "strife," than "study," and that the text contains "ambiguities" and "defects" is attested to by the instant case in which the Court did not agree on a construction of the Act. The provision for citizen participation in rule-making gives almost unlimited opportunity for sabotage, and the extension of judicial review may give so many citizens so many days in court that the government will have very few days out of court.

[285] *Wong Yang Sung v. McGrath,* 339 U.S. 33, 40–41, 70 S. Ct. 445, 450, 94 L. Ed. 616, 624 (1950).

Chapter 4

ENFORCEMENT OF ADMINISTRATIVE ACTION

Due process of law generally requires that administrative agencies cannot enforce their rules or orders but must rely upon the equity jurisdiction of the courts of law. A person whose rights are affected has the constitutional right to challenge the validity of the administrative action in a court, where the issue can be resolved according to traditional rules and principles of justice. Furthermore, regulatory statutes commonly provide for judicial enforcement of administrative rules and orders.

When an agency has made an order, ordinarily that agency alone is authorized to take proceedings to enforce compliance.[1] The Supreme Court has held with respect to the National Labor Relations Board that for the purpose of enforcing its orders

> . . . the Board is empowered to petition the Circuit Court of Appeals for a decree of enforcement. . . . When the Board has made its order, the Board alone is authorized to take proceedings to enforce it. . . . the Act gives no authority for any proceeding by a private person or group, or by any employee or group of employees, to secure enforcement of the Board's order. The vindication of the desired freedom of employees is thus confided by the Act, by reasons of recognized public interest, to the public agency the Act creates.[2]

Likewise, contempt proceedings for violating injunctions following upon determinations of the National Labor Relations

[1] Securities Act of 1933 and Securities Exchange Act of 1934, § 21, 15 *U.S.C.A.* §§ 21(a)(b)(c)(d), 78q(a), 78w(b); *Securities and Exchange Commission v. Okin,* 58 F. Supp. 20 (D.C.S.D.N.Y., 1944).

National Labor Relations Act of 1935, § 10(e), 29 *U.S.C.A.* § 160(e); *National Labor Relations Board v. Fickett-Brown Mfg. Co.,* 140 F. (2d) 883 (C.C.A. 5th, 1944).

Federal Trade Commission Act of 1914, §§ 5, 9, 10, 15 *U.S.C.A.* §§ 46, 49, 50; *United States v. Standard Education Society,* 55 F. Supp. 189 (D.C.N.D. Ill., 1943).

Interstate Commerce Act, 24 *Stat.* 383, § 11 (1887), 49 *U.S.C.A.* § 11 (1934); Board of Tax Appeals Act, 43 *Stat.* 336 (1924), 26 *U.S.C.A.* § 600 (1934); Longshoremen's and Harbor Workers' Compensation Act, 44 *Stat.* 1424–46 (1927), 33 *U.S.C.A.* § 901 (1934).

[2] *Amalgamated Utility Workers v. Consolidated Edison Co. of New York,* 309 U.S. 261, 265, 266, 60 S. Ct. 561, 563–64, 84 L. Ed. 738, 742 (1940).

Board can be instituted only by the Board and in the public interest.[3]

Some statutes provide that a party aggrieved by an administrative order may apply for judicial review within a prescribed period. At the end of that period, however, the order becomes self-enforcing,[4] that is, enforceable by the process of the agency or by courts in a purely formal proceeding "in which the aggrieved party need not be given notice, or cannot question the correctness of the administrative decision on any grounds other than those going to the jurisdiction of the tribunal." [5]

But a "reparation order," that is, an order for the payment of a money award, may require the beneficiary to bring the enforcement action, in which case the party against whom the order runs may challenge the validity of the order.

An administrative cease and desist order is essentially an injunction and it becomes so in law when sustained by a court. The order should, therefore, comply with the usual requisites for an injunction as to specificity in stating what is required or forbidden.[6] In most situations the issuing of an injunction to enforce an administrative order is discretionary with the court.[7] The court will first determine the validity of the order and then consider the question of compliance.[8]

A general order of affirmance by a court for an administrative cease and desist order is not in legal effect an *enforcement decree* embodying the prohibitions of the administrative order and enjoining

---

[3] *May Department Stores Co. v. National Labor Relations Board,* 326 U.S. 376, 388, 66 S. Ct. 203, 210, 90 L. Ed. 145, 156 (1946).

"Courts are not expected to start wheels moving or to follow up judgments. Courts neither have, nor need, sleuths to dig up evidence, staffs to analyze reports, or personnel to prepare prosecutions for contempts." *United States v. Morton Salt Co.,* 338 U.S. 632, 641, 70 S. Ct. 357, 363 (1950).

[4] Federal Trade Commission Act, 52 *Stat.* 111 (1938), 15 *U.S.C.A.* § 41 (Supp. 1939).

[5] Ernst H. Shopflocher, "Doctrine of Res Judicata in Administrative Law," 17 *Wisconsin Law Review* (1942), 12.

[6] *Hughes Tool Co. v. National Labor Relations Board,* 147 F. (2d) 69 (C.C.A. 5th, 1945) ; *General Motors Corp. v. National Labor Relations Board,* 150 F. (2d) 201 (C.C.A. 3d, 1945).

[7] *Hecht Co. v. Bowles,* 321 U.S. 321, 64 S. Ct. 587, 88 L. Ed. 754 (1944). *Bowles v. Lake Lucerne Plaza, Inc.,* 148 F. (2d) 967 (C.C.A. 5th, 1945) ; *Bowles v. Katz,* 61 F. Supp. 333 (D.C.E.D. Pa., 1945) ; *Bowles v. Harrison,* 61 F. Supp. 160 (D.C.W.D. Pa., 1945) ; *Porter v. Granite State Packing Co.,* 155 F. (2d) 786 (C.C.A. 1st, 1946) ; *Bowles v. Henry Lustig & Co., Inc.,* 155 F. (2d) 236 (C.C.A. 2d, 1946).

[8] *National Labor Relations Board v. Fickett-Brown Mfg. Co.,* 140 F. (2d) 883 (C.C.A. 5th, 1944) ; *Bowles v. Bonnie Bee Shop,* 55 F. Supp. 754 (D.C.W.D. Mo., 1944) ; *National Labor Relations Board v. Cheney California Lumber Co.,* 327 U.S. 385, 66 S. Ct. 553, 90 L. Ed. 739 (1946).

violation of an injunctive order of the court. A decree of enforcement should be of the general nature and form of a decree of injunction, definitely fixing the duties of the party against whom the cease and desist order was issued.[9] A court must affirm a cease and desist order before it will enforce it.[10] If there is a question whether the cease and desist order has been violated, the court will refer the matter to the agency for a finding of fact on that point.[11] When a court has entered an enforcement decree, it will not vacate it at the behest of the agency to permit the latter to correct an alleged error in its original order.[12]

A cease and desist order by the National Labor Relations Board directed not only to the respondent but also to the "successors and assigns" was upheld by the Supreme Court [13] despite the objection of three Justices that the order was an unwarranted threat against innocent third parties.[14] But the Board may not issue a blanket order against all violations of the Act; [15] the order must be limited to unfair practices of the kind originally committed.[16]

State courts are required under the Supremacy Clause (Article VI) of the Constitution to enforce federal regulations made under authority of valid law. Federal law is the "supreme law of the land" and "the judges in every State shall be bound thereby." Thus, a State court was required to assume jurisdiction of an action for treble damages for sales above ceiling prices established by the Emergency Price Control Act of 1942.[17] The Supreme Court ruled that

> The policy of the federal Act is the prevailing policy in every State. . . . It is conceded that this same type of claim arising under Rhode Island law would be enforced by that State's courts. . . . Under these circumstances the State courts are not free to refuse enforcement of petitioner's claims.[18]

[9] *Federal Trade Commission v. Fairyfoot Products Co.*, 94 F. (2d) 844 (C.C.A. 7th, 1938).

[10] *Federal Trade Commission v. Baltimore Paint and Color Works, Inc.*, 41 F. (2d) 474 (C.C.A. 4th, 1930).

[11] *Ibid.*

[12] *International Union of Mine, Mill and Smelter Workers, etc. v. Eagle-Picher Mining & Smelting Co.*, 325 U.S. 335, 65 S. Ct. 1166, 89 L. Ed. 1649 (1945).

[13] *Regal Knitwear Co. v. National Labor Relations Board*, 324 U.S. 9, 65 S. Ct. 478, 89 L. Ed. 661 (1945).

[14] 324 U.S. at 17, 65 S. Ct. at 482, 89 L. Ed. at 668.

[15] *General Motors Corp. v. National Labor Relations Board*, 150 F. (2d) 201 (C.C.A. 3d, 1945).

[16] *National Labor Relations Board v. Lipshutz*, 149 F. (2d) 141 (C.C.A. 5th, 1945).

[17] 56 *Stat.* 23, 50 *U.S.C.A.* App. § 901 *et sqq.*

[18] *Testa v. Katt*, 330 U.S. 386, 393–94, 67 S. Ct. 810, 814–15, 91 L. Ed. 967, 972 (1947).

The Investigating Power

In order to exercise effectively their legislative and judicial functions, administrative bodies must be able to obtain pertinent information and to enforce valid rules and orders. Agencies are authorized to conduct investigations and, in aid thereof, to summon witnesses and require the production of books, papers, contracts, agreements, and other documents. Investigations may be for the purpose of acquiring data to serve as a basis for the formulation of policies, or they may be preliminary steps in the process of enforcing administrative action, or they may merely be "hearings."

It has long been recognized that "the power of inquiry—with process to enforce it—is an essential and appropriate auxiliary to the legislative function." [19] This was so in England and America even before the Constitution was framed.[20] Process to enforce the legislative power of inquiry embraces the power to subpoena and to punish contumacious witnesses for contempt.[21] Either branch of the legislature may, by resolution, direct its presiding officer to command its sergeant at arms or his deputy to take the offending witness into custody and imprison him for the duration of the legislative session. The legislative power to punish for contempt is limited to acts which obstruct the performance of the duties of the legislature.[22]

Either house of Congress may delegate to one of its committees the power of inquiry, "with process to enforce it," [23] *but not its power to legislate.* On the other hand, Congress may delegate to an administrative agency *the power to legislate, together with the power of inquiry* but *without* "process to enforce it."

> Such a body could not, under our system of government, and consistently with due process of law, be invested with authority to compel obedience to its orders by a judgment of fine or imprisonment. Except in the particular instances enumerated in the Constitution, and considered in *Anderson v. Dunn, . . .* and *Kilbourn v. Thompson, . . .* of the exercise by either house of Congress of its right to punish disorderly behavior upon the part of its members, and to compel the attendance of witnesses and the production of papers in election and impeachment cases and in cases that may involve the existence of those bodies, the power to impose fine or imprisonment in order to compel the perform-

[19] *McGrain v. Daugherty*, 273 U.S. 135, 174, 47 S. Ct. 319, 328, 71 L. Ed. 580, 593 (1927).
[20] 273 U.S. at 175, 47 S. Ct. at 329, 71 L. Ed. at 593.
[21] *Jurney v. MacCracken*, 294 U.S. 125, 55 S. Ct. 375, 79 L. Ed. 802 (1935).
[22] *Kilbourn v. Thompson*, 103 U.S. 168, 190, 26 L. Ed. 377, 387 (1881).
[23] *McGrain v. Daugherty*, 273 U.S. 135, 47 S. Ct. 319, 71 L. Ed. 580 (1927).

ance of a legal duty imposed by the United States, can only be exerted, under the law of the land, by a competent judicial tribunal having jurisdiction in the premises.[24]

That is to say, even if "the power of inquiry—with process to enforce it—is an essential and appropriate auxiliary to the legislative function"[25] and Congress can delegate rule-making (legislative) power to an administrative body, the power so delegated does not include "process to enforce it."[26]

Moreover, "The power to punish for contempts is inherent in all courts; its existence is essential to the preservation of order in judicial proceedings, and to the enforcement of the judgments, orders and writs of the courts, and consequently to the due administration of justice."[27] And either house of Congress may, while exercising its *judicial* functions (such as deciding on the elections, returns, and qualifications of its members), require the attendance of witnesses and may punish contemnors of its authority—a power "in no wise inferior under like circumstances to that exercised by a court of justice."[28] But, an administrative tribunal may not punish for contempt of its authority, even though it exercises important delegated adjudicating powers.

If "the function of the contempt power is to remove impediments to the administration of justice, it is a narrow view which would distinguish between the administrative and judicial departments."[29] The courts evidently regard it as a loss of dignity to be classified with

[24] *Interstate Commerce Commission v. Brimson,* 154 U.S. 447, 485, 14 S. Ct. 1125, 1136, 38 L. Ed. 1047, 1060 (1894).

[25] Footnote 19, *supra.*

[26] "Cadwalader, District Judge . . . would further say that he very much doubted the power of congress to invest a commissioner with the authority in a proceeding originally instituted before him, to summarily commit a citizen for an alleged contempt. This was an exercise of the judicial power of the United States, which, under the constitution, could not be entrusted to an officer, appointed and holding his office in the manner in which these commissioners were appointed and held office." *Ex parte Doll.,* 7 Fed. Cas. 855, Case No. 3968 (1870).

[27] Mr. Justice Field in *Ex parte Robinson,* 19 Wall. 505, 22 L. Ed. 205 (1873). See also *Ex parte Grossman,* 267 U.S. 87, 45 S. Ct. 332, 69 L. Ed. 527 (1925); *Michaelson v. United States,* 266 U.S. 42, 45 S. Ct. 18, 69 L. Ed. 162 (1925); *In re Debs,* 158 U.S. 564, 15 S. Ct. 900, 39 L. Ed. 1092 (1895).

Some State courts have held that administrative agencies also possess inherent contempt power. See *In re Hayes,* 200 N.C. 133, 156 S.E. (2d) 791 (1931); *In re Sanford,* 236 Mo. 665, 139 S.W. 376 (1911); *Plunkett v. Hamilton,* 136 Ga. 72, 70 S.E. 781 (1911); *State ex rel. Dysart v. Cameron,* 140 Wash. 101, 248 Pac. 408 (1926).

[28] *Barry v. United States ex rel. Cunningham,* 279 U.S. 597, 616, 49 S. Ct. 452, 456, 73 L. Ed. 867, 873 (1929).

[29] "The Power of Administrative Agencies to Commit for Contempt," 35 *Columbia Law Review* (1935), 587.

administrative tribunals. To deny the contempt power to administrative bodies seems particularly artificial since the power is not *judicial,* either historically or in practice. The power descended from the English king (who did not limit it to judicial matters, but employed it to ensure respect for all departments of his government) to Parliament and thence to the American legislatures; its contemporaneous exercise by the courts was sustained in the first and final instance by necessity alone.[30] While the necessity argument has been generally used to justify the exercise of the contempt power by both legislatures and courts, its application to administrative bodies has been as generally rejected by courts and writers. But in its nature the contempt power is *administrative* rather than legislative or judicial—*it is a power used to enforce a law by whomsoever it is exercised.* It is expediency rather than logic, therefore, that denies the contempt power to administrative agencies.

It has been said that the doctrine that the power to punish for contempt "rests with the courts alone [except where the constitution expressly confers such power upon some other body or tribunal[31]] is based upon the fact that a party cannot be deprived of his liberty without a trial. To adjudge a person guilty of contempt for a refusal to answer questions, the tribunal must determine whether such questions are material, and whether it is a question which the witness is bound to answer; otherwise it cannot be determined that the witness is in contempt of its authority in refusing to answer."[32]

The trouble with this view of the matter is that the contempt power as exercised by courts is summary, and it is difficult to see how the recusancy of a witness can be a matter for trial.

While the federal courts will not permit federal officers or agencies to punish for contempt, a number of the States have conferred, either by express constitutional provision[33] or by statute,[34] the contempt

---

[30] See C. S. Potts, "Power of Legislative Bodies to Punish for Contempt," 64 *University of Pennsylvania Law Review* (1926), 691–725, 780–829; James M. Landis, "Constitutional Limitations on the Congressional Power of Investigation," 40 *Harvard Law Review* (1926), 153–221; W. Nelles, "The Summary Power to Punish for Contempt," 31 *Columbia Law Review* (1931), 956–74; William Blackstone, *Commentaries,* Bk. IV, chap. ix, Pt. II, §§ 2–5.

[31] *Ex parte Victor,* 220 Cal. 729, 32 P. (2d) 608 (1934).

[32] *Langenberg v. Decker,* 131 Ind. 471, 483, 31 N.E. 190, 194 (1892).

[33] California *Constitution,* Art. XII, §§ 22, 15, the Railroad Commission and the Workmen's Compensation Commission; Oklahoma *Constitution,* Art. IX, § 19, the Corporation Commission; Louisiana *Constitution,* Art. VI, § 4, the Public Service Commission; Virginia *Constitution,* Art. XII, § 15, the Corporation Commission.

[34] As examples: *New Jersey Stat. Ann.,* Title 54, c. 2, § 15 (1940), the Board of Tax Appeals; *Missouri Rev. Stat.,* c. 33, § 5123 (1944), Board of Tax Appeals, and *ibid.* (Ann.), c. 128, § 15346, Public Utilities Commission; *North Carolina Gen. Stat.,* c. 153, § 30 (1943), Board of County Commissioners, and *ibid.,* c. 62, § 13

power upon some of their officers or agencies.[35] When State administrative officers exercise the contempt power they are said to act judicially [36] or as courts.[37]

There are times and circumstances when it is necessary to use some summary method to enforce the commands of government, be they legislative, administrative, or judicial; but summary power is arbitrary and peculiarly susceptible to abuse and should be used only in the public interest and not to gratify personal ambition or vanity. "The claim of 'inherent power' is always invoked by every governmental agency which is reaching out for more power, as did King James and Charles the First, and unless the dynamism of this doctrine is restrained, it leads to absolutism." [38] And judicial absolutism is the least defensible since it is the least responsive to the general will. In the exercise of the contempt power, *one individual* acts as lawyer, judge, and jury. Such a power exists by grace of the governed; it is not *inherited* from either a King James or an equally odious Judge Jeffreys, nor yet from "a law of the nature of things." The "inherent" theory was logically rejected when Congress limited the power in 1831 [39] and when the Supreme Court applied the "clear and present danger" doctrine to its exercise.[40] The power is not personal to the judge but is an attribute of his office [41] and, thus, is conditioned by the enabling statute. An "inherent" power, not having its source in statute, would not be subject to the legislative will.

The accepted federal administrative procedure to compel testimony since *Interstate Commerce Commission v. Brimson* [42] is for the

---

(1943), Utilities Commission; New York, *McKinney's Con. Law Ann.*, Art. 13, § 134 (1943), Superintendent of Public Works; *Texas Rev. Civil Stat. Ann.*, Title 102, Art. 6024, Railroad Commission; *California Gen. Stat.*, c. 115, § 54, Utilities Commission; *Vermont Public Laws*, Title 28, § 6068, Public Service Commission; *Connecticut Gen. Stat.*, § 490 (1930), Board of Police Commissioners, and *ibid.*, § 2000 (1930), Board of Pardons.

[35] *Cf.* R. J. Tresolini, "The Use of Summary Contempt Powers by Administrative Agencies," *Dickinson Law Review* (June, 1950) ; R. Parker, "Contempt Procedure in the Enforcement of Administrative Orders," 40 *Illinois Law Review* (1946), 344 ff.

[36] *Vogel v. Corporation Commission,* 190 Okla. 110, 121 Pac. (2d) 586 (1942).

[37] *Pacific Coast Casualty Co. v. Pillsbury,* 171 Cal. 319, 153 Pac. 24 (1915) ; *Louisiana v. Meyers,* 171 La. 313, 131 So. 31 (1931).

[38] Justice Maxey in *Pennsylvania Anthracite Mining Co. v. Anthracite Miners,* 318 Pa. 401, 413–14, 178 Atl. 291, 296 (1935).

[39] Act of March 2, 1831, 4 *Stat.* 487, *Criminal Code,* 135, 35 *Stat.* 1113, 18 U.S.C.A. § 242.

[40] *Bridges v. California,* 314 U.S. 252, 62 S. Ct. 190, 86 L. Ed. 192 (1941) ; *Pennekamp v. Florida,* 328 U.S. 331, 66 S. Ct. 1029, 90 L. Ed. 1295 (1946) ; *Craig v. Harvey,* 331 U.S. 367, 67 S. Ct. 1249, 91 L. Ed. 1546 (1947).

[41] *Ex parte Grossman,* 267 U.S. 87, 45 S. Ct. 332, 69 L. Ed. 527 (1925).

[42] 154 U.S. 447, 14 S. Ct. 1125, 38 L. Ed. 1047 (1894).

agency, on recusancy of a witness, to apply to a court for an order requiring the witness to testify. Disobedience of the judicial order is punishable as contempt of court.[43] The pattern is found in Sections 9 and 10 of the Federal Trade Commission Act [44] which authorizes the Commission to require by subpoena

> . . . the attendance and testimony of witnesses and the production of all such documentary evidence relating to any matter under investigation. . . .
>
> Any of the district courts of the United States within the jurisdiction of which such inquiry is carried on may, in case of contumacy or refusal to obey a subpoena issued to any corporation or other person, issue an order requiring such corporation or other person to appear before the commission, or to produce documentary evidence if so ordered, or to give evidence touching the matter in question; and any failure to obey such order of the court may be punished by such court as a contempt thereof.

Section 10 imposes criminal penalties for refusal or neglect to obey the "subpoena or lawful requirement of the commission."

These sections have been incorporated in other statutes, such as the Fair Labor Standards Act [45] and the Administrative Procedure Act. The latter provides that agency subpoenas authorized by law may be issued to any party

> . . . upon a statement or showing of general relevance and reasonable scope of the evidence sought. Upon contest the court shall sustain any such subpena or similar process or demand to the extent that it is found to be in accordance with law and, in any proceeding for enforcement, shall issue an order requiring the appearance of the witness or the production of the evidence or data within a reasonable time under penalty of punishment for contempt in case of contumacious failure to comply.[46]

Any person required to testify shall be accorded the right of counsel, and any such person shall be entitled to retain or, on payment of

[43] See D. E. Lilienthal, "The Power of Governmental Agencies to Compel Testimony," 39 *Harvard Law Review* (1926), 694 ff.

[44] Act of September 16, 1914, 38 *Stat.* 717, 15 *U.S.C.A.* §§ 49, 50. At first the courts refused to enforce an administrative subpoena *duces tecum* on the ground that the agency was not a judicial body and that, therefore, to enforce the subpoena would be an exercise of nonjudicial power. *In re Pacific Railway Commission,* 32 Fed. 241, 249 (1887). In *Interstate Commerce Commission v. Brimson,* 154 U.S. 447, 14 S. Ct. 1125, 38 L. Ed. 1047 (1894), the Supreme Court held that the enforcement of an administrative subpoena was "judicial."

[45] Act of June 25, 1938, 52 *Stat.* 1060, § 9, 29 *U.S.C.A.* § 201 ff.

[46] Sec. 6(c). The legislature may provide for the delegation of the subpoena power. *Fleming v. Mohawk Wrecking Co.,* 331 U.S. 111, 67 S. Ct. 1129, 91 L. Ed. 1375 (1947); *Aponaug Mfg. Co. v. Bowles,* 162 F. (2d) (C.C.A. 5th, 1947).

costs, procure a copy or transcript of his testimony.[47] Officers presiding at a hearing (which may be the agency, one or more of its members, or one or more examiners appointed under Civil Service rules) have authority to issue subpoenas authorized by law.

While an administrative officer may issue a subpoena, "the Administrator has no power to compel obedience to the subpoena—such powers have historically resided in the courts as an appropriate exercise of a judicial function." [48] In general, courts will enforce a subpoena when the evidence sought is not "plainly incompetent or irrelevant to any lawful purpose" of the agency seeking the subpoena,[49] or when the court is assured that "it is not giving judicial sanction and force to unwarranted and arbitrary action, but that reasonable grounds exist for making the investigation." [50] Mr. Justice Rutledge, speaking for the Court in *Oklahoma Press Publishing Co. v. Walling*,[51] said:

> It is not necessary, as in the case of a warrant, that a specific charge or complaint of violation of law be pending or that the order be made pursuant to one. It is enough that the investigation be for a lawfully authorized purpose, within the power of Congress to command. This has been ruled most often perhaps in relation to grand jury investigations, but also frequently in respect to general or statistical investigations authorized by Congress. The requirement of "probable cause, supported by oath or affirmation," literally applicable in the case of a warrant is satisfied in that of an order for production, by the court's determination that the investigation is authorized by Congress, is for a purpose Congress can order, and the documents sought are relevant to the inquiry. Beyond this the requirement of reasonableness, including particularity in "describing the place to be searched, and the persons or things to be seized," also literally applicable to warrants, comes down to specification of the documents to be produced adequate, but not excessive, for the purposes of the relevant inquiry. Necessarily, as

[47] Sec. 6(a), (b).

[48] *Oklahoma Press Publishing Co. v. Walling,* 147 F. (2d) 658, 660 (C.C.A. 10th, 1945).

[49] *McGarry v. Securities and Exchange Commission,* 147 F. (2d) 389 (C.C.A. 10th, 1945).

[50] *Oklahoma Press Publishing Co. v. Walling,* 147 F. (2d) 658, 662 (C.C.A. 10th, 1945), quoting *Walling v. Benson,* 137 F. (2d) 501. For cases sustaining the administrative subpoena power see: (Securities and Exchange Commission) *Penfield Co. v. SEC,* 143 F. (2d) 746 (C.C.A. 9th, 1944); *SEC v. McGarry,* 56 F. Supp. 791 (D.C. Colo., 1944); (Administrator of the Wage and Hour Division) *Walling v. Detweiler Bros.,* 58 F. Supp. 201 (D.C.S.D. Idaho, 1944); (Price Administrator) *Bowles v. Curtis Candy Co.,* 55 F. Supp. 527 (D.C.W.D. Mo., 1944); *Bowles v. Joseph Denuncio Fruit Co.,* 55 F. Supp. 9 (D.C.W.D. Ky., 1944); *Bowles v. Chew* 53 F. Supp. 787 (D.C.N.D. Cal., 1944).

[51] 327 U.S. 186, 66 S. Ct. 494, 90 L. Ed. 614 (1946).

has been said, this cannot be reduced to formula; for relevancy and adequacy or excess in the breadth of the subpoena are matters variable in relation to the nature, purposes and scope of inquiry.[52]

When an agency applies to a court for an order to enforce an administrative subpoena, such an order

. . . does not issue as a matter of course. An administrative subpoena may be contested on the ground that it exceeds the bounds set by the Fourth Amendment against unreasonable search and seizure; that the inquiry is outside the scope of the authority delegated to the agency; that the testimony sought to be elicited is irrelevant to the subject matter of the inquiry; that the person to whom it is directed cannot be held responsible for the production of the papers.[53]

To the same effect, Mr. Justice Jackson said in *Fleming v. Mohawk Wrecking Co.* that the "Enforcement of such subpoenas by the courts is not and should not be automatic." [54]

If a court order is issued, a contempt proceeding for noncompliance with this order is a *civil* contempt proceeding, since the agency is seeking the production of evidence and the only sanction asked is a penalty to compel its production. That is, when a fine or imprisonment imposed on a contemnor is intended to be remedial by coercing him to do what he had refused to do, the remedy is for *civil contempt.* "Fine and imprisonment are then employed not to vindicate the public interest but as coercive sanctions to compel the contemnor to do what the law made it his duty to do." [55] The contemnor is not relieved of his duty to testify or produce relevant books or records by paying a fine—he can be imprisoned until he complies with the court's order.[56]

There are those who would take the subpoena power away from administrative agencies and vest it exclusively in the courts. Mr. Justice Murphy, who sometimes was more zealot than realist, regarded the administrative subpoena power as a "corrosion of liberty." In one of his frequent dissenting opinions he concluded:

---

[52] 327 U.S. at 209–10, 66 S. Ct. at 505–6, 90 L. Ed. at 629–30.

[53] Mr. Justice Frankfurter in *Penfield Co. of California v. Securities and Exchange Commission,* 330 U.S. 585, 604, 67 S. Ct. 918, 928, 91 L. Ed. 1117, 1130 (1947).

[54] 331 U.S. 111, 124, 67 S. Ct. 1129, 1136, 91 L. Ed. 1375, 1386 (1947).

[55] *Penfield Co. of California v. Securities and Exchange Commission,* 330 U.S. 585, 590, 67 S. Ct. 918, 921, 91 L. Ed. 1117, 1123 (1947).

[56] *Securities and Exchange Commission v. Penfield Co. of California,* 157 F. (2d) 65 (C.C.A. 9th, 1946).

To allow a non-judicial officer, unarmed with judicial process, to demand the books and papers of an individual is an open invitation to abuse of that power. It is no answer that the individual may refuse to produce the material demanded. Many persons have yielded solely because of the air of authority with which the demand is made, a demand that cannot be enforced without subsequent judicial aid. Many invasions of private rights thus occur without the restraining hand of the judiciary ever intervening.

Only by confining the subpoena power exclusively to the judiciary, can there be any insurance against this corrosion of liberty.[57]

The Justice's argument can be applied to the enforcement of every law before it is challenged and declared unconstitutional. Unquestionably "many persons" are deterred by fear of authority from challenging administrative action; but far more serious than the tendency to be unduly persuaded by "the air of authority" of the administrator is the bother and costliness and intricacy of judicial justice—considerations which make us rather "bear the ills we have than flee to others that we know not of."

If the evidence required is self-incriminating, both the Constitution and the law afford the witness complete immunity against prosecutions, federal or State.[58] The immunity, however, is from prosecution, not from testifying, and it attaches only when the testimony is compulsory.

The Fifth Amendment to the Constitution declares that no person "shall be compelled in any criminal case to be a witness against himself." The object of this provision in the Amendment, said the Supreme Court, "is to establish in express language and upon a firm basis the general principle of English and American jurisprudence, that no one shall be compelled to give testimony which may expose him to prosecution for crime." [59] Furthermore, it has been held that "compulsory extortion of a man's own testimony, or of his private papers, to connect him with a crime or a forfeiture of his goods" is an unreasonable search and seizure within the Fourth Amendment.[60] However, "The interdiction of the fifth amendment operates only where a witness is asked to incriminate himself—in

[57] *Oklahoma Press Pub. Co. v. Walling,* 327 U.S. 186, 219, 66 S. Ct. 494, 510, 90 L. Ed. 614, 635 (1946).

[58] *Wolf v. People of State of Colorado,* 338 U.S. 25, 69 S. Ct. 1359, 92 L. Ed. 1782 (1949); *Rochin v. People of California,* 342 U.S. 165, 72 S. Ct. 205, 96 L. Ed. 154 (1952). But *cf. Stefanelli v. Minard,* 342 U.S. 117, 72 S. Ct. 118, 96 L. Ed. 99 (1952).

[59] *Hale v. Henkel,* 201 U.S. 43, 66, 26 S. Ct. 370, 375, 50 L. Ed. 652, 662 (1906).

[60] *Boyd v. United States,* 116 U.S. 616, 6 S. Ct. 524, 29 L. Ed. 746 (1886).

other words, to give testimony which may possibly expose him to a criminal charge. But if the criminality has already been taken away, the amendment ceases to apply." [61] Criminality has been "taken away" by the various federal immunity acts, and a witness may, therefore, be required to testify even if his testimony is self-incriminating.[62] If the immunity acts in applicable cases did not make the Fifth Amendment inoperative, a witness would be his own judge as to what would incriminate him and could refuse to answer almost any question in a criminal proceeding.

The immunity to which a witness is entitled has reference to prosecution within the same jurisdiction and under the same sovereignty. That is, a person may not refuse to testify in a federal (or State) proceeding for the reason that his testimony might incriminate him under State (or federal) law.[63]

> . . . the authorities are numerous and very nearly uniform to the effect that, if the proposed testimony is material to the issue on trial, the fact that the testimony may tend to degrade the witness in public estimation does not exempt him from the duty of disclosure. A person who commits a criminal act is bound to contemplate the consequences of exposure to his good name and reputation, and ought not to call upon the courts to protect that which he himself esteemed to be of such little value. . . . The design of the constitutional privilege is not to aid the witness in vindicating his character, but to protect him against being compelled to furnish evidence to convict him of a criminal charge.[64]

The Immunity Act of June 30, 1906, extends to "a *natural* person who, in obedience to a subpoena, gives testimony under oath or produces evidence, documentary or otherwise, under oath." [65] Accordingly, a corporation cannot claim immunity by reason of the enforced testimony of its officers, nor can such officers refuse to testify in regard to the corperation or refuse to produce the books of the corporation on the ground that their acts would implicate the

[61] *Hale v. Henkel,* 201 U.S. at 67, 26 S. Ct. at 376, 50 L. Ed. at 662.

[62] An Act of June 25, 1948, 18 *U.S.C.A.* § 3486, reads: "No testimony given by a witness before either House, or before any committee of either House of Congress . . . shall be used as evidence in any criminal proceedings against him in any court, except in a prosecution for perjury committed in giving such testimony. But an official paper or record produced by him is not within the said privilege."

[63] *Hale v. Henkel,* 201 U.S. 43, 26 S. Ct. 370, 50 L. Ed. 652 (1906); *Jack v. Kansas,* 199 U.S. 372, 26 S. Ct. 73, 50 L. Ed. 234 (1905).

[64] *Brown v. Walker,* 161 U.S. 591, 605–6, 16 S. Ct. 644, 650, 40 L. Ed. 819, 824 (1896), sustaining immunity amendment of February 11, 1893, of the Interstate Commerce Act.

[65] 34 *Stat.* 798, c. 3920, 49 *U.S.C.A.* § 48.

employer corporation.[66] In reference to the immunity amendment of 1893 to the Interstate Commerce Act, a federal judge charged a jury as follows:

> You are also instructed that the Act of February 11, 1893, does not grant immunity from indictment and prosecution to a corporation even though its officers or agents have been compelled to appear before the grand jury and testify to facts which would tend to incriminate it, or produce books and papers of the corporation bearing upon the offense of which it is charged. The immunity of the statute is confined to the witness who gives his testimony, belongs only to him personally, and cannot, in the nature of the thing, be extended to include the corporation he represents.[67]

Furthermore, since a corporate officer holds corporate books subject to the corporate duty, he may be required to produce such books even though they contain personally incriminating matter.[68]

[66] The distinction between an individual and a corporation in respect to immunity was clearly drawn in *Hale v. Henkel,* 201 U.S. 43 at 74, 75 where the Court said: "We are of the opinion that there is a clear distinction in this particular between an individual and a corporation, and that the latter has no right to refuse to submit its books and papers for an examination at the suit of the State. The individual may stand upon his constitutional rights as a citizen. He is entitled to carry on his private business in his own way. His power to contract is unlimited. He owes no duty to the State or his neighbors to divulge his business, or to open his doors to an investigation, so far as it may serve to incriminate him. He owes no such duty to the State, since he receives nothing therefrom, beyond the protection of his life and his property. His rights are such as existed by the law of the land long antecedent to the organization of the State, and can only be taken from him by due process of law, and in accordance with the Constitution. Among his rights is a refusal to incriminate himself, and the immunity of himself and his property from arrest and seizure except under a warrant of the law. He owes nothing to the public so long as he does not trespass upon their rights.

"Upon the other hand, the corporation is a creature of the State. It is presumed to be incorporated for the benefit of the public. It receives certain special privileges and franchises, and holds them subject to the laws of the State and limitations of its charter. Its powers are limited by law. It can make no contract not authorized by its charter. Its rights as a corporation are only preserved to it as long as it obeys the laws of its creation. There is a reserve right in the legislature to investigate its contracts to find out whether it has exceeded its power. It would be a strange anomaly to hold that a State could not in the exercise of its sovereignty inquire how these franchises had been employed, and whether they had been abused, and demand the production of the corporate books and papers for that purpose."

[67] *In re Pooling Freights,* 115 Fed. 588, 590 (D.C.W.D. Tenn., 1902). See also *United States v. Swift,* 186 Fed. 1002 (D.C.N.D. Ill., 1911); *United States v. Armour,* 142 Fed. 808 (D.C.N.D. Ill., 1906); *Heike v. United States,* 227 U.S. 131, 33 S. Ct. 226, 57 L. Ed. 450 (1913).

[68] *Wilson v. United States,* 221 U.S. 361, 31 S. Ct. 538, 55 L. Ed. 771 (1911). Reaffirmed in *Essgee Co. of China v. United States,* 262 U.S. 151, 43 S. Ct. 514, 67 L. Ed. 917 (1923). See also *Wheeler v. United States,* 226 U.S. 478, 33 S. Ct. 158, 57 L. Ed. 309 (1913); *Grant v. United States,* 227 U.S. 74, 33 S. Ct. 190, 57 L. Ed. 423 (1913).

The Supreme Court has made the following summary of the cases relating to the immunity of corporate books and papers:

> Without attempt to summarize or accurately distinguish all of the cases, the fair distillation in so far as they apply merely to the production of corporate records and papers in response to a subpoena or order authorized by law and safeguarded by judicial sanction, seems to be that the Fifth Amendment affords no protection by virtue of the self-incrimination provision, whether for the corporation or for its officers; and the Fourth, if applicable, at the most guards against abuse only by way of too much indefiniteness or breadth in the things required to be "particularly described," if also the inquiry is one the demanding agency is authorized by law to make and the materials specified are relevant.[69]

The Administrative Procedure Act limits agency investigations to those "authorized by law."[70] This provision probably is intended to prevent what the courts have denounced as "fishing expeditions into private papers on the possibility that they may disclose evidence of crime."[71] In reference to the investigating power of the Federal Trade Commission Mr. Justice Holmes said:

> Anyone who respects the spirit as well as the letter of the Fourth Amendment would be loath to believe that Congress intended to authorize one of its subordinate agencies to sweep all our traditions into the fire, ... We do not discuss the question whether it [Congress] could do so if it tried, as nothing short of the most explicit language would induce us to attribute to Congress that intent. The interruption of business, the possible revelation of trade secrets and the expense that compliance with the commission's wholesale demand would cause are the least considerations. It is contrary to the first principles of justice to allow a search through all the respondents' records, relevant or irrelevant, in the hope that something will turn up. . . .
>
> The right of access given by the statute is to documentary evidence —not to all documents, but to such documents as are evidence.[72]

[69] *Oklahoma Press Pub. Co. v. Walling*, 327 U.S. 186, 208, 66 S. Ct. 494, 505, 90 L. Ed. 614, 629 (1946). See also *Wilson v. United States*, 221 U.S. 361, 31 S. Ct. 538, 55 L. Ed. 771 (1911). An unincorporated labor union is in the same position as a corporation. *United States v. White*, 322 U.S. 694, 64 S. Ct. 1248, 88 L. Ed. 1542 (1944). See *Shapiro v. United States*, 335 U.S. 1, 68 S. Ct. 1375 (1948) for the use of incriminating data in administrative records.

[70] Sec. 6(b).

[71] *Federal Trade Commission v. American Tobacco Co.*, 264 U.S. 298, 44 S. Ct. 336, 68 L. Ed. 696 (1924).

[72] 264 U.S. at 306, 44 S. Ct. at 337, 68 L. Ed. at 700–1. See also *Ellis v. Interstate Commerce Commission*, 237 U.S. 434, 444, 35 S. Ct. 645, 59 L. Ed. 1036 (1914). *Cf.* Milton Handler, "The Constitutionality of Investigations by the Federal Trade Commission," 38 *Columbia Law Review* (1928), 708 ff.; Albert Langeluttig, "Constitutional Limitations on Administrative Power of Investigation," 28 *Illinois Law Review* (1933), 508 ff.

But whether the examination of a record or document is "relevant" in the investigating stage is essentially a matter for administrative determination; the judicial power would seem to be limited properly to the question whether such material is admissible evidence in a proceeding before a court of law.

All private rights are subject to the paramount right of society to regulate them in the public interest. So it may be necessary to regard corporate records and reports as quasi-public documents, not immune under the Fourth and Fifth Amendments from inspection by authorized persons.[73]

A State exercises visitorial powers over corporations created under its laws or doing business within its borders.[74] A corporation is a creature of a State, vested with special privileges and franchises in the public interest. It may act as a corporation only so long as it obeys the laws of its creation, and the legislature necessarily has a reserved right to investigate a corporation's activities to determine if it has exceeded its powers under its charter.

> Visitation, in law, is the act of a superior or superintending officer, who visits a corporation to examine into its manner of conducting business, and enforce an observance of its laws and regulations.[75]

At common law this right of visitation was exercised by the King as to civil corporations. In the United States the legislature is the visitor of all corporations created by it for public purposes. This power normally is exercised through some administrative agency, such as a public utilities commission.[76]

Administrative Sanctions

The means employed by a state to enforce its laws are "sanctions." Violation of a law may be *punished* or its observance may be *rewarded*. Sanctions which punish crimes are *penal* and those which redress civil injuries are *civil*.

[73] *Bowles v. Curtis Candy Co.,* 55 F. Supp. 527 (D.C.W.D. Mo., 1944); *Bowles v. Joseph Denuncio Fruit Co.,* 55 F. Supp. 9 (D.C.W.D. Ky., 1944); *Bowles v. Chew,* 53 F. Supp. 787 (D.C.N.D. Cal., 1944).

[74] The right of the government to investigate corporations and to require them to produce corporate books and papers in aid of an investigation ". . . is involved in the reservation of the visitorial power of the State, and the authority of the National Government where the corporate activities are in the domain subject to the powers of Congress." *Wilson v. United States,* 221 U.S. 361, 382, 31 S. Ct. 538, 55 L. Ed. 771 (1911).

[75] *Guthrie v. Harkness,* 199 U.S. 148, 158, 26 S. Ct. 4, 7, 50 L. Ed. 130 (1905), citing J. Baxter in *First National Bank v. Hughes,* 6 Fed. 737, 740 (C.C.N.D. Ohio, 1881).

[76] *Ibid.;* 2 Bouvier's *Law Dictionary* (Rawle's third revision), p. 3404.

Sanctions for administrative rules and orders are defined by the Administrative Procedure Act as follows:

> "Sanction" includes the whole or part of any agency (1) prohibition, requirement, limitation, or other condition affecting the freedom of any person; (2) withholding of relief; (3) imposition of any form of penalty or fine; (4) destruction, taking, seizure, or withholding of property; (5) assessment of damages, reimbursement, restitution, compensation, costs, charges, or fees; (6) requirement, revocation, or suspension of a license; or (7) taking of other compulsory or restrictive action. "Relief" includes the whole or part of any agency (1) grant of money, assistance, license, authority, exemption, exception, privilege, or remedy; (2) recognition of any claim, right, immunity, privilege, exemption, or exception; or (3) taking of any other action upon the application or petition of, and beneficial to, any person.[77]

Administrative Imposition of Sanctions.—Penalties commonly are associated with criminal law and their imposition is regarded, therefore, as a judicial function. However, the imperative demand for effective administration of revenue, immigration, public utility, public welfare, and labor legislation has led to· administrative assessment of statutory penalties in many situations such as withholding benefits, damaging publicity, revocation of a privilege voluntarily granted, forfeiture of goods or their value, and the payment of fixed or variable sums of money. These penalties are regarded as remedial or civil, not criminal, sanctions; they are not subject to procedural rules governing criminal prosecutions and may, therefore, be imposed by administrative officers.[78] Nevertheless, the *judicial character* of assessing and applying remedial penalties is apparent. Judicial acceptance of this practice is, therefore, a concession to expediency and a compromise with consistency, for it means that a person can be adjudged guilty of a public wrong and penalized by a civil instead of a criminal procedure. To quote Mr. Justice Sutherland in another connection: "No mere exercise of the art of lexicography can alter the essential nature of an act or thing; and if an exaction be clearly a penalty it cannot be converted into a tax by the simple expedient of calling it such." [79] The Supreme Court has relied largely on the "plenary power of the Congress" over the subject matter in sustaining delegations of power to administrative agencies to impose sanctions.

[77] Sec. 2(f), 60 *Stat.* 237, 5 *U.S.C.A.* c. 19, § 1001(f).

[78] *Helvering v. Mitchell,* 303 U.S. 391, 58 S. Ct. 630, 82 L. Ed. 917 (1938).

[79] *United States v. La Franca,* 282 U.S. 568, 572, 51 S. Ct. 278, 280, 75 L. Ed. 551, 555 (1931).

But penalties may not "be enforced through the secret findings and summary action of executive officers. The guarantees of due process of law and trial by jury are not to be forgotten or disregarded." [80] That is, penalties are to be imposed only after notice and hearing. Also, administrative officers may not commit to prison. Imprisonment is a criminal offense (except in civil contempt proceedings) and belongs traditionally to the judicial process. Temporary confinement may be necessary to give effect to a legislative policy, such as an immigration statute, but such detention is not a punishment.[81]

Practically all the administrative "sanctions," including the "reliefs," authorized under the Administrative Procedure Act can be applied as penalties or punishments against persons who fail to conform to or comply with some legislative policy or standard. These sanctions are essentially remedial, but they are also deterrent, as are criminal penalties.

IMMIGRATION AND ALIENS. In *Oceanic Navigation Co. v. Stranahan* [82] the Court upheld a provision in the Immigration Act of 1903 [83] which authorized the Secretary of Treasury to impose fines on steamship companies bringing inadmissible aliens to the United States. The statute was regarded as an incident to the exercise by Congress of its plenary power to control immigration, and due process did not require that courts, rather than administrative officers, should be charged with determining the facts upon which the imposition of the fine depended. "In effect," said Mr. Justice White, "all the contentions pressed in argument concerning the repugnancy of the statute to the due process clause really disregard the complete and absolute power of Congress over the subject with which the statute deals." [84]

In *Lloyd Sabaudo Societa v. Elting* [85] the section of the Immigration Act of 1924 [86] corresponding to Section 9 of the Act of 1903, was challenged on the ground that "the imposition of the fines by administrative action is a denial of due process unless opportunity is afforded at some stage to test their validity in court by a trial of the

---

[80] *Lipke v. Lederer*, 259 U.S. 557, 562, 42 S. Ct. 549, 551, 66 L. Ed. 1061, 1065 (1922); *Regal Drug Co. v. Wardell*, 260 U.S. 386, 43 S. Ct. 152, 67 L. Ed. 318 (1922).
[81] *Wong Wing v. United States*, 163 U.S. 228, 16 S. Ct. 977, 41 L. Ed. 140 (1896).
[82] 214 U.S. 320, 29 S. Ct. 671, 53 L. Ed. 1013 (1909).
[83] 32 *Stat.* 1213, 1215, § 9.
[84] 214 U.S. at 343, 29 S. Ct. at 677, 53 L. Ed. at 1023.
[85] 287 U.S. 329, 53 S. Ct. 167, 77 L. Ed. 341 (1932).
[86] 43 *Stat.* 153, 166, c. 190, § 26; 8 *U.S.C.A.* § 145.

facts de novo." [87] The Court rejected the argument for judicial review of the facts *de novo,* on authority of the Stranahan case, but held that

> The action of the Secretary is, nevertheless, subject to some judicial review, as the courts below held. The courts may determine whether his action is within his statutory authority, . . . whether there was any evidence before him to support his determination, . . . and whether the procedure which he adopted in making it satisfies elementary standards of fairness and reasonableness, essential to the due administration of the summary proceeding which Congress has authorized. . . .
>
> We think it clear, despite language in the Stranahan case intimating a different view, that the statute, as it has been consistently construed administratively, contemplates that the Secretary should fairly determine, after a hearing and upon the evidence, the facts establishing its violation.[88]

Aliens may be deported by executive order, that is, by administrative and not by judicial proceedings, under the general immigration law.[89] The Supreme Court has held that deportation proceedings are civil in character, and therefore they are not governed by the constitutional provisions for the protection of persons accused of crime.[90] To adjudge an alien guilty of a deportable offense is certainly a judicial determination, and it is equally clear that to deport the alien is the imposition of a penalty.

Administrative decision as to deportation "shall be final,"

> . . . unless it be shown [through habeas corpus] that the proceedings were "manifestly unfair," were "such as to prevent a fair investigation," or show "manifest abuse" of the discretion committed to the executive officers by the statute, or that "their authority was not fairly exercised; that is, consistently with the fundamental principles of justice embraced within the conception of due process of law." [91]

---

[87] 287 U.S. at 335, 53 S. Ct. at 170, 77 L. Ed. at 346.

[88] 287 U.S. at 335–37, 53 S. Ct. at 170–71, 77 L. Ed. at 347.

[89] Act of 1917, 39 *Stat.* 874, 887, 889, 8 *U.S.C.A.* § 155(a).

[90] *United States v. Tod,* 263 U.S. 149, 44 S. Ct. 54, 68 L. Ed. 221 (1923) ; *Tiaco v. Forbes,* 228 U.S. 549, 33 S. Ct. 585, 57 L. Ed. 960 (1913). A naturalized alien whose citizenship is revoked and certificate of naturalization canceled in a denaturalization proceeding on the ground that he had procured it by fraud is deportable by order of the Attorney General under § 1 of the Espionage Act of May 10, 1920, 41 *Stat.* 593, 8 *U.S.C.A.* 157. *United States v. Shaughnessy,* 338 U.S. 521, 70 S. Ct. 329 (1950).

[91] *Kwock Jan Fat v. White,* 253 U.S. 454, 457–58, 40 S. Ct. 566, 567, 64 L. Ed. 1010, 1012 (1920). See also *Mahler v. Eby,* 264 U.S. 32, 44 S. Ct. 283, 68 L. Ed. 549 (1924) ; *Low Wah Suey v. Backus,* 225 U.S. 460, 32 S. Ct. 734, 56 L. Ed. 1165 (1912) ; *Tang Tun v. Edsell,* 223 U.S. 673, 32 S. Ct. 359, 56 L. Ed. 606 (1912) ; *McGrath v. Kristensen,* 340 U.S. 162, 71 S. Ct. 224, 229, 95 L. Ed. 165 (1950).

REVENUE. In the administration of the revenue laws it is common procedure to authorize revenue officers to penalize taxpayers found guilty of fraud or negligence in the payment of taxes. The penalty usually takes the form of an increased tax. An importer who undervalues the goods he imports may be penalized by an administrative assessment of extra duties,[92] and, "It is wholly immaterial whether they are called additional duties or penalties. Congress had the power to impose them under either designation or character." [93] In like manner, fraud in connection with the filing of a return and the payment of an income tax may be punished by increasing the taxpayer's tax. These penalties, said the Court, ". . . are provided primarily as a safeguard for the protection of the revenue and to reimburse the Government for the heavy expense of investigation and the loss resulting from the taxpayer's fraud." [94]

This "reimbursement theory" seems far-fetched, says Walter Gellhorn, "since there is no relationship between the amount of the penalty and the Government's cost." [95] But it serves, in connection with the theory of civil sanctions (and of the doctrine of *quasi*-power), to postpone the ultimate admission that administrative agencies do exercise *judicial* power.

PUBLIC SERVICE. In the public utility field, federal and State commissions have long exercised fairly broad powers to punish, by imposing money fines, those who violate their orders.

The Interstate Commerce Commission, the Federal Communications Commission, and the United States Shipping Board may issue orders, after hearings, fixing the amounts of damages due injured parties and directing their payment, as the result of violations by common carriers of the laws which apply to said carriers. Such orders are not enforceable by the issuing agency, but the beneficiary of an order may sue a noncomplying carrier in a federal district court (or State court), and in such an action the findings and order are prima facie evidence of the facts therein stated.[96]

A "cursory" examination of State public utility reports, says Walter Gellhorn,

---

[92] *Bartlett v. Kane,* 16 How. 263, 273–74, 14 L. Ed. 931 (1853).

[93] *Passavant v. United States,* 148 U.S. 214, 221, 13 S. Ct. 572, 575, 37 L. Ed. 426, 429 (1893).

[94] *Helvering v. Mitchell,* 303 U.S. 391, 401, 58 S. Ct. 630, 634, 82 L. Ed. 917, 923 (1938).

[95] *Administrative Law—Cases and Comments* (2d ed., The Foundation Press, Inc., Brooklyn, 1947), p. 330, note 72.

[96] Interstate Commerce Act, 24 *Stat.,* 379, 382–84, §§ 8, 9, 13, 16; Federal Communications Act of June 19, 1934, 48 *Stat.* 1064, §§ 209, 407.

. . . discloses a number of recorded instances of administrative imposition of penalties to enforce a declared policy. No doubt there are others, and surely there must be innumerable unreported cases. The recorded instances suggested three observations: 1. There is a considerable variety in the offences for which penalties have been imposed. 2. The Commissions have exercised a very marked degree of discretion in determining the penalties, if any, they will impose in particular cases. 3. The imposition of fines by administrators instead of by judges has not brought our democratic institutions tumbling down upon us.[97]

The Public Utility Holding Company Act of 1935,[98] Section 11(b), limits each holding company system to a single integrated and simplified system; requires the elimination of unnecessary holding companies and a reorganization of those which are unnecessarily complicated and overcapitalized; and directs the redistribution of voting power among security holders of holding and operating companies. The Securities and Exchange Commission, charged with the enforcement of these provisions, is not authorized to apply penalties for noncompliance; but, in directing a company to divest itself of property or to reorganize its capital structure (which may result in forced dissolution and liquidation of a corporation within a holding system), the Commission exercises a *margin of discretion* which unquestionably operates as a sanction. The practical significance of this administrative margin of discretion is appreciated when it is related to the dollar value of the property affected by the Commission's directives—the divestments to date total several billion dollars.[99] The power of Congress to delegate this regulatory power to the Commission has been upheld by the courts.[100]

Under the "affected with a public interest" doctrine, public utilities have been held to a far stricter public accountability than other businesses, but in *Nebbia v. New York*,[101] the Court rejected the traditional distinction between public and private business and held that all business is public and subject to regulation, limited only by the requirements of due process of law.

BANKING. The Home Owners' Loan Act [102] authorizes the Federal Home Loan Bank Board to regulate the reorganization, con-

---

[97] *Op. cit.*, pp. 336–37, citing cases.
[98] 49 *Stat.* 803, 15 *U.S.C.A.* § 79 *et sqq.*
[99] For the period from 1936 to July 1, 1946, the divestments totaled $8,051,375,752, according to the Commission's *Thirteenth Annual Report* (1948).
[100] *North American Co. v. Securities and Exchange Commission,* 327 U.S. 686, 66 S. Ct. 784, 90 L. Ed. 945 (1946); *American Power and Light Co. and Electric and Light Corp. v. Securities and Exchange Commission,* 329 U.S. 90, 67 S. Ct. 133, 91 L. Ed. 103 (1946).
[101] 291 U.S. 502, 54 S. Ct. 505, 78 L. Ed. 940 (1934).
[102] Act of June 13, 1933, as amended, 12 *U.S.C.A.* § 1464(d).

solidation, merger, or liquidation of building and loan associations, with power to appoint a conservator or receiver under rules to be made by the Board setting forth the grounds governing the appointment. In *Fahey v. Mallonee* [103] the grounds assigned for the appointment of a conservator for the Long Beach Federal Savings and Loan Association were that the Association "was conducting its affairs in an unlawful, unauthorized and unsafe manner, that its management was unsafe, that it was pursuing a course injurious to, and jeopardizing the interests of, its members, creditors, and the public." [104]

In thus adjudging the Association "guilty" of the offenses charged and penalizing it by placing it in the hands of a conservator, the Board undoubtedly exercised a power in its nature *judicial*. The Supreme Court held, however, that the Board exercised validly delegated power and that the provisions of the statute were "regulatory" not "penal." Therefore, the procedure was not violative of the due process clause, even though the regulations adopted by the Board provided for a hearing *after* the conservator takes possession instead of *before*. No provision was made for judicial review.

> This is drastic procedure. But the delicate nature of the institution and the impossibility of preserving credit during an investigation has made it an almost invariable custom to apply supervisory authority in this summary manner. It is a heavy responsibility to be exercised with disinterestedness and restraint, but in the light of the history and customs of banking we cannot say it is unconstitutional. [105]

The Court skirted the question of judicial review of the Board's determinations.

> We do not now decide whether the determination of the Board in such proceeding is subject to any manner of judicial review. The absence from the statute of a provision for court review has sometimes been held not to foreclose review. [106]

WAR POWERS. A citizen may be excluded from a defense plant and so deprived of his employment without notice, hearing, or counsel, and on mere uncorroborated suspicion. [107] During World War II, the War Relocation Authority, acting under the authority of the President, evacuated many persons of Japanese ancestry from the Pacific Coast to inland relocation centers, thereby depriving the evacuees temporarily of their homes and businesses. While sustain-

---

[103] 332 U.S. 245, 67 S. Ct. 1552, 91 L. Ed. 2030 (1947).
[104] 332 U.S. at 247, 67 S. Ct. at 1553, 91 L. Ed. at 2035.
[105] 332 U.S. at 253–54, 67 S. Ct. at 1556, 91 L. Ed. at 2039.
[106] 332 U.S. at 256, 67 S. Ct. at 1557, 91 L. Ed. at 2040.
[107] *Von Knorr v. Miles,* 60 F. Supp. 962 (D.C. Mass., 1945).

ing this procedure in general,[108] the Supreme Court ordered the release from a relocation center of an admittedly loyal citizen on the ground that the detention of such a person had no relation to the war effort.[109] In short, the *necessity* for the exercise of the war power may be a matter for judicial determination. On the Pacific Coast, curfew orders applicable to citizens of Japanese ancestry were upheld as valid regulations under the war powers.[110] The delegation of power to fix and define crimes and penalties under the second War Powers Act of 1942 [111] was upheld in cases involving criminal convictions for violations of rationing regulations.[112] On November 18, 1942, the President, as Commander-in-Chief, directed Montgomery Ward & Co., Inc., to obey an order of the National Labor Relations Board and sign a maintenance-of-membership contract with the CIO. Compliance under protest averted a judicial test of this executive order. The dispute with this company continued into 1944 when its plants were seized by the Secretary of War under an Executive order of December 27, 1944.[113] During 1945 the President directed the seizure of many other important industries in the course of labor disputes: two railroads, one utility, nine industrial companies, the transportation systems of two cities, the motor carriers in one city, a towing company, a butadiene plant, 251 bituminous coal mines, the mines of 365 anthracite coal companies, and 54 petroleum plants and pipe lines.[114]

REVOCATION OF LICENSES, PERMITS, BENEFITS. The revocation of a license is fixing a penalty. Two California cases upheld the authority of the State Board of Equalization to suspend or revoke liquor licenses, ruling that a lower court could not revoke a license which the Board had ordered suspended,[115] or revoke a license which the Board had refused to revoke.[116] The California courts have held

[108] *Korematsu v. United States,* 323 U.S. 214, 65 S. Ct. 193, 89 L. Ed. 194 (1944).

[109] *Ex parte Endo,* 323 U.S. 283, 65 S. Ct. 208, 89 L. Ed. 243 (1944).

[110] *Hirabayashi v. United States,* 320 U.S. 81, 93, 102–4, 63 S. Ct. 1375, 1386–87, 87 L. Ed. 1774, 1787–88 (1943).

[111] 56 *Stat.* 177, 50 *U.S.C.A.* (App.) § 633.

[112] *Randall v. United States,* 148 F. (2d) 234 (C.C.A. 5th, 1945), 325 U.S. 885, 65 S. Ct. 1579, 89 L. Ed. 2000; *Rose v. United States,* 149 F. (2d) 755 (C.C.A. 9th, 1945).

[113] Executive Order No. 9508, 3 *C.F.R.,* 1944 Supp., p. 104.

[114] Arthur T. Vanderbilt, "War Powers and Their Administration," in *1945 Annual Survey of American Law* (New York University School of Law, New York, 1946), pp. 271–72.

[115] *Reynolds v. State Board of Equalization,* 29 Cal. (2d) 137, 173 Pac. (2d) 551 (1946).

[116] *Covert v. State Board of Equalization,* 29 Cal. (2d) 125, 173 Pac. (2d) 545 (1946).

that the suspension of a certificate to act as a broker, for fraud and misrepresentation, "is highly penal in its nature." [117] The Postmaster General may issue postal fraud orders and so withdraw the privileges of the mails from persons who use the postal facilities to defraud; [118] or he may revoke a newspaper's second-class mail privileges for a number of reasons, such as violation of the Espionage Act.[119]

The Securities Act of 1933 requires the issuer of securities to file with the Securities and Exchange Commission a registration statement containing all material facts concerning the proposed issue and closes the mails and the channels of interstate commerce (with some exceptions) to securities which are not so registered.[120] Section 8(d) of the Act authorizes the Commission to issue a stop order suspending the effectiveness of a registration statement if and when it shall appear to the Commission that the registration statement contains any untrue statement of a material fact or omits any required material fact. This stop order is in the nature of an injunction, which operates to restrain a business organization from proceeding with its financing until it has complied with the requirements of the statute; and the proceedings have been said to be "somewhat analogous" to grand jury proceedings.[121]

> A stop order serves two purposes: first, it suspends the effectiveness of the registration statement and the license of the issuer to use the mails and the facilities of interstate commerce for the purposes recognized by the act; second, it operates as a warning to the investing public that the Commission has found that the statement is untrue or misleading and, therefore, unreliable.[122]

In *Jones v. Securities and Exchange Commission* [123] the Supreme Court ruled that the initiation of stop order proceedings by the Commission before there were any outstanding securities prevented the applicant's registration from becoming "effective," and that the Com-

[117] *Abrams v. Daugherty,* 60 Cal. App. 297, 212 Pac. 942 (1922), quoting *Schomig v. Keiser,* 189 Cal. 596, 209 Pac. 550, 551 (1922); *Dyment v. Board of Medical Examiners,* 57 Cal. App. 260, 266, 207 Pac. 409, 412 (1922).

[118] *American School of Magnetic Healing v. McAnnulty,* 187 U.S. 94, 23 S. Ct. 33, 41 L. Ed. 90 (1902).

[119] *Milwaukee Social Democratic Publishing Co. v. Burleson,* 255 U.S. 407, 41 S. Ct. 352, 65 L. Ed. 704 (1921); *Lewis Publishing Co. v. Morgan,* 229 U.S. 288, 33 S. Ct. 867, 57 L. Ed. 1190 (1913).

[120] 48 *Stat.* 74, 15 *U.S.C.A.* § 77(a) *et sqq.* Originally the administration of this Act was assigned to the Federal Trade Commission, but the Securities Exchange Act of 1934 (48 *Stat.* 881, 15 *U.S.C.A.* § 78(a) *et sqq.*) put the administration of both acts in the hands of the Securities and Exchange Commission.

[121] *In re Securities Exchange Commission,* 84 F. (2d) 316 (C.C.A. 2d, 1936).

[122] *Oklahoma-Texas Trust v. Securities and Exchange Commission,* 100 F. (2d) 888, 891 (C.C.A. 10th, 1939).

[123] 298 U.S. 1, 56 S. Ct. 654, 80 L. Ed. 1015 (1936).

mission could not prevent the withdrawal of an ineffective registration statement. Later, however, the Circuit Court of Appeals affirmed a stop order suspending a registration of securities which had been marketed when the stop order proceedings were commenced. The Commission had refused to permit the registrant to withdraw its registration statement.[124] In another case the Commission instituted stop order proceedings the day after the registration statement of the corporation registrant became effective. When the Commission refused the corporation's request for withdrawal, the registrant asked a district court to enjoin the Commission from continuing with the stop order proceedings. Injunction was denied, and this ruling was affirmed by the court of appeals.[125]

The Securities Exchange Act of 1934 [126] broadened the powers of the Commission, particularly by placing under its jurisdiction organized exchanges, brokers, dealers, and securities associations. For violations of the Act, the Commission may apply to the courts for injunctions, or it may refer cases to the Department of Justice, or it may issue orders of its own in some cases, denying, suspending, or revoking the registration of brokers and dealers, or suspending or expelling them from membership in the National Association of Securities Dealers, Inc.[127]

These orders apply penalties of far greater severity than the imposition of a money penalty, and they result from administrative findings (after notice and hearing, to be sure) that certain illegal and reprehensible acts have been committed, which may well destroy public confidence in the registrant's business integrity and ultimately force him out of business. The fact that very few of these Commission orders have been questioned in the courts would seem to justify the procedure and speak well for the Commission's administration of the law.[128] James M. Landis, writing of his experience as Chairman of the Commission, makes this significant comment:

[124] *Oklahoma-Texas Trust v. Securities and Exchange Commission,* 100 F. (2d) 888 (C.C.A. 10th, 1939).

[125] *Resources Corp. International v. Securities and Exchange Commission,* 103 F. (2d) 929 (C.A.D.C., 1939).

[126] 48 *Stat.* 881, 15 *U.S.C.A.* § 78 *et sqq.*

[127] Secs. 3, 19(a), 21(e)(f). For a summary of disciplinary proceedings under this Act see the current *Annual Report* of the Commission. From 1939 to 1947 inclusive there were 206 cases of revocation or suspension of registration as broker-dealer firms, and 11 cases of expulsion or suspension from NASD. Securities and Exchange Commission, *13th Annual Report* (1948). See also *The Work of the Securities Exchange Commission* (Government Printing Office, Washington, D.C., 1940), p. 3.

[128] Cases supporting Commission orders: *Charles Hughes & Co., Inc. v. Securities and Exchange Commission,* 139 F. (2d) 434 (C.C.A. 2d, 1943), revocation of

The ability to sell a substantial block of securities depends upon creation of a belief that the issue is, like Calpurnia, above suspicion. It depends further upon a wise choice as to the time for offering the securities to the public. The very institution of proceedings is frequently sufficient to destroy the former quality, for the Commission's allegation that some untruthfulness attends their registration is sufficient to create grave suspicion as to their merit. The threat to institute proceedings, furthermore, will mean delay and even though the proceedings may later be dismissed by the Commission, or eventually by a court, the time that elapses before such relief can be procured will have permanently chilled the market for the securities. Administrative adjudication in these cases is, to all intents and purposes, final. But more than this, the threat of initiating a proceeding, because of its tendency to assail the reputation of an issue and because it will mean delay, is sufficient in the normal case to bring compliance with the desire of the administrative.

. . . I advert to this power to prosecute primarily to emphasize the point that the charge of arbitrariness, which is commonly made against administrative action, usually appertains to the exercise of the power to prosecute rather than to the power to adjudicate. It is restraints upon the exercise of that power that in my judgment are of far greater significance than the creation of restraints upon the power to adjudicate. The nature of what these restraints can be, I have referred to before —professionalism in spirit, the recognition that arbitrariness in the enforcement of a policy will destroy its effectiveness, and freedom from intervening irrelevant considerations.[129]

Inspection, investigation, publicity, and prosecution are powerful sanctions for the effectuation of official policy, and these administrative weapons cannot be circumscribed by the procedural requirements of the judicial process. Different techniques of limitation are necessary. The greater the procedural flexibility, the greater the need for attention to personnel.

LABOR RELATIONS. The National Labor Relations Act [130] outlaws "unfair labor practices"; provides for filing, with the Labor Board, complaints of unfair practices against employers; and defines the remedial powers of the Board as follows: "The Board . . . shall issue and cause to be served on such person an order requiring such

registration for fraud; *Archer v. Securities and Exchange Commission,* 133 F. (2d) 795 (C.C.A. 8th, 1943), revocation of registration and expulsion from NASD, certiorari denied 319 U.S. 767; *Charles C. Wright v. Securities and Exchange Commission,* 134 F. (2d) 733 (C.C.A. 2d, 1943), expulsion from national securities exchanges.

[129] *The Administrative Process* (Yale University Press, New Haven, 1938), pp. 108–9, 110–11.

[130] Act of July 5, 1935, 49 *Stat.* 449, 29 *U.S.C.A.* § 151 *et sqq.*

person to cease and desist from such unfair labor practice and to take such affirmative action, including reinstatement of employees with or without pay, as will effectuate the policies of this Act." [131]

The "affirmative action" which the Board may take by virtue of the above provision is not limited to "reinstatement of employees with or without pay." Congress left "the adaptation of means to end to the empiric process of administration." And, "Because the relation of remedy to policy is peculiarly a matter for administrative competence, courts must not enter the allowable area of the Board's discretion." [132] More specifically, the Supreme Court has said that the Labor Act left to the Board "some scope for the exercise of judgment and discretion in determining, upon the basis of the findings, whether the case is one requiring affirmative action, and in choosing the particular affirmative relief." [133]

> The Act is essentially remedial. It does not carry a penal program declaring the described unfair labor practices to be crimes. The Act does not prescribe penalties or fines in vindication of public rights or provide indemnity against community losses as distinguished from the protection and compensation of employees. Had Congress been intent upon such a program, we cannot doubt that Congress would have expressed its intent and would itself have defined its retributive scheme. . . . We do not think Congress intended to vest in the Board a virtually unlimited discretion to devise punitive measures, and thus to prescribe penalties or fines which the Board may think would effectuate the policies of the Act. . . . We think that affirmative action . . . is action to achieve the remedial objectives set forth in the Act.[134]

The courts hold that reimbursement and back-pay orders of the Board are public, not private, remedies. A reimbursement order, said the Supreme Court,

> . . . is not a redress for a private wrong. Like a back-pay order, it does restore to the employees in some measure what was taken from them because of the Company's unfair labor practices. In this, both these types of monetary awards somewhat resemble compensation for private injury, but it must be constantly remembered that both are remedies created by statute—the one explicitly and the other implicitly in the concept of effectuation of the policies of the Act—which are designed

---

[131] *Ibid.*, Sec. 10(c), 15 *U.S.C.A.* § 160(c).

[132] Mr. Justice Frankfurter in *Phelps Dodge Corp. v. National Labor Relations Board*, 313 U.S. 177, 194, 61 S. Ct. 845, 852, 85 L. Ed. 1271, 1283 (1941).

[133] Mr. Justice Stone in *National Labor Relations Board v. Pennsylvania Greyhound Lines, Inc.*, 303 U.S. 261, 265, 58 S. Ct. 571, 574, 82 L. Ed. 831, 834 (1938).

[134] Mr. Chief Justice Hughes in *Republic Steel Corp. v. National Labor Relations Board*, 311 U.S. 7, 10–12, 61 S. Ct. 77, 79–80, 85 L. Ed. 6, 9–10 (1940).

to aid in achieving the elimination of industrial conflict. They vindicate public, not private rights. . . . For this reason it is erroneous to characterize this reimbursement order as penal or as the adjudication of a mass tort.[135]

"Back pay" is "remuneration," based upon the loss of wages which the employee has suffered from the employer's wrong. It ". . . is not a fine or penalty imposed upon the employer by the Board. Reinstatement and 'back pay' are for the 'protection of the employees and the redress of their grievances' to make them 'whole.' "[136] This would seem to say that a back-pay order *is* a "redress for a private wrong" or grievance. The Court reiterated that "The purpose of the 'back-pay' allowance is to effectuate the policies of the Labor Act for the preservation of industrial peace."[137]

But it is submitted that a back-pay order requires an employer to pay wages for work that was not done; he is not paying for "value received"—he is paying for his "folly," in violating the law—he is *punished,* fined, for his illegal act. This is an imposition of an administrative sanction, a penalty.

The levying of a fine by the New York State Industrial Commission against an employer who had failed to file payroll reports required by law, was upheld by the State Court of Appeals, reversing a ruling by the State Supreme Court to the effect that the Commission had made an error in law, on the ground that the error, if an error, was one of fact.[138] On the other hand, the Commissioner may penalize an employee by withholding benefit payments if he "has wilfully made a false statement or representation to obtain any benefit under the provisions of this article."[139]

It is fairly common practice to authorize administrative imposition of money penalties for violation of workmen's compensation laws. For example, under the Federal Longshoremen's and Harbor Workers' Act[140] the compensation commissioner may add a twenty

---

[135] Mr. Justice Murphy in *Virginia Electric Co. v. National Labor Relations Board,* 319 U.S. 533, 543, 63 S. Ct. 1214, 1220, 87 L. Ed. 1568, 1576 (1943). Mr. Justice Roberts, dissenting, said: ". . . the only effect of the order is *to redress a supposed private wrong* to employees which the evidence and findings indicate never was inflicted, and *to inflict drastic punishment* of the employer for its earlier violation of the statute by encouraging its employees to organize. Neither is within the competence of the Board, as this Court has repeatedly held." 319 U.S. at 550, 63 S. Ct. at 1223, 87 L. Ed. at 1579. Italics supplied.

[136] Mr. Justice Reed in *Social Security Board v. Nierotko,* 327 U.S. 358, 364–65, 66 S. Ct. 637, 641, 90 L. Ed. 718, 725 (1946).

[137] 327 U.S. at 363, 66 S. Ct. at 640, 90 L. Ed. at 724.

[138] *In re Rumsey Mfg. Co.,* 296 N.Y. 118, 71 N.E. (2d) 426 (1947).

[139] *New York Labor Law,* Art. 18, § 594.

[140] Act of March 4, 1937, 44 *Stat.* 1424, 33 *U.S.C.A.* § 901 *et sqq.*

per cent penalty to an award that is not seasonably paid.[141] Similar
provisions in State laws have been held not to violate due process or
the separation of powers.[142] The courts like to call these increases
"additional compensation" rather than "penalties," but increases from
twenty to fifty per cent are punitive, not compensatory.

Declaratory Orders to Mitigate Sanctions.—There has been a
long-felt need for *preventive* regulatory measures to replace *punitive*
ones. The Federal Trade Commission was created in response to this
demand for a more enlightened governmental policy in dealing with
business and industry. But the Commission was not authorized to
approve or disapprove in advance of execution any proposed business
transaction or activity, and so relieve the persons receiving such
approval from prosecution under the antitrust laws. To effect this
end, a bill was introduced in Congress in 1918, and reintroduced in
1919,[143] which provided that a person could apply to the Commission
for a license to engage in interstate or foreign commerce in accordance with a prospectus submitted to the Commission for approval.
If, after investigation, the Commission should be satisfied that the
business set forth would not violate the antitrust laws, it should grant
the license applied for, and such license should constitute a complete
defense to any prosecution or proceeding under the antitrust laws.
The bill did not become law.

The Attorney General's Committee on Administrative Procedure,
reporting in 1941,[144] included in its draft bill [145] a provision giving
each adjudicating agency

> . . . power to issue declaratory rulings concerning rights, status, and
> other legal relations arising under the statute or the several statutes
> committed to its administration or arising under its regulations, in
> order to terminate a controversy or remove an uncertainty.

Such a ruling should "have the same force and effect, and be binding
in the same manner, as a final order or other determination" of the
agency issuing it.

[141] *Arrow Stevedore Co. v. Pillsbury,* 88 F. (2d) 446 (C.C.A. 9th, 1937); *Candado Stevedoring Corp. v. Lowe,* 85 F. (2d) 119 (C.C.A. 2d, 1936).

[142] See Gellhorn, *op. cit.,* p. 335, citing: *Chicago Board of Education v. Industrial
Commission,* 351 Ill. 128, 184 N.E. 202 (1933); *Index Mines Corp. v. Industrial
Commission,* 82 Colo. 272, 259 Pac. 1036 (1927); *Clark v. Industrial Commission,*
197 Wis. 597, 222 N.W. 823 (1929); *Milwaukee Corrugating Co. v. Industrial Commission,* 197 Wis. 414, 222 N.W. 251 (1928); *Stockdale v. Industrial Commission,*
76 Colo. 494, 232 Pac. 669 (1929).

[143] *H. R. 1186,* bill by Representative Henry J. Steele. See Charles R. Michael,
"Trusts Again to the Fore," *New York Times,* Oct. 12, 1919.

[144] *Final Report* (1941), *S. Doc. No. 8,* 77th Cong., 1st Sess.

[145] Introduced in Congress as *S. 675,* 77th Cong., 1st Sess.

The essentials of the above provisions were incorporated in the Administrative Procedure Act of 1946 as follows:

> The agency is authorized in its sound discretion, with like effect as in the case of other orders, to issue a declaratory order to terminate a controversy or remove uncertainty.[146]

The power to issue a declaratory order is limited to an agency empowered by statute to adjudicate after opportunity for a hearing; and certain types of cases are excepted.[147]

Since the declaratory order is the administrative counterpart of the declaratory judgment, agency and court should be governed by the same basic principles. The chief use of the declaratory order will be to secure a binding administrative determination as to whether an intended action will expose the doer to administrative sanctions. A person should not be required to discover his legal rights by the trial and error method. The declaratory order is appropriate in a situation where the facts are susceptible of advance determination, as in a case involving status—such as a classification of property for tax purposes, or a finding that a proposed business operation would not be subject to the provisions of the antitrust laws—and where the relief is from sanctions of a public rather than a private nature, since the latter are remedies to which individuals are entitled as of legal right.

Summary Action

The dictum of the police power, that one must so use one's own as not to injure others, places important limitations and even burdens upon private right and makes the state the arbiter of these conflicting interests.

Where the primary social interests of health, safety, order, and morals are involved, summary action may be necessary to protect the public interest lest the well-known cliché about locking the barn after the horse is stolen apply here. Contaminated food must be confiscated before it is sold; a quack doctor must be barred from practice before he engages in some malpractice; salacious and seditious literature should be barred from the channels of trade; and so on.

Consequently, a "hearing before seizure and condemnation and destruction of food which is unwholesome and unfit for use, is not necessary," [148] since a protracted hearing might imperil the public

[146] 60 *Stat.* 239 § 5(d), 5 *U.S.C.A.* § 1004(d).
[147] Sec. 5, 5 *U.S.C.A.* § 1004.
[148] *North American Cold Storage Co. v. Chicago,* 211 U.S. 306, 315, 29 S. Ct. 101, 104, 53 L. Ed. 195, 199 (1908).

health. For the same reason, animals infected with contagious diseases may be summarily condemned and destroyed.[149] It is customary to authorize highway commissioners summarily to remove obstructions placed upon the public highways.[150] Unwholesome and dangerous trades, the burial of the dead, and the use of combustible building materials may all be interdicted by law and subjected to summary abatement in densely populated areas.[151] The ordinary trial procedure for one who maintains a public nuisance does not always remove the source of danger. Every moment's delay in the removal of the nuisance *may* expose the public to irreparable injury.

The legislative power to authorize summary administrative action is limited, however, by the constitutional injunction that a person may not be deprived of his property without due process of law. And under the rule of law only that which is *in fact* proscribed by statute is subject to summary administrative action. If a party cannot get a hearing in advance of the seizure and destruction of his property, he is entitled to a hearing after the taking. He must be afforded an opportunity to prove that there was no necessity for the seizure, or that what was condemned was not properly within the jurisdiction of the officers issuing the order.

It may be said that if the determination of a board of health as to a nuisance is not final and conclusive, then the members of the board, and all persons acting under their authority in abating the alleged nuisance, act at their peril; and so they do, and no other view of the law would give adequate protection to private rights. They should not destroy property, as a nuisance unless they know it to be such, and if there be doubt whether it be a nuisance or not, the board should proceed by action to restrain or abate the nuisance, and thus have the protection of a judgment for what it may do.

It may further be asked, what, under this view of the law is the remedy of the owner of property threatened with destruction or actually destroyed as a nuisance? He may have his action in equity to restrain the destruction of his property if the case be one where a court of equity under equitable rules has jurisdiction, or he may bring a common-law action against all the persons engaged in the abatement of the nuisance to recover his damages, and thus he will have due process of law; and if he can show that the alleged nuisance does not in fact exist, he will recover judgment, notwithstanding the ordinance of the board of health. Thus the views we take of these acts and similar acts confer-

[149] *Miller v. Horton,* 152 Mass. 540, 26 N.E. 100 (1891).
[150] *Hubbell v. Goodrich,* 37 Wis. 84 (1875).
[151] *King v. Davenport,* 98 Ill. 305 (1881); *Jackson v. Bell,* 143 Tenn. 452, 226 S.W. 207 (1920).

ring powers upon local officers to proceed summarily upon their own view and examination furnish adequate protection to boards of health, to the public and to property owners; and, while these views are not supported by all the decided cases upon the subject, they have the support of the best reasons and of ample authority.[152]

Goods, such as foods, that can be condemned under the police power, may be destroyed without compensation even if they have a small legitimate value.[153] But the owner may not be required to bear the loss when legitimate property is destroyed by error or otherwise. The destruction of such property constitutes a taking under eminent domain requiring compensation.

When a healthy horse is killed by a public officer, acting under a general statute, for fear that it should spread disease, the horse certainly would seem to be taken for public use, as truly as if it were seized to drag an artillery wagon. The public equally appropriate it, whatever they do with it afterwards.[154]

If the statute does not provide for compensation and if it should appear, at a hearing subsequent to the taking, that the property destroyed was not what the legislature had declared to be a nuisance, then the officer acting under the statute proceeds at his peril, as he would be personally liable for his *ultra vires* acts.

Furthermore, the power to abate summarily has been limited to goods of small value. Said Mr. Justice Brown in *Lawton v. Steele:*

But where the property is of little value, and its use for the illegal purpose is clear, the legislature may declare it to be a nuisance, and subject to summary abatement. . . . It is true there are several cases of a contrary purport. Some of these cases, however, may be explained upon the ground that the property seized was of considerable value . . . in others the court seems to have taken a more technical view of the law than the necessities of the case or an adequate protection of the owner required.[155]

---

[152] *People ex rel. Copcutt v. Board of Health of City of Yonkers,* 140 N.Y. 1, 8, 35 N.E. 320, 322 (1893).

[153] *North American Cold Storage Co. v. Chicago,* 211 U.S. 306, 29 S. Ct. 101, 53 L. Ed. 195 (1908).

[154] Judge Holmes in *Miller v. Horton,* 152 Mass. 540, 547, 26 N.E. 100, 102 (1891).

[155] 152 U.S. 133, 140, 143, 14 S. Ct. 499, 502–3, 38 L. Ed. 385, 390–91 (1894). See also *California Reduction Co. v. Sanitary Reduction Works,* 199 U.S. 306–22, 26 S. Ct. 100–5, 50 L. Ed. 204–11 (1905); *Gardner v. Michigan,* 199 U.S. 325, 331, 26 S. Ct. 106, 108, 50 L. Ed. 212, 216 (1905).

Accordingly, goods having little or no legitimate value, such as counterfeiting tools or slot machines useful only for law-breaking,[156] may be declared a public nuisance and destroyed without hearing or compensation; but an automobile used for illicit purposes may be confiscated but not destroyed. Said the Supreme Court of Nebraska:

> There is a clear and marked distinction between that species of property which can only be used for an illegal purpose, and which therefore may be declared a nuisance and summarily abated, and that which is innocent in its ordinary and proper use, and which only becomes illegal when used for an unlawful purpose. We know of no principle of law which justifies the seizure of property, innocent in itself, its forfeiture and the transfer of the right of property in the same from one person to another as a punishment for crime, without the right of a hearing upon the guilt or innocence of the person charged, before the forfeiture takes effect. If the property seized by a game keeper or warden [in this case a gun used illegally] were a public nuisance, such as provided for in section one, he had the right under the duties of his office at common law to abate the same without judicial process or proceeding. . . . but if the property is of such a nature that, though innocent in itself and susceptible of a beneficial use, it has been perverted to an unlawful use, and is subject to forfeiture to the state as a penalty, no person has a right to deprive the owner of his property, summarily, without affording opportunity for a hearing and without due process of law.[157]

But the power to prevent and abate nuisances is limited to the condemnation and destruction of that which in its nature, situation, or use is a nuisance *in fact*.[158]

The power to seize and destroy private property summarily is, generally, exercised for the protection of the public health, safety, and morals; but sometimes the purpose is to protect other property, as when trees or plants, infected with disease or pests, may be sprayed at the owner's expense or destroyed.[159]

Also, it seems well settled that a person's property may be seized for nonpayment of his taxes, upon the mere assessment of the commissioner of revenue, and without any judgment of any court against him. Governments cannot permit their claims for public taxes to become subjects of judicial controversy, said Mr. Justice Curtis in *Murray's Lessee v. Hoboken Land & Improvement Co.*[160] This is

[156] *Mullen & Co. v. Moseley*, 13 Idaho 457, 90 Pac. 986 (1907); *Police Commissioner v. Wagner*, 93 Md. 182, 48 Atl. 455 (1901).
[157] *McConnell v. McKillip*, 71 Nebr. 712–21, 99 N.W. 505–9 (1904).
[158] *City of Orlando v. Pragg*, 31 Fla. 111 (1893); *People v. Broad*, 216 Cal. 1, 12 P. (2d) 941 (1932).
[159] *Balch v. Glenn*, 85 Kan. 735, 119 Pac. 67 (1911).
[160] 18 How. 272, 282, 15 L. Ed. 372 (1855).

so because governments need to secure their revenues promptly.[161] The requirements of due process are satisfied if a full hearing is given on judicial review should a hearing be not accorded on the administrative level.[162]

[161] *Phillips v. Commissioner of Internal Revenue,* 283 U.S. 589, 595, 51 S. Ct. 608, 75 L. Ed. 1289 (1931) ; *Hagar v. Reclamation District,* 111 U.S. 701, 708, 4 S. Ct. 663, 28 L. Ed. 569 (1884).
[162] *Phillips v. Commissioner of Internal Revenue,* 283 U.S. 589, 596–97, 51 S. Ct. 608, 75 L. Ed. 1289 (1931).

Chapter 5

THE RULE OF LAW: THE DOCTRINE OF STATE IMMUNITY

The Common Law and Constitutional Immunity of the United States

Under the doctrine of the common law, a state is not responsible in its own courts for the tortious acts of its agents, since the sovereign could not be sued in his own courts without his consent. Said Mr. Justice Field:

> It is a familiar doctrine of the common law, that the sovereign cannot be sued in his own courts without his consent. The doctrine rests upon reasons of public policy; the inconvenience and danger which would follow from any different rule. It is obvious that the public service would be hindered, and the public safety endangered, if the supreme authority could be subjected to suit at the instance of every citizen and, consequently, controlled in the use and disposition of means required for the proper administration of the government. The exemption from direct suit is, therefore, without exception. This doctrine of the common law is equally applicable to the supreme authority of the nation, the United States. They cannot be subjected to legal proceedings at law or in equity without their consent; and whoever institutes such proceedings must bring his case within the authority of some act of Congress.[1]

[1] *The Siren,* 7 Wall. 152, 153–54, 19 L. Ed. 129, 130–31 (1869). "A sovereign is exempt from suit, not because of any formal conception of obsolete theory, but on the logical and practical ground that there can be no legal right against the authority that makes the law on which the right depends." Mr. Justice Holmes in *Kawanana-koa v. Polyblank,* 205 U.S. 349, 353, 27 S. Ct. 526–27, 51 L. Ed. 834, 836 (1907). See also Mr. Justice Holmes in *The Western Maid,* 257 U.S. 419, 433, 42 S. Ct. 159, 161, 66 L. Ed. 299, 303 (1922); *Robertson v. Sichel,* 127 U.S. 507, 515, 8 S. Ct. 1286, 1290, 32 L. Ed. 203, 206 (1888). ". . . it [the government] does not undertake to guarantee to any persons the fidelity of any of the officers or agents, whom it employs; since that would involve it, in all its operations in endless embarrassments, and difficulties, and losses, which would be subversive of the public interests. . . ." Joseph Story, *Commentaries on the Law of Agency* (5th ed.; Little, Brown & Co., Boston, 1857), § 319. For a comprehensive treatment of the subject see E. M. Borchard, *Theories of Governmental Responsibility in Tort* (in eight parts published under different titles), 34, 36 *Yale Law Journal* (1924, 1926); 28 *Columbia Law Review* (May, June, 1928). Also, J. M. Maguire, "State Liability in Tort," 30 *Harvard Law Review* (1916), 20 ff.

The immunity of the United States applies not only to suits by individuals, but to suits by one of the States as well. "It does not follow that because a state may be sued by the United States without its consent, therefore the United States may be sued by a state without its consent," said Mr. Chief Justice Fuller in *Kansas v. United States:* "Public policy forbids that conclusion." [2]

This exemption from judicial process extends to the property of the United States, since there is no distinction between suits against the state directly and suits against its property.[3] However

> . . . when the United States institute a suit, they waive their exemption so far as to allow a presentation by the defendant of the setoffs, legal and equitable, to the extent of the demand made or property claimed, and when they proceed *in rem,* they open to consideration all claims and equities in regard to the property libelled. They then stand in such proceedings, with reference to the rights of defendants or claimants, precisely as private suitors, except that they are exempt from costs and from affirmative relief against them, beyond the demand or property in controversy.[4]

Does the Constitution disturb the common-law immunity of the United States? That instrument, in the Fifth Amendment, declares that no person shall be deprived of life, liberty, or property without due process of law. This is not in the nature of a limitation upon the United States; it is a directive from the United States to its government, or agent. The importance of the clause, for the purposes of this discussion, is whether the United States withdrew its immunity from suit in all cases where a "person" claims that an act of the government deprives him of his life or liberty or property "without due process of law." Failure to distinguish between the *United States* and its *government* has confused the issue.

For example, the question of the legal responsibility of the United States arose out of the Joint Resolution of Congress of June 5, 1933, which declared that the "gold clauses" in private or public contracts obstructed "the power of Congress to regulate the value of the money of the United States," that they were "against public policy," and

---

[2] 204 U.S. 331, 342, 27 S. Ct. 388, 391, 51 L. Ed. 501, 513 (1907). Also *Minnesota v. Hitchcock,* 185 U.S. 373, 22 S. Ct. 650, 46 L. Ed. 954 (1902); *Oregon v. Hitchcock,* 202 U.S. 60, 26 S. Ct. 568, 50 L. Ed. 935 (1906).

[3] *United States v. Alabama,* 313 U.S. 274, 282, 61 S. Ct. 1011, 1014, 85 L. Ed. 1327, 1333 (1941). "A proceeding against property in which the United States has an interest is a suit against the United States." *Minnesota v. United States,* 305 U.S. 382, 386, 59 S. Ct. 292, 294, 83 L. Ed. 235, 240 (1939), where it was held that the United States has a real and direct interest in Indian lands, since it holds these lands as guardian.

[4] *The Siren,* 7 Wall. 152–54, 19 L. Ed. 129, 131 (1869).

that, therefore, they were henceforth void both as to existing and future contracts. The Resolution was held valid as applied to private contracts on the ground that gold clauses were contracts to pay in *money,* not in coin as a commodity or bullion; that, therefore, such contracts, if valid, would create a dual monetary system.[5]

But the Gold Clause Resolution was held invalid in so far as it applied to obligations of the United States, that is, government bonds. In an opinion in which there is much confusion as to the nature of sovereign power, the Court held that a government bond is an inviolable contract of the United States made by the Congress under the authority to borrow money on the credit of the United States. To say, as did Mr. Chief Justice Hughes, quoting Mr. Justice Strong in *Knox v. Lee,* that "The United States are as much bound by their contracts as are individuals" just is not true, not even morally speaking, since repudiation might conceivably be for the greater public good, and the state, not the individual, is the guardian of the public welfare. "When the United States," said the Chief Justice, "with constitutional authority, makes contracts, it has rights and incurs responsibilities similar to those of individuals who are parties to such instruments. There is no difference, . . . except that the United States cannot be sued without its consent." And "The fact that the United States may not be sued without its consent is a matter of procedure which does not affect the legal and binding character of its contracts."[6] But the fact that the United States cannot be sued without its consent is *not* a mere matter of procedure—it is a basic attribute of sovereignty. To say that there is a legal right without a legal remedy—that there is no difference between an obligation that is enforceable and one that is not—that sovereignty can bind but not unbind—are strange doctrines. Any agreement between the sovereign state and its people can bind the state only in a moral sense. Mr. Justice Stone, dissenting, was on much firmer ground when he said:

> I . . . do not join in so much of the opinion as may be taken to suggest that the exercise of the sovereign power to borrow money on credit, *which does not override the sovereign immunity from suit,* may nevertheless preclude or impede the exercise of another sovereign power,

---

[5] *Norman v. Baltimore & Ohio R. Co.,* 294 U.S. 240, 55 S. Ct. 407, 79 L. Ed. 885 (1935). But Mr. Justice McReynolds (Justices Butler, Sutherland, and Van Devanter concurring) denounced both the Resolution and the majority opinion, declaring that "The Constitution is gone." *New York Times,* Feb. 19, 1935.

[6] *Perry v. United States,* 294 U.S. 330, 351, 352, 354, 55 S. Ct. 432, 435, 436, 79 L. Ed. 912, 917, 918, 919 (1935). Cf. *Smyth v. United States,* 302 U.S. 329, 58 S. Ct. 248, 82 L. Ed. 294 (1937).

to regulate the value of money; or to suggest that although there is and can be no present cause of action upon the repudiated gold clause, its obligation is nevertheless, in some manner and to some extent, not stated, superior to the power to regulate currency which we now hold to be superior to the obligation of the bonds.[7]

As an aftermath of this ruling, the Fourth Federal Circuit Court of Appeals in Richmond held in April, 1937, that a holder of a government gold clause bond could not be required to surrender the bond when called unless the government was prepared to redeem at full gold value, and that the Treasury was obligated to pay the contractual three and one-half per cent interest rate on such bond.[8] It would be interesting to know how this court would enforce its judgment against the Treasury in the face of an act of Congress directing the Treasury to stop payment.

The gold clause decision led to considerable speculation here and abroad as to how foreign holders of United States (Liberty) bonds could collect in gold or its equivalent. Such persons might have assigned their holdings to their governments for collection through diplomatic channels, but a diplomatic agreement to pay in gold would require congressional approval; and an agreement to permit suit in the Supreme Court would have left the judgment of that Court unenforceable except by congressional action or by war. The bond issues were floated in the United States, not abroad, and called for payment of gold at the Treasury of the United States. Thus, even if they had been paid in gold coin, the bondholder would have been required to turn the gold back to the Treasury and would have received in return therefor an equivalent amount of currency based upon the devalued dollar.

Mr. Justice Stone's conclusion seems inescapable, therefore, that the invalidation of the gold clause in both private and public contracts or obligations was a constitutional exercise of the "sovereign power to regulate the value of money." The action was legal, no matter what may be said for its wisdom.[9]

---

[7] 294 U.S. at 361, 55 S. Ct. at 439, 79 L. Ed. at 922. Italics supplied.

[8] See *New York Times,* April 7, 1937.

[9] Referring to the decision in *Clearfield Trust Co. v. United States,* 318 U.S. 363, 369, 63 S. Ct. 573, 576, 87 L. Ed. 838, 843 (1943), Arthur T. Vanderbilt observes: "In a dictum which is as untrue in practice as the proposition is laudable in theory, the Supreme Court announced that the United States 'is not excepted from the general rules governing rights and duties . . . by the largeness of its dealings and its having to employ agents to do what if done by a principal in person would leave no room for doubt.'" "Administrative Law," *1943 Annual Survey of American Law* (New York University School of Law, New York, 1944), p. 102.

When is a suit against an officer of the United States a suit against the United States? If an individual applies to a court for a writ of injunction to restrain an officer from enforcing a law on the ground that the law would deprive him of his property without due process of law, is such a proceeding an action against the United States and can it be estopped by the rule of immunity? Obviously not since the courts have not hesitated to take jurisdiction in such cases to enjoin enforcement of "unconstitutional laws." A judicial inquiry into the legality of official action is not a suit against the state. Logically (under the American doctrine of judicial review), if not pragmatically, an unconstitutional statute, being null and void, is not an act of the United States and cannot confer any authority upon an officer. Therefore, a suit against an officer enforcing an unconstitutional statute is a suit against the officer as an individual and not a suit against the United States. But judicial review is built upon expediency and not logic, and so are the judicial rulings on the effect of unconstitutional statutes when vested rights are involved. The legal befuddlement on this point is most pronounced in connection with State action under the Fourteenth Amendment, which will be considered in subsequent pages.

Is an *ultra vires* act of a federal officer acting under a valid statute an act of the United States and so shielded from judicial process?

When the President ordered officers of the United States to seize and to hold, without compensation, a private estate for the use of the United States, a suit against the officers for recovery was held to be a suit against individuals and not against the United States. Said Mr. Justice Miller for the Court:

> The defense stands here solely upon the absolute immunity from judicial inquiry of anyone who *asserts* authority from the executive branch of the government, however clear it may be made that the executive possessed no such power. Not only no such power is given, but it is absolutely prohibited, both to the executive and the legislative, to deprive any one of life, liberty, or property without due process of law, or to take private property without just compensation. . . .
>
> Shall it be said, in the face of all this, and of the acknowledged right of the judiciary to decide in proper cases, statutes which have been passed by both branches of Congress and approved by the President to be unconstitutional, that the courts cannot give a remedy when the citizen has been deprived of his property by force, his estate seized and converted to the use of the government without lawful authority, without process of law, and without compensation, because the President has ordered it and his officers are in possession?
>
> If such be the law of this country, it sanctions a tyranny which has

no existence in the monarchies of Europe, nor in any other government which has a just claim to well-regulated liberty and the protection of personal rights.[10]

That is, while an action will not lie against property of the United States, an action will lie to determine ownership of property in issue; and if found not to be property of the United States, a suit for recovery is not against the United States.[11]

However, for the torts of its agents acting within a valid law the United States has assumed only a limited responsibility.[12] Congress has, from time to time, allowed suit for certain types of tort claims, such as patent infringment,[13] admiralty and maritime torts,[14] damage to oyster beds caused by dredging operations,[15] and injuries caused by federal corporations performing public functions.[16] In addition, the Small Tort Claims Act of 1922 [17] authorized heads of departments to certify claims not exceeding $1000 to Congress arising from the negligence of a government employee. In general, prior to the Federal Tort Claims Act of 1946, the injured individual was limited to two ineffective remedies: a private action against the officer for damages, and a private bill in Congress.

Liability by Consent

Consent for the United States to be sued by an individual can be given, it appears, only by an "act of Congress" and not by "any officer of the government." [18] The consent may apply to suits by States as well as by individuals.[19] A statute giving consent for the government to be sued, "since it is a relinquishment of a sovereign immunity, must be strictly interpreted." [20] Note the qualification for a

[10] *United States v. Lee,* 106 U.S. 196, 220, 221, 1 S. Ct. 240, 260, 261, 27 L. Ed. 171, 181, 182 (1882). See also *Langford v. United States,* 101 U.S. 341, 25 L. Ed. 1010 (1880).

[11] See also *Ickes v. Fox,* 300 U.S. 82, 96–97, 57 S. Ct. 412, 417, 81 L. Ed. 525, 531 (1937).

[12] *Cf.* Walter Gellhorn and C. Newton Schenck, "Tort Actions Against the Federal Government," 47 *Columbia Law Review* (1947), 722–41.

[13] 36 *Stat.* 851 (1910), 40 *Stat.* 705 (1918), 35 *U.S.C.A.* § 68 (1940).

[14] 41 *Stat.* 525 (1920), 46 *U.S.C.A.* §§ 741, 742 (1940) ; 43 *Stat.* 1112 (1925), 46 *U.S.C.A.* § 781 (1940).

[15] 49 *Stat.* 1049 (1935), 57 *Stat.* 553 (1943), 28 *U.S.C.A.* § 250a.

[16] *Keifer & Keifer v. Reconstruction Finance Corp.,* 306 U.S. 381, 59 S. Ct. 516, 83 L. Ed. 784 (1939).

[17] 42 *Stat.* 1066, 31 *U.S.C.A.* §§ 215–17 (1940). Repealed August 2, 1946.

[18] *The Davis,* 10 Wall. 15, 19 L. Ed. 875 (1870).

[19] *Minnesota v. Hitchcock,* 185 U.S. 373, 22 S. Ct. 650, 46 L. Ed. 954 (1902).

[20] *United States v. Sherwood,* 312 U.S. 584, 590, 61 S. Ct. 767, 771, 85 L. Ed. 1058 (1941).

governmental agency such as the Reconstruction Finance Corporation. "While it acts as a governmental agency . . . still its transactions are akin to those of private enterprises and the mere fact that
it is an agency of the government does not extend to it the immunity
of the sovereign." [21] Congress has full power, however, to endow
government corporations with immunity from suit or to determine the
extent of their liability; and if Congress authorizes an agency "to
sue and be sued," liability to suit is assumed.[22] But *Federal Crop Insurance Corp. v. Merrill* [23] seems to hold that a federal agency is
immune from suit *unless Congress provides otherwise.* Said Mr.
Justice Frankfurter:

> It is too late in the day to urge that the Government is just another
> private litigant, for purposes of charging it with liability, whenever it
> takes over a business theretofore conducted by private enterprise or
> engages in competition with private ventures. . . . The Government
> may carry on its operations through conventional executive agencies or
> through corporate forms especially created for defined ends.[24]

Court of Claims, 1855.—By an Act of February 24, 1855,[25]
Congress created a Court of Claims, consisting of three judges, with
jurisdiction to hear and determine all claims founded upon any national law, executive regulation, or contract with the government of
the United States, and claims referred to it by either house of Congress. Its decisions had no legal effect but were in the nature of
reports with findings and opinions to Congress, which required legislative approval and enforcement. An Act of March 3, 1863,[26] added
two judges and authorized the court to render judgments, with a
right of appeal to the Supreme Court when the amount in controversy exceeded $3,000. However, neither court could enforce its
judgment. Either court could do no more than certify its opinion to
the Secretary of the Treasury who, in his discretion, could include it
in his estimates of private claims, leaving final decision as to payment
with Congress. The provision for appeal to the Supreme Court was
held unconstitutional in *Gordon v. United States* [27] on the grounds
that (1) since the Court of Claims could not render valid judgments,

---

[21] *Reconstruction Finance Corp. v. J. G. Menihan Corp.,* 312 U.S. 81, 83, 61 S. Ct.
483, 486, 85 L. Ed. 595 (1941).
[22] *Federal Housing Administration v. Burr,* 309 U.S. 242, 60 S. Ct. 488, 84 L. Ed.
724 (1940).
[23] 332 U.S. 380, 68 S. Ct. 1, 92 L. Ed. 10 (1947).
[24] 332 U.S. at 383–84, 68 S. Ct. at 3.
[25] 10 *Stat.* 612.
[26] 12 *Stat.* 765, 766, c. 92, § 14, 28 *U.S.C.A.* § 241.
[27] 2 Wall. 561, 17 L. Ed. 921 (1865).

it was not, within the meaning of Article III of the Constitution, an "inferior court" from which appeal could lie to the Supreme Court; and (2) the "judicial power of the United States" confided to the Supreme Court could not be made subject to revision by the Treasury or Congress. Whereupon, Congress repealed the offending provision [28] and the appellate power of the Supreme Court has been exercised ever since.[29] Review is limited to questions of law. The findings of fact of the Court of Claims are "treated like the verdict of a jury." It is the duty of the Court of Claims to resolve conflicting inferences and to draw from the evidence the necessary conclusions of fact.[30]

The Tucker Act, 1887, redefined the jurisdiction of the Court of Claims as follows:

First. All claims (except for pensions) founded upon the Constitution of the United States or any law of Congress, or upon any regulation of an executive department, or upon any contract, expressed or implied, with the government of the United States, or for damages, liquidated or unliquidated, in cases not sounding in tort, in respect of which claims the party would be entitled to redress against the United States either in a court of law, equity, or admiralty if the United States were suable. . . . Second. All set-offs, counter-claims, claims for damages, whether liquidated or unliquidated, or other demands whatsoever on the part of the government of the United States against any claimant against the government in said court.[31]

The district courts of the United States were given concurrent jurisdiction with the Court of Claims where the amount of the claim does not exceed $10,000.[32]

Claims pending in any of the executive departments which involve controverted questions of law or fact may be referred, with the consent of the claimant, to the Court of Claims by the head of the department, provided, that the court has jurisdiction to render judgment thereon.[33] Also, either house of Congress may refer to the court, for investigation and determination of facts, any pending bill providing

[28] Act of March 17, 1866, 14 *Stat.* 9. See also Act of June 25, 1868, 15 *Stat.* 75.
[29] *Langford v. United States,* 101 U.S. 341, 25 L. Ed. 1010 (1880); *De Groot v. United States,* 5 Wall. 419, 18 L. Ed. 700 (1867); *United States v. Jones,* 119 U.S. 477, 7 S. Ct. 283, 30 L. Ed. 440 (1886).
[30] *United States v. Esnault-Pelterie,* 303 U.S. 26, 58 S. Ct. 412, 82 L. Ed. 625 (1938).
[31] Act of March 3, 1887, 24 *Stat.* 505, c. 359, § 1; March 3, 1911, c. 231, 36 *Stat.* 1168; *Judicial Code,* § 145, 28 *U.S.C.A.* § 251(1) and (2).
[32] *Judicial Code,* § 24(20), 28 *U.S.C.A.* § 41(20).
[33] *Judicial Code,* 148, 28 *U.S.C.A.* § 254.

for the payment of a claim against the United States (except for a pension).[34] The procedure is the same in all cases before the Court of Claims, except that the court renders a judgment on claims referred by an executive department, but merely reports its findings of fact on claims which Congress refers to it.

The jurisdiction of the Court of Claims and of the district courts under the Tucker Act is limited to judgments for money only—it does not embrace equitable relief by specific performance of a contract or the restitution of property.[35] This jurisdiction was further limited to cases of contract, express or implied, as distinguished from those founded in tort, thus distinguishing between actions *ex contractu* and actions *ex delicto,* "which is well understood in our system of jurisprudence."[36] Congress chose to assume liability only for the former actions; for the latter actions the officers were left personally liable under the "rule of law." The general rule adhered to by the federal courts prior to the Federal Tort Claims Act of 1946 was that, unless specific consent were given in some act of Congress, the United States government is not liable to suit for the torts, misconduct, misfeasances, or laches of its officers or employees.[37]

Thus, if the United States *claims title to* and its agents forcibly seize property which *in fact is private property,* the action of the officers is an unequivocal tort for which no action lies in the Court of Claims.[38] But if property to which the United States asserts no title is taken by its officers pursuant to an act of Congress, the taking is under eminent domain and there is an implied obligation to compensate the owner, which may be enforced by suit in the Court of Claims.[39]

An illegal collection of duties or taxes gives rise to a claim "founded" upon a "law of Congress" within the jurisdiction of the Court of Claims.[40] It appears that where a remedy is expressly provided by statute, the remedy is exclusive and there is no right of action in the Court of Claims;[41] but if no special remedy is provided,

---

[34] *Ibid.* Bowman Act of March 3, 1883, 22 *Stat.* 485.

[35] *United States v. Jones,* 131 U.S. 1, 9 S. Ct. 669, 33 L. Ed. 90 (1889). See also *United States v. Alire,* 6 Wall. 573, 18 L. Ed. 947 (1868) ; *Bonner v. United States,* 9 Wall. 156, 19 L. Ed. 666 (1870).

[36] *Langford v. United States,* 101 U.S. 341, 25 L. Ed. 1010 (1880).

[37] *Bigby v. United States,* 188 U.S. 400, 407, 23 S. Ct. 468, 471, 47 L. Ed. 519, 524 (1903) ; *John M. Flynn v. United States,* 65 Ct. Cl. 33 (1928).

[38] *Ibid.*

[39] *United States v. Great Falls Manufacturing Co.,* 112 U.S. 645, 5 S. Ct. 306, 28 L. Ed. 846 (1884).

[40] *Dooley v. United States,* 182 U.S. 222, 21 S. Ct. 762, 45 L. Ed. 1074 (1901).

[41] *Nicholl v. United States,* 7 Wall. 122, 19 L. Ed. 125 (1869).

the general laws which govern the Court of Claims may be resorted to for relief if any can be found applicable in the case.[42]

Attorney General Homer Cummings, in 1938, recommended to Congress a statute providing that the United States could be sued in tort for personal or property damages caused by the negligence of federal officers or employees.[43] A bill to that effect was introduced in the 76th Congress. This principle of responsibility was incorporated in the Legislative Reorganization Act of 1946 as Title IV, "Federal Tort Claims Act."

Federal Tort Claims Act, 1946.—On August 2, 1946, the Federal Tort Claims Act [44] was approved, providing for the adjustment of or suits on tort claims against the United States. The tort liability of the United States is limited to "damage to or loss of property or on account of personal injury or death *caused by the negligent or wrongful act or omission of an employee* of the Government while acting within *the scope of his office or employment,* under circumstances where the United States, if a private person, would be liable to the claimant for such damage, loss, injury, or death in accordance with the law of the place where the act or omission occurred." [45] The United States is made liable in respect to such claims "in the same manner, and to the same extent as private individual under like circumstances, except that the United States shall not be liable for interest prior to judgment, or for punitive damages." [46]

No liability is assumed for claims arising out of (1) an act of an employee "exercising due care, in the execution of a statute or regulation, whether or not such statute or regulation be valid"; (2) the exercise or failure to exercise a discretionary function, "whether or not the discretion involved be abused"; (3) "assault, battery, false imprisonment, false arrest, malicious prosecution, abuse of process, libel, slander, misrepresentation, deceit, or interference with contract rights"; (4) the postal, fiscal or military operations; (5) the operation of the Panama Canal and Tennessee Valley Au-

---

[42] *United States v. Kaufman,* 96 U.S. 567, 24 L. Ed. 792 (1878).

[43] *Annual Report Attorney General* (1938), p. 9. See Alexander Holtzoff, "Tort Claims Against the United States," 25 *American Bar Association Journal* (1939), 828 ff.

[44] 60 *Stat.* 843–47 (1946), as amended, 61 *Stat.* 722 (1947), 28 *U.S.C.A.* §§ 921–46.

[45] Secs. 403, 410, 28 *U.S.C.A.* §§ 921, 931(a). Italics supplied.

[46] Act, amended August 1, 1947, to permit residents of Alabama and Massachusetts to sue under the Act despite the rule in these states that wrongful death actions can result only in punishment. This amendment was made necessary by virtue of the "law of the place" doctrine. See *H. R. Rep. No. 748,* June 30, 1947, 80th Cong., 1st Sess., 61 *Stat.* 722.

See Dahelite vs U.S. + subsequent Congressional action for a response to this point of "the king can do no wrong" concept.

thority; (6) the imposition of a quarantine; (7) admiralty; and (8) residence abroad.[47]

Claims of \$1,000 or less may be determined and settled by the head of each federal agency or his designee for the purpose. Claims for more than \$1,000 must be taken to a United States district court, sitting without jury, which has exclusive jurisdiction to hear and render judgment on any tort claim against the United States. Appeal may be taken from an agency award to a district court; or the claimant may, upon fifteen days' notice in writing, withdraw the claim from the consideration of the agency and commence suit thereon in the district court, provided that the amount of the claim presented to the court shall not exceed the sum presented to the agency, unless based upon new evidence.

Acceptance of an agency award by a claimant constitutes a complete release by the claimant of any claim against the United States and against the employee whose act gave rise to the claim; and a judgment by a district court bars any action by the claimant, by reason of the same subject matter, against the employee whose act gave rise to the adjudicated claim.

Final judgments of the district courts in claims cases are subject to review by appeal either in (1) the circuit courts of appeals in the same manner and to the same extent as other judgments of the district courts; or (2) the Court of Claims of the United States, with the written consent of all the appellees. Appeals to the Court of Claims shall be taken within three months after the entry of the judgment of the district court. When acting as a court of appeals, the Court of Claims shall have the same powers and duties as a circuit court of appeals and shall be governed by the rules relating to appeals from a district court to a circuit court of appeals.

The Attorney General is authorized to arbitrate, compromise, or settle any claim cognizable under the Act, after the institution of a suit thereon, with the approval of the court in which the suit is pending. Any such settlement or any award made by an agency shall be paid by the head of the agency concerned out of appropriations made therefor.

Any claim against the United States is outlawed unless within one year after the claim accrued the claimant institutes proceedings either before an agency or a district court, except that the time to institute a suit in the district court is extended six months for all cases that originate before an agency.

Some federal courts have taken a strict construction view of the

---

[47] Sec. 421 (a–k), 28 *U.S.C.A.* § 943 (a–l).

Act. "We start with the principle from which there has been no deviation in our entire judicial history," said a district court, "that the sovereign's immunity to suit can only be waived by the sovereign himself in language which explicitly indicates such waiver. Statutes waiving immunity are construed not only strictly in favor of the Government, but narrowly and literally. And because a statute of this character creates both the right and the remedy, any limitation of the remedy is also a limitation of the right." [48] But the Supreme Court appears to have adopted a contrary view in *United States v. Aetna Casualty & Surety Co.,*[49] where Mr. Chief Justice Vinson said:

> In argument before a number of District Courts and Courts of Appeals, the Government relied upon the doctrine that statutes waiving sovereign immunity must be strictly construed. We think that the Congressional attitude in passing the Tort Claims Act is more accurately reflected by Judge Cardozo's statement in *Anderson v. Hayes Construction Co., 243 N.Y. 140, 147, 153 N.E. 28, 29:* "The exemption of the sovereign from suit involves hardship enough, where consent has been withheld. We are not to add to its rigor by refinement of construction, where consent has been announced." [50]

All suits for tort liability, regardless of their origin, must be prosecuted against the United States, not against an officer or agency.[51] In proceedings against the United States the governing law shall be "the law of the place where the act or omission occurred." [52] The right of subrogees, such as insurers, to sue the government under the Act, to obtain reimbursement for claims paid on the theory that such payment constitutes an assignment of legal rights, has had diverse interpretations.[53] Under a strict construction of the Act such claims have been denied on the grounds that subrogees are not specifically included and that insurers have been com-

[48] *Urate v. United States,* 7 *F.R.D.* 705, 706 (S.D. Cal., 1948). Also *Bates v. United States,* 76 F. Supp. 57 (D. Nebr., 1948).

[49] 338 U.S. 366, 70 S. Ct. 207, 94 L. Ed. 151 (1949).

[50] 338 U.S. at 383, 70 S. Ct. at 216, 94 L. Ed. at 161.

[51] R. M. Hulen, "Tort Claims Against the United States," 7 *F.R.D.* 689 (1948).

[52] Federal Tort Claims Act, 410(a); 28 *U.S.C.A.* § 931(a); *Spell v. United States,* 72 F. Supp. 731 (D.C. Fla., 1947); *Lachman v. Pennsylvania Greyhound Lines,* 160 F. (2d) 496 (D.C.A. 4th, 1947); *Burkhardt v. United States,* 70 F. Supp. 982 (D.C. Md., 1947), overruled, 165 F. (2d) 869 (C.C.A. 4th, 1947); R. C. Thomsen, " 'The Law of the Place' Provision of the Act," 33 *American Bar Association Journal* (1947), 959 ff.

[53] Subrogation is the act of putting one thing or person in place of another, such as the substitution of another person in the place of a claimant, to whose rights he succeeds in relation to the claim. See R. J. Flynn, "Torts—The Federal Tort Claims Act Does Not Exclude Suits Against the Government on Subrogated Claims," 37 *Georgetown Law Journal* (1948), 121 ff.

pensated already in the form of premiums.[54] Courts of appeals in several circuits, however, have upheld the right of subrogation,[55] and the Supreme Court ruled similarly in 1949.[56]

Generally, claims will not be allowed under the Act if other means of recompense are available, as where benefits have been accepted under the Federal Employees Compensation Act or the World War Veterans' Act.[57] The Act covers claims for injury or death of military personnel not incident to their service, provided claims paid under available acts are set off against the final recovery.[58]

The Constitutional Immunity of the Several States

State Immunity Under the Eleventh Amendment.—The Eleventh Amendment to the Constitution declares that "The judicial power of the United States shall not be construed to extend to any suit in law or equity, commenced or prosecuted against one of the United States by citizens of another State, or by citizens or subjects of any foreign state." This Amendment was intended to extend the rule of sovereign immunity to the several States, overruling *Chisholm v. Georgia*[59] where the Supreme Court held that for the

---

[54] For cases denying claims of subrogees see: *Bewick v. United States,* 74 F. Supp. 730 (N.D. Tex., 1947); *Old Colony Insurance Co. v. United States,* 74 F. Supp. 723 (S.D. Ohio, 1947); *Rusconi et al. v. United States,* 74 F. Supp. 669 (S.D. Cal., 1947); *Cascade Co., Montana v. United States,* 75 F. Supp. 850 (D. Mont., 1948); *Aetna Casualty Security Co. v. United States,* 76 F. Supp. 333 (E.D.N.Y., 1948).

[55] *Old Colony Insurance Co. v. United States,* 168 F. (2d) 931 (C.C.A. 6th, 1948); *Aetna Casualty & Surety Co. v. United States,* 170 F. (2d) 469 (C.C.A. 2d, 1948); *Yorkshire Insurance Co. v. United States,* 171 F. (2d) 374 (C.C.A. 3d, 1948). "Where an insurance company has indemnified the injured person for the loss that he has sustained because of the wrong, there is no reason in law or in common sense why it should not be subrogated pro tanto to the rights of the injured party, just as though the suit were against a private person. It is inconceivable that the fact that the injured party has insurance should affect his right to recover in tort against the government, or that the recovery for property damages should not go to the insurer to the extent that he has reimbursed the injured party rather than to the latter. Certainly, it could not have been intended either that recovery for a loss be denied because the injured party has been prudent enough to insure against it or that recovery be allowed where the insurer has paid the loss except for his reimbursement." *United States v. South Carolina State Highway Department,* 171 F. (2d) 893, 900 (C.C.A. 4th, 1948).

[56] *United States v. Aetna Casualty & Surety Co.,* 338 U.S. 366, 70 S. Ct. 207, 94 L. Ed. 151 (1949).

[57] *Wham v. United States,* 81 F. Supp. 126 (D.C.D.C., 1948); *White v. United States,* 77 F. Supp. 316 (D.C.N.J., 1948).

[58] *Brooks v. United States,* 337 U.S. 49, 69 S. Ct. 918, 93 L. Ed. 1200 (1949); *Samson v. United States,* 79 F. Supp. 406 (D.C.S.D.N.Y., 1948); *Jefferson v. United States,* 77 F. Supp. 706 (D. Md., 1948).

[59] 2 Dall. 419, 1 L. Ed. 440 (1793).

4. *Ultra vires acts.* Suits against State officers acting under *unconstitutional statutes* are not suits against the State but against the defendants as individuals within the meaning of the Eleventh Amendment.[76]

> . . . yet it is also true, in respect to the State itself, that whatever wrong is attempted in its name is imputable to its government, and not to the State, for, as it can speak and act only by law, whatever it does say and do must be lawful. That which, therefore, is unlawful because made so by the supreme law, the Constitution of the United States, is not the word or deed of the State, but it is the mere wrong and trespass of those individual persons who falsely speak and act in its name.[77]

In such cases the State is not made a party on the record, even though it may be the *real party* in that it might benefit from the acts of its officers. When a federal law is involved, the United States

> . . . deals with all persons within its territorial jurisdiction as individuals owing obedience to its authority. The penalties of disobedience may be visited upon them without regard to the character in which they assume to act, or the nature of the exemption they may plead in justification. Nothing can be interposed between the individual and the obligation he owes to the Constitution and laws of the United States, which can shield or defend him from their just authority, ... If, therefore, an individual, acting under the assumed authority of a State, as one of its officers, and under color of its laws, comes into conflict with the superior authority of a valid law of the United States, *he is stripped of his representative character,* and subjected in his person to the consequences of his individual conduct. The State has no power to impart to him any immunity from responsibility to the supreme authority of the United States.[78]

Whether a State is the actual party, within the prohibition of the Eleventh Amendment, is to be determined by the nature of the case rather than by the question whether the State is or is not named on the record. Whenever a State is an indispensable party to enable a court, under its rules of procedure, to grant the relief sought, the court will refuse to take jurisdiction. "But in the desire to do that justice, which in many cases the courts can see will be defeated by an unwarranted extension of this principle, they have in some instances gone a long way in holding the State not to be a necessary party,

[76] *Osborn v. Bank of the United States,* 9 Wheat. 738, 6 L. Ed. 204 (1824); *Mitchel v. Harmony,* 13 How. 115, 14 L. Ed. 75 (1851); *Bates v. Clark,* 95 U.S. 204, 24 L. Ed. 471 (1877); *Brown v. Huger,* 21 How. 305, 16 L. Ed. 125 (1859).

[77] *Poindexter v. Greenhow,* 114 U.S. 270, 290, 5 S. Ct. 903, 914, 29 L. Ed. 185, 192–93 (1885).

[78] *In re Ayers,* 123 U.S. 443, 507, 8 S. Ct. 164, 184, 31 L. Ed. 216, 230 (1887). Italics supplied.

though some interest of hers may be more or less affected by the decision." [79] This is presumably on the theory that where there is a right there must be a remedy. A State is a "necessary party defendant" whenever the rights of the State would be directly and adversely affected by the judgment or decree sought.[80]

In this connection an important distinction is drawn between suits to compel official performance of an obligation which belongs to the State in its political capacity, and suits to enjoin the performance of acts by State officers which violate and invade the personal and property rights of the plaintiffs under color of unconstitutional authority.[81]

It has been held that a State is an indispensable party in a proceeding in equity to secure possession of State property for the purpose of applying it to the payment of the State's debt due to the plaintiff. Such a proceeding is, therefore, proscribed by the Eleventh Amendment.[82] A suit to enforce a contract of a State is a suit against the State, for the reason that the officers, as individuals, are not parties to the contract and are not, therefore, capable in law of committing a breach of it. "There is no remedy for a breach of contract, actual or apprehended, except upon the contract itself, and between those who are by law parties to it." [83] Therefore, a contract of a State with individuals "is substantially without sanction, except that which arises out of the honor and good faith of the State itself, and these are not subject to coercion." [84]

So a mandamus will not lie to compel State officers to execute contracts repudiated by the State.[85] However,

> . . . where property or rights are enjoyed under a grant or contract made by a State, they cannot wantonly be invaded. Whilst the State cannot be compelled by suit to perform its contracts, any attempt on its part to violate property or rights acquired under its contracts may be judicially resisted; and any law impairing the obligation of contracts under which such property or rights are held is void and powerless to affect their enjoyment.[86]

[79] *Cunningham v. Macon and Brunswick R. Co.,* 109 U.S. 446, 451, 3 S. Ct. 292, 296, 27 L. Ed. 992, 994 (1883).

[80] *Schwing et al. v. Miles et al.,* 376 Ill. 436, 11 N.E. (2d) 944 (1937).

[81] *Pennoyer v. McConnaughy,* 140 U.S. 1, 16–18, 11 S. Ct. 699, 703–4, 35 L. Ed. 363, 367–68 (1891).

[82] *Cunningham v. Macon & Brunswick R. Co.,* 109 U.S. 446, 3 S. Ct. 292, 27 L. Ed. 992 (1883); *Christian v. Atlantic & N. C. R. Co.,* 133 U.S. 233, 10 S. Ct. 260, 33 L. Ed. 589 (1890).

[83] *In re Ayers,* 123 U.S. 443, 503, 8 S. Ct. 164, 182, 31 L. Ed. 216, 229 (1887).

[84] 123 U.S. at 505, 8 S. Ct. at 183, 31 L. Ed. at 229.

[85] *Louisiana v. Jumel,* 107 U.S. 711, 2 S. Ct. 128, 27 L. Ed. 448 (1883).

[86] *Hans v. Louisiana,* 134 U.S. 1, 20–21, 10 S. Ct. 504, 509, 33 L. Ed. 842, 849 (1890).

Accordingly, when a State agreed to accept interest coupons from its bonds in payment of State taxes and the State subsequently repudiated this agreement, the Supreme Court held that a proffer of coupons constituted payment, and it intervened to prevent the State from collecting the tax by forced sale of the defendant's property.[87] That is, a federal court will enjoin State officers from doing certain acts, authorized by State law, which would violate the litigant's contract with the State and work irreparable injury to his property.[88]

It would seem that affirmative relief will not be granted against a State officer by ordering him to perform an act which is forbidden by a State statute, even though this statute is unconstitutional.[89] But a mandamus proceeding to compel a State officer to perform a ministerial duty imposed by a State law which has not been repudiated by *de facto* legislative action does not violate the Eleventh Amendment.[90]

If a State sues an individual in one of its courts, the defendant may carry the case to a federal court on a writ of error, and such a proceeding is not a suit commenced or prosecuted against a State within the meaning of the Eleventh Amendment. "It is clearly in its commencement the suit of a State against an individual, which suit is transferred to this Court, not for the purpose of asserting any claim against the State, but for the purpose of asserting a constitutional defense against a claim made by a State."[91] The writ of error

> . . . does not in any manner act upon the parties; it acts only on the record. It removes the record into the supervising tribunal. Where, then, a State obtains a judgment against an individual, and the Court, rendering such judgment, overrules a defense set up under the constitution or laws of the United States, the transfer of this record into the supreme court, for the sole purpose of inquiring whether the judgment violates the constitution or laws of the United States, can, with no propriety, we think, be denominated a suit commenced or prosecuted against the State whose judgment is so far re-examined. Nothing is demanded from the State. No claim against it of any description is asserted or prosecuted. The party is not to be restored to the possession of anything. Essentially, it is an appeal on a single point; and the defendant who appeals from a judgment rendered against him, is never said to commence or prosecute a suit against the plaintiff who

[87] *Poindexter v. Greenhow,* 114 U.S. 270, 5 S. Ct. 903, 29 L. Ed. 185 (1885).

[88] *Pennoyer v. McConnaughy,* 140 U.S. 1, 11 S. Ct. 699, 35 L. Ed. 363 (1891).

[89] *Cunningham v. Macon & Brunswick R. Co.,* 109 U.S. 446, 454, 3 S. Ct. 292, 298, 27 L. Ed. 992, 995 (1883).

[90] *Rolston v. Missouri Fund Commissioners,* 120 U.S. 390, 411, 7 S. Ct. 599, 610, 30 L. Ed. 721, 728 (1887).

[91] *Cohens v. Virginia,* 6 Wheat. 264, 409, 5 L. Ed. 257, 293 (1821).

has obtained the judgment. The writ of error is given rather than an appeal, because it is the more usual mode of removing suits at common law; and because, perhaps, it is more technically proper where a single point of law, and not the whole case, is to be re-examined. But an appeal might be given, and might be so regulated as to effect every purpose of a writ of error. The mode of removal is form, and not substance. Whether it be by writ of error or appeal, no claim is asserted, no demand is made by the original defendant; he only asserts the constitutional right to have his defense examined by that tribunal whose province it is to construe the constitution and laws of the Union.[92]

Under the federal habeas corpus statute,[93] persons in the custody of State officers for alleged crimes against the State, have been discharged from such custody by federal judges on the ground that the imprisonment was in violation of the Constitution or laws of the United States. Likewise, the Judicial Code gives the right of removal to a federal court of any criminal prosecution begun in a State court against a federal revenue officer "on account of any act done under color of his office or of any such law [revenue]."[94] Such actions are not suits against States within the meaning of the Eleventh Amendment.[95]

One State may sue another State in the United States courts;[96] but a State may not, in its own name under the guise of a suit between States but actually on behalf of its citizens, act as a collecting agency for its citizens by suing another State to secure payment on delinquent State bonds. The evident purpose of the Eleventh Amendment, said Mr. Chief Justice Waite,

> . . . was to prohibit all suits against a State by or for citizens of other States, or aliens without the consent of the State to be sued, and in our opinion, one State cannot create a controversy with another State, within the meaning of that term as used in the judicial clauses of the Constitution, by assuming the prosecution of debts owing by the other State to its citizens.[97]

---

[92] 6 Wheat. at 410–11, 5 L. Ed. at 292–93.

[93] *Rev. Stat.* §§ 643, 753, *Comp. Stat.* 1901, p. 592.

[94] Act of March 3, 1911, 36 *Stat.* 1097, as amended, 28 *U.S.C.A.* § 76. Applied in *Tennessee v. Davis,* 100 U.S. 257, 25 L. Ed. 648 (1880).

[95] *Ex parte Milligan,* 4 Wall. 2, 18 L. Ed. 281 (1866); *In re Neagle,* 135 U.S. 1, 10 S. Ct. 658, 34 L. Ed. 55 (1890); *Kilbourn v. Thompson,* 103 U.S. 168, 26 L. Ed. 377 (1881).

[96] *Constitution,* Art. III, Sec. 2. *South Dakota v. North Carolina,* 192 U.S. 286, 24 S. Ct. 269, 48 L. Ed. 448 (1904); *Louisiana v. Texas,* 176 U.S. 1, 20 S. Ct. 251, 44 L. Ed. 347 (1900).

[97] *New Hampshire v. Louisiana,* 108 U.S. 76, 91, 2 S. Ct. 176, 184, 27 L. Ed. 656, 662 (1883).

In a case of this nature the suing State is not the real party. When, however, the State as *parens patriae* brings suit to protect the general health, safety, or property of its citizens from injurious action by another State, its interest is sufficient to make it the real party to the controversy.[98] And it has been held that where railroads are alleged to fix rates in restraint of trade in violation of the federal antitrust laws, and that such rates are injurious to a State's economy, the State, as *parens patriae,* is authorized to invoke the original jurisdiction of the Supreme Court in a suit for injunctive relief.[99]

State immunity does not apply to suits instituted by the United States against States in the Supreme Court, as such suits have been held to fall within the original jurisdiction of that Court.[100]

Waiver of State Immunity under the Eleventh Amendment.— A State may waive its immunity from suit under the Eleventh Amendment. As Congress alone may waive the immunity of the United States, it would seem that the State legislature alone may waive State immunity.[101]

The waiver of immunity may be conditioned and may be retracted as to cases not in process of adjudication.[102] If a State permits itself to be sued *in its own courts,* it does not, by implication, thereby waive its immunity under the Eleventh Amendment.[103]

Waiver of State Immunity in Its Own Courts.—The States, even more than the United States, have been reluctant to waive their immunity to suit in their own courts. A survey in 1939 indicated that nearly half of the States had no constitutional provisions respecting suits against the State; four State constitutions forbid such suits; but a considerable number make some arrangement for actions against the State by aggrieved individuals—the most common pro-

---

[98] *United States v. North Carolina,* 136 U.S. 211, 10 S. Ct. 920, 34 L. Ed. 336 (1890) ; *United States v. Texas,* 143 U.S. 621, 12 S. Ct. 488, 36 L. Ed. 285 (1892) ; *United States v. Michigan,* 190 U.S. 379, 23 S. Ct. 742, 47 L. Ed. 1103 (1903).

[99] *State of Georgia v. Pennsylvania Railroad Co.,* 324 U.S. 439, 65 S. Ct. 716, 89 L. Ed. 1051 (1945).

[100] *Georgia v. Tennessee Copper Co.,* 206 U.S. 230, 27 S. Ct. 618, 51 L. Ed. 1038 (1907) ; *Missouri v. Illinois,* 180 U.S. 208, 21 S. Ct. 331, 45 L. Ed. 497 (1901).

[101] *Galbes v. Girard,* 46 Fed. 500 (C.C.S.D. Cal., 1891).

[102] *Beers v. Arkansas,* 20 How. 527, 15 L. Ed. 991 (1858).

[103] *Smith v. Rackliffe,* 87 Fed. 964 (C.C.A. 9th, 1898) ; *Smith v. Reeves,* 178 U.S. 436, 20 S. Ct. 919, 44 L. Ed. 1140 (1900) ; *Chandler v. Dix,* 194 U.S. 590, 24 S. Ct. 766, 48 L. Ed. 1129 (1904) ; *Murray v. Wilson Distilling Co.,* 213 U.S. 151, 29 S. Ct. 458, 53 L. Ed. 742 (1909) ; *Ford Motor Company v. Department of Treasury of State of Indiana,* 323 U.S. 459, 65 S. Ct. 347, 89 L. Ed. 389 (1945).

vision being to the effect that the legislature shall make provision therefor by law.[104]

New York has assumed a limited liability for the acts of its officers. Section 12 of the Court of Claims Act [105] removed the defense of sovereignty in an action for damages for a wrongful act on the part of the State. That is, Section 12 *waived immunity from suit.* Section 12a, added in 1929,[106] *waived immunity from liability.* The section reads:

> The state hereby waives its immunity from liability for the torts of its officers and employees and consents to have its liability for such torts determined in accordance with the same rules of law as apply to an action in the supreme court against an individual or a corporation, and the state hereby assumes liability of such acts, and jurisdiction is hereby conferred upon the court of claims to hear and determine all claims against the state to recover damages for injuries to property or for personal injury *caused by the misfeasance or negligence of the officers or employees of the state while acting as such officer or employee.*[107]

Section 12a, according to the New York Court of Appeals,

> . . . constitutes a recognition and acknowledgment of a moral duty demanded by the principles of equity and justice. It includes only claims which appear to the judicial mind and conscience to be such as the Legislature may declare to be affected by a moral obligation and which the state should satisfy. . . . It declares that no longer will the state use the mantle of sovereignty to protect itself from such consequences as follow negligent acts of individuals. It admits that in such negligence cases the sovereign ought to and promises that in the future it will voluntarily discharge its moral obligations in the same manner as the citizen is forced to perform a duty which courts and Legislatures have so long held, as to him, to be a legal liability. It transforms an unenforceable moral obligation into an actionable legal right, and applies to the state the rule *respondent superior.*[108]

The Illinois constitution, Art. 4, Sec. 26, declares that "The State of Illinois shall never be made defendant in any court of law and equity." But the Illinois Court of Claims Act, Sec. 6(4) empowers the Court of Claims

---

[104] C. B. Nutting, "Legislative Practice Regarding Tort Claims Against the State," 4 *Missouri Law Review* (1939), 1 ff.

[105] *Laws of 1920,* c. 922.

[106] *Laws of 1929,* c. 467.

[107] Italics supplied.

[108] *Jackson v. State,* 261 N.Y. 134, 138, 184 N.E. 735, 736 (1933).

To hear and determine all claims and demands, legal and equitable, liquidated and unliquidated, *ex contractu* and *ex delicto,* which the State, as a sovereign commonwealth, should, in equity and conscience discharge and pay; . . . .

The courts of Illinois have held that the State is not liable, under the Court of Claims Act, for the negligence of its officers in the performance of governmental duties; and that the Act does not enlarge, or otherwise change, the existing liability of the State; but that it merely defines the jurisdiction of the Court of Claims, and limits that jurisdiction to claims in respect to which the State would be liable at law or equity if the State were suable.[109]

The Doctrine of State Immunity as a Rule of Political Action

The theoretical basis of the doctrine of state immunity may be admitted, but the assumptions of public policy advanced to support the doctrine as a rule of political action are questionable. The juristic entity, the state, can act only through agents. The moral and intellectual limitations of these agents are some of the hazards of political life. Therefore, when public officers act under color of law, sound reason requires that they shall be deemed to engage the responsibility of the community or state. It is unjust to hold the honest but mistaken officer responsible in private actions for tort; it is equally unjust to shift the burden of damage sustained to the shoulders of the helpless individual. The United States and the States have surrendered their sovereign immunity to some extent by permitting themselves to be sued in courts of claims, but the degree of liability is far too limited. The arbitrary or dishonest officer need not go unpunished, but his responsibility should be to the state and not to the individual.

There has been much erudite discussion of the theoretical and historical bases of the doctrine of state irresponsibility.[110] It has been argued with plausible learning that *fault* is personal; that it implies a breach of duty; that a sovereign state creates and is not subject to legal duties, and so cannot commit a fault or tort; that, therefore, an officer who commits a fault acts *ultra vires* and not as an agent of the state.

A distinction is commonly made between *corporate* and *governmental* functions of the government of a state. The former relate

---

[109] *Harry S. Kramer, Claimant, v. Illinois, Respondent,* 8 Ill. Ct. Cl. 31 (1934).
[110] See footnote 1 to this chapter.

to such activities as might be undertaken by a private corporation, for instance, the exercise of proprietary rights and the conclusion of contracts for material or services. Here the principles of private law are deemed properly applicable. Governmental functions pertain to acts of public authority, acts of sovereignty—in general, the exercise of legislative, executive, and judicial power. Here the rules of private law are held inapplicable. But an abstruse concept of sovereignty has little relation to reality in our world, and it is increasingly difficult to distinguish between corporate and governmental functions in the modern administrative state. Responsibility for "corporate" acts rests upon the same foundation as responsibility for "governmental" acts, namely the will of the state. The issue is not for the closet philosopher or the spinner of "gossamer distinctions"—it is one for the lawmaker, to be resolved according to the formula of social expediency. The views of Hobbes, Austin, or Bluntschli are interesting but not controlling. A "sovereign" state can with equal facility assume or not assume responsibility for the torts of its officers—it is a decision that involves the sovereign prerogative of choice. It is not necessary to resort to labored argument in order to justify tort responsibility. Through the law of municipal corporations, the creation of courts of claims, and the passage of limited torts claims acts, we have made inroads into the sovereign "immunity," but "we still have a long way to go to rid our law of the artifices, fictions, symbols and phrases which have served as excuses to make the group irresponsible." [111]

Under the French system of administrative law, state responsibility in tort has received its greatest extension. "In the process of developing this great body of administrative law (the *droit administratif*) the classical distinction between *actes de gestion publique* (administrative or 'corporate' acts) and *actes de puissance publique* or *actes d'autorité* ('governmental acts') has become overshadowed and immaterial, and while responsibility cannot be charged to the State, in the absence of legislation, for ordinary judicial or legislative acts or for certain high political acts, the acts of administrative officers inflicting special injury on individuals subject the State, almost without exception, to responsibility." [112] The state is not responsible for the *personal* acts or faults of the officer (*fautes personnelles*) but only for his *official* acts or faults (*fautes de service*). For his *personal faults* (acts outside the scope of the office and moti-

---

[111] E. M. Borchard, "Theories of Governmental Responsibility," 28 *Columbia Law Review* (1928), 603.

[112] *Ibid.*, p. 739.

vated by malice or passion), the functionary is accountable to the ordinary courts. But the Council of State (the highest administrative court) has interpreted "acts of authority" broadly so as to make a fault one of service whenever possible, thus supporting the view that the distinction between personal faults and faults of service is being abandoned.[113]

Governments in our day exercise a large number of commercial, industrial, and managerial functions which affect the rights of individuals. The assumption of these powers should carry correlative responsibilities. The question is not what a state *can* do, but what it *should* do—it is a question of *moral*, not *legal* responsibility. "Whether this immunity is an absolute survival of the monarchial privilege, or is a manifestation merely of power, or rests on abstract legal grounds, . . . it undoubtedly runs counter to modern democratic notions of the moral responsibility of the State." [114]   And again in *Larson v. Domestic & Foreign Commerce Corp.,* Mr. Justice Frankfurter, dissenting, said: " 'Sovereign immunity' carries an august sound. But very recently we recognized that the doctrine is in 'disfavor.' " [115]

[113] J. W. Garner, "Anglo-American and Continental European Administrative Law," 8 *New York University Law Quarterly Review* (1929), 387, 402, 411.

[114] Mr. Justice Frankfurter, dissenting in *Great Northern Life Insurance Co. v. Read,* 322 U.S. 47, 59, 64 S. Ct. 873, 879, 88 L. Ed. 1121 (1944). Two judges of the Utah Supreme Court, dissenting in *Bingham v. Board of Education of Ogden City,* 223 Pac. (2d) 432 (1941) held that the entire doctrine of sovereign immunity was unsound in principle and inconsistent with justice.

[115] 337 U.S. 682, 723, 69 S. Ct. 1457, 1478 (1949), citing *Federal Housing Administration v. Burr,* 309 U.S. 242, 245, 60 S. Ct. 488, 490, 84 L. Ed. 724 (1940).

Chapter 6

THE RULE OF LAW: THE LIABILITY
OF PUBLIC OFFICERS

The Anglo-American Rule of Law.—Under the Anglo-American *rule of law,* officers and citizens are subject to the same law in the same courts, and officers are personally liable for both official and personal faults in private actions for damages.[1] The state ordinarily assumes no responsibility for the tortious acts of its agents. William A. Robson has made this observation on the rule of law:

> The liability of the individual official for wrongdoing committed in the course of his duty, on which so much praise has been bestowed by English writers, is essentially a relic from past centuries when government was in the hands of a few prominent, independent, and substantial persons, so-called Public Officers, who were in no way responsible to ministers or elected legislatures or councils. . . . Such a doctrine is utterly unsuited to the twentieth-century state, in which the Public Officer has been superseded by armies of anonymous and obscure civil servants acting directly under the orders of their superiors, who are ultimately responsible to an elected body. The exclusive liability of the individual officer is a doctrine typical of a highly individual common law. It is of decreasing value today, and is small recompense for an irresponsible state. The doctrine has been abandoned, in whole or in part, by the more intelligent legal systems in the Continent.[2]

This phase of the rule of law—the doctrine that an officer is personally liable for his official as well as personal faults—resulted from the desire of the English Courts to protect private property rights. Since the King was immune from suit under the theory that he could do no wrong, the King's officer was the only party upon whom the courts could fix responsibility. In the United States the national and State governments inherited the immunity of the English Crown,

[1] *Cf.* J. H. Morgan, Introduction to Gleeson E. Robinson, *Public Authorities and Legal Liability* (University of London Press, London, 1925), pp. 49–51.

[2] "Report of the Committee on Ministers' Powers," 3 *Political Quarterly* (1932), 346, 357–58. Quoted by Walter Gellhorn, *Administrative Law—Cases and Comments* (2d ed., The Foundation Press, Inc., Brooklyn, 1947), pp. 298–99.

and they declined responsibility for the torts of their officers. Thus the American courts followed the practice of the English courts of holding the officers personally liable for their torts.

But official responsibility is subject to a number of practical qualifications. The administration of law frequently requires that a person's rights be put in jeopardy pending a determination of legal issues. Therefore, it is familiar practice to arrest, publicly charge, and imprison a person accused of crime, even though under our legal system he is deemed innocent until proved guilty. Similarly, property may be seized or impounded pending a judicial determination of legality. Temporary injunctions may prevent persons from exercising a privilege (as by a licensee, an office holder, or a striker) or enjoying the use of property. In each of these cases the action taken is *summary* but *temporary*, pending final determination of the issue on its merits upon notice and hearing.[3]

The conflicting problems presented to the courts by the rule of law have been described as:

> One, the protection of the individual against oppressive official action, and in the other, the protection of the whole people by protecting their officers against vindicative, and retaliatory damage suits, in order to insure their fearless and effective administration of the law.[4]

Liability to the Public.—CRIMINAL LIABILITY. Public officers, even more than other persons, are required to obey the law. A crime is an offense against the state. An officer, judicial or executive, cannot justify a wrong against the state by his position as officer of the state. At common law, nonfeasance and misfeasance in office are indictable offenses,[5] except that discretionary acts must be wilful or corrupt and the highest executive officers are excepted.[6] Furthermore, State and national laws impose criminal liability for specified acts of specified officers or of officers generally. A federal statute of 1825 provided for fine or imprisonment of "every officer of the United States who is guilty of extortion under color of his office."[7] Election officials have been punished for "fraud or delinquency" in connection with an election.[8] Judges may be held criminally liable for accepting bribes or receiving illegal fees; prosecuting attorneys for malicious prosecution, suppression of evidence, or removing pub-

---

[3] See Gellhorn, *op. cit.*, pp. 283–90, for cases.

[4] *Cooper v. O'Conner*, 99 F. (2d) 135, 137 (App. D.C., 1938).

[5] *Commonwealth v. Coyle*, 160 Pa. St. 36 (1894).

[6] Joel P. Bishop, *Criminal Law* (T. H. Flood & Co., Chicago, 1923), Vol. I, § 462.

[7] 4 *Stat.* 118; *United States v. Germaine*, 99 U.S. 508, 25 L. Ed. 482 (1879).

[8] *Ex parte Siebold*, 100 U.S. 371, 25 L. Ed. 717 (1880).

lic records; police officers for false imprisonment, extortion, assault, use of third degree, intimidation, and so on. Section 19 of the Federal Criminal Code makes it a criminal conspiracy for "two or more persons" to "conspire to injure, oppress, threaten, or intimidate any citizen in the free exercise or enjoyment of any right or privilege secured to him by the Constitution or laws of the United States." [9] Section 20 provides that "Whoever, _under color of any law,_ statute, ordinance, regulation, or custom, _wilfully_ subjects, or causes to be subjected, any inhabitant of any State, Territory, or District to the deprivation of _any rights, privileges, or immunities secured or protected by the Constitution and laws of the United States,_ . . . shall be fined not more than $1,000, or imprisoned not more than one year, or both." [10]

Section 19 originated in the Enforcement Act of 1870,[11] and Section 20 in the Civil Rights Act of 1866.[12] These Acts were designed to enforce the Thirteenth, Fourteenth, and Fifteenth Amendments. Section 20 materially broadened the scope of the Civil Rights Act— from a specific enumeration of civil rights to "any rights, privileges, or immunities secured or protected by the Constitution and laws of the United States."

The penalties under both Sections are applicable to _individuals._ The acts made punishable under Section 19 are _individual_ acts. Presumably, therefore, this Section does not include violations of the Fourteenth Amendment. Section 20, however, applies to acts committed "under color of any law," federal or State. This obviously has reference to acts taken by _public officers,_ both federal and State, since only _de facto_ or _de jure_ officers can act "under color of law."

In _United States v. Classic_ [13] the Supreme Court held that election officers in Louisiana, who falsely counted the ballots of qualified negro voters at a primary election, were guilty of conspiring under Section 19 and of wilfully depriving said voters within the meaning of Section 20 of the right to vote secured by Article I, Section 2, of the Constitution. Three dissenting Justices argued that "§19 lacks the requisite specificity necessary for inclusion of acts which interfere with the nomination of party candidates"; and, "It is not enough for us to find in the vague penumbra of a statute some offense about which Congress could have legislated and then to particularize it as

---

[9] Act of March 4, 1909, 35 _Stat._ 1092, c. 321, 18 _U.S.C.A._ § 241.
[10] _Ibid.,_ 18 _U.S.C.A._ § 242. Italics supplied.
[11] Act of May 31, 1870, 16 _Stat._ 141, c. 114, § 6.
[12] Act of April 9, 1866, 14 _Stat._ 27, § 2.
[13] 313 U.S. 299, 61 S. Ct. 1031, 85 L. Ed. 1368 (1941).

a crime because it is highly offensive. . . . Civil liberties are too dear to permit conviction for crimes which are only implied and which can be spelled out only by adding inference to inference." [14]

Does Section 20 apply to deprivations of rights protected by the Fourteenth Amendment? "The congressional purpose," said a United States district court, "obviously, is to assure enjoyment of the rights of citizens defined by the Fourteenth Amendment, *including the mandate that no State shall deprive any person of life, liberty, or property without due process of law. . . ."* [15] In 1945, this question came before the Supreme Court for full consideration for the first time in *Screws v. United States*,[16] when a majority of the Court held, against a well-reasoned dissent by three of the Justices,[17] that Section 20 established, in the words of the dissenters, "as federal crimes violations of the vast, undisclosed range of the Fourteenth Amendment." [18] Said Mr. Justice Rutledge in a concurring opinion:

> Historically, the section's function and purpose have been to secure rights given by the Amendment. From the Amendment's adoption until 1874, it was Fourteenth Amendment legislation. Surely when in that year the section was expanded to include other rights these were not dropped out.[19]

Since the Fourteenth Amendment applies to *State action* only, it follows from the above ruling that a State officer who acts "under color of law" *acts for the State;* and Congress may punish a State officer for performing an "act of the State" which violates the Fourteenth Amendment. The single act of the State officer at once engages the responsibility of his State under the Fourteenth Amendment and fixes his personal criminal liability under Section 20. That would seem to be a questionable constitutional doctrine, for not only does Section 20 punish an officer for the acts of his State, but it makes criminal a deprivation of rights under the undefined constitutional provisions of due process, equal protection, and privileges and

[14] 313 U.S. at 340, 331–32, 61 S. Ct. at 1049, 1045–46, 85 L. Ed. at 1391, 1386. Mr. Justice Douglas joined by Mr. Justice Black and Mr. Justice Murphy.

[15] *United States v. Trierweiler*, 52 F. Supp. 4, 5 (D.C.E.D. Ill., 1943). Italics supplied.

[16] 325 U.S. 91, 65 S. Ct. 1031, 89 L. Ed. 1495 (1945). Only three reported cases had considered Section 20 prior to the instant case: *United States v. Buntin*, 10 Fed. 730 (C.C.S.D. Ohio, 1882); *United States v. Stone*, 188 Fed. 836 (D.C.D. Md., 1911); *United States v. Classic*, 313 U.S. 299, 61 S. Ct. 1031, 85 L. Ed. 1368 (1941). It was assumed unnecessarily in the Classic case that "the scope of Section 20 was coextensive with the Fourteenth Amendment."

[17] Mr. Justice Roberts, Mr. Justice Frankfurter, and Mr. Justice Jackson.

[18] 325 U.S. at 157, 65 S. Ct. at 1061, 89 L. Ed. at 1532.

[19] 325 U.S. at 123–24, 65 S. Ct. at 1046, 89 L. Ed. at 1515.

immunities of United States citizens—provisions that are not and
can not be defined by Congress, but must be "argumentatively spelled
out through the judicial process" by changing majorities of the
Supreme Court.[20] *This is not punishment according to due process.*
As pointed out by the dissenting Justices:

> To base federal prosecutions on the shifting and indeterminate deci-
> sions of courts is to sanction prosecution for crimes based upon defini-
> tions made by courts. This is tantamount to creating a new body of
> federal criminal law.
>
> It cannot be too often emphasized that as basic a difference as any
> between our notions of law and those of legal systems not founded
> on Anglo-American conceptions of liberty is that crimes must be defined
> by the legislature. The legislature does not meet this requirement by
> issuing a blank check to courts for their retrospective finding that
> some act done in the past comes within the contingencies and conflicts
> that inhere in ascertaining the content of the Fourteenth Amendment
> by "the gradual process of judicial inclusion and exclusion." [21]

And the introduction of the term "wilfully" into Section 20 in
1909 did not add definiteness to the congressional definition of
criminal action, although the majority rested their decision thereon
Said Mr. Justice Douglas:

> The constitutional requirement that a criminal statute be definite
> serves a high function. It gives a person acting with reference to the
> statute fair warning that his conduct is within its prohibition. This
> requirement is met when a statute prohibits only "wilful" acts in the

---

[20] That indefiniteness is the chief characteristic of "due process" may be inferred
from the following observation by Mr. Justice Frankfurter:

"Due process of law thus conveys neither formal nor fixed nor narrow requirements. It is the compendious expression for all those rights which the courts must
enforce because they are basic to our free society. But basic rights do not become
petrified as of any one time, even though, as a matter of human experience, some
may not too rhetorically be called eternal verities. It is of the very nature of free
society to advance in its standards of what is deemed reasonable and right. Representing as it does a living principle, due process is not confined within a permanent
catalogue of what may at a given time be deemed the limits or the essentials of fundamental rights.

"To rely on a tidy formula for the easy determination of what is a fundamental
right for purposes of legal enforcement may satisfy a longing for certainty but ig-
nores the movements of a free society. It belittles the scale of the conception of due
process. The real clue to the problem confronting the judiciary in the application of
the Due Process Clause is not to ask where the line is once and for all to be drawn
but to recognize that it is for the Court to draw it by the gradual and empiric process
of 'inclusion and exclusion.'" *Wolf v. People of the State of Colorado,* 338 U.S. 25,
27, 69 S. Ct. 1359, 1361, 93 L. Ed. 1782 (1949).

[21] 325 U.S. at 152, 65 S. Ct. at 1059, 89 L. Ed. at 1530.

sense we have explained [that of acting with a "bad purpose" or "evil motive"]. One who does act with such specific intent is aware that what he does is precisely that which the statute forbids.[22]

To which Mr. Justice Roberts retorted:

> It is as novel as it is an inadmissible principle that a criminal statute of indefinite scope can be rendered definite by requiring that a person "wilfully" commit what Congress has not defined but which, if Congress had defined, could constitutionally be outlawed. . . .
>
> "Wilfully" doing something that is forbidden, when that something is not sufficiently defined according to the general conceptions of requisite certainty in our criminal law, is not rendered sufficiently definite by that unknowable having been done "wilfully." [23]

The net result of the Classic and Screws cases is to make it a federal crime for a State officer to violate a State law (for in both cases the acts complained of were in defiance of State law) and to subject the officer to punishment under both federal and State law. It would seem to be a dubious play on words to hold that an officer acts for the State when he clearly disobeys the commands of the State. Some official authentication would seem to be required to engage the responsibility of the State, such as a legislative act or a judicial decision or even failure, perhaps, to punish the officer. Until it can be fairly said that the State has *adopted* the action of the officer by some act of commission or omission, the officer would seem to be guilty of a *personal fault,* for which, *if it violates a national law,* Congress undoubtedly can prescribe a penalty. But can Congress punish *individuals* for *acts which the Constitution ascribes to States,* such as violations of the Fourteenth Amendment? If a *State* cannot commit a *crime,* can its officers do so *in the name of the State?* Is Section 20 as applied in the Screws case a joint legislative and judicial confession of lack of constitutional power to enforce a judgment against a State—a lack of power to coerce a State—despite the assertion (but not exertion) of such power in *Virginia v. West Virginia?* [24] No wonder Mr. Justice Frankfurter has found ". . . the state of the law regarding litigation brought formally against an official but intrinsically against the Government is . . . compounded of confusion and artificialities." [25]

[22] 325 U.S. at 103–4, 65 S. Ct. at 1036, 89 L. Ed. at 1504.
[23] 325 U.S. at 153–54, 65 S. Ct. at 1060, 89 L. Ed. at 1530, 1531.
[24] 246 U.S. 565, 38 S. Ct. 400, 62 L. Ed. 883 (1918).
[25] *Snyder v. Buck,* 340 U.S. 15, 22, 71 S. Ct. 93, 97 (1950). To add to the "confusion" noted above, *United States v. Williams,* 341 U.S. 70, 71 S. Ct. 581 (1951) held (four Justices dissenting) that the rights which Congress sought to protect under Sections 19 and 20 against interference by private individuals arise from the

CUSTODIAL RESPONSIBILITY. Many public officers have custody of public property or of persons in the care of the state. Such officers have special legal responsibilities. At common law an officer having property in his custody in his official capacity is a *bailee,* and the general rule of official obligation is that the officer shall perform his duties to protect and return such property to the bailor, honestly, faithfully, and to the best of his ability, but that he is not responsible for loss which does not result from his fault or negligence.

It is laid down by Justice Story that officers of courts having the custody of property of suitors are bailees, and liable only for the exercise of good faith and reasonable diligence, and not responsible for loss occurring without their fault or negligence. Trustees are only bound to exercise the same care and solicitude with regard to the trust property which they would exercise with regard to their own. Equity will not exact more of them. They are not liable for a loss by theft without their fault. But this exemption ceases when they mix the trust-money with their own, whereby it loses its identity, and they become mere debtors. Receivers, appointed by the court, though held to a stricter accountability than trustees, on account of their compensation, are nevertheless not liable for a loss without their fault; and they are entitled to manage the property and transact the business in their hands in the usual and accustomed way. A marshal appointed by a court of admiralty to take care of a ship and cargo is responsible only for a prudent and honest execution of his commission. . . . A postmaster is bound to exercise due diligence, and nothing more, in the care of matter deposited in the postoffice. He is not liable for a loss happening without his fault or negligence. . . .

In certain cases, it is true, a more stringent accountability is exacted; as in the case of a sheriff, in reference to prisoners held by him in custody, where the law puts the whole power of the county at his disposal and makes him liable for an escape in all cases, *except* where it is caused by an act of God or the public enemy. . . .

But the legislature can undoubtedly, at its pleasure, change the common-law rule of responsibility. And with regard to the public moneys, as they often accumulate in large sums in the hands of collectors, receivers, and depositories, and as they are susceptible of being embezzled and privately used without detection, and are often difficult of identification, legislation is frequently adopted for the purpose

relationship of the individual and the federal government and exclude those rights which the Constitution merely guarantees from interference by a State. Thus, an indictment against a police officer and employees of a private corporation for extorting confessions from other employees by the "third degree" was not sufficient to charge an offense under Sections 19 and 20 notwithstanding an allegation that the defendants acted under color of law.

of holding such officers to a very strict accountability. And in some cases they are spoken of as though they were absolute debtors for, and not simply custodians of, the money in their hands.[26]

To insure honest and faithful performance of custodial duties, the law ordinarily imposes criminal sanctions for unauthorized use of moneys entrusted to the care of the officer; and requires the posting of an official bond, under the terms of which the officer and his sureties are liable (to the amount of the bond) unless the officer is prevented from performing his duties by the law or by an overruling necessity, such as an act of God or of a public enemy.[27]

IMPEACHMENT. Public officers are subject to impeachment in accordance with federal and State constitutional provisions.[28] Impeachment may lie for offenses ranging from "any misdemeanor in office" [29] or "misconduct and maladministration in their offices" [30] to "treason, bribery, or other high crimes or misdemeanors." [31] In general, the Senate is constituted the high court of impeachment [32] and only "civil" officers are subject to impeachment. Thus, military officers and members of Congress, not being *civil officers,* are not impeachable under the federal Constitution.[33] Impeachment proceedings may be instituted even after the accused officer has resigned from office, since the object of impeachment is not only to remove the accused from office but also to disqualify him from holding office in the future.[34] Federal impeachment trials have not been limited to offenses

[26] *United States v. Thomas,* 15 Wall. 337, 342–45, 21 L. Ed. 89, 91–92 (1872).
[27] *Ibid.*
[28] Provided for in all the State Constitutions except Oregon. Impeachment under the federal Constitution is available against "the President, Vice-President and all civil officers of the United States."
[29] Constitution of South Carolina, see *The State ex parte v. O'Driscoll,* 2 Treadway's South Carolina Report 713 (1815).
[30] Constitution of Massachusetts, Part II, chap. i, § v, Art. 8. See *Opinion of the Justices,* 167 Mass. 599, 46 N.E. 118 (1897).
[31] United States *Constitution,* Art. II, Sec. 4.
[32] In Nebraska trial is by the courts upon charges preferred by the legislature. *Constitution,* Art. II, Sec. 17.
[33] Members of Congress are not "officers of the United States" since they are not appointed by the President, courts of law, or heads of departments. *United States v. Germaine,* 99 U.S. 508, 25 L. Ed. 482 (1879). In impeachment proceedings against Senator Blount in the United States Senate he was acquitted on the ground that he was not a civil officer of the United States. W. W. Willoughby, *The Constitutional Law of the United States* (Baker, Voorhis & Co., New York, 1929), Vol. III, p. 1449. That is, an officer of the United States is one who has been appointed in any of the modes prescribed in Article II, Sec. 2, Cl. 2 of the Constitution; any person in the employ of the United States not so appointed is not an officer of the United States. *Hoeppel v. United States,* 85 F. (2d) 237 (App. D.C., 1936) ; *Morgenthau v. Barrett,* 108 F. (2d) 481 (App. D.C., 1939).
[34] Willoughby, *op. cit.,* Vol. III, pp. 1448–49.

made penal by statute. That is, "high misdemeanors" are not necessarily indictable offenses but may include general misbehavior in office.[35] The House Committee recommending impeachment of District Judge English in 1926 made this sweeping statement:

> It is now, we believe, considered that impeachment is not confined alone to acts which are forbidden by the Constitution or Federal statutes. The better sustained and modern view is that the provision for impeachment in the Constitution applies not only to high crimes and misdemeanors as those words were understood at common law but also acts which are not defined as criminal and made subject to indictment, and also to those which affect the public welfare. Thus an official may be impeached for offenses of a political character and for gross betrayal of public interests. Also for abuses or betrayal of trusts, for inexcusable negligence of duty, for the tyrannical abuse of power, or, as one writer puts it, for "a breach of official duty by malfeasance, including conduct such as drunkenness, when habitual, or in the performance of official duties, gross indecency, profanity, obscenity, or other language used in the discharge of an official function, which tends to bring the office into disrepute, or for an abuse or reckless exercise of discretionary power as well as the breach of an official duty imposed by statute or common law." No judge may be impeached for a wrong decision.[36]

Conviction upon impeachment "shall not extend further than to removal from office, and disqualification to hold and enjoy any office of honor, trust or profit under the United States; but the party convicted shall nevertheless be liable and subject to indictment, trial, judgment, and punishment, according to law." [37] That is, judgment of impeachment cannot extend to fine or corporal punishment. "The offenders, offenses, court and punishment are all distinctly impressed with political features." [38]

Impeachment has not been a useful institution for popular control of official misconduct. It has been pretty well discredited by such disgraceful proceedings as the trials of Warren Hastings in England and President Johnson in the United States.[39] The Johnson trial

[35] David Y. Thomas, "The Law of Impeachment in the United States," 2 *American Political Science Review* (1908), 378 ff.

[36] Quoted by Willoughby, *op. cit.*, Vol. III, pp. 1449–50.

[37] *Constitution*, Art. I, Sec. 3, Cl. 7. Also the general rule in the States.

[38] Senator Davis, at trial of President Johnson, in the Senate of the United States, 1868. See F. J. Goodnow, *Selected Cases on the Law of Officers* (Callaghan & Co., Chicago, 1906), p. 287.

[39] Four State governors have been impeached: Sulzer of New York in 1913, Ferguson of Texas in 1917, Walton of Oklahoma in 1923, and Johnston of Oklahoma in 1929. Impeachment proceedings have been instituted against eleven federal officers (not including Senator Blount); nine federal judges; Secretary of War,

demonstrated that impeachment can be a dangerous political weapon in times of bitter partisanship.

Liability for Ministerial Acts.—Just as courts distinguish between *ministerial* and *discretionary* acts in the matter of equity relief, so they distinguish in the matter of liability. In general, officers are liable for their torts in the exercise of the former but not the latter.

> The duty is ministerial, when the law, exacting its discharge, prescribes and defines the time, mode and occasion of its performance, with such certainty that nothing remains for judgment or discretion. Official action, the result of performing a certain and specific duty arising from fixed and designated facts, is a ministerial act.[40]

For such an act it is "an undisputed rule" that an officer "is amenable to the law for his conduct, and is liable to any party specially injured by his acts of *misfeasance* or *nonfeasance*," [41] and good faith is not a defense.[42] "Where an officer injures another while performing *ministerial* duties, he is liable." [43] Moreover, "Where the issue is negligence, motives or good faith are immaterial." [44] Where a duty is imposed upon an officer by law, failure to act constitutes *nonfeasance*, and wrongful action *misfeasance*, for which not only the officer but his sureties are liable upon his official bond if a bond is required to insure the faithful performance of the office.[45]

> The rule is well settled, that where the law requires absolutely a ministerial act to be done by a public officer, and he neglects or refuses to do such act, he may be compelled to respond in damages to the extent of the injury arising from his conduct. There is an unbroken current of authorities to this effect. A mistake as to his duty and honest intentions will not excuse the offender.[46]

William W. Belknap (August 1, 1876); and President Andrew Johnson (May 26, 1868). All were acquitted except federal judges John Pickering (March 12, 1804), West H. Humphreys (June 26, 1862), Robert W. Archbold (January 13, 1913), and Halsted L. Ritter (April 17, 1936). The judges acquitted were Samuel Chase (March 1, 1805), James H. Peck (January 31, 1831), Charles Swayne (February 27, 1905), and Harold Louderback (May 24, 1933). Impeachment proceedings against Judge George W. English were dropped when he resigned his office (December 13, 1926).

[40] *Grider v. Talley,* 77 Ala. 422, 425 (1884).
[41] *Ibid.,* at 424.
[42] *Lowe v. Conroy,* 120 Wis. 151, 97 N.W. 942 (1904); *Pearson v. Zehr,* 138 Ill. 48, 29 N.E. 854 (1891).
[43] *Robinson v. Rohr,* 73 Wis. 436, 40 N.W. 668, 671 (1889).
[44] *Ibid.*
[45] *People ex rel. Kellogg v. Schuyler,* 4 N.Y. 173 (1850).
[46] *Amy v. Barkholder,* 11 Wall. 136, 138, 20 L. Ed. 101, 102 (1871).

Thus, liability has been sustained in cases involving negligent driving of a police car; [47] negligently shooting an innocent bystander while attempting to stop and search a truck suspected of transporting liquor; [48] and unnecessary clubbing while making an arrest.[49]

But an order issued by a superior officer, which presumably is valid because it relates to a subject matter within the jurisdiction of the superior, is a valid defense in an action for damages against the ministerial officer. Mr. Justice Field stated the rule as follows:

> . . . if the officer or tribunal possess jurisdiction over the subject-matter upon which judgment is passed, with power to issue an order or process for the enforcement of such judgment, and the order or process issued thereon to the ministerial officer is regular on its face, showing no departure from the law, or defect of jurisdiction over the person or property affected, then, in such cases, the order or process will give full and entire protection to the ministerial officer in its regular enforcement against any prosecution which the party aggrieved thereby may institute against him, although serious errors may have been committed by the officer or tribunal in reaching the conclusion or judgment upon which the order or process is issued.[50]

This rule is now generally followed. In *McCall v. McDowell* [51] it was pointed out that

> Between an order plainly legal and one palpably otherwise . . . there is a wide middle ground, where the ultimate legality and propriety of orders depends or may depend upon circumstances and conditions, of which it cannot be expected that the inferior is informed or advised. In such cases justice to the subordinate demands, and the necessities and efficiency of the public service require that the order of the superior should protect the inferior; leaving the responsibility to rest where it properly belongs—upon the officer who gave the command.[52]

The adoption of plans and specifications for public works by the proper officers is a *discretionary* (judicial) function; but when the same officers undertake to carry out such plans practically and to do

[47] *United States Fidelity & Guaranty Co. v. Samuels,* 116 Ohio St. 586 (1927).
[48] *Dean v. Brannon,* 139 Miss. 312, 104 So. 173 (1925).
[49] *Rice v. Lavin,* 199 Ky. 790 (1923).
[50] *Erskine v. Hohnboch,* 14 Wall. 613, 616–17, 20 L. Ed. 745, 747 (1872). But in *Tracy v. Swartwout,* 10 Pet. 80, 9 L. Ed. 354 (1836), a collector, a ministerial officer, acting under instructions of the Secretary of the Treasury, "who is expressly authorized to give instructions, as to the due enforcement of the revenue laws," was held liable for illegal acts and his "instructions, when not given in accordance with the law" did not "afford a justification."
[51] 1 Abb. (U.S.) 212 (1867).
[52] 1 Abb. at p. 222, quoted with approval in *Commonwealth v. Shortall,* 206 Pa. St. 165 (1903).

the work themselves, or to employ agents to execute the plans manually, then, if they are acting as public officers at all, they are merely *ministerial* officers and are liable to third persons for their negligence or misfeasance.[53] When a county judge excluded negroes from the jury on account of their color, his act was held to be ministerial, not judicial, and the judge was liable to prosecution under federal law.[54]

Liability for Discretionary Action.—Public officials must necessarily exercise discretionary powers. The *rule of law* is presumed to be government according to publicly declared rules, as opposed to government according to official discretion. But everywhere government is *by men*, and to these men must be left a "sovereign prerogative of choice," [55] a modicum of discretion. This is because some things cannot be done according to written rule, but must be left to the exercise of human judgment from case to case.

The general rule is that judicial officers are not liable to civil actions whilst exercising their judicial functions, however erroneously, negligently, or corruptly, so long as they act within the general scope of their jurisdiction. In *Bradley v. Fisher,* Mr. Justice Field said:

> Judges of courts of superior or general jurisdiction are not liable to civil actions for their judicial acts, even when such acts are in excess of their jurisdiction, and are alleged to have been done maliciously or corruptly. A distinction must be here observed between excess of jurisdiction and the clear absence of all jurisdiction over the subject-matter. Where there is clearly no jurisdiction over the subject-matter any authority exercised is an usurped authority, and for the exercise of such authority, when the want of jurisdiction is known to the judge, no excuse is permissible. . . .
>
> But for malice or corruption in their action whilst exercising their judicial functions within the general scope of their jurisdiction, the judges of these courts can only be reached by public prosecution in the form of impeachment, or in such other form as may be specifically prescribed.[56]

This freedom from personal liability is held to be essential to the independence of judges, who must be free to act upon their own convictions without fear of personal consequences. For the proper ex-

[53] *Robinson v. Rohr,* 73 Wis. 436, 40 N.W. 668 (1889).
[54] *Ex parte Virginia,* 100 U.S. 339, 25 L. Ed. 676 (1880).
[55] Oliver Wendell Holmes, *Collected Legal Papers* (Harcourt, Brace & Co., New York, 1920), p. 239.
[56] 13 Wall. 335, 351–52, 354, 20 L. Ed. 646, 651 (1872).

ercise of their judicial duties, judges are responsible to the public collectively and not to individuals, and the public has adequate remedies in the criminal statutes and in removal or impeachment proceedings.

In early federal cases involving the personal liability of *executive officers,* it was held that such officers were not punishable civilly for acts which required (by law) the exercise of opinion or judgment so long as they acted "honestly." This immunity resulted from the law which placed "a confidence in the opinion of the officer," not from the judicial nature of discretionary action.[57] Mr. Chief Justice Taney stated the doctrine thus:

> A public officer is not liable to an action if he falls into error in a case where the act to be done is not merely a ministerial one, but is one in relation to which it is his duty to exercise judgment and discretion, even though an individual may suffer by his mistake.[58]

The Chief Justice observed, in the instant case, that the officer "acted from a sense of public duty and without malice." [59] Later the Supreme Court observed that all "judicial officers, when acting on subjects within their jurisdiction, are exempted from civil prosecution for their acts"; and that since the position of a public officer invested with "discretionary powers" is in many respects "quasi-judicial," he "never has been, and never should be, made answerable for any injury, when acting within the scope of his authority, and not *influenced by malice, corruption, or cruelty."* [60]

Following the decision in *Bradley v. Fisher* [61] which emphatically established the immunity from civil actions of judges when acting judicially, the courts gradually adopted the doctrine that public officers (at least superior public officers) exercising discretionary powers act judicially and are, therefore, entitled to the personal immunity accorded judges.[62] Thus, in *Williams v. Weaver,* Mr. Justice Miller said that "an officer whose duty . . . is mainly judicial, is no more liable in damages personally for a mistaken construction of an

---

[57] *Crowell v. M'Fadon,* 8 Cranch 94, 98, 3 L. Ed. 499, 500 (1814); *Otis v. Watkins,* 9 Cranch 339, 3 L. Ed. 752 (1815).

[58] *Kendall v. Stokes,* 3 How. 87, 98, 11 L. Ed. 506, 512 (1845).

[59] 3 How. at 99, 11 L. Ed. at 512.

[60] *Wilkes v. Dinsman,* 7 How. 88, 129, 12 L. Ed. 618, 636 (1849). Italics supplied.

[61] 13 Wall. 335, 20 L. Ed. 646 (1872).

[62] See *Gottschalk v. Shepperd,* 65 N.D. 544, 260 N.W. 573 (1935); *Wasserman v. Kenosha,* 217 Wis. 223, 258, N.W. 857 (1935); *Hatfield v. Graham,* 73 W. Va. 759, 81 S.E. 533 (1914).

Act of Congress than he would be for mistaking the common law or a state statute." [63]   In *Spalding v. Vilas* the Court held

> . . . that the same general considerations of public policy and con-venience which demand for judges of courts of superior jurisdiction immunity from civil suits for damages arising from acts done by them in the course of the performance of their judicial functions, apply to a large extent to official communications made by *heads of executive departments* when engaged in the discharge of duties imposed upon them by law.[64]

A United States Attorney has been held to be "a quasi-judicial officer of the government," and, "The reasons for granting immunity to judges, jurors, attorneys, and executive officers of the govern-ment apply to a public prosecutor in the performance of the duties which rest upon him." [65]   In *Cooper v. O'Conner* [66] the court tended to extend the rule of judicial immunity to executive officers generally.

And, since personal or improper motives cannot be imputed to duly authorized official conduct, the general rule seems to be that public officers are not personally liable for *judicial* or *discretionary* acts, whatever their motives may be.[67]   In an early case a New York Court found that

> Where a duty judicial in nature is imposed upon a public officer, a private action will not be for misconduct or delinquency even if cor-rupt motives are charged. The same principle prevails where the party on whom the duty devolves, though not a judge, is clothed with discre-tionary powers to be exerted according to his sense of fitness and pro-priety. If such officers act corruptly, they are liable to impeachment or indictment.[68]

And a federal court said more recently:

> . . . if the act complained of was done within the scope of the offi-cer's duties as defined by law, the policy of the law is that he shall not be subjected to the harassment of civil litigation or be liable for civil damages because of a mistake of fact occurring in the exercise of his judgment or discretion, or because of erroneous construction and appli-

---

[63] 100 U.S. 547, 548, 25 L. Ed. 708, 709 (1880).
[64] 161 U.S. 483, 498, 16 S. Ct. 631, 637, 40 L. Ed. 781, 785 (1896). Italics supplied.
[65] *Yaselli v. Goff,* 12 F. (2d) 396, 404 (1926).
[66] 99 F. (2d) 135 (App. D.C., 1938).
[67] *Spalding v. Vilas,* 161 U.S. 483, 498, 16 S. Ct. 631, 637, 40 L. Ed. 781, 785 (1896).
[68] *Wilson v. Mayor,* 1 Denio (N.Y.) 595, 16 N.Y. Com. L. 906 (1845). Also, *Gottschalk v. Shepperd,* 65 N.D. 544, 260 N.W. 573 (1935); *Wasserman v. Kenosha,* 217 Wis. 223, 258 N.W. 857 (1935).

cation of the law. . . . It is now generally recognized that, as applied to some officers at least, even the absence of probable cause and the presence of malice or other bad motives are not sufficient to impose liability upon such an officer who acts within the general scope of his authority.[69]

As in the case of judicial officers, a distinction is drawn between administrative action which is manifestly or palpably *ultra vires* and "action having more or less connection with the general matters committed by law" to administrative control or supervision.[70] Thus a judge would be liable for damages resulting from the issuance of a void, pretended process, one unknown to the law, or from the issuance of a warrant on a complaint alleging facts which in no conceivable form could constitute an offense.[71] Similarly, a prosecuting attorney is answerable for damages resulting from an act performed outside the scope of his duties, as where he acts on a report submitted to him by a private investigator not verified by the prosecuting attorney, and arrests an innocent person without warrant.[72] A police officer is liable for the use of excessive force in making an arrest, and for using the "third degree" after arrest.[73]

The liability in many of these cases is more theoretical than real. It has been said that "a great majority of arrests by police officers are illegal in their inception, continuance, or termination."[74] Yet relatively few suits are brought against police officers. The average police officer probably is unable to pay substantial judgments, and this is equally true for most "inferior" public officers. And judges are inclined to give the officer the benefit of the doubt, particularly in cases involving persons with criminal records. In this the judge is aided by community opinion which too often is apathetic to, if it does not actually condone, police violence. Occasionally a Screws case[75] arouses our sense of civic responsibility, only to be relegated shortly to the lawbooks as classroom material. Clearing the channels of judicial and executive justice requires organized leadership, which is the special business of the legal profession.

Both judicial and administrative officers are liable for tortious ministerial acts. But the distinction drawn between *judicial* and

---

[69] *Cooper v. O'Conner*, 99 F. (2d) 135, 138, 140 (App. D.C., 1938).

[70] *Spalding v. Vilas*, 161 U.S. 483, 16 S. Ct. 631, 40 L. Ed. 781 (1896).

[71] "Judges," *American Jurisprudence*, Sec. 49.

[72] *Schneider v. Shepherd*, 192 Mich. 82 (1916).

[73] Leon Thomas David, *The Tort Liability of Public Officers* (Public Administration Service, Chicago, 1940), p. 60.

[74] Sam B. Warner, "The Uniform Arrest Act," 28 *Virginia Law Review* (January, 1942), 315.

[75] *Screws v. United States*, 325 U.S. 91, 65 S. Ct. 1031, 89 L. Ed. 1495 (1945).

ministerial action often has been artificial and arbitrary; and there is a tendency to label administrative action as "judicial" when an officer acts in good faith,[76] or even to disregard the judicial concept and rely upon public necessity as a defense, as did the New Jersey court when it said, "We think it not unreasonable to require him [the citizen] . . . to depend for redress upon the sense of justice of the public, rather than upon the right of action against public officers who have acted, as they thought, for the public weal in a matter of public duty."[77] Some statutes and ordinances confer a blanket immunity upon officers who act in good faith and without malice in the performance of their official duties.[78]

For example, a mayor ordering the destruction of a building to prevent the spread of a conflagration was held to act "judicially," and so without legal liability in a private suit for damages.[79] Likewise the adoption by a municipality of a plan for a sewerage system is "quasi-judicial" and "not subject to revision by a court or jury in a private action for not sufficiently draining a particular lot of land."[80] The imposition of a quarantine by health officers is a judicial act for which they are not personally liable "however erroneous or mistaken the action may be, provided there be no malice or wrong motive present."[81] An officer charged with the construction and maintenance of highways "is not personally liable for errors of judgment, or for acts done within the scope of his authority, unless it appears that the particular acts complained of were not only unnecessary, but were done corruptly, or maliciously."[82] At common law an election officer is not liable for wrongfully withholding from an elector the right to vote, unless malice is alleged and proved; this appears to be the general rule in the United States.[83] But an officer is not liable for a wrongful assessment of taxes, resulting from an erroneous construction and application of a statute in relation to

[76] *Beeks v. Dickinson County,* 131 Iowa 244, 108 N.W. 311 (1906).

[77] *Valentine v. Englewood,* 76 N.J.L. 509, 522, 71 Atl. 344, 349 (1908); *Cooper v. O'Conner,* 99 F. (2d) 135 (App. D.C., 1938); Gellhorn, *op. cit.,* pp. 301–2.

[78] See Building Code of the City of New York, *Administrative Code,* Sec. C., 26–204 I.

[79] *American Print Works v. Lawrence,* 23 N.J.L. 590, 600 (1851).

[80] *Johnston v. District of Columbia,* 118 U.S. 19, 21, 6 S. Ct. 923, 924, 30 L. Ed. 75, 76 (1885).

[81] *Beeks v. Dickinson County, Iowa,* 131 Iowa 244, 247, 108 N.W. 311, 312 (1906).

[82] *Wilbrecht v. Babcock,* 179 Minn. 263, 265, 228 N.W. 916 (1930); *Packard v. Voltz,* 94 Iowa 277, 62 N.W. 757 (1895).

[83] *Wheeler v. Patterson,* 1 N.H. 88, 8 Am. Dec. 41 (1817); *Jenkins v. Waldron,* 11 Johns. (N.Y.) 114, 6 Am. Dec. 359 (1814). *Contra: Lincoln v. Hapgood,* 11 Mass. 350 (1814).

matters committed by law to his control or supervision, even though his error be described as arbitrary, capricious, and malicious.[84]

There are persuasive reasons for the aforementioned rule. If an officer were to be held liable for injuries resulting from a mistake in judgment, as in the construction of sewers,[85] or the building of side-walks,[86] the courts would be exercising engineering judgment.

Exceptions to the general rule have been made where "there is otherwise no remedy for the injury because of the "very old and just maxim of the law" that "where there is a wrong, there is a remedy" —exceptions made by denominating the official acts "ministerial," [87] or by blunt refusal to extend judicial immunity to "quasi-judicial officers" where private property is involved, such as a summary destruction of property under health laws.[88]

But an officer

> . . . for any wanton or malicious abuse of legal process which is set on foot for the oppression of a citizen, must be held liable to the same or possibly to a greater extent than a private individual, still there must be undoubted evidence of malice, oppression, or wanton prosecution, with the absence of all probable cause or excuse, to hold a public officer liable for errors in the execution of his duties.[89]

In short, an officer is liable for a gross abuse of discretionary power.[90] False imprisonment and malicious prosecution are all-too-common forms of abuse of discretion. They are doubly reprehensible in that they breach both civil liberty and a public trust. But courts have considerable difficulty in determining whether the accused officer was in fact wilfully malicious or honestly mistaken or merely stupid. A strict enforcement of the rule of personal liability in these cases may lead to laxity in the enforcement of law, and the public generally will suffer; on the other hand, too much judicial leniency will encourage official carelessness, arbitrariness, and brutality which will not only jeopardize our freedom, but will breed public contempt for both the law and its officers. The following statement presents one horn of this dilemma:

[84] *Standard Nut Margarine Co. v. Mellon,* 63 App. D.C. 339, 72 F. (2d) 557, 559 (1934).
[85] *Atchison v. Challiss,* 9 Kan. 603 (1872).
[86] *Urquhart v. Ogdensburg,* 91 N.Y. 67 (1883).
[87] *McCord v. High,* 24 Iowa 336 (1868).
[88] *Lowe v. Conroy,* 120 Wis. 151, 97 N.W. 942 (1904).
[89] *Goodwin v. Guild,* 94 Tenn. 486, 491–92 (1895).
[90] *Kinneen v. Wells,* 144 Mass. 496, 11 N.E. 916 (1887); *Pike v. Megoun,* 44 Mo. 491 (1869).

✱ another way of saying "expertise" - the specialty of admin.

Actions for malicious prosecution are regarded by law with jealousy and they ought not to be favored but managed with great caution. Their tendency is to discourage prosecution for crime as they expose the prosecutor to civil suits, and the love of justice may not always be strong enough to induce individuals to commence prosecutions when, if they fail, they may be subjected to the expense of litigation, if they be not mulcted in damages. Suits by which the complainant in a criminal prosecution is made liable to an action for damages, at the suit of the person complained of, are not to be favored in law, as they have a tendency to deter men who know of the breaches of the law from prosecuting offenders thereby endangering the order and peace of the community.[91]

In regard to the granting of liquor licenses by judges of the Court of Quarter Sessions, the Supreme Court of Pennsylvania called attention to the distinction between discretion and arbitrary power in the following:

We have decided repeatedly, in language too plain to be misunderstood, that the granting of a license to sell liquor by retail rests in the sound discretion of the court below. . . . This discretion, however, is a legal discretion, to be exercised wisely, and not arbitrarily. A judge who refuses all applications for license, unless for cause shown, errs as widely as the judge who grants all applications. In either case, it is not the exercise of judicial discretion, but of arbitrary power.[92]

The social implications of the use and misuse of discretion vary with the type of officer or agency intrusted with discretion. Law enforcement officers—officers charged with the duty of punishing violators of the law—are subject to considerable pressure from without and from within. The public expects a prosecuting attorney, for example, to be *active;* his success is too often measured by the number of convictions to his credit. If he has political ambitions he may institute proceedings against, and even secure convictions of, innocent persons, for no better reason than to add "notches to his shooting iron." To the same end he may use his office to persecute the unpopular and to protect the powerful members of the community. Abuse of discretion by law enforcement officers constitutes misfeasance or malfeasance for which they may be removed from office.

Regulatory agencies are charged with the duty of directing and promoting social objectives, often involving the promotion or inhibition of social change. They were created by legislatures in response to pressures for changes in existing social relationships.

[91] *Van Sant v. American Express Co.,* 158 F. (2d) 924, 931 (C.C.A. 3d, 1946).
[92] *In re Sparrow,* 138 Pa. 116, 124, 20 Atl. 711, 712 (1890).

Thus, public utility and factory legislation resulted from pressures from farmers and shippers and consumers and employees for protection against the abuses of monopoly. These agencies operate, therefore, in cross currents of pressures from vested and group interests. If they misuse the discretionary powers vested in them, they not only destroy private rights, but they may perpetuate or create social maladjustments and so arrest the orderly process of social change.

Liability for Ultra Vires Acts.—An officer who acts in excess of his statutory authority acts at his peril. Thus, if health officers destroy food which they adjudge unfit for human use within the interdiction of the health laws,

> The *ex parte* finding of the health officers as to the fact is not in any way binding upon those who own or claim the right to sell the food. If a party cannot get his hearing in advance of the seizure and destruction, he has the right to have it afterward, which right may be claimed upon the trial in an action brought for the destruction of his property; and in that action those who destroyed it can only successfully defend if the jury shall find the fact of unwholesomeness, as claimed by them.[93]

To permit a jury of laymen to overrule a finding based upon scientific laboratory tests by medical officers, including the State bacteriologist, and to make the technicians liable for damages on the basis of such an uninformed verdict would seem to be due process in reverse.[94] This is to pervert the rule of law into the rule of ignorance, and to expose the public health to the mercy of local prejudice. To apply the jury system to technological determinations, not involving life or liberty, is an unrealistic concept of justice. To hold that neither technical competence nor good faith [95] is a good defense in an action against an officer for damages, is to encourage official laxity on the one hand and to discourage recruitment of competent officers on the other hand.

The doctrine of *Miller v. Horton* [96] has received too general acceptance. In that case Judge Oliver Wendell Holmes held that unless the legislature provides compensation for the owner of property erroneously damaged or destroyed by an officer, the officer is personally liable even if he acts in good faith. This is based on the

---

[93] Mr. Justice Peckham in *North American Cold Storage Co. v. City of Chicago*, 211 U.S. 306, 315–16, 29 S. Ct. 101, 104, 53 L. Ed. 195, 199–200 (1908).

[94] *Lowe v. Conroy*, 120 Wis. 151, 97 N.W. 942 (1904).

[95] *Pearson v. Zehr*, 138 Ill. 48, 29 N.E. 854 (1891).

[96] 152 Mass. 540, 26 N.E. 100 (1891).

principle that where there is a right there must be a remedy; so if the principal cannot be held liable, the agent will.

In an early case it was held that even when a ministerial officer acts in good faith and under instructions from a superior, he is not exonerated from the payment of damages for an injury resulting from his act if his instructions are found not to have been authorized by law.[97] His act has no legal justification. "Some personal inconvenience," said Mr. Justice McLean, "may be experienced by an officer who shall be held responsible in damages for illegal acts done under instructions of a superior; but, as the government in such cases is bound to indemnify the officer, there can be no eventual hardship."[98] But suppose the government is not "bound to indemnify the officer"— would the luckless officer be any less liable? Obviously not. The ruling in the instant case was qualified by a later decision which exonerated an officer acting under orders which his superior presumably had authority to make and enforce.[99]

Liability for Acts Under Unconstitutional Statute.[100]—An individual suffers a loss or injury through the enforcement of a legislative act which later is held unconstitutional. Who should bear the loss, the individual, the enforcing officer, or the state? The real wrongdoer is the legislature, not the enforcing officer. But the legislature represents the state, and the state cannot be sued without its consent. According to the void *ab initio* theory, the traditional theory of American courts,

> An unconstitutional act is not a law; it confers no rights; it imposes no duties; it affords no protection; it creates no office; it is, in legal contemplation, as inoperative as though it had never been passed.[101]
>
> When a statute is adjudged to be unconstitutional it is as if it had never been. Rights cannot be built under it; contracts which depend upon it for their consideration are void; it constitutes no protection to

---

[97] *Tracy v. Swartwout*, 10 Pet. 80, 9 L. Ed. 354 (1836).

[98] 10 Pet. at 98–99.

[99] *Erskine v. Hohnbach*, 14 Wall. 613, 20 L. Ed. 745 (1872).

[100] See O. P. Field, *The Effect of an Unconstitutional Statute* (University of Minnesota Press, Minneapolis, 1935); G. N. Crocker, "The Tort Liability of Public Officers Who Act Under Unconstitutional Statute," 2 *Southern California Law Review*, 236 ff.; L. T. David, "Tort Liability of Public Officers," 12 *Southern California Law Review*, 368 ff.; R. J. Moore, Jr., "Liability of Public Officers Acting Under Unconstitutional Statutes—Federal Rule," 22 *Virginia Law Review*, 316 ff.; M. P. Rapacz, "Protection of Officers Who Act Under Unconstitutional Statute," 11 *Minnesota Law Review* (1927), 585 ff.

[101] Mr. Justice Field in *Norton v. Shelby County*, 118 U.S. 425, 442, 6 S. Ct. 1121, 1125, 30 L. Ed. 178, 186 (1886).

one who has acted under it, and no one can be punished for having refused obedience to it before the decision was made.[102]

Therefore, officers are personally liable when enforcing unconstitutional statute, for "All persons are presumed to know the law, and if they act under an unconstitutional enactment of the legislature, they do so at their own peril and must take the consequences.[103]

This is the only *logical* theory of judicial review. But the exercise of judicial review has been characterized by expediency rather than by logic. Obviously the void *ab initio* doctrine would result in endless litigation and countless inequitable decisions. So the courts have compromised with logic and today the general rule is more honored in its "exceptions." In the apt words of Thomas Reed Powell "the law is full of collateral devices and doctrines that keep it from behaving as badly as it sometimes talks." [104]

Modern judicial practice varies from mere qualification to complete rejection of the void *ab initio* doctrine. Mr. Chief Justice Hughes made the following observation respecting the practical application of the doctrine:

> The courts below have proceeded on the theory that the Act of Congress, having been found to be unconstitutional, was not a law; that it was inoperative, conferring no rights and imposing no duties, and hence affording no basis for the challenged decree. . . It is quite clear, however, that such broad statements as to the effect of a determination of unconstitutionality must be taken with qualifications. The actual existence of a statute, prior to such a determination, is an operative fact that may have consequences which cannot justly be ignored. The past cannot always be erased by a new judicial declaration. The effect of the subsequent ruling, as to invalidity may have to be considered in various aspects,—with respect to particular relations, individual

---

[102] Thomas M. Cooley, *A Treatise on the Constitutional Limitations Which Rest Upon the Legislative Powers of the States of the American Union* (8th ed.; Little Brown & Co., Boston, 1927), Vol. I, p. 382. In *Chicago, Indianapolis & Louisville Ry. Co. v. Hackett,* 228 U.S. 559, 566, 33 S. Ct. 581, 584, 57 L. Ed. 966, 969 (1912), the Supreme Court said, in considering the effect of an Act of Congress on a State statute: "That Act was therefore as inoperative as if it had never been passed, for an unconstitutional Act is not a law, and can neither confer a right or immunity nor operate to supersede any existing valid law." *Dr. John Hopkins, Plaintiff in Error v. Clemson Agricultural College,* 221 U.S. 636, 643, 31 S. Ct. 654, 657, 55 L. Ed. 890, 895 (1911): "But a void act is neither a law nor a command. It is a nullity. It confers no authority. It affords no protection. Whoever seeks to enforce unconstitutional statutes, or to justify under them, or to obtain immunity through them, fails in his defense and in his claim of exemption from suit."

[103] *Sumner v. Beeler,* 50 Ind. 341–42, 19 Am. Rep. 718–19 (1875).

[104] Book Review, 48 *Harvard Law Review* (1935), 1271.

and corporate, and particular conduct, private and official. Questions of rights claimed to have become vested, of status, of prior determinations deemed to have finality and acted upon accordingly, of public policy in the light of the nature both of the statute and of its previous application, demand examination. These questions are among the most difficult of those which have engaged the attention of courts, state and federal, and it is manifest from numerous decisions that an all-inclusive statement of a principle of absolute retroactive invalidity cannot be justified.[105]

The preceding extract suggests two of the "collateral devices" employed by courts to qualify the void *ab initio* theory: the case to case theory and the presumption of validity theory. According to the former, a statute may not be wholly void or void in all situations or for all purposes—the constitutionality of the statute must be determined case by case,

> . . . for even unconstitutional statutes may not be treated as though they had never been written. They are not void for all purposes and to all persons.[106]

In *Dahnke-Walker Milling Co. v. Bondurant* the Court held that a judgment refers to litigated questions and the parties involved, and is not a device for establishing rules of general import. "A statute may be invalid as applied to one set of facts and yet valid as applied to another."[107]

It would be more accurate to say that a statute may be *inapplicable* "as applied to one set of facts" and *applicable* "as applied to another," since, as the statute is presumed to be valid, it should be so construed as to make it inapplicable to a "set of facts" which, if applicable, would make it unconstitutional. The case to case theory of constitutionality leaves public officers and judges of inferior courts without a known criterion to govern their actions, and the result is official confusion. The degree of administrative liability varies from State to State and from court to court.

Practical necessity has induced an increasing number of courts to adopt the view that a statute is presumed to be valid until declared invalid by a court of competent jurisdiction. In the words of a Connecticut Court:

[105] *Chicot County Drainage District v. Baxter State Bank,* 308 U.S. 371, 374, 60 S. Ct. 317, 318–19, 84 L. Ed. 329, 332–33 (1940).

[106] Mr. Justice Stone dissenting in *Frost v. Corporation Commission of Oklahoma,* 278 U.S. 515, 552, 49 S. Ct. 235, 248, 73 L. Ed. 483, 501–2 (1929).

[107] 257 U.S. 282, 289, 42 S. Ct. 106, 108, 66 L. Ed. 239, 243 (1921).

Every law of the legislature, however repugnant to the constitution, has not only the appearance and semblance of authority, *but the force of law.* It cannot be questioned at the bar of private judgment, and if thought unconstitutional resisted, but must be received and obeyed, as to all intents and purposes law, until questioned in and set aside by the courts.[108]

That is to say, whether a statute is constitutionally valid is a "judicial question" for courts to determine, and therefore a public officer cannot be charged with the duty of determining the constitutional validity of a statute before acting in reliance thereon.[109] And since courts frequently disagree on questions of constitutionality, it would be ironic for the same courts to hold that an enforcing officer is "presumed to know the law." The obvious injustice of such a ruling is summed up in the following observations of a Utah judge:

The older cases seem to hold that an unconstitutional law afforded no protection to officers who acted under it. . . . The evils of such a holding, however, were apparent, since it is by no means easy oft times for even a trained lawyer to tell whether or not a law is unconstitutional. The Judges of the Supreme Courts of the various States and of the United States are frequently divided in their opinion on the question of whether a law should or should not be held unconstitutional. To make the sheriff and his deputies, who are not supposed to be lawyers, act at their peril . . . would certainly work a great injustice to these officers, and tend to work against public policy for the reason that the officers would always be hesitant in carrying out the directions of the statutes and the orders of the courts.[110]

Goodwin v. Guild [111] involved an action for false imprisonment and malicious prosecution against a mayor who had caused the arrest of plaintiff under an ordinance which was subsequently held invalid. The court held:

It is evident that this void ordinance could not justify the arrest of the plaintiff and his prosecution, still, it was the duty of the mayor, as the chief executive of the city, to see its ordinances enforced, and, so long as he acted in good faith, and with no malice or improper motive, he cannot be held personally liable for a mere error in judgment. If he took advantage of his official position to oppress the plaintiff, either

---

[108] *State v. Carroll*, 38 Conn. 449, 472 (1871). Italics supplied.

[109] *Gordon v. O'Conner*, 183 Okla. 82, 80 P. (2d) 322 (1938); *Gladstone et al. v. Galton*, 145 F. (2d) 742 (C.C.A. 9th, 1944).

[110] *Allen v. Holbrook, Sheriff et al.*, 103 Utah 319, 325–26, 135 P. (2d) 242, 245 (1943).

[111] 94 Tenn. 486 (1895).

from ill will towards him, or because of any other improper motive, he would be liable.[112]

Under the presumption of validity rule, a finance officer who pays out public money in reliance upon an unconstitutional statute is not personally liable.[113] Assessors are not held liable for illegal assessments under an unconstitutional statute, as they are held to exercise quasi-judicial power.[114] A State tax collector has been held liable to suit for a tax paid under protest and collected under an invalid statute on the theory that the payment was involuntary;[115] but he is not liable for money collected without protest, since such payments are deemed to be voluntary.

A judicial officer is not liable for false arrest and imprisonment under an unconstitutional statute, provided he has jurisdiction.[116] An officer serving process under an unconstitutional statute "was not protected by an unconstitutional act if he was acting on his own volition but was protected if he was acting under order of a court of competent jurisdiction."[117]

> . . . when a court of competent jurisdiction issues process based upon a statute, the mere issuing of process is a sufficient declaration of the constitutionality of that statute as to afford protection to an officer who in good faith serves the process [even if the statute is later held unconstitutional by a higher court].[118]

Furthermore, under the ministerial officer rule,[119] until a statute has been held unconstitutional, a writ of mandamus may be asked to compel performance of the statute, yet the courts are divided as to whether the officer may raise the question of constitutionality in such a proceeding. Logically, "a ministerial officer of the government may not ordinarily resist compliance with, or decline the enforcement of,

---

[112] 94 Tenn. at 490.

[113] Annotation, "Liability of Public Officer With Respect to Money Paid Out in Reliance Upon an Unconstitutional Statute," 118 *American Law Review,* 787. There are "no cases wherein public officers have been held liable for paying out public money in reliance upon an unconstitutional statute."

[114] 52 *American Jurisprudence,* 1035.

[115] *Scottish Union and National Insurance Co. v. Herriot,* 109 Iowa 606, 80 N.W. 665 (1899).

[116] 31 *American Jurisprudence,* 721.

[117] *Allen v. Holbrook,* 103 Utah 319, 329, 135 P. (2d) 242, 247 (1943).

[118] 103 Utah at 329.

[119] "A ministerial officer is liable in damages to a party having 'special and direct interest' for any injury caused by his (1) nonfeasance, i.e., omission—'neglect or refusal'—to do an act he ought to do; (2) misfeasance, i.e., negligence in doing what he may do; (3) malfeasance, i.e., doing an act he ought not to do." James Hart, *An Introduction to Administrative Law* (F. S. Crofts & Co., New York, 1940), p. 447, citing Meechem in *Law of Public Officers,* §§ 664, 665.

a statute, upon the ground of his view that the act is unconstitutional or otherwise invalid." [120] But many courts will permit an officer to raise the constitutional issue when the performance of a ministerial duty involves his personal interests or liability,[121] or the violation of his oath of office,[122] or the disbursement of public funds,[123] or where he has secured the advice of a public law officer, such as the attorney general.[124] In *State ex rel. Johnson, Attorney General v. Baker*[125] the issue was the obtaining of a writ of mandamus to compel the auditor to pay warrants drawn by State officials. The court held that since the auditor acted on her own without consulting the attorney general, the mandamus would issue; but had she secured and followed an opinion of the law officer she would have been protected, even though the opinion was later found to be erroneous. On the broad issue involved, the court made the following comment:

> In short, respondent admits her refusal to issue warrants (of payment) and justifies it by reason of her great doubts as to the constitutionality of the statute in question, and in effect, asks for an advisory opinion from this court as to its constitutionality, since, as she alleges, if she issues the warrants, and the statute is unconstitutional she will have violated her duty under her oath of office and become liable on his official bond. . . . The court may not render advisory opinions. . . .
>
> The question as to the right of ministerial officers, such as the state auditor, to raise the point that an enactment under which they are required to act is unconstitutional and therefore invalid, is one that fre-

---

[120] *O'Shields v. Caldwell*, 207 S.C. 194, 216, 35 S.E. (2d) 184, 193 (1945).

[121] ". . . it appears from consideration of the authorities that the ministerial officer rule is subject to the exception that a governmental officer may raise the question of the constitutionality of an act *when his personal interests are affected,* whether adversely or otherwise, and *that he is protected from liability by it only when he acts in good faith and with due care.*" *O'Shields v. Caldwell*, 207 S.C. 194, 219, 35 S.E. (2d), 184, 194 (1945). Italics supplied. *Utah v. Candland*, 36 Utah 406, 104 Pac. 285 (1909); *State ex rel. Pierce v. Slusher*, 119 Ore. 141, 248 Pac. 358 (1926).

[122] "Several of the later cases have held that where fulfillment of an officer's duty under a statute would or might cause a violation of his oath of office, and especially where the disposition of public moneys is involved, his official capacity enables him to raise the question of the constitutionality of the state." Annotation, "Unconstitutionality of Statute as Defense to Mandamus Proceedings," 129 *American Law Review* (1940), 941. For citation of cases see *ibid.*, pp. 947–50.

[123] "Notwithstanding these various conflicting views, it is generally held that the constitutionality of a statute authorizing disbursement of public funds may be questioned by the officer on whom the duty of disbursement is imposed, although there is also authority to the contrary." *Corpus Juris Secundum*, Vol. XVI, p. 175.

[124] *Department of State Highways v. Baker*, 69 N.D. 702, 290 N.W. 257 (1940); *Commonwealth v. Mathues*, 210 Pa. 372, 59 Atl. 961 (1904); *State ex rel. Equality Building Association v. Brown*, 334 Mo. 781, 68 S.W. (2d) 55 (1934).

[125] 74 N.D. 244, 21 N.W. (2d) 355 (1945).

quently has been before the courts, and there is a diversity of holding in the decisions touching that question. . . .

And it seems to us it would be a harsh and unconsciable doctrine to apply that where a ministerial officer acts in good faith and in compliance with the mandate of a statute that is subsequently held to be invalid, he becomes responsible under his oath on his official bond; to hold in other words, that every such officer who is required to subscribe to the official oath in order to qualify performs his statutory duty in every case at his peril.[126]

The *de facto* doctrine further qualifies the void *ab initio* theory. To protect the interests of the public and of individuals, the proceedings of a *de facto* office and the acts of a *de facto* officer are as valid and binding as are those of a *de jure* office or of a *de jure* officer. This practice is a simple matter of policy and necessity.

An officer *de facto* is one whose acts though not those of a lawful officer, the law, upon principles of policy and justice, will hold valid so far as they involve the interests of the public and third persons, where the duties of the office are exercised, ...

Fourth, under color of an election or appointment by or pursuant to a public unconstitutional law before the same is adjudged to be such. . . .

If, then, the law of the legislature, which creates an office and provides an officer to perform its duties, must have the force of law until set aside as unconstitutional by the courts, it would be absurd to say that an officer so provided had no color of authority. But on this question we need not reason. There is an irresistible current of authority in this country which determines it.[127]

And the Supreme Court has added the weight of its authority: "As to third parties, at least he was an officer *de facto*; and if an officer *de facto*, the same validity and the same presumptions attached to his actions as to those of an officer *de jure*."[128]

Thus a *de facto* officer has been compelled to perform the duties of the office he assumed;[129] and a *de facto* officer is liable for either a tortious or a criminal act committed by him in the discharge of the functions of his office.[130]

---

[126] 74 N.D. at 247–49, 256, 21 N.W. at 358–59, 362–63.

[127] *State v. Carroll*, 38 Conn. 449, 471–72, 473–74 (1871). Also *Oliver v. The Mayor*, 63 N.J.L. 634 (1899); *State v. Gardner*, 54 Ohio St. 24 (1896).

[128] *Nofire v. United States*, 164 U.S. 657, 661, 17 S. Ct. 212–13, 41 L. Ed. 588, 590 (1896).

[129] *State v. Supervisors*, 21 Wis. 280 (1866).

[130] *Boone County v. Jones*, 54 Iowa 699 (1880); *Longacre v. State*, 3 Miss. 637 (1837).

It appears that a majority of the State courts continue to apply the void *ab initio* rule. A review of the cases in 1927 led to the following conclusion:

> By the great weight of authority a public officer who acts under a statute which has subsequently been declared unconstitutional cannot successfully rely on the statute as a defense to a suit brought against him to recover damages caused by the attempted enforcement of the statute. Sheriffs, Constables, Justices of the Peace and other inferior officers, even when acting in a judicial capacity, have been held liable in damages to parties injured by the attempted enforcement of unconstitutional statutes. Nevertheless, there are a number of well reasoned cases holding that the officer who has acted in good faith in enforcing such statutes is not liable.[131]

The following categorical rejections of the void *ab initio* doctrine may be taken as representative of the minority view. A New Jersey judge in *Lang v. Bayonne* said:

> Notwithstanding the great weight which the opinion of so distinguished a jurist carries, notwithstanding that Norton v. Shelby County has been frequently cited with approval in other jurisdictions, I am unable to accept as sound the doctrine upon which it is rested, namely that an unconstitutional law is void ab initio, and affords no protection for acts done under its sanction.[132]

And in *State v. Gardner,* an Ohio judge spoke even more emphatically:

> To say, then, that a statute, which by all presumptions, is valid and constitutional until set aside as invalid by judicial authority, cannot in the meantime, confer any right, impose any duty, afford any protection, but is inoperative as though it had never been passed, is at least startling. To say that a statute which purports to create a constitutional office, duly enacted by our general assembly, and duly promulgated, enjoins no duty of respect or obedience by the people, and affords no corresponding right or protection, and that all who undertake to enforce its demands do so at their peril, and at the risk of being deemed trespassers and usurpers, in case it shall be finally decided to be unconstitutional, by a bare majority, perhaps of the court of last resort, no matter what public necessities existed for its enforcement, nor what public approval and acquiescence there may have been, nor for how long a term of years, and no matter how many holdings of intermediary

----

[131] Max P. Rapacz, "Protection of Officers Who Act Under Unconstitutional Statutes," 2 *Minnesota Law Review* (1927), 585. For illustrative cases see: *Kelly v. Bemis,* 4 Gray 83, 70 Mass. 83 (1855); *Kinneen v. Wells,* 144 Mass. 497, 11 N.E. 916 (1887); *Cartwright v. Canode,* 138 S.W. 792 (1911).

[132] 74 N.J.L., 455, 68 Atl. 90 (1907).

courts there may have been sustaining its constitutionality, is to invite riot, turmoil and chaos. It is not the law in Ohio.[133]

Nevertheless, the Supreme Court has stated the prevailing doctrine of official liability as follows:

The many claims of immunity from suit have therefore been uniformly denied, where the action was brought for injuries done or threatened by public officers. If they were indeed agents, acting for the State, they—though not exempt from suit—could successfully defend by exhibiting the valid power of attorney or lawful authority under which they acted. But if it appears that they proceeded under an unconstitutional statute, their justification failed and their claim of immunity disappeared on the production of the void statute. Besides, neither a State nor an individual can confer upon an agent authority to commit a tort so as to excuse the perpetration. In such cases the law of agency has no application—the wrongdoer is treated as a principal and individually liable for the damages inflicted, and subject to injunction against the commission of acts causing irreparable injury.[134]

Mechem

The constitutional basis for the suability of officers enforcing unconstitutional statutes was stated as follows by Mr. Justice Peckham:

The act to be enforced is alleged to be unconstitutional; and if it be so, the use of the name of the State to enforce an unconstitutional act to the injury of complainants is a proceeding without the authority of, and one which does not affect, the State in its sovereign or governmental capacity. It is simply an illegal act upon the part of a state official in attempting, by the use of the name of the State, to enforce a legislative enactment which is void because unconstitutional. If the act which the state Attorney General seeks to enforce be a violation of the Federal Constitution, the officer, in proceeding under such an enactment, comes into conflict with the superior authority of the Constitution, *and he is in that case stripped of his official or representative character and is subjected in his person to the consequences of his individual conduct.*[135]

The problems arising out of the enforcement of an unconstitutional statute place the courts on the proverbial horns of a dilemma. On the one hand, the statute was not unconstitutional as of the time of its enforcement, *since no court had so held.* It was not merely *presumed* to be valid, *it was valid in law,* binding every citizen and governmental agency, save the courts under the practice of judicial

NB dilemma

[133] 54 Ohio St. 24, 48, 42, N.E. 999, 1004–5 (1896).

[134] *Hopkins v. Clemson College,* 221 U.S. 636, 643, 31 S. Ct. 654, 656–57, 55 L. Ed. 890, 894 (1911).

[135] *Ex parte Young,* 209 U.S. 123, 159–60, 28 S. Ct. 441, 454, 52 L. Ed. 714, 729 (1908). Italics supplied.

review. Therefore, the enforcing officer did not administer an unconstitutional law. On the other hand, if the statute is later held unconstitutional, it is so because it conflicts with a provision of the Constitution which was the same at the time the law was enacted as it is when the court renders its decision. The court merely declares *authoritatively* that there *is,* and hence there *always was,* a repugnancy between the law and the Constitution. The decision is necessarily retroactive. This is the juristic theory of *constitutional supremacy.* Accordingly, the statute *never was law,* and the officer who administered the statute did not act in the capacity of an officer and he did not enforce a law—his act was not only without legal force, it was *illegal* if it resulted in injury to individuals or to the public.

Under the "presumption of validity doctrine," the court, in its discretion, decides when and under what circumstances its ruling on the constitutionality of a legislative act shall have retroactive effect and when prospective. If the nullifying judicial decision has prospective force only, the court gives legal effect to acts that were not authorized by any *law* of the legislature. The court legislates retroactively. Also, the court does what it says the legislature cannot do, it enforces the provisions of a statute which is repugnant to the Constitution. The theory of every government which has framed a written constitution, said Mr. Chief Justice Marshall, "must be that an act of the legislature, repugnant to the constitution, is void." [136] Moreover, "How immoral," he declared, to impose an oath on the judges "if they were to be used as the instruments, and the knowing instruments, for violating what they swear to support!" [137]

Judicial discretion in this connection is a dispensing power that places the Court above the Constitution, but it is a power that necessarily results from the exercise of the power of judicial review. In the last analysis the Supreme Court of the United States is not only "A Constitutional convention in continuous session," [138] but it frequently exercises "powers of a super-legislature," [139] which should find its justification in public policy rather than in constitutional dogma. To apply the void *ab initio* doctrine to the honest administration of an unconstitutional statute is to rob Peter to pay Paul—it protects one individual at the expense of another, and the real

---

[136] *Marbury v. Madison,* 1 Cranch 137, 177, 2 L. Ed. 60, 73 (1803).

[137] 1 Cranch at 180.

[138] Woodrow Wilson, quoted by E. S. Corwin, "Curbing the Court," 85 *The Annals of the American Academy of Political and Social Science* (May, 1936), 49.

[139] Mr. Justice Brandeis dissenting in *Burns Baking Co. v. Bryan,* 264 U.S. 505, 534, 44 S. Ct. 412, 421, 68 L. Ed. 813, 836 (1924).

offender, the state, perpetrates the injustice. Since justice is the business of law, the state should assume responsibility for its own misdeeds. The ancient cliché that the king can do no wrong lost its respectability long ago.

It would seem that the declaratory judgment device might be used rather extensively in situations involving enforcement of statutes of questionable constitutionality. An officer should neither have the discretion to refuse enforcement, nor should he be liable for enforcement. If in doubt, let the officer seek a declaratory judgment from a court, particularly while the rule of personal liability prevails.

Liability for Acts of Subordinates.—A public officer is not responsible for the misfeasances or positive wrongs, or for the nonfeasances or negligences, or omissions of duty of any person properly employed by him in the discharge of his official duties.[140] To hold an officer responsible for the acts of his subordinates ". . . would be to establish a principle which would paralyze the public service. Competent persons could not be found to fill positions of the kind, if they knew that they would be held liable for all the torts and wrongs committed by a large body of subordinates, in the discharge of duties which it would be utterly impossible for the superior officer to discharge in person."[141]

Since the relation of superior to inferior officer is not that of master and servant, the doctrine of *respondent superior* does not apply;[142] but if the former directs or encourages, or personally co-operates in, the negligent act of the latter, he must answer for the subordinate's wrong—and "cooperation may be inferred from acquiescence where there is power to restrain."[143]

But a sheriff has been held liable to a statutory penalty for the failure of his deputy to execute a summons, on the theory that in legal contemplation the deputy and the sheriff "were one officer, so far as third persons are concerned, as to all questions of civil responsibility."[144] And if an inferior officer enforces an illegal order of his superior where the order is presumably valid, the latter is responsible.[145]

[140] *Robertson v. Sichel,* 127 U.S. 507, 8 S. Ct. 1286, 32 L. Ed. 203 (1887); *Keenan v. Southworth,* 110 Mass. 474, 14 Am. Rep. 613 (1872); *Smyer v. United States,* 273 U.S. 333, 47 S. Ct. 375, 71 L. Ed. 667 (1927).
[141] *Robertson v. Sichel,* 127 U.S. at 515, 8 S. Ct. at 1290, 32 L. Ed. at 206.
[142] *Robinson v. Rohr,* 73 Wis. 436 (1889).
[143] *Dowler v. Johnson,* 225 N.Y. 39, 43, 121 N.E. 487, 488 (1918).
[144] *Rogers v. Carroll,* 111 Ala. 610, 20 So. 602–3 (1896).
[145] *McCall v. McDowell,* 1 Abb. (U.S.) 212, cited with approval in *Commonwealth v. Shortall,* 206 Penn. St. 165 (1903).

Chapter 7

JUDICIAL PROCESSING OF ADMINISTRATIVE ACTION

The Doctrine of the Supremacy of the Law as the Basis for Judicial Review

The "rule of law" means, said Dicey,

> . . . in the first place, that no man is punishable or can be lawfully made to suffer in body or goods, except for a distinct breach of law *established in the ordinary legal manner before the ordinary courts of law*.[1]

The same idea is implicit in the statement by Mr. Justice Brandeis to the effect that

> The supremacy of the law demands that there shall be opportunity to have some *court* decide whether an erroneous rule of law was applied; and whether the proceeding in which facts were adjudicated was conducted regularly.[2]

That is, the rule of law means the supremacy of that law which is enforced in courts of justice. John Dickinson translates the rule of law into constitutional theory as follows:

> Administrative justice has been fitted into the governmental system of the United States—but, without that independence or finality which characterizes the traditional arms of state. The "rule of law" has been restated to require judicial control of administrative action: ". . . every citizen is entitled . . . to call into question in such a court the legality of any act done by an administrative official."[3]

The rule of law has the necessary effect of elevating the courts to a position of ultimate supremacy over the administrative hierarchy. In England the "supreme law" which the courts enforce is, in the

[1] Albert V. E. Dicey, *Law of the Constitution* (8th ed., The Macmillan Co., New York, 1923), p. 183. Italics supplied.

[2] *St. Joseph Stock Yards Co. v. United States*, 298 U.S. 38, 84, 56 S. Ct. 720, 740, 80 L. Ed. 1033, 1058 (1936). Italics supplied.

[3] *Administrative Justice and the Supremacy of the Law* (Harvard University Press, Cambridge, Mass., 1927), p. 35. See also Roscoe Pound, "Justice According to Law," 13 *Columbia Law Review* (December, 1913), 696 ff.

last analysis, the law of Parliament.   But judges, no less than officers of the Crown, are governed by this law—they can *enforce* but they cannot *overrule* the law.   Judicial review of administrative action is limited, therefore, to questions of statutory and common law construction.   If the challenged act is authorized by statute, the courts have no choice but to support it, no matter how arbitrary or capricious they regard it.   Anything authorized by law is "due process of law" —the *effect* of the law is not a matter for judicial concern.   In short, judicial review of administrative action in England is relatively simple.

But in the United States the supremacy of the law means not only administrative adherence to statutes but, in addition, administrative action, and the statute under which such action is taken, must conform to the Constitution.   This means that administrative policy is largely determined by judges trained in the technique of common law legal reasoning.

In the common law sense, the rule of law is consistent only with a laissez faire economy and a laissez faire state where government is but one of several competing power structures.   Government did not create law, it discovered and declared "the law of nature."   Even such eminent jurists as Coke and Blackstone gave obeisance to the doctrine of natural law.

> The law of nature, being coeval with mankind and dictated by God himself, is of course superior in obligation to any other.   It is binding over all the globe in all countries, and at all times; no human laws are of any validity, if contrary to this; and such of them as are valid derive all their force, and all their authority, mediately or immediately, from this original.[4]

But our Supreme Court substituted the Constitution for the law of nature as the fundamental and supreme law; and under the doctrine of the separation of powers the legislature became, in theory, the sole creator of new law.   "Sovereign" power is centralized in the state, with the government exercising powers of agency *within* the Constitution as its commission.   Furthermore, *public service* has become the basis of this state, as in truth it is of all modern states.   What, then, has happened to the rule of law?   It has become a rule of political action—a standard of conduct for those entrusted with the power to govern.   This does not mean that in the service state *law* has been replaced by unrestrained administration.   A service state is not necessarily, or even properly, a national socialist state

[4] Sir William Blackstone, *Commentaries* (Postrait Edition; Strahan and Woodfall, London, 1793), Vol. I, pp. 40–41.

or a Marxian state where the administration of things will replace the rule of law over men. As long as men actively choose to be free, government will be their servant and not their master. Nevertheless, as the state's public service functions grow there is a corresponding growth in administrative machinery, and contacts between the government and the individual increase, multiplying the opportunities for friction and arbitrariness and making the need for effective controls even more imperative.

American thinking on methods of control centers on judicial review. Our faith in our "day in court" is a basic article in our political ideology. If our courts have failed us, it is largely because we have ascribed to our judges a knowledge and a wisdom which by the nature of things they do not and cannot possess and because we have permitted or required them to assimilate to the judicial function the power to govern. In our effort to counter executive absolutism through the establishment of judicial controls, we may do no more than to substitute one form of centralized authority for another. The judicial and administrative processes are not competing elements of social control—they are related "instrumentalities of justice." A "cardinal principle" to be kept in mind by courts, said Mr. Justice Stone, is

> . . . that in construing a statute setting up an administrative agency and providing for judicial review of its action, court and agency are not to be regarded as wholly independent and unrelated instrumentalities of justice, each acting in the performance of its prescribed statutory duty without regard to the appropriate function of the other in securing the plainly indicated object of the statute. Court and agency are the means adopted to attain the prescribed end, and so far as their duties are defined by the words of the statute, those words should be construed so as to attain that end through co-ordinated action. Neither body should repeat in this day the mistake made by the courts of law when equity was struggling for recognition as an ameliorating system of justice; neither can rightly be regarded by the other as an alien intruder, to be tolerated if must be, but never to be encouraged or aided by the other in the attainment of the common aim.[5]

Here Mr. Justice Stone "practiced" what he "preached" earlier in his devastating dissenting opinion in *United States v. Butler*[6] when he pointed out that "Courts are not the only agency of government that must be assumed to have capacity to govern," and he warned against an ". . . interpretation of our great charter of government

---

[5] *United States v. Morgan,* 307 U.S. 183, 191, 59 S. Ct. 795, 799–800, 83 L. Ed. 1211, 1217 (1939).
[6] 297 U.S. 1, 56 S. Ct. 312, 80 L. Ed. 477 (1936).

which proceeds on any assumption that the responsibility for the preservation of our institutions is the exclusive concern of any one of the three branches of government, or that it alone can save them from destruction." [7]

Equally realistic is Mr. Justice Frankfurter's comment in the Pottsville Broadcasting Co. case: [8]

> But courts are not charged with general guardianship against all potential mischief in the complicated tasks of government. The present case makes timely the reminder that "legislatures are ultimate guardians of the liberties and welfare of the people in quite as great a degree as the courts." . . . Congress which creates and sustains these [administrative] agencies must be trusted to correct whatever defects experience may reveal. Interference by the courts is not conducive to the development of habits of responsibility in administrative agencies. Anglo-American courts as we now know them are themselves in no small measure the product of a historic process.[9]

The Great Judicial Writs as Instruments for Control of Administrative Action

The methods of review prescribed by a statute are controlling, subject only to constitutional requirements. In the absence of a specified statutory procedure, the common law remedies are available. But the great judicial writs have only limited use as instruments for control of administrative action. Consequently, injunction, mandamus, prohibition, quo warranto, or certiorari will not issue where there is an adequate legal remedy, and even so the jurisdiction of the several courts, particularly federal courts, to issue the writs is limited considerably. Federal courts have full power to issue writs of habeas corpus,[10] but no such general jurisdiction exists as to the writs of mandamus, certiorari, prohibition, and quo warranto. The District Courts for the District of Columbia inherited the power to issue the writ of mandamus from the common law of Maryland,[11] and federal courts have been authorized to issue the writ by statute in specified cases.[12] Rule 81(b) of the Federal Rules of Civil Pro-

---

[7] 297 U.S. at 87, 88, 56 S. Ct. at 329, 80 L. Ed. at 449, 500.

[8] *Federal Communications Commission v. Pottsville Broadcasting Co.,* 309 U.S. 134, 60 S. Ct. 437, 84 L. Ed. 656 (1940).

[9] 309 U.S. at 146, 60 S. Ct. at 443, 84 L. Ed. at 663–64.

[10] *Rev. Stat.,* §§ 751–53, 28 *U.S.C.A.* §§ 451–53 (1934).

[11] *Kendall v. United States,* 12 Peters 524, 9 L. Ed. 1181 (1838); *United States ex rel. McBride v. Schurz,* 102 U.S. 378, 26 L. Ed. 167 (1880).

[12] Act of June 7, 1922, 42 *Stat.* 624, 49 *U.S.C.A.* § 19(1) (1934); Act of August 9, 1935, 49 *Stat.* 548, 49 *U.S.C.A.* § 305(g). The Administrative Procedure Act of June 11, 1946, Sec. 10(e) provides that the reviewing court shall, among other things, "compel agency action unlawfully withheld or unreasonably delayed."

cedure abolishes the writ of mandamus as such and substitutes relief "by appropriate action or by appropriate motions under the practice prescribed in these rules." [13] Presumably this rule does not affect statutes which specifically authorize the use of mandamus. And, "It is doubtful whether even the District of Columbia courts can issue certiorari to bring up the record of proceedings before an administrative tribunal or officer. . . . And no cases have been found where prohibition, . . . or quo warranto has issued from a lower Federal court. To fill the gap thus left in the process of judicial review of administrative action, the federal courts have extended the scope of equitable relief." [14]

Prohibition.—The writ of prohibition is seldom used to control administrative action. It does not lie against an administrative body to prevent purely *administrative* or *ministerial* acts. Its principal function is to restrain inferior courts from proceeding in matters over which they have no jurisdiction or from exceeding their jurisdiction, but it is available to prevent *judicial* action by an agency in the States.

> A writ of *prohibition* does not lie to a *ministerial officer* to stay the execution of process in his hands. It is directed to a *court* in which some action or legal proceeding is pending, and to the party who prosecutes the suit, and commands the one not to hold, and the other not to follow, the plea. It stays both the court and the party from proceeding with the suit. The writ was framed for the purpose of keeping inferior courts within the limits of their own jurisdiction, without encroaching upon other tribunals.[15]

Prohibition is an extraordinary remedy which lies within the discretion of the court, and it will not issue where the grievance can be

[13] New York also has abolished the writ of mandamus, if not the remedy, in favor of a smplified application for relief by petition. *Civil Practices Act of September 1, 1937,* Chap. 526, Art. 78, § 1283.

[14] Walter Gellhorn, *Administrative Law, Cases and Comments* (2d ed., The Foundation Press, Inc., Brooklyn, 1947), pp. 881–82.

[15] *The People v. Supervisors,* 1 Hill, N.Y. 195 (1841). In *Hathaway Bakeries, Inc. v. Labor Relations Commission,* 316 Mass. 136, 139, 55 N.E. (2d) 254, 255 (1944), the Supreme Judicial Court of Massachusetts said: "A writ of prohibition lies to restrain a court or quasi-judicial body from acting outside its jurisdiction against one who has not submitted thereto and where there is no other adequate remedy. The writ does not lie to correct errors committed by a tribunal having jurisdiction over a subject matter and the parties, but its function is to prevent the court from proceeding to a decision where the court has no power to make any decision at all. If the tribunal possesses jurisdiction, then the writ cannot be invoked by one who has been harmed by a decision, whether that decision was right or wrong."

redressed by ordinary proceedings in law or equity or by appeal.[16] It lies only to prevent the commission of an act; it is not used to correct errors in completed proceedings.[17]

Quo Warranto.—In modern practice a quo warranto proceeding is in the form of an information issued in the name of the public prosecutor, either ex officio or on the relation of some private person (who, in most jurisdictions, must show that he has some claim to the office), for the purpose of trying title to office or the right to exercise a franchise. Such a proceeding is brought in the name of and on behalf of the people and is not primarily in the interest of any individual, but it is intended to protect the public generally against the unlawful usurpation of offices and franchises. At common law the state's attorney is not *required* to institute quo warranto proceedings on request of a claimant to an office;[18] but there are statutory modifications of this rule, as in Illinois where it is made a *duty* enforceable by mandamus if the claimant presents a proper petition with evidence of the facts necessary to support his claim.[19] Informations at the relation of private persons can be filed only by leave of the court—they are not granted as a matter of course but depend upon the discretion of the court.[20]

Quo warranto is properly a civil remedy, even though at times the proceedings may be criminal in form,[21] as where an ouster is accompanied with a fine.[22] Ordinarily it is used only to oust from office or to recover for the state a franchise illegally held; it is not employed to test the validity of an action by one exercising the powers of an office or the privileges of a franchise.[23] That is, it is not generally available to protect private rights against administrative action.[24]

---

[16] *Culver Contracting Corp. v. Humphrey,* 268 N.Y. 26, 196 N.E. 627 (1935); *People v. Westbrook,* 89 N. Y. 152 (1882); *State ex rel. Harrison v. Perry,* 113 Ohio St. 641, 150 N.E. 78 (1925).

[17] *United States v. Hoffman,* 4 Wall. 158, 18 L. Ed. 354 (1866).

[18] *People ex rel. v. Fairchild,* 67 N.Y. 334 (1876); *State Railroad Commission v. People ex rel.,* 44 Colo. 345, 98 Pac. 7 (1908).

[19] *People ex rel. Post v. Healy, State's Atty.,* 231 Ill. 629, 83 N.E. 453 (1907); *People ex rel. Raster v. Healy, State's Atty.,* 230 Ill. 280, 82 N.E. 599 (1907).

[20] *State ex rel. McIlhany, etc. v. Stewart et al.,* 32 Mo. 379 (1862).

[21] *People ex rel. Drainage Commissioners,* 282 Ill. 514, 118 N.E. 742 (1918); *People ex rel. Blair et al.,* 339 Ill. 57, 170 N.E. 680 (1930).

[22] *Standard Oil Co. v. Missouri,* 224 U.S. 270, 32 S. Ct. 406, 56 L. Ed. 760 (1912).

[23] *State v. Evans,* 3 Ark. 585, 36 Am. Dec. 468 (1841). Contra: *People ex rel. Congress v. Board of Education of City of Quincy,* 101 Ill. 308, 40 Am. Rep. 196 (1882); *Shanley v. People,* 225 Ill. 579, 80 N.E. 277 (1907); *State v. Topeka,* 30 Kan. 653, 2 Pac. 587 (1883).

[24] *Attorney General v. Sullivan,* 163 Mass. 446, 40 N.E. 843 (1895).

Habeas Corpus.—The writ of habeas corpus, unlike quo warranto, is primarily for the vindication of private rights—it is used for the relief of an individual against unlawful detention by an officer.[25] It is in the nature of a writ of error to examine the legality of the commitment. But,

It cannot be used as a mere writ of error. Mere error in the judgment or proceedings, under and by virtue of which a party is imprisoned, constitutes no ground for the issue of the writ. Hence, upon a return to a *habeas corpus,* that the prisoner is detained under a conviction and sentence by a court having jurisdiction of the cause, the general rule is, that he will be instantly remanded. No inquiry will be instituted into the regularity of the proceedings, unless, perhaps, where the court has cognizance by writ of error or appeal to review the judgment. In such a case, if the error be apparent and the imprisonment unjust, the appellate court may, perhaps, in its discretion, give immediate relief on *habeas corpus,* and thus save the party the delay and expense of a writ of error. . . . But the general rule is that a conviction and sentence by a court of competent jurisdiction is lawful cause of imprisonment, and no relief can be given by *habeas corpus.*

The only ground on which this court, or any court, without some special statute authorizing it, will give relief on *habeas corpus* to a prisoner under conviction and sentence of another court is the want of jurisdiction in such court over the person or the cause, or some other matter rendering its proceedings void.[26]

The writ is used to relieve confinement under either civil or criminal process. The restraint must be physical, not merely moral. And, "Wives restrained by husbands, children withheld from the proper parent or guardian, persons held under arbitrary custody by private individuals, as in a madhouse, as well as those under military control, may all become proper subjects of relief by the writ of *habeas corpus.*" [27]

But while it is true that

. . . habeas corpus cannot be used as a means of reviewing errors of law and irregularities—not involving the question of jurisdiction— occurring during the course of trial; and the "writ of habeas corpus

---

[25] For use of habeas corpus in immigration cases see: *Ng Fung Ho v. White,* 259 U.S. 276, 42 S. Ct. 492, 66 L. Ed. 938 (1922) ; *Mahler v. Eby,* 264 U.S. 32, 43, 44 S. Ct. 283, 287, 68 L. Ed. 549 (1924) ; *Wong Yang Sung v. McGrath,* 339 U.S. 33, 70 S. Ct. 445, 94 L. Ed. 616 (1950).

[26] *Ex parte Siebold,* 100 U.S. 371, 375, 25 L. Ed. 717, 718–19 (1880). *People ex rel. Tweed v. Liscomb,* 60 N.Y. 559 (1875) ; *United States ex rel. Mason v. Hunt,* 16 F. Supp. 285 (D.C.W.D.N.Y., 1936) ; *Ex parte Watkins,* 3 Pet. 193, 7 L. Ed. 650 (1830) ; *Knewal v. Egan,* 268 U.S. 442, 45 S. Ct. 552, 69 L. Ed. 1036 (1925).

[27] *Wales v. Whitney,* 114 U.S. 564, 571, 5 S. Ct. 1050, 1053, 29 L. Ed. 277, 279 (1884).

cannot be used as a writ of error." [28] These principles, however, must be construed and applied so as to preserve—not destroy—constitutional safeguards of human life and liberty. . . . Congress has expanded the rights of a petitioner for habeas corpus [29] and the ". . . effect is to substitute for the bare legal review that seems to have been the limit of judicial authority under the common-law practice, . . . a more searching investigation, in which the applicant is put upon his oath to set forth the truth of the matter respecting the causes of his detention, and the court, upon determining the actual facts is to 'dispose of the party as law and justice require.' "

. . . it results that under the sections cited a prisoner in custody pursuant to the final judgment of a state court of criminal jurisdiction may have a judicial inquiry in a court of the United States into the very truth and substance of the causes of his detention, although it may be necessary to look behind and beyond the record of his conviction to a sufficient extent to test the jurisdiction of the state court to proceed to judgment against him.[30]

Thus, when the petitioner was convicted and sentenced without the assistance of counsel, to which he was entitled by the Sixth Amendment, and he contended that he was ignorant of his right to counsel and incapable of preserving his legal and constitutional rights during trial,[31] the Supreme Court held that if his contentions were true in fact it necessarily followed that no legal procedural remedy was available to grant relief for a violation of his constitutional rights unless the courts protected his rights by habeas corpus. And, "To deprive a citizen of his only effective remedy would not only be contrary to the 'rudimentary demands of justice' but destructive of a constitutional guarantee specifically designed to prevent injustice." [32]

The Court held further that

Where a defendant, without counsel, acquiesces in a trial resulting in his conviction and later seeks release by the extraordinary remedy of *habeas corpus,* the burden of proof rests upon him to establish that he did not competently and intelligently waive his constitutional right to assistance of counsel. If in a habeas corpus hearing, he does meet

---

[28] Quoting from *Woolsey v. Best,* 299 U.S. 1, 2, 57 S. Ct. 2, 81 L. Ed. 3 (1936).
[29] 28 *U.S.C.A.,* Chap. 14, §§ 451 *et sqq.*
[30] *Johnson v. Zerbst, Warden,* 304 U.S. 458, 465–66, 58 S. Ct. 1019, 1023–24, 82 L. Ed. 1461, 1467 (1938), quoting with approval from *Frank v. Magnum,* 237 U.S. 309, 330, 331, 35 S. Ct. 582, 588, 59 L. Ed. 969, 981 (1915).
[31] Petitioner claimed that, "after conviction — he was unable to obtain a lawyer; was ignorant of the proceedings to obtain a new trial or appeal, . . . and that he did not possess the requisite skill or knowledge to conduct an appeal, . . . as a practical matter, it was not possible for him to obtain relief by appeal." 304 U.S. at 467.
[32] 304 U.S. at 467, 58 S. Ct. at 1024, 82 L. Ed. at 1468.

this burden and convinces the court by a preponderance of evidence that he neither had counsel nor properly waived right to counsel, it is the duty of the court to grant the writ.[33]

To maintain the supremacy of national over State law, a federal officer is not amenable to State courts for his official acts, and he may be discharged from State custody by habeas corpus.[34] But the Supreme Court will not issue habeas corpus in favor of a person held under a State commitment until such person has exhausted the judicial remedy provided by the State.[35]

Certiorari.—It has been noted that "The writ of certiorari has a variety of uses and has suffered from confusion."[36] That confusion results largely from the fact that the office of the writs of certiorari, mandamus, and error are often much the same.[37]

Certiorari is a discretionary writ, whereas the writ of error is one of right. The latter is the normal procedure for review of proceedings in inferior law courts having general common law jurisdiction. In order to relieve the Supreme Court of much of its appellate jurisdiction, Congress, by the Webb Act of 1916[38] and the Judges Bill Act of 1925,[39] substituted certiorari for the writ of error as the method of securing review by the Supreme Court of all the reviewable decisions (except in a few cases) of State courts, the Circuit Court of Appeals of the District of Columbia, and the Federal Circuit Courts of Appeals.

In the States certiorari is used to a considerable extent to secure judicial review of administrative action of a judicial or quasi-judicial nature. The use of this writ for the review of federal administrative action seems to be more limited than in the States, due in part to the greater deference given by federal courts to administrative expertising. According to the New York Court of Appeals:

A writ of certiorari is appropriate to review the judicial or semi-judicial action of inferior courts or of public officers or bodies exercising,

---

[33] 304 U.S. at 468–69, 58 S. Ct. at 1025, 82 L. Ed. at 1468–69.

[34] *In re Neagle,* 135 U.S. 1, 10 S. Ct. 658, 34 L. Ed. 55 (1890) ; *Reed v. Madden,* 87 F. (2) 846 (C.C.A., 8th, 1937).

[35] *Mooney v. Holohan,* 294 U.S. 103, 55 S. Ct. 340, 79 L. Ed. 791 (1935).

[36] Kenneth C. Sears, *Cases and Materials on Administrative Law* (West Publishing Co., St. Paul, 1938), p. 61, note 22.

[37] In Oregon certiorari is also called a writ of review. *Burnett v. Douglas County,* 4 Ore. 388 (1873). In New York it has even been substituted for habeas corpus. *People ex rel. Semenoff v. Nagle,* 118 Misc. 476, 194 N.Y.S. 602 (1922).

[38] Act of September 6, 1916, 39 *Stat.* 726.

[39] Act of February 13, 1925, 43 *Stat.* 936.

under the laws, judicial functions, and there is no authority unless it is expressly given by statute sanctioning its use for any other purpose.[40]

And to the same general effect the Supreme Court of Illinois has said:

> The general rule seems to be that this writ lies only to inferior tribunals and officers exercising judicial functions, and the act to be reviewed must be judicial in the nature, and not ministerial or legislative. . . . But it is not essential that the proceedings should be strictly and technically "judicial," in the sense in which that word is used, when applied to courts of justice. It is sufficient if they are what is sometimes termed "quasi judicial." The body or officers acting need not constitute a court of justice in the ordinary sense. If they are invested by the legislature with the power to decide on the property rights of others, they act judicially in making their decision, whatever may be their public character.[41]

But while State courts generally agree that certiorari will issue to review only judicial and not administrative action, there is no agreement as to what constitutes judicial and administrative action for the purposes of the writ. Further, some courts hold that the sole office of the writ of certiorari is to certify the record of an inferior tribunal for review, and that the only question before the reviewing court is whether, on the basis of the facts set forth in the record, the inferior tribunal had jurisdiction.[42] This was the common law office of the writ. But to other courts, certiorari is practically a writ of error—it reaches *all* errors of law,[43] even "jurisdictional facts." [44]

Certiorari will not issue where there exists another method for review of the administrative action complained of, such as an action for damages against the officer.[45] The office of the writ is not that of a restraining order; its purpose is to annul, not to prohibit; therefore, it will lie only to review completed or final action.[46] Ordinarily it is

[40] *In re Standard Bitulithic Co.*, 212 N.Y. 179, 182, 105 N.E. 967–68 (1914).

[41] *Commissioners of Mason & Tazewell Special Drainage District v. Griffin et al.*, 134 Ill. 330, 25 N.E. 995, 997 (1890).

[42] *Carroll v. Hueston et al.*, 341 Ill. 531, 173 N.E. 657 (1930).

[43] *People ex rel. Cook v. Board of Police of the Metropolitan Police District of the State of New York*, 39 N.Y. 506 (1868). The writ of certiorari has now been abolished for most purposes by New York. Review is now on application for relief by petition. *Civil Practice Act of 1937*, Chap. 526, § 1283. *Hayford v. Municipal Officers of City of Bangor*, 102 Me. 340, 66 Atl. 731 (1907); *Jackson v. People*, 9 Mich. 111 (1860).

[44] *State ex rel. Milwaukee Medical College v. Chittenden*, 127 Wis. 468 (1906).

[45] *People ex rel. Copcutt v. Board of Health of City of Yonkers*, 140 N.Y. 1, 35 N.E. 320 (1893); *Hartman v. Wilmington*, 15 Del. 215 (1894).

[46] *In re Gauld*, 122 Cal. 18, 54 Pac. 272 (1898).

not a remedy for wrongs in tax proceedings.[47] In the regulatory field, rate-making is generally regarded as a legislative, not a judicial, function and therefore is not reviewable on certiorari.[48]

When an application was made to the Supreme Court of the District of Columbia for a writ of certiorari to review a fraud order of the Postmaster General, issued after notice and hearing, the petition was dismissed for want of jurisdiction. This ruling was affirmed by the Court of Appeals of the District on the ground that the evidence supported the order, without reference to the issue of jurisdiction. On further appeal to the Supreme Court, Mr. Justice Lamar said for that Court:

> This case is the first instance, as far as we can find, in which a Federal Court has been asked to issue a writ of certiorari to review a ruling by an executive officer of the United States Government. . . . The modern decisions cited to sustain the power of the court to act in the present case are based on state procedure and statutes that authorize the writ to issue not only to inferior tribunals, boards, assessors and administrative officers, but even to the Chief Executive of a State in proceedings where a quasi-judicial order has been made. But none of these decisions are in point in a Federal jurisdiction where no statute has been passed to enlarge the scope of the writ at common law.
>
> In ancient times it was used to compel the production of a record for use as evidence; more often to supplement a defective record in an appellate court, but later, to remove, before judgment . . . a record from a court without jurisdiction and with a view of preventing error rather than of correcting it. When later its scope was enlarged so as to make it serve the office of a writ of error, certiorari was granted only in those instances in which the inferior tribunal had acted without jurisdiction, or in disregard of statutory provisions. But in those cases the writ ran to boards . . . officers, tribunals and inferior judicatures, whose finding and decisions, even though erroneous, had the quality of a final judgment, and there being no right of appeal or other method of review, the extraordinary writ of certiorari was resorted to from necessity to afford a remedy where there would otherwise have been a denial of justice. But in all these cases it ran from court to court— including boards, officers, or tribunals having a limited statutory jurisdiction, but whose judgments would be conclusive unless set aside.[49]

Although the Postmaster General in the instant case acted in a quasi-judicial capacity in that he issued his order after notice and

[47] *Whitbeck v. Common Council of Hudson,* 50 Mich. 86, 14 N.W. 708 (1883); *Eddy v. Township of Lee,* 73 Mich. 123, 40 N.W. 792 (1888).
[48] *Cumberland Telephone & Telegraph Co. v. State ex rel. Potter, Atty. Gen.,* 135 Miss. 835, 100 So. 378 (1924).
[49] *Degge v. Hitchcock,* 229 U.S. 162, 169–72, 33 S. Ct. 639, 640–41, 57 L. Ed. 1135, 1137 (1913).

hearing to the persons immediately affected, the statute under which he acted was passed primarily for the benefit of the public at large.

That fact gave an administrative quality to the hearing and to the order and was sufficient to prevent it from being subject to review by writ of certiorari. The Postmaster General could not exercise judicial functions, and in making the decision he was not an officer presiding over a tribunal where his ruling was final unless reversed. *Not being a judgment, it was not subject to appeal, writ of error, or certiorari.* Not being a judgment, in the sense of a final adjudication, the appellants were not concluded by his decision, for had there been an arbitrary exercise of statutory power or a ruling in excess of the jurisdiction conferred, they had the right to apply for and obtain appropriate relief in a court of equity. . . .

To hold that the writ could issue either before or after an administrative ruling would make the dispatch of business in the Departments wait on the decisions of the courts and not only lead to consequences of the most manifest inconvenience, but would be an invasion of the Executive by the Judicial branch of the Government.[50]

Mandamus.—Any generalization on the use of the writ of mandamus must be qualified by the "rule of diversity" in State judicial procedure. At common law, mandamus was a high prerogative writ issued in the name of the King, and the proceeding did not partake of the nature of a suit between parties. It was not an action by the relator, and the writ was not a summons requiring a party to appear and plead. Nor was it a writ of right; and the return could not be traversed or controverted by the relator but had to be taken as absolutely true, however false it might be in its statement of fact.

But the common law procedure and the nature of the writ have been changed by statute both in England and in the United States. In its present form, in the United States, it is a writ issued in the name of the state and directed to an individual, a corporation, or an inferior court, requiring them to do some particular thing which appertains to their office or duty. The writ is either *alternative* or *peremptory.* The former, usually issued at the commencement of a legal action, directs a party to take a specified action or show cause why he should not; the latter, issued after a hearing, commands a performance in accordance with the court's decree, without alternative. The peremptory writ will ordinarily issue in the first instance if only questions of law are involved; but if there are any questions of fact, the alternative writ is employed first in order to give the respondent an opportunity to show cause why he should not perform the act in issue. The alternative writ is not merely a writ as

[50] 229 U.S. at 171–72, 33 S. Ct. at 641, 57 L. Ed. at 1137–38. Italics supplied.

formerly, which could not be traversed or denied, but it is also a pleading. Issues are now made up by the writ and the return, and a trial may be had on these issues as in any civil action. In most of the States, a proceeding by mandamus is now considered a *civil action* by and between the real parties thereto—the relator and the respondent—and it is considered almost as much an *action of right* as any other civil action.[51]

However, the Supreme Court and some Federal Circuit Courts have held that an action for a writ of mandamus is not a suit of a civil nature at common law or in equity within the meaning of the acts of Congress creating and defining the jurisdiction of the Circuit Courts, and that such courts have no jurisdiction of such an action except in aid of a jurisdiction previously acquired.[52]

The thing to be done may consist of a single act or of a series of continuing acts, but each must be specific in nature—courts will not enforce performance of duties generally, such as the enforcement of general laws.[53] Furthermore, the duty to be performed must be ministerial, not discretionary or judicial.[54]

> The office of the writ of mandamus is, in general, to compel the performance of mere ministerial acts prescribed by law. It lies, however, also to subordinate judicial tribunals, to compel them to act where it is their duty to act, but never to require them to decide in a particular manner. It is not, like a writ of error or appeal, a remedy for erroneous decisions.[55]

[51] *State of Kansas ex rel. Atchison, Topeka & Santa Fe R. Co. v. Board of County Commissioners,* 11 Kan. 66 (1873); *Western Union Telegraph Co. v. State of Indiana ex rel. Hammond Elevator Co., et al.,* 165 Ind. 492, 76 N.E. 100 (1905).

[52] *Rosenbaum v. Bauer,* 120 U.S. 450, 7 S. Ct. 633, 30 L. Ed. 743 (1887); *Mystic Milling Co. v. Chicago, M. & St. P. Ry. Co.,* 132 F. 289 (C.C.N.D., Iowa, 1904).

[53] *People ex rel. Bartlett v. Dunne,* 219 Ill. 346, 76 N.E. 570 (1906); *Walsh v. LaGuardia,* 269 N.Y. 437, 199 N.E. 652 (1936). "Mandamus will not lie to compel a general course of official conduct, as it is impossible for a court to oversee the performance of such duties." *State ex rel. Hawes v. Brewer,* 39 Wash. 65, 80 Pac. 1001 (1905), quoted with approval in *State ex rel. Beardslee v. Landes, Mayor, et al.,* 149 Wash. 570, 571, 271 Pac. 829, 830 (1928).

[54] *Roberts, Treasurer v. United States,* 176 U.S. 221, 20 S. Ct. 376, 44 L. Ed. 443 (1900). For a discussion of the use of mandamus to control administrative discretion, see pp. 284–91.

[55] *People ex rel. Sheppard v. Dental Examiners,* 110 Ill. 180 (1884). Also, *Work v. United States ex rel. Rives,* 267 U.S. 175, 45 S. Ct. 252, 69 L. Ed. 561 (1925). *Safeway Stores, Inc. v. Brown,* 138 F. (2d) 278 (U.S.E.C.A., 1943) at p. 280: "Under such circumstances mandamus will lie where an inferior tribunal or agency refuses to act even though the act required involves the exercise of judgment and discretion. . . . Of course, in such a case the decree of the court would merely require the Administrator to exercise his discretionary power with respect to the protest without any direction as to the manner in which his discretion should be exercised."

So when the Interstate Commerce Commission refused to act from a mistaken interpretation of its powers under the Commerce Act, the Supreme Court affirmed a peremptory writ of mandamus by the Court of Appeals of the District of Columbia directing the Commission "to take jurisdiction of said cause and proceed therein as by law required." [56]

A mandamus proceeding is in substance a *personal* action. The writ seeks to enforce the *personal obligation* of the individual to whom it is addressed, even when he is an officer and the duty to be enforced is an official one. The writ cannot be directed to the office. It follows that on the death or retirement of the original defendant, the writ must abate in the absence of a statutory provision to the contrary; otherwise a successor in office may be mulcted in costs for the faults of his predecessor.[57] But a writ that has been directed to the officers of a corporation does not abate with the retirement of such officers, for the corporation is responsible for the acts of its officers, and the law can reach the corporation only through its officers—the corporation has perpetual succession, it cannot die or retire from office.[58]

Mandamus is a discretionary writ. It will not issue where there is a plain, speedy, and adequate remedy at law; and it is the *inadequacy* not the mere absence of other legal remedies, that generally determines the propriety of issuing a writ of mandamus. Many courts refuse the writ when it will not serve a useful purpose; [59] or where it would be ineffectual, as where the defendants cannot perform the duty; [60] or where the act in issue is expressly prohibited by statute,[61] or judicial decree.[62]

---

[56] *Interstate Commerce Commission v. United States, ex rel. Humboldt S. S. Co.,* 224 U.S. 474, 478, 32 S. Ct. 556, 56 L. Ed. 849, 851 (1911).

[57] *United States ex rel. Lewis v. Boutwell,* 17 Wall. 604, 21 L. Ed. 721 (1873).

[58] *Leavenworth County Commissioners v. Sellew,* 99 U.S. 624, 25 L. Ed. 333 (1879).

[59] *People ex rel. v. Green,* 356 Ill. 651, 190 N.E. 808 (1934); *County Commissioners v. Jacksonville,* 36 Fla. 196 (1895); *Rosenthal v. State Board of Canvassers,* 50 Kan. 129, 32 Pac. 129 (1893).

[60] *People ex rel. Bailey v. Supervisors of Greene County,* 12 Barb (N.Y.) 217 (1851); *County Commissioners v. Jacksonville, supra.*

[61] *Matter of Dr. Bloom, Dentist, Inc.,* 259 N.Y. 358, 364, 182 N.E. 16, 17 (1932): "Generally but not always the City Clerk's duties are ministerial, yet surely he could not be compelled to perform an act which would result in crime, fraud, or even public deception. He cannot be coerced into participating in transactions which are forbidden by law. While his power to exercise discretion is extremely limited, he is not, on the facts before us, entirely without some measure of it." Also, *City of Fostoria v. State ex rel.,* 125 Ohio St. 1, 180 N.E. 371 (1932); *People ex rel. v. Village of Oak Park,* 356 Ill. 154, 190 N.E. 286 (1934).

[62] *Ohio and Indiana Railroad Co. v. Commissioners,* 7 Ohio St. 278 (1857).

The court, in its discretion, may refuse mandamus to compel the doing of an idle act, . . . or to give a remedy which would work a public injury or embarrassment . . . just as, in its sound discretion, a court of equity may refuse to enforce or protect legal rights, the exercise of which may be prejudicial to the public interest.[63]

A peremptory writ of mandamus will be granted only to enforce a *clear* legal right—not to enforce rights of doubtful inference from statutes of uncertain meaning.[64] If the relator has slept upon his rights for an unreasonable time a court may refuse the writ.[65]

Out of deference to the doctrine of the separation of powers, the writ of mandamus will not issue to the President; and the better rule seems to be that it will not lie to a governor,[66] although some State courts hold that the governor, like other officers in the discharge of mere ministerial duties, is subject to the writ.[67]

There is a rule in some States that where the public interest is involved, a court may act upon the relation and motion of a private citizen if redress is required and mandamus is the proper remedy; but in other States an individual citizen cannot be heard as a relator and on his own motion unless he can show that he has some personal interest in the subject matter of complaint which is not common to all other citizens of the State.[68]

Injunction.—The injunction is an equity writ restraining a defendant in an equity proceeding or suit from doing an act which the court deems to be unjust or inequitable as regards the rights of some other party to the suit or proceeding. Injunctions may be classified as: *ex parte restraining orders, temporary* or *interlocutory,* and *permanent.* An ex parte restraining order is issued at the beginning of the suit on the basis of proof presented by the plaintiff alone, without opportunity for the defendant to be heard in rebuttal or to cross-examine. Obviously this remedy is used only in very

[63] *United States ex rel. Greathouse v. Dern,* 289 U.S. 352, 360, 53 S. Ct. 614, 617, 77 L. Ed. 1250, 1255 (1933). Also, *Duncan Townsite Co. v. Lane,* 245 U.S. 308, 38 S. Ct. 99, 62 L. Ed. 309 (1917); *Asbury Park v. Christmas,* 78 F. (2d) 1003 (C.C.A. 3d, 1935); *Application of Lingreen,* 232 N.Y. 59, 133 N.E. 353 (1921).

[64] *Wilbur v. United States,* 281 U.S. 206, 50 S. Ct. 320, 74 L. Ed. 809 (1930); *Miguel v. McCarl,* 291 U.S. 442, 54 S. Ct. 465, 78 L. Ed. 901 (1934); *United States ex rel. Girard Trust Co. v. Helvering,* 301 U.S. 540, 57 S. Ct. 855, 81 L. Ed. 1272 (1937); *Colonial Beacon Oil Co., Inc. v. Finn,* 245 App. Div. 459, 283 N.Y. Supp. 384 (3d Dept., 1935).

[65] *People ex rel. Gas Light Co. v. Common Council of Syracuse,* 78 N.Y. 56 (1879).

[66] *State v. Drew,* 17 Fla. 67 (1879); *People v. Morton et al.,* 156 N.Y. 136 (1898).

[67] *Magruder v. Swann, Governor,* 25 Md. 173 (1866); *State v. Chase,* 5 Ohio St. 528 (1856); *People v. Bissell,* 19 Ill. 229 (1857).

[68] *People ex rel. Drake v. Regents of the University of Michigan,* 4 Mich. 98 (1856), citing cases.

urgent cases. A temporary injunction is issued after notice to the plaintiff and a preliminary hearing to both parties and forbids or restrains the doing of acts which the court believes to be prejudicial to a decision of the case on the merits. A permanent injunction is issued after a full hearing and the case has been decided on the merits. Injunctions may also be classified as mandatory (affirmative) and preventive or prohibitory (negative).

The injunction has many and varied uses, the most common being the prevention of irreparable injury to private property, "irreparable" including inadequacy of legal remedy. Wrongs to personality, such as injury to reputation or restraint of body, are receiving increasing equity protection. Injunction has also been used freely to restrain violations of criminal statutes where the threatened criminal act would also result in irreparable injury to private right, such as the use of injunctions to prevent industrial strikes, stop public meetings of subversive elements (syndicalists, communists), and to abate an increasing number of public nuisances. Abuse of equity relief in these cases has led to charges of "government by injunction."

Injunction is also widely used against administrative action, ostensibly to prevent irreparable injury to private right, but actually to obtain judicial review. This has become regular procedure in federal and most State jurisdictions. Administrative law is concerned with the use of the injunction for the control of administrative action.[69]

The distinction between a mandatory injunction and mandamus is not clear. In fact, it appears that no distinction between these remedies is made in States where law and equity are administered by the same courts [70]—the choice of remedy is discretionary with the courts. In a Kentucky case involving an application for a mandatory injunction to compel election commissioners, who had refused to issue a certificate of nomination, to reconvene and issue the certificate, the court said:

> The further suggestion has been made that mandamus and not a mandatory injunction is the proper remedy in a case like this. We think either of these remedies, whichever is more available and will more speedily accomplish the desired result, may be resorted to, and the plaintiff may elect which he will pursue.[71]

[69] For a discussion equity to control administrative discretion see pp. 283–290.

[70] "High, in discussing interlocutory mandatory injunctions, declares that in those States where the distinctions between law and equity have been abolished (having reference only to distinctions between courts of law and courts of chancery) a mandatory injunction is not to be distinguished from a mandamus. 1 High on Injunctions, p. 6." *City of Dallas et al. v. McElroy,* 254 S.W. 599, 601 (Texas Civil Appeals, 1923).

[71] *Hays et al. v. Combs,* 177 Ky. 355, 361, 197 S.W. 788, 790 (1917).

To the same effect a Kansas court has held that "The difference in the procedure [between mandamus and mandatory injunction] lies chiefly in the names given the process issued." [72] The similarity of the remedies has been recognized also by the federal courts. [73] A common form of the mandatory injunction enjoins one officer from interfering with some other officer in performing a ministerial duty, which the latter is commanded to perform; [74] or, it may be a left-handed mandamus, enjoining an officer from refusing to perform a ministerial duty, [75] or enjoining an inferior officer from carrying out an order of his superior. [76] It is a discretionary writ, [77] which ordinarily will issue when, in the opinion of the court, speedy action is necessary and mandamus is inadequate or incomplete. [78]

It is common knowledge that a suit in equity does not lie where there is a plain adequate and complete remedy at law. "But the legal remedy must be as complete, practical and efficient as that which equity will afford." [79] Thus, the right to challenge the constitutionality of a State statute in an enforcement proceeding is not an adequate legal remedy if the risks involve heavy penalties, such as fine, imprisonment, and loss of property. Such risks effectively deter interested parties from securing an adjudication of their rights, and equity is a proper remedy. [80] Technically, a taxpayer or a licensee has a legal remedy for the payment of an illegal tax or fee by paying under protest and then suing to recover. In most cases this remedy is worthless, as it is cheaper and less onerous to pay and submit to the exaction than to protest and recover. Nevertheless equity will not interfere, except that a considerable number of complainants with the same grievance arising from the same cause may be allowed to sue together to avoid a multiplicity of suits. If, in such a situation, the complainants are required to pay the illegal tax and to resort to courts of law to recover the amounts so paid, the business of the courts will be obstructed by numerous actions of the same character, and the

---

[72] *Bissey et al. v. City of Marion et al.,* 104 Kan. 311, 314, 178 Pac. 611, 612 (1919).

[73] *Miguel v. McCarl,* 291 U.S. 442, 54 S. Ct. 465, 78 L. Ed. 901 (1934); *Warner Valley Stock Co. v. Smith,* 165 U.S. 28, 17 S. Ct. 225, 41 L. Ed. 621 (1897).

[74] *Dallas et al. v. McElroy, supra; Miguel v. McCarl, supra.*

[75] *Wilson v. Bowers,* 14 F. (2d) 976 (S.D.N.Y., 1924); *Moor v. Texas & N. O. R. Co.,* 75 F. (2d) 386 (C.C.A. 5th, 1935).

[76] *American School of Magnetic Healing v. McAnnulty,* 187 U.S. 94, 23 S. Ct. 33, 47 L. Ed. 90 (1902).

[77] *McNulty v. National Mediation Board,* 18 F. Supp. 494 (D.C.N.D.N.Y., 1936).

[78] *Scott et al. v. Singleton,* 171 Ky. 117, 188 S.W. 302 (1916).

[79] *Terrace et al. v. Thompson,* 263 U.S. 197, 214, 44 S. Ct. 15, 17, 68 L. Ed. 255, 274 (1923); *Matthews v. Rodgers,* 284 U.S. 521, 52 S. Ct. 217, 76 L. Ed. 447 (1932).

[80] *Terrace et al. v. Thompson,* 263 U.S. 197, 44 S. Ct. 15, 68 L. Ed. 255 (1923).

costs to the persons prosecuting the suits will be greater than the amount recovered. To prevent such large scale injustice equity will intervene.

> . . . where as here an ordinance of a city imposes an unauthorized and illegal tax, which affects in the same way a large number of its residents, who have a community of interest in the controlling principle involved, the decision of which will determine their separate property rights, the method of enforcement of the ordinance being drastic, the legal relief afforded to an individual being attended with expense out of proportion to the amount involved and practically not worth pursuing, but in combination relief in equity being complete, a representative action may be maintained by one or more aggrieved persons in behalf of themselves and others similarly situated and appropriate relief by injunction may be given.[81]

If the financial condition of a taxing unit is such that recovery of taxes paid under protest is doubtful, an injunction will lie to restrain collection of the tax.[82]

Equity is increasingly invoked to aid the enforcement of so-called police power laws with criminal penalties, particularly the abatement of public nuisances. The office of the writ of injunction in this connection is well stated by a Kentucky court as follows:

> It is freely admitted that equity will not enjoin the commission of a crime as such. As for instance, it will not enjoin one from carrying concealed deadly weapons or from committing any other crime, whether it be a felony or misdemeanor, where nothing else is involved except the commission of the crime, but where the chief purpose of the statute is to provide for the public welfare by regulating (not prohibiting) some already lawful calling and only provides a penalty for refusing to comply with such regulations, and which penalty is enacted as a punishment for such refusal, we can discover no logical reason why a court in administering the laws of its jurisdiction would be powerless to *prevent* the doing of the prohibited act merely because a penalty (only nominal in this case) is attached for a refusal to comply with the regulation.[83]

Conversely, equity will enjoin the enforcement of public welfare laws which do not in fact serve a legitimate purpose of the police power. Health and other sanitary authorities may be restrained from

---

[81]*Fairley v. City of Duluth et al.,* 150 Minn. 374, 383, 185 N.W. 390, 393 (1921).

[82] *Stewart Dry Goods Co. v. Lewis et al.,* 287 U.S. 9, 53 S. Ct. 68, 77 L. Ed. 135 (1932).

[83] *Kentucky State Board of Dental Examiners v. Payne,* 213 Ky. 382, 389, 281 S.W. 188, 191 (1926).

summarily abating property,[84] from taking action which threatens to create a nuisance,[85] or from acting fraudulently or oppressively.[86]

To come within the equity jurisdiction the rights in danger must be rights of persons or property. Equity is concerned with civil, not political, rights. Therefore, equity relief does not lie against the exercise of political, governmental, or sovereign power. Executive power is political, and under the constitutional separation of powers the President or a governor is free from judicial control in the performance of his executive powers. "Courts have no power over his person, and they cannot commit him for a disobedience of judicial process. For errors, if any, of law or of fact in the proceeding now pending before him [the removal of Mayor Walker by Governor Roosevelt], he is responsible, not to the courts, but to the people, and to his own conscience." [87] The reason for executive immunity from judicial process was explained by the Supreme Court in a case involving the enforcement of the Military Reconstruction Act of 1867 as follows:

> The Congress is the Legislative Department of the government; the President is the Executive Department. Neither can be restrained in its action by the Judicial Department, though the acts of both, when performed, are, in proper cases, subject to its cognizance.
>
> The impropriety of such interference will be clearly seen upon consideration of its possible consequences.
>
> Suppose the bill filed and the injunction prayed for [to restrain President Johnson from enforcing the Reconstruction Acts of 1867] allowed. If the President refuses obedience, it is needless to observe that the court is without power to enforce its process. If, on the other hand, the President complies with the order of the court and refuses to execute the acts of Congress, is it not clear that a collision may occur between the Executive and Legislative Departments of the government? May not the House of Representatives impeach the President for such action? And in that case could this court interfere, in behalf of the President, thus endangered by compliance with its mandate, and restrain by injunction the Senate of the United States from sitting as a court of impeachment? Would the strange spectacle be offered to the public world of an attempt by this court to arrest proceedings in that court?
>
> These questions answer themselves.[88]

[84] *Babcock v. Buffalo*, 56 N.Y. 268 (1874) ; *Rogers v. Barker,* 31 Barb. (N.Y.) 447 (1860).

[85] *Thompson v. Kimbrough,* 23 Tex. Civ. App. 350, 57 S.W. 328 (1900) ; *Baltimore v. Fairfield Improvement Co.,* 87 Md. 352, 39 Atl. 1081 (1898).

[86] *Chase v. Middleton,* 123 Mich. 647, 82 N.W. 612 (1900).

[87] *Donnelly v. Roosevelt,* 144 Misc. 525, 532, 259 N.Y.S. 356, 364–65 (1932).

[88] *Mississippi v. Johnson,* 4 Wall. 475, 500, 18 L. Ed. 437, 441 (1866). Also *Georgia v. Stanton,* 6 Wall. 50, 18 L. Ed. 721 (1867). But the Supreme Court of

Courts will not review, therefore, except to determine limits of jurisdiction, administrative acts such as the location of a political boundary,[89] the calling out of the militia,[90] the recognition of a foreign government,[91] the deportation of an enemy alien,[92] or the enforcement of a State election law where the basis for the suit is not a private wrong but a wrong suffered by the State as a polity.[93] Said Mr. Jus-

---

Wisconsin rejected the reasoning in the above federal cases as applied to the chief executive of the State, holding that it would constitute treason, "as it were," for the Governor to resist a proper writ. *Ekern v. McGovern,* 154 Wis. 157, 142 N.W. 595 (1913). *Query:* Did the Supreme Court abandon its traditional "hands off political questions" policy in *Youngstown Co. v. Sawyer,* decided June 3, 1952, when in a 6 to 3 decision it ruled that President Truman's executive order directing Secretary Sawyer to seize the steel mills to avert a strike was an unconstitutional usurpation of legislative power and enjoined enforcement thereof? The decision poses the question whether (the merits of the issue aside) the Court did not, in the name of constitutional separation of powers, itself violate that principle by assuming authority over the President in the exercise of the undefined executive power conferred upon him in Article II of the Constitution. *Lest we forget:* "So may judicial power be abused." Mr. Justice Stone in *United States v. Butler,* 297 U.S. 1, 87, 56 S. Ct. 312, 328, 80 L. Ed. 477, 499 (1936).

[89] *Foster v. Neilson,* 2 Pet. 253, 7 L. Ed. 415 (1829).

[90] *Martin v. Mott,* 12 Wheat. 19, 29, 30, 6 L. Ed. 537, 540 (1827) ; *Luther v. Borden,* 7 How. 1, 45, 12 L. Ed. 581 (1849). "By virtue of his duty to 'cause the laws to be faithfully executed,' the Executive is appropriately vested with the discretion to determine whether an exigency requiring military aid for that purpose has arisen. His decision to that effect is conclusive." But "what are the allowable limits of military discretion, and whether or not they have been overstepped in a particular case, are judicial questions." *Sterling v. Constantin,* 287 U.S. 378, 399, 401, 53 S. Ct. 190, 196, 77 L. Ed. 375, 386, 387 (1932).

[91] *United States v. Pink,* 315 U.S. 203, 230, 62 S. Ct. 552, 565, 86 L. Ed. 796, 817–18 (1942) ; *Jones v. United States,* 137 U.S. 202, 11 S. Ct. 80, 34 L. Ed. 961 (1890).

[92] *United States v. Watkins,* 159 F. (2d) 650, 653 (C.C.A. 2d, 1947). "The exclusion of aliens is a fundamental act of sovereignty. The right to do so stems not alone from legislative power, but is inherent in the executive power to control the foreign affairs of the nation. . . . When Congress prescribes a procedure concerning the admissibility of aliens, it is not dealing alone with a legislative power. It is implementing an inherent executive power." *United States v. Shaughnessy,* 338 U.S. 537, 542, 70 S. Ct. 309, 312, 94 L. Ed. 317, 324 (1950).

[93] *Colegrove et al. v. Green et al.,* 328 U.S. 549, 552, 66 S. Ct. 1198, 1199, 90 L. Ed. 1432, 1434 (1946). See *Cook v. Fortson,* 329 U.S. 675, 67 S. Ct. 21, 91 L. Ed. 596 (1946), and *South v. Peters,* 339 U.S. 276, 70 S. Ct. 641 (1950) involving Georgia's "County unity" plan for nomination of Governor; *Sanders v. Wilkins,* 152 F. (2d) 235 (C.C.A. 4th, 1945), involving Virginia's poll tax; *Wood v. Broom,* 287 U.S. 1, 53 S. Ct. 1, 77 L. Ed. 131 (1932), the Mississippi apportionment act. The right to vote, to hold office, to run for office, and to have a candidate to vote for, are political, not civil, rights and are not protected against invasion by equity. *MacDougall et al. v. Green et al.,* 335 U.S. 281, 69 S. Ct. 1, 93 L. Ed. 3 (1948) ; *Blackman et al. v. Stone et al.,* 17 F. Supp. 102 (D.C.S.D. Ill., 1936). But State courts have used the injunction to prevent frauds against the election laws. *Pierce et al. v. Superior Court of Los Angeles County,* 1 Cal. (2d) 759, 37 P. (2d) 453 (1934) ; *Aichele v. People ex rel. Lowry,* 40 Colo. 482, 90 Pac. 1122 (1907) ; *Spriggs v. Clark,* 45 Wyo. 62, 14 P. (2d) 667 (1932).

tice Frankfurter: "It is hostile to a democratic system to involve the judiciary in the politics of the people. And it is not less pernicious if such judicial intervention in an essentially political contest be dressed up in the abstract phrases of the law." [94]

Furthermore, a court of equity does not have jurisdiction over the prosecution, the punishment, or the pardon of crimes or misdemeanors, or over the appointment or removal of public officers. These matters lie within the domain of the courts of common law or of the executive department of the government. Accordingly, equity will not intervene to restrain a criminal prosecution or to prevent the removal of a public officer; [95] except that in removal proceedings a court of equity can require the removing officer to keep within his jurisdiction, such as granting a hearing where required by statute; [96] and except that "where property rights will be destroyed, unlawful interference by criminal proceedings under a void law or ordinance may be reached and controlled by a decree of a court of equity." [97]

> It is settled beyond controversy that a court of equity has no jurisdiction to interfere with prosecutions for criminal offenses, and it makes no difference whether the prosecution is under a statute which applies to the State at large or under an ordinance which is in force only in a particular municipality. *Courts of equity deal only with civil and property rights,* and their powers do not extend to determining what laws or ordinances are valid or invalid unless such determination is incidental to the protection of rights recognized by courts of equity alone.[98]

Furthermore,

> It is equally well settled that a court of equity has no jurisdiction

[94] 328 U.S. at 553–54, 66 S. Ct. at 1200, 90 L. Ed. at 1434. And "Federal courts consistently refuse to exercise their equity powers in cases posing political issues arising from a state's geographical distribution of electoral strength among its political subdivisions." *South v. Peters,* 339 U.S. 276, 277, 70 S. Ct. 641, 642 (1950).

[95] *In re Sawyer,* 124 U.S. 200, 8 S. Ct. 482, 31 L. Ed. 402 (1888); *State ex rel. Derwort v. Hummel,* 146 Ohio 618, 67 N.E. (2d) 540 (1946); *Creek Nation v. United States,* 318 U.S. 629, 638–40, 63 S. Ct. 784, 789–90, 87 L. Ed. 1046, 1052–54 (1943); *White, Collector, et al. v. Berry,* 171 U.S. 366, 18 S. Ct. 917, 43 L. Ed. 199 (1898).

[96] *State ex rel. Churchill, Atty. Gen. v. Hay,* 45 Neb. 321, 63 N.W. 821 (1895); *State ex rel. Loomis v. Dahlem,* 37 Wyo. 498, 263 Pac. 708 (1927).

[97] *Dobbins v. City of Los Angeles,* 195 U.S. 223, 241, 25 S. Ct. 18, 22, 49 L. Ed. 169, 177 (1904), citing, *Davis & F. Mfg. Co. v. Los Angeles,* 189 U.S. 207–18, 23 S. Ct. 498, 47 L. Ed. 778–80 (1903).

[98] *City of Chicago v. Chicago City Ry. Co.,* 222 Ill. 560, 570, 78 N.E. 890, 892 (1906), italics supplied; *Kelly & Co. v. Conner,* 122 Tenn. 339, 123 S.W. 622 (1909); *Lindsey v. Drane,* 154 Tenn. 458, 285 S.W. 705 (1926).

over the appointment and removal of public officers, whether the power of removal is vested, as well as that of appointment, in executive or administrative boards or officers, or is intrusted to a judicial tribunal. The jurisdiction to determine the title to a public office belongs exclusively to the courts of law, and is exercised either by *certiorari,* error, or appeal, or by a writ of *quo warranto,* . . . according to the circumstances of the case, and the mode of procedure established by common law or by statute.[99]

The general rule is that an injunction will not be granted against the collection of taxes, "unless it clearly appears, not only that the tax is illegal, but that the owner of the property taxed has no adequate remedy by the ordinary processes of the law, and that there are special circumstances bringing the case under the recognized head of equity jurisdiction." [100] The reason for this rule is that since the levy of a tax is legislative and not judicial, a court which enjoins the enforcement of an invalid tax cannot render justice by substituting a valid tax—and taxes are essential to the maintenance of government. Ordinarily the taxpayer has ample remedy, either by action against the officer collecting the tax or against the body to whom the tax is paid.

Equity, however, will enjoin an intentionally discriminatory valuation of property for tax purposes. The discrimination must be more than sporadic, due to mistake or other accidental causes. A court of equity "can interfere only when it is made clear that there is, with respect to certain species of property, systematic, intentional, and unlawful under-valuations for taxation by the taxing officers, which necessarily effect an unjust discrimination against the species of property of which the complainant is an owner." [101] Also, the enforcement of confiscatory rates by regulatory commissions will be enjoined; [102] and a tax collector [103] or a regulatory agency [104] will be restrained from proceeding under an unconstitutional law to prevent irreparable injury to private property.

[99] *In re Sawyer,* 124 U.S. 200, 212, 8 S. Ct. 482, 488, 31 L. Ed. 402, 406 (1888).

[100] *Pittsburgh etc. Railway v. Board of Public Works of West Virginia,* 172 U.S. 32, 37, 19 S. Ct. 90, 92, 43 L. Ed. 354, 356 (1898).

[101] *Taylor et al. v. Louisville & Nashville R. Co.,* 88 Fed. 350, 373 (C.C.A. 6th, 1898).

[102] *Reagan v. Farmers' Loan & Trust Co.,* 154 U.S. 362, 14 S. Ct. 1047, 38 L. Ed. 1014 (1894) ; *Prout v. Starr,* 188 U.S. 537, 23 S. Ct. 398, 47 L. Ed. 584 (1903).

[103] *Poindexter v. Greenhow,* 114 U.S. 270, 5 S. Ct. 903, 29 L. Ed. 185 (1885).

[104] *McNeill v. Southern R. Co.,* 202 U.S. 543, 26 S. Ct. 722, 51 L. Ed. 1142 (1906).

The Scope of Judicial Review

It has been a mistake to regard the executive and judicial departments as independent and opposed branches of government in an elaborate scheme of constitutional checks and balances. They are related instrumentalities for the effectuation of public policy formulated by the legislative branch. The administrator and judge are partners in the business of law enforcement. Justice is the cooperative responsibility of government. Judicial review of administrative action should not be regarded as a form of "control" but rather as a step in an integrated process of common achievement, the administration of justice. Judicial review is at best only a means to an end— an end that is not being served by an endless jockeying for power and prestige. The methods of agency and court are different, but they are complementary not antagonistic; and since the duties of both are largely determined by statute, it is for the legislature, within constitutional limitations, to define their respective jurisdictions.

Mr. Justice Frankfurter, the Supreme Court's specialist in administrative law, is of the opinion that

> Except in those rare instances, as in a claim of citizenship in deportation proceedings, when a judicial trial becomes a constitutional requirement because of "The difference of security of judicial over administrative action," . . . whether judicial review is available at all and, if so, who may invoke it, under what circumstances, in what manner, and to what end, are questions that depend for their answer upon the particular enactment under which judicial review is claimed. . . . Apart from the text and texture of a particular law in relation to which judicial review is sought "judicial review" is a mischievous abstraction. There is no such thing as a common law of judicial review in the federal courts. The procedural provisions in more than a score of these regulatory measures prove that the manner in which Congress has distributed responsibility for the enforcement of its laws between courts and administrative agencies runs a gamut all the way from authorizing a judicial trial de novo of a claim determined by the administrative agency to denying all judicial review and making administrative action definitive. . . .
>
> However useful judicial review may be, it is for Congress and not for this Court to decide when it may be used—except when the Constitution commands it.[105]

[105] *Stark v. Wickard,* 321 U.S. 288, 312–13, 314, 64 S. Ct. 559, 572, 573, 88 L. Ed. 733, 749, 750 (1944). In dissenting opinion.

Where the statute prescribes a procedure for review the courts are not likely to recognize any other, unless the prescribed procedure is not constitutional "due process." [106]

General Jurisdiction to Review Administrative Action.—Judicial review of an administrative proceeding may be indirect through a common-law action for damages. This is so where the statute does not make any special provision for review, and parties must resort to such common-law remedies as injunction or habeas corpus. Such actions ordinarily are tried before a jury, and there is a tendency to reexamine all questions, including questions of fact, which have a bearing on the officer's liability. This procedure subjects the findings of administrative experts to the judgment of a lay jury. With the growth of regulatory agencies, provision was made by statute for direct appellate review of the *judicial actions* of these administrative bodies. This is in the nature of an appeal and, therefore, appellate procedure applies. In this kind of proceeding the whole case ordinarily is not open for revision. Only "questions of law" are supposed to be open to review. Findings of fact should not be questioned or disturbed. Direct review is applicable only to cases where the agency has made a formal investigation or held a hearing and made a finding which constitutes a record for the reviewing court to act upon. If the administrative action has been summary, the old indirect method of review by an action for damages is the only available remedy. Direct review may be by certiorari, the traditional common-law method of removing proceedings from an inferior to a superior court for review, or by statutory forms of injunction, which are substantially appellate in character and so are governed by appellate procedure. Injunction proceedings are used almost universally in the federal administrative system.

The right to nonstatutory review by federal courts results from the vesting of "the judicial power" in such courts by Article III of the Constitution, and "the silence of Congress as to judicial review is not necessarily to be construed as a denial of the power of the federal courts to grant relief in the exercise of the *general jurisdiction* which Congress has conferred upon them." [107] The framers of the Constitution recognized "the judicial power" as a separate governmental function and reposed it in a third, independent and coordinate

---

[106] *Securities and Exchange Commission v. Andrews,* 88 F. (2d) 441 (C.C.A. 2d, 1937). See B. P. McAllister, "Statutory Roads to Review of Federal Administrative Orders," 28 *California Law Review* (1940), 129 ff.

[107] *Estep v. United States,* 327 U.S. 114, 120, 66 S. Ct. 423, 426, 90 L. Ed. 567, 571 (1946). Italics supplied.

branch. "Inherent" in the "judicial power" is authority to decide cases according to the law, in the last analysis according to the fundamental and superior law, the Constitution.[108] Administrative decisions, therefore, which affect constitutional rights cannot be made final, for that "would spell executive absolutism, a concept unknown to our law. . . . If the judiciary has no power in such matter, the only practical restraint would be the self-restraint of the executive branch. Such a result is foreign to our concept of the division of the powers of government." [109]

Nevertheless, judicial opinion is divided, and the decisions of the Supreme Court do not seem to be wholly consistent on the question of reviewability of administrative action taken under a statute which does not specifically provide for review. In general,

> Where an Act fails to provide for review of preliminary rulings determining status in preparation for subsequent action, or performing administrative duties which were not final in character, such rulings have not been considered as subject to review by virtue of general statutory review provisions. The reason that review is not allowed at such a stage is that the rulings or orders are only preparation for future effective action. *The Rochester Telephone Corporation case . . . .* teaches that where this otherwise abstract determination of status has instantaneous, final effect, such determination comes under general statutory review provisions.[110]

But it was also stated in the same case :

> Congress has long delegated to executive officers or executive agencies the determination of complicated questions of fact and of law. And where no judicial review was provided by Congress this Court has often refused to furnish one even where questions of law might be involved. [Citing cases] . . .
>
> All constitutional questions aside, it is for Congress to determine how the rights which it creates shall be enforced. . . .
>
> Generalizations as to when judicial review of administrative action may or may not be obtained are, of course, hazardous. Where Congress has not expressly authorized judicial review, the type of problem in-

---

[108] This is the doctrine of *Marbury v. Madison,* 1 Cranch 137, 2 L. Ed. 60 (1803).

[109] *Fleming v. Moberly Milk Products Co.,* 160 F. (2d) 259, 265 (App. D.C., 1947). Mr. Justice Stone used similar language in reference to *judicial discretion* in *United States v. Butler,* 297 U.S. 1, 78, 79, 56 S. Ct. 312, 325, 80 L. Ed. 477, 495 (1936).

[110] Mr. Justice Reed, dissenting, in *Switchmen's Union v. Board,* 320 U.S. 297, 313, 64 S. Ct. 95, 103 88 L. Ed. 61, 70–71 (1943). For nonreviewability of tentative action see *Delaware & Hudson Co. v. United States,* 266 U.S. 438, 45 S. Ct. 153, 69 L. Ed. 369 (1925); for intermediary action, *Federal Power Commission v. Edison Co.,* 304 U.S. 375, 58 S. Ct. 963, 82 L. Ed. 1408 (1938).

volved and the history of the statute in question become highly relevant in determining whether judicial review may be nonetheless supplied.[111]

Butte, A. & P. Ry. Co. v. United States,[112] arose out of federal operation of the railroads during World War I. Congress provided compensation to carriers for losses attributable to government control and directed the Interstate Commerce Commission to ascertain the amount of such losses and authorized the Secretary of the Treasury to draw warrants upon the Treasury for the amounts certified by the Commission. The United States instituted suit to recover payments made to the Butte Company on the theory that the money had been disbursed on an erroneous construction of the statute. The Court held that authority to interpret the statute was "essential to the performance of the duty imposed upon the Commission," and since "Congress did not provide a method of review," both the government and the carrier were "remediless whether the error be one of fact or of law." [113]

In *Switchmen's Union v. Board,*[114] the National Mediation Board had made a certification of representatives for collective bargaining under the Railway Labor Act.[115] A suit for cancellation was brought in the District Court, and that court upheld the decision of the Board and this decision was affirmed by the Circuit Court of Appeals. On appeal, the Supreme Court ruled that the District Court did not have power to review the action of the Board, by virtue of its general jurisdiction under the Judicial Code [116] "in face of the special circumstances which obtain here." Relying on the ruling in the Butte Railway case discussed above, the Court now said:

> In the present case the authority of the Mediation Board in election disputes to interpret the meaning of "craft" as used in the statute is no less clear and no less essential to the performance of its duty. The statutory command that the decision of the Board shall be obeyed is no less explicit. Under this Act Congress did not give the Board discretion to take or withhold action, to grant or deny relief. It gave it no enforcement functions. It was to find the fact and then cease. Congress prescribed the command. Like the command in the *Butte A. & P. Ry.* case it contained no exception. Here as in that case the intent

[111] 320 U.S. at 303, 301, 64 S. Ct. at 98, 97, 88 L. Ed. at 65, 64.
[112] 290 U.S. 127, 54 S. Ct. 108, 78 L. Ed. 222 (1933).
[113] 290 U.S. at 143, 54 S. Ct. at 112, 78 L. Ed. at 228.
[114] 320 U.S. 297, 64 S. Ct. 95, 88 L. Ed. 61 (1943).
[115] Section 2, Ninth, 44 *Stat.* 577, 48 *Stat.* 1185, 45 *U.S.C.A.* § 152.
[116] Act of March 3, 1911, Sec. 24(8), 28 *U.S.C.A.* § 41(8).

seems plain—the dispute was to reach its last terminal point when the administrative finding was made. There was to be no dragging out of the controversy into other tribunals of law.[117]

This conclusion, said the Court, is reinforced by the fact that while Congress did provide for judicial review of two types of orders or awards under Sections 3 and 9 of the Act, it omitted any provision for review under Section 2 (applicable in the instant case), thereby drawing a line of distinction. "And the inference is strong from the history of the Act that that distinction was not inadvertent. The language of the Act read in the light of that history supports the view that Congress gave administrative action under § 2, Ninth a finality which it denied administrative action under the other sections of the Act." [118] In short, administrative finality may be inferred or implied as well as expressly conferred.

Nevertheless, a year later, in *Stark v. Wickard,*[119] the Court reached the opposite conclusion in a case involving an essentially similar legal situation. Here certain milk producers challenged a marketing order made by the Secretary of Agriculture by authority of the Agricultural Marketing Agreement Act of 1937.[120] The Act provides specifically for judicial review of such orders in the case of milk handlers, but is silent as to producers and consumers. The Court proceeded to deduce "from the statutes and precedents" that Congress had recognized "the applicability of judicial review in this field" and that therefore "it is not to be lightly assumed that the silence of the statute bars from the courts an otherwise justiciable issue." And, "When . . . definite personal rights are created by federal statute, similar in kind to those customarily treated in courts of law, the silence of Congress as to judicial review is, at any rate in the absence of an administrative remedy, not to be construed as a denial of authority to the aggrieved person to seek appropriate relief in the federal courts in the exercise of their general jurisdiction." [121]

But Mr. Justice Frankfurter, dissenting, appears to have the better of the argument. After pointing out that "only the other day we found the implications of the Railway Labor Act . . . to be such that courts could not even exercise the function of keeping the Na-

---

[117] 320 U.S. at 305, 64 S. Ct. at 99, 88 L. Ed. at 66.

[118] 320 U.S. at 306, 64 S. Ct. at 99, 88 L. Ed. at 67. Mr. Justice Reed, Mr. Justice Roberts, and Mr. Justice Jackson dissented.

[119] 321 U.S. 288, 64 S. Ct. 559, 88 L. Ed. 733 (1944).

[120] 50 *Stat.* 246, 7 *U.S.C.A.* §§ 601 *et sqq.*

[121] 321 U.S. at 309, 64 S. Ct. at 570–71, 88 L. Ed. at 747–48. Opinion by Mr. Justice Reed.

tional Mediation Board within its statutory authority," [122] he proceeded:

> Provision for judicial remedies for consumers and producers is significantly absent. Such omission is neither inadvertent nor surprising. It would be manifestly incongruous for an Act which specifically provides that no order shall be directed at producers to give to producers the right to attack the validity of such an order in court. . . .
>
> An elaborate process of implications should not be invented to escape the plain meaning of § 8c(15), and to dislocate a carefully formulated scheme of enforcement. . . .
>
> The Court is thus adding to what Congress has written a provision for judicial relief of producers. And it sanctions such relief in a case in which petitioners have no standing to sue on any theory.[123]

But in a case involving the power of a reviewing court to stay the order under review, in the absence of an express grant of such staying power, Mr. Justice Frankfurter, for the Court, found "controlling considerations" which "compel the assumption that Congress would not, *without clearly expressing such a purpose,* deprive the Court of Appeals of its customary power to stay orders under review," [124]

He continued:

> The search for significance in the silence of Congress is too often the pursuit of a mirage. We must be wary against interpolating our notions of policy in the interstices of legislative provisions. Here Congress said nothing about the power of the Court of Appeals to issue stay orders under § 402(b). But denial of such power is not to be inferred merely because Congress failed specifically to repeat the general grant of auxiliary powers to the federal courts. . . . The power to stay was so firmly imbedded in our judicial system, so consonant with the historic procedures of federal appellate courts, that there was no necessity for the Court of Appeals to justify its settled practice.[125]

Section 10 of the Administrative Procedure Act makes *any administrative action* reviewable provided (1) a person's legal rights are affected adversely, (2) there is no other adequate remedy in any court, and (3) review is not in terms precluded, either by specific prohibition or by grant of administrative discretion.

---

[122] 321 U.S. at 313, 64 S. Ct. at 572–73, 88 L. Ed. at 750, referring to *Switchmen's Union v. National Mediation Board,* 320 U.S. 297, 64 S. Ct. 95, 88 L. Ed. 61 (1943).

[123] 321 U.S. at 317, 319, 64 S. Ct. at 574, 575, 88 L. Ed. at 752, 753.

[124] *Scripps-Howard Radio v. Federal Communications Commission,* 316 U.S. 4, 11, 62 S. Ct. 875, 880, 86 L. Ed. 1229, 1235 (1942). Italics supplied.

[125] 316 U.S. at 11, 13, 62 S. Ct. at 880, 881, 86 L. Ed. at 1235, 1236.

In the States, common-law remedies are available in the absence of statutory provisions to the contrary, and the courts will apply the common-law remedies when the statutes are merely silent as to review. "Whether an act expressly provides for an appeal is of no consequence. If an administrative officer undertakes to perform any unauthorized act, an action will lie in court enjoining, prohibiting, or mandating him in the performance of administrative acts." [126]

When an agency institutes a proceeding for the enforcement of one of its orders the court may, ordinarily, review the validity of the order. This may take the form of an indictment for refusal to obey an order,[127] or a petition for an enforcement decree.[128] Thus, when the National Labor Relations Board petitions for enforcement under §10(e) of the Labor Act, "The party proceeded against is entitled to raise all pertinent questions and to obtain any affirmative relief that is appropriate." [129]

Questions of Law.—The scope of judicial review of administrative action is determined, therefore, in part by statute and in part by the courts in reference to the common law and Article III and the due process clauses of the Constitution. An administrative rule or order which raises a question of law is ordinarily subject to judicial review on both substantive and jurisdictional grounds.[130] *"When dealing with constitutional rights* (as distinguished from privileges accorded by the Government, United States v. Babcock, 250 U.S. 328, 331) *there must be the opportunity of presenting,* at some time, *to some court, every question of law raised,* whatever the nature of the right invoked or the status of him who claims it." [131] Except in special cases this rule applies whether the applicant seeks the protection of a constitutional, statutory, or common-law right.

---

[126] *Financial Aid Corp. v. Wallace,* 216 Ind. 114, 23 N.E. (2d) 472 (1939). For a further citation of cases see Carl McFarland and Arthur T. Vanderbilt, *Cases on Administrative Law* (Mathew Bender & Co., Inc., Albany and New York, 1947), note, p. 949.

[127] *Estep v. United States,* 327 U.S. 114, 66 S. Ct. 423, 90 L. Ed. 567 (1946).

[128] *Amalgamated Workers v. Edison Co.,* 309 U.S. 261, 60 S. Ct. 561, 84 L. Ed. 738 (1940).

[129] *Ford Motor Co. v. Labor Board,* 305 U.S. 364, 370, 59 S. Ct. 301, 305, 83 L. Ed. 221, 228 (1939).

[130] *Gonzales v. Williams,* 192 U.S. 1, 24 S. Ct. 177, 48 L. Ed. 317 (1904); *Gegiow v. Uhl,* 239 U.S. 3, 36 S. Ct. 2, 60 L. Ed. 114 (1915); *Interstate Commerce Commission v. Union Pacific R.R.,* 222, U.S. 541, 32 S. Ct. 690, 56 L. Ed. 308 (1912). *Cf.* A. M. Tollefson, "Administrative Finality," 29 *Michigan Law Review* (May, 1931), 839 ff., for cases.

[131] Mr. Justice Brandeis (in a concurring opinion) in *St. Joseph Stock Yards Co. v. United States,* 298 U.S. 38, 73, 56 S. Ct. 720, 735, 80 L. Ed. 1033, 1052 (1936). Italics supplied.

Statutory provision respecting judicial review of administrative action varies from no mention of the matter to positive prohibition. Some statutes merely provide that "orders" shall be reviewable; some that an "aggrieved person" or person "adversely affected" by an order may bring suit; some specify what may be reviewed; some confine review to "questions of law"; some deny the right of review; some provide that the order shall be prima facie evidence; and others require judicial enforcement of orders.

Section 10 of the Administrative Procedure Act [132] provides that

> Except so far as (1) statutes preclude judicial review or (2) agency action is by law committed to agency discretion—
>
> . . . Any person suffering legal wrong because of *any agency action,* or adversely affected or aggrieved by such action within the meaning of any relevant statute, shall be entitled to judicial review, thereof.
>
> . . . Every agency action made reviewable by statute and *every final agency action for which there is no other adequate remedy in any court* shall be subject to judicial review.
>
> . . . So far as necessary to decision and where presented the reviewing court shall decide all relevant questions of law, interpret constitutional and statutory provisions, and determine the meaning or applicability of the terms of any agency action. It shall (A) compel agency action unlawfully withheld or unreasonably delayed; and (B) hold unlawful and set aside agency action, findings, and conclusions found to be (1) arbitrary, capricious, an abuse of discretion, or otherwise not in accordance with law; (2) contrary to constitutional right, power, privilege, or immunity; (3) in excess of statutory jurisdiction, authority, or limitations, or short of statutory right; (4) without observance of procedure required by law; (5) unsupported by substantial evidence in any case subject to the requirements of sections 7 and 8 or otherwise reviewed on the record of an agency hearing provided by statute; or (6) unwarranted by the facts to the extent that the facts are subject to trial de novo by the reviewing court. In making the foregoing determinations the court shall review the whole record or such portions thereof as may be cited by any party, and due account shall be taken of the rule of prejudicial error.

In the above situations the ruling principle is an attempt to separate questions of law from questions of fact and to confine judicial review to the former. This is true even when the courts invade the fact-finding field, as when they review jurisdictional facts and determine what constitutes "substantial evidence," since jurisdiction in these cases is based upon the questionable assumption that the issues

---

[132] Public Law 404, Chap. 324, 79th Cong., 2d Sess. 60 *Stat.,* 243, 5 *U.S.C.A.* § 1009. Italics supplied.

involved are legal and not factual. The judicial attitude may be
summed up as follows:

> The power usually delegated to administrative agencies is of three
> (3) general patterns: (1) quasi judicial power, to determine controver-
> sies; (2) legislative power, such as rate and rule making; or (3) the
> power to act merely in an advisory capacity to the Legislative or Ex-
> ecutive branch of the Government. It is generally understood that as
> to agencies coming within the first two classifications, there is an under-
> lying power in the Courts to scrutinize the acts of such jurisdiction,[133]
> even though no right of review is given by statute. As to administra-
> tive tribunals falling within the third classification, it is settled law
> that the Courts have no inherent power to interfere with, or review, the
> acts of such an agency and unless the right of review is especially given
> by statute Courts are without jurisdiction to control the action taken
> by the said agency. The National War Labor Board is an administra-
> tive tribunal within the last classification.[134]

To the same general effect Mr. Justice Frankfurter has said:

> Generally speaking, judicial review of administrative orders is lim-
> ited to determining whether errors of law have been committed. . . .
> Because of historical differences in the relationship between adminis-
> trative bodies and reviewing courts and that between lower and upper
> courts, a court of review exhausts the power when it lays bare a mis-
> conception of law and compels correction.[135]

But, "on matters of law, unmixed, reviewing courts are free to
substitute their own judgment for that of the administrators, although great weight must be given to administrative judgment." [136]
However, an administrative determination of a "question of law"
is not to be overruled unless the mistake in law is "clear cut," at least
in tax cases.

[133] Cf. Hannegan v. Esquire, Inc., 327 U.S. 146, 66 S. Ct. 456, 90 L. Ed. 586
(1946); Chenery Corp. v. Securities and Exchange Commission, 154 F. (2d) 6
(App. D.C., 1946).

[134] May Department Stores Co. v. Brown, 60 F. Supp. 735, 738 (D.C.W.D. Mo.,
1945).

[135] Scripps-Howard Radio v. Federal Communications Commission, 316 U.S. 4,
10, 62 S. Ct. 875, 880, 86 L. Ed. 1229, 1234 (1942). "Unless in some specific
respect there has been prejudicial departure from requirements of the law or
abuse of the Commission's [Interstate Commerce Commission] discretion, the reviewing court is without authority to intervene. It cannot substitute its own view
concerning what should be done, whether with reference to competitive considerations or others, for the Commission's judgment upon matters committed to its determination, if that has support in the record and the applicable law." United
States v. Pierce Auto Freight Lines, Inc., 327 U.S. 515, 535, 66 S. Ct. 687, 698,
90 L. Ed. 821, 835 (1946).

[136] Agnew v. Board of Governors of Federal Reserve System, 153 F. (2d) 785,
789 (App. D.C., 1946).

Congress did not authorize review of all legal questions upon which the Tax Court passed. It merely allowed modification or reversal if the decision of the Tax Court is "not in accordance with law." But if a statute upon which the Tax Court unmistakably has to pass allows the Tax Court's application of the law to the situation before it as a reasonable one—if the situation could, without violence to language, be brought within the terms under which the Tax Court placed it or be kept out of the terms from which that Court kept it—the Tax Court cannot in reason be said to have acted "not in accordance with law." In short, there was no "clear-cut mistake of law" but a fair administration of it.[137]

Statutory construction is "a question of law" and thus a judicial function. Interpretation by the agency charged with the administration of a statute will be given great weight, particularly if the terms of the statute are ambiguous, but such construction is not controlling upon the courts. Administrative rulings and interpretations, said the Supreme Court, "while not controlling upon the courts by reason of their authority, do constitute a body of experience and informed judgment to which courts and litigants may properly resort for guidance."[138] Administrative interpretation which tends to restrict civil liberty, as for example the establishment of censorship, is presumed to be erroneous unless the language of the statute is not susceptible of a different construction. Thus, when the Postmaster General revoked the second-class permit of *Esquire Magazine* on the ground that it was not "devoted to literature" within the second-class classification of the postal laws,[139] and held that "A publication to enjoy these unique mail privileges . . . is under a positive duty to contribute to . . . the public welfare," the Supreme Court reversed the Postmaster General. The Court found that "a requirement that literature or art conform to some form prescribed by an official smacks of an ideology foreign to our system."[140] Properly construed the standards prescribed by the statute referred to the format of the publication and to the nature of its contents and not to their quality. If, however, the interpretation of a given statute is "peculiarly within

[137] Mr. Justice Frankfurter in *Bingham's Trust v. Commissioner of Internal Revenue*, 325 U.S. 365, 381–82, 65 S. Ct. 1232, 1240, 89 L. Ed. 1670, 1681 (1945).
[138] *Mabee v. White Plains Publishing Co.*, 327 U.S. 178, 182, 66 S. Ct. 511, 513, 90 L. Ed. 607, 611 (1946); quoting from *Skidmore v. Swift & Co.*, 323 U.S. 134, 140, 65 S. Ct. 161, 164 (1945). Other cases: *Roland Electric Co. v. Walling*, 326 U.S. 657, 66 S. Ct. 413, 90 L. Ed. 383 (1946); *Boutell v. Walling*, 327 U.S. 363, 66 S. Ct. 631, 90 L. Ed. 786 (1946); *Social Security Board v. Nierotko*, 327 U.S. 358, 368–70, 66 S. Ct. 637, 643, 90 L. Ed. 718, 727–28 (1946).
[139] 20 *Stat.* 359 (1879), 48 *Stat.* 928 (1934), 39 *U.S.C.A.* § 226.
[140] *Hannegan v. Esquire, Inc.*, 327 U.S. 146, 150, 158, 66 S. Ct. 456, 458, 462, 90 L. Ed. 586, 589, 593 (1946).

the competence" of an administrative tribunal, even statutory construction may be entrusted to such tribunal. In respect to the jurisdiction of the Tax Court it has been said:

> To hold that the Circuit Courts of Appeals, and eventually this Court, must make an independent examination of the meaning of every word of tax legislation, no matter whether the words express accounting, business, or other conceptions peculiarly within the special competence of the Tax Court, is to sacrifice the effectiveness of the judicial scheme designed by Congress especially for tax litigation to an abstract notion of "law" derived from the merely historic function of courts generally to construe documents, including legislation.[141]

Administrative construction of administrative regulations is controlling unless plainly erroneous or inconsistent.[142] And interpretative bulletins issued by an agency have been held to constitute official interpretation of statute or regulation.[143] Failure to exercise power conferred upon an agency by a statute "neither extinguishes power granted nor establishes that the agency to which it is given regards itself as impotent."[144]

An administrative statutory construction which involves the jurisdiction of the interpreting agency, is subject to judicial review. In reviewing the legality of an administrative action, a court will con-

---

[141] Mr. Justice Frankfurter (joined by Mr. Justice Roberts and Mr. Justice Jackson) in a concurring opinion in *Bingham's Trust v. Commissioner of Internal Revenue*, 325 U.S. 365, 380, 65 S. Ct. 1232, 1240, 89 L. Ed. 1670, 1680-81 (1945). In *Unemployment Compensation Commission of Alaska v. Aragan*, 329 U.S. 143; 153–54, 67 S. Ct. 245, 250, 91 L. Ed. 136, 145 (1946), it was held in regard to a finding by the Commission that a labor dispute was in "active progress" within the meaning of the Alaska Unemployment Compensation Act of 1937, 1939: "To sustain the Commission's application of this statutory term, we need not find that its construction is the only reasonable one or even that it is the result we would have reached had the question arisen in the first instance in judicial proceedings. The 'reviewing court's function is limited.' All that is needed to support the Commission's interpretation is that it has 'warrant in the record' and a 'reasonable basis in law.' "

[142] *Bowles v. Mannie & Co.*, 155 F. (2d) 129 (C.C.A. 7th, 1946); *Superior Packing Co. v. Porter*, 156 F. (2d) 193 (C.C.A. 8th, 1946).

[143] *Bridgeman v. Ford, Bacon & Davis Co.*, 64 F. Supp. 1006 (E.D. Ark., 1946); *Damutz v. Pinchbeck, Inc.*, 66 F. Supp. 667 (D. Conn., 1946).

[144] Mr. Justice Rutledge for the majority in *United States v. American Union Transport*, 327 U.S. 437, 454, 66 S. Ct. 644, 653 (note 18), 90 L. Ed. 772 (1946). But Mr. Justice Frankfurter, Mr. Justice Black, and Mr. Justice Douglas, dissenting, said: "Just as assumption of jurisdiction by an administrative agency for a long period of time goes a long way to prove that powers exercised were impliedly given, . . . a consistent and unexplained failure to exercise power not obviously conferred by legislation may be equally persuasive that the power claimed was never conferred. It is not to be presumed that for decades officials were either ignorant of the duties with which Congress charged them or derelict in their enforcement." *Ibid.*, at 459.

sider not only the question of statutory authority but also that of the constitutionality of the statute under which the action is taken. In a case involving the legality of an order by the Oklahoma Civil Service Commission, the Supreme Court, through Mr. Justice Reed, said:

> Was the order within the competency of the Commission? That question of competency included the issue of the constitutionality of the basis for the order, § 12(a). Only if the statutory basis for an order is within constitutional limits can it be said that the resulting order is legal. To determine that question, the statutory review must include the power to determine the constitutionality of § 12(a).[145]

Questions of Law vs. Questions of Fact.—Legislators and judges assume the separability of questions of law and questions of fact. It is common procedure to provide by statute that administrative findings of fact shall be conclusive upon the courts but that all questions of law shall be subject to judicial review. But as John Dickinson has pointed out:

> In truth the distinction between "questions of law" and "questions of fact" really gives little help in determining how far the courts will review; and for the good reason that there is no fixed distinction. They are not mutually exclusive *kinds* of questions, based upon a difference of subject-matter. Matters of law grow downward into roots of fact, and matters of fact reach upward, without a break, into matters of law. . . . It would seem that when the courts are unwilling to review, they are tempted to explain by the easy device of calling the question one of "fact," and when otherwise disposed, they say that it is a question of "law." [146]

And in *Dobson v. Commissioner,*[147] Mr. Justice Jackson observed that

> Perhaps the chief difficulty in consistent and uniform compliance with the congressional limitation upon court review lies in the want of a certain standard for distinguishing "questions of law" from "questions of fact." This is the test Congress has directed, but its difficulties in practice are well known and have been the subject of frequent comment. Its difficulty is reflected in our labelling questions as "mixed questions of law and fact" and in a great number of opinions distinguishing "ultimate facts" from evidentiary facts.

[145] *Oklahoma v. United States Civil Service Commission,* 330 U.S. 127, 138, 67 S. Ct. 544, 551, 91 L. Ed. 794, 803–4 (1947).
[146] *Administrative Justice and the Supremacy of Law in the United States* (Harvard University Press, Cambridge, Mass., 1927), p. 55.
[147] 320 U.S. 489, 64 S. Ct. 239, 88 L. Ed. 248 (1943).

It is difficult to lay down rules as to what should or should not be reviewed in tax cases except in terms so general that their effectiveness in a particular case will depend largely upon the attitude with which the case is approached.[148]

Thus, findings of "circumstantial facts" by the Board of Tax Appeals, when supported by substantial evidence, were held to be conclusive upon the courts, but

In addition to and presumably upon the basis of these findings, the board made its "ultimate finding." And upon that determination it ruled that the transaction was not within the nonrecognition provisions of section 202(b). The ultimate finding is a conclusion of law or at least a determination of a mixed question of law and fact. It is to be distinguished from the findings of a primary, evidentiary, or circumstantial facts. It is subject to judicial review and, on such review, the court may substitute its judgment for that of the board.[149]

Referring again to *Dobson v. Commissioner* in later cases, Mr. Justice Frankfurter commented to the effect that the Court "was not unaware that 'questions of fact' and 'questions of law' were legal concepts around which dialectic conflicts have been fought time out of mind." [150] And

The Court made a brave effort in *Dobson v. Commissioner, . . .* to meet some of the difficulties of the present distribution of judicial authority in tax cases by lodging practical finality in a Tax Court decision unless it involves a "clear-cut mistake of law." . . . An attempt to give adequate scope to such a doctrine of judicial abstention by dealing with the practicalities of tax matters instead of relying on the grab-bag concepts of "law" and "fact" as a basis of review has not, however, commended itself to the Court.[151]

The distinction is especially tenuous in cases attempting to differentiate questions of mixed law and fact, jurisdictional, quasi-juris-

[148] 320 U.S. at 500–1, 64 S. Ct. at 246, 88 L. Ed. at 255–56. *Cf.* R. E. Paul, "Dobson v. Commissioner: the Strange Ways of Law and Fact," 57 *Harvard Law Review* (1944), 753 ff.

[149] Mr. Justice Butler in *Helvering v. Tex-Penn Oil Co.,* 300 U.S. 481, 491, 57 S. Ct. 569, 574, 81 L. Ed. 755, 762 (1937). James Hart describes the "circumstantial" or "evidentiary" facts as the "findings from evidence of the *occurrence of historical events:* what the persons involved in the situation said, what acts they committed, what papers they drew up and signed, etc., wholly aside from the legal inferences to be drawn from such events." *An Introduction to Administrative Law* (F. S. Crofts & Co., New York, 1940), pp. 389–90.

[150] *Bingham's Trust v. Commissioner of Internal Revenue,* 325 U.S. 365, 378, 65 S. Ct. 1232, 1239, 89 L. Ed. 1670, 1679 (1945).

[151] Dissenting in *Burton-Sutton Oil Co. v. Commissioner of Internal Revenue,* 328 U.S. 25, 37–38, 66 S. Ct. 861, 868, 90 L. Ed. 1062, 1070 (1946).

dictional, and constitutional fact. The spinning of legal formalism is a highly skilled art.

Messrs. McFarland and Vanderbilt point out that

> Two things should be noted respecting questions of law in the field of judicial review of administrative action. The first is that there are several well and long defined categories, which are formal and easily enumerated. The second is that questions of law do not exist apart from facts. . . . Most cases involve so-called "mixed" questions of "law and fact," although there are, of course, cases in which one or the other are stressed. Discretion also plays an important part, but many things are called discretion which are hardly more than the exercise of conferred authority. Law, fact, and discretion come together in many cases. . . . How they are unraveled and treated as a matter of language may depend upon the preferences of the judge writing the opinion. There is no mechanical rule whereby they may be distinguished in all cases. The turn of a sentence converts one into the other in judicial opinions, or it is simply assumed that certain things are matters of fact while others are subjects of law or discretion. . . . On the other hand terms, like "law," "fact," and "discretion" nevertheless serve as tools for thinking and working. In the strenuous study and hard work of judicial review they are brought into close relation. That is a situation that is not peculiar to administrative law. If the ultimate quest for certainty could succeed and if results could be made to flow automatically, this and other fields of the law would be quite different than the nature of human institutions has made them.[152]

Determinations by the Tax Court as to whether payments made on certain corporate obligations are "dividends" or "interest" for tax purposes, were held not to be "clear-cut questions of law" for judicial determination. Admitting that both Congress and the courts were "well aware of the difficulties in drawing a line between questions of fact and questions of law," the Court held that the Tax Court were "experts in tax affairs" whose "usefulness lies primarily in their ability to examine relevant facts of business to determine whether or not they come under statutory language." [153] Mr. Justice Rutledge, dissenting, was of the opinion that the Tax Court had held payments "dividends" in one case and "interest" in another when the facts in each case were essentially alike. "When this occurs, in my opinion, a 'clear cut' question of law is presented, arising above

---

[152] Carl McFarland and Arthur T. Vanderbilt, *Cases and Materials on Administrative Law* (Matthew Bender & Co., Albany and New York, 1947), pp. 966, 967.

[153] *John Kelley Co. v. Commissioner of Internal Revenue*, 326 U.S. 521, 527, 529, 66 S. Ct. 299, 302, 304, 90 L. Ed. 278, 282, 283 (1946).

the rubric of 'expert administrative determination.' The more apt characterization would be 'expert administrative fog.' " [154]

Mixed Questions of Law and Fact.—Judicial opinion is divided on the issue of reviewing administrative decisions involving questions of *mixed law and fact*. A preponderance of State opinion appears to favor review, on the theory that the question of fact is not separable from the question of law which is controlling. The federal cases do not fall into two clearly distinguishable groups. Where, in the opinion of any particular court, the questions of law and of fact are not separable, the deciding factor seems to have been the relative importance of the questions—the more important assimilates the other. Mr. Justice Brandeis stated the rule as follows:

> . . . where what purports to be a finding upon a question of fact is so involved with and dependent upon questions of law as to be in substance and effect a decision of the latter, the Court will, in order to decide the legal question, examine the entire record, including the evidence if necessary, as it does in cases coming from the highest court of a State.[155]

But conversely,

> Even though the finding determines a mixed question of law and fact, the finding is conclusive unless the court is able "to so separate the question as to see clearly what and where the mistake of law is." [156]

[154] 326 U.S. at 533, 66 S. Ct. at 306, 90 L. Ed. at 285.

[155] *St. Joseph Stock Yards Co. v. United States,* 298 U.S. 38, 74, 56 S. Ct. 720, 735, 80 L. Ed. 1033, 1053 (1936). Also, *Helvering v. Tex-Penn Oil Co.,* 300 U.S. 481, 57 S. Ct. 569, 81 L. Ed. 755 (1937); *United States v. Idaho,* 298 U.S. 105, 56 S. Ct. 690, 80 L. Ed. 1070 (1936). *Cf.* R. M. Cooper, "Administrative Justice and the Role of Discretion," 47 *Yale Law Journal* (1938), 577 ff. In *Interstate Commerce Commission v. Union Pacific Railroad,* 222 U.S. 541, 547, 32 S. Ct. 108, 110–11, 56 L. Ed. 308, 311 (1912), Mr. Justice Lamar summed up as follows: "There has been no attempt to make an exhaustive statement of the principle involved, but in cases thus far decided, it has been settled that the orders of the Commission are final unless (1) beyond the power which it could constitutionally exercise; or (2) beyond its statutory power; or (3) based upon a mistake of law. *But questions of fact may be involved in the determination of questions of law,* so that an order, regular on its face, may be set aside if it appears that (4) the rate is so low as to be confiscatory and in violation of the constitutional prohibition against taking property without due process of law; or (5) if the Commission acted so arbitrarily and unjustly as to fix rates contrary to evidence, or without evidence to support it; or (6) if the authority therein involved has been exercised in such an unreasonable manner as to cause it to be within the elementary rule that the substance and not the shadow, determines the validity of the exercise of power." Italics supplied.

[156] *United States v. Esnault-Pelterie,* 303 U.S. 26, 29, 58 S. Ct. 412, 414, 82 L. Ed. 625, 628 (1938). To the same effect see *Marquez v. Frisbie,* 101 U.S.

The former statement would seem to mean that an administrative ruling on a mixed question of law and fact is *not conclusive* unless the question of fact is clearly separable from the question of law, and then it is conclusive only as to the finding of fact. But according to the latter statement the administrative ruling *is conclusive* as to both law and fact unless the question of law is clearly separable from that of fact. This view of the matter is supported by the ruling in the Dobson case to the effect that a decision of the Tax Court is conclusive upon the courts unless it involves *"a clear-cut mistake of law."* It follows that in most cases involving a mixed question of law and fact, the administrative decision is subject to the substantial evidence rule—it "is conclusive if supported by substantial evidence." This view of the scope of judicial review in this type of case is fortified by later decisions of the Supreme Court. In *Cardillo v. Liberty Mutual Co.,*[157] the Court assimilated the scope of review to that over administrative findings of fact and applied the substantial evidence rule to a finding by the Deputy Commissioner in a compensation case under the Longshoremen's and Harbor Workers' Compensation Act. The inference drawn by the Deputy Commissioner from the facts (as found by him) involved a construction of a provision of the statute (namely, what constitutes an injury "arising out of and in the course of employment") and was admittedly "vital to the validity of the order subsequently made." This type of administrative finding was held to be a mixed question of law and fact and conclusive upon the court in *Marra Bros. v. Cardillo.*[158]

On the other hand, an agency may not finally decide the limits of its statutory power. That is a judicial question. Accordingly, when the Federal Social Security Board refused to credit "back pay" as "wages" within the meaning of the National Labor Relations Act, the Supreme Court held that the ruling was erroneous and beyond the

---

473, 476, 25 L. Ed. 800, 801 (1879) to the effect that "This means, and it is a sound principle, that where there is a mixed question of law and fact, and the Court cannot so separate it as to see clearly where the mistake of law is, the decision of the tribunal to which the law has confided the matter is conclusive." Also *Bates & Guild Co. v. Payne,* 194 U.S. 106, 24 S. Ct. 595, 48 L. Ed. 894 (1904); A. M. Tollefson, "Administrative Finality," 29 *Michigan Law Review* (1931), 839.

[157] 330 U.S. 469, 67 S. Ct. 801, 91 L. Ed. 1028 (1947). Also *Gray v. Powell,* 314 U.S. 402, 62 S. Ct. 326, 86 L. Ed. 301 (1941).

[158] 154 F. (2d) 357 (C.C.A. 3d, 1946). But cf. *Helvering v. Tex-Penn Oil Co.,* 300 U.S. 481, 491, 57 S. Ct. 569, 574, 81 L. Ed. 755, 762 (1937). In *Hurley v. Lowe,* 168 F. (2d) 553, 556 (App. D.C., 1948), the court said that even if the court is of the opinion that "the Deputy Commissioner was in error as to the legal content of the term 'in the course of employment' in the statute, we cannot say that his view is 'forbidden by the law' or without any reasonable basis."

permissible limits of administrative interpretation; [159] and Mr. Justice Butler said in another case that the "ultimate finding" of an agency was "a conclusion of law or at least a determination of a mixed question of law and fact" and was "subject to judicial review." [160]   It is not easy to distinguish this case from the cases discussed in the preceding paragraph.

Constitutional Fact.—In the field of economic regulation, where private rights are affected directly, the courts have not been willing to accept administrative findings as conclusive. All *constitutional facts* must be determined ultimately by the courts. Thus the facts of *citizenship* or *alienage*,[161] and especially of a *deprivation of liberty or property without due process of law,* are for judicial determination. In *Ohio Valley Water Co. v. Ben Avon Borough,*[162] the public service law of Pennsylvania had been construed by the State Supreme Court to mean that on appeal to that court from a ruling of the State Public Service Commission, the court must accept the Commission's findings of fact if supported by evidence. The United States Supreme Court held the law, so interpreted, contrary to the due process clause of the Fourteenth Amendment, ruling that unless the courts could substitute their judgment for that of the Commission on questions of fact (the valuation of the Company's property) the plaintiff company would be denied its day in court. Speaking for the majority of the Court Mr. Justice McReynolds said:

> The order here involved prescribed a complete schedule of maximum future rates and was legislative in character. . . . In all such

[159] *Social Security Board v. Nierotko,* 327 U.S. 358, 66 S. Ct. 637, 90 L. Ed. 718 (1946).

[160] *Helvering v. Tex-Penn Oil Co.,* 300 U.S. 481, 491, 57 S. Ct. 569, 574, 81 L. Ed. 755, 762 (1937); and see *Bogardus v. Commissioner of Internal Revenue,* 302 U.S. 34, 58 S. Ct. 61, 82 L. Ed. 32 (1937), where the Supreme Court divided five to four on the questions whether a ruling by the Board of Tax Appeals was a determination of fact and therefore final, or of law, or of mixed law and fact, and therefore subject to judicial review. The Board had ruled that a distribution of profits by a corporation to its employees, *in order to avoid taxation,* was not a tax-free gift but income and, therefore, subject to tax. Five justices held that the payment was intended to be compensation for services, even though made without consideration; that intent was controlling; that intent was a question of fact; and that, therefore, the finding of the Board should be conclusive and not subject to judicial review.

[161] *Ng Fung Ho v. White,* 259 U.S. 276, 284–85, 42 S. Ct. 492, 495, 66 L. Ed. 938, 943 (1922): "To deport one who so claims to be a citizen obviously deprives him of liberty, ... It may result also in loss of both property and life, or of all that makes life worth living. Against the danger of such deprivation without the sanction afforded by judicial proceedings, the Fifth Amendment affords protection in its guarantee of due process of law."

[162] 253 U.S. 287, 40 S. Ct. 527, 64 L. Ed. 908 (1920).

cases, if the owner claims confiscation of his property will result, the state must provide a fair opportunity for submitting that issue to a *judicial* tribunal *for determination upon its independent judgment as to both law and facts;* otherwise the order is void because in conflict with the due process clause, Fourteenth Amendment.[163]

Mr. Justice Brandeis dissented, saying:

> The claim that the rates are confiscatory rested wholly on the contention that the property was undervalued; and on that question the contention is that the court failed to give due weight to the evidence adduced by the company and that the processes by which the Commission arrived at the value it fixed differed from that often pursued by courts and administrative bodies. . . . The objections to the valuation made by the company *raise no questions of law but concern pure matters of fact;* and the finding of the Commission, affirmed by the highest court of the State, is conclusive upon this court.[164]

In a later valuation case the Court, after citing with approval the doctrine of the Ben Avon Borough case, proceeded to weigh the evidence, and then reversed a State court and held the order of the State Commission confiscatory, since, among other matters, "The court failed to give *proper* consideration . . . to the testimony of the company's valuation engineer . . . that the property in his opinion, was worth $900,000." [165]

In *St. Joseph Stock Yards Co. v. United States* [166] the Supreme

---

[163] 253 U.S. at 289, 40 S. Ct. at 528, 64 L. Ed. at 914. Italics supplied. New York appears to follow the ruling in this case. See *Staten Island Edison Corp. v. Maltbie,* 296 N.Y. 374, 382, 73 N.E. (2d) 705, 708 (1947).

[164] 253 U.S. at 299, 40 S. Ct. at 532, 64 L. Ed. at 918. Italics supplied.

[165] *Bluefield Waterworks and Improvement Co. v. Public Service Commission of West Virginia,* 262 U.S. 679, 692, 43 S. Ct. 675, 678, 67 L. Ed. 1176, 1182 (1923). Italics supplied.

[166] 298 U.S. 38, 56 S. Ct. 720, 80 L. Ed. 1033 (1936). To the same effect see *Interstate Commerce Commission v. Illinois Central R. Co.,* 215 U.S. 452, 30 S. Ct. 155, 54, L. Ed. 280 (1910); *I.C.C. & United States v. Louisville and Nashville R. Co.,* 227 U.S. 88, 33 S. Ct. 185, 57 L. Ed. 431 (1931); *Interstate Commerce Commission v. Union Pacific R.R.* 222 U.S. 541, 32 S. Ct. 108, 56 L. Ed. 308 (1912). In *Interstate Commerce Commission v. Alabama Midland Ry. Co.,* 168 U.S. 144, 175, 18 S. Ct. 45, 52, 42 L. Ed. 414, 426 (1897), the Court pointed out that "It has been uniformly held by the several circuit courts and the circuit court of appeals, in such cases, that they are not restricted to the evidence adduced before the Commission, not to a consideration merely of the power of the Commission to make the particular order under question, but that additional evidence may be put in by either party, and that the duty of the Court is to decide, as a court of equity, upon the entire body of evidence." In *East Tennessee V. & G. R. Co. v. Interstate Commerce Commission,* 181 U.S. 1, 27, 21 S. Ct. 516, 526, 45 L. Ed. 719, 729 (1901), the Court declined "to assume to exert its *original* judgment on the facts" but required "the *previous* enlightened judgment of the commission upon such subjects" (italics supplied); that is, the function of the court was not to take original jurisdiction but to review orders of the Commission.

Court reviewed an order by the Secretary of Agriculture, issued under authority of the Packers and Stockyards Act of 1921, fixing the rates for services rendered in stockyards. The order was upheld by a unanimous Court, but the Justices did not agree as to the main issue in the case, namely, the finality of the Secretary's conclusion as to the facts. A majority, speaking through the Chief Justice, held that while the Secretary's findings of fact in the instant case were reasonable, not arbitrary or capricious, they could not be conclusive under the due process clause, even if they were based upon an elaborate examination of the evidence. "Under our system," said Mr. Chief Justice Hughes, "there is no warrant for the view that the judicial power of a competent court can be circumscribed by any legislative arrangement designed to give effect to administrative action going beyond the limits of constitutional authority. This is the purport of the decisions above cited with respect to the exercise of an independent judicial judgment upon the facts where confiscation is alleged." [167] On the other hand, three of the Justices,[168] in a concurring opinion, supported the ruling of the District Court [169] to the effect that inasmuch as the procedure was fair, and the conclusions were supported by evidence, the Secretary's findings of fact were final. Said Mr. Justice Brandeis:

> If in a judicial review of an order of the Secretary his findings supported by substantial evidence are conclusive upon the reviewing court in every case where a constitutional issue is not involved, why are they not conclusive when a constitutional issue is involved? Is there anything in the Constitution which expressly makes findings of fact by a jury of inexperienced laymen, if supported by substantial evidence, conclusive, that prohibits Congress making findings of fact by a highly trained and especially qualified administrative agency likewise conclusive, provided they are supported by substantial evidence? [170]

But in *Railroad Commission of Texas v. Rowan & Nichols Oil Co.*[171] a majority of the Court refused to review an order of the Texas Railroad Commission which the District Court and the Court of Appeals had found to be confiscatory within the due process of law clause of the Fourteenth Amendment. Mr. Justice Frankfurter, speaking for the majority, said that the question was

[167] 298 U.S. at 52, 56 S. Ct. at 726, 80 L. Ed. at 1042 (1936).

[168] Mr. Justice Brandeis, Mr. Justice Stone, and Mr. Justice Cardozo.

[169] *St. Joseph Stock Yards Co. v. United States,* 11 F. Supp. 322 (W.D. Mo., 1935).

[170] Mr. Justice Brandeis concurring in *St. Joseph Stock Yards Co. v. United States,* 298 U.S. 38, 73, 56 S. Ct. 720, 735, 80 L. Ed. 1033, 1052 (1936).

[171] 310 U.S. 573, 60 S. Ct. 1021, 84 L. Ed. 1368 (1940) ; 311 U.S. 570, 61 S. Ct. 343, 85 L. Ed. 358 (1941).

. . . whether the state action complained of has transgressed whatever restrictions the vague contours of the Due Process Clause may place upon the exercise of the state's regulatory power. A controversy like this always calls for fresh reminder that courts must not substitute their notions of expediency and fairness for those which have guided the agencies to whom the formulation and execution of policy have been entrusted. . . .

Certainly in a domain of knowledge still shifting and growing, and in a field where judgment is therefore necessarily beset by the necessity of inferences bordering on conjecture even for those learned in the art, it would be presumptuous for courts, on the basis of conflicting expert testimony, to deem the view of the administrative tribunal, acting under legislative authority, offensive to the Fourteenth Amendment. . . .

The record is redolent with familiar dogmatic assertions by experts equally confident of contradictory contentions. These touch matters of geography and geology and physics and engineering. . . .

Plainly these are not issues for our arbitrament.[172]

This opinion, according to Mr. Justice Roberts, with whom concurred Mr. Chief Justice Hughes and Mr. Justice McReynolds, "announces principles with respect to the review of administrative action challenged under the due process clause directly contrary to those which have been established." [173]

Jurisdictional Fact.—The question of administrative jurisdiction is a complex one. Suppose a health officer summarily destroys foodstuffs offered for sale on the ground that such goods are unwholesome and contaminated within the proscriptions of a pure food law or a meat inspection act.[174] Suppose further that the owner of the goods sues the officer for damages alleging (1) that the statute does not authorize summary destruction but only the confiscation (pending a hearing) of condemned foods, and (2) that even if the statute does empower the officer to destroy unwholesome foods, the action in this case was *ultra vires* since the goods destroyed were not *in fact* unwholesome. Which of these issues may a court properly determine? Since the first is a matter of statutory construction it is a question of *law* which clearly falls within the jurisdiction of a court. The second issue poses the question: did the *fact* (the unwholesome quality of the goods) exist upon which the authority of the officer depended? The issue, in short, involves the determination of a question of *jurisdictional fact*. Should judicial review of this question be limited to the

[172] 310 U.S. at 580, 581–82, 583, 60 S. Ct. at 1024, 1025, 84 L. Ed. at 1373, 1374.
[173] 310 U.S. at 585, 60 S. Ct. at 1026, 84 L. Ed. at 1375.
[174] See Meat Inspection Act of March 4, 1907, 34 *Stat.* 1260, 21 *U.S.C.A.* § 72.

administrative procedure involved, or should the court grant a trial *de novo* and determine the jurisdictional fact upon its own independent evaluation of the evidence? If questions of jurisdictional fact are held to be inseparable from questions of law, the entire federal and State administrative systems are brought under the surveillance of the judiciary. And that is the general effect of the ruling in *Crowell v. Benson.*[175] The case involved the question whether a Federal District Court could grant a trial *de novo* in the matter of certain jurisdictional facts already examined and determined by the deputy commissioner under the Longshoremen's and Harbor Workers' Compensation Act.[176] The question, said the Chief Justice, is

> . . . whether the Congress may substitute for constitutional courts, in which the judicial power of the United States is vested, an administrative agency . . . for the final determination of the existence of the facts upon which the enforcement of the constitutional rights of the citizen depend. The recognition of the utility and convenience of administrative agencies for the investigation and finding of facts within their proper province, and the support of their authorized action, does not require the conclusion that there is no limitation of their use, and that the Congress could completely oust the courts of all determinations of fact by vesting the authority to make them with finality in its own instrumentalities or in the Executive Department. That would be to sap the judicial power as it exists under the Federal Constitution, and to establish a government of a bureaucratic character alien to our system, whenever fundamental rights depend . . . upon the facts, and finality as to facts becomes in effect finality in law.[177]

[175] 285 U.S. 22, 52 S. Ct. 285, 76 L. Ed. 598 (1932).

[176] Act of March 4, 1927, 44 *Stat.* 1424, c. 509, 33 *U.S.C.A.* §§ 901–50.

[177] 285 U.S. at 56, 57, 52 S. Ct. at 294, 295, 76 L. Ed. at 616. See *Ng Fung Ho v. White,* 259 U.S. 276, 284, 42 S. Ct. 492, 495, 66 L. Ed. 938, 942–43 (1922) where the Court reviewed an administrative determination of the *jurisdictional fact of alienage:* "Jurisdiction in the executive to order deportation exists only if the person arrested is an alien. The claim of citizenship is thus a denial of an essential jurisdictional fact. The situation bears some resemblance to that which arises where one against whom proceedings are being taken under the military law denies that he is in the military service. It is well settled that in such a case a writ of habeas corpus will issue to determine the status."

The "fact of citizenship" appears to be the only reviewable fact in deportation proceedings. In *Kessler v. Strecker,* 307 U.S. 22, 34–35, 59 S. Ct. 694, 700, 83 L. Ed. 1082, 1090 (1939), Mr. Justice Roberts observed: "The proceeding for deportation is administrative. If the hearing was fair, if there was evidence to support the finding of the Secretary, and if no error of law was committed, the ruling of the Department must stand and cannot be corrected in judicial proceedings. If, on the other hand, one of the elements mentioned is lacking, the proceeding is void and must be set aside. A district court cannot upon *habeas corpus,* proceed *de novo,* for the function of investigation has not been conferred upon it but upon the Secretary of Labor. Only in the event an alleged alien asserts his United States citizenship in the hearing before the Department, and supports his claim by substantial evidence, is he entitled to a trial *de novo* of that issue in the district court." *Query:*

The Chief Justice conceded Congress constitutional power to prescribe the measure of the employer's liability and to leave to the conclusive determination of the deputy commissioner "the questions of fact as to the circumstances, nature, extent and consequences of the injuries sustained by the employee for which compensation is to be made in accordance with the prescribed standards." [178] But, "A different question is presented where the determinations of fact are fundamental or 'jurisdictional,' in the sense that their existence is a condition precedent to the operation of the statutory scheme." [179] In the instant case the constitutional authority of Congress to impose liability was limited (1) to injuries which occur upon the navigable waters of the United States and (2) to injuries sustained by persons in fact employed by the respondent employer. These are questions of jurisdictional fact, said the Court, which Congress cannot withdraw from the jurisdiction of the courts without doing violence to the due process clause. The ruling rests, therefore, partly upon the due process clause and partly upon the essential nature of the federal judicial power.

Mr. Justice Brandeis,[180] dissenting, held that

> The primary question . . . is not whether Congress provided, or validly could provide, that determination of fact by the deputy commissioner should be conclusive upon the district court. The question is: Upon what record shall the district court's review of the order of the deputy commissioner be based? The courts below held that the respondent was entitled to a trial *de novo;* that all the evidence introduced before the deputy commissioner should go for naught; and that the respondent should have the privilege of presenting new, and even entirely different, evidence in the district court. . . . To permit a contest *de novo* in the district court of an issue tried, or triable, before the deputy commissioner will, I fear, gravely hamper the effective administration of the Act. . . . Persistence in controversy will be encouraged and since the advantage of prolonged litigation lies with the party able to bear heavy expenses, the purpose of the Act will be in part defeated.[181]

Nevertheless, the cases involving the doctrines of "jurisdictional fact" have been decided by a divided Court. In *Ohio Valley Water Co. v. Ben Avon Borough,*[182] three Justices dissented; in

Does this mean that a departmental finding of alienage is conclusive upon the courts if supported by substantial evidence?

[178] 285 U.S. at 54, 52 S. Ct. at 293, 76 L. Ed. at 614.
[179] 285 U.S. at 54, 55, 52 S. Ct. at 294, 76 L. Ed. at 614–15.
[180] Mr. Justice Stone and Mr. Justice Roberts concurred.
[181] 285 U.S. at 66, 94, 52 S. Ct. at 298, 309, 76 L. Ed. at 621, 637.
[182] 253 U.S. 287, 40 S. Ct. 527, 64 L. Ed. 908 (1920).

Crowell v. Benson,[183] three Justices dissented; in *St. Joseph Stock Yards Co. v. United States,*[184] three Justices again dissented and Justice Roberts indicated a dissent; in *Baltimore & Ohio R.R. Co. v. United States,*[185] four Justices said they would not support the majority on the issue. The minority view has prevailed in a number of more recent cases, and findings of "jurisdictional fact" are now pretty generally governed by the substantial evidence rule. Thus, whereas in the previously cited case, *Crowell v. Benson,* a ruling of a deputy commissioner that a certain person was an "employee" within the Longshoremen's and Harbor Workers' Compensation Act was held to involve a determination of a "jurisdictional fact" which was subject to judicial review, in *Gray v. Powell*[186] the Court sustained the provision of the Bituminous Coal Act of 1937[187] which left to the Director of the Bituminous Coal Division the determination of who constitutes a "producer" under the Act. Again, in *National Labor Relations Board v. Hearst Publications, Inc.,*[188] the Court ruled that the Board's determination that specified persons are "employees" within the National Labor Relations Act is to be accepted by the courts if it has warrant in the record and a reasonable basis in law. Furthermore, the Court ruled that the Board is not limited to the common-law meaning of "employee," but that the term is to be understood with reference to the purpose of the Act and the underlying economic facts. In *Cardillo v. Liberty Mutual Co.,*[189] the substantial evidence rule was applied to a finding by the deputy commissioner that a particular injury was one "arising out of and in the course of employment" within the provisions of the Longshoremen's and Harbor Workers' Compensation Act: "If supported by evidence and not inconsistent with the law, the deputy commissioner's inference that an injury did or did not arise out of and in the course of

[183] 285 U.S. 22, 52 S. Ct. 285, 76 L. Ed. 598 (1932).

[184] 298 U.S. 38, 56 S. Ct. 720, 80 L. Ed. 1033 (1936).

[185] 279 U.S. 781, 49 S. Ct. 492, 73 L. Ed. 954 (1929).

[186] 314 U.S. 402, 62 S. Ct. 326, 86 L. Ed. 301 (1941). "Unless we can say that a set of circumstances deemed by the Commission to bring them within the concept 'producer' is so unrelated to the tasks entrusted by Congress to the Commission as in effect to deny a sensible exercise of judgment, it is the Court's duty to leave the Commission's judgment undisturbed." 314 U.S. at 413, 62 S. Ct. at 333, 86 L. Ed. at 310. Mr. Justice Roberts dissented, holding that the question was one of statutory construction, which, "under all relevant authorities, is subject to court review." 314 U.S. at 418, 62 S. Ct. at 336, 86 L. Ed. at 313.

[187] 50 *Stat.* 72 § 4A, 15 *U.S.C.A.* §§ 828 *et sqq.* (1940).

[188] 322 U.S. 111, 131, 64 S. Ct. 851, 861, 88 L. Ed. 1170, 1185 (1944); *National Labor Relations Board v. Gluek,* 144 F. (2d) 847 (C.C.A. 8th, 1944); *Fleming v. Demerritt Co.,* 56 F. Supp. 376 (D.C. Vt., 1944), Fair Labor Standards Act; *La Lone v. United States,* 57 F. Supp. 947 (D.C.E.D. Wash., 1944), Social Security Act.

[189] 330 U.S. 469, 67 S. Ct. 801, 91 L. Ed. 1028 (1947).

employment is conclusive." [190] In *Packard Co. v. National Labor Relations Board* [191] a ruling by the Board that foremen were "employees" within the meaning of the Act was upheld, since "there is clearly substantial evidence in support of the determination that foremen are an appropriate unit . . ." [192] for bargaining purposes.

Abandonment of the doctrine of "jurisdictional fact" unquestionably limits judicial control over administrative action, and to many people this represents a dangerous overdeference to administrative fact-finding. But, on the other hand,

> It is not the province of a court to absorb the administrative functions to such an extent that the executive or legislative agencies become mere fact finding bodies deprived of the advantages of prompt and definite action.[193]

And if it is the clear intent of the statute to entrust the finding of jurisdictional facts to an agency, it would seem to be an invasion of the legislative function for courts to interfere with the effectuation of the policy of the law where no question of constitutionality is raised. To interpolate judicial review would, in many situations, encourage obstruction and delay through dilatory court proceedings and disrupt legislative schemes which require speedy formulation and enforcement of a large number of orders.

Mr. Justice Frankfurter indicated the "morass" into which the courts have blundered in attempting to apply the jurisdictional fact rule when he said:

> Analysis is not furthered by speaking of such findings as "jurisdictional" and not even when—to adopt a famous phrase—jurisdictional is softened by a quasi. "Jurisdiction" competes with "right" as one of the most deceptive of legal pitfalls. The opinions in *Crowell v. Benson,* . . . and the casuistries to which they have given rise bear unedifying testimony of the morass into which one is led in working out problems of judicial review over administrative decisions by loose talk about jurisdiction.[194]

[190] 330 U.S. at 477, 67 S. Ct. at 806, 91 L. Ed. at 1036. The doctrine of *Crowell v. Benson* is not followed in New York where the substantial evidence rule is applied to questions of jurisdictional fact. For cases see Bernard Schwartz, "Administrative Law," 24 *New York University Law Quarterly Review* (December, 1949), 1036–38.

[191] 330 U.S. 485, 67 S. Ct. 789, 91 L. Ed. 1040 (1947).

[192] 330 U.S. at 491, 67 S. Ct. at 793, 91 L. Ed. at 1050. Mr. Justice Douglas, dissenting, held that foremen were "allied with management," not with the "employees." 330 U.S. at 494, 496, 67 S. Ct. at 794, 795, 91 L. Ed. at 1052, 1053.

[193] *Gray v. Powell,* 314 U.S. 402, 412, 62 S. Ct. 326, 333, 86 L. Ed. 301, 310 (1941).

[194] Mr. Justice Frankfurter dissenting (Mr. Justice Reed and Mr. Justice Jackson concurring) in *City of Yonkers v. United States,* 320 U.S. 685, 695, 64 S. Ct. 327, 332–33, 88 L. Ed. 400, 406 (1944).

And in the Estep case [195] Mr. Justice Frankfurter again spoke of ". . . the casuistic difficulties spawned by the doctrine of 'jurisdictional fact,' " [196] and added:

> In view of the criticism which that doctrine, as sponsored by *Crowell v. Benson,* . . . brought forth and of the attritions of that case through later decisions one had supposed that the doctrine had earned a deserved repose.[197]

The Substantial Evidence Rule.—The facts found by an administrative agency may be (1) *prima facie* evidence [198] or (2) they may be made conclusive "when supported by evidence" [199] or "by the weight of the evidence" [200] or by "the preponderance of the evidence." [201]

EVOLUTION OF THE SUBSTANTIAL EVIDENCE RULE. At first the Supreme Court was reluctant to accept these statutory provisions at their face value. "Supported by evidence" meant "substantial evi-

[195] *Estep v. United States,* 327 U.S. 114, 66 S. Ct. 423, 90 L. Ed. 567 (1946).
[196] 327 U.S. at 142, 66 S. Ct. at 437, 90 L. Ed. at 584. [197] *Ibid.*
[198] See Interstate Commerce Act of 1887, 24 *Stat.* 379, 385, § 16, 49 *U.S.C.A.* § 16(2); Hepburn Act of 1906, 34 *Stat.* 584, § 5, 49 *U.S.C.A.* § 1.
[199] The Securities and Exchange Act of June 6, 1934, 48 *Stat.* 881, 901, c. 404, § 25a, 15 *U.S.C.A.* § 78y (1934), provides that "The Commission shall . . . file such . . . finding, . . . which, if supported by substantial evidence, shall be conclusive."
The National Labor Relations Act of July 5, 1935, 49 *Stat.* 449, 454, § 10(2), 29 *U.S.C.A.* §§ 151, 160(e) provides that findings of the National Labor Relations Board as to facts "if supported by evidence, shall be conclusive."
The Fair Labor Standards Act of June 25, 1938, 52 *Stat.* 1060, 1065, c. 676, § 10(a), 29 *U.S.C.A.* § 210, provides in part: "The review by the court shall be limited to questions of law, and findings of fact by the Administrator when supported by substantial evidence shall be conclusive."
The Federal Trade Commission Act of September 26, 1914, 38 *Stat.* 717, § 5, 15 *U.S.C.A.* § 45c, declares that the "findings of the Commission as to the facts, if supported by evidence, shall be conclusive."
The Tariff Act of June 17, 1930, 46 *Stat.* 793, 19 *U.S.C.A.* § 1337(c), provides that the findings of the Commission "if supported by evidence, shall be conclusive."
The Federal Communications Act of June 19, 1934, 48 *Stat.* 1064, 1094, 47 *U.S.C.A.* § 402e, provides: "That the review by the court (Court of Appeals of the District of Columbia) shall be limited to questions of law and that findings of fact by the Commission, if supported by substantial evidence, shall be conclusive unless it shall clearly appear that the findings of the Commission are arbitrary or capricious."
Similar provisions are found in Federal Alcohol Administration Act of 1935, 49 *Stat.* 978, 27 *U.S.C.A.* § 204L; Federal Power Commission Act of 1935, 49 *Stat.* 860, 16 *U.S.C.A.* § 825; Federal Social Security Act of August 14, 1935, 49 *Stat.* 620 c. 531, 53 *Stat.* 1369, § 205(c) and (g); Radio Act of February 23, 1927, 44 *Stat.* 1166, 47 *U.S.C.A.* § 96, as amended July 1, 1930, 46 *Stat.* 844, 47 *U.S.C.A.* § 96; Bituminous Coal Act of April 26, 1937, 50 *Stat.* 72, 85, § 4–A.
[200] The Commodity Exchange Act of 1922, 42 *Stat.* 1002, 7 *U.S.C.A.* § 9 (Supp. 1939).
[201] The Walsh-Healey Act of 1936, 49 *Stat.* 2038, 41 *U.S.C.A.* § 39 (Supp. 1939).

dence." What constituted "substantial evidence" was a *question of law,* since a finding not so supported is capricious and arbitrary and not due process. "Substantial evidence is more than a mere scintilla. It means such relevant evidence as a *reasonable* mind might accept as adequate to support a conclusion." [202] But "reasonable" minds, administrative and judicial, may differ as to what evidence is "relevant" and "adequate," and that mind is likely to be most reasonable which is best informed. Whenever a majority opinion of the Court differs with a finding of fact by an administrative agency, the latter is, inferentially, not of "reasonable mind." Thus, in the Columbian Enameling case the Court by a five to two decision overruled a finding by the Labor Board that the company had refused to bargain collectively with its employees—there was not "substantial evidence" to support the Board.[203] In the Sands case the Labor Board had concluded from the evidence that the company had locked out, discharged, and refused employment to its employees because they were members of the Mechanics Educational Society of America Union and had engaged in concerted activities for the purpose of collective bargaining. *"We think,"* said Mr. Justice Roberts for the Court, "the conclusion has no support in the evidence and is contrary to the entire and uncontradicted evidence or record." [204]

More recently the Court was more inclined to accept the legislative mandate in respect to the finality of administrative determinations of fact. Dissenting in the Columbian Enameling and Stamping Company case, Mr. Justice Black said: "Courts should not—*as here*— substitute *their appraisal of the evidence* for that of the board. The

[202] *Consolidated Edison Co. v. National Labor Relations Board,* 305 U.S. 197, 229, 59 S. Ct. 206, 217, 83 L. Ed. 131, 140 (1938). Italics supplied.

"But what is 'substantial' evidence? Is the existence of substantial evidence in favor of the decisions reached to be determined by examining the *quantum* of evidence on that side only, or by viewing it against the background of all the evidence? Most lawyers would agree that the latter is meant. This means, in practical effect, that the court will have to weigh the evidence, and the line is a vague one, in practice, between doing so to determine whether the evidence that supports the decision is *substantial,* and doing so to determine the *preponderance* of the evidence. It is thus apparent that the formula gets its meaning from the way in which the courts choose to apply it." Hart, *op. cit.,* pp. 384–85; also see note 149 *supra.*

[203] *National Labor Relations Board v. Columbian Enameling & Stamping Co.,* 306 U.S. 292, 59 S. Ct. 501, 83 L. Ed. 660 (1939).

[204] *National Labor Relations Board v. Sands Manufacturing Co.,* 306 U.S. 332, 339, 59 S. Ct. 508, 512, 82 L. Ed. 682, 687 (1939). Italics supplied. See also *Washington, Virginia & Maryland Coach Co. v. National Labor Relations Board* 301 U.S. 142, 57 S. Ct. 648, 81 L. Ed. 965 (1937) ; *Swayne & Hoyt, Ltd. v. United States,* 300 U.S. 297, 57 S. Ct. 478, 81 L. Ed. 659 (1937) ; *National Labor Relations Board v. Pennsylvania Greyhound Lines, Inc.,* 303 U.S. 261, 58 S. Ct. 571, 82 L. Ed. 831 (1938).

Labor Board [and others] . . . were all created to deal with problems of regulation of ever-increasing complexity in the economic fields of trade, finance and industrial conflicts. Congress thus sought to utilize procedures more expeditious and administered by more specialized and experienced experts than courts had been able to afford. *The decision here tends to nullify this Congressional effort."* [205] In *Federal Communications Commission v. Pottsville Broadcasting Co.,*[206] Mr. Justice Frankfurter, for a unanimous court,[207] said in part:

> To be sure, the laws under which these agencies operate prescribe the fundamentals of fair play. They require that interested parties be afforded an opportunity for hearing and that judgment must express a reasoned conclusion. But to assimilate the relation of these administrative bodies and the courts to the relationship between lower and upper courts is to disregard the origin and purposes of the movement for administrative regulation and at the same time to disregard the traditional scope, however far-reaching, of the judicial process. *Unless these vital differentiations between the functions of judicial and administrative tribunals are observed, courts will stray outside their province and read the laws of Congress through the distorting lenses of inapplicable legal doctrine.* . . .
>
> On review the Court may thus correct errors of law and on remand the Commission is bound to act upon the correction. . . . But an administrative determination in which is imbedded a legal question open to judicial review does not impliedly foreclose the administrative agency, after its error has been corrected, from enforcing the legislative policy committed to its charge. . . .
>
> But courts are not charged with general guardianship against all potential mischief in the complicated tasks of government. The present case makes timely the reminder that "legislatures are ultimate guardians of the liberties and welfare of the people in quite as great a degree as the courts.". . . Congress which creates and sustains these agencies must be trusted to correct whatever defects experience may reveal. Interference by the courts is not conducive to the development of habits of responsibility in administrative agencies.[208]

Mr. Justice Black, delivering another unanimous opinion in *National Labor Relations Board v. Waterman Steamship Corp.* said:

> In that Act [The National Labor Relations Act], Congress provided,

---

[205] 306 U.S. at 301, 59 S. Ct. at 505–6, 83 L. Ed. at 666 (1938). Italics supplied.
[206] 309 U.S. 134, 60 S. Ct. 437, 84 L. Ed. 656 (1940).
[207] "Justice McReynolds concurs in the results." 309 U.S. 134, 146, 60 S. Ct. 437, 443, 84 L. Ed. 656, 664 (1940).
[208] 309 U.S. at 143–46, 60 S. Ct. at 442, 443, 89 L. Ed. at 662–63 (1940). Italics supplied.

"The findings of the Board, as to the facts, if supported by evidence, shall be conclusive." It is of paramount importance that courts not encroach upon this exclusive power of the Board if effect is to be given the intention of Congress to apply an orderly, informed and specialized procedure to the complex administrative problems arising in the solution of industrial disputes. As it did in setting up other administrative bodies, Congress has left questions of law which arise before the Board —but not more—ultimately to the traditional review of the judiciary. *Not by accident, but in line with a general policy, Congress has deemed it wise to entrust the finding of facts to these specialized agencies. It is essential that courts regard this division of responsibility which Congress as a matter of policy has embodied in the very statute from which the Court of Appeals derives its jurisdiction to act.* And therefore, charges by public agencies constitutionally created—such as the Board—that their duly conferred jurisdiction has been invaded so that their statutory duties cannot be effectively fulfilled, raise questions of high importance.[209]

The point of view expressed in these later cases appears to have been adopted in the Opp Cotton Mills case, where Mr. Justice Stone said, after holding that the findings of fact by the administrator under the Fair Labor Standards Act of 1938 were supported by substantial evidence: "Any different conclusion would require us to substitute our judgment of the weight of the evidence and the inferences to be drawn from it for that of the Administrator which the statute forbids." [210] Similarly,

Administrative finality is not, of course, applicable only to agency findings of "fact" in the narrow, literal sense. The Commission's findings as to valuation, *which are based upon judgment and prediction,* as well as upon "facts," like the valuation findings of the Interstate Commerce Commission in reorganizations under § 77 of the Bankruptcy Act, . . . are not subject to reexamination by the court unless they are not supported by substantial evidence or were not arrived at "in accordance with legal standards." [211]

[209] *National Labor Relations Board v. Waterman Steamship Corp.,* 309 U.S. 206, 208, 209, 60 S. Ct. 493, 495, 496, 84 L. Ed. 704, 706–7 (1940), sustaining § 10(e) of *National Labor Relations Act,* 49 *Stat.* 449, 29 *U.S.C.A.* § 160, which provides that the findings of the Board as to the facts "if supported by evidence, shall be conclusive." Italics supplied. To the same effect see *National Labor Relations Board v. Pennsylvania Greyhound Lines, Inc.,* 303 U.S. 261, 271, 58 S. Ct. 571, 576, 82 L. Ed. 831 (1938) ; *National Labor Relations Board v. Falk Corp.,* 308 U.S. 453, 461, 60 S. Ct. 307, 311, 84 L. Ed. 396, 400 (1940).

[210] *Opp Cotton Mills, Inc., et al. v. Administrator of Wage and Hour Division of Department of Labor,* 312 U.S. 126, 156, 61 S. Ct. 524, 538, 85 L. Ed. 624, 642 (1941).

[211] *Securities and Exchange Commission v. Central-Illinois Securities Commission et al.,* 338 U.S. 96, 126, 69 S. Ct. 1377, 1393, 93 L. Ed. 1836, 1862 (1949). Italics supplied.

The jury-trial rules have been applied to administrative findings. "Substantial evidence . . . must be enough to justify, if the trial were to a jury, a refusal to direct a verdict when the conclusion sought to be drawn from it is one of fact for the jury." [212] Likewise, "A good rule for weighing the evidence to ascertain whether it is adequate for the purpose mentioned is to compare it with the evidence necessary to sustain a verdict of a jury on a similar issue." [213]

But according to the New York "residuum rule" an administrative tribunal need not actually be limited by the jury-trial rules, nevertheless, there must be found somewhere in the mass of evidence accepted enough evidence acceptable by jury-trial rules to sustain the finding.

> There must be in the record some evidence of a sound, competent and recognizedly probative character to sustain the findings and award made, else the findings must in fairness be set aside by (the) court.[214]

Slight, even speculative evidence was held sufficient to sustain administrative orders predicated upon a finding of rate discrimination,[215] value for the purpose of railroad reorganization,[216] and requirements for food standards.[217] In the matter of deportation proceedings :

> Congress has committed the conduct of deportation proceedings to an administrative officer, the Attorney General, with no provision for direct review of his action by the courts. Instead it has provided that his decision shall be "final," 8 U.S.C. § 155, as it may constitutionally do. . . . Only in the exercise of their authority to issue writs of habeas corpus, may courts inquire whether the Attorney General has exceeded his statutory authority or acted contrary to law or the Constitution. . . . And when the authority to deport the alien turns on a determination of fact by the Attorney General, the courts, as we have said, are without authority to disturb his finding if it has the support of *evidence of any probative value.*[218]

[212] *National Labor Relations Board v. Columbian Enameling and Stamping Co.,* 306 U.S. 292, 300, 59 S. Ct. 501, 505, 83 L. Ed. 660, 665 (1939).

[213] *National Labor Relations Board v. Bell Oil and Gas Co.,* 98 F. (2d) 406, 410 (C.C.A. 5th, 1938).

[214] *Matter of Carroll v. Knickerbocker Ice Co.,* 218 N.Y. 435, 440 (1916), quoting Justice Woodward of the Appellate Division.

[215] *Barringer & Co. v. United States,* 319 U.S. 1, 7–8, 63 S. Ct. 967, 971–72, 87 L. Ed. 1171, 1177–78 (1943).

[216] *Group of Institutional Investors v. Chicago, Milwaukee R. R. Co.,* 318 U.S. 523, 539–43, 63 S. Ct. 727, 737–39, 87 L. Ed. 959, 993–96 (1943).

[217] *Federal Security Administrator v. Quaker Oats Co.,* 318 U.S. 218, 226–27, 229, 63 S. Ct. 589, 594, 595, 87 L. Ed. 724, 729–30, 731 (1943).

[218] Mr. Chief Justice Stone, dissenting, in *Bridges v. Wixon,* 326 U.S. 135, 167, 65 S. Ct. 1443, 1458, 89 L. Ed. 2103, 2122 (1945). Italics supplied.

In another opinion in the same case, it was stated that

> In these *habeas corpus* proceedings we do not review the evidence beyond ascertaining that there is *some evidence* to support the deportation order.[219]

The Supreme Court will not disturb findings by an expert administrative agency so long as there is a rational basis for the findings, even if the Court would have made a different appraisal of the evidence,[220] or even though the evidence permitted conflicting inferences.[221]

The inferences and conclusions to be drawn from the evidence is for the agency, not for the courts. "We are not free to exercise our independent judgment on the evidence," said a federal court, "but must limit ourselves to the rather perfunctory duty of determining whether there was any reasonable evidence upon which the [National Labor Relations] Board may have reached the conclusion it did." [222]

> Congress entrusted the Board [National Labor Relations Board], not the Courts, with the power to draw inferences from the facts. . . . *The Board, like other expert agencies dealing with specialized fields . . . has the function of appraising conflicting and circumstantial evidence, and the weight and credibility of testimony.*[223]

Thus, where evidence, pro and con, is produced on the issue of accident or suicide in a claim for compensation under the Longshore-

---

[219] Mr. Justice Douglas, for the majority, *ibid.,* 326 U.S. at 149, 65 S. Ct. at 1450, 89 L. Ed. at 2113. Italics supplied. Also *Colorado-Wyoming Gas Co. v. Federal Power Commission,* 324 U.S. 626, 634, 65 S. Ct. 850, 854, 89 L. Ed. 1235, 1241 (1945).

[220] *United States v. Wabash R.R.,* 321 U.S. 403, 64 S. Ct. 752, 88 L. Ed. 827 (1944).

[221] *Norton v. Warner Co.,* 321 U.S. 565, 568, 64 S. Ct. 747, 749, 88 L. Ed. 931, 935 (1944).

Sec. 19(a) of the Longshoremen's and Harbor Workers' Compensation Act (44 *Stat.* 1424, 33 *U.S.C.A.* §§ 901 *et sqq.*) gives the Deputy Commissioner "full power and authority to hear and determine all questions in respect of" claims for compensation. And Sec. 21(b) empowers the Federal District Courts to suspend or set aside compensation orders if "not in accordance with law." The Supreme Court has held that it was the duty of a District Court to give effect to an award if there was evidence to support it and that the findings of the Commissioner were conclusive even though the evidence permitted conflicting inferences. *South Chicago Coal & Dock Co. v. Bassett,* 309 U.S. 251, 60 S. Ct. 544, 84 L. Ed. 732 (1940).

[222] *National Labor Relations Board v. Servel, Inc.,* 149 F. (2d) 542, 544 (C.C.A. 7th, 1945); *Federal Communications Commission v. WOKO,* 329 U.S. 223, 67 S. Ct. 213, 91 L. Ed. 204 (1946). For a list of typical cases see *1946 Annual Survey of American Law* (New York University School of Law, New York, 1947), p. 229, note 199.

[223] *National Labor Relations Board v. Link-Belt Co.,* 311 U.S. 584, 597, 61 S. Ct. 358, 365, 85 L. Ed. 368, 378 (1941).

men's and Harbor Workers' Compensation Act, and the evidence "permits an inference either way upon the question of suicide, the Deputy Commissioner and he alone is empowered to draw the inference; his decision as to the weight of the evidence may not be disturbed by the court." [224] And even on "questions of law the experienced judgment of the Labor Board is entitled to great weight," where specialized knowledge or experience is required.[225] The findings of the National Labor Relations Board even brought forth the following comment:

> Though it may strain our credulity, if it does not quite break it down, we must accept it; and in the case at bar, regardless of what might have been our own conclusion, we are not prepared to say that no rational person could have come to the same conclusion.[226]

And according to Mr. Chief Justice Stone,[227] "when there is evidence more than a scintilla, and not unbelievable on its face, *it is for the administrative officer to determine its credibility and weight.*" [228] That is, courts will not pass upon the credibility of witnesses appearing before an administrative tribunal: "Even assuming that some of the testimony . . . was prejudiced or biased as contended, if the [Federal Trade] Commission wished to rely upon such testimony, we may not intervene whatever our thought." [229] Nor, will courts set aside an administrative finding as against the weight of the evidence. More is required. The error must be one of law, such as the misconstruction of a term of the act.[230] In a draft board classification case the court limited its jurisdiction to determining whether the classification had "no basis in fact" [231] and drew a sharp dissent from Mr. Justice Murphy who said, in part:

> I object to the standard of review whereby the draft board classification is to be sustained unless there is no evidence to support it. Less

---

[224] *Del Vecchio v. Bowers,* 296 U.S. 280, 287, 56 S. Ct. 190, 193, 80 L. Ed. 229, 232 (1935).

[225] *Medo Photo Supply Corp. v. National Labor Relations Board,* 321 U.S. 678, 681, 64 S. Ct. 830, 832 note, 88 L. Ed. 1007, 1010 (1944).

[226] *National Labor Relations Board v. Columbia Products Corp.,* 141 F. (2d) 687, 688 (C.C.A. 2d, 1944).

[227] Mr. Justice Roberts and Mr. Justice Frankfurter concurring.

[228] *Bridges v. Wixon,* 326 U.S. 135, 178, 65 S. Ct. 1443, 1463, 89 L. Ed. 2103, 2128 (1945). Italics supplied.

[229] *Jacob Siegel Co. v. Federal Trade Commission,* 150 F. (2d) 751, 754 (C.C.A. 3d, 1944).

[230] *Norton v. Warner Co.,* 321 U.S. 565, 569, 64 S. Ct. 747, 750, 88 L. Ed. 935 (1944). For federal cases see, *1945 Annual Survey of American Law* (New York University School of Law, New York, 1946), pp. 216, 217, notes 172 and 173.

[231] *Cox v. United States,* 332 U.S. 442, 68 S. Ct. 115, 92 L. Ed. 59 (1947).

than a substantial amount of evidence is thus permitted to legalize the classification.[232]

It follows that the courts do not try the matter *de novo,* but are limited to the agency record.[233] The courts are not authorized "to make findings . . . and substitute them for those of the [Federal Power] Commission." [234]

But an "arbitrary or capricious finding" is not "supported by substantial evidence" and is not conclusive upon the courts.

> The provision that the Commission's [Federal Radio Commission] finding of fact, if supported by substantial evidence, shall be conclusive unless it clearly appears that the findings are arbitrary or capricious, cannot be regarded as an attempt to vest in the Court [Court of Appeals] an authority to revise the action of the Commission from an administrative standpoint and to make an administrative judgment. A finding without substantial evidence to support it—an arbitrary or capricious finding—does violence to the law. It is without the sanction of the authority conferred. And an inquiry into the facts before the Commission, or order to ascertain whether its findings are thus vitiated, belongs to the judicial province and does not trench upon, or involve the exercise of, administrative authority. Such an examination is not concerned with the weight of evidence or with the wisdom or expediency of the administrative action.[235]

If a person affected by an administrative order is given an opportunity to object to the agency before the effective date of the order, it would appear that the order becomes final and binding if no objection is raised prior to such date. The Court "will not listen to an objection that the charge has been laid in an arbitrary manner when an administrative remedy for the correction of defects or inequalities has been given by the statute and ignored by the objector." [236] Thus, an initiating rate order of the Interstate Commerce Commission

> . . . is equivalent, in essence, to an ex parte order to the carriers to show cause why the designated routes and rates should not be established. The effect of that order was simply to put upon the rail carriers the necessity, within a comparatively brief period, of either availing themselves of the right to file the routes and rates and appear and

[232] 332 U.S. at 457, 68 S. Ct. at 122, 92 L. Ed. at 72.
[233] *Holland v. Altmeyer,* 60 F. Supp. 954 (D.C. Minn., 1945).
[234] *Colorado-Wyoming Gas Co. v. Federal Power Commission,* 324 U.S. 626, 634, 65 S. Ct. 850, 854, 89 L. Ed. 1235, 1241 (1945).
[235] *Federal Radio Commission v. Nelson Bros. Bond & Mortgage Co.,* 289 U.S. 266, 276–77, 53 S. Ct. 627, 633, 77 L. Ed. 1166, 1174 (1933).
[236] *Utley v. St. Petersburg,* 292 U.S. 106, 109–10, 54 S. Ct. 593, 595, 78 L. Ed. 1155, 1158 (1923).

be heard in opposition thereto (the operation of the order in the mean-
time being held in abeyance), or of suffering them to go into effect by
default.[237]

To understand the effect of the substantial evidence rule, writes
Arthur T. Vanderbilt,

> . . . one must look into the workings of the system of review by
> *certiorari* in the Supreme Court. If an administrative decision is clearly
> without basis in the record and the lower courts hold it invalid, the
> Government may not attempt to carry the case up to the Supreme Court
> or the latter may refuse to review it, even if requested by application
> for writ of *certiorari*. The result of this process is that cases where
> the agencies might be reversed seldom reach the Supreme Court, and
> accordingly reversals of administrative agencies there are rare. Super-
> ficially it appears from the Supreme Court reports that the agencies are
> almost always right, for nearly all reversals of agencies in the lower
> courts are in turn reversed by the Supreme Court. This result, it
> may be fairly assumed, has, in turn, the effect of dissuading original
> courts of review from upsetting administrative orders in any but the
> most extreme cases. Nor does this one-sided process of selectivity in
> the *certiorari* process end here; because of the disinclination of the
> Supreme Court to review cases of private wrong as distinguished from
> cases in which public agencies seek review, the failure of lower courts
> to exercise their full powers of judicial review is rarely subjected to
> correction by the Supreme Court. The substantial evidence rule and
> the certiorari process are the mill stones which threaten to crush the
> life out of judicial review as a reality, while preserving its form.[238]

Occasionally a judge raises an objection to the curtailment of
judicial review under the substantial evidence rule. An extreme view
was voiced by Circuit Judge Waller:

> Give a partisan examiner or board the right to fix the facts and the
> right to declare the law may well be but as "sounding brass or a tin-
> kling cymbal.". . . If the judicial power is vested in the courts in all
> cases and controversies mentioned in Section 2 of Article III; if re-
> view by a Federal Court of the decision of a board is a case or con-
> troversy; if the judicial power is the power to administer justice; and
> if in the administration of justice it is necessary first to know the truth,
> how can Congress constitutionally withhold from the courts on review
> the right to be satisfied as to facts.[239]

---

[237] *United States v. Illinois Central R. Co.,* 291 U.S. 457, 463, 54 S. Ct. 471, 473,
78 L. Ed. 909, 917 (1934).

[238] "Administrative Law," *1942 Annual Survey of American Law* (New York
University School of Law, New York, 1943), p. 101.

[239] *National Labor Relations Board v. Robbins Tire & Rubber Co.,* 161 F. (2d)
798, 804 (C.C.A. 5th, 1947).

Underlying this view of the judicial power is the fatal assumption that courts are "the only agency of government that must be assumed to have capacity to govern," [240] and it ascribes to judges a technical knowledge and a consecration to the service of justice which unfortunately they cannot and do not possess.

THE SUBSTANTIAL EVIDENCE RULE AND THE ADMINISTRATIVE PROCEDURE AND LABOR MANAGEMENT RELATIONS ACTS. The legislative histories of the Walter-Logan Bill, the Administrative Procedure Act, and the Labor Management Relations Act indicate that Congress was dissatisfied with the restricted application of the "substantial evidence" test described in the preceding pages. Charges of judicial abdication were linked with charges of administrative absolutism. The Administrative Procedure Act of 1946 provides that the reviewing court shall hold unlawful and set aside agency action, findings, and conclusions *found to be unsupported by substantial evidence, and in making these determinations the court shall review the whole record* or such portions thereof as shall be cited by any party.[241] Similarly the Labor Management Relations Act of 1947 (Taft-Hartley Act) provides that "The findings of the Board with respect to questions of fact *if supported by substantial evidence on the record considered as a whole* shall be conclusive." [242] Accordingly, ". . . the standard of proof specifically required of the Labor Board by the Taft-Hartley Act is the same as that to be exacted by courts reviewing every administrative action subject to the Administrative Procedure Act." [243] Is this "standard of proof" a new formula for judicial review of administrative action, altering the substantial evidence rule as heretofore applied by the courts?

The Supreme Court has held that the above Acts direct Courts of Appeals to assume more responsibility now for the reasonableness and fairness of administrative decisions than they have done in the past—*the evidence must appear substantial when viewed on the record as a whole.*[244] But the Court concedes that

> . . . the requirement for canvassing "the whole record" in order to ascertain substantiality does not furnish a calculus of value by which a reviewing court can assess the evidence. Nor was it intended to

[240] Mr. Justice Stone in *United States v. Butler,* 297 U.S. at 87, 56 S. Ct. at 329, 80 L. Ed. at 499 (1936).

[241] Sec. 10(e), 60 *Stat.* 237, 243–44, 5 *U.S.C.A.* § 1009(e).

[242] 61 *Stat.* 148, 29 *U.S.C.A.* § 160(e). Italics supplied.

[243] *Universal Camera Corp. v. National Labor Relations Board,* 340 U.S. 474, 487, 71 S. Ct. 456, 464, 95 L. Ed. 304, 312 (1951).

[244] *Universal Camera Corp. v. National Labor Relations Board,* 340 U.S. 474, 71 S. Ct. 456, 95 L. Ed. 304 (1951); *National Labor Relations Board v. Pittsburgh S. S. Co.,* 340 U.S. 498, 71 S. Ct. 453, 95 L. Ed. 318 (1951).

negative the function of the Labor Board as one of those agencies presumably equipped or informed by experience to deal with a specialized field of knowledge, whose findings within that field carry the authority of an expertness which courts do not possess and therefore must respect. Nor does it mean that even as to matters not requiring expertise a court may displace the Board's choice between two fairly conflicting views, even though the court would justifiably have made a different choice had the matter been before it *de novo*. Congress has merely made it clear that a reviewing court is not barred from setting aside a Board decision when it cannot conscientiously find that the evidence supporting that decision is substantial, when viewed in the light that the record in its entirety furnishes, including the body of evidence opposed to the Board's view.[245]

That is to say, Congress prescribed an "uncritical" formula for judicial review, in the application of which the Courts of Appeals (charged with the primary responsibility of enforcing the Labor Board's orders) have somewhat more discretion than formerly. Congress did not make any radical change in the substantial evidence rule; rather the statutory provisions under discussion are expressions of disapproval of the manner in which the courts were applying their own standard. Mr. Justice Frankfurter, speaking for the Court, pointed out that

> Since the precise way in which courts interfere with agency findings cannot be imprisoned within any form of words, new formulas attempting to rephrase the old are not likely to be more helpful than the old. There are no talismanic words that can avoid the process of judgment. The difficulty is that we cannot escape, in relation to this problem, the use of undefined defining terms.
>
> Whatever changes were made by the Administrative Procedure and Taft-Hartley Acts are clearly within the area where precise definition is impossible. Retention of the familiar "substantial evidence" terminology indicates that no drastic reversal of attitude was intended.[246]

The "uncritical" nature of the new standard was brought into the open in *O'Leary v. Brown-Pacific-Maxon, Inc.*,[247] where three dissenting Justices held that the deputy commissioner's findings of fact for compensation under the Longshoremen's Compensation Act, was "false" and had "no scintilla of evidence or inference to support it," and that the majority opinion avoided the ruling in the Universal Camera Corp. case by finding "facts where there are no facts, on the whole record or any piece of it."

[245] *Universal Camera Corp. v. National Labor Relations Board,* 340 U.S. at 488, 71 S. Ct. at 465, 95 L. Ed. at 313.

[246] 340 U.S. at 489, 71 S. Ct. at 465, 95 L. Ed. at 313.

[247] 340 U.S. 504, 509, 510, 71 S. Ct. 470, 473, 95 L. Ed. 341, 344, 345 (1951).

Judicial Review of Rule-Making.—Administrative legislation is subject to judicial supervision in a number of ways: (1) the courts can control the degree of delegation of legislative power to administrative and executive agencies through the requirement and application of an "appropriate standard"; (2) they may hold the agency to the terms of the statutory grant; (3) they may set aside a rule as contrary to constitutional right, power, or immunity, or (4) for failure to observe procedure required by law.

Many of the legislative standards prescribed for the guidance of administrative action are necessarily in such general and flexible terms as "unfair methods of competition," "reasonable rates," "fair value," "fair return," "public convenience and necessity," "adequate facilities and services," "safe," "wholesome," "expedient," "necessary," "reciprocally unequal and unreasonable," "any manipulative or deceptive device or contrivance," and "undue and unreasonable advantage." The application of these general standards calls for the exercise of judgment in finding the required facts or acquiring the necessary information by persons possessing specialized or technical knowledge or skills. It embraces the regulation of public utilities, banks and banking, agriculture, labor relations, the licensing of occupations, competitive business practices, theaters, schools, and so on into all the byways of our social existence.[248]

An administrative agency may be authorized to define a statutory standard by rule and regulation. Thus, the Federal Trade Commission Act authorized the Commission to restrain "unfair methods of competition" and impliedly empowered it to define what constitutes unfair methods.[249] But, the Supreme Court said: "The words 'unfair

---

[248] "Today, the state acts also as doctor, nurse, teacher, insurance organizer, house builder, sanitary engineer, chemist, railway controller, supplier of gas, water and electricity, town planner, pensions distributor, provider of transport, hospital organizer, road-maker, and in a large number of other capacities." Committee on Ministers' Powers, *Minutes of Evidence* (1932), Vol. II, p. 52. Memorandum by W. A. Robson; quoted by F. F. Blachly and Miriam Oatman, *Administrative Legislation and Adjudication* (Brookings Institution, Washington, D.C., 1940), p. 2; also see p. 274 for a list of matters regulated by the national government.

A special committee on administrative law of the American Bar Association has estimated that ". . . the total volume of administrative legislation now in force greatly exceeds the total legislative output of Congress since 1789." *American Bar Association Reports, 1934,* p. 555.

[249] See *Report of the Committee on Interstate Commerce,* June 13, 1914, 63d Cong., 2d Sess., No. 597: "The Committee gave careful consideration to the question as to whether it would attempt to define the many and variable unfair practices which prevail in commerce, and to forbid their continuance, or whether it would, by general declaration condemning unfair practices, *leave it to the Commission to determine what practices were unfair.* It concluded that the latter course would be better." Italics supplied.

methods of competition' are not defined by the statute and their exact meaning is in dispute. It is for the courts, not the Commission, ultimately to determine as a matter of law what they include." [250] Further, the Federal Trade Commission, the Interstate Commerce Commission, and Federal Communications Commission, are authorized to enforce compliance with the prohibitions of the Clayton Act.[251] Nevertheless, the courts have asserted the authority to decide what constitutes price discrimination within the meaning of Section 2,[252] price maintenance [253] and exclusive agency contracts [254] within Section 3, and intercompany stock acquisition within Section 7 [255] of the Clayton Act, thus largely taking over the functions of the Federal Trade Commission.[256]

[250] *Federal Trade Commission v. Gratz,* 253 U.S. 421, 427, 40 S. Ct. 572, 575, 64 L. Ed. 993, 996 (1920). Also, *Federal Trade Commission v. Algona Lumber Co.,* 291 U.S. 67, 54 S. Ct. 315, 78 L. Ed. 655 (1934), reversing 64 F. (2d) 618 (C.C.A., 1933); *Federal Trade Commission v. Standard Education Society,* 302 U.S. 112, 58 S. Ct. 113, 82 L. Ed. 141 (1937); *Federal Trade Commission v. Winsted Hosiery Co.,* 258 U.S. 483, 42 S. Ct. 384, 66 L. Ed. 729 (1922). Cf. *Federal Trade Commission v. R. F. Keppel & Bros., Inc.,* 291 U.S. 304, 54 S. Ct. 423, 78 L. Ed. 814 (1934); and see Milton Handler, "Unfair Competition," 21 *Iowa Law Review* (1936), 175 ff.

[251] Act of October 15, 1914, 38 *Stat.* 730, 734, § 11, 15 *U.S.C.A.* § 21.

[252] *Mennen Co. v. Federal Trade Commission,* 288 Fed. 774 (C.C.A. 2d, 1923); *National Biscuit Co. v. Federal Trade Commission,* 299 Fed. 733 (C.C.A. 2d, 1924).

[253] *Beech Nut Packing Co. v. Federal Trade Commission,* 264 Fed. 885 (C.C.A. 2d, 1920), modified by *Federal Trade Commission v. Beech Nut Packing Co.,* 257 U.S. 441, 42 S. Ct. 150, 66 L. Ed. 307 (1922); *Cream of Wheat Co. v. Federal Trade Commission,* 14 F. (2d) 40 (C.C.A. 8th, 1926); *Moir v. Federal Trade Commission,* 12 F. (2d) 22 (C.C.A. 1st, 1926); *Federal Trade Commission v. American Tobacco Co.,* 274 U.S. 543, 47 S. Ct. 663, 71 L. Ed. 1193 (1927).

[254] *Butterick Co. v. Federal Trade Commission,* 4 F. (2d) 910 (C.C.A. 2d, 1925); *Q. R. S. Music Co. v. Federal Trade Commission,* 12 F. (2d) 730 (C.C.A. 7th, 1926); *Federal Trade Commission v. Curtis Publishing Co.,* 260 U.S. 568, 43 S. Ct. 210, 67 L. Ed. 408 (1923); *Pearsell Butter Co. v. Federal Trade Commission,* 292 Fed. 720 (C.C.A. 7th, 1923).

[255] *Swift & Co. v. Federal Trade Commission,* 272 U.S. 554, 47 S. Ct. 175, 71 L. Ed. 405 (1926); *Aluminum Co. of America v. Federal Trade Commission,* 284 Fed. 401 (C.C.A. 3d, 1922); *Arrow-Hart Electric Co. v. Federal Trade Commission,* 291 U.S. 587, 54 S. Ct. 532, 78 L. Ed. 1007 (1934); *Vivaudou, Inc. v. Federal Trade Commission,* 54 F. (2d) 273 (C.C.A. 2d, 1931); *International Shoe Co. v. Federal Trade Commission,* 280 U.S. 291, 50 S. Ct. 89, 74 L. Ed. 431 (1930).

[256] "The definition of unfair competition by administrative legislation is incomparably superior to definition by administrative decision. The method of judicial exclusion and inclusion does not permit of a sustained, consistent, comprehensive, and speedy attack upon the trade practice problem. The case by case determination takes years to cover even a narrow field; it leaves wide lacunae; false starts are difficult to correct and the erroneous decision is just as prolific as a sound ruling in begetting a progeny of subordinate rules. . . . The fusion of law and economics, the detailed investigations and hearings, and the precise formulation of rules, all of which are so essential to a proper regulation of competition, are not feasible when law making is but a by product of the adjustment of controversies. The combination of the two functions may have been justified when knowledge of the workings of

More recently ". . . there has been an ever-growing dependency by the court upon the findings of administrative commissions generally, even when factual issues are not too clearly disassociated from questions of law." Therefore, "the judgment of the Commission as to what practices are to be deemed unfair, is of weight." [257] In *Federal Trade Commission v. Cement Institute,*[258] the Court said: "We sustain the [Federal Trade] Commission's holding that concerted maintenance of the basing point delivered price system is an unfair method of competition. . . . In so doing we give great weight to the Commission's conclusion, as this Court has done in other cases." [259]

This manhandling of the Federal Trade Commission is not an exceptional arrogation of judicial power; the Interstate Commerce Commission has also been buffeted from court to court. J. C. Blaisdell sums up the case against judicial interference as follows: "The history of the Interstate Commerce Commission, which is probably the most important federal commission for industrial control, has been a struggle marked by empowering acts of Congress, followed by a series of court decisions limiting the powers of the Commission, followed in turn by further acts of Congress strengthening the Commission. . . . Its power was gained only after half a century of conflict with the courts, during which it has again and again been necessary for Congress to intervene on the side of the Commission." [260]

The Attorney General's Committee pointed out that until recently, judicial review of administrative regulations could be had only collaterally, in actions brought to enforce them, in injunction suits to prevent their enforcement, in habeas corpus actions to obtain release from arrests for violation, or in private actions in which the results turned upon the effect of regulations. In such an action, the issue may

---

competition was sparse and objectives ill-defined. It can no longer be justified today. It would be little short of criminal to reply upon so inefficient a method of law making when more scientific and expeditious devices are available." Milton Handler, "Unfair Competition," 31 *Iowa Law Review* (January, 1936), 175, 259.

[257] *Hastings Mfg. Co. v. Federal Trade Commission,* 153 F. (2d) 253, 258 (C.C.A. 6th, 1946).

[258] 333 U.S. 683, 68 S. Ct. 793, 92 L. Ed. 1010 (1948).

[259] 333 U.S. at 720, 68 S. Ct. at 812, 92 L. Ed. at 1044.

[260] *The Federal Trade Commission* (Columbia University Press, New York, 1932), p. 323. See also Carl McFarland, *Judicial Control of the Federal Trade Commission and the Interstate Commerce Commission, 1920–1930* (Harvard University Press, Cambridge, Mass., 1933), p. 96: "In connection with all cases, the courts determine the sufficiency of the pleadings, . . . what shall constitute proof and what conclusions shall be drawn from the evidence, when the matter is of public interest, and what amounts to interference with competition, and when monopoly exists or is fostered."

be either the validity of a regulation as a whole or the legality of applying it to the person who is challenging it, in the same way that an
attack upon a statute may involve either the constitutionality of the
measure as a whole or the constitutionality of applying it to a particular party.[261]

The issues thus presented are of the kind traditionally decided by
the courts, questions of law. More recent statutes have opened up
new areas for judicial review by requiring that administrative regulations shall be based upon findings of fact, adduced from evidence
made of record at a hearing, and that a reviewing court may set aside
such regulations, not only for failure to conform to constitutional
and statutory requirements, but also for failure of the findings of fact
to be supported by substantial evidence in the record.

Rule-making involves the exercise of discretion in the choice and
formulation of policy, and the required fact-finding may involve
many complicated and highly technical questions. To require a public
hearing on such questions and to embody the evidence into a record
may be feasible if not profitable; but to subject such a record to review and evaluation by judges would seem to be more mischievous
than useful. The Attorney General's Committee on Administrative
Procedure cautioned:

> Undoubtedly the appraisal of evidence bearing upon such question
> and the formulation of findings upon the evidence lie peculiarly within
> administrative competence. It seems unlikely that advantage will be
> gained from exposing this process to the scrutiny of judges untrained
> in the subject matter of regulations. It should be enough that the
> administrative authorities are required, in case their regulations are
> called in question before a court, to demonstrate that they come ration-
> ally within the statutory authorization. For these reasons the opera-
> tion of existing statutes which provide for the detailed type of judi-
> cial review upon administrative records should be carefully watched
> before other similar measures are enacted. The Commission does not
> recommend the general application or extension of this type of court
> review of regulations.[262]

That Congress has a broad discretion in circumscribing court
review of administrative rule-making is now freely conceded by the
Supreme Court. In a decision enforcing jurisdictional limitations
placed upon court review of a rate order of the Interstate Commerce

---

[261] *Administrative Procedure in Government Agencies, S. Doc. No. 8,* 77th Cong.,
1st Sess. (1941), p. 115.

[262] *Administrative Procedure in Government Agencies, S. Doc. No. 8,* 77th Cong.,
1st Sess. (1941), p. 119.

Commission by the Urgent Deficiencies Act, Mr. Justice Rutledge said:

> The limitations exemplify settled Congressional policy concerning the relations of rate-making bodies and reviewing courts. Not only is rate-making essentially legislative in the first instance. The policy of judicial restraint is one having regard for the expertise of special agencies charged with performing the rate-making function and for the inherent actual, as well as legal, disability of courts to execute that function.[263]

[263] *United States v. Jones,* 336 U.S. 641, 652, 69 S. Ct. 787, 793–94, 93 L. Ed. 938, 946 (1949). See also *United States v. Griffin,* 303 U.S. 226, 58 S. Ct. 601, 82 L. Ed. 764 (1938).

Chapter 8

LIMITATIONS OF JUDICIAL CONTROL OF THE ADMINISTRATIVE PROCESS

Judicial Self-Restraint in the Review of Administrative Action

The Negative Order Doctrine.—In *Procter & Gamble Co. v. United States* [1] the Supreme Court ruled that a so-called "negative order" of the Interstate Commerce Commission was not reviewable by the Commerce Court. The Commission had dismissed a complaint by the Procter & Gamble Company to set aside demurrage rules adopted by the National Association of Railroad Commissioners. It was held that only "affirmative orders" were reviewable. Presumably a "negative" order (as distinguished from an "affirmative" order) is one that does not have "the legal effect of changing the status quo, permitting what was previously not allowed or compelling what was previously not required." [2] For example, an order of the Interstate Commerce Commission denying an application by a railroad company for a certificate of public necessity and convenience to extend its lines was held to be a nonreviewable "negative" order, because: "It is not susceptible of violation and cannot call for enforcement. It does not finally adjudicate the railway's standing; nor does it enjoin it to do or refrain from doing anything. The penalties provided . . . are prescribed not for violation of an order of the Commission, but for violation of the provisions of the statute." [3]

[1] 225 U.S. 282, 32 S. Ct. 761, 56 L. Ed. 1091 (1912). The United States Commerce Court was created in 1910 with jurisdiction to review decisions of the Interstate Commerce Commission, but was legislated out of existence in 1913, a victim of politics.

[2] *Rochester Telephone Co. v. United States,* 307 U.S. 125, 140, note 24, 59 S. Ct. 754, 762, note 24, 83 L. Ed. 1147 (1939). Prior to this case, the "negative order" cases involved action by the Interstate Commerce Commission, except in *United States v. Corrick,* 298 U.S. 435, 56 S. Ct. 829, 80 L. Ed. 1263 (1936), which involved action by the Secretary of Agriculture under the Packers and Stockyards Act, 7 U.S.C.A. §§ 181 *et sqq.*

[3] *Piedmont & Northern Ry. v. United States,* 280 U.S. 469, 477, 50 S. Ct. 192, 194, 74 L. Ed. 551, 555 (1930). *United States v. Griffin,* 303 U.S. 226, 234, 58 S. Ct. 601, 605, 82 L. Ed. 764, 769 (1938): "The order . . . here assailed, does not command either the Government or the Railroad to do anything. . . . The order assailed, being a refusal to change the existing status, was a 'negative' order. The Dis-

This doctrine was rejected, however, in *Rochester Telephone Co. v. United States* [4] where it was held that it is the *effect,* not the *form,* of an administrative action that determines its reviewability. Therefore, a "negative" order by the Federal Communications Commission classifying the Rochester Telephone Company as a common carrier subject to the orders of the Telephone Division of the Commission was reviewable upon application by the company for a court order and decree setting aside the order of the Commission on the ground that the Commission's threat to enforce its order put the company to the hazard of irreparable injury. The Commission's denial of the complainant's assertion of a legal right, the right of exemption from the provisions of the Federal Communications Act, gave rise to a constitutional "case" or "controversy"; and the requirements of equity were satisfied, since to disregard the Commission's adverse action entailed a threat of oppressive penalties. An action before the Commission is akin to an inclusive equity suit in which all relevant claims are adjusted. Thus an order of the Commission dismissing a complaint on the merits and maintaining the status quo is not different from an order directing some change in status.

Furthermore, the negative order doctrine was intended to carry out the purposes of the Federal Communications Act [5] by a clarification of the relations between administrative bodies and the courts; but, said the Court, "The considerations of policy for which the notions of 'negative' and 'affirmative' orders were introduced, are completely satisfied by proper application of the combined doctrines of primary jurisdiction and administrative finality." [6] The primary jurisdiction doctrine requires that, before a court can be invoked, the regulatory agency must first pass upon matters requiring technical knowledge.[7] The doctrine of administrative finality limits judicial review to questions of constitutional power, statutory authority, and

---

trict Court lacked jurisdiction to set it aside, and should have dismissed the bill." In *Shannahan v. United States,* 303 U.S. 596, 599, 58 S. Ct. 732, 734, 82 L. Ed. 1039, 1041 (1938), an order by the Interstate Commerce Commission denying an application for a rehearing was held to be "as clearly 'negative' as orders by which the Commission refuses to take requested action. . . . As such, it is not reviewable under the Urgent Deficiences Act."

[4] 307 U.S. 125, 59 S. Ct. 754, 83 L. Ed. 1147 (1939). Also *United States v. Maher,* 307 U.S. 148, 59 S. Ct. 768, 83 L. Ed. 1162 (1939); *Federal Power Commission v. Pacific Power & Light Co.,* 307 U.S. 156, 59 S. Ct. 766, 83 L. Ed. 1180 (1939).

[5] 48 *Stat.* 1064 (1934), 50 *Stat.,* 189 (1937), 47 *U.S.C.A.* §§ 151 *et sqq.*

[6] *Rochester Telephone Co. v. United States,* 307 U.S. at 142, 59 S. Ct. at 763, 83 L. Ed. at 1159 (1939).

[7] *Texas and Pac. Ry. Co. v. Abilene Cotton Oil Co.,* 204 U.S. 426, 27 S. Ct. 350, 51 L. Ed. 553 (1907).

the basic prerequisites of proof—otherwise the orders of the agency are incontestable.[8] Although these doctrines evolved in relation to the Interstate Commerce Commission, they have become general rules of administrative law.

In rejecting the "negative order doctrine," Mr. Justice Frankfurter said for the majority of the Court:

> . . . the opinion in *Procter & Gamble v. United States* gave authority to a doctrine which harmonizes neither with the considerations which induced it nor with the course of decisions which have purported to follow it. Subsequent cases have made it abundantly clear that "negative order" and "affirmative order" are not appropriate terms of art. Thus, the court has had occasion to find that while an order was "negative in form" it was "affirmative in substance." "Negative" has really been an obfuscating adjective in that it implied a search for a distinction—non-action as against action—which does not involve the real considerations on which rest, as we have seen, the reviewability of Commission orders, within the framework of its discretionary authority and within the general criteria of justiciability. "Negative" and "affirmative," in the context of these problems, is as unilluminating and mischief-making a distinction as the outmoded line between "nonfeasance" and "misfeasance". . . . We conclude, therefore, that any distinction, as such, between "negative" and "affirmative" orders, as a touchstone of jurisdiction to review the Commission's orders, serves no useful purpose, and insofar as earlier decisions have been controlled by this distinction, they can no longer be guiding.[9]

Primary Jurisdiction Doctrine—The Exhaustion of Administrative Remedies.—In *Myers V. Bethlehem Shipbuilding Corp.*[10] the Supreme Court held that a federal district court did not have equity jurisdiction to enjoin the National Labor Relations Board from holding a hearing upon a complaint which it filed against an employer alleged to be engaged in unfair labor practices prohibited by the National Labor Relations Act.[11] Since the procedure before the Board was appropriate and adequate review by the circuit court of

[8] *Interstate Commerce Commission v. Illinois Central R.R.*, 215 U.S. 452, 470, 30 S. Ct. 155, 160, 54 L. Ed. 280, 288 (1910) ; *Interstate Commerce Commission v. Union Pacific R.R.*, 222 U.S. 541, 32 S. Ct. 108, 56 L. Ed. 308 (1912).

[9] *Rochester Telephone Co. v. United States,* 307 U.S. at 140–42, 143, 59 S. Ct. at 762–63, 764, 83 L. Ed. at 1158–59, 1160. Mr. Justice Butler, concurring, said, "There is no occasion to review earlier decisions dealing with affirmative and negative administrative orders and obviously none to overrule any of them or to repudiate or impair the doctrine they establish. The Court's discussion, extraneous to the issue involved, confuses rather than clarifies." 307 U.S. at 147–48, 59 S. Ct. at 765–66, 83 L. Ed. at 1162.

[10] 303 U.S. 41, 58 S. Ct. 459, 82 L. Ed. 683 (1938).

[11] Act of July 5, 1935, 49 *Stat.*, 449, 29 *U.S.C.A.* §§ 151 *et sqq.*

appeals had been provided, it was necessary to exhaust the administrative remedy before resort could be had to the courts. The Court spoke of

> . . . the long-settled rule of judicial administration that no one is entitled to judicial relief for a supposed or threatened injury until the prescribed administrative remedy has been exhausted.
>
> Obviously, the rule requiring exhaustion of the administrative remedy cannot be circumvented by asserting that the charge on which the complaint rests is groundless and that the mere holding of the prescribed administrative hearing would result in irreparable damage. Lawsuits also often prove to have been groundless; but no way has been discovered of relieving a defendant from the necessity of a trial to establish the fact.[12]

Again, in *National Labor Relations Board v. Hearst Publications, Inc.*,[13] the Court ruled that the power of the circuit court of appeals to review decisions by the Board was limited by the substantial evidence rule—"the Board's determination that specific persons are 'employees' under the Act is to be accepted if it has 'warrant in the record' and a reasonable basis in law." [14] In consequence, many issues are not determined by a court on the merits but are disposed of finally by an agency.[15]

The exhaustion of administrative remedies rule "does not require merely the *initiation* of prescribed administrative procedures. It is one of *exhausting* them, that is, of pursuing them to their appropriate conclusion and, correlatively, of awaiting their final outcome before seeking judicial intervention." [16]

The primary jurisdiction doctrine recognizes *de facto* the judicial character of administrative adjudication, and for its purposes incorporates administrative tribunals into the judicial hierarchy. It

[12] 303 U.S. at 50–52, 58 S. Ct. at 463–64, 82 L. Ed. at 644. Also *United States v. Euzicka*, 329 U.S. 287, 67 S. Ct. 207, 91 L. Ed. 290 (1946) ; *Macauley v. Waterman Steamship Corp.*, 327 U.S. 540, 66 S. Ct. 712, 90 L. Ed. 839 (1946) ; *United States v. Joseph A. Holpuch Co.*, 328 U.S. 234, 66 S. Ct. 1000, 90 L. Ed. 1192 (1946) ; *Illinois Commerce Commission v. Thomson*, 318 U.S. 675, 686, 63 S. Ct. 834, 840, 87 L. Ed. 1075, 1082 (1943) ; *White v. TVA*, 58 F. Supp. 776 (D.C.E.D. Tenn., 1945) ; *Bowles v. Batson*, 61 F. Supp. 839 (D.C.W.D.S.C., 1945) ; *United States v. Wood*, 61 F. Supp. 175 (D.C. Mass., 1945) ; *Shigeru Fuji v. United States*, 148 F. (2d) 298 (C.C.A. 10th, 1945). See also, R. Berger, "The Exhaustion of Administrative Remedies," 48 *Yale Law Journal* (1939), 981–1006; and 44 *Michigan Law Review*, 1035 ff.

[13] 322 U.S. 111, 64 S. Ct. 851, 88 L. Ed. 1170 (1944).

[14] 322 U.S. at 131–32, 64 S. Ct. at 860–61, 88 L. Ed. at 1185.

[15] For this reason the Supreme Court of New Jersey rejected the primary jurisdiction rule in *Ward v. Keenan*, 3 N.J. 298, 70 Atl. (2d) 77 (1949).

[16] *Aircraft & Diesel Equipment Corp. v. Hirsch*, 331 U.S. 752, 767, 67 S. Ct. 1493, 1500, 91 L. Ed. 1796, 1806 (1947).

applies to review of agency cases the same orderly procedure that prevails for the review of court cases; and it is closely related to the chancery rule that a litigant has no standing in equity if he has an adequate legal remedy.

The exhaustion of remedies rule extends to questions of law as well as of fact. In the Myers case, Mr. Justice Brandeis said that "because the rule is one of judicial administration—not merely a rule governing the exercise of discretion—it is applicable to proceedings at law as well as suits in equity." [17] The rule thus relieves the courts of much needless litigation and secures for them the assistance of specialized tribunals for the preliminary examination of many technical matters.

There are some exceptions to the rule. It is not necessary, for example, to pursue and so exhaust an administrative remedy that would be futile.[18] The equitable jurisdiction of the federal courts has been exercised where there has been an inadequate administrative remedy and a threatened or impending irreparable injury resulting from delay in following the prescribed procedure.[19] However,

> Where the intent of Congress is clear to require administrative determination, either to the exclusion of judicial action or in advance of it, a strong showing is required, both of inadequacy of the prescribed procedure and of impending harm, to permit short-circuiting the administrative process. Congress' commands for judicial restraint in this respect are not lightly to be disregarded.[20]

The exhaustion rule, it has been held, does not automatically require that judicial review must always be denied where an administrative rehearing is authorized but not sought. That is, where a rehearing *may* be granted but is *not mandatory* and the statute provides judicial review, an application for a rehearing is not required before judicial review.[21] If, however, a rehearing or review is a matter of

[17] *Myers v. Bethlehem Shipbuilding Corp.*, 303 U.S. 41, note 9, 58 S. Ct. 459, note 9, 82 L. Ed. 688 (1938).

[18] *Publicker Industries, Inc. v. Anderson*, 68 F. Supp. 532 (D.D.C., 1946).

[19] *Oklahoma Natural Gas Co. v. Russell*, 261 U.S. 290, 43 S. Ct. 353, 67 L. Ed. 659 (1923); *Pacific Telephone & Telegraph Co. v. Kuykendall*, 265 U.S. 196, 44 S. Ct. 553, 68 L. Ed. 975 (1924); *Porter v. Investors' Syndicate*, 286 U.S. 461, 52 S. Ct. 617, 76 L. Ed. 1226 (1932); *Hillsborough v. Cromwell*, 326 U.S. 620, 66 S. Ct. 445, 90 L. Ed. 358 (1946); *Wallace v. Hines*, 253 U.S. 66, 40 S. Ct. 435, 64 L. Ed. 782 (1920).

[20] *Aircraft & Diesel Equipment Corp. v. Hirsch*, 331 U.S. 752, 773–74, 67, S. Ct. 1493, 1504, 91 L. Ed. 1796, 1809 (1947). See also *Natural Gas Pipeline Co. of America v. Slattery*, 302 U.S. 300, 58 S. Ct. 199, 82 L. Ed. 276 (1937).

[21] *Prendergast v. New York Tel. Co.*, 262 U.S. 43, 46, 48, 43 S. Ct. 466, 468, 469, 67 L. Ed. 853, 856 (1923).

right, and stay therein is automatic, it may be required as a pre-requisite to judicial review.[22] Some statutes provide that no proceeding to review an agency order shall be brought by any person unless such person has made an application to the agency for a rehearing thereon. This procedure gives the agency an opportunity to correct its errors preliminary to judicial relief.

Under the Selective Service Training Act [23] a registrant was held not entitled to judicial review of a board's classification until and unless he had registered, since at the time of his registration he was entitled to another physical examination which might result in a change of classification or even rejection. This administrative remedy had to be exhausted before judicial relief could be had.[24] When the Act was amended to eliminate medical examination upon reporting for registration, the Court held that, since the selectee could take no further action to change his status, the administrative remedy had been exhausted and an order by a draft board to report to a work camp was reviewable by a court.[25]

Where a State court is authorized by law to *review and to amend* administrative orders, the exhaustion of remedies rule requires a litigant to seek the aid of the State court before he is entitled to relief in a federal court.[26] This is on the theory that the proceeding before the State court is administrative, not strictly judicial, in character; as far as the litigant is concerned, action by the court is necessary to complete the administrative act. The exhaustion rule is thus correlated to the rule that courts will review only final administrative action.

Presumption of Administrative Validity.—The frequently stated rule governing judicial consideration of legislation is that the legislation is presumed to be constitutional and "only if no construction can save the act from this claim of unconstitutionality are we

[22] *Levers v. Anderson,* 326 U.S. 219, 222, 66 S. Ct. 72, 73, 90 L. Ed. 26, 29 (1945), citing *United States v. Abilene & So. Ry. Co.,* 265 U.S. 274, 280-82, 44 S. Ct. 565, 566, 567, 68 L. Ed. 1016, 1019, 1020 (1924).

[23] Act of September 16, 1940, 54 *Stat.* 885, 50 *U.S.C.A.* (App.) §§ 301 ff.

[24] *Falbo v. United States,* 320 U.S. 549, 64 S. Ct. 346, 88 L. Ed. 305 (1944). *Swaczyk v. United States,* 156 F. (2d) 17 (C.C.A. 1st, 1946); *Rusk v. United States,* 154 F. (2d) 763 (C.C.A. 5th, 1946); *Hudson v. United States,* 157 F. (2d), 782 (C.C.A. 10th, 1946).

[25] *Gibson v. United States,* 329 U.S. 338, 67 S. Ct. 301, 91 L. Ed. 331 (1946).

[26] *Porter, Auditor v. Investors' Syndicate,* 286 U.S. 461, 52 S. Ct. 132, 76 L. Ed. 1226 (1932); *J. B. Schermerhorn, Inc. v. Holloman,* 74 F. (2d) 265 (C.C.A. 10th, 1934); *Kansas City Southern Ry. Co. v. Cornish,* 65 F. (2d) 671 (C.C.A. 10th, 1933); *Prentis v. Atlantic Coast Line,* 211 U.S. 210, 29 S. Ct. 67, 53 L. Ed. 150 (1908).

willing to reach that result." [27] Mr. Justice Sutherland asserted, in
Adkins v. Children's Hospital: "This Court, by an unbroken line of
decisions from Chief Justice Marshall to the present day, has steadily
adhered to the rule that every possible presumption is in favor of the
validity of an act of Congress until overcome beyond rational
doubt." [28] This same rule of presumed regularity and validity applies
to administrative rules; [29] that is, an administrative determination is
prima facie correct; and the burden of proof to show error is on the
attacker. [30] The administrator is presumed to have considered all the
evidence, [31] followed regular procedure, [32] acted in good faith, [33] and not
oppressively, [34] and reached conclusions based upon and supported by
the facts. [35] The presumption of regularity may be rebutted by the
evidence, [36] but judicial deference to administrative judgment weighs
heavily in favor of the validity of the regulation. [37]

In *Federal Power Commission v. Hope Natural Gas Co.,* Mr.
Justice Douglas pointed out that

[27] *Screws v. United States,* 325 U.S. 91, 100, 65 S. Ct. 1031, 1035, 89 L. Ed. 1495,
1502 (1945); *Ashwander v. Tennessee Valley Authority,* 297 U.S. 288, 348, 56
S. Ct. 466, 483, 80 L. Ed. 688, 712 (1936).

[28] 261 U.S. 525, 544, 43 S. Ct. 394, 396, 67 L. Ed. 785, 790 (1923).
To the same effect: "A decent respect for a coordinate branch of the government
demands that the judiciary should presume, until the contrary is clearly shown, that
there has been no transgression of power by Congress — all the members of which
act under the obligation of an oath of fidelity to the Constitution." Mr. Justice
Strong in *Legal Tender Cases,* 12 Wall. 457, 531, 20 L. Ed. 287, 305 (1870). See
also *Sinking Fund Cases,* 99 U.S. 700, 718, 25 L. Ed. 496 (1878); *Trade Mark
Cases,* 100 U.S. 82, 96, 25 L. Ed. 550 (1879); *Nicol v. Ames,* 173 U.S. 509, 514,
19 S. Ct. 522, 43 L. Ed. 786 (1899).

[29] *Pacific States Box & Basket Co. v. White,* 296 U.S. 176, 56 S. Ct. 159, 80
L. Ed. 138 (1935); *Boske v. Comingore,* 177 U.S. 459, 20 S. Ct. 701, 44 L. Ed. 846
(1900).

[30] *Fleming v. Commissioner of Internal Revenue,* 153 F. (2d) 361 (C.C.A. 5th,
1946); *Gaylord v. Commissioner of Internal Revenue,* 153 F. (2d) 408 (C.C.A. 9th,
1946); *Friese v. Jones,* 156 F. (2d) 454 (C.C.A. 10th, 1946).

[31] *Watson Bros. Transportation Co., Inc. v. United States,* 59 F. Supp. 762 (D.C.
Nebr., 1945).

[32] *Bowles v. Glick Bros. Lumber Co.,* 146 F. (2d) 566 (C.C.A. 9th, 1945); *Hagen
v. Porter,* 156 F. (2d) 362 (C.C.A. 9th, 1946); *Bowles v. Sachnoff,* 65 Supp. 538
(W.D. Pa., 1946).

[33] *Fair Store Co. v. Board of Revision of Hamilton County,* 145 Ohio St. 231,
61 N.E. (2d) 209 (1945).

[34] *Bowles v. Northwest Poultry and Dairy Products Co.,* 153 F. (2d) 32 (C.C.A.
9th, 1946).

[35] *Bailey Farm Dairy Co. v. Jones,* 61 F. Supp. 209 (D.C.E.D. Mo., 1945); *Halibut Producers Cooperative v. Porter,* 157 F. (2d) 332 (E.C.A., 1946); *Bowles v.
Weiss,* 66 F. Supp. 366 (W.D. Pa., 1946).

[36] *Hughes v. Commissioner of Internal Revenue,* 153 F. (2d) 712 (C.C.A. 5th,
1946); *Halibut Producers Cooperative v. Porter,* 157 F. (2d) 332 (E.C.A., 1946).

[37] *Cities Service Gas Co. v. Federal Power Commission,* 155 F. (2d) 694 (C.C.A.
10th, 1946); *Gardner v. United States,* 67 F. Supp. 230 (D.N.J., 1946).

. . . the Commission's order does not become suspect by reason of the fact that it is challenged. It is the product of expert judgment which carries a presumption of validity. And he who would upset the rate order under the Act carries the heavy burden of making a convincing showing that it is invalid because it is unjust and unreasonable in its consequences.[38]

Only Final Administrative Action Is Reviewable.—Closely related to the rule that administrative remedies must be exhausted before one may seek relief in the regular courts is the further rule that generally only *final* administrative action is reviewable. Courts should not concern themselves with preliminary or intermediate administrative action or with action which has not finally determined a legal right. The Administrative Procedure Act makes reviewable,

> Every agency action made reviewable by statute and every *final* agency action for which there is no other adequate remedy in any court. . . . Any preliminary, procedural, or intermediate agency action or ruling not directly reviewable shall be subject to review upon the review of the final agency action.[39]

To review intermediate orders would afford "opportunity for constant delays in the course of the administrative proceeding for the purpose of reviewing mere procedural requirements or interlocutory directions." [40]

In *Myers v. Bethlehem Shipbuilding Corp.*,[41] the Supreme Court held that a district court did not have equity jurisdiction to enjoin the National Labor Relations Board from holding a hearing on a complaint issued by the Board against the corporation. The latter alleged, among other things, that the hearing would cause it irreparable injury, because of the expense, loss of good will, and so on. The contention that the district court had jurisdiction to enjoin the holding of the hearing, said the Court, " . . . is at war with the long settled rule of judicial administration that no one is entitled to judicial relief for *a supposed or threatened injury* until the prescribed administrative remedy has been exhausted." [42]

[38] 320 U.S. 591, 602, 64 S. Ct. 281, 288, 88 L. Ed. 333, 345 (1944).
[39] Sec. 10(c), 5 *U.S.C.A.* 1009(c). Italics supplied. " 'Final' action includes any effective agency action for which there is no other adequate remedy in any court." *Report of the Committee on the Judiciary, United States Senate on S. 7, S. Rep. No. 752,* 79th Cong., 1st Sess. (1945), p. 27.
[40] *Federal Power Commission v. Metropolitan Edison Co.,* 304 U.S. 375, 383–84, 58 S. Ct. 963, 967, 82 L. Ed. 1408, 1414 (1938).
[41] 303 U.S. 41, 58 S. Ct. 459, 82 L. Ed. 638 (1938).
[42] 303 U.S. at 50–51, 58 S. Ct. at 463, 82 L. Ed. at 644. Italics supplied.

In *United Employees Association v. National Labor Relations Board,*[43] a certification by the Board of a union as the exclusive employee representative for collective bargaining was held not subject to review, since it was not a final and binding order but merely a certification of a fact which if ignored, had no operative effect without further proceedings.

The Supreme Court has held that an allegation that an administrative regulation will produce irreparable injury gives a right of judicial review. When the Federal Communications Commission promulgated regulations announcing the principles to be applied in the future in the exercise of the Commission's licensing power, a broadcasting system charged that many of their affiliates, fearing the loss of their licenses as a result of the new regulations, threatened to cancel and repudiate their affiliation contracts, thus seriously impairing the system's ability to conduct its business. Suit was brought in the southern district of New York to enjoin enforcement of the order. That court dismissed the complaint for want of jurisdiction but stayed the Commission's order pending direct appeal to the Supreme Court. The latter held that the appellant was entitled to judicial review (in a plenary suit in equity) under Section 402(a) of the Communications Act of 1934[44] and the Urgent Deficiencies Act[45] and continued the stay on terms to be settled by the district court.[46] The appellant, said the Court, was entitled to bring suit to enjoin enforcement of regulations which threatened wholesale cancellations of its contracts. An announcement of future policy is an exercise of delegated legislative power, which, until amended, is controlling alike upon the Commission and all others whose rights may be affected by the execution of that policy. The regulation promulgating the policy applies to all who are within its terms without further or future administrative action—in fact, it operates to control such action and to determine in advance the rights of those affected by it. The regulation is final administrative action giving rise to a right to judicial review. Mr. Justice Frankfurter's dissent calls attention again to the unsettled and uncertain state of our administrative law, as well as to shifting divisions within the Court:

> To argue that irreparable injury implies reviewability is, in effect, to contend that there must be a remedy because the plaintiff claims serious damage. . . .

[43] 96 F. (2d) 875 (C.C.A. 3d, 1938).
[44] 48 *Stat.* 1093, 47 *U.S.C.A.* § 402(a).
[45] 38 *Stat.* 220, 28 *U.S.C.A.* § 47.
[46] *Columbia Broadcasting System, Inc. v. United States,* 316 U.S. 407, 62 S. Ct. 1194, 86 L. Ed. 1563 (1942).

This case illustrates anew the influence of a particular instance of felt hardship in derailing legal principles from customary tracks. But this is not an isolated case. If threatened damage through general pronouncement of policy for future administrative action, even if cast in the formal language of a regulation, is to give rise to equitable review apart from the rule that judicial review is premature because of want of administrative finality, the same basis of irreparable harm which is here equated to jurisdiction will bear rich litigious fruit in the case of "regulations" issued by the Securities and Exchange Commission which are damaging in their immediate repercussions to stock exchange and holding companies, or regulations announced by the Treasury for the guidance of taxpayers but which adversely affect business interests, or regulations by the Federal Power Commission, etc. . . .

Hardship may well come through action of an administrative agency. But to slide from recognition of a hardship to assertion of jurisdiction is once more to assume that only the courts are the guardians of the rights and liberties of the people. In denying that it had power to review the action of the Federal Communications Commission because that body had not yet determined a legal right, the court below, as Judge Learned Hand's opinion abundantly proves, was not respecting a rule of etiquette. On the contrary, it merely recognized that the federal courts are entrusted with the correction of administrative errors or wrongdoing only to the extent of Congressional authorization. To say that the courts should reject the doctrine of administrative finality and take jurisdiction whenever action of an administrative agency may seriously affect substantial business interests, regardless of how intermediate or incomplete the action may be, is, in effect, to imply that the protection of legal interests is entrusted solely to the courts.[47]

Administrative Discretion.—A reading of the judicial decisions indicate that

> . . . there is a different significance to the term "discretion" in the various sectors of the administrative process. In making procedural judgments or in framing rules of practice agencies have one kind of discretion; in deciding questions of law they are said to have another type; in determining issues of fact, still another. Then again there is said to be degrees of discretion, the term "absolute discretion" being in effect indistinguishable from the harsher term "arbitrary authority." Courts call agency action "final" or "not subject to review" when they refrain from disturbing it, but "capricious" when they find it unlawful. But, while there may be no ready formula, this is not to say that the courts are themselves arbitrary or capricious, or that there is no ra-

---

[47] 316 U.S. at 441–42, 446–47, 62 S. Ct. at 1211, 1213–14, 86 S. Ct. at 1583, 1584, 1586 (1942). Mr. Justice Reed and Mr. Justice Douglas concurred. The minority view in this case seems to be the majority view in *Eccles v. Peoples Bank*, 333 U.S. 426, 68 S. Ct. 641, 92 L. Ed. 1153 (1948).

tional distinction in the cases. Words like "discretion" or "final" are legal shorthand, just as "arbitrary" and "capricious" are.

In its essentials discretion means no more than the necessary room in which to work, to proceed, to find facts, to frame remedies, and the like. Otherwise the official duty is called "ministerial.". . . The federal courts themselves are careful to find two things before leaving matters to "administrative discretion"—first, authority to act and, secondly, reasonableness in the specific action involved.[48]

While the courts are not necessarily "arbitrary or capricious" in reviewing administrative discretion, they sometimes are, and they transcribe their "legal shorthand" without providing a key or manual that is intelligible to laymen.

The purpose of judicial control of the administrative process is to maintain law as the agency for the control of administrative discretion. But

> This end is not furthered by the mere substitution of the opinion of the judges for the opinion of administrative experts as to issues and matters peculiar to individual cases. Such substitution does not subordinate discretion to law; it simply sets the discretion of an unqualified agency in the place of a qualified one. It piles one discretionary authority on top of another. The subordination of discretion to law means its subordination to rules of a stable character and of general application. Therefore the first consideration which should go toward determining the scope of judicial control is that it should be limited so far as possible to the enforcement of general rules. The discretion of the judges will be sufficiently employed in evolving and applying such rules, without attempting to revise expert determinations of special questions of fact. Evaluations of evidence and conclusions of fact are essentially a matter for administrative discretion as distinguished from law, and, when so understood, clearly belong, even under the rule of law, to the officials. The courts, if left free to revise administrative determinations on no more accurate grounds than their private opinions as to the facts of particular cases, not merely will substitute untrained for technical judgments, but will also inevitably overlook that laborious development of general rules which under a sound division of labor is their proper task.[49]

The general principle governing judicial review of administrative discretion was stated by Mr. Justice Story as follows:

---

[48] Carl McFarland and Arthur T. Vanderbilt, *Cases and Materials on Administrative Law* (Matthew Bender & Co., Inc., Albany and New York, 1947), pp. 466, 467.

[49] John Dickinson, "Judicial Control of Official Discretion," 22 *American Political Science Review* (May, 1928), 297–98.

Whenever a statute gives a discretionary power to any person, to be exercised by him, upon his own opinion of certain facts, it is a sound rule of construction, that the statute constitutes him the sole and exclusive judge of the existence of those facts. . . . It is no answer, that such a power may be abused, for there is no power which is not susceptible of abuse. The remedy for this, as well as for all other official misconduct, if it should occur, is to be found in the constitution itself. In a free government, the danger must be remote, since, in addition to the high qualities which the Executive must be presumed to possess, of public virtue and honest devotion to the public interests, the frequency of elections, and the watchfulness of the representatives of the nation, carry with them all the checks which can be useful to guard against usurpation or wanton tyranny.[50]

Accordingly the orthodox rule is that the writ of mandamus will not lie to direct the performance of a discretionary power or duty in any particular manner.[51] If the manner of performance is prescribed by statute or if something is not left to official judgment, then the duty is ministerial, not discretionary, and is enforceable by mandamus. However, if public or private rights are involved, an officer may not have discretion as to *whether* he shall act but only as to *how* he shall act.

Mandamus is employed to compel the performance, when refused, of a ministerial duty, this being its chief use. It also is employed to compel action, when refused, in matters involving judgment or discretion, but not to direct the exercise of judgment or discretion in a particular way nor to direct the retraction or reversal of action already taken in the exercise of either.[52]

And also to the same effect:

[50] *Martin v. Mott,* 12 Wheat. 19, 31–32, 6 L. Ed. 541 (1827).

[51] See *Wilson v. Eureka City,* 173 U.S. 32, 19 S. Ct. 317, 43 L. Ed. 603 (1899), quoting from *In re Flaherty,* 105 Cal. 558 (1895), and listing a considerable number of cases sustaining the exercise of unregulated administrative discretion. Also *Decatur v. Paulding,* 14 Pet. (39 U.S.) 497, 10 L. Ed. 559 (1840) ; *Gaines v. Thompson,* 7 Wall. (74 U.S.) 347, 19 L. Ed. 62 (1869) ; *United States ex rel. Riverside Oil Co. v. Hitchcock,* 190 U.S. 316, 324–25, 23 S. Ct. 698, 702, 47 L. Ed. 1074 (1903) ; *Wilbur v. United States,* 60 App. D.C. 326 (1931) ; *Tidal Osage Co. v. West,* 58 App. D.C. 327 (1929) ; *Pittsburgh and West Virginia Ry. Co. v. Interstate Commerce Commission,* 54 App. D.C. 34 (1923) ; *Bates and Guild Co. v. Payne,* 194 U.S. 106, 24 S. Ct. 595, 48 L. Ed. 894 (1904) ; *United States ex rel. Dunlap v. Black,* 128 U.S. 40, 9 S. Ct. 12, 32 L. Ed. 354 (1888).

[52] *Wilbur v. United States,* 281 U.S. 206, 218, 50 S. Ct. 320, 324, 74 L. Ed. 809, 816 (1930). Also *People ex rel. Sheppard v. Illinois State Board of Dental Examiners,* 110 Ill. 180, 185 (1884) ; *United States ex rel. Louisville Cement Co. v. Interstate Commerce Commission,* 246 U.S. 638, 38 S. Ct. 408, 62 L. Ed. 914 (1918) ; *Interstate Commerce Commission v. Humboldt S. S. Co.,* 224 U.S. 474, 32 S. Ct. 556, 56 L. Ed. 849 (1912).

A subordinate body can be directed to act, but not how to act, in a matter as to which it has the right to exercise its judgment. The character of the duty, and not that of the body or officers, determines how far performance of the duty may be enforced by mandamus. Where a subordinate body is vested with power to determine a question of fact, the duty is judicial, and though it can be compelled by mandamus to determine the fact, it can not be directed to decide in a particular way, however clearly it be made to appear what the decision ought to be.[53]

Section 10(e) of the Administrative Procedure Act directs the reviewing court to "compel agency action unlawfully withheld or unreasonably delayed." This in terms would seem to apply to unreasonable delays in the exercise of discretionary as well as ministerial power.

Every officer exercises judgment and discretion in interpreting the statutes which it is his duty to enforce. But this is reviewable discretion, since statutory construction is a "question of law." If the administrative reading of the statute is erroneous, the officer may be restrained from acting under it; or he may be required, by writ of mandamus, to perform some act which he mistakenly believed to be discretionary, or outside his jurisdiction, but which, upon a correct interpretation of the law, is a ministerial duty.[54] Refusal to act from a misunderstanding of the law is not an exercise of discretion, said Mr. Justice McKenna, in a case in which the Interstate Commerce Commission *refused to take jurisdiction* of a complaint for what it believed to be a want of statutory power.[55] And when the Commission actually took jurisdiction, heard the case, and decided as a matter of law that it was without power or authority in the premises, the Supreme Court held:

If *beyond peradventure* the Act does not confer upon the Commission the power invoked by a complainant, the writ will not be granted. . . . If on the other hand power and authority are plainly found in the Act, and the commission erroneously refuses to exercise such power and authority, mandamus is the appropriate remedy to compel that body to

[53] *People v. Common Council of Troy,* 78 N.Y. 33, 39 (1879). To same effect see *Powers v. Bowles,* 144 F. (2d) 491 (E.C.A., 1944).

[54] *Roberts, Treasurer v. United States ex rel. Valentine,* 176 U.S. 211, 20 S. Ct. 376, 44 L. Ed. 443 (1900). *Cf. American Casualty Ins. Co. v. Tyler,* 60 Conn. 448, 462, 22 Atl. 494, 495 (1891): "The construction of a statute is not a ministerial act; it is the exercise of judgment."

[55] *Interstate Commerce Commission v. United States ex rel. Humboldt S. S. Co.,* 224 U.S. 474, 32 S. Ct. 556, 56 L. Ed. 849 (1912). The Motor Carrier Act of 1935, Sec. 205(h) specifically authorizes the District Courts of the United States to enforce by mandatory injunction the Commission's taking of jurisdiction if the Commission issues a negative order solely because of a supposed lack of power and the Court finds that the Commission has such power. 49 *Stat.* 550, 49 *U.S.C.A.* § 304(h).

proceed and to hear the case upon the merits. The fact that the complaint has been heard and, after hearing, the Commission has refused to enter an order because in its opinion no authority for such action is conferred by the statute, will not avail with the courts to prevent mandamus to correct a plain error of the Commission in renouncing jurisdiction.[56]

But,

> Where the matter *is not beyond peradventure clear* we have invariably refused the writ, even though the question was one of law as to the extent of the statutory power of an administrative officer or body.[57]

If the provisions of a statute are clear and precise, the language is controlling—no administrative construction thereof is required, and, therefore, no discretion in relation thereto is conferred. "There can be no construction where there is nothing to construe." [58]

The usual rule is that the use of "may" in a statute confers discretion, and "shall" prescribes a ministerial duty; but "may" is mandatory when the grant of power relates to something which the public interest requires should be done.[59] Negative language makes the statute mandatory.[60]

> The conclusion to be deduced from the authorities is, that where power is given to public officers, in the language of the act before us ["may, if deemed advisable"], or in equivalent language—whenever the public interest or individual rights call for its exercise—the language used, though permissive in form, is in fact peremptory. What they are empowered to do for a third person the law requires shall be done. The power is given not for their benefit, but for his. It is placed with the depository to meet the demands of right, and to prevent a failure of justice. It is given as a remedy to those entitled to invoke its aid, and who would otherwise be remediless.[61]

Where a statute gives an agency discretion as to means or methods of enforcement, the courts will not interfere with the exercise of a choice of remedies so long as the remedy selected is authorized by the

[56] *United States ex rel. Chicago Great Western Railroad v. Interstate Commerce Commission,* 294 U.S. 50, 61, 55 S. Ct. 326, 330, 79 L. Ed. 752, 759–60 (1935). Italics supplied.

[57] 294 U.S. at 63, 55 S. Ct. at 331, 79 L. Ed. at 761. Italics supplied.

[58] *United States v. Shreveport Grain Co.,* 287 U.S. 77, 83, 53 S. Ct. 42, 44, 77 L. Ed. 175, 179 (1932), quoting *United States v. Hartwell,* 6 Wall. 385, 396, 18 L. Ed. 830, 832 (1868).

[59] *People ex rel. Reynolds v. Buffalo,* 140 N.Y. 300, 35 N.E. 485 (1893) ; *Pierson v. People ex rel. Walter,* 204 Ill. 456, 68 N.E. 383 (1903).

[60] *Connecticut Mutual Life Insurance Co. v. Wood,* 115 Mich. 444, 74 N.W. 656 (Mich. 1897) ; *Hurford v. Omaha,* 4 Nebr. 336 (1876).

[61] *Supervisors v. United States,* 4 Wall. 435, 446–47, 18 L. Ed. 419, 423 (1866).

law. Our courts do not enforce the German rule of "the mildest means." In *American Power & Light Co. v. Securities and Exchange Commission,* the Supreme Court held:

> In view of the rational basis of the Commission's choice, the fact that other solutions might have been selected becomes immaterial. The Commission is the body which has the statutory duty of considering the possible solutions and choosing that which it considers most appropriate to the effectuation of the policies of the Act. Our review is limited solely to testing the propriety of the remedy from the standpoint of the Constitution and the statute. We would be impinging upon the Commission's rightful discretion were we to consider the various alternatives in the hope of finding one that we consider more appropriate.[62]

THE LICENSING POWER. The granting of licenses is commonly left to administrative discretion. It may be argued that an applicant who claims he is entitled to a license under a proper construction of the statute is entitled to a judicial determination of the issue and, in case of a favorable decision, to a court order directing the licensing authority to issue the license. Judicial opinion, however, is to the contrary.

> In many of these cases the language of the law or ordinance authorizing the granting of the license is that, upon the doing of certain things, the licensing officer or body shall grant the license; but the decisions are to the effect that, nevertheless, a discretion exists in such officer or body, and that they will not be compelled to issue a license when in their discretion, reasonably and fairly exercised, the license has been refused.[63]

The Supreme Court has said concerning the licensing power of the Federal Communications Commission:

> . . . it is the Commission, not the courts, which must be satisfied that the public interest will be served by renewing the license. And the fact that we might not have made the same determination on the same facts does not warrant a substitution of judicial for administrative discretion since Congress has confined that problem to the latter. We agree that this is a hard case, but we cannot agree that it should be allowed to make bad law.[64]

---

[62] 329 U.S. 90, 118, 67 S. Ct. 133, 148, 91 L. Ed. 103, 122 (1946).

[63] *Harrison, Mayor et al. v. People ex rel. Raben,* 222 Ill. 150, 153, 78 N.E. 52, 53 (1906), citing cases. Not infrequently statutes make the issuing of licenses a ministerial duty.

[64] *Federal Communications Commission v. WOKO, Inc.,* 329 U.S. 223, 229, 67 S. Ct. 213, 216, 91 L. Ed. 190, 208–9 (1946).

Thus it has been held that a State legislature may clothe the secretary of state with authority to "determine whether it is either 'against public policy' or 'otherwise objectionable' that the state should permit any certain corporation to be organized under the laws of the commonwealth, and receive sanction and permission of the sovereign powers to exist and to operate." [65] This authority is discretionary, not ministerial. The New York Supreme Court said in reference to the refusal of the Commissioner of Licenses of New York City to issue a license:

> Only if the action of the License Commissioner was arbitrary, capricious or unreasonable may this court interfere with his discretion in issuing licences. Whether the court agrees or disagrees with the ultimate result, or whether a different decision may have been reached, is of no consequence if the record permitted scope for the exercise of discretion.[66]

ABUSE OF DISCRETION. But does not the denial of judicial review in cases involving discretion leave the complaining party without remedy? Judge Cooley answered that question as follows:

> Practically, there are a great many such cases, but theoretically, there are none at all. All wrongs, certainly, are not redressed by the judicial department. A party may be deprived of a right by a wrong verdict, or an erroneous ruling by a judge, and, though the error may be manifest to all others than those who are to decide upon his rights, he will be without redress. A person lawfully chosen to the legislature may have his seat given by the House to another, and be thus wronged without remedy. A just claim against the state may be rejected by the board of auditors, and neither the Governor nor the Courts can give relief. A convicted person may conclusively demonstrate his innocence to the Governor, and still be denied a pardon. In which one of these cases could the denial of redress by the proper tribunal constitute any ground for interference by any other authority? The law must leave the final decision upon every claim and every controversy somewhere, and, when that decision has been made, it must be accepted as correct. The presumption is just as conclusive in favor of executive action as in favor of judicial. The party applying for action, which, under the Constitution and laws, depends on the executive discretion, or is to be determined by the executive judgment, if he fails to obtain it, has sought the proper remedy and must submit to the decision.[67]

[65] *Lloyd v. Ramsay,* 192 Iowa 103, 113, 183 N.W. 333, 337 (1921).
[66] *Erwich Bowling Center v. Canella,* 82 N.Y.S. (2d) 192, 193 (1948).
[67] *People ex rel. Sutherland v. Governor,* 29 Mich. 320, 330–31, 18 Am. Rep. 89 (1874).

Discretion is *informed discretion*. An officer must not act "corruptly or maliciously," [68] that is, discretionary power implies the exercise of a sound judgment, based upon substantial and relevant evidence.[69]

> . . . if a discretionary power is exercised with manifest *injustice,* the courts are not precluded from commanding its due exercise. They will interfere, where it is clearly shown that the discretion is *abused.* Such abuse of discretion will be controlled by *mandamus.* A public officer or inferior tribunal may be guilty of so gross an abuse of discretion, or such an evasion of positive duty as to amount to a virtual refusal to perform the duty enjoined, or to act at all in contemplation of law. In such a case *mandamus* will afford a remedy.[70]

Unless, however, the action taken is not obviously arbitrary, the courts will not interfere.[71] Arbitrary action is an abuse of discretion.

> It would be arbitrary, in the proper sense of the term, for an official to act in the teeth of a statute or stubbornly to refuse to act at all where a statute commands action, but where he essays to exercise the jurisdiction conferred upon him, though his errors may be subject to subsequent correction, they cannot be enjoined as an arbitrary exercise of authority. To hold otherwise would render orderly administrative procedure impossible.[72]

Section 10(e) of the Administrative Procedure Act subjects to judicial review all administrative conclusions found to be "arbitrary, capricious, an abuse of discretion, or otherwise not in accordance with law."

Constitutional and Statutory Limitations

Cases and Controversies.—To bring an administrative order before a constitutional court there must be a bona fide "case" or "controversy" within the meaning of Article III, Section 2, of the Consti-

[68] *Wilbrecht v. Babcock,* 179 Minn. 263, 264–65, 228 N.W. 916 (1930).

[69] *Vajtauer v. Commissioner of Immigration,* 273 U.S. 103, 47 S. Ct. 302, 71 L. Ed. 560 (1927) ; *Kwock Jan Fat v. White,* 253 U.S. 454, 40 S. Ct. 566, 64 L. Ed. 1010 (1920) ; *Tang Tun v. Edsell,* 223 U.S. 673, 32 S. Ct. 359, 56 L. Ed. 606 (1912).

[70] *Illinois State Board of Dental Examiners v. Cooper,* 123 Ill. 227, 241, 13 N.E. 201, 202 (1887). Italics supplied. See also *Harrison, Mayor v. Raben,* 222 Ill. 150, 78 N.E. 52 (1906) ; *In re Sparrow,* 138 Pa. St. 116, 20 Atl. 711 (1890). "The propriety of the remedy of *mandamus,* in the event that an abuse of discretion is proved, is clear. While *mandamus* will not lie to compel the exercise of discretion in a particular manner, it will lie to correct an abuse of discretion, ..." *Landsborough v. Kelly,* 1 Cal. (2d) 739, 744, 37 Pac. (2d) 93, 95 (1934).

[71] *Northwestern Electric Co. v. Federal Power Commission,* 321 U.S. 119, 64 S. Ct. 461, 88 L. Ed. 596 (1944).

[72] *Adams v. Nagle,* 303 U.S. 532, 543, 58 S. Ct. 687, 693, 82 L. Ed. 999, 1007 (1938).

tution. "A 'case' or 'controversy' within the meaning of Article III requires adverse parties with substantial interests at stake whose interests are threatened with imminent invasion of valuable rights in an actual controversy involving concrete issues whose solution will result in a determination of legal rights or a redress of wrongs before a court with power to determine finally the issues between the parties." [73] In *Liberty Warehouse Co. v. Grannis* [74] the Supreme Court summed up as follows:

> . . . it is not open to question that the judicial power vested by Article III of the Constitution in this Court and the inferior courts of United States established by Congress thereunder, extends only to "cases" and "controversies" in which the claims of litigants are brought before them for determination by such regular proceedings as are established for the protection and enforcement of rights, or the prevention, redress, or punishment of wrongs; and that their jurisdiction is limited to cases and controversies presented in such form, with adverse litigants, that the judicial power is capable of acting upon them, and pronouncing and carrying into effect a judgment between the parties, and does not extend to the determination of abstract questions or issues framed for the purpose of invoking the advice of the court without real parties or a real case. [75]

[73] Note, "The Reviewability of Negative Administrative Orders," 53 *Harvard Law Review* (November, 1939), 102, quoted by F. F. Blachly and Miriam Oatman, *Federal Regulatory Actions and Control* (The Brookings Institution, Washington, D.C., 1940), p. 118. See also Joseph Story, *Commentaries on the Constitution* (5th ed., Little, Brown and Co., Boston, 1891), §§ 1637–58; Reynolds Robertson and F. R. Kirkham, *Jurisdiction of the Supreme Court of the United States* (West Publishing Co., St. Paul, Minn., 1936), pp. 410, 413, 414. "By cases and controversies are intended the claims of litigants brought before the courts for determination by such regular proceedings as are established by law or custom for the protection or enforcement of rights, or the prevention, redress, or punishment of wrongs. Whenever the claim of a party under the Constitution, laws, or treaties of the United States takes such a form that the judicial power is capable of acting upon it, then it has become a case. The term implies the existence of present or possible adverse parties whose contentions are submitted to the court for adjudication." *In re Pacific Railway Commission,* 32 Fed. 241, 255 (1887), quoted with approval in *Muskrat v. United States,* 219 U.S. 346, 357, 31 S. Ct. 250, 254, 55 L. Ed. 246, 250 (1911). For the practice in the States see *Drake v. Regents of University of Michigan,* 4 Mich. 98 (1856). Also, *Ashwander v. Tennessee Valley Authority,* 297 U.S. 288, 56 S. Ct. 466, 80 L. Ed. 688 (1936); *United States v. West Virginia,* 295 U.S. 463, 55 S. Ct. 789, 79 L. Ed. 1546 (1935); *Osborn v. Bank of the United States,* 22 U.S. 738, 818, 6 L. Ed. 204, 223 (1824); *Prentis v. Atlantic Coast Line Co.,* 211 U.S. 210, 29 S. Ct. 67, 53 L. Ed. 150 (1908); *Aetna Life Insurance Co. v. Haworth,* 300 U.S. 227, 57 S. Ct. 461, 81 L. Ed. 617 (1937).

[74] 273 U.S. 70, 47 S. Ct. 282, 71 L. Ed. 541 (1927).

[75] 273 U.S. at 74, 47 S. Ct. at 283, 71 L. Ed. at 544. But *cf.* E. M. Borchard, "Declaratory Actions as 'Cases' or 'Controversies,'" 36 *Yale Law Journal* (1927), 845–53.

Section 10 of the Administrative Procedure Act [76] gives "any person suffering *legal wrong* because of any agency action, or *adversely affected or aggrieved* by such action within the meaning of any relevant statute," the right to judicial review by constitutional courts. "The phrase 'legal wrong' means such a wrong as is specified in subsection (e) of this section. It means that something more than mere adverse personal effect must be shown—that is, that the adverse effect must be an illegal effect. The law so made relevant is not just constitutional law but any and all applicable law." [77]

To have standing in court, a party must show an injury or threat to *a particular right of his own,* as distinguished from the public's interest in the administration of law. Thus, the legislature may prescribe the conditions for the letting of government contracts and may leave the administration thereof to the executive branch free from interference by the judiciary. Unless so provided by statute, a bidder does not have a standing in court, either for the purpose of questioning the conditions upon which an award is made [78] or for the purpose of challenging the manner in which administrative discretion is exercised in making the award. [79]

A State, as well as an individual, may be the party aggrieved and may maintain an action for judicial review. In a case involving an order of the United States Civil Service Commission which had the effect of withholding federal highway funds from the State of Oklahoma for alleged violation of the Hatch Act, the Supreme Court said:

> Congress has power to fix the conditions for review of administrative orders. By providing for judicial review of the orders of the Civil Service Commission, Congress made Oklahoma's right to receive funds a matter of judicial cognizance. Oklahoma's right became legally enforceable. Interference with the payment of the full allotment of federal highway funds to Oklahoma made the statutory proceeding to set aside the order a case or controversy between Oklahoma and the Commission whose order Oklahoma was authorized to challenge. . . . A reading of § 12 [Hatch Act] will show the special interest Oklahoma had in preventing the exercise of the Civil Service Commission's power to direct that Oklahoma's fund be withheld. . . . It was named as the employer affected by § 12(a). Notices were sent to it. Funds allotted to Oklahoma were to be withheld under certain conditions. It was a "party aggrieved." [80]

[76] Act of June 1, 1946, 60 *Stat.* 237, 5 *U.S.C.A.* §§ 1001–11.
[77] United States Senate, *Report of the Committee on the Judiciary, on S. 7,* 79th Cong., 1st Sess., *S. Rep. No. 752,* p. 261.
[78] *Perkins v. Lukens Steel Co.,* 310 U.S. 113, 60 S. Ct. 869, 84 L. Ed. 1108 (1940).
[79] *O'Brien v. Carney,* 6 F. Supp. 761 (D.C., Mass., 1934); *Champion Coated Paper Co. v. Joint Committee on Printing,* 47 App. D.C. 141 (1917).
[80] *Oklahoma v. United States Civil Service Commission,* 330 U.S. 127, 137, 67 S. Ct. 544, 550–51, 91 L. Ed. 794, 803 (1947).

But when the State of Massachusetts sought to enjoin enforcement of the Federal Maternity Act, the Court denied federal jurisdiction because the Act did not impose any burden on or infringe any right of the State. To invoke the power of the Court to declare a statute unconstitutional, the party "must be able to show, not only that the statute is invalid, but that he has sustained or is immediately in danger of sustaining some direct injury as the result of its enforcement, and not merely that he suffers in some indefinite way in common with people generally." [81]

In re Summers [82] was a case where relief was sought in a State court against the action of a Committee on Character and Fitness in rejecting an application for admission to the practice of law. The Court held as follows: "we think the consideration of the petition by the Supreme Court, the body which has authority itself by its own act to give the relief sought, makes the proceeding adversary in the sense of a true case or controversy." [83] And a denial of relief by the State court is reviewable under Article III, Section 2, of the Constitution if a federal question is raised. The petitioner claimed that in being excluded from the practice of law on the ground that he was a conscientious objector, the State committee and court had violated the due process clause of the Fourteenth Amendment which secured to him the protection of the First Amendment.

Accordingly, the licensing power of the States may be subjected to judicial supervision under "the vast, undisclosed range" of the due process clause of the Fourteenth Amendment.

The Federal Declaratory Judgment Act of 1934 [84] empowered the federal courts to grant declaratory judgments in "cases of actual controversy," a proceeding that has not been used extensively for the review of administrative action.[85] The act is not applicable unless the court otherwise has jurisdiction of the subject matter and the parties.[86] The power "to make a declaratory decree does not authorize a court of equity by declaration to stop, or interfere with administrative pro-

---

[81] *Massachusetts v. Mellon,* 262 U.S. 477, 488, 43 S. Ct. 597, 601, 67 L. Ed. 1078, 1085 (1923).

[82] 325 U.S. 561, 65 S. Ct. 1307, 89 L. Ed. 1795 (1945).

[83] 325 at 568, 65 S. Ct. at 1312, 89 L. Ed. at 1801.

[84] Act of June 14, 1934, 48 *Stat.* 955, c. 512, 28 *U.S.C.A.* § 400.

[85] *Cf.* E. M. Borchard, *Declaratory Judgments* (Banks Baldwin Law Publishing Co., Cleveland, Ohio, 1934); E. M. Borchard, "Declaratory Judgments in Administrative Law," 11 *New York University Law Quarterly Review* (1933), 139–82; H. Oliphant, "Declaratory Rulings," 24 *American Bar Association Journal* (1938), 7–9; *Aetna Life Insurance Co. v. Haworth,* 300 U.S. 227, 57 S. Ct. 461, 81 L. Ed. 617 (1937); *United States v. West Virginia,* 295 U.S. 463, 55 S. Ct. 789, 79 L. Ed. 1546 (1935); *Myers v. Bethlehem Shipbuilding Corp.,* 303 U.S. 41, 58, S. Ct. 459 82 L. Ed. 638 (1938).

[86] *Putnan et al. v. Ickes et al.,* 78 F. (2d) 223 (App. D.C., 1935).

ceedings at a point where it would not, under settled principles, have interfered with or stopped them under its power to enjoin." [87] And, "the test for determining whether a federal court has authority to make a declaration such as is here asked, is whether the controversy 'would be justiciable in this Court if presented in a suit for injunction.' " [88] A declaratory judgment will be denied where a special statutory procedure for determining the issue has been provided.

In *Perkins v. Elg* [89] the Court of Appeals of the District of Columbia held that a person threatened with deportation as an alleged alien ". . . is entitled to a declaration of her political status, for her rights as a citizen are valuable rights,—certainly no less valuable than property rights,—and an actual and vital controversy exists between her and the government in relation to them. The right to be immune from threats of deportation and from the declarations of public officials that she is an alien and subject to arrest is, we think, a right within the declaratory judgment act entitling Miss Elg to prosecute this suit." [90] Accordingly, the Secretary of Labor and the Commissioner of Immigration were enjoined from carrying out a *threat to deport her.* This court declined, however, to enjoin the Secretary of State from refusing to issue her a passport for the reason that she was an alien, since the issuance of passports is a discretionary act. The Supreme Court affirmed the decree of the district court, but modified the decree to include the Secretary of State, not so as to interfere with the exercise of the Secretary's discretion with respect to the issue of a passport, but simply to preclude the denial of a passport on the sole ground that Miss Elg was not an American citizen.[91]

The declaratory judgment device is, perhaps, most effective when used by an officer to secure judicial determination of his powers, when he does not wish to risk liability under an ambiguous statute or one of questionable constitutionality. In short, the declaratory judgment is not effective for testing or reviewing administrative action after it has been taken. But, "Public officers should have the right to have their legal duties judicially determined. In this way only can the dis-

[87] *Bradley Lumber Co. v. National Labor Relations Board,* 84 F. (2d) 97, 100 (C.C.A. 5th, 1936).

[88] *Colegrove v. Green,* 328 U.S. 549, 552, 66 S. Ct. 1198, 1199, 90 L. Ed. 1432, 1433 (1946).

[89] 99 F. (2d) 408, 169 App. D.C. 175 (1938). The petitioner, Mary Elizabeth Elg, was held to be an American citizen.

[90] *Ibid.,* at 414.

[91] *Perkins v. Elg,* 307 U.S. 325, 349–50, 59 S. Ct. 884, 896, 83 L. Ed. 1320, 1334 (1939). In *McGrath v. Kristensen,* 340 U.S. 162, 71 S. Ct. 224, 95 L. Ed. 165 (1950), the Court held that an alien is not required to await the traditional remedy of habeas corpus after his arrest for deportation because of ineligibility for citizenship but may seek a declaratory judgment to determine his eligibility.

astrous results of well intentioned but illegal acts be avoided with certainty." [92]

Statutory Limitations.—The Supreme Court has conceded that "except when the Constitution requires it, judicial review of administrative action may be granted or withheld as Congress chooses." [93] But,

> *In the absence of statutory prescription to the contrary,* review of administrative adjudications begins in the courts of original jurisdiction with opportunities for appellate review in the appellate courts. This is true whether the review is sought by a bill to enjoin enforcement of the administrative order or by an action for damages against the officer involved, or by a suit for declaratory judgment, or in a case between parties in which the order is relied upon, or by any other of the common law remedies.[94]

Section 10 of the Administrative Procedure Act provides for judicial review of "agency action" unless "the statute reflects an intent that they are not reviewable." [95] It appears that the Congressional "intent" to preclude review may be implied as well as expressly stated.[96]

The World War Veterans Act of 1933 provided that "All decisions rendered by the Administrator of Veterans' Affairs under

---

[92] *Wingate, Surrogate, v. Flynn, Secretary of State,* 249 N.Y.S. 351, 354, 139 Misc. 779, 781 (1931).

[93] *Estep v. United States,* 327 U.S. 114, 120, 66 S. Ct. 423, 426, 90 L. Ed. 567, 572 (1946). "I have no doubt," said Mr. Justice Frankfurter in *Radio Corp. of America v. United States,* 312 U.S. 412, 423, 71 S. Ct. 806, 811 (1951), "that if Congress chose to withdraw all court review from the Commission's orders it would be constitutionally free to do so."

"When judicial review is available and under what circumstances, are questions (apart from whatever requirements the Constitution may make in certain situations) that depend on the particular Congressional enactment under which judicial review is authorized." *National Labor Relations Board v. Cheney California Lumber Co.,* 327 U.S. 385, 388, 66 S. Ct. 553, 554, 90 L. Ed. 739, 741 (1946).

"It will hardly be suggested that the Constitution requires judicial review of a reparation order by the Commission. Such a notion is precluded by *Cary v. Curtis,* 3 How. 236, 11 L. Ed. 576, and the whole unfolding of administrative law during the hundred years since that decision." *Ibid.,* 337 U.S. at 446, 69 S. Ct. at 1421.

[94] *Administrative Procedure in Government Agencies, Report of the Committee on Administrative Procedure* (Government Printing Office, Washington, D.C., 1941), *S. Doc. No. 8,* 77th Cong., 1st Sess., pp. 92–93. Italics supplied. *Scripps-Howard Radio v. Federal Communications Commission,* 316 U.S. 4, 11, 15, 62 S. Ct. 875, 880, 882, 86 L. Ed. 1229, 1235, 1237 (1942); *Stark v. Wickard,* 321 U.S. 288, 310, 64 S. Ct. 559, 571, 88 L. Ed. 733, 748 (1944).

[95] *Unger v. United States,* 79 F. Supp. 281, 286 (E.D. Ill., 1948). Also *Ludecke v. Watkins,* 335 U.S. 160, 68 S. Ct. 1429, 92 L. Ed. 1881 (1948).

[96] *Attorney General's Manual on the Administrative Procedure Act,* p. 136.

the provisions . . . of this title . . . shall be final and conclusive on all questions of law and fact, and no other official or court of the United States shall have jurisdiction to review by mandamus or otherwise any such decision." [97]

The Selective Training and Service Act of 1940 [98] entrusted the administration of the Selective Service System to civilian local boards. The Act made no provision in terms for judicial review of the actions of the local or appeal boards but provided that "decisions of such local boards shall be final except where an appeal is authorized and is taken in accordance with such rules and regulations as the President may prescribe." [99]

> Thus we start with a statute which makes no provision for judicial review of the actions of the local boards or the appeal agencies. That alone, of course, is not decisive. For the silence of Congress as to judicial review is not necessarily to be construed as a denial of the power of the federal courts to grant relief in the exercise of the general jurisdiction which Congress has conferred upon them. . . . Apart from constitutional requirements, the question whether judicial review will be provided where Congress is silent depends on the whole setting of the particular statute and the scheme of regulation which is adopted.[100]

If the local boards act outside their jurisdiction, the courts can grant relief.

> The provision making the decisions of the local boards "final" means to us that Congress chose not to give administrative action under this Act the customary scope of judicial review which obtains under other statutes. *It means that the courts are not to weigh the evidence to determine whether the classification made by the local boards was justified.* The decisions of the local boards made in conformity with the regulations are final even though they may be erroneous. The question of jurisdiction of the local board is reached *only if there is no basis in fact* for the classification which it gave to the registrant.[101]

Again in another case, it was held that

> Whether there was "no basis in fact" for the classification is not a question to be determined by the jury on an independent consideration of the evidence. The concept of a jury passing independently on an

[97] Act of March 20, 1933, 48 *Stat.* 9, § 5, 38 *U.S.C.A.* § 705. See also Federal Power Commission Regulation No. 15, 16 *U.S.C.A.* § 803. Sustained in *Barnett v. Hines,* 105 F. (2d), 96 (App. D.C., 1939), certiorari denied 308 U.S. 573 (1939), on the ground that a gratuity was involved.

[98] Act of September 6, 1940, 54 *Stat.* 885, 50 *U.S.C.A.* (App.) §§ 301 *et sqq.*

[99] Sec. 10(a) ; 50 *U.S.C.A.* (App.) § 310(a)(1).

[100] *Estep v. United States,* 327 U.S. 114, 119–20, 66 S. Ct. 423, 426, 90 L. Ed. 567, 571–72 (1946).

[101] 327 U.S. at 122–23, 66 S. Ct. at 427, 90 L. Ed. at 573. Italics supplied.

issue previously determined by an administrative body or reviewing the action of an administrative body is contrary to settled federal administrative practice; the constitutional right to jury trial does not include the right to have a jury pass on the validity of an administrative order.[102]

But Mr. Justice Frankfurter, although concurring in the decision, held in the Estep case that

> . . . Congress did not say that "the decision of such local boards *when properly acting under their authority* shall be final." It said simply and unqualifiedly "the decisions of such local boards shall be final."[103]

And, "One need not italicize 'final' to make final mean final."[104]   To interpolate judicial review is "to disrupt a whole scheme of legislation under which millions of orders need promptly to be made and promptly to be respected."[105]

The Emergency Price Control Act of 1942[106] limited judicial review to a special Emergency Court of Appeals, with a right of appeal from this court to the Supreme Court.[107]   Every other court, federal or State, was prohibited from passing upon the validity of any price or rent regulation.   On these and other procedural provisions of the Act, Arthur T. Vanderbilt comments: "In all of these procedural devices, the Act is quite without precedent.   Not only does it provide strange methods, but it uses terms unfamiliar to American jurisprudence.   Throughout the procedural aspects of the Act runs a studied effort to comply with the form of constitutional requirements while withholding the substance."[108]

But the power of Congress thus to define and limit the jurisdiction of inferior federal courts was sustained by the Supreme Court.

> The Congressional power to ordain and establish inferior courts includes the power "of investing them with jurisdiction either limited, concurrent, or exclusive, and of withholding jurisdiction from them in the exact degrees and character which to Congress may seem proper for the public good.". . . In the light of the explicit language of the Constitution and our decisions, it is plain that Congress has power to

[102] *Cox v. United States,* 332 U.S. 442, 452–53, 68 S. Ct. 115, 120, 92 L. Ed. 59, 69 (1947).

[103] 327 U.S. at 142, 66 S. Ct. at 436, 90 L. Ed. at 584.

[104] 327 U.S. at 136, 66 S. Ct. at 434, 90 L. Ed. at 580.

[105] 327 U.S. at 142, 66 S. Ct. at 436, 90 L. Ed. at 583.

[106] Act of June 30, 1942, 56 *Stat.* 23, 50 *U.S.C.A.* (App.) §§ 901 *et sqq.*

[107] *Ibid.,* 56 *Stat.* 31, 204, 50 *U.S.C.A.* (App.) § 924.

[108] "War Powers and Their Administration," *1942 Annual Survey of American Law* (New York University School of Law, New York, 1943), p. 151.

provide that the equity jurisdiction to restrain enforcement of the Act, or of regulations promulgated under it, be restricted to the Emergency Court, and, upon review of its decisions, to this court.[109]

Since only the Emergency Court (and the Supreme Court on appeal) had jurisdiction to consider the validity of a price regulation, the unconstitutionality of such a regulation could not be set up as a defense in a criminal prosecution under the Act.[110] But in such a proceeding the constitutionality of the Act could be challenged, provided the attack upon the validity of the Act was not for the purpose of making an indirect attack upon some regulation made thereunder.[111]

The court review thus afforded under the Emergency Price Control Act was characterized by Mr. Justice Roberts in a dissenting opinion in the Yakus case as

> . . . a solemn farce in which the Emergency Court of Appeals, and this court, on certiorari, must go through a series of motions which look like judicial review but in fact are nothing but a catalogue of reasons why, under the scheme of the Act, the courts are unable to say that the Administrator has exceeded the discretion vested in him.[112]

Certification of a bargaining representative by the National Mediation Board,[113] or by the National Labor Relations Board,[114] has been held not subject to judicial review except in the limited case of enforcing the certification and, presumably, on a showing that the Board has acted unlawfully.[115] The Labor Board has two principal functions under the Labor Act:[116] the certification of an appropriate unit of employees for collective bargaining, and the issuing of orders

---

[109] *Lockerty v. Phillips*, 319 U.S. 182, 187–88, 63 S. Ct. 1019, 1022–23, 87 L. Ed. 1339, 1343 (1943). Also *Taylor v. Bowles*, 147 F. (2d) 824 (C.C.A. 9th, 1945); *Bowles v. Meyers*, 149 F. (2d) 440 (C.C.A. 4th, 1945); *United States v. George F. Fish, Inc.*, 154 F. (2d) 798 (C.C.A. 2d, 1946); *Crary v. Porter*, 157 F. (2d) 410 (C.C.A. 8th, 1946); *Martini v. Porter*, 157 F. (2d) 35 (C.C.A. 9th, 1946); *United States v. Tantleff*, 155 F. (2d) 27 (C.C.A. 2d, 1946); *Cooper v. Anderson*, 156 F. (2d) 564 (App. D.C., 1946).

[110] *Yakus v. United States*, 321 U.S. 414, 64 S. Ct. 660, 88 L. Ed. 834 (1944).

[111] *Case v. Bowles*, 327 U.S. 92, 98, 66 S. Ct. 438, 441, 90 L. Ed. 552, 558 (1946).

[112] 321 U.S. at 458, 64 S. Ct. at 683, 88 L. Ed. at 866.

[113] *Switchmen's Union of N. A. v. National Mediation Board*, 320 U.S. 297, 64 S. Ct. 95, 88 L. Ed. 61 (1943); *Order of Railway Conductors v. National Mediation Board*, 141 F. (2d) 366 (App. D.C., 1944).

[114] *American Federation of Labor v. National Labor Relations Board*, 308 U.S. 401, 60 S. Ct. 300, 84 L. Ed. 347 (1940); *Millis v. Inland Empire District Council*, 144 F. (2d) 539 (App. D.C., 1944).

[115] *Inland Empire District Council v. Millis*, 325 U.S. 697, 65 S. Ct. 1316, 89 L. Ed. 1887 (1945).

[116] 49 *Stat.* 449, §§ 9, 10, 29 *U.S.C.A.* §§ 151–66.

to prevent unfair labor practices. Only the latter are reviewable.[117] A jurisdictional or interunion dispute is not reviewable under the Railway Labor Act [118] and the Declaratory Judgment Act.[119]

Section 19 of the Immigration Act of 1917 [120] provides that decisions of the Attorney General in deportation proceedings "shall be final." It has been held, however, that this does not preclude review under Section 10 of the Administrative Procedure Act.[121]

A railway mail service pay order of the Interstate Commerce Commission is not reviewable under the Railway Mail Service Pay Act of 1916 [122] or the Urgent Deficiencies Act of 1913.[123] A suit under the latter Act to set aside such an order is not primarily one against the Commission, but against the United States, and authority to sue the United States has not been specifically conferred by the Railway Mail Service Pay Act.[124]

Legislative authority to determine the conditions under which resort may be had to the courts includes the power to specify the persons entitled to court review.

> In awarding a review of an administrative proceeding Congress has power to formulate the conditions under which resort to the courts may be had. The persons accorded a right to obtain review are, therefore, to be ascertained from the terms of the statute. Congress might here have provided that only parties to the administrative proceeding should have standing to obtain court review.[125]

[117] *American Federation of Labor v. National Labor Relations Board,* 308 U.S. 401, 60 S. Ct. 300, 84 L. Ed. 347 (1940). Courts differ as to whether the Labor Management Relations Act of 1947 [61 *Stat.* 136 (1947), 29 *U.S.C.A.* (App.) § 141] broadened the scope of judicial review of the orders of the National Labor Relations Board. *Cf. National Labor Relations Board v. Caroline Mills,* 167 F. (2d) 212, 213 (5th Cir., 1948) with *National Labor Relations Board v. Austin Co.,* 165 F. (2d) 592, 595 (7th Cir., 1947).

[118] 44 *Stat.* 577, 48 *Stat.* 1185, 45 *U.S.C.A.* §§ 151 *et sqq. General Committee, etc., of Brotherhood of Locomotive Engineers v. Missouri-Kansas Railroad,* 320 U.S. 323, 64 S. Ct. 146, 88 L. Ed. 76 (1943).

[119] 48 *Stat.* 955, 28 *U.S.C.A.* § 400.

[120] 39 *Stat.* 889 (1917), 8 *U.S.C.A.* § 155.

[121] *United States ex rel. Trinler v. Carusi,* 166 F. (2d) 457, 461 (3d Cir., 1948); *United States v. Miller,* 79 F. Supp. 643 (S.D.N.Y., 1948); *Scholnick v. Clark,* 81 F. Supp. 298, 300 (D.C.D.C., 1948).

[122] Act of July 28, 1916, 59 *Stat.* 412, 425–30, c. 216, § 5, 39 *U.S.C.A.* § 551.

[123] Act of October 22, 1913, 38 *Stat.* 208, 219, 220, c. 32, 28 *U.S.C.A.* § 41 (28).

[124] *United States v. Griffin,* 303 U.S. 226, 58 S. Ct. 601, 82 L. Ed. 764 (1938). The order may be triable in the Court of Claims if confiscation or error of law is alleged.

[125] *American Power & Light Co. v. Securities and Exchange Commission,* 325 U.S. 385, 389, 90, 65 S. Ct. 1254, 1257, 89 L. Ed. 1683, 1687 (1945). Also *Schenley Distillers Corp. v. United States,* 326 U.S. 432, 435, 66 S. Ct. 247, 248, 90 L. Ed. 181, 183 (1946).

The authority of civil courts to review decisions of military tribunals under the Articles of War is limited to the question of jurisdiction.

> If the military tribunals have lawful authority to hear, decide and condemn, their action is not subject to judicial review merely because they have made a wrong decision on disputed facts. Correction of their errors of decision is not for the courts but for the military authorities which are alone authorized to review their decisions.[126]

Mr. Justice Murphy, dissenting, summed up his view of judicial authority over military commissions or tribunals as follows:

> As I understand it, the following issues in connection with war criminal trials are reviewable through the use of the writ of habeas corpus: (1) whether the military commission was lawfully created and had authority to try and to convict the accused of a war crime; (2) whether the charge against the accused stated a violation of the laws of war; (3) whether the commission, in admitting certain evidence, violated any law or military command defining the commission's authority in that respect; and (4) whether the commission lacked jurisdiction because of a failure to give advance notice to the protecting power as required by treaty or convention.[127]

The jurisdiction of a military tribunal is limited by the "open court" doctrine of the Milligan case,[128] which is that military courts cannot supplant the civil courts where the latter are open and able to function, since the Constitution embraces the principle of the supremacy of the civil law.[129]   In the Duncan case Mr. Justice Murphy observed:

> The so-called "open court" rule of the Milligan case, to be sure, has been the subject of severe criticism, especially by military commentators. That criticism is repeated by the Government in these cases. It is said that the fact that courts are open is but one of many factors relevant to determining the necessity and hence the constitutionality of military trials of civilians. The argument is made that however adequate the "open court" rule may have been in 1628 [Petition of Right] or 1864 [Milligan case] it is distinctly unsuited to modern warfare conditions where all the territories of a warring nation may be in combat zones or imminently threatened with long-range attack even while civil courts are operating. Hence if a military commander, on the basis of his conception of military necessity, requires all civilians accused of crime

---

[126] *In re Yamashita,* 327 U.S. 1, 8, 23, 66 S. Ct. 340, 344–45, 351, 90 L. Ed. 499, 505–6, 513 (1946).

[127] 327 U.S. at 31, 66 S. Ct. at 355, 90 L. Ed. at 518.

[128] *Ex parte Milligan,* 71 U.S. 2, 18 L. Ed. 281 (1886).

[129] *Duncan v. Kahanamoku,* 327 U.S. 304, 66 S. Ct. 606, 90 L. Ed. 688 (1946).

to be tried summarily before martial law tribunals, the Bill of Rights must bow humbly to his judgment despite the unquestioned ability of the civil courts to exercise their criminal jurisdiction.

The argument thus advanced is as untenable today as it was when cast in the language of the Plantagenets, the Tudors and the Stuarts. It is a rank appeal to abandon the fate of all our liberties to the reasonableness of the judgment of those who are trained primarily for war. It seeks to justify military usurpation of civilian authority to punish crime without regard to the potency of the Bill of Rights. It deserves repudiation.[130]

But Mr. Justice Burton, dissenting, said:

. . . I am obliged to dissent from the majority of this Court and to sound a note of warning against the dangers of over-expansion of judicial control into the fields allotted by the Constitution to agencies of legislative and executive action. . . .

For a court to recreate a complete picture of the emergency is impossible. That impossibility demonstrates the need for a zone of executive discretion within which courts must guard themselves with special care against judging past military action too closely by the inapplicable standards of judicial, or even military, hindsight. The nature of judicial authority is largely negative as contrasted with the generally positive nature of the executive authority, and it is essential that the opportunity for well directed positive action be preserved and vigorously used if the Government is to serve the best interests of the people.[131]

The jurisdiction of military tribunals extends to members of the armed forces, those directly connected with such forces, enemy belligerents, prisoners of war, other persons charged with violating the laws of war, civilians in occupied enemy territory or territory regained from an enemy where civil government cannot and does not function, and civilians interfering with a necessary military function at a time when there is danger from insurrection or war.[132]

Judicial review of decisions of the Tax Court is more limited than is review of district court decisions. Judge Learned Hand has made the following observation on the scope of the court's jurisdiction:

. . . if the case were an appeal from a district court, we should have no alternative but to reverse. But the Supreme Court has repeatedly admonished us (in so many decisions that it would be idle to repeat them), that our power to review a ruling of the Tax Court is very much

[130] 327 U.S. at 328–29, 66 S. Ct. at 617–18, 90 L. Ed. at 702–3.
[131] 327 U.S. at 338, 343, 66 S. Ct. at 622, 624, 90 L. Ed. at 708, 710. Mr. Justice Frankfurter concurred.
[132] 327 U.S. at 313–14, 66 S. Ct. at 610–11, 90 L. Ed. at 694, citing cases.

more limited than in the case of a district court. As we understand it, before we may substitute our own interpretation of a provision of the Revenue Act, not only must a naked question of law detach itself from the nexus of law and fact in the record as a whole; but we must conclude that the Tax Court has been indubitably wrong in its decision of the question which emerges: reasonable differences in legal opinion we are to resolve in its favor. . . . That finality [of the orders of the Tax Court] depends, as we understand, upon the added competency which inevitably follows from concentration in a special field. Why, if that be so, we—or indeed even the Supreme Court itself—should be competent to fix the measure of the Tax Court's competence, and why we should ever declare that it is wrong, is indeed an interesting inquiry, which happily it is not necessary for us to pursue.[133]

The Second Renegotiation Act [134] gave the Tax Court "exclusive jurisdiction" to review and redetermine, upon appeal by any aggrieved contractor, any order of the War Contracts Price Adjustment Board,[135] and "such determination shall not be reviewed or redetermined by any court or agency." In *Macauley v. Waterman S. S. Corp.,*[136] the Supreme Court upheld the exclusive jurisdiction of the Tax Court to determine whether a given contract was subject to the Act. The Court said:

> The legislative history of the Renegotiation Act . . . shows that Congress intended the Tax Court to have *exclusive jurisdiction to decide questions of fact and law,* which latter include the issue raised here of whether the contracts in question are subject to the Act.[137]

Also, the Tax Court has been held to have exclusive jurisdiction to determine the amount of excessive profits.

> We think, therefore, that the statute places exclusive and unreviewable jurisdiction in the Tax Court to determine the amount of excessive profits, including both questions of law and fact in such determination, ...[138]

Even inconsistent conclusions by the Tax Court upon similar states of fact are not reviewable.[139]

---

[133] *Brooklyn Nat. Corp. v. Commissioner of Internal Revenue,* 157 F. (2d) 450, 452 (C.C.A. 2d, 1946).

[134] In 1943 Revenue Act, 58 *Stat.* 78 (1944), as amended 59 *Stat.* 294 § 403(e)(1) (1945), 50 *U.S.C.A.* (App.) § 1191(e)(1).

[135] *Ibid.,* § 403(d)(1), 50 *U.S.C.A.* (App.) § 1191(d)(1).

[136] 327 U.S. 540, 66 S. Ct. 712, 90 L. Ed. 839 (1946).

[137] 327 U.S. at 544, 66 S. Ct. at 714, 90 L. Ed. at 842. Italics supplied.

[138] *United States Electrical Motors, Inc. v. Jones,* 153 F. (2d) 134, 136 (App. D.C., 1946). Italics supplied.

[139] *John Kelley Co. v. Commissioner of Internal Revenue,* 326 U.S. 521, 66 S. Ct. 299, 90 L. Ed. 278 (1946).

Section 9 of the Interstate Commerce Act [140] provides that any person who claims to be damaged by any common carrier may either make complaint to the Commission or bring suit for damages in any district court of the United States with competent jurisdiction; however, such person may not pursue both remedies but must elect which one he will adopt. The Supreme Court has held that if a shipper elects to make complaint to the Commission, a reparation order by the Commission is not final but is subject to judicial review. Section 9 of the Act merely bars *initiation* of action by both Commission and court.[141] This ruling, said Mr. Justice Frankfurter in dissent, overrules four uniform decisions of the Court [142] and ". . . is to mutilate the whole scheme of the Interstate Commerce Act by disregarding the distribution of authority Congress saw fit to make between the Commission and the courts for the enforcement of the Act." [143]

[140] 49 *U.S.C.A.* § 9.

[141] *United States v. Interstate Commerce Commission,* 337 U.S. 426, 69 S. Ct. 1410, 93 L. Ed. 1451 (1949).

[142] *Standard Oil Co. v. United States,* 283 U.S. 235, 51 S. Ct. 429, 75 L. Ed. 999 (1931); *Brady v. United States,* 283 U.S. 804, 51 S. Ct. 559, 75 L. Ed. 1424 (1931); *Allison & Co. v. United States,* 296 U.S. 546, 57 S. Ct. 175, 80, L. Ed. 387 (1935); *Ashland Coal & Ice Co. v. United States,* 325 U.S. 840, 65 S. Ct. 1573, 89 L. Ed. 1966 (1945).

[143] 337 U.S. at 445–46, 69 S. Ct. at 1421. Mr. Justice Jackson and Mr. Justice Burton concurring.

Chapter 9

GOVERNMENT BY AGENCY OR GOVERNMENT BY LAWSUIT

Government by Agency

The concern expressed by Charles E. Hughes in 1931, over the opportunities for oppression inherent in the prevailing tendency to extend administrative power, is still shared by many of his fellow citizens. Mr. Hughes then pointed out that

> A host of controversies as to provisional rights are no longer decided by courts. Administrative authority, within a constantly widening sphere of action, and subject only to the limitations of certain broad principles, establishes particular rules, finds the facts, and decides as to particular rights. The power of administrative bodies to make findings of fact which may be treated as conclusive, if there is evidence both ways, is a power of enormous consequence. An unscrupulous administrator might be tempted to say, "Let me find the facts for the people of my country, and I care little who lays down the general principles." We all recognize that the development has been to a great extent a necessary one. . . . Experience, expertness, and continuity of supervision, which could only be had by administrative agencies in a particular field, have come to be imperatively needed. But these new methods put us to new tests, and the serious question of the future is whether we have enough of the old spirit which gave us our institutions to save them from being overwhelmed.[1]

In other words, legislative declaration of "general principles," the provision in a statute for an "adequate standard," is not a sufficient check on administrative discretion if administrative bodies have the power to "find the facts." On the other hand, Elihu Root, while admitting that "the powers that are committed to these regulatory agencies . . . carry with them great and dangerous opportunities of oppression and wrong," observed that "such agencies furnish protection to rights and obstacles to wrongdoing which under our social

[1] *New York Times,* February 13, 1931, p. 18. For statistics on the volume of business in administrative agencies, see *Administrative Procedure in Government Agencies, S. Doc. No. 8,* 77th Cong., 1st Sess. (1941), pp. 314–26.

and industrial conditions cannot be practically accomplished by the old and simple procedure of legislatures and courts." [2]

Since the introduction of the constitutional doctrine of dual federalism during the Chief Justiceship of Roger Taney,[3] the prevailing judicial philosophy has been one of constitutional limitations, reflecting the traditional American distrust of government—a distrust that has yielded only to economic and military necessity. American individualism, nurtured on unlimited natural resources, went into reverse in the depression period of the 1930's, and the period during and after World War II may well make the conversion permanent. A new order of life is in the making. We have discarded laissez faire and we are building a service state, with its potentialities for both good and evil.

In building our defenses against absolutism in government, it is in the best American tradition to depend upon legal rather than political safeguards, to use the "rule of law" rather than the ballot as the principal weapon, to curtail administration by the use of constitutional and statutory "don'ts" to be enforced by the judiciary. Accordingly, almost any serious discussion of administrative reform is weighted with suggestions for bringing the administrative process under closer judicial supervision.

This is not to say that the defects of bureaucracy can be corrected by increasing the legal control over administration but rather to call attention to the emphasis currently placed upon this aspect of the problem, an emphasis which is diverting public attention from seeking structural and personnel antidotes. Furthermore, this preoccupation with the legality of administrative action is often at the expense of efficiency. On the one hand, strict adherence to rules gives rigidity to administration by introducing legal formalism and red tape. On the other hand, the "rule of law" not only restrains improper administrative action but often excuses laxity in law enforcement, since official zeal for the public welfare pales before the fear of legal responsibility for *ultra vires* acts, a responsibility that is at once personal and political.

Criticism of the administrative process is centered upon the consolidation of governmental functions, particularly the commingling of the judicial with the other governmental powers. Montesquieu voiced the common fear of tyranny by the concentration of powers

---

[2] Speaking before the American Bar Association. See American Bar Association, *Report*, Vol. LXI (1916), p. 368.

[3] See E. S. Corwin, *The Twilight of the Supreme Court* (Yale University Press, New Haven, 1934), chap. i.

when he said, "It is the highest masterpiece of legislation to know how to place properly the judicial power. But it could not be in worse hands than in those of the person to whom the executive power had been already committed." [4]

The irrational extreme to which critics of the administrative process will go is illustrated by the following example of constitutional Toryism:

> An amendment should be passed forbidding Congress to delegate to any person, board, commission, or department any authority of a legislative or judicial nature, and, particularly any power to make rules and regulations with the force of law, and any power to sit in judgment in the execution of its own rules. The curse of commerce and industry in the United States today is this *alien institution* of an administrative agency which is both law-maker and judge, summoning whom it pleases, when it pleases, to Washington with his private books and papers for a hearing and, by the findings on the facts, concluding such person before the courts. It is wholly arbitrary and despotic.[5]

For a number of years prominent lawyers and a Committee on Administrative Law of the American Bar Association have been warning the American people against the growth of "administrative absolutism," pointing out that administration violates the time-honored separation of governmental powers by commingling in single agencies the essentially different legislative, executive, and judicial powers. A single agency may make legislative rules and regulations and then investigate, prosecute, and judge violations thereof, a procedure which is said to be unwise, unworkable, and contrary to sound principles of justice.[6] "The blending of these functions," said the New York Bar Association, "is the very definition of totalitarianism—the consolidation of power in him who governs." [7] A bill,

---

[4] Charles de Secondat, *The Spirit of the Laws,* Book XI, chap. xi, in *Oeuvres Complètes de Montesquieu* (Garnier Frères, Paris, 1876), Vol. III, p. 30. Functionally, however, Montesquieu did not separate the judicial from the executive powers. See Chapter 2, note 13 *supra*.

[5] Sterling E. Edmunds, *The Federal Octopus* (The Mitchie Co., Charlottesville, Va., 1933), p. 141. Italics supplied.

[6] See addresses by O. R. McGuire before Indiana Bar Association, February 5, 1938, in 13 *Indiana Law Review,* 433, 464; before California State Bar, September 22, 1939, in 11 *Annual Proceedings, California State Bar,* 19, 33; and before Oregon State Bar, September 29, 1939, in 18 *Oregon Law Review* (December, 1939), No. 1. See also reports by the Special Committee on Administrative Law, American Bar Association, in the Association's annual *Reports* since 1934; *Administrative Law, Hearings before Subcommittee No. 4 of the Committee of the Judiciary House of Representatives,* on H.R. 4236, H.R. 6198, and H.R. 6324, 76th Cong., 1st Sess., March 17 and April 5, 1939.

[7] *Lawyer Service Letter No. 104* (August 14, 1945).

designed to correct this and other alleged evils of administrative bureaucracy, the Logan-Walter Bill, was sponsored by the American Bar Association in 1939, passed by the Congress in November, 1940, but vetoed by the President on December 18, 1940.[8] The lawyers were more successful in 1946 when the President signed their Administrative Procedure Act,[9] which critics have pronounced "destructive and malicious" and "adopted with the purpose of impeding and confusing administration and thus weakening important government controls and adding to the incomes of the lawyers sponsoring it through the American Bar Association." [10]

[8] The Logan-Walter Bill was introduced in the Senate by Senator Logan on January 17, 1939 (*S. 915*) and in the House by Representative Celler on February 16, 1939 (*H.R. 4236*). The Bill, as introduced, was drawn by the Committee on Administrative Law of the American Bar Association and approved by the Association at its Chicago meeting January 9–10, 1939. See 25 *American Bar Association Journal* (February, 1939). For the Veto Message, see *H. R. Doc. No. 986*, 76th Cong., 3d Sess. The veto was upheld by a House vote of 153 for overriding and 127 for sustaining it.

The following remark in re the Logan-Walter Bill, by O. R. McGuire, chairman of the Special Committee on Administrative Law of the American Bar Association which framed the Bill, probably represented the views of many of the sponsors of that Bill: "I think you may readily see that the American Bar bill presents the eternal conflict between two different theories of government: One, the American theory of a tripartite government, each with a check upon the other two and none overbalancing the others. The other, the parliamentary theory of government, in which the Executive, for the time being, is the dominating force and which could but result in this country in forcing the acceptance of the Roman theory in which the Executive becomes supreme—a reversion to the primitive type of government resulting in the condition obtaining in Germany, Italy, and Russia today." *Administrative Law, Hearings before Subcommittee No. 4*, p. 4. It would be interesting to know where the author of the above statement got his misinformation on the nature of parliamentary government.

Although, presumably, the mature result of study and investigation by the Special Committee on Administrative Law of the American Bar Association from 1933 to 1939, the Logan-Walter Bill reflected only a superficial understanding of the problem of administrative law, and the reports of the Special Committee bear many of the earmarks of political propaganda. *Cf.* L. L. Jaffe, "Invective and Investigation in Administrative Law," 52 *Harvard Law Review* (1939), 1221 ff.; James M. Landis, "Crucial Issues in Administrative Law—The Walter-Logan Bill," 53 *Harvard Law Review* (1940), 1077 ff.

[9] Act of June 11, 1946, *Public Law 404*, chap. 324, 79th Cong., 2d Sess., 60 *Stat.* 237, 5 *U.S.C.A.* §§ 1001–11 (1950).

[10] F. F. Blachly and Miriam E. Oatman, "Sabotage of the Administrative Process," 6 *Public Administration Review* (1946), 227. The authors quote the following from J. P. Callahan, "Industries Hail Curb on Agencies," *New York Times*, Sunday, July 21, 1946, Sec. 3, p. 1: "Utility, rail and numerous other industries . . . are celebrating the recent passage of the Administrative Procedure Act. . . . When the . . . bill became law last month, corporation counsel and company officials looked back on more than ten years of continuous effort . . . to remove the 'onerous' problems that beset companies appearing before these agencies. . . . Passage of the bill was considered a major victory for the American Bar Association, sponsor for the measure."

That administrative agencies have grown up in defiance of the American theory of tripartite government was also the view of the President's Committee on Administrative Management, reporting in 1937. The Committee found that:

> The Executive Branch of the Government . . . has thus grown up without plan or design . . . commissions have been given broad powers to explore, formulate, and administer policies of regulation; they have been given the task of investigating and prosecuting business misconduct; they have been given powers, similar to those exercised by courts of law, to pass in concrete cases upon the rights and liabilities of individuals under the statutes. They are in reality miniature independent governments . . . . They constitute a headless "fourth branch" of the Government, a haphazard deposit of irresponsible agencies and uncoordinated powers. They do violence to the basic theory of the American Constitution that there should be three major branches of the Government and only three. The Congress has found no effective way of supervising them, they cannot be controlled by the President, and they are answerable to the courts only in respect to the legality of their activities . . . . There is a conflict of principle involved in their makeup and functions . . . . The evils resulting from this confusion of principles are insidious and far-reaching. . . . The discretionary work of the administrator is merged with that of the judge. Pressures and influences properly enough directed toward officers responsible for formulating and administering policy constitute an unwholesome atmosphere in which to adjudicate private rights. But the mixed duties of the commissions render escape from these subversive influences impossible. . . . Furthermore, the same men are obliged to serve both as prosecutors and as judges. This not only undermines judicial fairness; it weakens public confidence in that fairness.[11]

The Secretary of Labor's Committee on Administrative Procedure reported in 1940:

> A genuinely impartial hearing, conducted with critical detachment, is psychologically improbable if not impossible, when the presiding officer has at once the responsibility of appraising the strength of the case and of seeking to make it as strong as possible. Nor is complete divorce between investigation and hearing possible so long as the presiding inspector has the duty himself of assembling and presenting the results of the investigation.[12]

---

[11] The President's Committee on Administrative Management, *Report with Special Studies* (Government Printing Office, Washington, D.C., 1937), pp. 32–40.

[12] The Immigration and Naturalization Service, 77 (*Mimeo.*, 1940); quoted in *Wong Yang Sung v. McGrath,* 339 U.S. 33, 44, 70 S. Ct. 445, 451, 94 L. Ed. 616 (1950).

In a supplementary statement three members of the Attorney General's Committee on Administrative Procedure,[13] speaking of the consolidation of functions in administrative agencies, said:

> The agency which prescribes rules is also the investigator, the prosecutor, the judge, and to a large extent the appellate tribunal. . . . Moreover, . . . agencies are empowered to act in several of these capacities at a single stage of proceedings. As investigator, an administrative agency, after making its own rules and regulations, may often summon witnesses and examine them in secret—a privilege otherwise accorded only to grand juries and denied to such important public officers as the Attorney General and the officials of the Department of Justice. It may, under some statutes, "visit" or inspect premises without a warrant—a power accorded no other public agency except a judge or a jury, and then only after a case has been instituted and the parties appraised of the charges against them. It may threaten the imposition of penalties if its demands for information are not met—a power otherwise accorded only to judges, and then only after valid subpoenas had issued. It may threaten to impose regulations—a power otherwise accorded only to Congress. It may threaten to prosecute and to judge—a power otherwise divided between the Department of Justice and the courts. It may threaten to withhold benefits—a prerogative otherwise accorded to Congress. Though this is not the normal course of administration, the exercise of such power is restrained only by human forbearance.[14]

In the same vein, the eminent Roscoe Pound has made the following indictment of the administrative process:

> Perhaps the worst feature of administrative procedure, as it has developed since 1900, results from combining or not differentiating the receiving of complaints, investigation of them, bringing and conducting a prosecution upon them, advocacy before the agency itself by its own subordinates in the course of the prosecution and adjudication. Thus the adjudication becomes one by or with the advice and assistance of those who investigated, prosecuted, and were advocates for the prosecution. Such things are in clear derogation of the fundamental maxims of justice that no one is to be judge in his own case.[15]

[13] The Committee consisted of twelve members, under the chairmanship of Dean Acheson. Four (Judge Groner filed separate recommendations) accepted the major outlines of the Committee Report but favored greater separation of the administrative and judicial functions and broader judicial review. The Committee issued a voluminous final report under the full title, *Administrative Procedure in Government Agencies—Report of the Committee on Administrative Procedure, appointed by the Attorney General, at the Request of the President, to Investigate the Need for Procedural Reform in Various Administrative Tribunals and to Suggest Improvement Therein. S. Doc. No. 8,* 77th Cong., 1st Sess. (1941).

[14] *Ibid.,* p. 204.

[15] "Proposed Legislation as to Federal Administrative Procedure," 20 *Indiana Law Journal* (October, 1944), 45. See also address by Roscoe Pound before Phi

The President's Committee on Administrative Management recommended in 1937 an overhauling of the whole executive branch of the national government, placing the 100-odd agencies under twelve major departments (adding Social Welfare and Public Works to the existing departments and changing Interior to Conservation). Each of the regulatory agencies was to be divided into (1) an *administrative section,* as a bureau or division in the appropriate department and responsible to the Secretary of the department and through him to the President; and (2) a *judicial section,* "in" a department only for housekeeping purposes and independent of the department and the President with respect to its work and its decisions. The administrative section would formulate rules and regulations, initiate action, investigate complaints, hold preliminary hearings, and prepare the formal record of cases to be heard and decided by the judicial section which would sit as an independent and impartial body for the determination of questions affecting the public interest and private rights.[16]

The Logan-Walter Bill provided that the head of every agency should "designate three employees of his agency" to act as an intra-agency board to hear and determine administrative appeals from decisions of any officer or employee of the agency. Limited judicial powers and judicial procedure were prescribed for the board, which would thus become the judicial section of the agency.[17]

The Attorney General's Committee found that the commingling of the functions of prosecutor and judge, of investigation and advocacy and decision in the same person or persons is "plainly undesirable"; and the Committee held that this commingling was "avoidable and should be avoided by appropriate internal division of labor." The Committee also made the point that it is a mistake to conceive of "an agency as a collective person" and to conclude that because an agency initiates action and renders decision, the same person is doing both, since internal separation of the two functions is possible. Accordingly, the Committee recommended the appointment of specially qualified "hearing commissioners" in each regulatory agency to exercise the judicial functions of the agency and subject to review by an agency tribunal.[18]

On the other hand, F. F. Blachly and Miriam Oatman concluded that

---

Beta Symposium, February 20, 1939, 5 *Vital Speeches* (March, 1939), 342; and speech before American Bar Association in the Association's *Report* for 1941.

[16] President's Committee on Administrative Management, *op. cit.,* p. 41.

[17] *S. 915,* 76th Cong., 1st Sess., § 4.

[18] *Administrative Procedure in Government Agencies,* pp. 55–61.

. . . there are relatively few instances where the independent regulatory boards and commissions exercise a prosecuting function in connection with their main activities. The question of separating the functions of prosecution and adjudication, therefore, seldom arises in a practical way. Where prosecution and adjudication are in the same hands, there appear to be sound reasons for continuing the mixture of functions and permitting appeal to the courts to ensure regularity and to prevent abuses.[19]

Blachly and Oatman point out, further, that the functions of regulatory agencies are primarily legislative. Therefore, these agencies should remain, as now, independent and responsible to Congress and answerable to the courts for their judicial functions; they should not be incorporated into the executive departments and made responsible to the President; nor is a separation of their functions advisable, "since each part of their work now strengthens each other part." [20] Also,

. . . it appears that the "tendencies toward administrative absolutism" so feared by certain promoters of the Bar Association bill [Logan-Walter Bill] are largely non-existent. . . . Arbitrary rule-making for administrative convenience is a charge that cannot be proved. . . . The accompanying charge of "perfunctory routine" is a matter of opinion. . . . The "uncontrolled discretion in interpreting the law and in finding the facts" are partly imaginary and partly a result of the constitutional separation of powers. . . . No progress would be made by seeking to substitute a real and all-pervading judicial absolutism for the imaginary "administrative absolutism" which is charged but not proved by supporters of the judicial formula.[21]

While admitting that the exercise by a single agency of the initiation and decision of complaints is susceptible of abuse, James M. Landis concludes that "Reasons of great weight, however, have made for that fusion," and that, despite a number of disadvantages, ". . . the net balance would still seem to favor leaving adjudication with the administrative. The necessity for coordinating enforcement with policy is still so urgent as not to lead lightly toward the divorcement of these functions." [22] Furthermore, ". . . the charge of arbitrariness, which is commonly made against administrative action, usually appertains to the exercise of the power to prosecute rather

[19] *Federal Regulatory Action and Control* (The Brookings Institution, Washington, D.C., 1940), p. 158, and see chap. ix for an analysis and criticism of the recommendations of the President's Committee on Administrative Management.

[20] *Ibid.*, p. 182. Also *cf.* chaps. ix, x, xi.

[21] *Ibid.*, pp. 227–30.

[22] *The Administrative Process* (Yale University Press, New Haven, 1938), pp. 101, 106.

than to the power to adjudicate. It is restraints upon the exercise of that power that in my judgment are of far greater significance than the creation of restraints upon the power to adjudicate." [23] These restraints must be largely self-imposed through the development of a "professionalism of spirit" and a "recognition that arbitrariness in the enforcement of a policy will destroy its effectiveness." [24] Another factor that makes for "rightness" in the settlement of claims is the independence of the agency from executive control; and Landis does not favor the incorporation of "independent agencies" into the executive departments, for, "Interposing the head of a department between the active administrative official and the public means insulating the administrative official from the public and consequently depriving him of a sounding-board for his views." [25]

The Administrative Procedure Act separates the judicial from the other agency functions by providing that the officers who preside at the taking of the evidence must make the decision or recommended decision in the case. Such officers shall not consult with any person or party on any fact in issue unless notice and opportunity for all parties to participate is given, except in the disposition of customary ex parte matters; nor shall such officers be made responsible to or subject to the supervision of prosecuting officers. The latter may not participate in the decision except as witnesses or counsel in public proceedings.[26]

Is our quest for efficiency leading us to administrative absolutism? Are we trying to save democracy from totalitarianism by inoculating the one with the virus of the latter? Is the administrative process fundamentally an undemocratic process in that it combines in one agency the functions of "prosecutor, legislator and judge"? Should and can these functions be segregated in accordance with the doctrine of the separation of powers? Or, are the faults of administration greatly exaggerated by the legal profession in an effort to preserve for the judiciary ancient and outgrown prerogatives? Legalists, fearing "government by agency" complain that "What is done officially is the law," [27] and "What these officials do about disputes is, to my mind, the law itself." [28] There is implied in these statements the charge that "What is done officially" is not necessarily what the

[23] *Ibid.*, p. 110.
[24] *Ibid.*, p. 111.
[25] *Ibid.*, p. 114.
[26] Sec. 5(c).
[27] Roscoe Pound, *Administrative Law: Its Growth, Procedure, and Significance* (University of Pittsburgh Press, Pittsburgh, 1942), p. 18.
[28] Karl N. Llewellyn, *The Bramble Bush* (Oceana Publications, Inc., New York, 1951), p. 12.

statutes prescribe and that, since a large majority of administrative decisions are not modified or even reviewed by courts, a large part of the law is made by administrators not legislators. However, the legal fraternity does not see anything sinister in judicial legislation. Reasoning from the same premise that "What is done officially is the law," John Chipman Gray concludes

> . . . that the Law is made up of the rules for decision which the courts lay down; that all such rules are Law; that rules of conduct which the courts do not apply are not Law; that the fact that the courts apply rules is what makes them Law; that there is no mysterious entity "The Law" apart from these rules; and that the judges are rather the creators than the discoverers of the Law.[29]

That is, "all the Law is judge-made law." [30]

Uncontrolled administrative discretion is totalitarianism, but control of administrative action by the ordinary courts of law can mean the substitution of uninformed for informed discretion. As an example (fortunately not a common one), a majority of the Supreme Court denounced as a "Star Chamber" proceeding an investigation by the Securities and Exchange Commission into the correctness of the registration statement of an appellant, *after appellant had withdrawn his application in order to stop the investigation.*[31] The ruling drew this stinging rebuke from Mr. Justice Cardozo: "To permit an offending registrant to stifle an inquiry by precipitate retreat in the eve of his exposure is to give immunity to guilt; to encourage falsehood and evasion; to invite the cunning and unscrupulous to gamble with detection. . . . The statute and its sanctions become the sport of clever knaves." [32] If this analysis of the effect of the Court's decision is correct, that decision was an exercise of *arbitrary* power par excellence.

There is always the possibility that discretion will be abused, but there is also a fair chance that the better informed person will exercise the sounder discretion. A surgeon may make a mistake which may cost a patient his life, but the patient's chance to survive would not be enhanced if the operation were performed by a Doctor of Divinity, even if the latter's intelligence quotient were higher than that of the man of medicine. On the other hand, the Hippocratic oath is neither

[29] *The Nature and Sources of the Law* (The Macmillan Co., New York, 1927), p. 121.

[30] *Ibid.,* p. 125.

[31] *Jones v. Securities and Exchange Commission,* 298 U.S. 1, 56 S. Ct. 654, 80 L. Ed. 1015 (1936).

[32] 298 U.S. at 32, 56 S. Ct. at 664, 665, 80 L. Ed. at 1029. Mr. Justice Stone and Mr. Justice Brandeis concurred.

a guaranty of skill nor a complete safeguard against malpractice, any more than the oath of office insures efficiency and honesty in the public service. Training in scientific method and testing under the watchful eye of a critical and demanding public will give meaning to the official oath. The recruitment of more bona fide experts would speed the professionalization of the public service—the development of traditions of technical efficiency, ethical conduct, and self-discipline —so that administrative expertising would refute the charge of being a mere fiction. But the administrative problem is as broad as life itself; it cannot be solved through the use of mechanical devices *only,* such as the reclassification of functions, the reshuffling of agencies, the testing of personnel, constitutional guarantees, and judicial review. These devices relate to *how to do* what *we want to do.* What we *want to do* is basic, since it determines the administrative pattern—defines the objectives and fixes the limits of administrative action.

We found that we could not function adequately through a strict tripartite departmental separation of governmental powers. So we devised the administrative process, which "represents an assemblage of rights normally exercisable by government as a whole." [33] But we have not set up a satisfactory system for the control of administration. Such control as exists is exercised largely by the judicial courts, a not-too-happy solution. The President's Committee "somewhat hysterically" [34] urged the redistribution of administrative agencies among the three departments and the dissolution of the administrative process to the extent that the judicial would be separated from the other functions. "Its sweeping condemnation of the process seems to proceed almost upon the mystical hypothesis that the number 'four' bespeaks evil or waste as contrasted with some beneficence emanating from the number 'three.' The desirability of four, five or six 'branches' of government would seem to be a problem determinable not in the light of numerology but rather against a background of what we now expect government to do." [35]

Government by Lawsuit

The Constitution limits the judicial power to "cases" and "controversies." Judicial review of administrative action means, therefore, that important and far-reaching policies of government are subjected to the lawsuit method of evaluation, a fairly narrow, individual, and

[33] Landis, *op. cit.,* p. 15.
[34] *Ibid.,* p. 47.
[35] *Ibid.*

legalistic procedure. Furthermore, questions growing out of these public policies are argued by lawyers and decided by lawyers. The decision in the case is "guided by the learning and limited by the understanding of a single profession—the law." [36] The views of other interested professions, classes, or persons reach the court only through lawyers at the bar. The questions raised before the court in these cases are all too often less concerned with jurisprudence than with politics, economics, sociology, finance, engineering, medicine, and other technical fields of learning. Even if judges were qualified by training (which they are not) to evaluate this technological data, the "case" procedure does not lend itself to bringing the data before the court. Since most of this technical information lies outside the personal knowledge of the judge, the judge cannot take judicial notice of its existence, even if it were proper to do so. "The test of the judicial process," said James M. Landis, "traditionally is not the fair disposition of the controversy; it is the fair disposition of the controversy *upon the record as made by the parties.*" [37] For all practical purposes a judge is limited to the record in the case—it is not his function to make independent investigations in order to find the *best* solution.

The more flexible administrative process is better adapted to resolve the issues, for its aim is to decide controversies ". . . as 'rightly' as possible, independently of the formal record the parties themselves produce. The ultimate test of the administrative is the policy that it formulates; not the fairness as between parties of the disposition of a controversy on a record of their own making." [38] It is both the right and the duty of the agency to make independent investigations, to point out defects in the law, and to recommend changes therein. Administrative adjudication, like equity, is an adaptation of the judicial process to situations where the conventional legal procedure tends to defeat rather than to promote the ends of justice. In his message vetoing the Logan-Walter Bill, President Franklin D. Roosevelt pointed out that the movement for administrative adjudication had

> . . . its origin in the recognition even by the courts themselves that the conventional processes of the court are not adapted to handling controversies in the mass. Court procedure is adapted to the intensive investigation of individual controversies. But it is impossible to subject

[36] Robert H. Jackson, *The Struggle for Judicial Supremacy* (Alfred A. Knopf, New York, 1941), p. 291.

[37] *Op. cit.,* p. 38.

[38] *Ibid.,* 39.

the daily routine of fact-finding in many of the agencies to court procedure. Litigation has become costly beyond the ability of the average person to bear. Its technical rules of procedure are often traps for the unwary and technical rules of evidence often prevent common sense determinations on information which would be regarded as adequate for any business decision. The increasing cost of competent legal advice and the necessity of relying upon lawyers to conduct court proceedings have made all laymen and most lawyers recognize the inappropriateness of intrusting routine processes of government to the outcome of never-ending lawsuits.[39]

Nevertheless,

. . . a large part of the legal profession has never reconciled itself to the existence of the administrative tribunal. Many of them prefer the stately ritual of the courts, in which lawyers play all the speaking parts, to the simple procedure of administrative hearings which a client can understand and even participate in. Many of the lawyers prefer that decision be influenced by a shrewd play upon technical rules of evidence in which the lawyers are the only experts, although they always disagree. Many of the lawyers still prefer to distinguish precedent and to juggle leading cases rather than to get down to the merits of the efforts in which their clients are engaged. For years such lawyers have led a persistent fight against the administrative tribunal.[40]

The President's criticism of the lawyers' delaying tactics in dealing with the administrative tribunal is not without basis in fact. Even Justices of the Supreme Court have not been able to conceal their impatience, when faced with cases of administrative adjudication, and not so much at the *miscarriage* as at the *misplacement* of justice. Thus, the majority opinion in *Jones v. Securities and Exchange Commission*[41] led the scholarly Mr. Justice Cardozo to observe in a dissenting opinion:

A Commission which is without coercive powers, which cannot arrest or amerce or imprison though a crime has been uncovered or even punish for contempt, but can only inquire and report, the propriety of every question in the course of the inquiry being subject to the supervision of the ordinary courts of justice, *is likened with denunciatory fervor to the Star Chamber of the Stuarts.* Historians may find hyperbole in the sanguinary simile.[42]

[39] Message of December 18, 1940, *H. R. Doc. No. 986*, 76th Cong., 3d Sess., 86 *Congressional Record*, Pt. 12, p. 13942.
[40] *Ibid.*, at 13942–43.
[41] 298 U.S. 1, 56 S. Ct. 654, 80 L. Ed. 1015 (1936).
[42] 298 U.S. at 33, 56 S. Ct. at 665, 80 L. Ed. at 1030. Mr. Chief Justice Stone and Mr. Justice Brandeis joined in the dissent. Italics supplied.

In another case, Mr. Justice Jackson has reminded his associates that

> We must not disguise the fact that sometimes, especially early in the history of the federal administrative tribunal, the courts were persuaded to engraft judicial limitations upon the administrative process. The courts could not go fishing, and so it followed neither could anyone else. Administrative investigations fell before the colorful and nostalgic slogan of "no fishing expeditions." It must not be forgotten that the administrative process and its agencies are relative newcomers in the field of law and that it has taken and will continue to take experience and trial and error to fit this process into our system of judicature. More recent views have been more tolerant of it than those which underlay many older decisions.[43]

Mr. Justice Frankfurter has expressed a similar view repeatedly, as for example:

> The extent to which administrative agencies are to be entrusted with the enforcement of federal legislation is for Congress to determine. Insofar as the actions of these agencies come under the scrutiny of judicial review, it is the business of the courts to respect the distribution of authority that Congress makes as between administrative and judicial tribunals. Of course courts must hold the administrative agencies within the confines of their Congressional authority. But in doing so they should not even unwittingly assume that the familiar is the necessary and demand of the administrative process observance of conventional judicial procedures when Congress has made no such exactions. Since these agencies deal largely with the vindication of public interest and not the enforcement of private rights, this Court ought not to imply hampering restrictions, not imposed by Congress, upon the effectiveness of the administrative process. One reason for the expansion of administrative agencies has been the recognition that procedures appropriate for the adjudication of private rights in the courts may be inappropriate for the kind of determinations which administrative agencies are called upon to make.[44]

Since law enforcement is channelled through the courts, the American bar plays a stellar role in the shaping of the law. A study of the role of lawyers in formulating law [45] ". . . shows that the

---

[43] *United States v. Morton Salt Co.,* 338 U.S. 632, 642, 70 S. Ct. 357, 363–64, 94 L. Ed. 401, 410 (1950).

[44] Mr. Justice Frankfurter dissenting in *Ashbacker Radio Corp. v. Federal Communications Commission,* 326 U.S. 327, 334–35, 66 S. Ct. 148, 152, 90 L. Ed. 108 (1945).

[45] B. R. Twiss, *Lawyers and the Constitution* (Princeton University Press, Princeton, 1942).

development of American Constitutional Law during the period from 1875 to 1935 was, . . . the work of a small group of lawyers, whose clients were great financial and business concerns—in short, of the aristocracy of the American Bar, the founders and principal figures." [46] Bishop Hoadley's much-quoted statement in a sermon preached in 1717 might have been addressed to our judiciary when he said that "whoever hath an *absolute authority* to *interpret* any written or spoken laws, it is *he* who is truly the Law-giver to all intents and purposes, and not the person who first wrote or spoke them." [47]

It is this favored position in our triadic system that the lawyers are reluctant to share with the administrators. The field of constitutional law is preeminently the domain of the lawyers, and laymen should not be permitted to trespass, according to Edward J. Phelps, a leader of the bar in his day and president of the Bar Association in 1880. He lamented that ". . . it is too true, that this constitution of ours . . . has become more and more a subject to be hawked about the country, debated in the newspapers, discussed from the stump, elucidated by pothouse politicians, and dung-hill editors, scholars in the science of government who have never found leisure for the graces of English grammar, or the embellishments of correct spelling." [48] And John Randolph Tucker, another prominent member of the bar at the time when government regulation of business was in its chrysalis stage, spoke of the "American Bar" as ". . . that priestly tribe to whose hands are confided the support and the defense of this Ark of the Covenant of our fathers [the Constitution], the security of which against the profane touch of open and covert foes is the noblest function and the most patriotic purpose of our great profession." [49]

These are fairly representative views of the lawyer's mission as defender of the Constitution and the American way of life. [50] The study and practice of law has a conservatizing influence. The lawyer deals with old authorities and with precedents. Furthermore, the judges of our courts are drawn largely from the ranks of the most successful in the profession, and these are mostly corporation lawyers. These factors create judicial predilections which are reflected in court decisions and have an important bearing upon judicial review of legislative and administrative action. The legal tradition is op-

[46] *Ibid.*, "Foreword" by Edward S. Corwin, p. x.
[47] Quoted by Gray, *op. cit.*, p. 125.
[48] *American Bar Association Reports* (1879), p. 190.
[49] *Ibid.*, Vol. XV (1892), p. 213, quoted by Twiss, *op. cit.*, p. 149.
[50] See Twiss, *op. cit., passim.*

posed to change, and it is individualistic.[51] If this conservatism is made a shield for civil liberty, the public applauds; but if it blocks a national legislative program, such as the recovery program of the first Franklin D. Roosevelt administration, there may be dangerous political repercussions.

Thus we may have in truth government by judicial process, government by lawsuit. Judicial control of administration by means of undefinable constitutional terms such as "due process of law," when that term by judicial legislation applies to substantive as well as procedural law, is government by judicial decree, since the function of the administrative process is "to effectuate the purposes of the law." Control is not limited to confining the administrator to "the purposes of the law"; it extends to the very "purposes" which the law would effectuate. In a simple equity proceeding, involving no more than the "right" of an unscrupulous dealer to sell sick chickens to an unsuspecting public, a court can restrain enforcement of a law designed to protect the public health and thus set bounds to the legislative authority to safeguard the general welfare. To attempt to explain and to justify such a use of judicial power by a "slide-rule" theory of judicial review [52] is but to use pious phrases to camouflage the essentially legislative and constituent nature of the power. When the court mentally lays a challenged statute beside the invoked provision of the Constitution, it measures them with a "rule" of its own devising, a rule marked with gradations of alternative principles of construction and alternative lines of precedent: the opposed principles of nationalism and of dual federalism.[53] This gives the court the

[51] A typical expression of judicial laissez faire is found in a dissenting opinion by Mr. Justice Brewer in *Budd v. New York,* 143 U.S. 517, 551, 12 S. Ct. 468, 478, 36 L. Ed. 247, 258 (1892) to this effect: "The paternal theory of government is to me odious. The utmost possible liberty to the individual, and the fullest possible protection to him and his property, is both the limitation and duty of government. If it may regulate the price of one service, which is not a public service, or the compensation for the use of one kind of property which is not devoted to a public use, why may it not with equal reason regulate the price of all service, and the compensation to be paid for the use of all property? And if so, 'Looking Backward' is nearer than a dream."

[52] Mr. Justice Roberts restated this orthodox theory of judicial review in *United States v. Butler,* 297 U.S. 1, 62, 56 S. Ct. 312, 318, 80 L. Ed. 477, 487 (1936): "When an act of Congress is appropriately challenged in the courts as not conforming to the constitutional mandate, the judicial branch of the Government has only one duty—to lay the article of the Constitution which is invoked beside the statute which is challenged—and to decide whether the latter squares with the former. All the court does, or can do, is to announce its considered judgment upon the question." This would make judicial review a purely mechanical process, not involving judicial judgment or discretion.

[53] *Cf.* Edward S. Corwin, *The Twilight of the Supreme Court* (Yale University Press, New Haven, 1934), chap. i.

"prerogative of choice," and that choice is governed by the social philosophy of the prevailing majority. On this point Robert E. Cushman has said:

> In applying these vague and general clauses of the Constitution to concrete cases the Court has the opportunity, and it embraces the opportunity, of giving effect to its hunches, its predilections, and its prejudices. In interpreting due process of law it may read into the Constitution either a progressive social philosophy or a Mid-Victorian theory of "rugged individualism." In setting the limits to the commerce power it may swing the balance toward an aggressive federal centralization or toward an equally vigorous protection of state rights. In my judgment the legislative power which the Supreme Court now wields in the exercise of its power of judicial review of legislation is far greater than can be soundly adjusted to the principles of democratic government.[54]

The result, in the words of Edward S. Corwin, is that

> The concept of "a government of laws" simmers down, therefore, under the Constitution to a power in the Supreme Court which is without statable limits to set the metes and bounds of political authority in both the nation and the states.[55]

Since, therefore, judicial control of administration is part and parcel of the general power of judicial review, the relation of court to agency has important political implications. The Supreme Court appears to see no inconsistency between its reiterated insistence that constitutional courts cannot exercise nonjudicial functions and the exercise of judicial review in an essentially political manner. The shop-worn myth that the Constitution and not the Court vetoes legislative policy no longer deceives the informed; for obviously "the Constitution is what the judges say it is." [56]   To subject the formulation and execution of broad public policies to vicarious proceedings in ordinary courts of law has apparent disadvantages.[57]   Not only is the

---

[54] "The Role of the Supreme Court in a Democratic Nation," Edward James Lecture at the University of Illinois, March 9, 1938. Reprinted in H. M. Bishop and Samuel Hendel, *Basic Issues of American Democracy* (Appleton-Century-Crofts, Inc., New York, 1948), p. 181.

[55] *Op. cit.,* p. 122.

[56] Charles Evans Hughes, *Addresses and Papers* (1st ed., G. P. Putnam's Sons, New York, 1908), p. 139 (2d ed.; p. 185).

[57] The limitations of the judicial process in supervising administrative action has been repeatedly recognized by the judges of our courts, as for example, when Mr. Justice Frankfurter said in reference to fixing and allocating allowables for the East Texas oil field by the Texas Railroad Commission: "Presumably that body, . . . possesses an insight and aptitude which *can hardly be matched by judges who are called upon to intervene at fitful intervals. . . . When we consider the limiting conditions of litigation—the adaptability of the judicial process only to issues*

basis of decision in a private law action very narrow, but any decision at all must await the bringing of a suit in a proper *case* or *controversy*. Thus law enforcement is on probation pending the judicial determination at some indeterminate time of some indeterminate issue, which may not be of public interest or concern save as it may serve to defeat the legislative will. Until a congressional policy has received the approval of the Supreme Court, its administrative effectuation remains in a state of suspended animation, a condition that is not conducive to orderliness and stability in our society. Nor is this problem solved by an exemplary forbearance on the part of a particular Court. A dormant power can be reasserted. The self-restraint exercised by the present Court is not pleasing to the legal profession generally. A leader of the bar comments:

> Although the Supreme Court has continued to minimize judicial review, the lawyers of the country, if we may judge from expressions of opinion at annual meetings and in bar journals, have been increasingly interested in strengthening it, and occasionally a state court has taken a decided stand.[58]

One is moved to inquire whether this is not a bread and butter interest. This fear that the courts are losing their control over government is not a recent phenomenon. The legal profession, or at least a substantial part of it, has always "viewed with alarm" any weakening in the court's resistance to social change. The Charles River Bridge case,[59] which weakened the doctrine of the Dartmouth College case,[60] was received with abuse by the old guard members of the legal fraternity of 1837. "The rights of property were gone, the Court was gone, the Constitution was gone. *There was great fear that lawyers would never again enjoy the pleasure of seeing legislation declared unconstitutional.*"[61] Mr. Justice Story had written a doleful dissent: "There will not, I fear, even in our day, be any case

---

definitely circumscribed and susceptible of being judged by the techniques and criteria within the special competence of lawyers—it is clear that the Due Process Clause does not require the feel of the expert to be supplanted by an independent view of judges on the conflicting testimony and prophecies and impressions of expert witnesses." *Railroad Commission v. Rowan & Nichols Oil Co.,* 311 U.S. 570, 575–76, 61 S. Ct. 343, 346, 85 L. Ed. 358, 362 (1941).

[58] Arthur T. Vanderbilt (Chief Justice of the New Jersey Supreme Court), in *1942 Annual Survey of American Law* (New York University School of Law, New York, 1943), p. 101.

[59] *Charles River Bridge v. Warren Bridge,* 11 Pet. 420, 9 L. Ed. 773 (1837).

[60] *Dartmouth College v. Woodward,* 4 Wheat. 518, 4 L. Ed. 629 (1819).

[61] James F. Byrnes in an address before the Assembly of the American Bar Association, July 12, 1939. 25 *American Bar Association Journal* (August, 1939), 667–69.

in which a law of a State or of Congress will be declared unconstitutional; for the old constitutional doctrines are fast fading away, and a change has come over the public mind from which I auger little good." [62]

In our own day, when the Supreme Court failed to invalidate the Congressional Gold Clause Resolution of June 5, 1933,[63] the intransigent Mr. Justice McReynolds, speaking for himself and Justices Butler, Sutherland, and Van Devanter, declared that "the Constitution is gone" and expressed the "shame" and "humiliation" of the minority.[64] Later, when the Court sustained the Social Security Act of August 14, 1935, Mr. Justice McReynolds asserted that the majority opinion opened the way for the "practical annihilation" of the theory that "the Constitution, in all its provisions, looks to an indestructible Union, composed of indestructible States." [65]

Executive Justice vs. Judicial Justice

Is one then to conclude that executive justice is incompatible with judicial justice, that the former denies a citizen his "day in court" and thus does violence to the American conception of justice?

No rational person can assume that mere access to the judicial courts is a guaranty of justice. Such an assumption makes no allowance for human infirmity. The voluminous dissenting opinions of our judges bear eloquent testimony to the fallibility of even our higher courts, and the records of our "inferior" courts too often show erratic, misinformed, and indefensible standards of law.[66] Altogether too much reliance is placed on judicial review, and not enough on political action, as a means of enforcing responsibility in government.

Executive justice is oriented to statute law—to the protection and promotion of public rights. Judicial justice is oriented to the common

---

[62] Quoted by Byrnes, *ibid.*

[63] *Norman v. Baltimore & O. R. Co.,* 294 U.S. 240, 55 S. Ct. 407, 79 L. Ed. 885 (1935).

[64] *New York Times,* February 19, 1935. In a "gold clause" case in 1937, Mr. Justice McReynolds in an oral dissent, charged the government with fraud and the majority of the court with condoning fraud. *New York Times,* December 14, 1937.

[65] *Steward Machine Co. v. Davis,* 301 U.S. 548, 599, 57 S. Ct. 883, 896, 81 L. Ed. 1279, 1297 (1937). Mr. Justice Butler, Mr. Justice Sutherland, and Mr. Justice Van Devanter also dissented.

[66] *Cf.* Jerome Frank, *Courts on Trial* (Princeton University Press, Princeton, 1949); Morton Sontheimer, "Our Reeking Halls of Justice," *Collier's* (April 2 and 9, 1949); Howard Whitman, "Behind the Black Robes," *Woman's Home Companion* (February, 1948).

law—to the protection of private rights.[67] In this difference lies the essential weakness of the ordinary courts in dealing with the administrative process—a maladjustment in professional objective, equipment, and technique. Herein, too, lies the implanted seed of executive absolutism. The exaltation of the social interest, if not restricted to legitimate "welfare government," may lead to the deification of the state and government by discretion—that is, a police state.

Judicial review means "rule by the legal order." The legal order is *government by rule;* it is legalistic determinism; it is concerned with *legal security;* it tends to be static; it is opposed to experimentation; it standardizes conduct. While *equity* supplements the legal order by giving it an ethical quality, which is of the spirit rather than the letter of the law, the *administrative process* adapts the legal order to social growth. Judicial and executive justice are, therefore, complementary processes—the separation is departmental, not functional.

Theoretically both court and agency are instruments of the legislative process, since they are charged with the administration of law. This relationship is conditioned, as we have seen, by the Constitution which purports to set up three "independent and coequal" departments. *Marbury v. Madison*[68] successfully challenged this "separation of powers" by assuming for the judiciary the power to restrain "unconstitutional exercise of power" by the legislative and executive branches. The judicial "check" served well enough until the emergence of the service state, when, because of the conservative nature of the judicial process, it was found that judicial application of the due process clause to legislative and administrative action often resulted in curtailing rather than giving direction to social experimentation. "This Court," said Mr. Justice Brandeis in 1932, "has the power to prevent an experiment. We may strike down the statute which embodies it on the ground that, *in our opinion,* the measure is arbitrary, capricious or unreasonable. *We have power to do this, because the due process clause has been held by the Court applicable to matters of substantive law as well as to matters of procedure."*[69]

Many judges have been aware of the essentially undemocratic nature of their legislative function and have labored to shift the ulti-

---

[67] "One reason for the expansion of administrative agencies has been the recognition that procedures appropriate for the adjudication of private rights in the courts may be inappropriate for the kind of determinations which administrative agencies are called upon to make." Mr. Justice Frankfurter dissenting in *Ashbacker Radio Co. v. Federal Communications Commission,* 326 U.S. 327, 335, 66 S. Ct. 148, 152, 90 L. Ed. 108, 114 (1945).

[68] 1 Cranch 137, 2 L. Ed. 60 (1803).

[69] *New State Ice Co. v. Liebman,* 285 U.S. 262, 311, 52 S. Ct. 371, 387, 76 L. Ed. 747, 771 (1932). Dissenting opinion. Italics supplied.

mate responsibility for public policy from the judiciary to the political branches of the government. Since 1937, the Supreme Court has curtailed its legislative activities to such an extent that many lawyers have become alarmed lest they and their clients have fewer days in court. Mr. Justice Frankfurter pointed out the nondemocratic character of courts as policy makers when he said:

> In the day-to-day working of our democracy it is vital that the power of the *nondemocratic organ of our Government* be exercised with rigorous self-restraint. *Because the powers exercised by this Court are inherently oligarchic,* Jefferson all his life thought of the Court as "an irresponsible body" and "independent of the nation itself." *The Court is not saved from being oligarchic* because it professes to act in the service of humane ends. As history amply proves, the judiciary is prone to misconceive the public good by confounding private notions with constitutional requirements, and such misconceptions are not subject to legitimate displacement by the will of the people except at too slow a pace.[70]

In considering a working relationship between court and agency, therefore, Mr. Justice Stone's observation in the fourth Morgan case [71] bears reiteration:

> . . . in construing a statute setting up an administrative agency and providing for judicial review of its action, court and agency are not to be regarded as wholly independent and unrelated instrumentalities of justice, each acting in the performance of its prescribed statutory duty without regard to the appropriate function of the other in securing the plainly indicated objects of the statute. Court and agency are the means adopted to attain the prescribed end, and so far as their duties are defined by the words of the statute, those words should be construed so as to attain that end through coordinated action.[72]

[70] *American Federation of Labor v. American Sash and Door Co.,* 335 U.S. 538, 555–56, 69 S. Ct. 260, 266–67, 93 L. Ed. 222, 232 (1949). Italics supplied.
[71] *United States v. Morgan,* 307 U.S. 183, 59 S. Ct. 795, 83 L. Ed. 1211 (1939).
[72] 307 U.S. at 191, 59 S. Ct. at 799, 83 L. Ed. at 1217.

Chapter 10

CONGRESSIONAL SUPERVISION OF THE
FEDERAL ADMINISTRATIVE PROCESS

Congress, the Source of Administrative Power

Congressional control of administration is primary. Congress is the source of administration. Administrative agencies are created and their duties and powers are defined by Congress. There have been some "emergency" and "war-time" exceptions. President Wilson, during World War I, created a War Industries Board, a War Labor Board, and a Committee on Public Information; and during World War II, President Roosevelt created numerous agencies without benefit of specific congressional authorization, such as the Board of Economic Warfare, the National Housing Agency, the National War Labor Board, the War Production Board, the Office of Civilian Defense, and the War Manpower Commission.[1] These agencies were created under authority of the "commander-in-chief" powers of the President, and their legality was not questioned by Congress. Their "directives" were "informatory" or "at most advisory" and consequently were "judicially unenforceable and unreviewable."[2]

Support for executive creation of agencies may be derived, also, from a board doctrine of implied powers—the theory that Article II of the Constitution contains an undefined grant of power.[3] The specifically enumerated powers of the President are referred to some-

---

[1] Edward S. Corwin, *Total War and the Constitution* (Alfred A. Knopf, New York, 1947), pp. 51–52, lists thirty-five "executive agencies" which "were of purely Presidential creation." See also Arthur T. Vanderbilt, "War Powers and Their Administration," *1942 Annual Survey of American Law* (New York University School of Law, New York, 1943), pp. 106–231; also the 1943, 1944, 1945, 1946, and 1947 issues of the *Annual;* C. A. Berdahl, *War Powers of the Executive in the United States* ("Studies in the Social Sciences," University of Illinois, Urbana, Ill., 1920), p. 117.

[2] *Employers Group of Motor Freight Carriers v. National Labor Relations Board,* 143 F. (2d) 145 (App. D.C., 1944). But, according to Edward S. Corwin, at least some of these agencies exercised "governing" rather than "advisory" powers. *Op. cit.,* pp. 54–55.

[3] See 10 *Ops. Att'y Gen.,* 74; 37 *ibid.,* 496, 593; 39 *ibid.,* 344, 348; 40 *ibid.,* 83.

times as "prerogative powers," while the duty to "take care that the laws be faithfully executed" vests "implied powers." [4] The latter have been held to include broad emergency powers. President Lincoln justified some of his actions on this basis. He said:

> I understand that my oath to preserve the Constitution to the best of my ability, imposed upon me the duty of preserving by every indispensable means, that government, that Nation of which the Constitution was the organic law. . . . I felt that measures, otherwise unconstitutional, might become lawful, by becoming indispensable to the preservation of the Union. Right or wrong, I assumed this ground, and now avow it.[5]

President Theodore Roosevelt held the even broader view that the executive power was limited only by specific restrictions and prohibitions in the Constitution or imposed by Congress in the exercise of its constitutional powers. Evidently, President Franklin D. Roosevelt also acted on this constitutional theory of presidential powers. But President Taft took issue with his predecessor and asserted that

> Mr. Roosevelt ascribing an undefined residuum of power to the President is an unsafe doctrine. . . . The mainspring of such a view is that the Executive is charged with responsibility for the welfare of

[4] *In re Neagle,* 135 U.S. 1, 10 S. Ct. 658, 34 L. Ed. 55 (1890).
For statements by Attorneys-General on the implied power of the Executive, see Cummings to the President, April 23, 1934, 37 *Ops. Att'y Gen.,* 496, upholding the validity of the Presidential creation of a Committee on National Land Problems; Cummings to the President, June 30, 1934, justifying creation by the President of the Quetico-Superior Committee to advise on the establishment of a wilderness sanctuary for wildlife in Minnesota; Jackson to the President, April 2, 1941, 40 *ibid.,* 41, Biddle to the President, April 22, 1944, 40 *ibid.,* 312, Murphy to the President of Senate, Oct. 4, 1939, 39 *ibid.,* 344, 348. Rita W. Nealon, *Contributions of the Attorneys General to the Constitutional Development of the American Presidency* (Unpublished Doctoral Dissertation, New York University, 1949), pp. 71–72. *The Opinions of the Attorney General* cited above is the edition of the Government Printing Office, Washington, D.C.
[5] Quoted in N. J. Small, *Some Presidential Interpretations of the Presidency* (Johns Hopkins University Studies in Historical and Political Science, Johns Hopkins Press, Baltimore, 1932), p. 35.
President Jefferson appears to have held a view similar to President Lincoln. Referring to a question "whether circumstances do not sometimes occur, which make it a duty in officers of high trust, to assume authorities beyond the law," Jefferson said: "To lose our country by a scrupulous adherence to written law, would be to lose the law itself, with life, liberty, property, and all those who are enjoying them with us; thus absurdly sacrificing the end to the means; . . . . The officer who is called to act on this superior ground, does indeed risk himself on the justice of the controlling powers of the Constitution, and his station makes it his duty to incur that risk. But those controlling powers, and his fellow citizens generally, are bound to judge according to the circumstances under which he acted." Jefferson to Colvin, September 20, 1810, *Writings* (Ford ed.), Vol. IX, pp. 279–80. Nealon, *op. cit.,* pp. 76–77.

all the people in a general way, that he is to play the part of a Universal Providence and set all things right, and that anything that in his judgment will help the people he ought to do, ...[6]

The effectiveness of congressional control of the administration is conditioned materially by the "strength" of the President. As leader of his party and director of administration, the President's influence with Congress normally is intimate and compelling, as has been demonstrated repeatedly.

The Spending Power.—It is commonly assumed that the Budget is Congress' "ace in the hand" in dealing with intransigent officials and agencies. An intelligent supervision of the administration through budget control, presupposes a knowledge of government operations and a freedom from pressure politics to which Congress cannot always lay claim. Nevertheless, the determination of general public policy and the taxing and spending to effectuate that policy are the inescapable responsibilities of the elected representatives of the people in a democratically organized society.

Congress may use the spending power to influence administration in a number of ways. It may restrain and curtail administrative activities by cutting appropriations; it may circumscribe materially the freedom of action of the spending agency by making conditional grants; and it may penalize nonconforming officers or agencies by withholding funds. Such uses of Treasury moneys, however, are limited by their effect upon continuing and essential services. In dealing with the executive department, the Congress may not condition appropriations so as to interfere with the constitutional powers of the President. In the opinion of Attorney General Mitchell:

> Congress may not, by conditions attached to appropriations, provide for a discharge of the functions of Government in a manner not authorized by the Constitution. If such a practice were permissible, Congress could subvert the Constitution. It might make appropriations on condition that the executive department abrogate its functions. It might, for example, appropriate money for the War Department on condition that the direction of military operations be conducted by some person designated by the Congress, thus requiring the President to abdicate his functions as Commander-in-Chief.[7]

[6] *Our Chief Magistrate and His Powers* (Columbia University Press, New York, 1916), pp. 144–45. But as Chief Justice, Mr. Taft supported broad implied executive powers. *Cf. Myers v. United States,* 272 U.S. 52, 47 S. Ct. 21, 71 L. Ed. 160 (1926).

[7] Attorney General Mitchell to President Hoover, January 24, 1933, 37 *Ops. Att'y Gen.,* 56, 61. Nealon, *op. cit.,* p. 255.

In 1943 Congress attempted to force the removal of three federal employees, alleged to be "disloyal" by the House Committee on Un-American Activities (Dies Committee), by withholding their salaries and barring them from holding any federal government job unless reappointed with the consent of the Senate.[8] The Supreme Court ruled that the challenged statutory provision (Section 304 of the Urgent Deficiency Act of 1943) was a bill of attainder forbidden by the Constitution, since it clearly accomplished the punishment of named individuals without a judicial trial, thereby rejecting argument by counsel for Congress to the effect that the issue was not subject to judicial review since it involved simply an exercise of the plenary Congressional powers over appropriations.[9]

This incident further illustrates how the Congress can use its financial powers to influence executive action. The offending Section 304 originated in the House as a rider to an important appropriation bill; it was rejected five times by the Senate, which yielded only when it became clear that the House would sacrifice the bill rather than withdraw the rider; and it was approved by the President with this protest: "The Senate yielded, as I have been forced to yield, to avoid delaying our conduct of the war. But I cannot so yield without placing on record my view that this provision is not only unwise and discriminatory, but unconstitutional." [10]

A similar move against Secretary of State Acheson was voted by House Republicans in a party conference, July 25, 1951, in the form of an amendment to the pending State, Justice, and Commerce Departments appropriation bill. The amendment was devised to force Secretary Acheson to resign by cutting off his salary. The amendment provided that

> None of the money appropriated in this act shall be paid to the head of any executive department who, within a period of five years preceding his appointment, was a partner in, or a member of, a professional firm which derived any part of its income from representing or acting for a foreign government, or who, acting as an individual, derived income from such representation, unless submitted or resubmitted by the President to the Senate for confirmation.[11]

[8] Urgent Deficiencies Act of July 12, 1943, 57 *Stat.* 431, 450, § 304.

[9] *United States v. Lovett,* 328 U.S. 303, 66 S. Ct. 1073, 90 L. Ed. 1252 (1946). Mr. Justice Frankfurter and Mr. Justice Reed dissented, holding that Section 304 was not a bill of attainder but a fiscal measure merely preventing the disbursal of money to pay respondents' salaries. *Cf.* G. J. Norville, "Bill of Attainder a Rediscovered Weapon Against Discriminatory Legislation," 26 *Oregon Law Review* (1947), 78 *et sqq.*

[10] *United States v. Lovett,* 328 U.S. 303, 313, 66 S. Ct. 1073, 1077, 90 L. Ed. 1252 (1946).

[11] *New York Herald Tribune,* July 26, 1951, p. 1.

Prior to his appointment to the State Department, Mr. Acheson's law firm had represented some foreign governments in connection with legal claims before some federal agencies. David Lawrence commented that

> Many reputable law firms here do this kind of work. To penalize any citizen and prevent him from holding public office because he once was employed in his profession by a particular type of client would be as unfair as for labor groups to ask Congress to declare by law that nobody should ever be appointed to the Federal bench who had been employed by a law firm representing a corporation. There is no limit to the injustice which that precedent would create.[12]

In like manner, however, the President can be coerced into accepting *valid* restrictions upon executive and administrative action.

The Investigating Power.—The chief device for implementing the legislative process is the investigating power. As technology continues to complicate the work of legislation, requiring an increasing delegation of legislative power to administrators, the investigating power is becoming ever more important as a political technique for the supervision of administrative action. The procedure is limited by the doctrine of the separation of powers, and its usefulness is qualified by its susceptibility to abuse.[13] On the debit side of the ledger, the congressional investigating committee has been called "a composite detective agency, grand jury, prosecuting attorney, judge and public hangman"; [14] it is largely uncontrolled by legal rules as to competency of witnesses, relevancy of documents, and procedure in general.

[12] *Ibid.,* p. 4. The amendment was rejected by a 171–81 vote of the House, July 26, 1951. *New York Times,* July 27, 1951, p. 1.

[13] Some representative discussions of the congressional investigating power are: Marshall E. Dimock, *Congressional Investigating Committees* (Johns Hopkins Press, Baltimore, 1929); Earnest Eberling, *Congressional Investigations* (Columbia University Press, New York, 1928); Martin N. McGeary, *The Development of Congressional Investigative Power* (Columbia University Press, New York, 1940); George B. Galloway, *Congress at the Crossroads* (Thomas Y. Crowell Co., New York, 1948); G. M. Fay, "A Prosecutor's View of Congressional Investigations," 19 *Pennsylvania Bar Association Journal* (April, 1948), 258 ff.; G. Meader, "Limitation of Congressional Investigation," 47 *Michigan Law Review* (April, 1949), 775 ff.; G. D. Morgan, "Congressional Investigation and Judicial Review," 37 *California Law Review* (December, 1949), 556 ff.; George B. Galloway, "The Investigative Function of Congress," 21 *American Political Science Review* (1927), 47–70; Jack Gose, "The Limits of Congressional Investigating Power," 10 *Washington University Law Review* (1935), 61 ff.

[14] Walter Lippmann, "The Senate Inquisition," 84 *Forum* (1930), 131. Also note "Many inquiries have been mere fishing excursions actuated by political malevolence or determined by the exigencies of an election campaign or bent upon gratifying personal animosities or casting reflection upon an opposite administration." Galloway, "The Investigative Function of Congress," *loc. cit.,* p. 67.

When John Stuart Mill observed that "the proper office of a representative assembly is to watch and control the government," [15] he may have been a better prophet than he knew.

Originally, the congressional investigating power was regarded as purely legislative, not judicial; that is, it was used to implement a "clear and precise legislative purpose." [16] Today, however, this power is not limited to securing information relating to legislative measures before one of the houses; select committees are engaged in all manner of investigations into the affairs and conduct of individuals and of government agencies. Many of the investigations are more judicial than legislative. "The power to investigate is at least as great as the power to legislate, and is probably necessarily greater," said a federal court in *United States v. Johnson.*[17] And in *United States v. Bryan,*[18] Judge Heltzaff observed that

> If the subject under scrutiny may have any possible relevancy and materiality, no matter how remote, to some possible legislation, it is within the power of the Congress to investigate the matter. Moreover, the relevancy and materiality of the subject matter must be presumed. The burden is on one who maintains the contrary to establish his contention. It would be intolerable if the judiciary were to intrude into the activities of the legislative branch of the Government, and virtually stop the progress of its investigation, which is intended to secure information that Congress deems necessary and desirable in the proper exercise of its functions, unless the lack of materiality and relevancy of the subject matter is clear and manifest.[19]

Two Justices of the Supreme Court declared, prior to appointment to the Court, for judicially uncontrolled Congressional investigations. In 1924, Felix Frankfurter wrote:

> The power of investigations should be left uncontrolled and the method and forms of such investigations should be left for the determination of Congress and its committees as each situation arises.[20]

[15] *Representative Government* ("Everyman's Library," E. P. Dutton Co., New York), p. 239.

[16] *Kilbourn v. Thompson,* 103 U.S. 168, 26 L. Ed. 377 (1881). In *Barry v. United States ex rel. Cunningham,* 279 U.S. 597, 49 S. Ct. 452, 73 L. Ed. 867 (1929), the Supreme Court concluded that either house of Congress could require the attendance of witnesses to aid in determining the qualifications of its members. The instant case involved a Senate inquiry into the election and qualifications of William S. Vare as Senator from Pennsylvania.

[17] 167 F. (2d) 82 (C.C.A. 2d, 1947); certiorari denied 333 U.S. 837 (1948).

[18] 72 F. Supp. 58 (D.C., 1947); aff'd 167 F. (2d) (App. D.C., 1948). Also *Barsky v. United States,* 167 F. (2d) 241 (App. D.C., 1948); certiorari denied 334 U.S. 843 (1948).

[19] 72 F. Supp., at 61.

[20] "Hands of the Investigation," 38 *New Republic* (May, 1924), 329.

Hugo Black in 1936 declared in the Senate:

> I will state very frankly that in my judgment if any judge ever issues
> an injunction to prevent delivery of papers that are sought by this body
> through subpoena, the Congress should immediately enact legislation
> taking away that jurisdiction from the courts. Congress creates the
> jurisdiction of these courts.[21]

Moreover, ". . . *the power of inquiry, with process to enforce it,*
is an essential and appropriate auxiliary to the legislative function." [22]
This power of either house to punish for contempt has been referred
to as "essential and inherent" [23] by the Supreme Court. Punishment
by Congress is limited to imprisonment for the remainder of the legislative session.[24] In addition to "its own process," that is, the subpoena
and contempt powers, Congress provided in 1857 that a witness who
should refuse to answer questions or produce papers before one of
its committees would be guilty of a misdemeanor and punishable by
fine or imprisonment upon conviction of contumacy before a court
of law.[25] The Supreme Court has held that "Punishment, purely as
such, through contempt proceedings, legislative or judicial, is not
precluded because punishment may *also* be inflicted for the same act
as a statutory offense." [26] This is not double jeopardy. The Court
said in *In re Chapman:* [27]

> . . . the contumacious witness is not subject to jeopardy twice for
> the same offense, since the same act may be an offense against one
> jurisdiction and also an offense against another; and indictable statu-
> tory offenses may be punished as such, while the offender may likewise
> be subjected to punishment for the same acts as contempts, the two
> being *diverso intuiti,* and capable of standing together.[28]

[21] *Congressional Record* (1936), Vol. LXXX, p. 3329.
[22] Mr. Justice Van Devanter in *McGrain v. Daugherty,* 273 U.S. 135, 174, 47
S. Ct. 319, 328, 71 L. Ed. 580, 593 (1927). Italics supplied.
[23] *In re Chapman,* 166 U.S. 661, 17 S. Ct. 667, 41 L. Ed. 1154 (1897).
[24] *Anderson v. Dunn,* 6 Wheat. 204, 19 L. Ed. 242 (1831).
[25] The Act provides that any person, who having been summoned as a witness
by the authority of either House of Congress, to give testimony or to produce
papers upon any matter under inquiry before either House, or any committee of
either House of Congress, wilfully makes default, or, having appeared, refuses to
answer any question pertinent to the inquiry, shall be deemed guilty of a misdemeanor, punishable by a fine of not more than $1000 nor less than $100, and
imprisonment in a common jail for not less than one month nor more than twelve
months. Act of January 24, 1857, 11 *Stat.* 155, c. 19, 52 *Stat.* 942, § 1942, 2
U.S.C.A. § 192 (1946), *Rev. Stat.* § 102.
[26] *Jurney v. MacCracken,* 294 U.S. 125, 151, 55 S. Ct. 375, 380, 79 L. Ed. 802,
808 (1935). Italics supplied.
[27] 166 U.S. 661, 17 S. Ct. 677, 41 L. Ed. 1154 (1897).
[28] 166 U.S. at 672, 17 S. Ct. at 681, 41 L. Ed. at 1159–60.

Since, under the Fifth Amendment, no person can "be compelled in any criminal case to be a witness against himself," Congress has provided that no testimony given by a witness before either house, or before a committee thereof, shall be used as evidence in any criminal proceedings against him in any court, except for perjury in giving such testimony; but that an official paper or record produced by the witness is not within this privilege.[29] But "No witness is privileged to refuse to testify or produce any paper upon the ground that his testimony to such fact may tend to disgrace him or otherwise render him infamous." [30] Furthermore, a refusal to answer creates in the public mind a presumption of guilt, making the value of the constitutional protection against giving self-incriminating testimony somewhat dubious.

While Congress cannot compel disclosures of information for the purpose of aiding in the prosecution of a pending suit against a witness, pertinent and freely made disclosures in aid of the legislative function may also be used in such a suit.[31] The contempt power is merely a means to an end, it "does not embrace punishment for contempt as punishment." [32]

The legislative power to punish contumacious witnesses stems from early English Parliamentary practice and was exercised by Congress as early as 1814.[33] The use of the contempt power against nonmembers was upheld by the Supreme Court in 1821 in a case involving an attempt to bribe members of the House [34] and again in

[29] Act of June 25, 1948, 62 *Stat.* 833, c. 645, 18 *U.S.C.A.* § 3486.

[30] 52 *Stat.* 942, 2 *U.S.C.A.* § 193. If a witness answers an incriminating question without claiming immunity, his testimony can be used against him. *United States v. De Lorenzo,* 151 F. (2d) 122 (1945).

[31] *Sinclair v. United States,* 279 U.S. 263, 49 S. Ct. 268, 73 L. Ed. 692 (1929).

[32] *Marshall v. Gordon,* 243 U.S. 521, 542, 37 S. Ct. 448, 453, 61 L. Ed. 881 (1917). Mr. Chief Justice White.

[33] For early cases see A. C. Hinds, *Precedents of the House of Representatives . . .,* 59th Cong. 2d Sess., *H. R. Doc. No. 355* (1907), Vol. II, pp. 1047–1142; Vol. III, pp. 1–78. In *McGrain v. Daugherty,* 273 U.S. 135, 175, 47 S. Ct. 319, 329, 71 L. Ed. 580, 593 (1927) the Court said: "A legislative body cannot legislate wisely or effectively in the absence of information respecting the conditions which the legislation is intended to affect or change; and where the legislative body does not itself possesses the requisite information—which not infrequently is true—recourse must be had to others who do possess it. Experience has taught that mere requests for such information often are unavailing, and also that information which is volunteered is not always accurate or complete; so some means of compulsion are essential to obtain what is needed. All this was true before and when the Constitution was framed and adopted. In that period the power of inquiry—with enforcing process—was regarded and employed as a necessary and appropriate attribute of the power to legislate—indeed, was treated as inhering in it."

[34] *Anderson v. Dunn,* 6 Wheat. 204, 5 L. Ed. 242 (1821).

1881 in a case involving a contumacious witness.[35] In the latter case, however, the court limited the power to testimony "required in a matter into which the House has jurisdiction to inquire. . . . neither of these bodies possesses the general power of making inquiry into the private affairs of citizens." [36]

In principle this limitation upon the congressional investigating power is salutary, but courts have found it difficult to enforce. In fact, it would appear that "the sky is the limit" to the investigating power of Congress. Operating under the cloak of constitutional immunity [37] and in the name of public service, members of the Congress may indulge their prejudices, their "yens" for publicity, and even their passions. A public officer has no defense against these "slings and arrows of outrageous fortune": the immunity rule bars an action for libel, and the doctrine of the separation of powers bars resort to equity.[38] An officer whose political or economic views are displeasing to some influential or demogogic Senator or Representative may find himself attacked on the floor of the Congress or investigated by one of its committees. And although no misfeasance or malfeasance or ground for impeachment is uncovered, the officer's usefulness may be destroyed and he may be persecuted out of office. The effect is government by terrorism. An observer of many Congressional investigations has pointed out that

> The Congress of the United States is always investigating somebody, in private life or in the bureaucratic life of the Government, but nobody is investigating Congress. So it is that fear pervades the scene. There are members of the Supreme Court of the United States who are afraid, even in private gatherings, to give but the faintest voice to the swollen apprehension and vast misgiving at what seems to be happening to due process, not just for the alleged Communists in the State Department but for a man who is said by somebody, on the basis of something whispered to him by somebody, to be, maybe, a "Five Per Center," or a "fixer," of some kind or another.

[35] *Kilbourn v. Thompson,* 103 U.S. 168, 26 L. Ed. 377 (1881).

[36] 103 U.S. at 190, 26 L. Ed. at 387. Similarly, the Court has held that an administrative agency may not engage in "fishing expeditions" into the private affairs of individuals or organizations on the off-chance that it may discover breaches of the law. *Federal Trade Commission v. American Tobacco Co.,* 264 U.S. 298, 44 S. Ct. 336, 68 L. Ed. 696 (1924).

For a criticism of the Kilbourn decision see James M. Landis, "Constitutional Limitations on the Congressional Power of Investigation," 40 *Harvard Law Review* (1926), 153 ff.; C. S. Potts, "Power of Legislative Bodies to Punish for Contempt," 74 *University of Pennsylvania Law Review* (1926), 691–725, 780–829.

[37] *United States Constitution,* Art. I, Sec. 5.

[38] *Hearst v. Black,* 87 F. (2d) 68 (App. D.C., 1936).

High officials of the Government of the United States live in a kind of psychotic terror. . . .

Men in the State Department trim their reports, and their views, in fear of the present, or of another, Senator McCarthy. Men in other bureaus, who ordinarily would be dealing hard-headedly in hard goods (like munitions) trim their activities. A gentleman in this endeavor who used to earn $150,000 in private life, and is now privileged to work for the Government for $15,000, looks over his shoulder before he accepts a highball with an old free-enterprising friend in the Mayflower bar. Who knows but what this enterpriser may be a wolf in a Brooks Brothers coat—in short, as they say, an "influence peddler." [39]

In the legislative forum the accuser is limited only by his conscience and by public opinion, and the latter has been calloused by years of antibureaucracy propaganda. An officer may be summoned before an investigating committee for no better purpose than to destroy public confidence in him and his associates. To this end a member of Congress may resort to unfair newspaper publicity, as when J. Parnell Thomas, chairman of the House Un-American Committee in the 80th Congress, discussed the suspicions of his committee in public lectures and in magazine articles. Even more pernicious is the current "guilt by association" doctrine, employed against a number of officers of the Department of State in the recent congressional onslaught on that Department. Congress would be well advised to take official notice of a warning by Mr. Justice Rutledge to the effect that: "Guilt with us remains individual and personal, even as respects conspiracies. It is not a matter of mass application." [40]

The implications of this un-American "guilt by association" theory were touched upon by Dr. Philip Jessup, Ambassador at Large, in a statement in the Senate concerning charges of Communism made by Senator McCarthy of Wisconsin:

It is impossible for anyone to estimate the harmful effect that these innuendoes have had on the success of my mission and the foreign policy of the United States. . . . It is a question of the utmost gravity when an official holding the rank of Ambassador at Large of the United States of America is held up before the eyes of the rest of the world as a liar and traitor.[41]

[39] William S. White, "An Inquiry into Congressional Inquiries," *New York Times Magazine,* March 23, 1952, Sec. 6, pp. 11, 25.

[40] *Kotteakos v. United States,* 328 U.S. 750, 772, 66 S. Ct. 1239, 1252, 90 L. Ed. 1557, 1571 (1946).

[41] *New York Times,* March 31, 1950, p. 24.

Anyone who is summoned before the bar of Congress to answer questions pertaining to his official [42] conduct can test the legality of the legislative procedure only by gambling on a prison term should he make the wrong guess: he must refuse to obey the subpoena, be convicted of contempt, and then petition for a writ of *habeas corpus;* or, if indicted under the 1857 Act,[43] he must defend the case on its merits in a criminal suit. That is not American justice.

Congress has made extensive investigations of the executive branch, ostensibly in aid of the legislative function, but more particularly to disclose irregular or corrupt practices. No national administration has escaped the congressional probers, the inquiry extending, in more than twenty cases, to the President himself. Congressional investigations uncovered General Wilkinson's treasonable acts in the Burr Conspiracy of 1810, the Crédit Mobilier scandal in 1872, the Teapot Dome oil scandal of the Harding administration, the tax scandal in the Truman administration, and led to the impeachment proceedings against President Johnson and Secretary Belknap.

The first comprehensive congressional investigation of the executive branch was made by the Cockrell Committee (1887–89) created in response to a resolution by Senator Francis M. Cockrell of Missouri which called for a committee of five "to inquire into and examine the methods of business and work in the Executive Departments of the Government." [44] The investigation was carried on by means of letters directed to the heads of the departments and bureau and division chiefs, and through personal visits or tours of inspection. While the inquiry did not uncover anything more serious than a

---

[42] It appears that Congress may even probe into the private affairs of private persons. In 1947 ten persons employed as writers by the movie industry refused to answer the question, "Are you a member of the Communist Party?" put to them by the Committee on Un-American Activities. All ten were cited for contempt of Congress. They claimed privacy for their political beliefs under the First Amendment. The Court of Appeals of the District of Columbia sustained the Committee. *Lawson and Trumble v. United States,* 176 F. (2d) 49 (D.C. Cir., 1949) ; certiorari denied 339 U.S. 934 (1950), rehearing denied 339 U.S. 992 (1950). But since the Smith Act (54 *Stat.* 671, 18 *U.S.C.A.* § 2385) makes it a crime to be a member of an organization which advocates the overthrow of the government by force, a witness may reasonably fear that criminal charges may be brought against him if he admits such membership, and the Supreme Court has held that a witness before a federal grand jury and a federal court may refuse to admit membership in the Communist Party. *Blau v. United States,* 340 U.S. 159, 71 S. Ct. 223, 95 L. Ed. 175 (1950). See also, *United States v. Josephsen,* 165 F. (2d) 82 (C.C.A.N.Y., 1947), certiorari denied 333 U.S. 838 (1948), rehearing denied, 333 U.S. 858 (1948), 335 U.S. 899 (1948). The constitutionality of the Smith Act was upheld in *Dennis v. United States,* 341 U.S. 494, 71 S. Ct. 857, 95 L. Ed. 865 (1951).

[43] 52 *Stat.* 942, § 192, 2 *U.S.C.A.* § 192. See p. 331 above.

[44] *Cong. Rec.,* 49th Cong., 2d Sess. (1887), Vol. XVIII, pt. 3, p. 2535.

certain amount of inefficiency, it established a precedent for over-all congressional responsibility for the national administration.

Since then there have been a number of such broad investigations,[45] but for the most part the inquiries have been limited to specified services or agencies. The Senate Committee to Investigate National Defense, created on March 1, 1941, may be taken as an example of an exemplary investigating committee.[46] The committee was unusually harmonious, as evidenced by the absence of a minority report. Its investigations were factual and objective, and it treated witnesses fairly and with proper consideration. Its recommendations were contributing factors in decisions which materially improved our war production and procurement program.[47]

But not all investigating committees have been as fortunate in their objectives, personnel, or procedures. Too often the hearings have degenerated into recriminating squabbles and a jockeying for partisan advantage. In 1938 the House created the Committee on Un-American Activities, the Dies Committee.[48] This Committee conducted a series of investigations and made lists of people and organizations which it considered subversive.[49] Statutory provisions followed which barred any person who was a member of any organization that advocated the overthrow of our form of government from holding a federal job.[50] Under these acts the Federal Bureau of Investigation made wholesale investigations of federal employees. On February 1, 1943, Representative Dies, the Chairman of the Un-American Activities Committee, in a speech on the floor of the House, named and attacked 39 employees of the government as "irresponsible, unrepre-

[45] For example, the Byrd Committee of the Senate (established in pursuance of Senate Resolution No. 217, 74th Cong., 2d Sess., January 9, 1936) was "authorized to make a full and complete study of all of the activities of the departments, agencies, bureaus, boards and commissions, and all other agencies of the executive branch of the government with a view to determining whether the activities of any such agency conflict with or overlap the activities of any other agency and whether, in the interest of simplification, efficiency and economy, any of such agencies, officers and employees thereof, should be coordinated with other agencies or abolished."

[46] Commonly known as the Truman Committee from March 1, 1941, to August 11, 1944, and as the Mead-Kilgore Committee from August 11, 1944, to July 11, 1948.

[47] Cf. Final Report, No. 440, 80th Cong., 2d Sess.; Harry A. Toulmin, Diary of Democracy; The Investigating Committee (R. R. Smith, New York, 1947).

[48] H.R. 1282, 83 Cong. Rec. 7568–87.

[49] H.R. Rep. No. 1, 77th Cong., 1st Sess.; H.R. Rep. No. 2748, 77th Cong., 2d Sess.; Hearings before the Committee on Un-American Activities, "Investigation of the Office of Price Administration," 79th Cong., 1st Sess. (1945); ibid., "Investigation of Un-American Propaganda Activities in the United States (Communist Party)," 79th Congress, 1st Sess. (1945), 79th Cong., 2d Sess. (1946).

[50] Hatch Act, 53 Stat. 1148, 1149, § 9A, 18 U.S.C.A. § 61i; Emergency Relief Appropriations Act of 1941, 54 Stat. 611, §§ 15(f), (17b), 15 U.S.C.A. §§ 721–28 and note.

sentative, crackpot, radical bureaucrats" affiliated with "communist-front organizations," and proposed their removal from public office.[51] The Cox Committee, a Select Committee of the House formed in 1943 to investigate the Federal Communications Commission,[52] engaged the Commission in an acrimonious two-year dogfight. It was less of an investigation than a sparring contest between Edward E. Cox of Georgia, the chairman of the Committee, and James L. Fly, the chairman of the Commission.[53]

As a result of the investigation, Congress amended the Communications Act of 1934 prohibiting certain coercive practices affecting licensees; the appropriations for the Commission were reduced drastically; and there were a number of resignations within the Commission. The investigation was clearly within the legislative function, but a more objective committee might have produced more constructive results.

A clear case of the unwise use, if not the misuse, of congressional power was the investigation by the joint Senate Armed Services and Foreign Relations Committees into the dismissal by President Truman, on April 11, 1951, of General Douglas MacArthur from his commands in the Far East. The hearings opened on May 3, when General MacArthur appeared before the investigators to defend his own position and to attack the military and foreign policies of the United Nations and of the President in the Orient.[54] It was the opening act of a political melodrama directed by the critics of the administration with the General as the hero and the President and the Secretary of State as the villains in the play. The prologue had been the General's dramatic speech before the Congress and a series of

---

[51] *United States v. Lovett,* 328 U.S. 303, 308–9, 66 S. Ct. 1073, 1075, 90 L. Ed. 1252 (1946).

[52] Organized in January, 1943, in pursuance of *H.R. Res. 21,* 78th Cong., 1st Sess., introduced by Representative Cox on January 6, 1943.

[53] Mr. Cox charged on the floor of the House that ". . . of all the bureaucrats who have sought to smear Congress this man Fly is the worst. His pursuit of me has been nothing but blackmail. . . . His whole outfit now is a nest of 'reds' . . . . This Commission as run by Fly is the nastiest nest of rats to be found in the entire country." *Cong. Rec.,* 78th Cong., 1st Sess., p. 235. On the other hand, the Committee hearings were described as a "terrifying example of lynch law by a Congressional committee." See "Smearing the FCC," 109 *New Republic* (August 23, 1943), 237. Robert D. Leigh, Director of the Commission's Foreign Broadcast Intelligence Service from 1942 to 1944, charged that the Cox Committee "offers one of the worst examples of substandard Congressional behavior in recent years" and that publication of its full record would "reveal cases of the grossest inquisitorial malpractice." See also "Politicians v. Bureaucrats," 190 *Harper's Magazine* (January, 1945), 97, 100, 102.

[54] The hearings ended on June 25, 1951. They covered all our Asian policies since 1944. The panel consisted of 26 Senators. An estimated 2,045,000 words went into the record. *New York Times,* June 26, 1951, p. 1.

triumphant parades that dwarfed Caesar's return from his foreign wars.

The probing went on for weeks. Day after day our top military leaders were questioned by Senators some of whom seemed to have but one aim in mind: to vindicate General MacArthur and to discredit his superiors. The investigation was not intended to serve a proper legislative purpose, but to provide political capital for the 1952 national election. The folly of the proceedings should have become apparent when the highest ranking military leaders supported the President and criticized General MacArthur's strategy as endangering our national security. General Omar N. Bradley, Chairman of the Joint Chiefs of Staff, testified that the Joint Chiefs had recommended General MacArthur's dismissal. General George C. Marshall, Secretary of Defense, said that General MacArthur would have the nation follow his counsel "even at the expense of losing our Allies and wrecking the coalition of free peoples throughout the world." [55]

The investigation created national hazards. The *New York Times* editorially pointed out one of these hazards as follows:

> The Senate hearings on the dismissal of General MacArthur are spreading on the record not only the broad outlines of our foreign policies but also some of the most secret information we possess regarding our estimates of the enemy's plans, resources and the disposition of his armed forces, as well as of our war plans in Korea. What is more, some of the information is provided in material which is not only secret but is also in a form which, if released without careful paraphrasing, could endanger this country's secret codes and cryptographic systems by making it easier to break them.
>
> It is true, of course, that the hearings, despite solid Republican opposition, are conducted in "closed sessions," and that the published record is censored for security. But even the published record contains enough to lend weight to Secretary Marshall's statement that he feels sometimes as though he were compelled to act as a sort of intelligence agent for the Soviet Government, revealing our conclusions, recommendations and proposed actions, without receiving anything of the kind in return. Furthermore, besides the censored published record, there is the uncensored record which must pass through all too many hands. Just how secret anything can or will remain, once it is known to twenty-five Senators, is a question on which previous experience provides no great assurance.

[55] *New York Times*, May 13, 1951, Sec. 4, p. 1. See also General Bradley's statement: "Frankly, in the opinion of the Joint Chiefs of Staff, this [MacArthur] strategy would involve us in the wrong war, at the wrong place, at the wrong time, and with the wrong enemy." *Ibid.*, May 20, 1951, Sec. 4, p. 1.

The danger of perilous leaks is obvious, and the present reports of "new secret weapons" for winning the Korean war suggest that the leaks may have begun. This is a situation which calls for a deep sense of personal responsibility on the part of every member of the Senate committees; for what is at stake is the security of our country and the lives of our soldiers in the field.[56]

And General Bradley expressed deep anxiety over the revelation of high United States military plans as a result of the hearings. In answer to some obvious partisan baiting, the General retorted:

I think it is very harmful to our security and to our country and to our future security to have to pass on to Russia all of our intentions, all of our thoughts, and all of our capabilities.

I would be perfectly willing to come up here before your Appropriations Committee and advocate a very large appropriation to buy similar information on Russia, and I think what you say is probably very true: that we are unnecessarily inciting Russia to war—maybe not unnecessarily—but it becomes necessary because of the nature of these hearings very largely.[57]

The Senators appeared to forget that in debating our foreign policy in this manner in time of war, they revealed information which concerned the common security of the United Nations.

In addition to jeopardizing our national safety, a practical effect of the investigation was to condone insubordination in the armed services and thus to subordinate civil to military authority. It is a revealing commentary on the character of the hearings that a general of the army found it necessary to remind the investigators that our Constitution is founded on the supremacy of the civil law. The Joint Chiefs felt, said General Bradley, that "General MacArthur's actions were continuing to jeopardize the civilian control over the military authorities." [58]

Congress thus often engages in ventilation investigations—the objective is not to legislate but to expose facts and opinions to public view and criticism. Inquiries of this kind frequently are political and punitive in nature, and equally often the investigating committee does not observe even rudimentary principles of due process in its procedure. The chief offender in this respect has been the committee investigating un-American activities. A public servant who is disloyal to his trust is a man without honor, but there is little choice

[56] Editorial, "The Senate and Security," May 11, 1951.
[57] New York Times, May 23, 1951, p. 30.
[58] New York World-Telegram and Sun, May 21, 1951, p. 2. Cf. Speech by General Douglas MacArthur before the Massachusetts legislature, July 25, 1951, New York Times, July 26, 1951, p. 12.

between one who sells his country's secrets and one who prostitutes her justice in the name of national security. "Security," said Mr. Justice Jackson, "is like liberty in that many are the crimes committed in its name." [59]

Fortunately, an investigation that gives publicity to the investigated publicizes the investigator as well and thus may result in curbing abuses by both. The excesses of the Dies Committee aroused much public resentment and caused its successor to "tone down" its activities. [60] The brutal procedure of this Committee was largely responsible, too, for various proposals for a code of procedure to govern congressional investigations. Resolutions to this end were introduced in Congress, [61] proposing that a person whose reputation was brought into question in the course of a congressional investigation should have the right to testify in his own behalf; to have counsel; to call and cross examine witnesses; and to file with the committee, as part of the record, a sworn statement concerning the testimony. No formal action has been taken by Congress in regard to these resolutions, even though they represent a minimum of protection for a person whose good name is in issue.

A legislative investigating committee should operate under flexible rules of procedure, but such rules should have due regard for basic

---

[59] Dissenting in *United States v. Shaughnessy*, 338 U.S. 537, 551, 70 S. Ct. 309, 317, 94 L. Ed. 317, 328 (1950).

[60] "Nothing in recent years has been as un-American as the conduct of the hearings of the congressional committee on un-American activities." Walter Gellhorn, "Report on a Report of the House Un-American Activities," 56 *Harvard Law Review* (1947), 1193.

[61] *S. Con. Res. 44*, 80th Cong., 2d Sess. (February 25, 1948); *H.R. Con. Res. 3*, 81st Cong., 1st Sess. (January 3, 1949); *H.R. Con. Res. 24*, 81st Cong., 1st Sess. (February 2, 1949); *H.R. 74*, 81st Cong., 1st Sess. (January 3, 1949); *H.R. 191*, 81st Cong., 1st Sess. (January 3, 1949); *H.R. 824*, 81 Cong., 1st Sess. (January 5, 1949); *S. Con. Res. 2*, 81st Cong., 1st Sess. (January 5, 1949).·

Speaking before a Conference of Chief Justices of the State Courts on September 13, 1951, Senator Herbert R. O'Conor, chairman of the Senate Crime Investigating Committee, proposed a code of fair conduct for congressional investigating committees, as follows:

"1. Advance notice to witnesses of charges against them, with ample time to prepare answers.

"2. The right of witnesses to consult counsel on their rights during examination.

"3. The right to submit written questions for the cross-examination of an accusing witness at public hearings.

"4. The right to a reasonable time to answer charges by appearing in person or by filing answers in writing.

"5. The right of non-witnesses to reply to statements derogatory to their character or conduct.

"6. Requirement of approval by a committee majority for any public statement about executive hearings that affects a citizen's character or reputation." *New York Times,* September 14, 1951.

principles of justice and for the constitutional separation of powers. The legislature has the unquestioned power to acquire information as the basis for legislation and to "follow up" such legislation by inquiring into the usefulness and effectiveness of the agency created to effectuate the legislative policy; but when the legislature inquires into matters which lie within the constitutional discretion of the executive branch, such as the formulation of military and foreign policies, the separation of powers, doctrine imposes limitations which the investigators are bound to respect.

Investigation of the administration has become one of the chief functions of the Congress. In fact so much time is given to investigation that the primary legislative function is neglected. Key members of the Congress spend so much time at hearings that they have little time for anything else. Furthermore, membership on an investigating committee gives more publicity, and hence more political prestige, than membership on a legislative committee. As of March 22, 1952, the Eighty-Second Congress, with several months to go, had instituted 225 distinct inquiries, in addition to the regular hearings on pending bills and had authorized funds for these hearings to the approximate amount of $4,100,000.[62] These inquiries also consume much time of executive officers at the expense of their duties, as well as at the expense of the Treasury. Congress could profit by setting up nonpartisan commissions, similar to the British commissions of inquiry, and investing them with all the authority now exercised by congressional investigating committees. Also, Congress could make greater use of existing research organizations, such as The Brookings Institution, thereby insuring more scientific findings and freeing members of Congress for the business of legislating.

Congress cannot direct the President to produce documents or papers affecting action by himself or of one of the department heads when acting as his representative. Not infrequently, Presidents have directed a Secretary or other high official not to comply with a congressional request for records. President Washington set a precedent in 1796 when he declined to give the House certain documents relating to the Jay Treaty.[63] Should Congress threaten a department head or other executive officer with contempt for failure to comply with a request for documents, the President may take personal pos-

[62] C. P. Trussell, "Congress Inquiries at Peak," *New York Times,* March 23, 1952, Sec. 1, p. 1. *Cf.* Arthur Krock, "Many Investigations Slow up Legislation," *New York Times,* June 17, 1951, Sec. 4, p. E3.

[63] James D. Richardson, *Messages and Papers of the Presidents,* Vol. I, pp. 194–96. For refusals of Presidents to comply with congressional requests for documents or papers see: Monroe (*Ibid.,* Vol. II, p. 278); Jackson (*Ibid.,* Vol III, pp. 36, 133–34); Cleveland (*Ibid.,* Vol. VIII, pp. 377–78).

session of the papers and defy congressional action. When the Senate in 1909 tried to get certain documents from the head of the Bureau of Corporations bearing on alleged violation of the Sherman Antitrust Act by the Tennessee Coal and Iron Company, President Roosevelt took charge of these papers and challenged the Senate to get them "through my impeachment." The President later explained the incident in this typically Rooseveltian manner:

> I really had a very disagreeable two days. The Senate called for certain papers in the Bureau of Corporations this week and on Thursday ordered Herbert Knox Smith to transmit all papers on a certain subject in his office. He came to see me and to tell me that most of the papers were given in a confidential way; that if they were made public no end of trouble would ensue. I ordered Smith to get a decision from the Attorney General that these papers should not be made public, and yesterday the Committee on Judiciary of the Senate summoned Herbert Knox Smith before it and informed him that if he did not at once transmit those papers the Senate would order his imprisonment at once or the committee would. As soon as he reported this to me I ordered him in writing to turn over to me all the papers in the case, so that I could assist the Senate in the prosecution of its investigation.
>
> I have those papers in my possession, and last night I informed Senator Clark of the Judiciary Committee what I had done. I told him also that the Senate should not have those papers and that Herbert Knox Smith had turned them over to me. The only way the Senate or the Committee can get those papers now is through my impeachment, and I so informed Senator Clark last night.[64]

Attorneys General have consistently held that investigative reports are confidential documents of the executive branch and that it lies in the discretion of the President to decide whether congressional or public access thereto would be in the public interest. Mr. Jackson stated his own view, and that of several of his predecessors, as follows:

> It is the position of the Department of Justice, restated now with the approval and at the direction of the President, that all investigative reports are confidential documents of the executive department and that congressional or public access thereto would not be in the public interest. This accords with conclusions reached by a long line of predecessors in the office of Attorney General and with the position taken by the President from time to time since Washington's administration.[65]

[64] Quoted in A. Butt, *Letters,* edited by L. F. Abbott (Doubleday, Page and Co., New York, 1924), p. 305, and in Nealon, *op. cit.,* pp. 248–49.

[65] Attorney General Jackson to Representative Vinson, April 30, 1941, 40 *Ops. Att'y Gen.* No. 8, pp. 3–4, citing opinions by former Attorneys General. Nealon, *op. cit.,* p. 251.

This can be taken as good law on matters relating to the constitutional powers of the President. It has not been judicially determined whether the congressional subpoena power extends to the statutory duties of department heads and other executive officers where the President has directed that the required information be withheld. If "executive officers" are "arms" of the President and "administrative officers" are "arms" of the Congress, as was held in the Humphrey case,[66] it would seem, applying the doctrine of the Myers case,[67] that when Congress in the exercise of its discretion confers powers upon *executive officers* such powers are subject to presidential rather than congressional supervision and control. These cases will need further judicial clarification. The line between executive and legislative power is not easily drawn in relation to a legal formula—it is rather a matter for compromise and adjustment in the political arena.

In dealing directly with the President, the congressional subpoena power is no greater certainly than is the subpoena power of the judiciary; and courts will not require the production of papers if, in the opinion of the Chief Executive, it would be contrary to the public interest to do so.[68] Mr. Chief Justice Marshall, in an unguarded

[66] *Humphrey's Executor v. United States,* 295 U.S. 602, 55 S. Ct. 869, 79 L. Ed. 1611 (1935).

[67] *Myers v. United States,* 272 U.S. 52, 47 S. Ct. 21, 71 L. Ed. 160 (1926). According to this case, it would seem that Congress cannot confer *conditional* powers upon the President without violating the principle of the separation of powers. Moreover, "The ordinary duties of officers prescribed by statute come under the general administrative control of the President by virtue of the general grant to him of the executive power, and he may properly supervise and guide their construction of the statutes under which they act in order to secure that unitary and uniform execution of the laws which Article 2 of the Constitution evidently contemplated in vesting general executive power in the President alone." 272 U.S. at 135, 47 S. Ct. at 31, 71 L. Ed. at 173.

[68] *Totten v. United States,* 92 U.S. 105, 23 L. Ed. 605 (1876); *Kilbourn v. Thompson,* 103 U.S. 168, 26 L. Ed. 377 (1880); *Vogel v. Cruaz,* 110 U.S. 311, 4 S. Ct. 12, 28 L. Ed. 158 (1884); *In re Quarles and Butler,* 158 U.S. 532, 15 S. Ct. 959, 39 L. Ed. 1080 (1895); *Boske v. Comingore,* 177 U.S. 459, 20 S. Ct. 701, 44 L. Ed. 846 (1900).

The Supreme Court has held that the head of an executive department may require his subordinates to decline to produce department records called for in a *subpoena duces tecum* in a judicial proceeding. However, the Court did not decide whether the department head could be compelled to disclose information in his department. *Boske v. Comingore,* 177 U.S. 459, 20 S. Ct. 701, 44 L. Ed. 846 (1900); *United States v. Ragen,* 340 U.S. 462, 71 S. Ct. 416, 95 L. Ed. 417 (1951). Said Mr. Justice Frankfurter in concurring opinion in the Ragen case: "To hold now that the Attorney General is empowered to forbid his subordinates, though within a court's jurisdiction, to produce documents and to hold later that the Attorney General himself cannot in any event be procedurally reached, would be to apply a fox-hunting theory of justice that ought to make Bentham turn in his grave." 71 S. Ct. at 422.

moment, issued a *subpoena duces tecum* for President Jefferson to produce a paper required by the Court in the Aaron Burr trial. But the President did not give the subpoena any notice beyond writing to the district attorney and stating emphatically that he did not propose to obey the summons. Thereupon Colonel Burr himself moved for compulsory process to compel the President to appear. This was a legitimate motion if the Court was right in holding the President amenable to subpoena. However, the Chief Justice obviously realized his error, for he took no further step to enforce his process.[69] The inability of the Supreme Court to enforce its process against the President was admitted in *Mississippi v. Johnson*[70] and *Stanton v. Georgia*.[71] The issue came to a dramatic head in *Ex Parte Merryman*.[72] Mr. Chief Justice Taney issued an attachment against General George Cadwalader, who was acting under orders of the President, for a contempt in refusing to produce the body of John Merryman according to the command of the writ of *habeas corpus*. In the marshal's return to the writ of attachment, he stated that he had not been permitted to enter the gate to Fort McHenry and so could not serve the writ as commanded. Whereupon the Chief Justice recorded a well-reasoned argument in support of the legality of his position but admitted that he was powerless to proceed further, beyond directing that a copy of the record and opinion in the case be sent to the President with this injunction: "It will then remain for that high officer, in fulfillment of his constitutional obligation to 'take care that the laws be faithfully executed,' to determine what measures he will take to cause the civil process of the United States to be respected and enforced."[73]

The issue was revived during the Senate inquiry into Senator McCarthy's charges of Communist influence in the Department of State when President Truman refused to turn over to the Senate the confidential loyalty files on the persons accused; and again during the General MacArthur investigation when General Bradley refused to disclose confidential conversations with the President, and the committee sustained the General by an 18 to 8 vote. While it is not likely that the Supreme Court will attempt to restrain improper congres-

---

[69] *Cf*. Argument by Attorney General Stanbery in *State of Mississippi v. Johnson,* 4 Wall. 475, 18 L. Ed. 437 (1867) ; David Robertson, *The Trial of Aaron Burr* (J. Cockcroft & Co., New York, 1875), pp. 180–82.

[70] 4 Wall. 475, 18 L. Ed. 437 (1867).

[71] 6 Wall. 50, 18 L. Ed. 721 (1867).

[72] *Taney's Reports,* 246 (C.C. Md., 1861), J. B. Thayer, *Cases in Constitutional Law* (George H. Kent, Cambridge, Mass., 1895), Vol. II, pp. 2361, 2373–74.

[73] Thayer, *op. cit.,* p. 2374.

sional investigations,[74] it is even less likely that that Court will give legal aid to such inquiries. Congress could, of course, resort to impeachment to enforce its process; but it is not conceivable that such drastic proceedings would avail for mere refusal to obey a congressional subpoena.

The Power to Resolve.—In addition to the legislative powers to create and to spend, Congress, or a group of Congressmen, can influence executive or administrative action through *resolutions,* expressing its opinion—and even demanding action therewith—on matters that lie within the constitutional discretion of the executive branch. For example, the House Republicans, on December 15, 1950, adopted "overwhelmingly" a resolution declaring that "It is completely obvious that Secretary Acheson and the State Department under his leadership have lost the confidence of the American people and cannot regain it," and calling on the President to replace the Secretary, to conduct "a thorough housecleaning in the State Department," and to make "changes in personnel and policies responsible for this lack of confidence." [75] The "resolvers" neglected to point out that the loss of "confidence of the American people" was largely of their own making—that they had long subjected the Department to an acrimonious barrage of criticism for the express purpose of destroying public confidence in its policies and its personnel. The campaign against the State Department was a frontal attack upon the foreign policy of the Administration, including actions by the United Nations and the use of American troops in Korea and Europe. Early in January, 1951, formal resolutions were introduced in Congress purporting to limit the President's constitutional powers as commander-in-chief of the army and navy: one by Representative Coudert forbidding the use of military funds for United States troops abroad without the consent of Congress, and another by Senator Wherry declaring that it is the "sense of the Senate" that United States troops should not be sent to Europe until "*the formulation of a policy by Congress.*"

In this case, the issue between the executive and legislative branches did not involve a declaration of war or the raising and equipping of armed forces—matters clearly within the competence of Congress. The controversy related to the carrying out of interna-

[74] Said Judge Prettyman in *Barsky v. United States,* 167 F. (2d) 241 (App. D.C., 1948), certiorari denied 334 U.S. 843 (1948) : "The remedy for unseemly conduct, if any, by committees of Congress is for Congress or the people . . . the courts have no authority to speak or act upon the conduct by the legislative branch so long as the bounds of power and pertinence are not exceeded."

[75] See report by Jack Steele, *New York Herald Tribune,* December 16, 1950.

tional obligations under the Constitution, laws, and treaties of the United States. When the Congress passed the United Nations Participation Act on December 20, 1945 [76] the obligations of the Charter of the United Nations became part of the law of the land. When the United Nations resolved to intervene in Korea, it became the duty of the President to "take care" that this resolution, in so far as it obligated the United States, "be faithfully executed." When the Senate approved the North Atlantic Treaty on July 21, 1949,[77] it pledged itself under Article 5 to "such action as it deems necessary, including the use of armed force, to restore and *maintain* the security of the North Atlantic area." This is a direction to the President to use such means as had been provided by law to fulfill these treaty obligations. The disposition of *existing* United States armed forces within the terms of this Treaty lies within the constitutional prerogative of the President. The Senate could have withheld its consent to the Treaty, and the Congress can repudiate its obligations thereunder by failing to provide the necessary "armed force"; but the Constitution and international law assume that the Chief Executive can and will use such means as are provided already by Congress.

These congressional resolutions clearly were intended to establish, as a constitutional rule, the power of Congress to dictate foreign policy and thus make the role of the President largely ministerial. Senator Taft obligingly offered "to sit down with the President or anyone else on the majority side to work out a constructive program which will have the consistent and unanimous support of the people." But the critics of the Administration's policy were hopelessly divided on the "proper" policy. "Confusion worse confounded" resulted at home and abroad, demonstrating the futility of managing foreign affairs from the public hustings. The conduct of foreign relations— the *federative* function, that is, "the executive in respect to things dependent on the law of nations," according to Locke and Montesquieu [78]—necessarily *belongs* to the head of state. The *initiative* lies

[76] *Public Law 264,* 79th Cong., 1st Sess.

[77] Ratified by the President on July 24, 1949, and proclaimed on August 24, 1949.

[78] "In every government there are three sorts of power: the legislative, the executive, in respect to things dependent on the law of nations, and the executive in regard to things that depend on the civil law.

"By virtue of the first, the prince or magistrate enacts temporary or perpetual laws, and amends or abrogates those that have been already enacted. By the second, he makes peace or war, sends or receives embassies, establishes the public security, and provides against invasion. By the third, he punishes crimes, or determines the disputes that arise between individuals. The latter we shall call the judiciary power, and the other simply the executive power of the state." Baron de Montesquieu, *The Spirit of the Laws,* trans. by Thomas Nugent (Hafner Publishing Co., New York, 1949), pp. 185–86.

with the President. "The President," said John Marshall, "is the sole organ of the nation in its external relations, and its sole representative with foreign nations." [79] The following observations by Mr. Justice Sutherland in the Curtiss-Wright Export Corp. case [80] is pertinent to the controversy here discussed:

> It is important to bear in mind that we are here dealing not alone with an authority vested in the President by an exertion of legislative power, but with such an authority plus the very delicate, plenary, and exclusive power of the President as the sole organ of the federal government in the field of international relations—a power which does not require as a basis for its exercise an act of Congress, ... It is quite apparent that if, in the maintenance of our international relations, embarrassment—perhaps serious embarrassment—is to be avoided and success for our aims achieved, congressional legislation . . . must often accord to the President a degree of discretion and freedom from statutory restriction which would not be admissible were domestic affairs alone involved. Moreover, he, not Congress, has the better opportunity of knowing the conditions which prevail in foreign countries, and especially is this true in time of war.[81]

The issue in the Truman-Congress controversy may be said to have been raised by the pro-French Republicans of 1793 when they charged that President Washington's Neutrality Proclamation of that year was an "usurpation by the President of authority granted to the Congress." To regularize Washington's procedure, Congress passed a neutrality act in June, 1794. The echo of this charge was heard in the Senate in 1951 when Senator Taft accused President Truman of usurping authority "in violation of the laws and the Constitution, when he sent troops to Korea." Senate opposition forced President Tyler to abandon his plan to give military aid to the Republic of Texas. When General Beauregard fired on Fort Sumter, President Lincoln, by wedding the "commander-in-chief" clause to the clause that makes it the duty of the President "to take care that the laws be faithfully executed,"

> . . . embodied the State militias into a volunteer army of 300,000 men, added 23,000 men to the Regular Army and 18,000 to the Navy, paid out two millions from unappropriated funds in the Treasury to persons unauthorized to receive it, closed the Post Office to "treasonable correspondence," subjected passengers to and from foreign coun-

---

[79] Quoted in *United States v. Curtiss-Wright Export Corp.*, 299 U.S. 304, 319, 57 S. Ct. 216, 220, 81 L. Ed. 255, 262 (1936).

[80] *Ibid.*

[81] 299 U.S. at 319–20, 57 S. Ct. at 221, 81 L. Ed. at 262–63.

tries to new passport regulations, proclaimed a blockade of the Southern ports, suspended the writ of habeas corpus in various places, caused the arrest of persons "who were represented to him" as being engaged in or contemplating "treasonable practices"—and all this for the most part without the least statutory authorization.[82]

Congress subsequently "legalized" these acts.

In 1890 Congress passed a resolution asking the President to negotiate an arbitration treaty with Great Britain. President Cleveland acted accordingly, but after a bitter partisan fight the Senate voted against ratification of the treaty in May, 1898.[83] In 1896 Congress passed a concurrent resolution extending the rights of belligerency to Cuban insurgents, and two years later, a powerful group in Congress tried to force United States intervention by pressing for a resolution calling for recognition of Cuban independence. President Cleveland refused to cooperate. But when the battleship, *U.S.S. Maine,* was blown up in Havana harbor on February 15, 1898, the "Congress, entirely out of hand, adopted joint resolutions, on April 17, calling upon Spain to withdraw from Cuba and authorizing the President to use our forces to compel her to do so." [84] President McKinley had recommended "forcible intervention, but recognition of neither belligerency nor independence." [85]

In 1917, before the United States declared war upon Germany, President Wilson asked Congress for authority to arm our merchant ships. A Senatorial filibuster killed the measure, but the President proceeded to arm the ships under his implied powers. Again in the 1920's, when Mexico threatened to confiscate American oil properties, the Senate, probably mindful of the occupation of Vera Cruz and the dispatching of General Pershing and his expeditionary force into Mexico by orders of President Wilson and without prior Congressional consent, adopted a resolution urging President Coolidge to arbitrate the threatened confiscation of American property by the Mexican Government; and Senator Frazier offered a resolution (pigeonholed by the Senate Foreign Relations Committee) which declared that "It is the sense of the Senate that the President should

[82] E. S. Corwin, *Total War and the Constitution* (Alfred A. Knopf, New York, 1947), p. 16.

[83] The Hay-Pauncefote Treaty of 1897. *Congressional Record* (1898), Vol. XIV, p. 279. For other resolutions of this nature see Samuel B. Crandall, *Treaties, their Making and Enforcement* (2d ed., John Byrne and Co., Washington, D.C., 1916), pp. 73–74.

[84] Carl R. Fish, *American Diplomacy* (Henry Holt & Co., New York, 1915), p. 416.

[85] *Ibid.*

not exercise the powers of Commander-in-Chief of the Army and Navy to send any of the armed forces of the nation into Mexico, or to mobilize troops on the Mexican border, or to assemble fighting units in waters adjacent to Mexico, while the Congress of the United States is not in session, but that if and when he contemplates such action, he shall immediately summon Congress in special session, and communicate to it the reason for such proposed military action." [86]

Resolutions of this nature are not legal directives, but the President may not feel free to ignore them if their sponsors succeed in marshalling public opinion behind them. They emphasize the essential unity of the war and foreign relations powers and the infirmity of the principle of the separation of powers when applied to these matters. The foreign relations and war powers relate to "external sovereignty" and they are, by implication and by their inherent nature, vested completely in the national government.[87] The constitutional references thereto prescribe areas for executive and legislative cooperation and not competition.

Congressional resolutions may strengthen as well as embarrass the President. For example, while the United States was pressing the United Nations for a declaration condemning Communist China as an aggressor in Korea, the House and Senate passed resolutions supporting the American position. The Senate resolutions not only declared Communist China an aggressor but opposed admitting the Communist China Government to membership in the United Nations.[88] Neither the American delegation nor the United Nations took any official notice of these resolutions, but member states were reminded that American aid—military, financial, and economic—depends upon the appropriation power of Congress.

[86] Roger Stuart, "Vague Constitution Sparks Foreign Policy Debate," *New York World-Telegram and Sun,* January 20, 1951, p. 15.

[87] See *United States v. Curtiss-Wright Export Corp.,* 299 U.S. at 317–18, 57 S. Ct. at 219, 81 L. Ed. at 261 (1936), where Mr. Justice Sutherland said: "A political society cannot endure without a supreme will somewhere. Sovereignty is never held in suspense. . . . It results that the investment of the Federal government with the powers of external sovereignty did not depend upon the affirmative grants of the Constitution. The powers to declare and wage war, to conclude peace, to make treaties, to maintain diplomatic relations with other sovereignties, if they had never been mentioned in the Constitution, would have vested in the Federal government as necessary concomitants of nationality."

[88] The Senate Resolutions, adopted on January 23, 1951, read: "Resolved, that it is the sense of the Senate that the United Nations should immediately declare Communist China an aggressor in Korea."

"Resolved that it is the sense of the Senate that the Communist China Government should not be admitted to membership in the United Nations as the representative of China." The House adopted a resolution similar to the former on January 19, 1951. See *New York Times,* January 24, 1951, pp. 1, 3.

Amendment and Rejection of Treaties by the Senate.—The Constitution gives the President power "by and with the advice and consent of the Senate, to make treaties." The Senate always has assumed that the power to advise and to consent includes the power to amend or reject. In support of broad Senatorial powers, it is urged that the power "to make treaties" involves both *negotiation* and *ratification* and that a treaty is not completely negotiated until the President and Senate are in agreement as to its terms. Therefore, the power to "consent" to the terms of a treaty is not limited to the acceptance or rejection thereof, but includes the right to amend or change. In short, the Senate stands "on a perfect equality with the President in the making of treaties." [89]

According to an analysis by Royden J. Dangerfield in 1933, the Senate had amended 152 treaties, divided into 44 political treaties, 45 treaties dealing with commercial and individual rights, 46 law enforcing treaties, and 17 multilateral treaties.[90] On a percentage basis, the Senate amended 21 per cent of all treaties to which it gave its advice and consent. Of the changes made (1) in the 44 political treaties, 13 were insignificant, 14 moderate, and 17 vital; (2) in the 45 treaties dealing with commercial and individual rights, 26 were insignificant, 12 moderate, and 7 vital; (3) in the 46 law enforcing treaties, 42 were insignificant, 2 moderate, and 2 vital; and (4) in the 17 multilateral treaties, 8 were insignificant, 7 moderate, 2 vital.

Many of the important treaties amended by the Senate were proposed by "strong" Presidents (Cleveland, Theodore Roosevelt, Wilson) and Secretaries of State that did not "get along" with the Senate (Hay, Marcy, Seward, Fish, and Bayard),[91] suggesting that in these cases the Senate was probably motivated as much by pique and a desire to assert its authority as by a sense of responsibility to the American people. Many of these amendments are in the nature of "strike" legislation: the President and the other contracting government are given the choice of accepting the changes or getting along without the treaty. Coming as they do after a treaty which, to all intents and purposes, has been negotiated, amendments are embarrassing to the President and are not calculated to promote international cooperation. The mischievous effect of this practice was touched upon by George Canning, the British Foreign Minister, in a

[89] Senator Henry Cabot Lodge, *Sen. Doc. No. 104*, 57th Cong., 1st Sess., p. 5.
[90] *In Defense of the Senate* (University of Oklahoma Press, Norman, Okla., 1933), chap. vi. *Cf.* Denna F. Fleming, *The Treaty Veto of the American Senate* (G. P. Putnam's Sons, New York, 1930), chap. iii.
[91] See Dangerfield, *op. cit.*, Tables on pp. 173, 174.

letter in 1824 to Richard Rush, the American Minister to England, when he said:

> The knowledge that the Constitution of the United States renders all their diplomatic compacts liable to this sort of revision undoubtedly precludes the possibility of taking exception at any particular instance in which that revision is exercised; but the repetition of such instances does not serve to reconcile to the practice the feelings of the other contracting party whose solemn ratification is thus rendered to no avail, and whose concessions in negotiation having been made (as all such concessions must be understood to be made) conditionally, are thus accepted as positive and absolute, while what may have been the stipulated price of those concessions is withdrawn.[92]

For whatever reasons, 51 of the treaties amended by the Senate were not ratified. Among these were some of the most important treaties negotiated by the United States, including 12 arbitration treaties.[93] These amendments admittedly handicapped the cause of arbitration in the United States. Mr. Dangerfield, while generally defending the Senate, accounts for the amendments to the 12 arbitration treaties as follows:

> (1) The Senate, ever jealous of its prerogatives, refused to permit the President to pledge in advance that the United States would arbitrate a particular type of dispute, unless each individual case was to be submitted to the Senate for approval. In debate the Senators cried the Treaties violated the Constitution of the United States, meaning the Treaties violated something even more sacred, namely, the constitution of the United States Senate, and the sacerdotal prerogatives of that body. (2) The relationship existing between the President and the Senate, and between the Secretary of State and the Senate, were important factors in the fight over the Hay Treaties. Roosevelt's exercise of the "big stick" methods in his relations with Congress helped line the Senate against him. (3) In the Taft-Knox Treaties the Roosevelt-Taft feud over the Presidency was a great factor in the fight. Roosevelt helped secure the defeat of an already tottering Administration. It is, of course, regrettable that factors such as these should affect foreign policy.[94]

In the exercise of its "consent" power, the Senate has vetoed a considerable number of treaties,[95] the most important of which were

[92] *American State Papers, Foreign Affairs,* Vol. V, p. 365; Fleming, *op. cit.,* pp. 41–42; Dangerfield, *op. cit.,* pp. 206–7.

[93] Ten Hay Treaties signed in 1904–5 and two Taft-Knox Treaties signed in 1911. President Roosevelt and President Taft refused to accept the Senate amendments.

[94] *Op. cit.,* p. 189. Of the 152 treaties amended by the Senate, 101 were later proclaimed. *Ibid.,* p. 152.

[95] According to Dangerfield, *op. cit.,* p. 215, the Senate had defeated 62 treaties submitted to it as of 1933. See also Fleming, *op. cit.,* chaps. iv–vii.

the Olney-Pauncefote Compulsory Arbitration Treaty signed with Great Britain on January 11, 1897, and defeated by the Senate on May 5, 1898, and the Treaty of Versailles signed on June 28, 1919, and rejected by the Senate on March 19, 1920. According to Allan Nevins, Secretary Olney gave several reasons for the defeat of the former treaty:

> One reason was that the Senate was steadily asserting itself as the dominant power in the Government; it was aggressively encroaching on the other branches, and when it dealt with a treaty, it insisted that "it must be either altogether defeated or so altered as to bear the unmistakable Senate stamp—and thus be the means both of humiliating the executive and of showing to the world the greatness of the Senate." Second among reasons for the defeat Olney placed the irritation of the silverite Senators against Great Britain as the most conspicuous and efficient supporter of the gold standard; and he quoted Mr. Lodge's violent speech on the subject as showing how this spirit had infested even the Eastern members. As a third explanation he mentioned the unfortunate behavior of Mr. Bayard, who was apparently "unable to understand that to conciliate one country by a process which simultaneously alienates another is not the best way to make the two countries friends." He believed that Bayard's continuous gush over England and the English, with its implied comparisons to the disadvantage of America, has caused a resentment which had not a little to do with the downfall of the treaty.[96]

Whether President Wilson or Senator Lodge was the villain in the play, as is variously claimed by the partisans of the two leaders, the fact remains that what a group of "wilful men" in the Senate did to the Treaty of Versailles was sheer vandalism. Even before the Treaty was negotiated on March 4, 1919, Senator Lodge's "Round Robin," signed by more than thirty Senators, served notice on the world that the Senate would defeat the Treaty if it contained the League Covenant. The Senate did not consider the Treaty on its merits—it debated President Wilson, not the Treaty.

> Senator Lodge declared privately that he had studied the mind of the President, had proposed reservations which he was confident the President would reject, and that he was prepared to add to them if it were necessary, his purpose being to have the League rejected, but to throw on the President the onus of its rejection.[97]

[96] Based on a letter from Secretary Olney to Henry White, May 8, 1897, in Allan Nevins, *Henry White* (Harper & Bros., New York, 1930), pp. 125–26; Dangerfield, *op. cit.,* p. 217.

[97] Charles P. Howland (ed.), *Survey of American Foreign Relations, 1928* (Yale University Press, New Haven, 1928), p. 272.

It is disturbing to contemplate that but for the vindictiveness of one Senator, the Treaty might have been ratified, and that other important treaties may have a similar fate.

It is difficult to measure the effect upon our foreign policy of the Senate's participation in the making of treaties. Statistically, the Senate "tampered" in the making of 234 treaties between 1788 and 1928, including in this group some of the most important treaties signed by the United States.[98] The Senate's attitude has kept the United States in the rear of the movement for the pacific settlement of international disputes; it has repeatedly blocked reciprocity treaties; and it may well be the judgment of history that but for the Senate the United States would have assumed her place of responsibility in the League of Nations and World War II might have been averted.

In giving its "advice and consent" to treaties, the Senate acts as a legislative body, not as a bipartisan advisory council. A legislative chamber is a public forum where partisanship, jealousy, personal ambition, sectionalism, and pressure politics have free play. Thus much of our foreign policy is shaped in a "house divided against itself," and a house where not infrequently foreign governments are the unhappy victims of domestic dissension. The Senate has unquestionably limited the scope of American foreign policy. It is largely responsible for the chief characteristic of that policy in the past—isolationism.[99]

Since a treaty is a part of the "supreme law of the land," and since most treaties require Congressional appropriations and other implementing legislation, treaties should be negotiated by the President and approved by a majority vote of both houses of Congress.[100] A mere one-third of the Senate should not have its present power to control and to shape our foreign policy.

[98] Dangerfield, *op. cit.,* pp. 256–57.

[99] In a stinging criticism of the Senate, Lindsay Rogers said in part: "The art of imagining dire possibilities if American isolation is abandoned was so successfully nurtured in the League debates of 1919 that more horrendous international goblins were seen in the World Court proposals. These fears did not come from transitory Senatorial nightmares; the phobia was more serious. It results in part from ignorance of foreign politics and international relations, and from inexpertise in discussing them." *The American Senate* (Alfred A. Knopf, New York, 1926), p. 74.

[100] *Cf.* Quincy Wright, *The Control of American Foreign Relations* (The Macmillan Co., New York, 1922), p. 368; J. W. Garner, *American Foreign Policies* (New York University Press, New York, 1928), p. 30.

TABLE OF CASES

Abrams v. Dougherty, 79, 145
Adams v. Nagle, 290
Adkins v. Children's Hospital, 280
Aetna Casualty & Surety Co. v. United States, 168
Aetna Life Insurance Co. v. Haworth, 291, 293
Agnew v. Board of Governors of Federal Reserve System, 242
Aichele v. People ex rel. Lowry, 231
Aircraft & Diesel Equipment Corp. v. Hirsch, 277, 278
Alabama v. United States, 95
Allen v. Holbrook et al., 204, 205
Allison & Co. v. United States, 303
Alton and Southern R. R. v. Commerce Commission, 78
Aluminum Co. of America v. Federal Trade Commission, 270
Amalgamated Utility Workers v. Consolidated Edison of New York, 123, 240
American Casualty Ins. Co. v. Tyler, 286
American Chain and Cable Co. v. Federal Trade Commission, 109
American Federation of Labor v. American Sash and Door Co., 324
American Federation of Labor v. National Labor Relations Board, 298, 299
American Insurance Co. v. Canter, 111
American Power and Light Co. v. Securities Exchange Commission, 53, 69, 142, 288, 299
American Print Works v. Lawrence, 197
American School of Magnetic Healing v. McAnnulty, 145, 228
American S. S. Co. v. Wickwire Spencer Steel Co., 107
Amy v. Barkholder, 191
Anderson v. Dunn, 331, 332
Aponang Mfg. Co. v. Bowles, 130
Archer v. Securities Exchange Commission, 147

Arizona Grocery Company v. Atchison, Topeka & Santa Fe Ry., 54, 104
Arrow-Hart Electric Co. v. Federal Trade Commission, 270
Arrow-Stevedore Co. v. Pillsbury, 141
Asbury Park v. Christmas, 226
Ashbacker Radio Corporation v. Federal Communications Commission, 317, 323
Ashland Coal & Ice Co. v. United States, 303
Ashwander et al. v. Tennessee Valley Authority et al., 280, 291
Associated Industries v. Industrial Welfare Commission, 67
Atchison v. Challiss, 198
Atchison, Topeka & Santa Fe R. R. v. United States, 99
Attorney General v. Sullivan, 217
Ayers, In re, 173, 174

Babcock v. Buffalo, 230
Backus v. United States, 107
Bailey Farm Dairy Co. v. Jones, 280
Bailey, People ex rel. v. Supervisors of Greene County, 225
Bakelite Corporation, Ex parte, 111, 113, 115, 117
Baker, Earl W. & Co. v. Maples, 79
Balch v. Glenn, 154
Baldwin, Trustees v. Scott County Milling Co., 105
Baltimore v. Fairfield Improvement Co., 230
Baltimore & Ohio R. R. Co. v. United States, 256
Barkan, Application of, 86
Barnett v. Hines, 296
Barringer & Co. v. United States, 262
Barry v. United States ex rel. Cunningham, 127, 330
Barsky v. United States, 330, 345
Bartlett, People ex rel. v. Dunne, 224
Bartlett v. Kane, 141
Bates v. Clark, 173
Bates v. United States, 167

Bates & Guild Co. v. Payne, 249, 285
Beardslee, State *ex rel.* v. Landes, Mayor *et al.*, 224
Beech Nut Packing Co. v. Federal Trade Commission, 270
Beeks v. Dickinson County, Iowa, 197
Beers v. Arkansas, 177
Beley v. Naphtali, 106
Benner v. Porter, 116
Bersoff v. Donaldson, 76
Bewick v. United States, 168
Bigby v. United States, 164
Bi-Metallic Investment Co. v. State Board of Equalization, 65, 81
Bingham v. Board of Education of Ogden City, Utah, 171, 181
Bingham's Trust v. Commissioner of Internal Revenue, 243, 244, 246
Bissey *et al.* v. City of Marion *et al.*, 228
Blackman *et al.* v. Stone *et al.*, 231
Blair v. Commissioner of Internal Revenue, 107
Blau v. United States, 335
Bluefield Waterworks & Improvement Co. v. Public Service Commission of West Virginia, 251
Bogardus v. Commissioner of Internal Revenue, 250
Bonner v. United States, 164
Boone County v. Jones, 207
Boske v. Comingore, 280, 343
Boutell v. Walling, 243
Bowles v. Batson, 277
Bowles v. Bonnie Bee Shop, 124
Bowles v. Chew, 131, 137
Bowles v. Curtis Candy Co., 131, 137
Bowles v. Glick Bros. Lumber Co., 280
Bowles v. Harrison, 124
Bowles v. Henry Lustig & Co. Inc., 124
Bowles v. Jos. Denuncio Fruit Co., 131, 137
Bowles v. Katz, 124
Bowles v. Lake Lucerne Plaza, Inc., 124
Bowles v. Mannie & Co., 244
Bowles v. Meyers, 298
Bowles v. Northwest Poultry & Dairy Products Co., 280
Bowles v. Sachnoff, 280
Bowles v. Weiss, 280
Bowles v. Willingham, 50, 67
Boyd v. United States, 133
Bradley v. Fisher, 194
Bradley Lumber Co. v. National Labor Relations Board, 294
Brady v. United States, 303

Bragg v. Weaver, 66
Brahy v. Federal Radio Commission, 78, 79
Bratton v. Chandler, 69
Bridgeman v. Ford, Bacon & Davis Co., 244
Bridges v. California, 129
Bridges v. Wixon, 81, 90, 262, 264
Brinkley v. Hassig, 118
Brooklyn Nat. Corp. v. Commissioner of Internal Revenue, 302
Brooks v. United States, 168
Brougham v. Blanton Mfg. Co., 105, 106, 107
Brown v. Huger, 173
Brown v. Walker, 134
Budd v. New York, 319
Buffalo v. Hawks, 80
Burkhardt v. United States, 167
Burnet v. Porter, 107
Burnett v. Douglas County, 220
Burns Baking Co. v. Bryan, 210
Burton-Sutton Oil Co. v. Commissioner of Internal Revenue, 246
Butte, Anaconda & Pacific Ry. Co. v. United States, 107, 237
Butterick Co. v. Federal Trade Commission, 270
Buttfield v. Stranahan, 49, 55

California Reduction Co. v. Sanitary Reduction Works, 153
Candado Stevedoring Co. v. Lowe, 150
Cardillo v. Liberty Mutual Co., 249, 256
Carl Zeiss, Inc. v. United States, 79
Carmichael v. Southern Coal & Coke Co., 23
Carroll v. Hueston *et al.*, 221
Carter v. Bowles, 50
Carter v. Carter Coal Co., 83
Cartwright v. Canode, 208
Cascade Co., Montana v. United States, 168
Case v. Bowles, 298
Case v. Michigan Liquor Control Commission, 91
Central of Georgia R. Co. v. Wright, 68
Central Pacific R. v. Gallatin, 39
Chamber of Commerce v. Federal Trade Commission, 80
Champion Coated Paper Co. v. Joint Committee on Printing, 292
Chandler v. Dix, 177
Chapman, *In re,* 331
Charles Hughes & Co., Inc. v. Securities and Exchange Commission, 146

Charles C. Wright v. Securities Exchange Commission, 147

Charles River Bridge v. Warren Bridge, 321

Chase v. Middleton, 230

Chenery Corp. v. Securities Exchange Commission, 242

Chicago, B. & Q. R. R. v. United States, 104

Chicago Board of Education v. Industrial Commission, 150

Chicago Great Western Ry., United States ex rel. v. Interstate Commerce Commission, 287

Chicago, Indianapolis & Louisville Ry. Co. v. Hackett, 202

Chicago, M. & St. P. Ry. Co. v. Minnesota, 67

Chicot County Drainage District v. Baxter State Bank, 203

Chiquita Mining Co. Ltd. v. Commissioner, 105

Chisholm v. Georgia, 168

Christian v. Atlantic & N. C. R. Co., 174

Churchill, Atty. Gen., State ex rel. v. Hay, 232

Cia. Mexicana De Gas v. Federal Power Commission, 91

Cities Service Gas Co. v. Federal Power Commission, 280

City of Chicago v. Chicago City Ry. Co., 232

City of Dallas et al. v. McElroy, 227

City of Fostoria v. State ex rel., 225

City of Newburgh v. Park Filling Station, 86

City of New Orleans v. Paine, 108

City of Orlando v. Pragg, 154

City of Yonkers v. United States, 96, 97, 257

Clark v. Industrial Commission, 150

Clark Distilling Co. v. West Maryland Railroad, 49

Clearfield Trust Co. v. United States, 159

Coe v. Aamons Fertilizer Works, 68

Cohens v. Virginia, 175

Colegrove et al. v. Green et al., 231, 294

Coles County v. Allison, 171

Colonial Beacon Oil Co., Inc. v. Finn, 226

Colorado-Wyoming Gas Co. v. Federal Power Commission, 263, 265

Columbia Broadcasting System Inc. v. United States, 282

Commissioners of Mason & Tazewell Special Drainage District v. Griffin et al., 221

Commonwealth v. Coyle, 183

Commonwealth v. Mathues, 206

Commonwealth v. Shortall, 192, 211

Commonwealth v. Sisson, 66

Commonwealth of Virginia, Ex parte, 170

Congress, People ex rel. v. Board of Education of City of Quincy, 217

Connecticut Mutual Life Insurance Co. v. Wood, 287

Consolidated Edison Co. v. National Labor Relations Board, 89, 90, 93, 259

Consolidated Mines of California v. Securities Exchange Commission, 86

Continental Petroleum Co. v. United States, 107

Cook v. Fortson, 231

Cook, People ex rel. v. Board of Police of the Metropolitan District of State of New York, 221

Cooper v. Anderson, 298

Cooper v. O'Connor, 183, 195, 196, 197

Cooper, Ex parte, 111

Copcutt, People ex rel. v. Board of Health of City of Yonkers, 153, 221

County Commissioners v. Jacksonville, 225

Covert v. State Board of Equalization, 144

Cox v. Cox, 86

Cox v. United States, 264, 297

Craig v. Harney, 129

Crary v. Porter, 298

Cream of Wheat Co. v. Federal Trade Commission, 270

Creek Nation v. United States, 232

Crowell v. Benson, 254, 256, 257

Crowell v. M'Fadon, 194

Culver Contracting Corp. v. Humphrey, 217

Cumberland T. & T. Co. v. State ex rel. Potter, Atty. Gen., 222

Cunningham v. Macon & Brunswick R. Co., 174, 175

Dahnke-Walker Milling Co. v. Bondurant, 203

Damutz v. Pinchbeck, Inc., 244

Dartmouth College v. Woodward, 321

Dation v. Ford Motors Co., 68

Davis & F. Mfg. Co. v. Los Angeles, 232

Davis, The, 161

Dean v. Brannon, 192

Debs, In re, 127

Decatur v. Paulding, 285
Degge v. Hitchcock, 222
DeGroot v. United States, 112, 163
Delaware & Hudson Co. v. United States, 236
Del Vecchio v. Bowers, 264
Dennis v. United States, 335
Department of State Highways v. Baker, 206
Derwort, State ex rel. v. Hummel, 232
Direct Realty Co. v. Porter, 87
Dobbins v. City of Los Angeles, 232
Dobson v. Commissioner of Internal Revenue, 107, 245, 246
Dodd et al. v. Francisco et al., 103
Doll, Ex parte, 127
Donnelly Garment Co. v. National Labor Relations Board, 89
Donnelly v. Roosevelt, 230
Dooley v. United States, 164
Dowler v. Johnson, 211
Dr. Johns Hopkins, Plaintiff in Error v. Clemson Agricultural College, 169, 202, 209
Draffen v. City of Paduah, 81
Drake, People ex rel. v. Regents of University of Michigan, 226
Duncan v. Kahanamoku, 300
Duncan Townsite Co. v. Lane, 226
Dunlap, United States ex rel. v. Black, 285
Dyment v. Board of Medical Examiners, 145
Dysart, State ex rel. v. Cameron, 127

Earl W. Baker & Co. v. Maples, 79
East Tennessee, V. & G. R. Co. v. Interstate Commerce Commission, 251
Eastern-Central Motor Carriers Ass'n. v. United States, 95
Eccles v. Peoples Bank, 283
Eddy v. Township of Lee, 222
Eisler v. Clark, 77
Ekern v. McGovern, 231
Ellis v. Interstate Commerce Commission, 136
Employers Group of Motor Freight Carriers v. National Labor Relations Board, 325
Endo, Ex parte, 144
Equality Building Ass'n, State ex rel. v. Brown, 206
Erskine v. Hohnboch, 192, 201
Ervien v. United States, 19
Erwich Bowling Center v. Canella, 289
Essgee Co. of China v. United States, 135

Estep v. United States, 234, 240, 258, 295, 296
Estes v. Union Terminal Co., 80
Evans v. Gore, 115

Fahey v. Malonee, 85, 143
Fairchild v. Hughes, 117
Fair Store Co. v. Board of Revision of Hamilton County, 280
Fairley v. City of Duluth et al., 229
Falbo v. United States, 279
Farmers Live Stock Commission v. United States, 118
Federal Communications Commission v. Pottsville Broadcasting Co., 56, 106, 215, 260
Federal Communications Commission v. WJR, The Goodwill Station, 101
Federal Communications Commission v. WOKO, Inc., 263, 288
Federal Crop Insurance Corporation v. Merrill, 162
Federal Housing Administration v. Burr, 162, 181
Federal Power Commission v. Edison Co., 236
Federal Power Commission v. Hope Natural Gas Co., 98, 280
Federal Power Commission v. Metropolitan Edison Co., 281
Federal Power Commission v. Pacific Power and Light Co., 275
Federal Radio Commission v. General Electric Co., 114
Federal Radio Commission v. Nelson Brothers Bond and Mortgage Co., 265
Federal Security Administrator v. Quaker Oats Co., 262
Federal Trade Commission v. Algona Lumber Co., 270
Federal Trade Commission v. American Tobacco Co., 136, 270, 333
Federal Trade Commission v. Baltimore Paint & Color Works, Inc., 125
Federal Trade Commission v. Beech Nut Packing Co., 270
Federal Trade Commission v. Cement Institute, 85, 93, 271
Federal Trade Commission v. Curtis Publishing Co., 270
Federal Trade Commission v. Fairyfoot Products Company, 125
Federal Trade Commission v. Gratz, 79, 270
Federal Trade Commission v. R. F. Keppel and Bro. Inc., 270

Pennsylvania Greyhound Lines Inc., 148, 259, 261

National Labor Relations Board v. Pittsburgh S. S. Co., 267

National Labor Relations Board v. Robbins Tire and Rubber Co., 266

National Labor Relations Board v. Sands Mfg. Co., 259

National Labor Relations Board v. Servel, Inc., 263

National Labor Relations Board v. T. W. Phillips Gas & Oil Co., 81

National Labor Relations Board v. Waterman Steamship Corp., 260, 261

National Licorice Co. v. National Labor Relations Board, 79

Natural Gas Pipeline Co. of America v. Slattery, 278

Neagle, *In re,* 176, 220, 326

Nebbia v. New York, 142

New Hampshire v. Louisiana, 176

New State Ice Co. v. Liebman, 323

Ng Fung Ho White, 219, 250, 254

Nicholl v. United States, 164

Nickey v. Mississippi, 66

Nicol v. Ames, 280

Noble v. Union River Logging R. R. Co., 103, 107

Nofire v. United States, 207

Norman v. Baltimore & Ohio R. Co., 158, 322

North American Co. v. Securities Exchange Commission, 142

North American Cold Storage Co. v. Chicago, 151, 153, 200

North Carolina v. United States, 94, 95

Northwestern Electric Co. v. Federal Power Commission, 290

Norton v. Shelby County, 201

Norton v. Warner Co., 263, 264

Norwegian Nitrogen Products Co. v. United States, 56, 68, 86

O'Brien v. Carney, 292

Oceanic Navigation Co. v. Stranahan, 139

O'Donoghue v. United States, 115, 116

Ohio Bell Telephone Co. v. Commission, 91

Ohio & Indiana R. Co. v. Commissioners, 225

Ohio Valley Water Co. v. Ben Avon Borough, 250, 255

Oklahoma v. United States Civil Service Commission, 245, 292

Oklahoma Natural Gas Co. v. Russell, 278

Oklahoma Operating Company v. Love, 54

Oklahoma Press Publishing Co. v. Walling, 131, 133, 136

Oklahoma-Texas Trust Co. v. Securities Exchange Commission, 145, 146

Old Colony Insurance Co. v. United States, 168

Old Colony Trust Company *et al.* v. Commissioner of Internal Revenue, 107, 113

O'Leary v. Brown-Pacific-Maxon, Inc., 268

Oliver v. The Mayor, 170, 207

Opp Cotton Mills, Inc. *et al.* v. Administrator of Wage and Hour Division of Department of Labor, 261

Order of Railway Conductors v. National Mediation Board, 298

Oregon v. Hitchcock, 157

Osborn v. Bank of the United States, 173, 291

O'Shields v. Caldwell, 206

Otis v. Watkins, 194

Pacific Coast Casualty Co. v. Pillsbury, 129

Pacific Ry. Commission, *In re,* 130, 291

Pacific States Box & Basket Co. v. White, 280

Pacific Telephone & Telegraph Co. v. Kuykendall, 278

Packard v. Voltz, 197

Packard Co. v. National Labor Relations Board, 257

Panama Refining Co. v. Ryan, 49, 71

Passavant v. United States, 141

Paulsen v. Portland, 69

Pearsell Butter Co. v. Federal Trade Commission, 270

Pearson v. Zehr, 191, 200

Pelham Hall Co., v. Hassett, 107

Penfield Co. of California v. Securities Exchange Commission, 132

Penfield Co. v. Securities Exchange Commission, 131

Pennekamp v. Florida, 129

Pennoyer v. McConnaughy, 174, 175

Pennsylvania Anthracite Mining Co. v. Anthracite Miners, 129

People v. Bissell, 226

People v. Broad, 154

People v. Common Council of Troy, 286

People v. Morton, *et al.*, 226
People v. Supervisors, 216
People v. Westbrook, 217
People *ex rel.* v. Fairchild, 217
People *ex rel.* v. Green, 225
People *ex rel.* v. Village of Oak Park, 225
People *ex rel.* Bailey v. Supervisors of Greene County, 225
People *ex. rel.* Bartlett v. Dunne, 224
People *ex rel.* Blair *et al.*, 217
People *ex rel.* Congress v. Board of Education of City of Quincy, 217
People *ex rel.* Cook v. Board of Police of the Metropolitan District of State of New York, 221
People *ex rel.* Copcutt v. Board of Health of City of Yonkers, 153, 221
People *ex rel.* Drainage Commissioners, 217
People *ex rel.* Drake v. Regents of University of Michigan, 226
People *ex rel.* Gas Light Co. v. Common Council of Syracuse, 226
People *ex rel.* Kellogg v. Schuyler, 191
People *ex rel.* Lodes v. Dep't of Health of City of New York, 101
People *ex rel.* Post v. Healy, State's Attorney, 217
People *ex rel.* Raster v. Healy, State's Attorney, 217
People *ex rel.* Reynolds v. Buffalo, 287
People *ex rel.* Semenoff v. Nagle, 220
People *ex rel.* Sheppard v. Illinois State Board of Dental Examiners, 224, 285
People *ex rel.* Sutherland v. Governor, 289
People *ex rel.* Tweed v. Liscomb, 218
People to use of State Board of Health v. McCoy, 102
Perkins v. Elg, 294
Perkins v. Lukens Steel Co., 292
Perry v. United States, 158, 159
Phelps Dodge Corp. v. National Labor Relations Board, 89, 148
Phillips v. Commissioner of Internal Revenue, 155
Piedmont & Northern Ry. v. United States, 274
Pierce, State *ex rel.* v. Slusher, 206
Pierce *et al.* v. Superior Court of Los Angeles County, 231
Pierson v. People *ex rel.* Walter, 287
Pike v. Megoun, 198
Pittsburgh etc. Railway v. Board of Public Works of West Virginia, 233

Pittsburgh C. C. & St. L. Ry. Co. v. Backus, 68, 81
Pittsburgh & West Virginia Ry. Co. v. Interstate Commerce Commission, 285
Plunkett v. Hamilton, 127
Plymouth Coal Co. v. Pennsylvania, 48, 55
Poindexter v. Greenhow, 173, 175, 233
Police Commissioners v. Wagner, 154
Pollock, *In re*, 106
Pooling Freights, *In re*, 135
Porter v. Granite State Packing Co., 124
Porter, Auditor v. Investors' Syndicate, 278, 279
Postum Cereal Co. v. California Fig Nut Co., 114, 117
Powers v. Bowles, 286
Prendergast v. New York Tel. Co., 278
Prentis v. Atlantic Coast Line Co., 39, 104, 279, 291
Proctor & Gamble Co. v. United States, 274
Prout v. Starr, 233
Publicker Industries, Inc. v. Anderson, 278
Putnam *et al.* v. Ickes *et al.*, 293

Q. R. S. Music Co. v. Federal Trade Commission, 270
Quarles and Butler, *In re*, 343

Radio Corporation of America v. United States, 295
Railroad Commission of Texas v. Rowan & Nichols Oil Co., 252, 321
Railroad Commissioners v. Columbia, N. & L. R. Co., 69
Randall v. United States, 144
Ranke v. Michigan Corporation & Securities Commission, 87
Reagan v. Farmers' Loan & Trust Co., 55, 233
Reconstruction Finance Corp. v. Denver & Rio Grande Western R. R., 92
Reconstruction Finance Corporation v. J. G. Menihan Corporation, 162
Reed v. Madden, 220
Regal Drug Co. v. Wardell, 139
Regal Knitwear Co. v. National Labor Relations Board, 125
Reilly v. Pinkus, 99
Republic Steel Corp. v. National Labor Relations Board, 148

Resources Corp. International v. Securities Exchange Commission, 146
Reynolds v. State Board of Equalization, 144
Rice v. Lavin, 192
Riverside Oil Co., United States *ex rel.* v. Hitchcock, 285
Roberts, Treasurer v. United States *ex rel.* Valentine, 224, 286
Robertson v. Sichel, 156, 211
Robinson, *Ex parte,* 127
Robinson v. Rohr, 191, 193, 211
Rochester Telephone Co. v. United States, 274, 275, 276
Rochin v. People of California, 133
Rogers v. Barker, 230
Rogers v. Carroll, 211
Roland Electric Co. v. Walling, 243
Rolston v. Missouri Fund Commissioners, 175
Roop, United States *ex rel.* v. Douglass, 103
Rose v. United States, 144
Rosenbaum v. Bauer, 224
Rosenthal v. State Board of Canvassers, 225
Rumsey Mfg. Co., *In re,* 149
Runkle v. United States, 42
Rusconi *et al.* v. United States, 168
Rusk v. United States, 279

Safeway Stores Inc. v. Brown, 224
Sager v. Parker, 88
St. Joseph Stock Yards Co. v. United States, 48, 212, 240, 248, 251, 252, 256
Samson v. United States, 168
Sanborn, *In re,* 112
Sanders v. Wilkins, 231
Sanford, *In re,* 127
Sawyer, *In re,* 232, 233
Scales v. Texas Liquor Control Board, 91
Schechter Poultry Corp. v. United States, 52, 71
Schenley Distillers Corp. v. United States, 299
Schermerhorn, J. B., Inc. v. Holloman, 279
Schmidt, *In re,* 91
Schneider v. Shepherd, 196
Scholnick v. Clark, 299
Schomig v. Keiser, 145
Schwing *et al.* v. Miles *et al.,* 174
Scott *et al.* v. Singleton, 228
Scottish Union & National Insurance Co. v. Herriot, 205

Screws v. United States, 172, 196, 280
Scripps-Howard Radio v. Federal Communications Commission, 239, 242, 295
Securities and Exchange Commission, *In re,* 86, 145
Securities and Exchange Commission v. Andrews, 235
Securities and Exchange Commission v. Central Illinois Securities Commission *et al.,* 261
Securities and Exchange Commission v. Chenery Corp., 95
Securities and Exchange Commission v. McGarry, 131
Securities and Exchange Commission v. Okin, 123
Securities and Exchange Commission v. Penfield Co. of California, 132
Segal and Smith, *In re,* 83
Semenoff, People *ex rel.* v. Nagle, 220
Shanley v. People, 217
Shannahan v. United States, 275
Shapiro v. United States, 136
Sheppard, People *ex rel.* v. Illinois State Board of Dental Examiners, 224, 285
Shigeru Fuji v. United States, 277
Siebold, *Ex parte,* 183, 218
Siegel, Jacob & Co. v. Federal Trade Commission, 264
Simpson v. Shepard, 53
Sinclair v. United States, 332
Sinking Fund Cases, 280
Siren, The, 156, 157
Skidmore v. Swift & Co., 243
Skinner & Eddy Corporation v. United States, 104
Smith v. Rackliffe, 177
Smith v. Reeves, 177
Smith v. United States, 95
Smyer v. United States, 211
Smyth v. United States, 158
Snyder v. Buck, 187
Social Security Board v. Nierotko, 149, 243, 250
South v. Peters, 231, 232
South Chicago Coal & Dock Co. v. Bassett, 263
South Dakota v. North Carolina, 176
Spalding v. Vilas, 195, 196
Sparrow, *In re,* 199, 290
Spaulding v. Douglas Aircraft Co., 51, 70
Spell v. United States, 167

Spokane Hotel Co. v. Younger, 67
Spriggs v. Clark, 231
Springer v. Philippine Islands, 47, 48
Standard Bitulithic Co., *In re*, 221
Standard Nut Margarine Co. v. Mellon, 198
Standard Oil Co. v. Missouri, 217
Standard Oil Co. v. United States, 56, 303
Stanton v. Georgia, 344
Stark v. Wickard, 234, 238, 295
State v. Board of Commissioners, 87
State v. Carroll, 171, 204, 207
State v. Chase, 226
State v. Dierberger, 171
State v. Drew, 226
State v. Evans, 217
State v. Gardner, 170, 207, 208
State v. Supervisors, 207
State v. Topeka, 217
State Board of Health, People to use of v. McCoy, 102
State Board of Milk Control, State *ex rel.* v. Newark Milk Co., 65
State Corporation Commission of Kansas v. Wichita Gas Co., 104
State of Kansas *ex rel*. A. T. & S. F. R. Co. v. Board of County Commissioners, 224
State Railroad Commission v. People *ex rel.*, 217
State *ex parte* v. O'Driscoll, 189
State *ex rel*. Beardslee v. Landes, Mayor *et al.*, 224
State *ex rel*. Churchill, Attorney General v. Hay, 232
State *ex rel*. Derwort v. Hummel, 232
State *ex rel*. Dysart v. Cameron, 127
State *ex rel*. Equality Building Ass'n v. Brown, 206
State *ex rel*. Harrison v. Perry, 217
State *ex rel*. Hawes v. Brewer, 224
State *ex rel*. Johnson, Attorney General v. Baker, 206
State *ex rel*. Loomis v. Dahlem, 232
State *ex rel*. McIlhany, etc. v. Stewart *et al.*, 217
State *ex rel*. Milwaukee Medical College v. Chittenden, 221
State *ex rel*. Pierce v. Slusher, 206
State *ex rel*. State Board of Milk Control v. Newark Milk Co., 65
Staten Island Edison Corp v. Maltbie, 251
Stefanelli v. Minard, 133
Sterling v. Constantine, 231

Steward Machine Co. v. Davis, 23, 322
Stewart Dry Goods Co. v. Lewis *et al.*, 229
Stockdale v. Industrial Commission, 150
Stone v. United States, 107
Stuart v. Palmer, 68
Summers, *In re*, 293
Sumner v. Beeler, 202
Sunshine Anthracite Coal Co. v. Adkins, 44, 54, 84
Superior Packing Co. v. Porter, 244
Supervisors v. United States, 287
Swaczyk v. United States, 279
Swayne & Hoyt, Ltd. v. United States, 259
Swift & Co. v. Federal Trade Commission, 270
Switchmen's Union of N. A. v. National Mediation Board, 236, 237, 239, 298

Tait, Collector v. Western Maryland Ry., 107
Takeo Tadano v. Manney, 82
Tang Tun v. Edsell, 140, 290
Taylor *et al.* v. Louisville & Nashville R. Co., 233
Taylor v. Bowles, 298
Tennessee v. Davis, 176
Terrace *et al.* v. Thompson, 228
Testa v. Katt, 125
Texas & Pacific Ry. Co. v. Abilene Cotton Oil Co., 275
Thompson v. Kimbrough, 230
Tiaco v. Forbes, 140
Tidal Osage Co. v. West, 285
Tisi, United States *ex rel*. v. Tod, 85
Toledo, P. & W. R. R. v. Stover, 97
Tonningsen v. Commissioner of Internal Revenue, 107
Toombs v. Citizens Bank, 69
Totten v. United States, 343
Tracy v. Swartout, 192, 201
Trade Mark Cases, 280
Trinler, United States *ex rel*. v. Carusi, 299
Tweed, People *ex rel*. v. Liscomb, 218
Twibill v. Federal Shipbuilding Co., 91

Unemployment Commission of Alaska v. Aragan, 244
Unger v. United States, 295
Union Bridge Co. v. United States, 56
United Employees Association v. National Labor Relations Board, 282
United Fruit Co. v. Pillsbury, 107

United States v. Abilene and So. Ry. Co., 91, 279

United States v. Aetna Casualty & Surety Co., 167, 168

United States v. Alabama, 157

United States v. Alire, 164

United States v. American Sheet & Tin Plate Co., 107

United States v. American Union Transport, 244

United States v. Armour, 135

United States v. Baltimore and Ohio R. Co., 67, 71, 94

United States v. Bryan, 330

United States v. Buntin, 185

United States v. Butler, 17, 25, 26, 27, 214, 231, 236, 267, 319

United States v. Carolina Carriers Corp., 96

United States v. Chicago, M., St. P. & P. R. Co., 95

United States v. Classic, 172, 184, 185

United States v. Coe, 111

United States v. Corrick, 274

United States v. Curtiss-Wright Export Corporation, 347, 349

United States v. DeLorenzo, 332

United States v. Eliason, 42

United States v. Esnault-Pelterie, 163, 248

United States v. Euzicka, 277

United States v. George F. Fish, Inc., 298

United States v. Germaine, 183, 189

United States v. Great Falls Mfg. Co., 164

United States v. Great Northern R. Co., 107

United States v. Griffin, 273, 274, 299

United States v. Grimaud, 35, 47, 55

United States v. Hartwell, 287

United States v. Hoffman, 217

United States v. Idaho, 248

United States v. Illinois Central R. Co., 67, 266

United States v. Interstate Commerce Commission, 303

United States v. Johnson, 330

United States v. Jones, 112, 163, 164, 273

United States v. Joseph A. Holpuch Co., 277

United States v. Josephson, 335

United States v. Kaufman, 165

United States v. LaFranca, 138

United States v. Lee, 161

United States v. Lovett, 328, 337

United States v. Maher, 275

United States v. Michigan, 177

United States v. Miller, 299

United States v. Morgan, 100, 214, 324

United States v. Morton Salt Co., 124, 317

United States v. North Carolina, 177

United States v. Pierce Auto Freight Lines, 92, 99, 242

United States v. Pink, 231

United States v. Ragen, 343

United States v. Rosenberg, 50

United States v. Shaughnessy, 78, 86, 140, 231, 340

United States v. Sherwood, 112, 161

United States v. Shreveport Grain Co., 48, 56, 287

United States v. South Carolina State Highway Dept., 168

United States v. Standard Education Society, 123

United States v. Stone, 185

United States v. Swift, 135

United States v. Tantleff, 298

United States v. Texas, 177

United States v. Thomas, 189

United States v. Throckmorton, 103

United States v. Todd, 140

United States v. Trierweiler, 185

United States v. Wabash R. R., 263

United States v. Watkins, 77, 231

United States v. West Virginia, 291, 293

United States v. White, 136

United States v. Willard Tablet Co., 105, 107

United States v. Williams, 187

United States v. Wood, 277

United States v. Yount, 64

United States Electrical Motors, Inc. v. Jones, 302

United States Fidelity & Guaranty Co. v. Samuels, 192

United States ex rel. Chicago Great Western Railroad v. Interstate Commerce Commission, 287

United States ex rel. Dunlap v. Black, 285

United States ex rel. Girard Trust Co. v. Helvering, 226

United States ex rel. Greathouse v. Dern, 226

United States ex rel. Lewis v. Boutwell, 225

United States ex rel. Louisville Cement Co. v. Interstate Commerce Commission, 285

United States *ex rel.* Mason v. Hunt, 218

United States *ex rel.* McBride v. Schurz, 215

United States *ex rel.* Riverside Oil Co. v. Hitchcock, 285

United States *ex rel.* Roop v. Douglass, 103

United States *ex rel.* Strachey v. Reimer, 107

United States *ex rel.* Tisi v. Tod, 85

United States *ex rel.* Trinler v. Carusi, 299

United States, *In re,* 77

Universal Camera Corp. v. National Labor Relations Board, 267, 268

Urate v. United States, 165

Urquhart v. Ogdensburg, 198

Utah v. Candland, 206

Utley v. St. Petersburg, 265

Vajtauer v. Commissioner of Immigration, 90, 290

Valentine v. Englewood, 197

Van Sant v. American Express Co., 199

Varney v. Warehime, 52

Victor, *Ex parte,* 128

Virginia, *Ex parte,* 193

Virginia v. West Virginia, 187

Virginia Electric Co. v. National Labor Relations Board, 149

Vivaudou, Inc. v. Federal Trade Commission, 270

Vogel v. Corporation Commission, 129

Vogel v. Cruaz, 343

Von Knorr v. Miles, 143

Waddell v. United States, 107

Wales v. Whitney, 218

Wallace v. Hines, 278

Wallace Corporation v. National Labor Relations Board, 105

Walling v. Detweiler Brothers, 131

Walsh v. LaGuardia, 224

Ward v. Keenan, 277

Warner Valley Stock Co. v. Smith, 228

Washington, Virginia and Maryland Coach Co. v. National Labor Relations Board, 259

Wasserman v. Kenosha, 194, 195

Watkins, *Ex parte,* 218

Watson Bros. Transportation Co., Inc. v. United States, 280

Wayman v. Southard, 36, 46

West v. Standard Oil Co., 106

Western Maid, The, 156

Western Union Telegraph Co. v. Industrial Commission of Minnesota, 67

Western Union Telegraph Co. v. State of Indiana *ex rel.* Hammond Elevator Co., *et al.,* 224

Wham v. United States, 168

Wheeler v. Patterson, 197

Wheeler v. United States, 135

Whitbeck v. Common Council of Hudson, 222

White v. Tennessee Valley Authority, 277

White v. United States, 168

White, Collector, *et al.* v. Berry, 232

Wilbrecht v. Babcock, 197, 290

Wilbur v. United States, 108, 226, 285

Wilcox, H. F. Oil & Gas Co. v. Walker, 80

Wilkes v. Dinsman, 194

Williams v. United States, 42, 111, 112, 172

Williams v. Weaver, 194

Willing v. Chicago Auditorium Association, 117

Wilson v. Bowers, 228

Wilson v. Eureka City, 285

Wilson v. Mayor, 195

Wilson v. United States, 135, 136, 137

Wingate, Surrogate v. Flynn, Sec. of State, 295

Wolf v. People of the State of Colorado, 133, 186

Wong So Wan, *Ex parte,* 77

Wong Wing v. United States, 139

Wong Yang Sung v. Clark, 76

Wong Yang Sung v. McGrath, 76, 77, 106, 122, 218, 308

Wood v. Broom, 231

Woods v. Cloyd W. Miller Co., 51, 52

Woodworth v. Kales, 104

Woolsey v. Best, 219

Work v. United States *ex rel.* Rives, 224

Wright, Charles C. v. Securities Exchange Commission, 147

Wuchter v. Pizzuti, 68

Yakus v. United States, 50, 298

Yamashita, *In re,* 300

Yamataya, Kaoru v. Fisher, 69

Yanish v. Wixon, 76

Yaselli v. Goff, 195

Yorkshore Insurance Co. v. United States, 168

Young, *Ex parte,* 209

Zeiss, Carl, Inc. v. United States, 79

INDEX OF NAMES

Abbotson, Martin, 9
Acheson, Dean, 328
Adams, John, 34
Allen, C. K., 9
Appleby, P. H., 11

Baikie, E. J., 16, 24
Beck, J. M., 8
Berdahl, C. A., 325
Berger, R., 277
Bishop, H. M., 320
Bishop, J. P., 171, 183
Bitterman, H. J., 16
Blachly, F. F., 60, 63, 121, 269, 291, 307, 311
Black, Hugo, 331
Blackstone, William, 128, 213
Bondy, William, 39, 46
Bontecou, Eleanor, 46
Borchard, E. M., 156, 180, 293
Bradley, O. N., 338, 339
Brady, R. A., 15
Bratter, H., 9
Brown, Nona, 7
Bular, D. C., 120
Butt, A., 342
Byrnes, J. F., 321

Caldwell, L. G., 120
Callahan, J. P., 307
Canning, George, 350–51
Carr, C. T., 46
Cole, T., 9
Comer, J. P., 46
Commager, H. S., 9
Cooley, T. M., 68, 202
Cooper, R. M., 248
Corwin, E. S., 16, 57, 58, 210, 305, 318, 319, 320, 325, 348
Cox, E. E., 337
Crandall, S. B., 348
Crocker, G. N., 201
Cushman, R. E., 320

Dangerfield, R. J., 59, 350, 351, 353
David, L. T., 196, 201

Davis, K. C., 39
de Secondat, Charles, 306
Dicey, A. V. E., 212
Dickinson, John, 8, 37, 110, 212, 245, 284
Dies, Martin, 336
Dimock, M. E., 8, 329
Dixon, F. M., 9
Duff, P. W., 35, 46
Duguit, Leon, 8, 37

Eberling, Earnest, 329
Edmunds, S. E., 306
Elson, Peter, 31

Fairlie, J. A., 37
Fay, G. M., 329
Field, O. P., 201
Finer, Herman, 38
Fish, C. R., 348
Fleming, D. F., 59, 350
Fly, J. L., 337
Flynn, R. J., 167
Frank, Jerome, 322
Frankfurter, Felix, 6, 11, 46, 330
Friedrich, C. J., 8, 9

Galloway, G. B., 329
Garner, J. W., 181, 353
Gellhorn, Walter, 63, 101, 141, 142, 150, 161, 182, 183, 216, 340
Gettell, R. G., 34, 38
Gooch, R. K., 38
Goodnow, Frank, 18, 38, 190
Gose, Jack, 329
Gray, J. C., 313, 318
Green, Frederick, 40
Gregory, N. K., 104
Griswold, E. N., 104

Hamilton, Alexander, 36
Handler, Milton, 270–71
Hart, James, 8, 205, 246, 259
Hendel, Samuel, 320
Hewart, Gordon, 8
Hibbard, B. H., 19, 30
Hinds, A. C., 332

369

Hoar, G. F., 59
Holtzoff, Alexander, 165
Hood, A. A., 9
Howland, C. P., 352
Hughes, C. E., 320
Hulen, R. M., 167
Hyde, H. K., 8

Jackson, R. H., 109, 315
Jaffe, L. L., 120, 307
Jaretzki, Alfred, Jr., 121
Jefferson, Thomas, 326
Jessup, Philip, 334

Key, V. O., 16
Kiplinger, W. M., 9
Kirkham, F. R., 291
Kluttz, J., 9
Krock, Arthur, 341

Landis, J. M., 44, 46, 71, 116, 128, 146,
 147, 307, 311, 314, 315, 333
Langeluttig, Albert, 136
Laski, Harold, 8, 9
Lawrence, David, 329
Leigh, R. D., 337
Lilienthal, D. E., 130
Lincoln, Abraham, 326
Lippman, Walter, 329
Locke, John, 3, 33, 38
Lodge, H. C., 350
Ludlow, Louis, 9

MacArthur, Douglas, 337, 339
MacDonald, A. F., 16
Madison, James, 33, 34
Maguire, J. M., 156
Marshall, G. C., 338
Marx, F. M., 9, 14
Mason, A. T., 9
McAllister, B. P., 235
McFarland, Carl, 247, 271, 284
McGeary, M. N., 329
McGuire, O. R., 119, 120, 306, 307
Meader, G., 329
Merriam, C. E., 34
Mill, J. S., 330
Mitchell, P. A., 327
Montesquieu, Baron de, 33, 346
Moore, R. J., 201
Morgan, G. D., 329
Morgan, J. H., 182

Nathanson, N. L., 72
Nealon, Rita, 326

Nelles, W., 128
Nevins, Allan, 352
Nutting, C. B., 178

Oatman, Miriam, 60, 63, 269, 291, 307,
 311
Oliphant, H., 293
O'Mahoney, J. C., 9
Outland, G. E., 9

Paine, Thomas, 38
Parker, Reginald, 103, 129
Paul, R. E., 246
Phelps, E. J., 318
Pinney, Harvey, 8
Potts, C. S., 128, 333
Pound, Roscoe, 212, 309, 312
Powell, T. R., 37

Rapacz, M. P., 201, 208
Richardson, J. D., 341
Robertson, David, 344
Robertson, Reynolds, 291
Robson, W. A., 269
Rogers, Lindsey, 353
Roosevelt, F. D., 315, 316
Roosevelt, Theodore, 326, 342
Root, Elihu, 304
Rosenberry, M. B., 8, 45
Rush, Richard, 351

Schenck, C. N., 161
Schwartz, Bernard, 65, 76, 77
Sears, K. C., 220
Sellers, Ashley, 121
Shopflocker, E. H., 104, 124
Small, N. J., 326
Smith, E. S., 100
Southeimer, Morton, 322
Stason, E. B., 9
Steele, Jack, 345
Story, Joseph, 156
Stuart, Roger, 349
Studenski, Paul, 16, 24
Sullivan, L., 9
Summers, H. W., 9

Taft, W. H., 326, 327
Thomas, D. Y., 190
Thomas, J. P., 334
Thomsen, R. C., 167
Tresolini, R. J., 129
Trussell, C. P., 341
Tucker, J. R., 318
Tuttrup, R. R., 101
Twiss, B. R., 317

Vanderbilt, A. T., 72, 144, 159, 247, 266, 284, 297, 321, 325
von Bauer, F. T., 104

Warner, S. B., 196
Warren, George, 72
Whalen, R. G., 15
White, Howard, 58
White, L. E., 45

White, W. S., 334
Whiteside, H. E., 35, 46
Whitman, Howard, 322
Willoughby, W. F., 36, 41
Willoughby, W. W., 41, 189
Wilson, James, 34
Wilson, Woodrow, 210
Wiltse, C. M., 9
Wright, Quincy, 353

INDEX OF SUBJECTS

Adjudication
  definition, 62
  procedural due process, 63
  statutory procedural requirements, 74–78
Administration
  federal bureaucracy, 6
  place in constitutional scheme, 33
  public vs. private, 10–11
Administrative Action
  See also *Administrative Procedure*
  adjudication, 62
  criticism of, 304–14
  discretionary action, 283
  enforcement of, 123
  final action reviewable, 281
  forms of, 60
  investigating power, 126
  legislation, 60
  rule making, 60
Administrative Adjudication
  See also *Adjudication; Administrative Procedure; Findings*
  must rest on evidence in record, 91
Administrative Court
  See also *Federal Administrative Court*
  proposals for, 118–20
Administrative Legislation
  adjudicatory procedure, 73
  administrative procedure, 73
  definition, 61
  discretionary procedure, 72
  hearing prior to action not required, 65, 70
  judicial review of, 269
  legislative and judicial action distinguished, 65–70
  publication, 73
  statutory procedural requirements, 70–74
Administrative Power
  not distinguishable from executive power, 36, 40
Administrative Procedure
  adjudication, 62
  hearing, 81

notice, 78
notice and hearing as due process, 63
rehearings, 98
res judicata, 103
right to cross examination, 99
rule making, 60
sanctions, 137
statutory requirements, 70–78
Administrative Procedure Act
  a lawyer's law, 121
  adjudication, 74
  hearing officers, 75
  order defined, 62
  rule defined, 61
Administrative Process, 60
  See also *Administrative Action; Administrative Procedure*
Administrative Rule Making
  See *Rule Making*
Administrative Sanctions
  See also *Sanctions*
  banking laws, under, 142
  civil not penal, in law, 138–39
  immigration laws, under, 139
  labor laws, under, 47
  penal in nature, 139–50
  public service laws, under, 141
  revenue laws, under, 141
  revocation of licenses, 144
  war powers, in exercise of, 143
Administrative Tribunals, 106, 117
  combine legislative, executive, and judicial powers, 118
  no contempt power, 127
  objective differs from that of judicial courts, 110
Administrative Validity
  resumption of, 279
Aliens, 139
  administrative exclusion of, 78, 86–87

Bias
  See *Hearing*
Big Government
  democracy, effect on, 32

Bureaucracy
"administrative lawlessness?" 8–13
federal, 6
indictment of, 12
bureaucrat not responsive to public
criticism, 12
hierarchy a loose federation, 13
leads to managed economy, 14
results in red tape, 14
meaning of, 8–10

Certiorari
annuls, does not prohibit, 221
discretionary writ, 220
will issue to review only judicial administrative action, 221
Congressional Control of Administration
amendment and rejection of treaties,
350
Congress source of administrative
power, 325
investigating power, 329
power to resolve, 345–50
spending power, 327
Constitutional Courts
created under Article III of Constitution, 110–11
exercise judicial power only, 111
Contempt
administrative in nature, 128
federal agencies may not exercise, 127
Court of Claims, 162
legislative court, 112
Court of Customs and Patent Appeals
legislative court, 113
Courts
administrative tribunals, 117
categories, 117
Claims, 112
classification, 110
constitutional, 110–11, 117
Customs, 112
Customs Appeals, 113
District of Columbia, 113–16
legislative, 110–11, 117
Tax, 113
Criminal Liability, 183
Cross Examination
right to, 99
Custodial Responsibility, 188
Customs Court
legislative court, 112–13

De Facto Doctrine, 207
Declaratory Orders, 150

Delegation of Powers
administrative absolutism, 306
doctrine of nondelegation, 45
only quasi power may be delegated,
48–50
Direct Federal Aid, 25
Discretionary Action
liability for, 193
District of Columbia Courts
constitutional courts, 113–16
Due Process
notice and hearing, 63
refusal to hear evidence not due process, 89

Evidence
deciding officer to hear, 87
duty to hear, 87–88
flexible procedure, 92
hearsay, 90–91
improper admission, 90
judicial notice of facts, 92
must appear in record, 91
refusal to hear not due process, 89
Executive Justice, 322
Exhaustion of Administrative Remedies
applies to questions of law and fact,
278

Federal Administrative Court
proposals for, 118–20
Federal Aid, 25
See *Federal Direct Aid; Federal
Grants-in-Aid*
Federal Declaratory Judgment Act, 293
Federal Direct Aid
agriculture, to, 26
business enterprises, through, 30
Old-Age Reserve Account, 29
subsidies to private business, 31
veterans, to, 28
workers, to, 28
Federal Grants-in-Aid
conditional grants, 22–28
education, to, 18
effect on States, 24
grants to States, 22
highway construction, for, 19
social field, 20
Federal Public Health Service, 21
Federal Security Agency, 21
Federal Tort Claims Act
limited liability, 165
strictly construed, 167
subrogees, rights of, 167

Federal Welfare Government
grants-in-aid, 16–28
Findings
based on evidence of record, 94
jurisdictional, 96
required for review, 95
shall set forth criteria which guide
agency, 98

General Welfare
direct aid, 25
grants-in-aid, 16
meaning of, 16–17
Government by Agency
consolidation of functions, 304
Government by Law Suit, 314–22

Habeas Corpus
not a writ of error, 218
used primarily to vindicate private
rights, 218
Hearing
concentration of functions not bias, 85
duty to hear evidence, 87
findings, 94
general prerequisites, 81
impartial forum, 83
informal, 81
prejudgment not bias, 84
preliminary investigation distinguished, 86
requisite fundamentals, 82
tentative reports, 93
when impractical, 86
Hoover Commission
bureaucracy, on, 7, 13
government business enterprises, on,
30
grants-in-aid, on, 25

Immigration, 139
hearing, 76
Immunity Acts, 134–35
corporate officers not immune, 135–36
corporations not immune, 134–35
from prosecution, not from testifying,
133
Impeachment, 189
Injunction
equity concerned with civil not political rights, 230–33
ex parte restraining orders, temporary
or interlocutory, and permanent, 226
increasingly invoked to aid or restrain
police power, 229–30
lies to prevent irreparable injury, 227

mandatory injunction and mandamus
distinguished, 227
used widely against administrative action, 227
Investigating Power
abuse of, 333–34, 336–40
Administrative Procedure Act, 136
contempt power, 127–29
immunity of witnesses, 133

Judicial Action
legislative action distinguished, 64
Judicial Review
See also *Judicial Writs*
abuse of discretion, 289
administrative discretion, 283
administrative interpretation of statute
reviewable, 286
basis for, 212
cases and controversies, 290, 314
circumstantial facts, 246
constitutional fact, 250
constitutional limitations of, 290
decisions of military tribunals, 300
exhaustion of administrative remedies,
276
Federal Declaratory Judgment Act,
293
final administrative action reviewable,
281
government by lawsuit, 314–22
instruments of control, 215
jurisdictional fact, 253, 256–57
legislative standards, 269
licensing, 288
limitations of, 274
mixed questions of law and fact, 248,
249
negative order doctrine, 274–76
parties with standing in court, 292
presumption of administrative validity,
279
primary jurisdiction doctrine, 276
questions of law, 240
questions of law vs. questions of fact,
245
rule making, 269
statutory limitations on, 295–304
substantial evidence rule, 258
supremacy of law as basis of, 212
Tax Court, 301
Judicial Writs
See also *Judicial Review*
certiorari, 220
habeas corpus, 218
injunction, 226

instruments of control, 215
mandamus, 223
prohibition, 216
quo warranto, 217
Justice
executive vs. judicial, 322

Labor Relations, 147, 148
Legislation
See *Rule Making*
judicial action distinguished, 64
rate making, 67
Legislative Courts
created in exertion of a delegated
power, 111
may exercise other than judicial
power, 111
Liability
official, 182
Licenses
granting of, 101
"privilege" and "property" categories,
101
revocation of, 101, 144
Licensing
judicialized procedure required, 102

Mandamus
alternative or peremptory, 223
discretionary writ, 225
governed by "rule of diversity," 223
lies to enforce ministerial acts only,
224
will not lie to control discretion, 285
Ministerial Acts
liability for, 191
proceeding a personal action, 225

Negative Order Doctrine, 274
Notice
assessment proceedings, 80
by publication, 80
notice and pleading, 78
preciseness of, 78–79
tax proceedings, 80
to a class, 80
what constitutes, 78
Notice and Hearing
as due process, 63
legislative and judicial action distinguished, 64
statutory requirements—rule making,
70
when implied, 69

Official Liability, 182
acts of subordinates, 211
acts under unconstitutional statute, 201
criminal, 183
custodial, 188
de facto doctrine, 207
discretionary acts, 193
impeachment, 189
liability to public, 183
ministerial acts, 191
presumption of validity rule, 205
ultra vires acts, 200
void *ab initio* doctrine, 201

Primary Jurisdiction Doctrine, 276, 277
Prohibition
does not lie to prevent administrative
acts, 216
Public Service, 141

Quasi Power
quasi power doctrine a fiction, 55–58
Quo Warranto
civil remedy, 217
generally not available to protect private rights, 217

Rehearings, 98
Reports
tentative, 93–94
Res Judicata, 103–9
applicable to administrative adjudication only, 104
continuing jurisdiction, 104–6
continuing jurisdiction ceases when
court takes jurisdiction of an order,
108
continuing jurisdiction in public interest, 105
continuing jurisdiction when private
rights are not affected, 106
immigration and naturalization service, applicable to, 106
not applicable to decisions of Labor
Board, 105
tax decisions, applicable to, 107
Rule of Law, 109, 182
doctrine of state immunity, 156
official liability, 182
Rule Making
See *Administrative Legislation*

Sanctions
See *Administrative Sanctions*
administrative imposition of, 138

Sanctions (*Continued*)
Administrative Procedure Act, provisions for, 138
administrative sanctions civil not penal, 138–39
declaratory orders, 150
Separation of Powers
constitutional separation departmental not functional, 34–45
doctrine of quasi power, 45
doctrine of non-delegation, 35, 45
powers distinguished, 37–45
representative views, 33–34
Social Security Act, 20
Spending Power, 327
State Immunity
common law on, 156
constitutional, 156
criticism of doctrine of, 179
States, of the, 168
United States, immunity of, 157
States, The
immunity of, 168
immunity limited by Fourteenth Amendment, 169
responsibility for acts of officers, 170–73
abuse of power, 171
acts of *de facto* officers, 170
acts pursuant to valid law, 171
ultra vires acts, 173
waiver of immunity, 177
Statutory Procedural Requirements
adjudication, 74
rule making, 70
adjudicatory procedure, 73
administrative procedure, 73
discretionary procedure, 72
Subpoena Power
administrative officer cannot enforce, 131
Administrative Procedure Act, provision for, 130
administrative subpoenas, enforced by courts, 130–32
compulsory incriminatory evidence not admissible evidence, 133

hearing officers, power to issue, 75
relevancy of evidence, 136–37
Substantial Evidence Rule
Administrative Procedure Act, effect of, 267
arbitrary finding, not supported by, 265
effect of, 266
evolution of, 258
jury trial rules applied, 262
Labor Management Act, effect of, 267
New York "residium rule," 262
Summary Action
day in court guaranteed, 152
officer liable for *ultra vires* acts, 152–53
property of considerable value must be abated, 154
property of small value may be destroyed, 154

Tort Claims Act, 165
Tucker Act, 163

Ultra Vires Acts
liability for, 200
Unconstitutional Statute
presumption of validity rule, 205
void *ab initio* doctrine, 201
United States
Court of Claims, 162
immunity to suit, 157
attribute of sovereignty, 156
liability by consent, 161
liability for contract, 162
liability for torts, 165
suits against United States officer, 160

Walter Logan Bill, 120
War Powers, 143
Welfare Government, Federal, 16
Witness
immunity of, 133–37